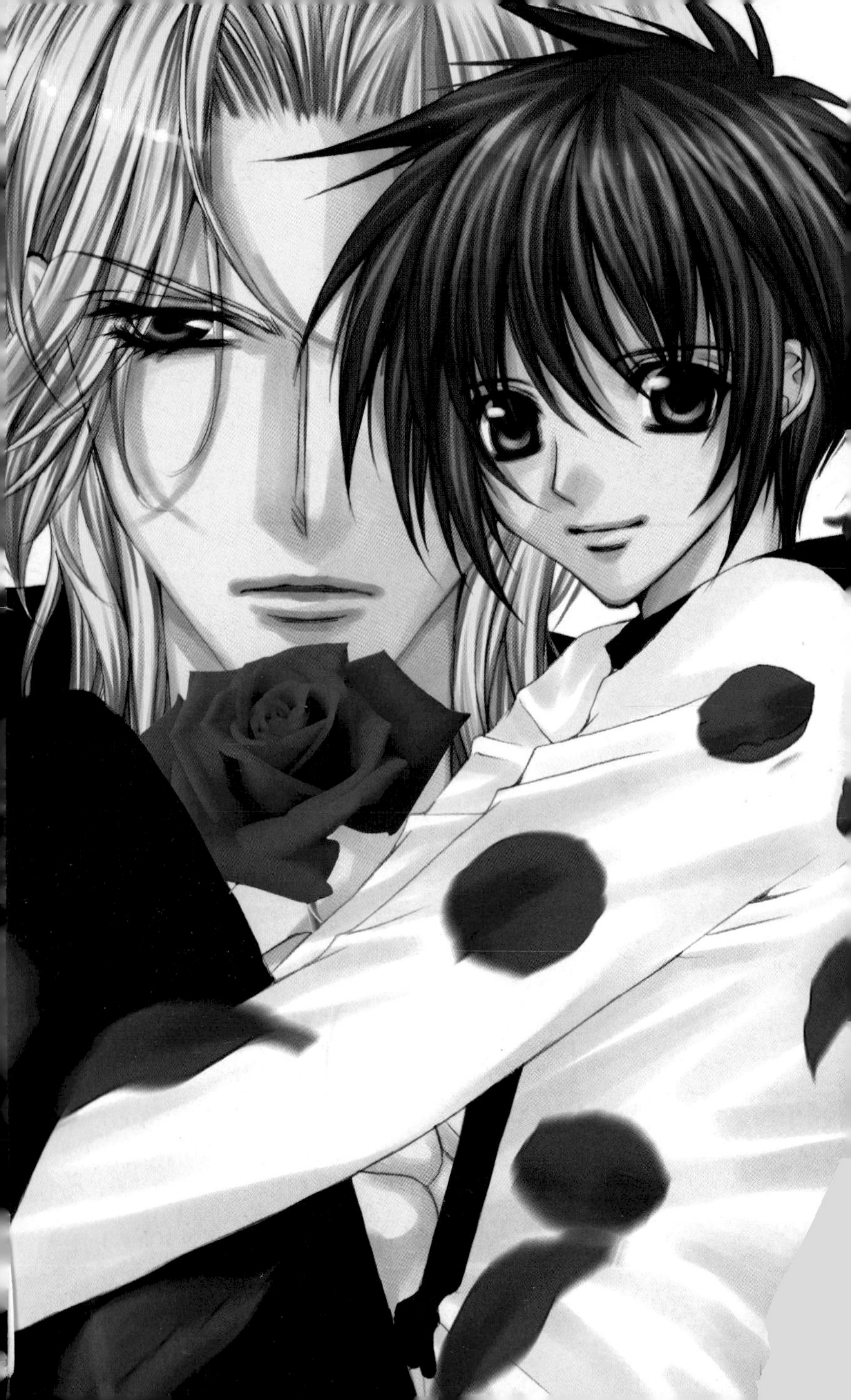

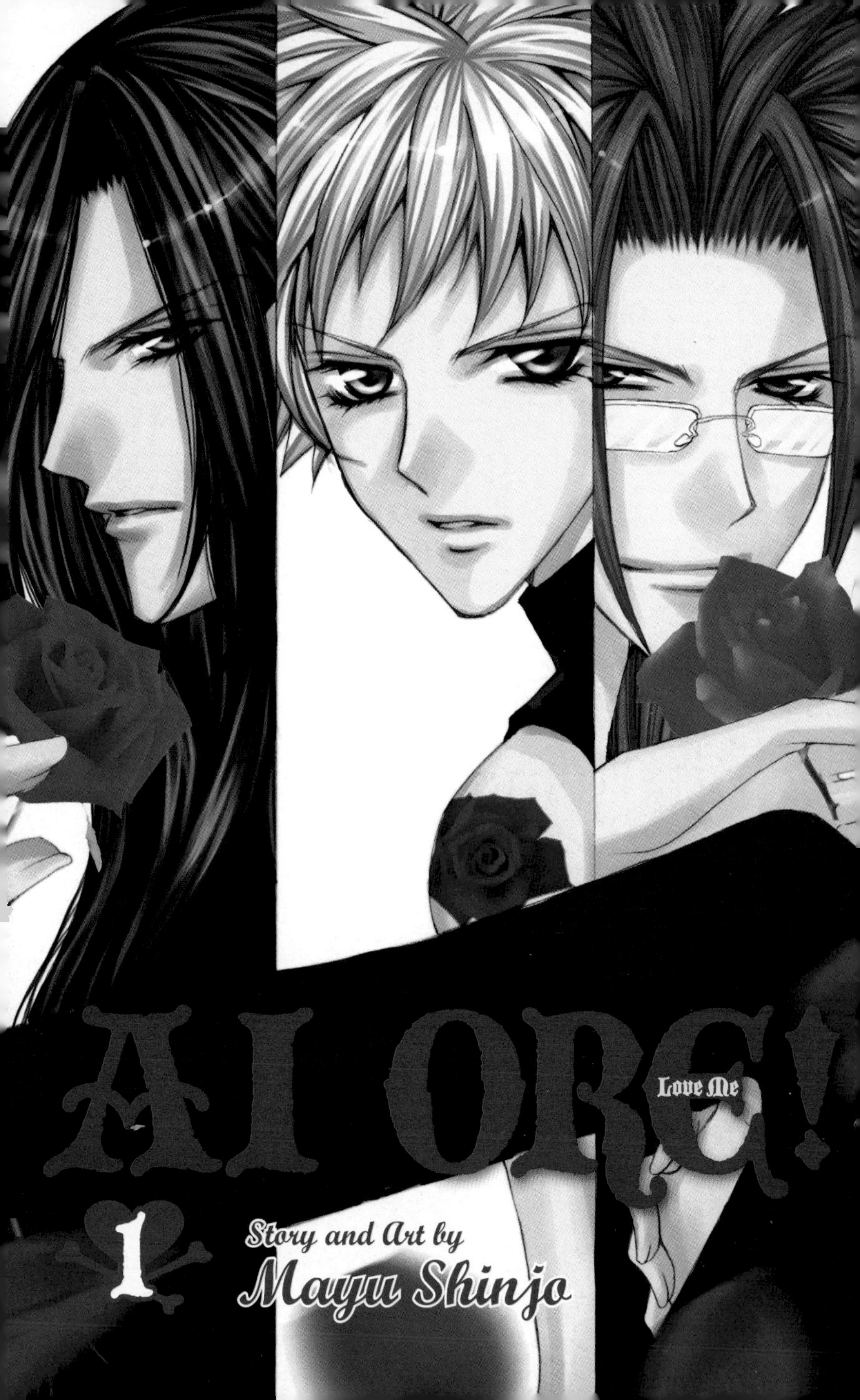

AI ORE!
Love Me
1
Story and Art by
Mayu Shinjo

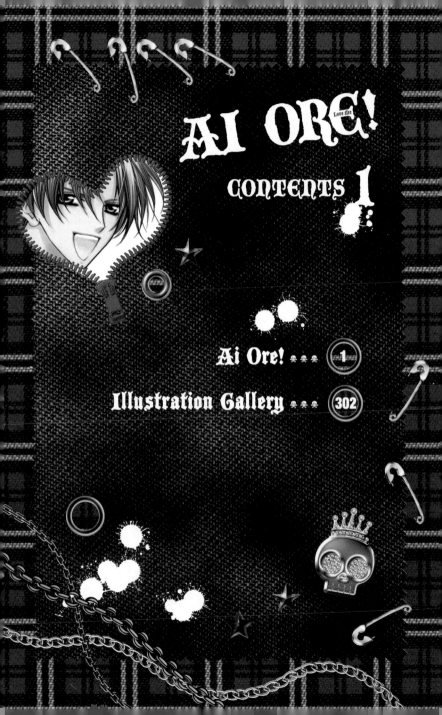

AI ORE! Love Me!

CONTENTS 1

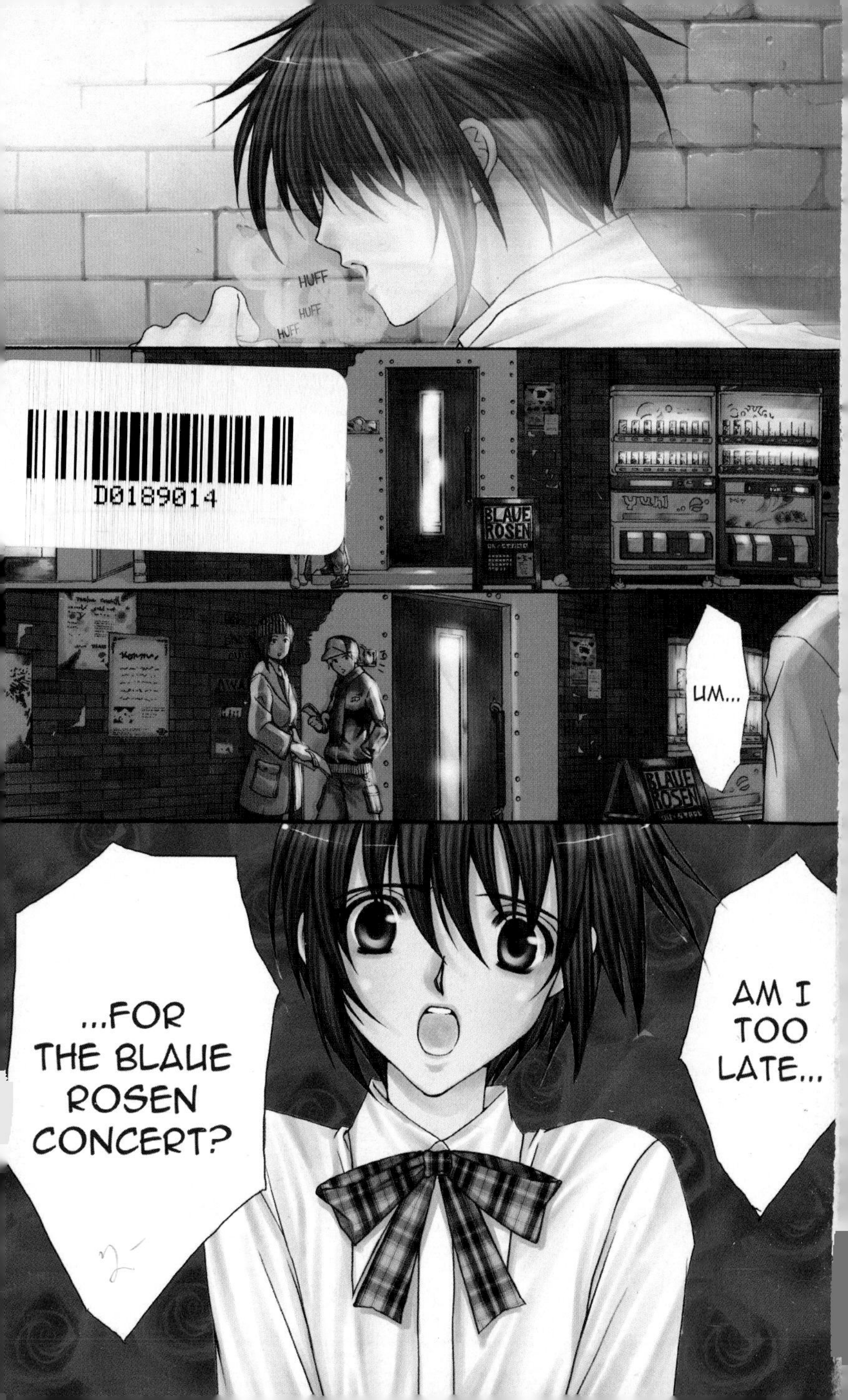
HUFF
HUFF
HUFF
BLAUE ROSEN
BLAUE ROSEN
UM...
AM I TOO LATE...
...FOR THE BLAUE ROSEN CONCERT?

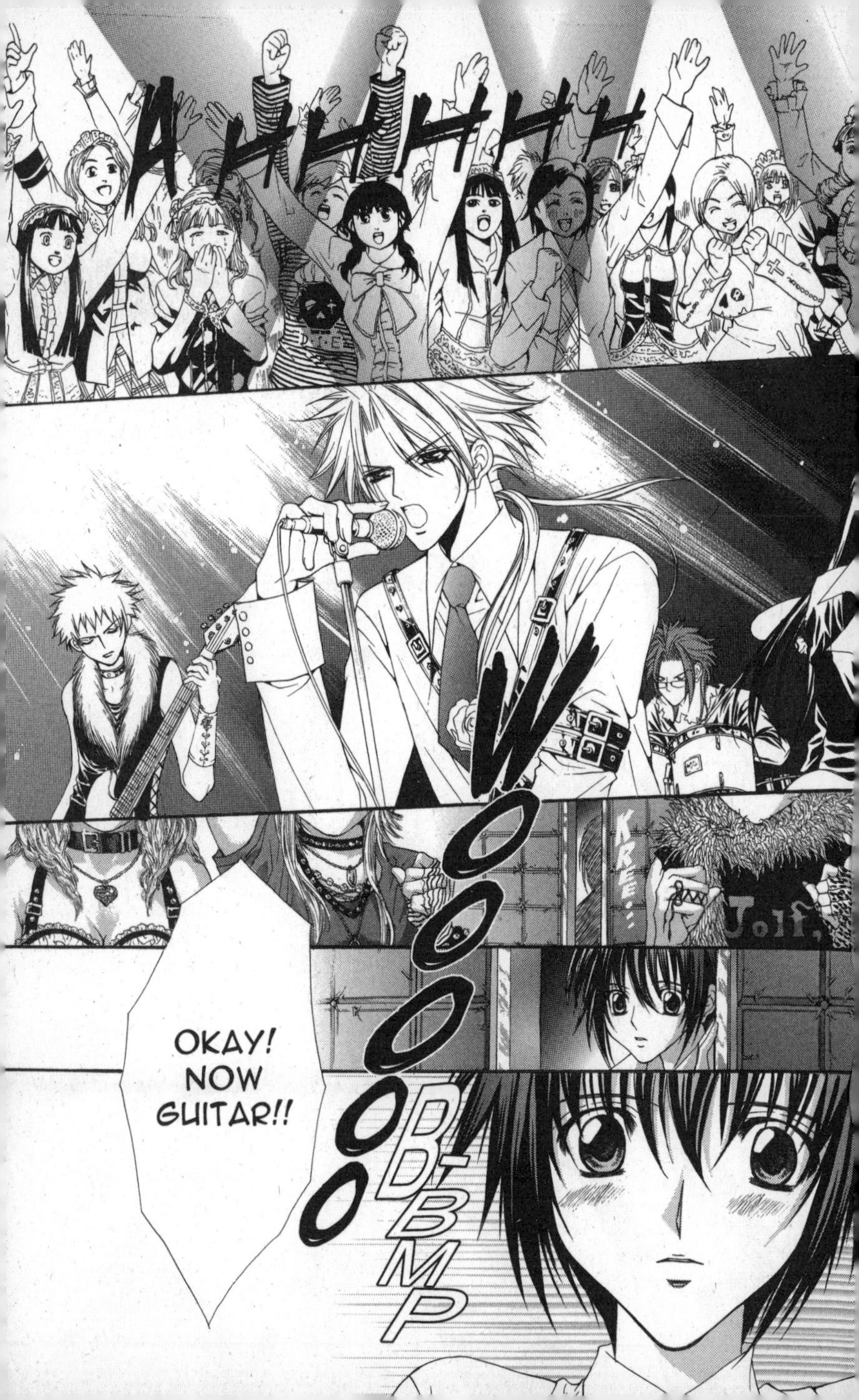
AHHHHHH
WOOOOOO
OKAY! NOW GUITAR!!
D-DBMP

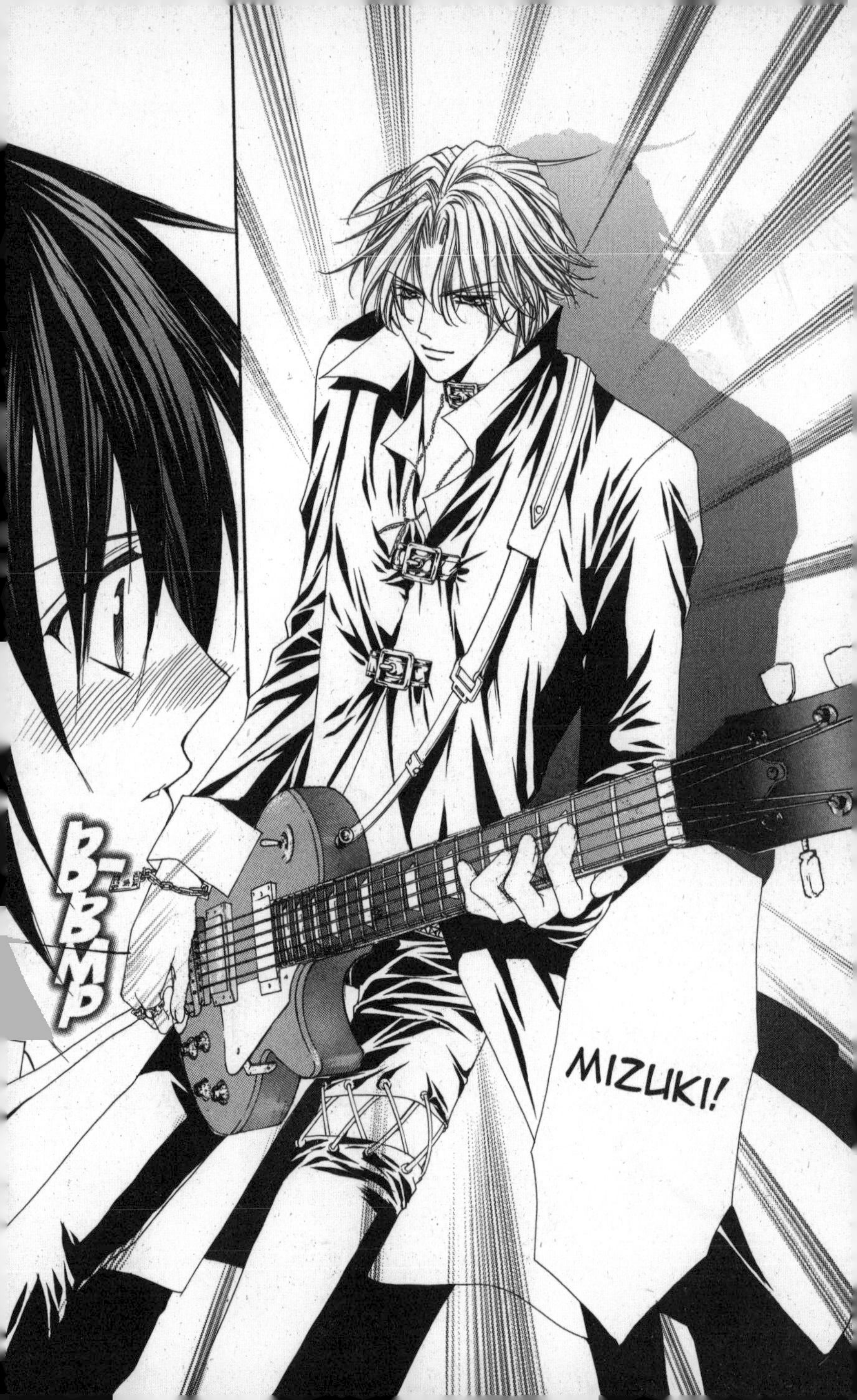
MIZUKI!
B-BUMP

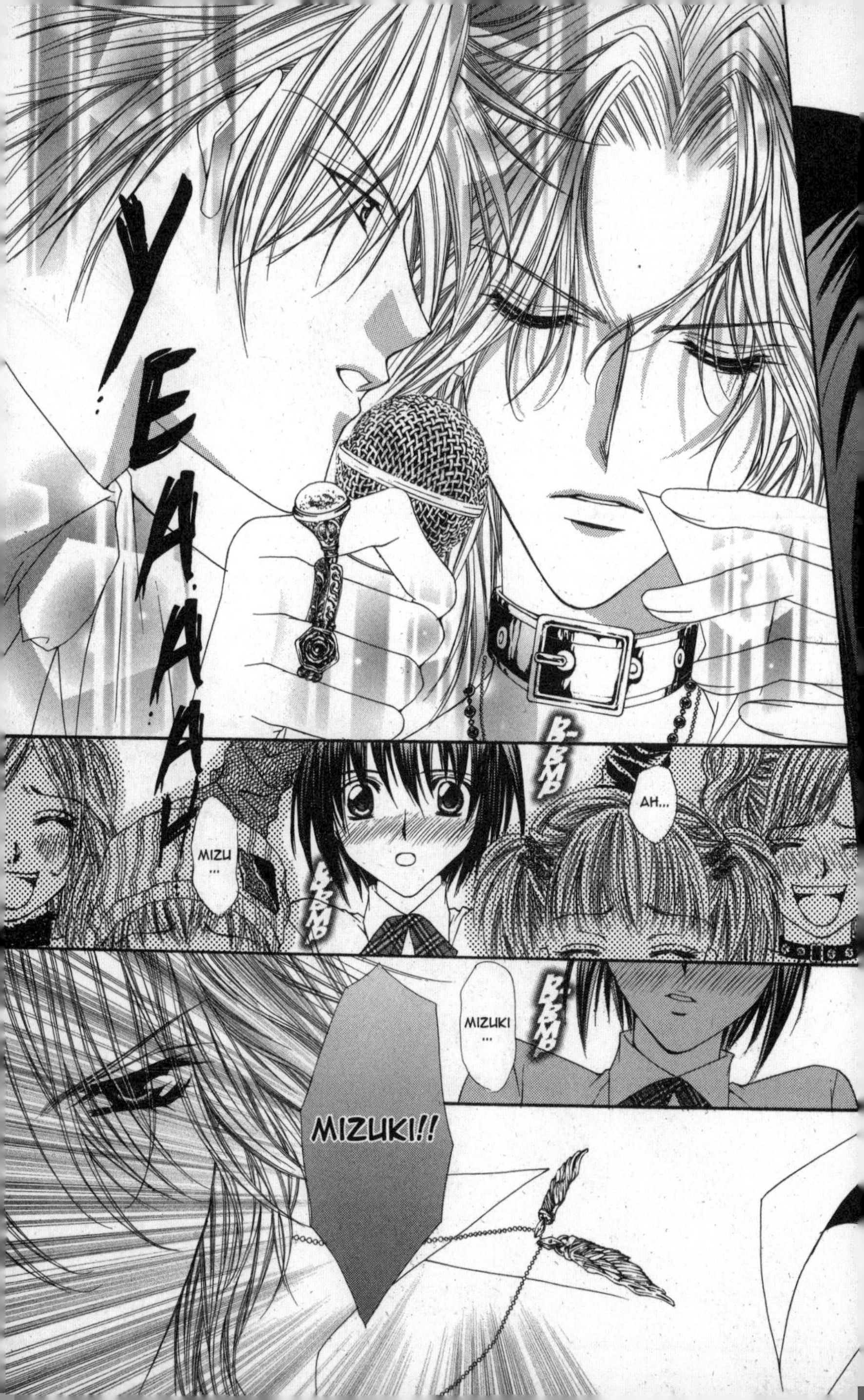
YEAAAAH
AH...
B-BMP
MIZU...
B-BMP
B-BMP
MIZUKI...
MIZUKI!!

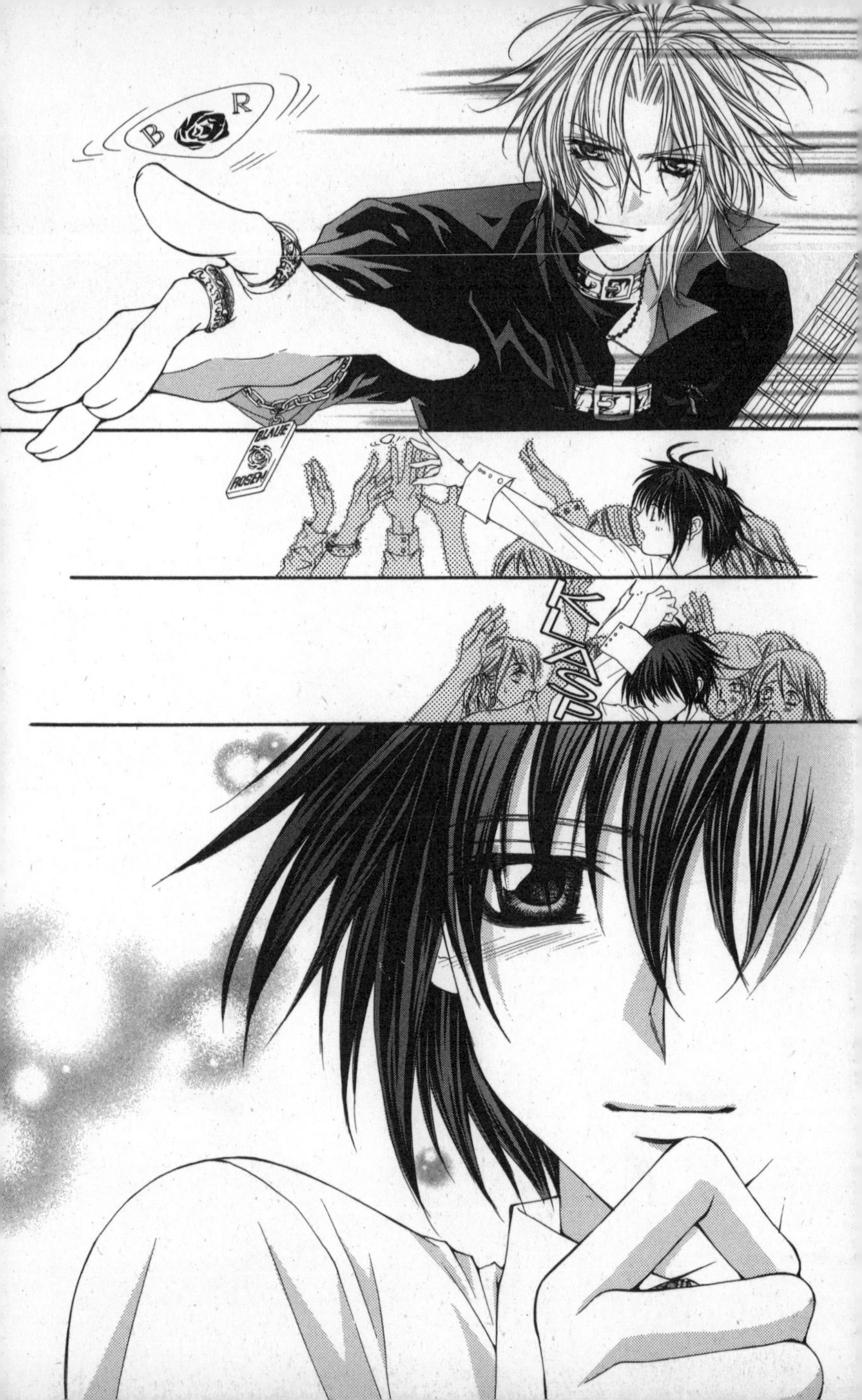
B R
BLAUE ROSEN
KLASP

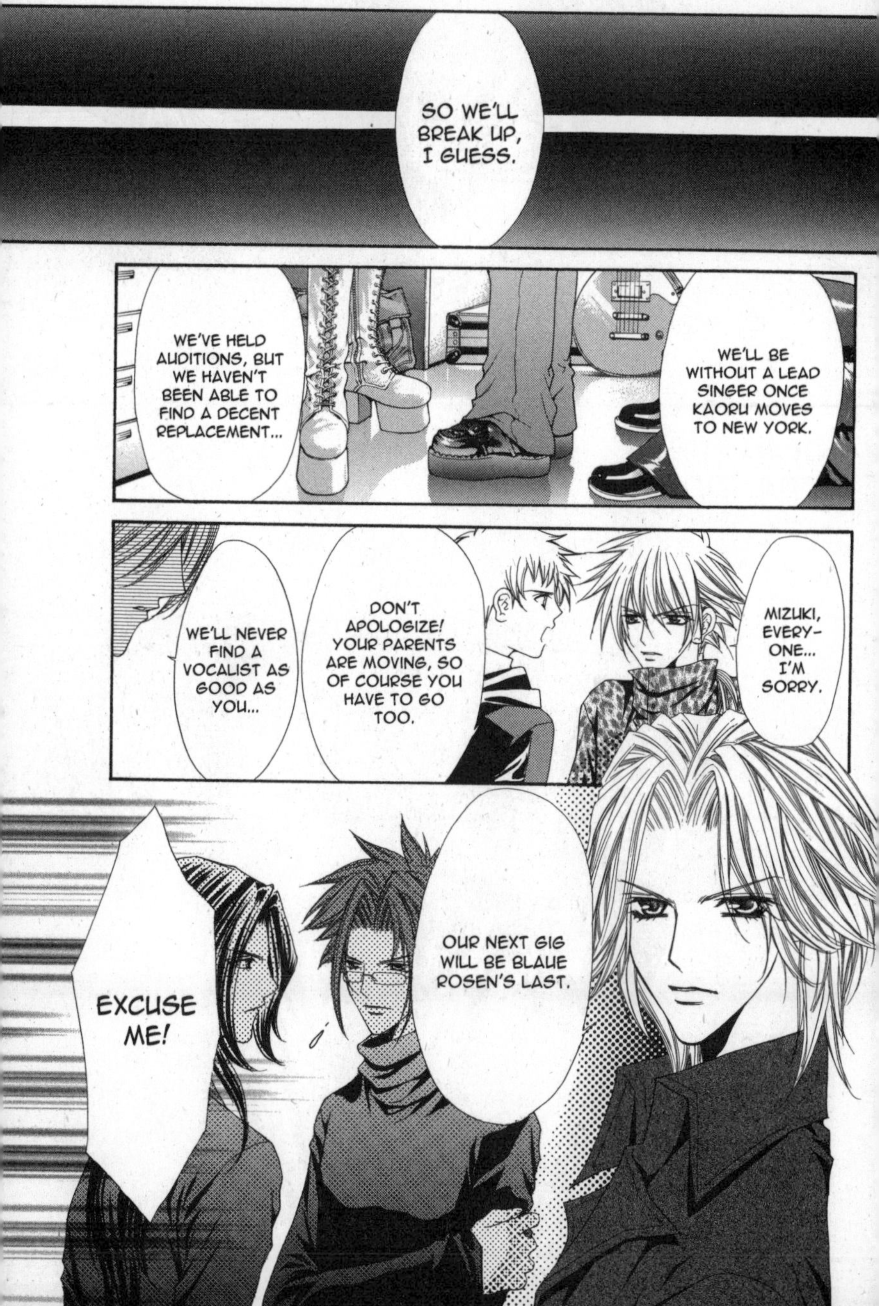
SO WE'LL BREAK UP, I GUESS.
WE'LL BE WITHOUT A LEAD SINGER ONCE KAORU MOVES TO NEW YORK.
WE'VE HELD AUDITIONS, BUT WE HAVEN'T BEEN ABLE TO FIND A DECENT REPLACEMENT...
MIZUKI, EVERY-ONE... I'M SORRY.
DON'T APOLOGIZE! YOUR PARENTS ARE MOVING, SO OF COURSE YOU HAVE TO GO TOO.
WE'LL NEVER FIND A VOCALIST AS GOOD AS YOU...
OUR NEXT GIG WILL BE BLAUE ROSEN'S LAST.
EXCUSE ME!

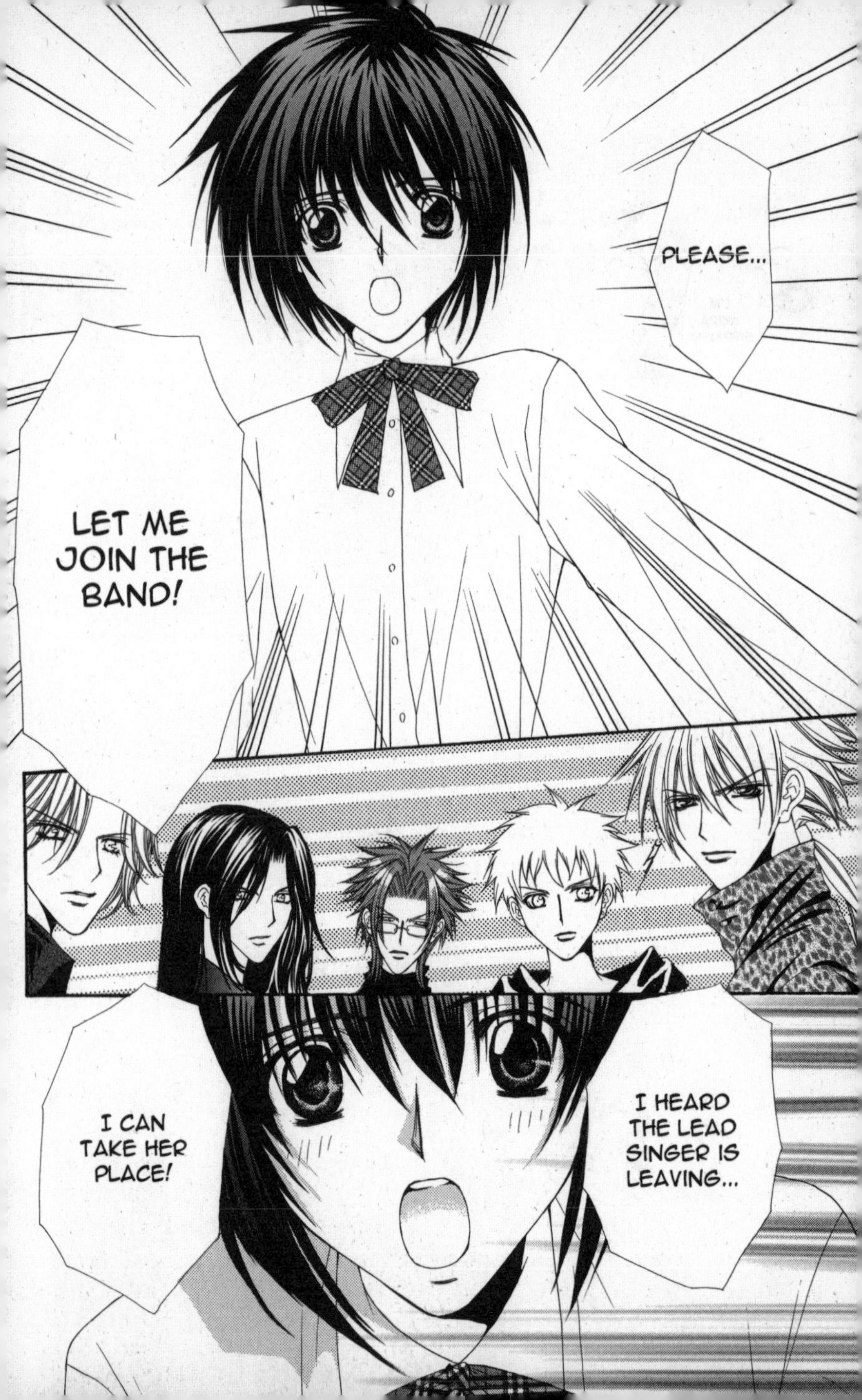
PLEASE...
LET ME JOIN THE BAND!
I HEARD THE LEAD SINGER IS LEAVING...
I CAN TAKE HER PLACE!

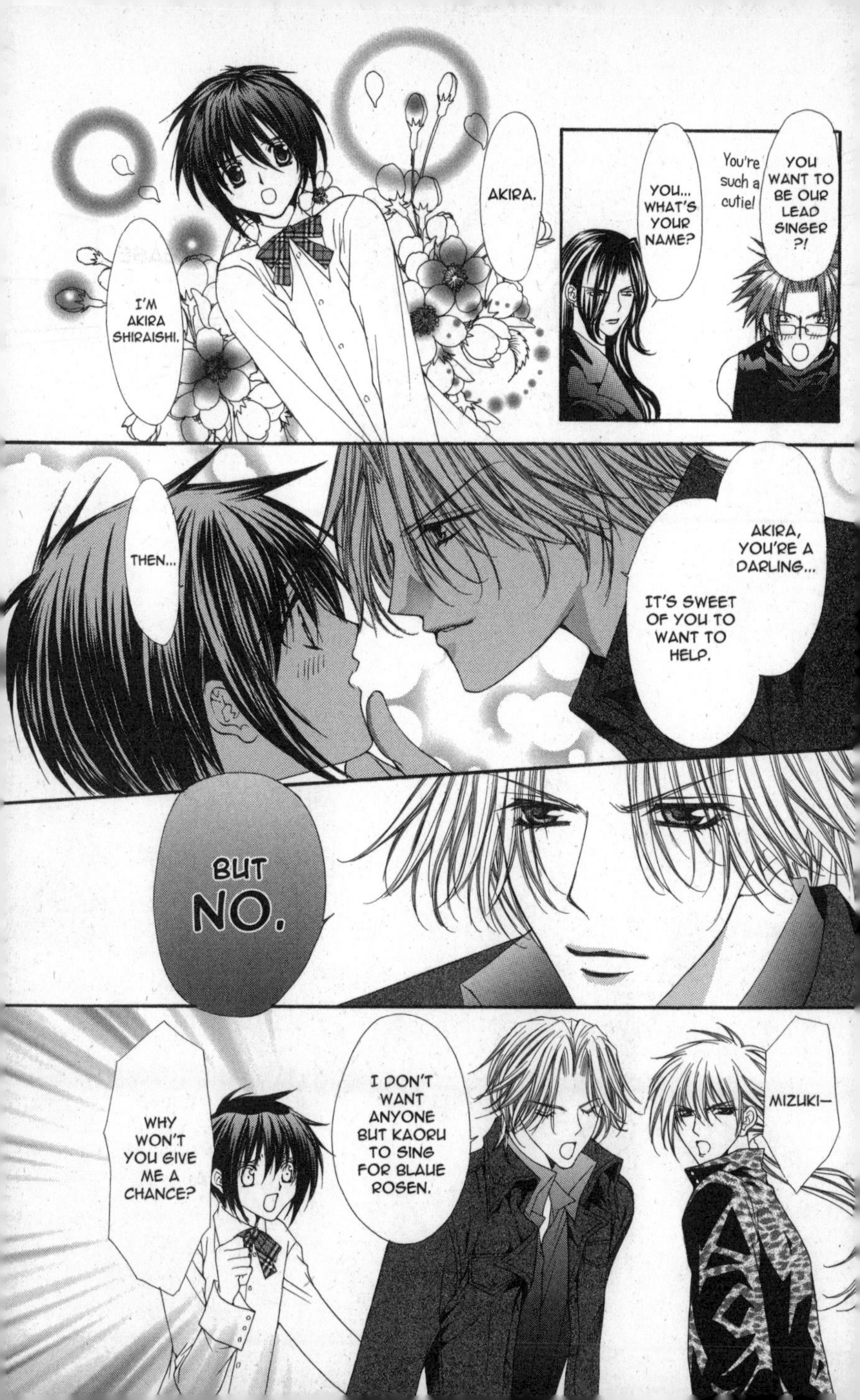
YOU WANT TO BE OUR LEAD SINGER ?!
You're such a cutie!
YOU... WHAT'S YOUR NAME?
AKIRA.
I'M AKIRA SHIRAISHI.
AKIRA, YOU'RE A DARLING...
IT'S SWEET OF YOU TO WANT TO HELP.
THEN...
BUT NO.
MIZUKI—
I DON'T WANT ANYONE BUT KAORU TO SING FOR BLAUE ROSEN.
WHY WON'T YOU GIVE ME A CHANCE?

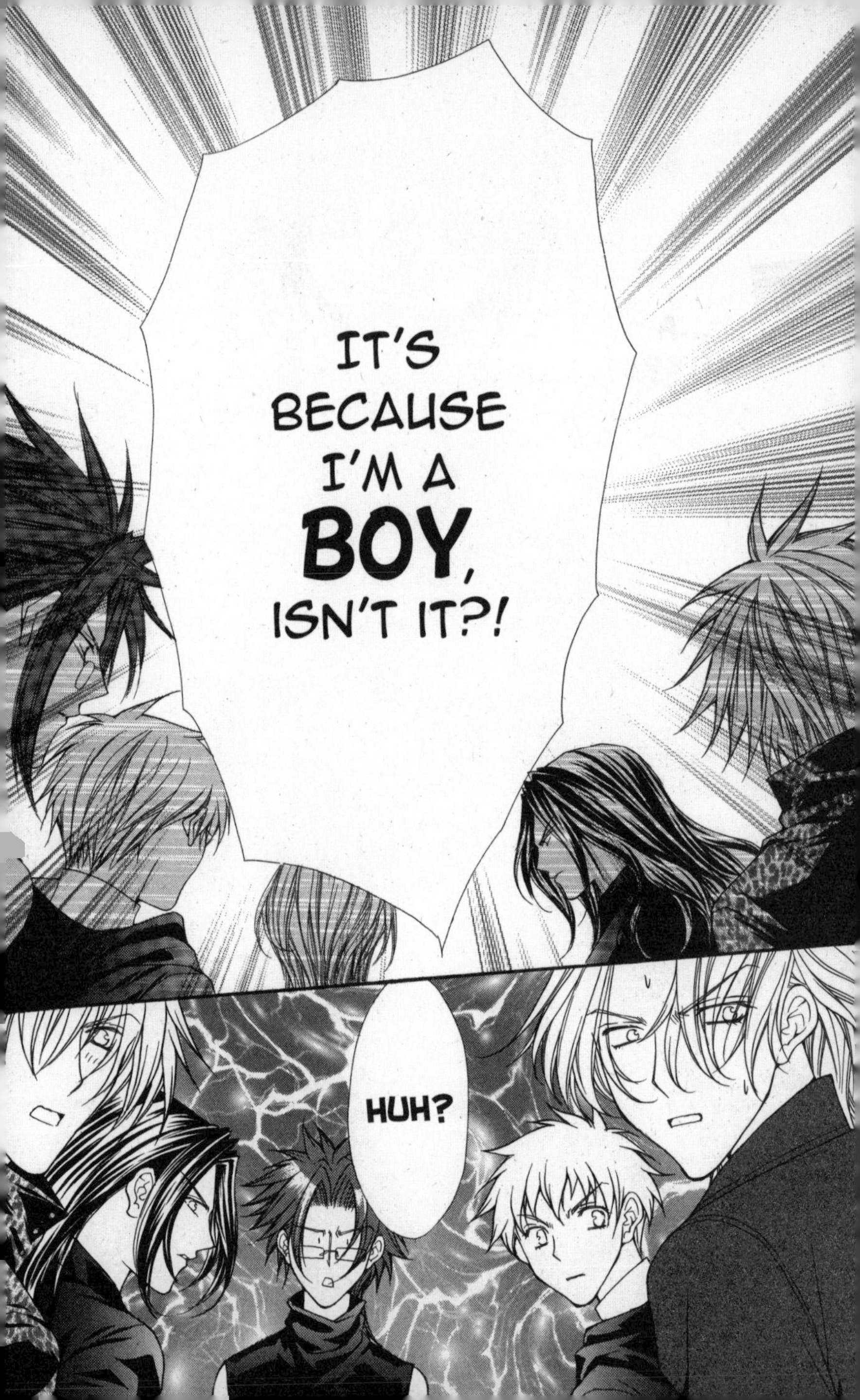
IT'S BECAUSE I'M A BOY, ISN'T IT?!
HUH?

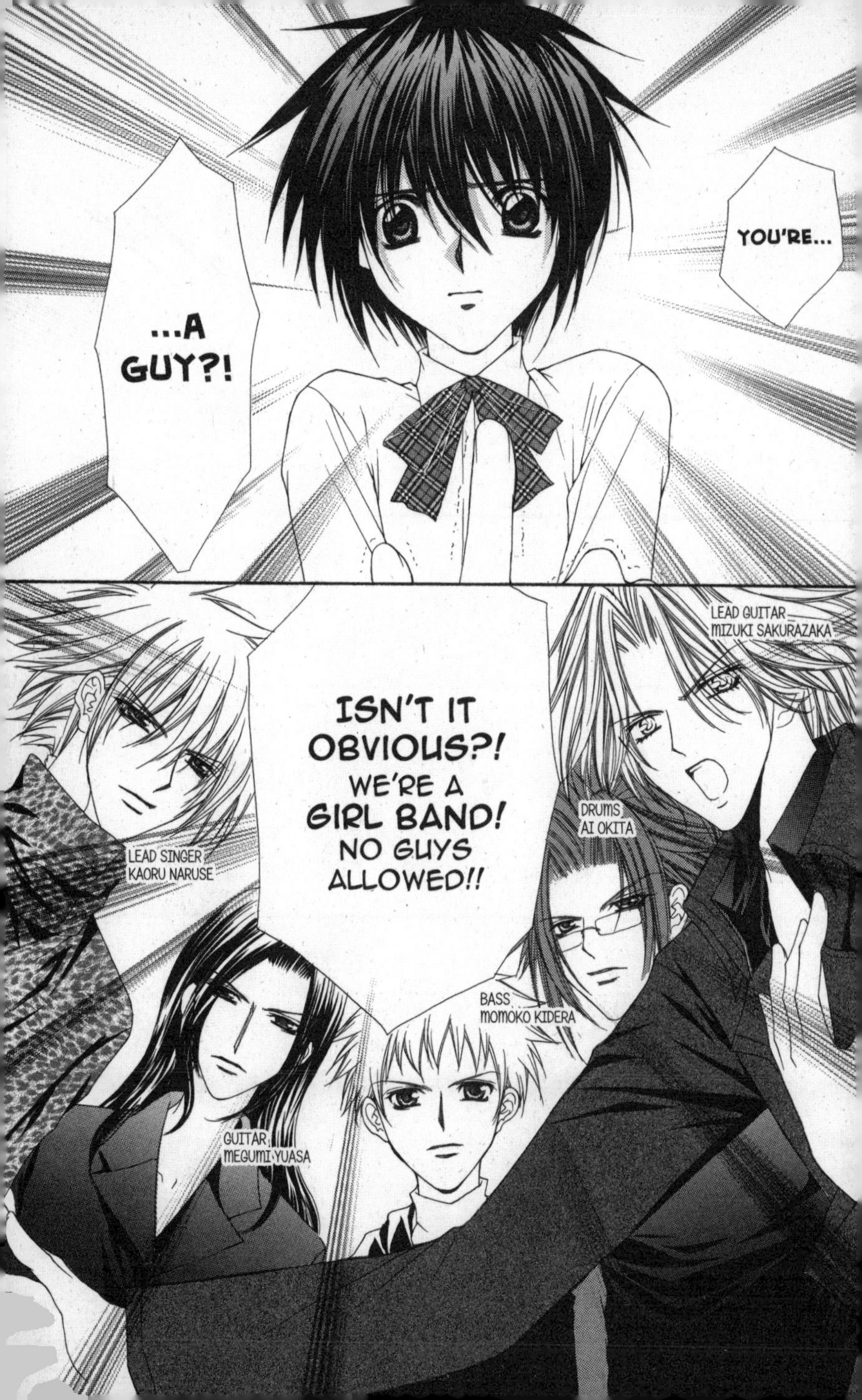
YOU'RE...
...A GUY?!
LEAD GUITAR MIZUKI SAKURAZAKA
ISN'T IT OBVIOUS?! WE'RE A GIRL BAND! NO GUYS ALLOWED!!
DRUMS AI OKITA
LEAD SINGER KAORU NARUSE
BASS MOMOKO KIDERA
GUITAR MEGUMI YUASA

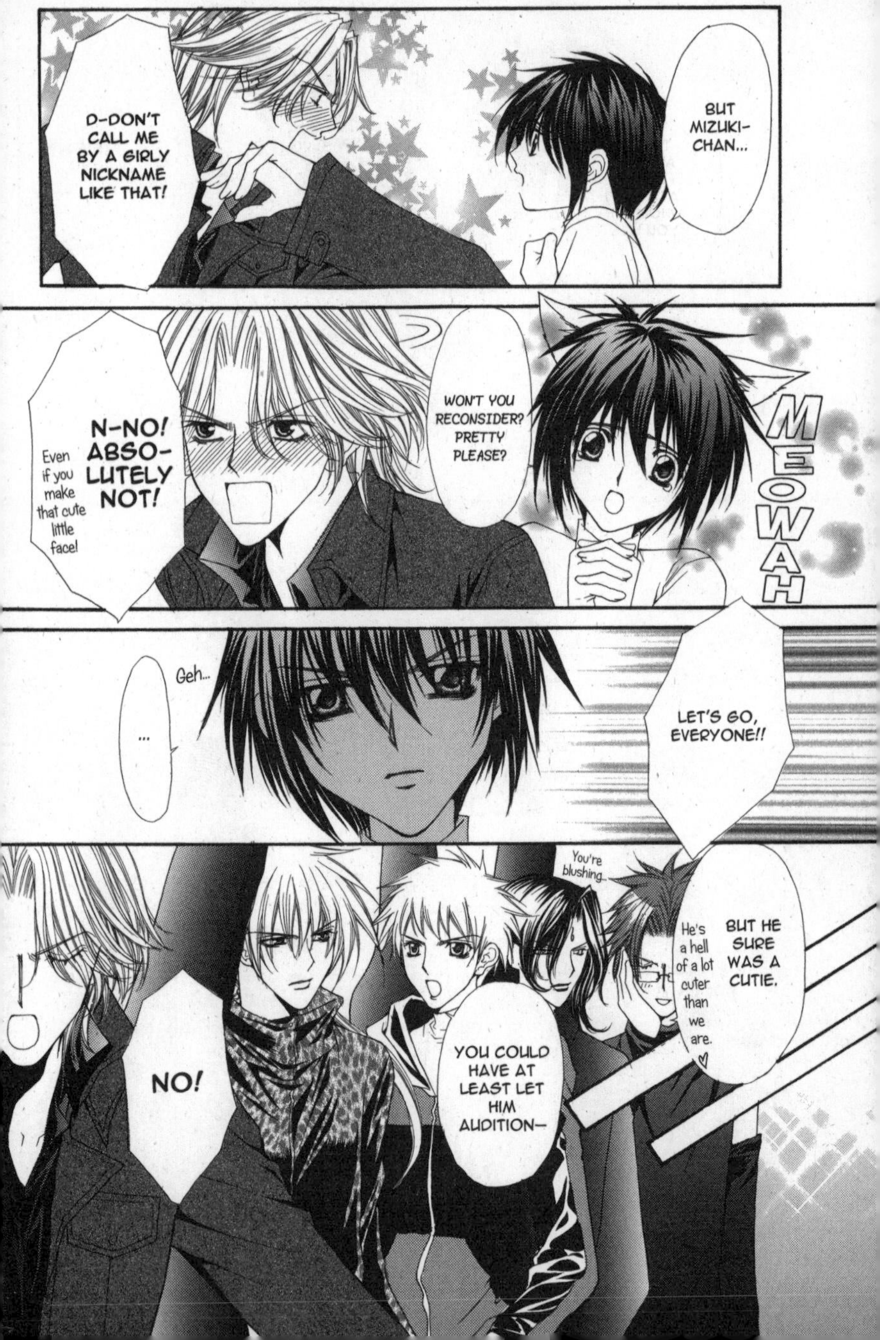
BUT MIZUKI-CHAN...
D-DON'T CALL ME BY A GIRLY NICKNAME LIKE THAT!
MEOWAH
WON'T YOU RECONSIDER? PRETTY PLEASE?
N-NO! ABSO-LUTELY NOT!
Even if you make that cute little face!
LET'S GO, EVERYONE!!
Geh...
...
BUT HE SURE WAS A CUTIE.
He's a hell of a lot cuter than we are. ♡
You're blushing...
YOU COULD HAVE AT LEAST LET HIM AUDITION–
NO!

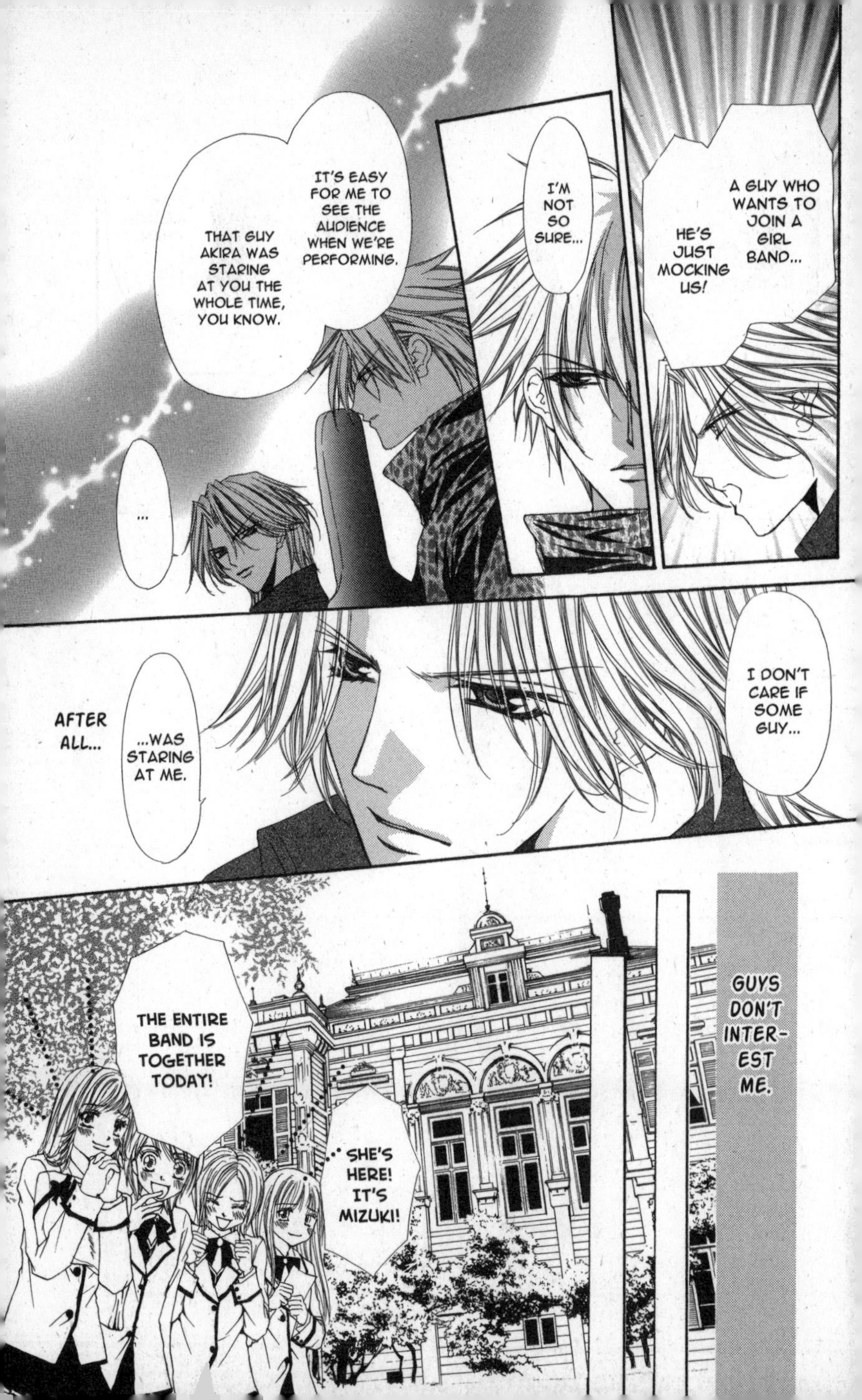
A GUY WHO WANTS TO JOIN A GIRL BAND...
HE'S JUST MOCKING US!
I'M NOT SO SURE...
IT'S EASY FOR ME TO SEE THE AUDIENCE WHEN WE'RE PERFORMING.
THAT GUY AKIRA WAS STARING AT YOU THE WHOLE TIME, YOU KNOW.
...
I DON'T CARE IF SOME GUY...
...WAS STARING AT ME.
AFTER ALL...
GUYS DON'T INTER-EST ME.
THE ENTIRE BAND IS TOGETHER TODAY!
SHE'S HERE! IT'S MIZUKI!

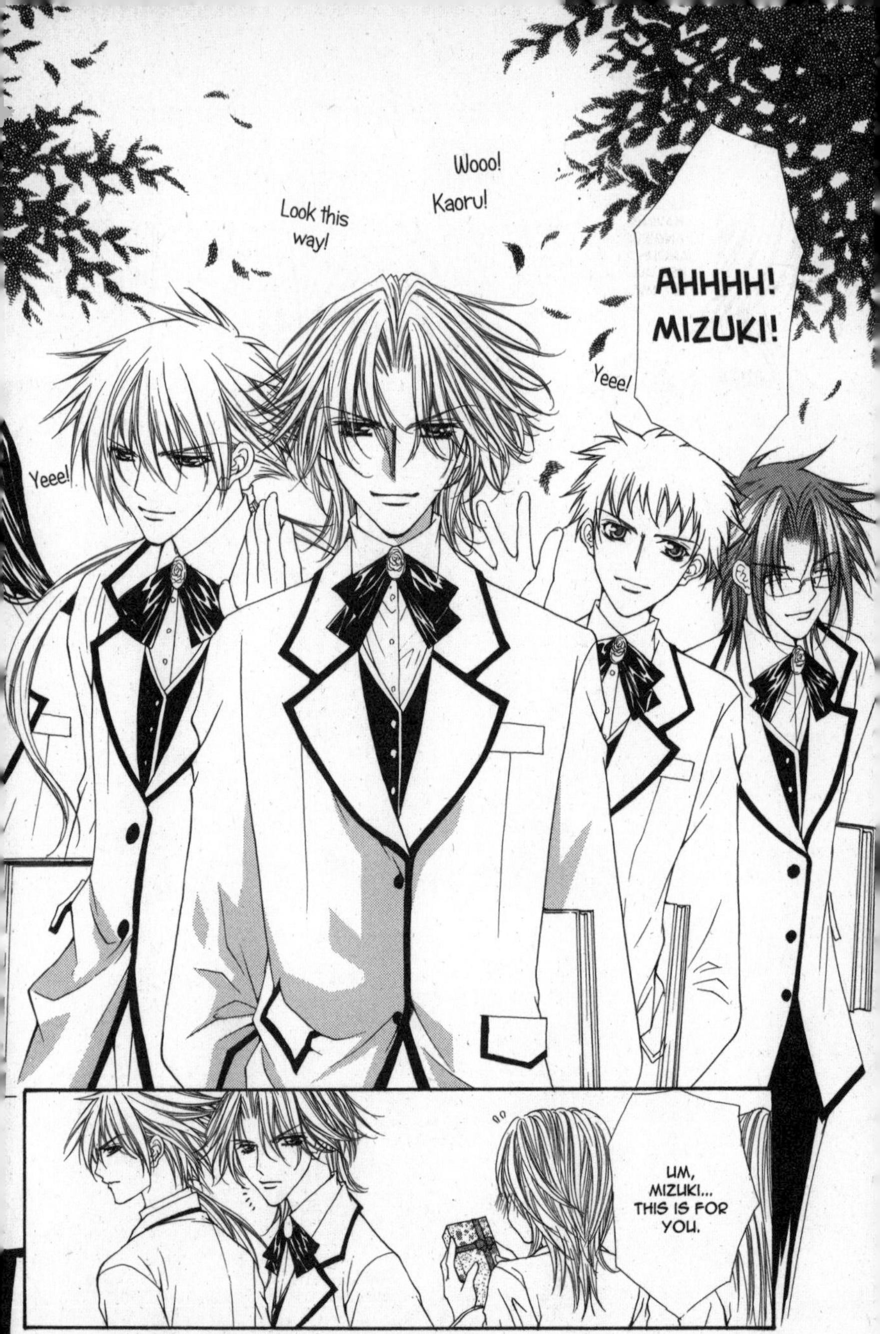
AHHHH! MIZUKI!
Yeee!
Wooo!
Kaoru!
Look this way!
Yeee!
UM, MIZUKI... THIS IS FOR YOU.

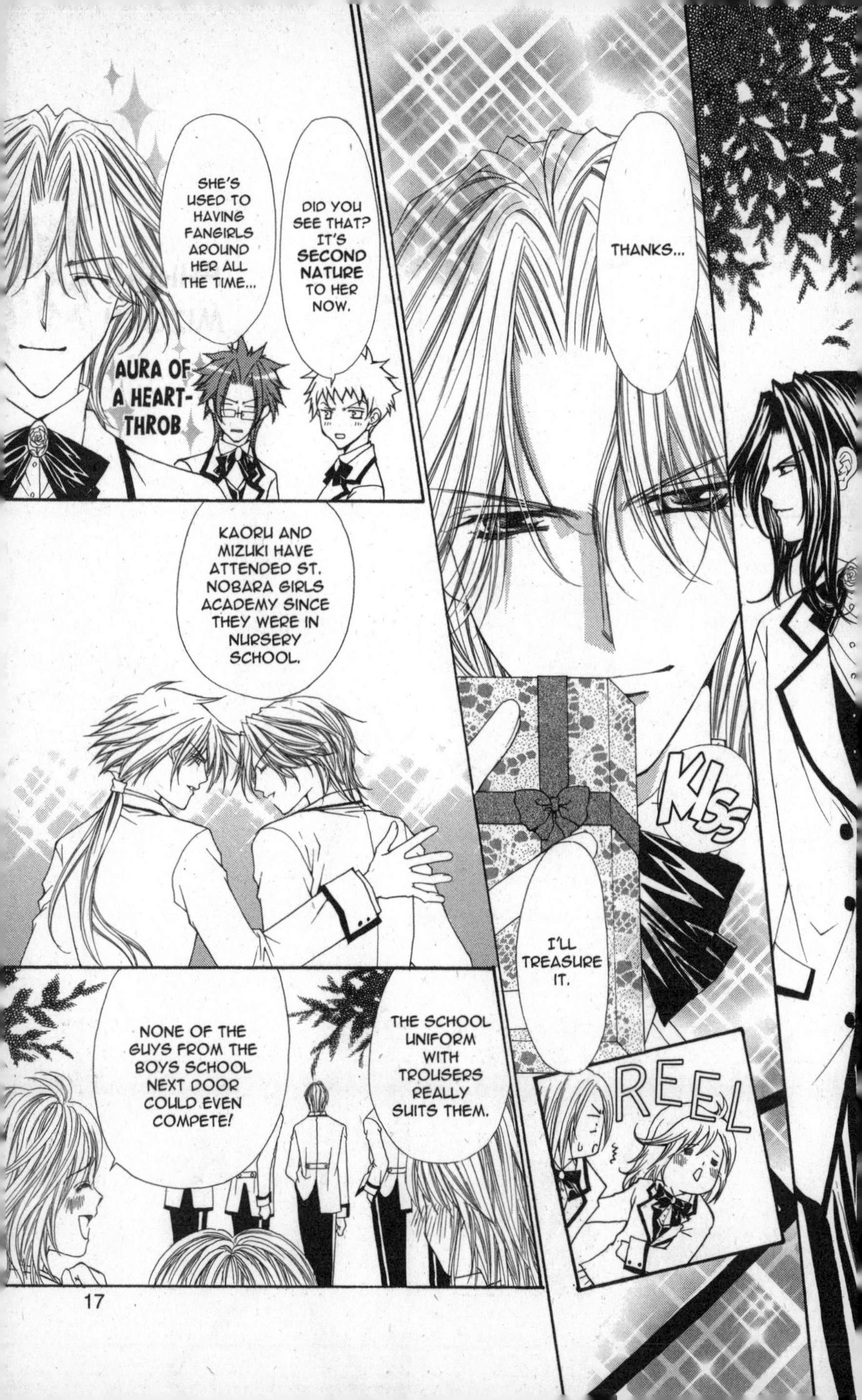
THANKS...
KISS
I'LL TREASURE IT.
REEL
DID YOU SEE THAT? IT'S SECOND NATURE TO HER NOW.
SHE'S USED TO HAVING FANGIRLS AROUND HER ALL THE TIME...
AURA OF A HEART-THROB
KAORU AND MIZUKI HAVE ATTENDED ST. NOBARA GIRLS ACADEMY SINCE THEY WERE IN NURSERY SCHOOL.
THE SCHOOL UNIFORM WITH TROUSERS REALLY SUITS THEM.
NONE OF THE GUYS FROM THE BOYS SCHOOL NEXT DOOR COULD EVEN COMPETE!

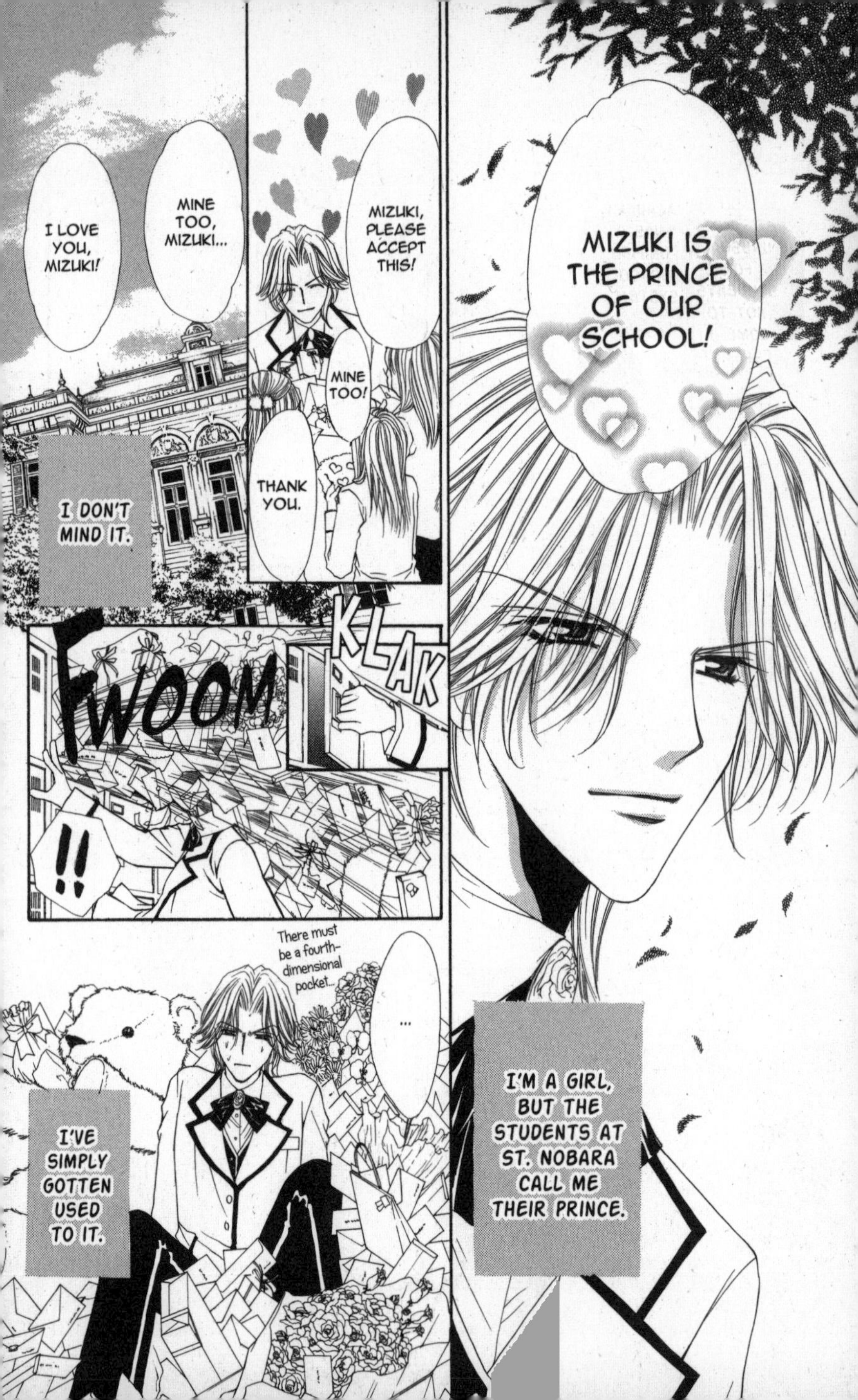
MIZUKI IS THE PRINCE OF OUR SCHOOL!
I'M A GIRL, BUT THE STUDENTS AT ST. NOBARA CALL ME THEIR PRINCE.
MIZUKI, PLEASE ACCEPT THIS!
MINE TOO!
THANK YOU.
MINE TOO, MIZUKI...
I LOVE YOU, MIZUKI!
I DON'T MIND IT.
KLAK
FWOOM
!!
There must be a fourth-dimensional pocket...
...
I'VE SIMPLY GOTTEN USED TO IT.

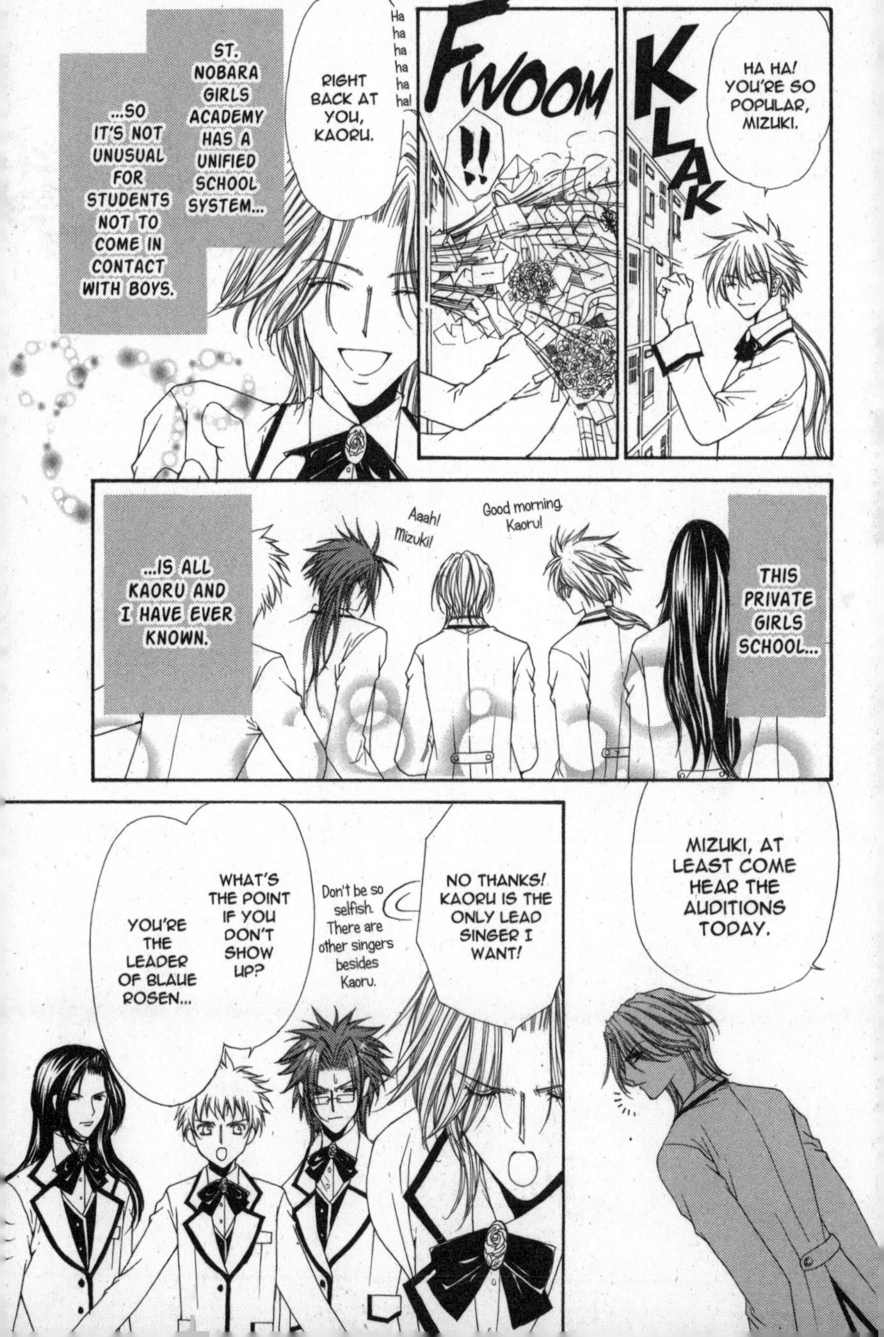
HA HA! YOU'RE SO POPULAR, MIZUKI.
KLAK
FWOOM
!!
Ha ha ha ha ha ha!
RIGHT BACK AT YOU, KAORU.
ST. NOBARA GIRLS ACADEMY HAS A UNIFIED SCHOOL SYSTEM...
...SO IT'S NOT UNUSUAL FOR STUDENTS NOT TO COME IN CONTACT WITH BOYS.
THIS PRIVATE GIRLS SCHOOL...
Good morning. Kaoru!
Aaah! Mizuki!
...IS ALL KAORU AND I HAVE EVER KNOWN.
MIZUKI, AT LEAST COME HEAR THE AUDITIONS TODAY.
NO THANKS! KAORU IS THE ONLY LEAD SINGER I WANT!
Don't be so selfish. There are other singers besides Kaoru.
WHAT'S THE POINT IF YOU DON'T SHOW UP?
YOU'RE THE LEADER OF BLAUE ROSEN...

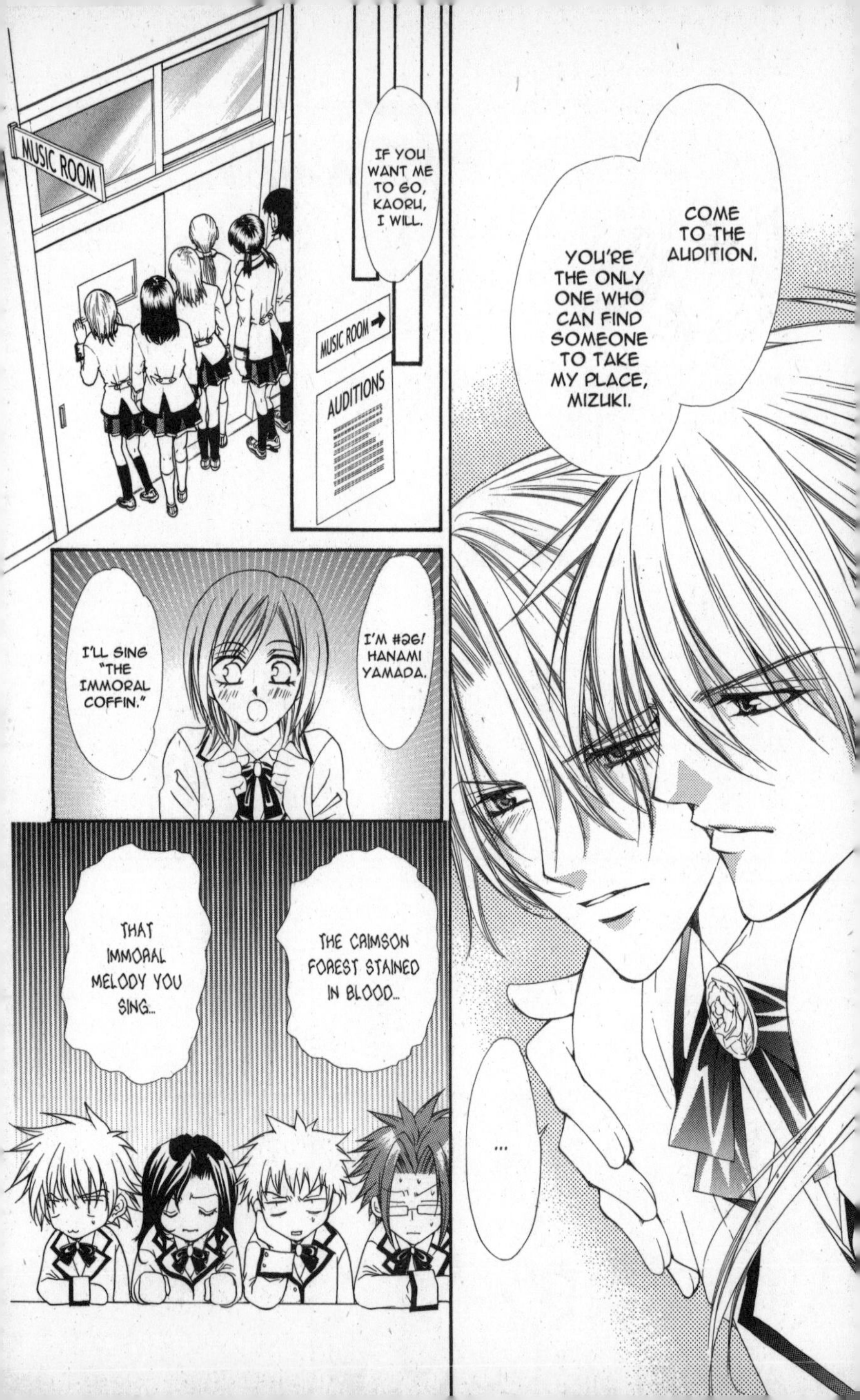
COME TO THE AUDITION.
YOU'RE THE ONLY ONE WHO CAN FIND SOMEONE TO TAKE MY PLACE, MIZUKI.
...
IF YOU WANT ME TO GO, KAORU, I WILL.
MUSIC ROOM
MUSIC ROOM →
AUDITIONS
I'M #26! HANAMI YAMADA.
I'LL SING "THE IMMORAL COFFIN."
THE CRIMSON FOREST STAINED IN BLOOD...
THAT IMMORAL MELODY YOU SING...

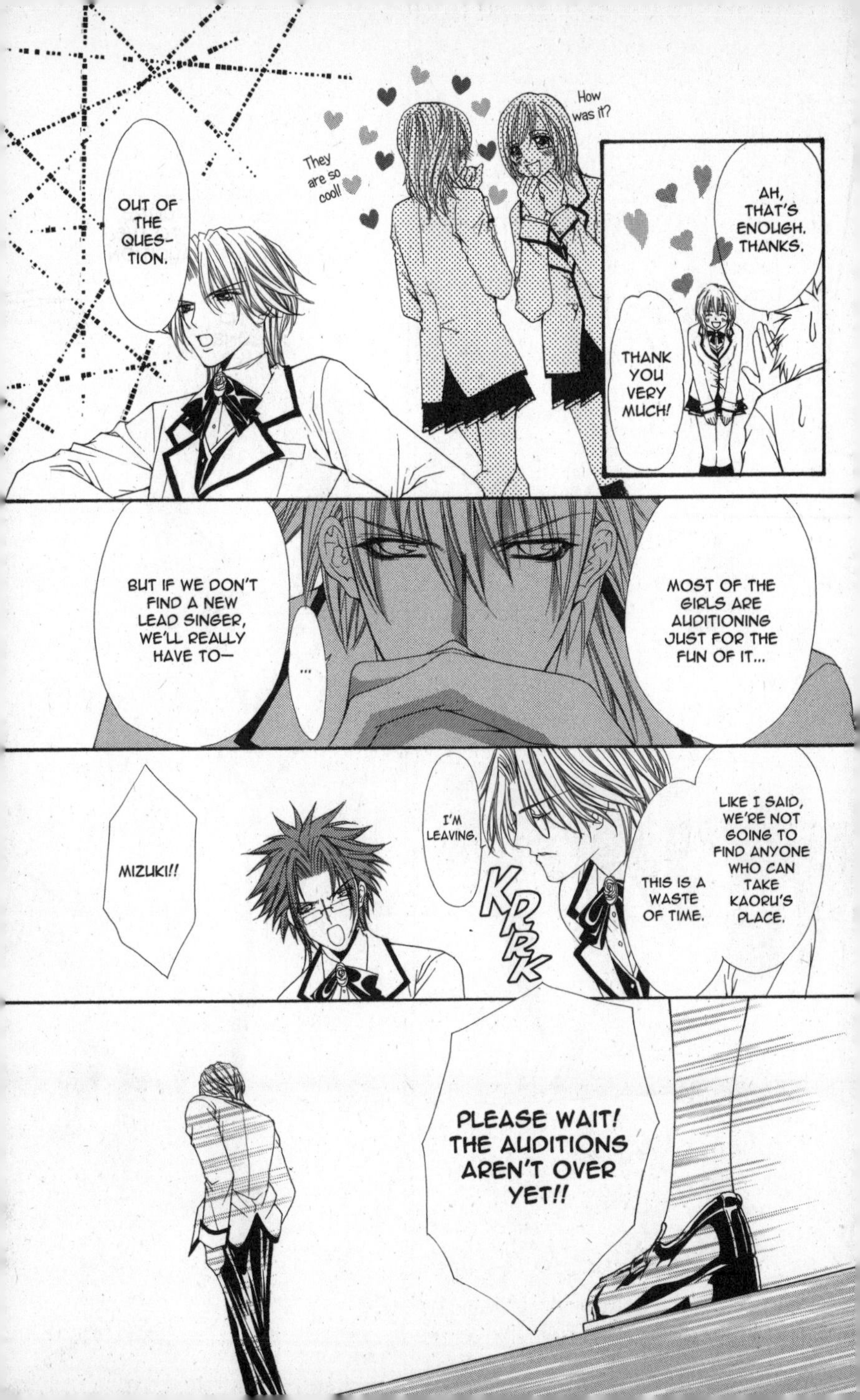
AH, THAT'S ENOUGH. THANKS.
THANK YOU VERY MUCH!
How was it?
They are so cool!
OUT OF THE QUESTION.
MOST OF THE GIRLS ARE AUDITIONING JUST FOR THE FUN OF IT...
...
BUT IF WE DON'T FIND A NEW LEAD SINGER, WE'LL REALLY HAVE TO—
LIKE I SAID, WE'RE NOT GOING TO FIND ANYONE WHO CAN TAKE KAORU'S PLACE.
THIS IS A WASTE OF TIME.
KRRK
I'M LEAVING.
MIZUKI!!
PLEASE WAIT! THE AUDITIONS AREN'T OVER YET!!

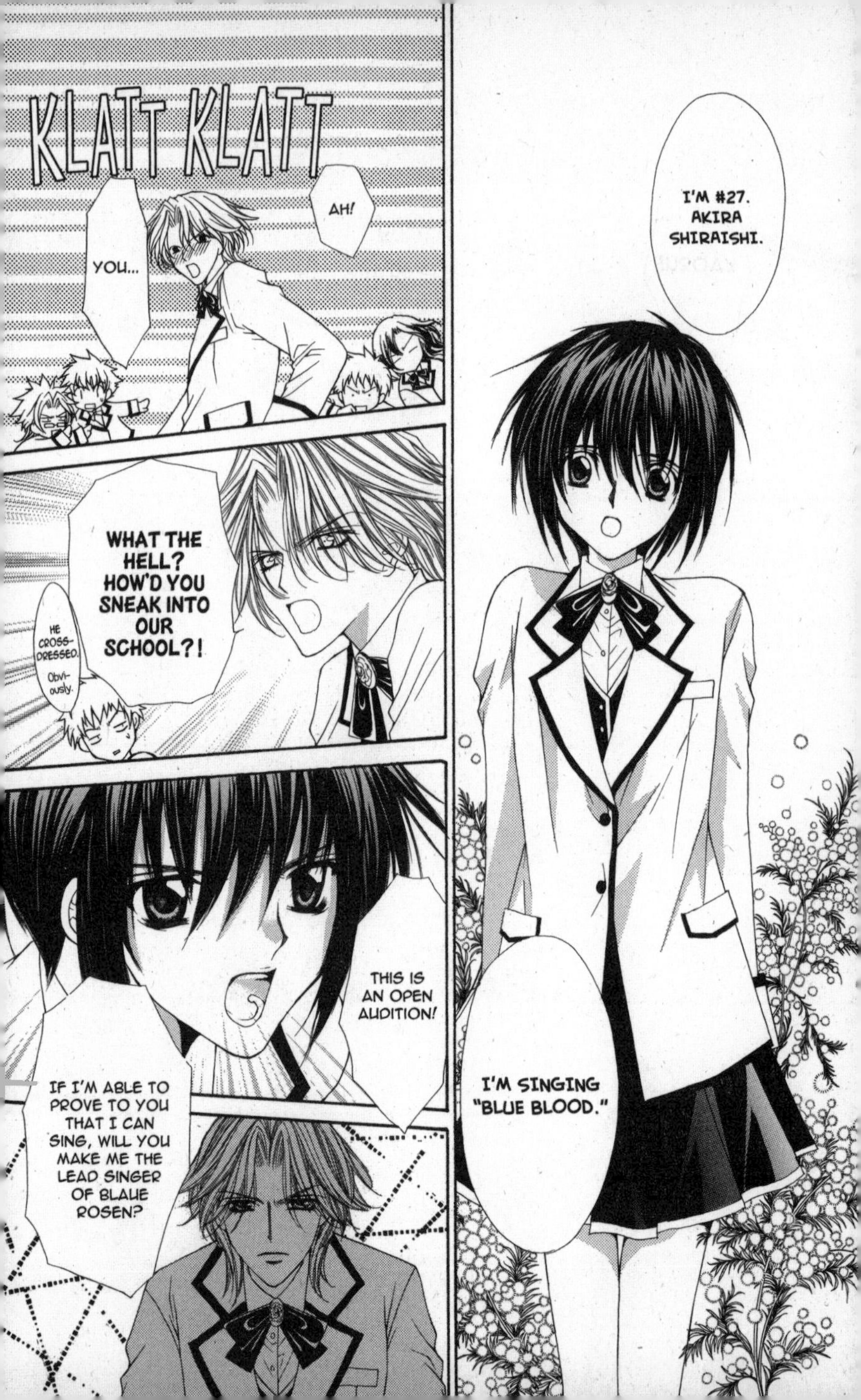
I'M #27. AKIRA SHIRAISHI.
I'M SINGING "BLUE BLOOD."
KLATT KLATT
AH!
YOU...
WHAT THE HELL? HOW'D YOU SNEAK INTO OUR SCHOOL?!
HE CROSS-DRESSED. Obviously.
THIS IS AN OPEN AUDITION!
IF I'M ABLE TO PROVE TO YOU THAT I CAN SING, WILL YOU MAKE ME THE LEAD SINGER OF BLAUE ROSEN?

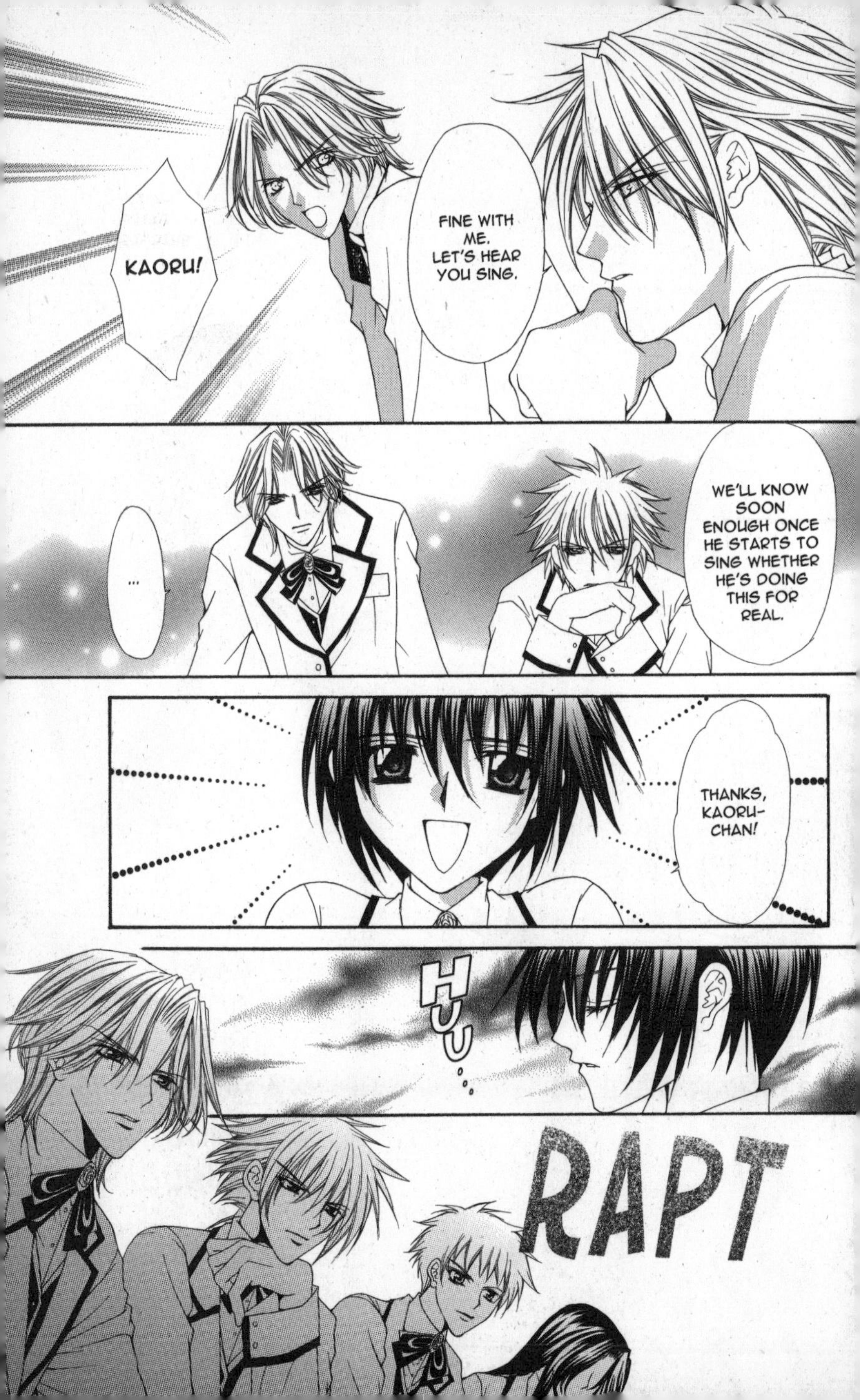
FINE WITH ME. LET'S HEAR YOU SING.
KAORU!
WE'LL KNOW SOON ENOUGH ONCE HE STARTS TO SING WHETHER HE'S DOING THIS FOR REAL.
...
THANKS, KAORU-CHAN!
HUU...
RAPT

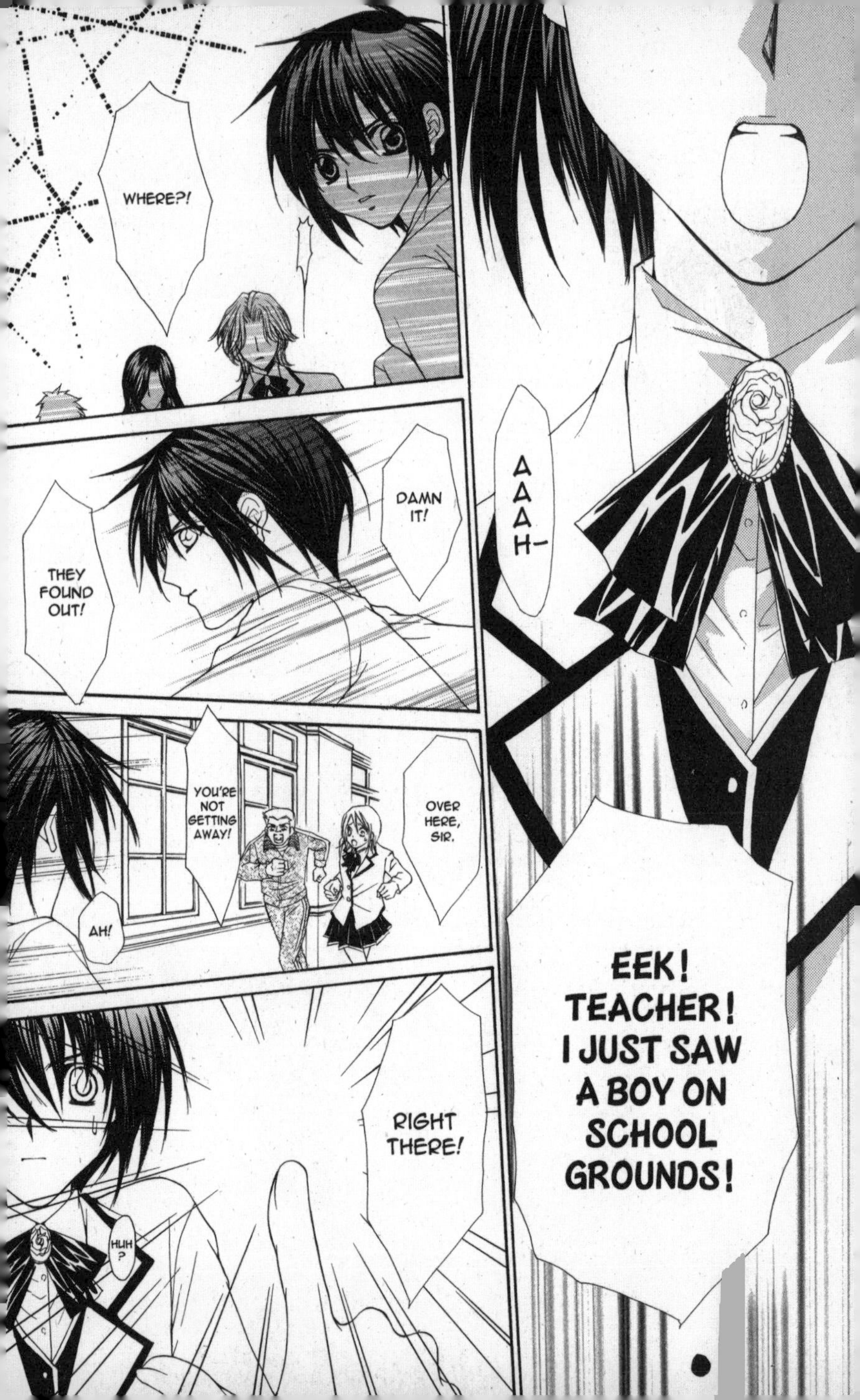
AAAH—
EEK! TEACHER! I JUST SAW A BOY ON SCHOOL GROUNDS!
WHERE?!
DAMN IT!
THEY FOUND OUT!
OVER HERE, SIR.
YOU'RE NOT GETTING AWAY!
AH!
RIGHT THERE!
HUH?

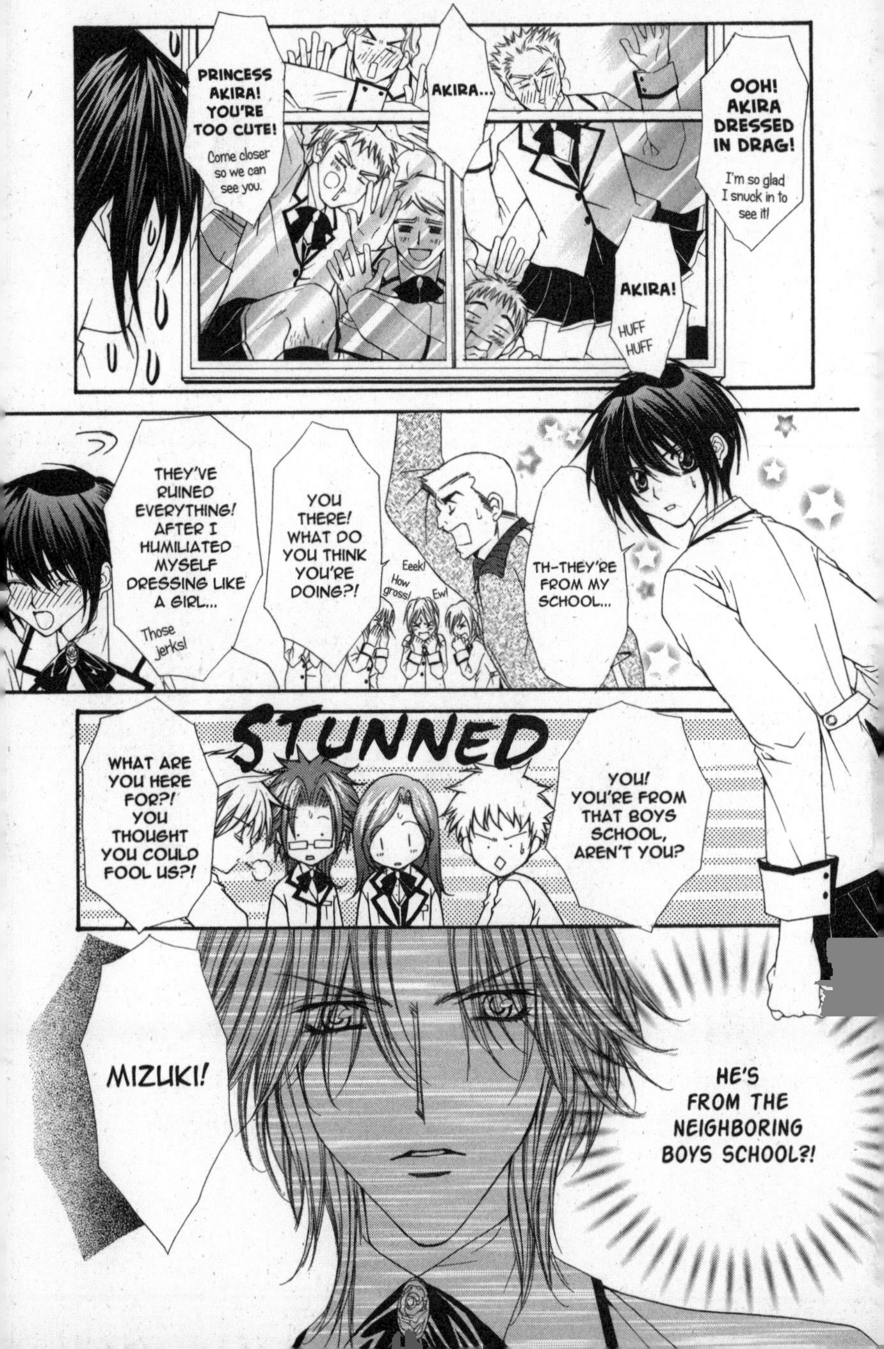
OOH! AKIRA DRESSED IN DRAG!
I'm so glad I snuck in to see it!
AKIRA...
PRINCESS AKIRA! YOU'RE TOO CUTE!
Come closer so we can see you.
AKIRA!
HUFF HUFF
TH-THEY'RE FROM MY SCHOOL...
YOU THERE! WHAT DO YOU THINK YOU'RE DOING?!
Eeek!
Ew!
How gross!
THEY'VE RUINED EVERYTHING! AFTER I HUMILIATED MYSELF DRESSING LIKE A GIRL...
Those jerks!
YOU! YOU'RE FROM THAT BOYS SCHOOL, AREN'T YOU?
STUNNED
WHAT ARE YOU HERE FOR?! YOU THOUGHT YOU COULD FOOL US?!
HE'S FROM THE NEIGHBORING BOYS SCHOOL?!
MIZUKI!

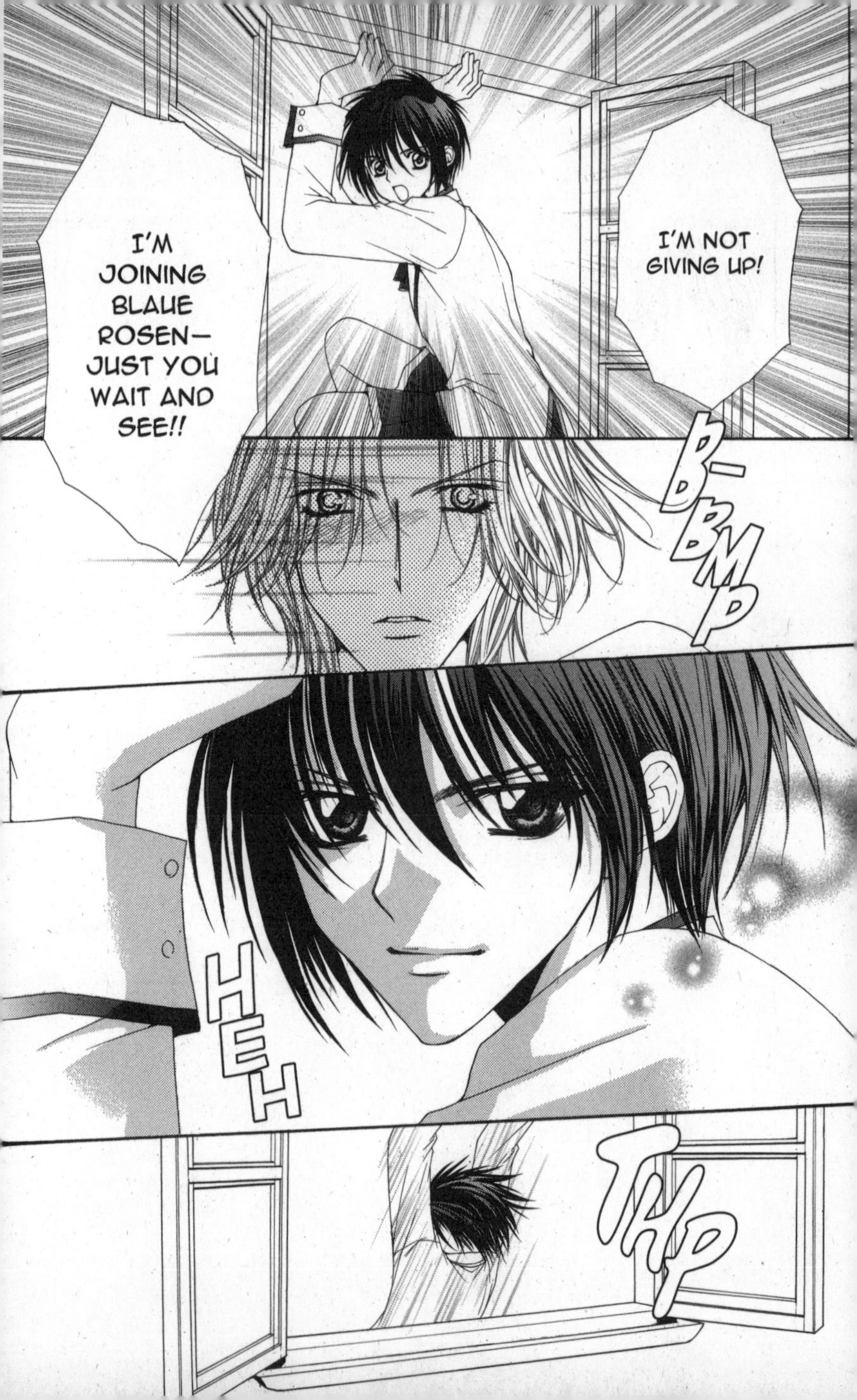
I'M NOT GIVING UP!
I'M JOINING BLAUE ROSEN—JUST YOU WAIT AND SEE!!
B-BMP
HEH
THP

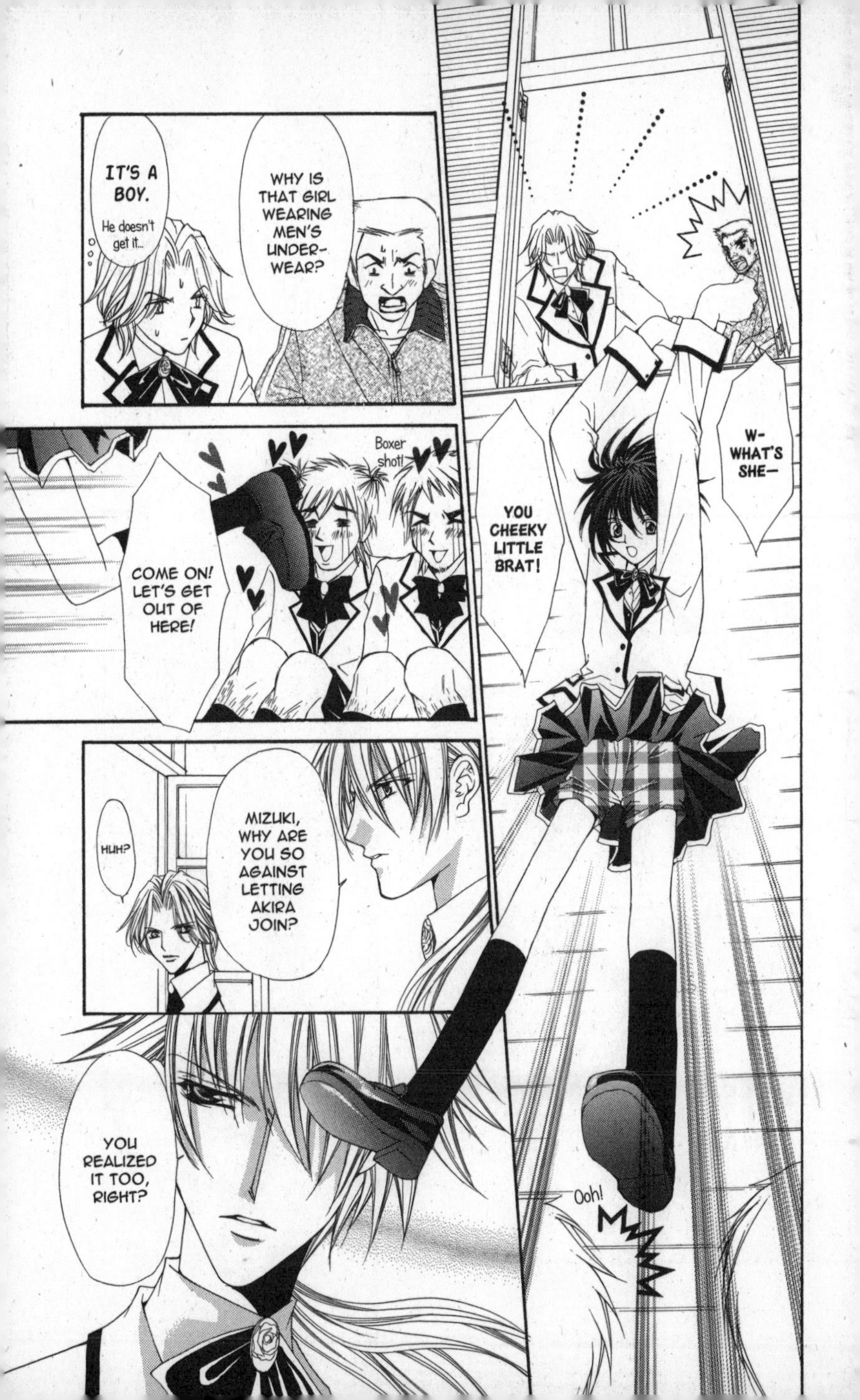

W-WHAT'S SHE—
YOU CHEEKY LITTLE BRAT!
Ooh!
WHY IS THAT GIRL WEARING MEN'S UNDER-WEAR?
IT'S A BOY.
He doesn't get it...
Boxer shot!
COME ON! LET'S GET OUT OF HERE!
MIZUKI, WHY ARE YOU SO AGAINST LETTING AKIRA JOIN?
HUH?
YOU REALIZED IT TOO, RIGHT?

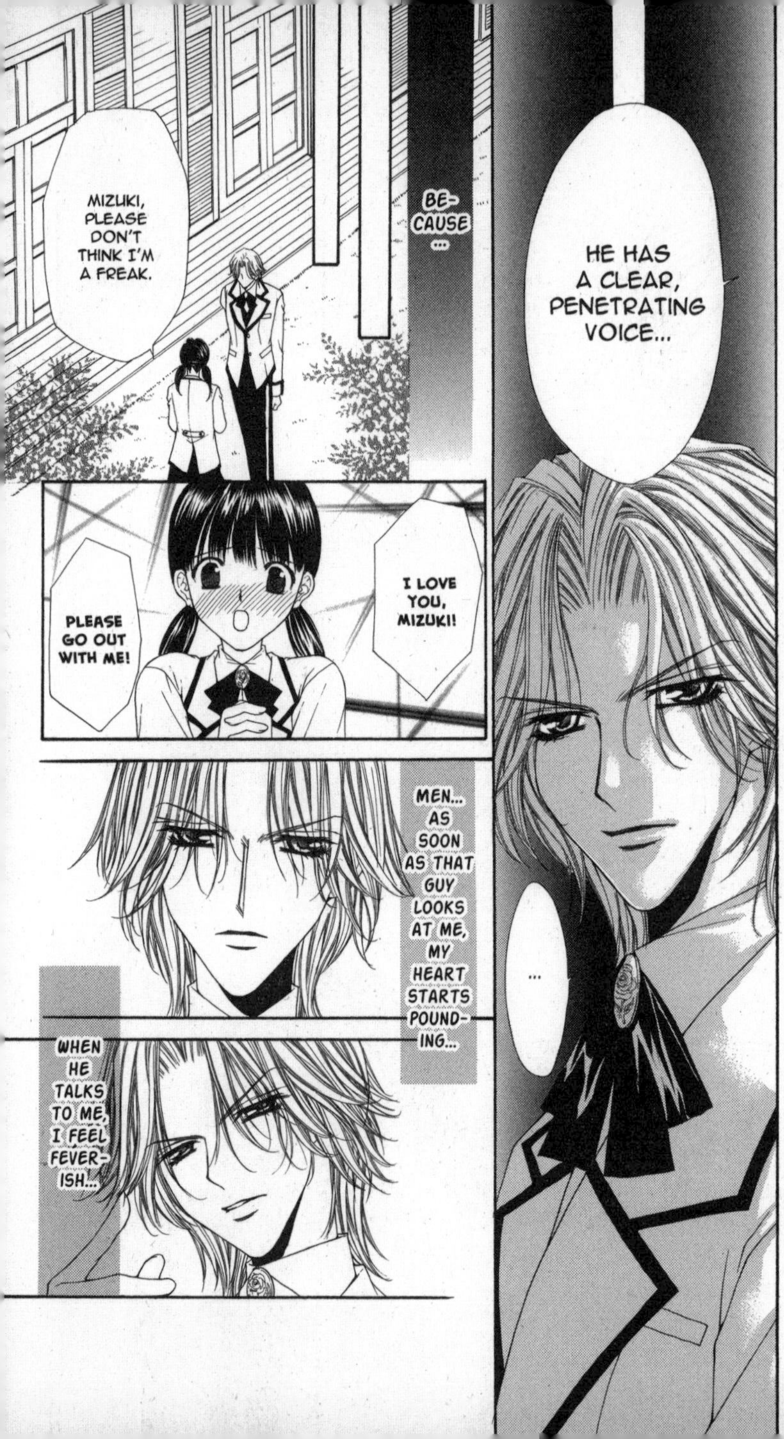
HE HAS A CLEAR, PENETRATING VOICE...
...
BE-CAUSE...
MIZUKI, PLEASE DON'T THINK I'M A FREAK.
I LOVE YOU, MIZUKI!
PLEASE GO OUT WITH ME!
MEN... AS SOON AS THAT GUY LOOKS AT ME, MY HEART STARTS POUNDING...
WHEN HE TALKS TO ME, I FEEL FEVERISH...

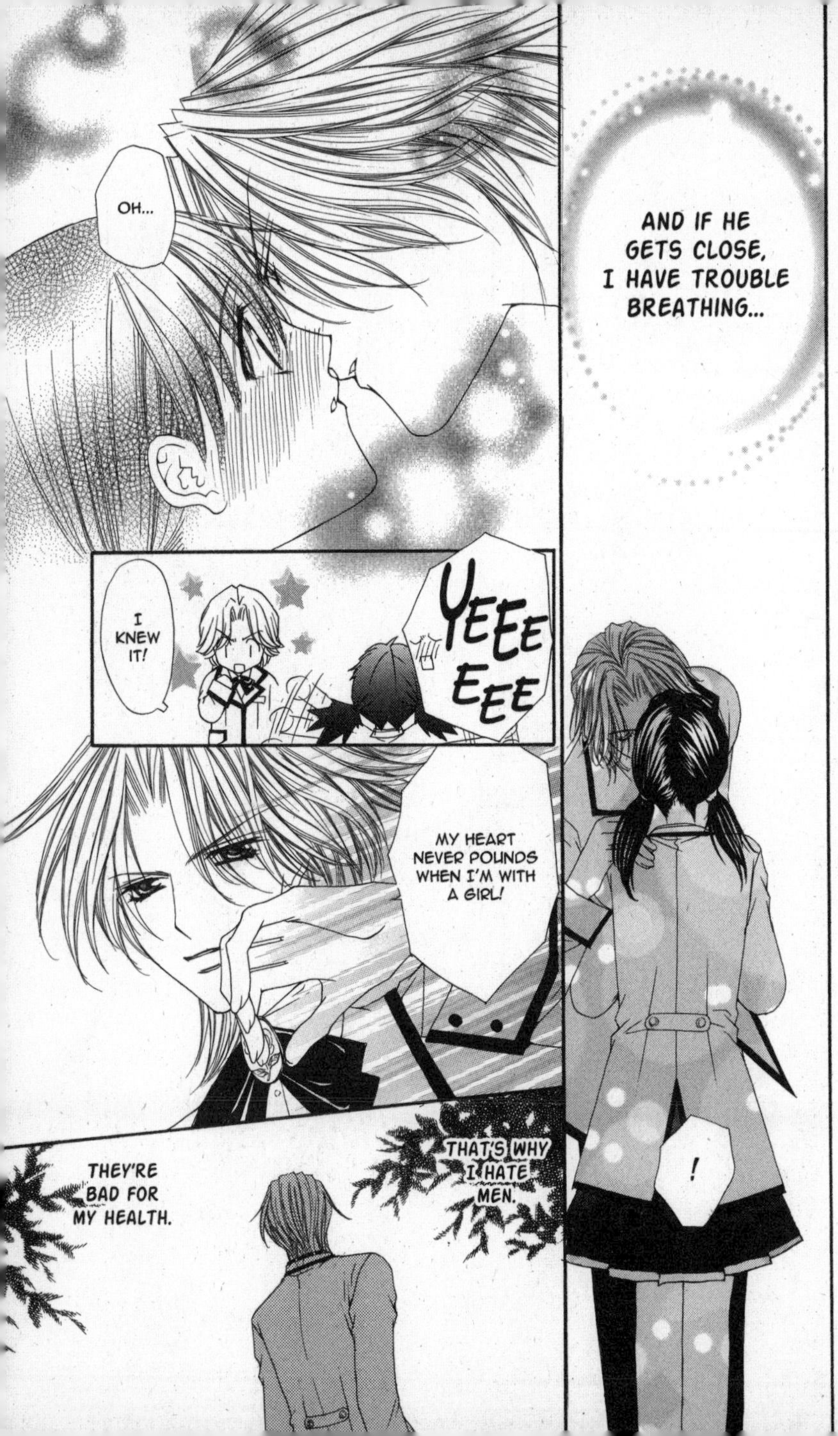
AND IF HE GETS CLOSE, I HAVE TROUBLE BREATHING...
!
OH...
YEEEEEE
I KNEW IT!
MY HEART NEVER POUNDS WHEN I'M WITH A GIRL!
THAT'S WHY I HATE MEN.
THEY'RE BAD FOR MY HEALTH.

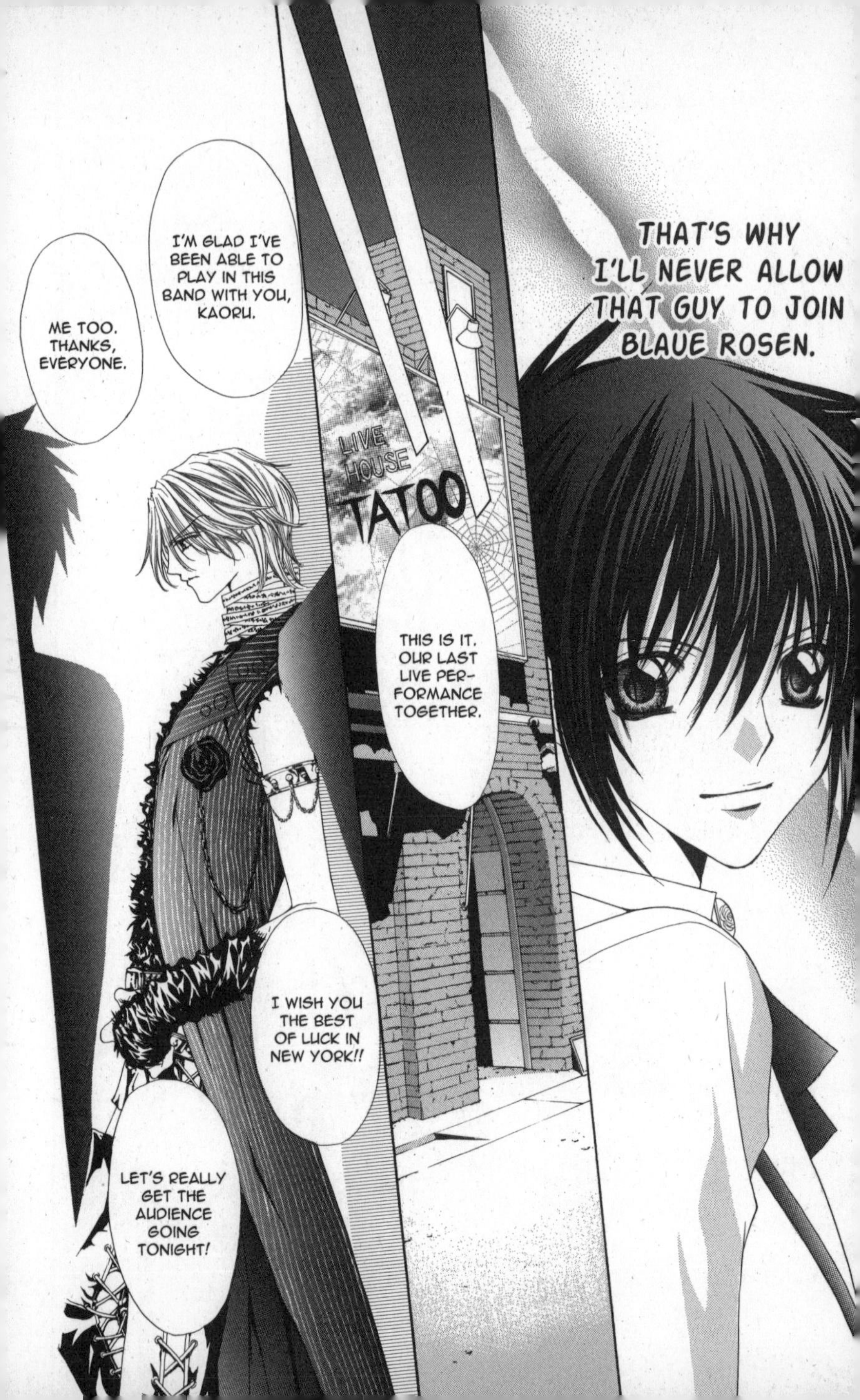
THAT'S WHY I'LL NEVER ALLOW THAT GUY TO JOIN BLAUE ROSEN.
LIVE HOUSE TATOO
THIS IS IT. OUR LAST LIVE PER-FORMANCE TOGETHER.
I'M GLAD I'VE BEEN ABLE TO PLAY IN THIS BAND WITH YOU, KAORU.
ME TOO. THANKS, EVERYONE.
I WISH YOU THE BEST OF LUCK IN NEW YORK!!
LET'S REALLY GET THE AUDIENCE GOING TONIGHT!

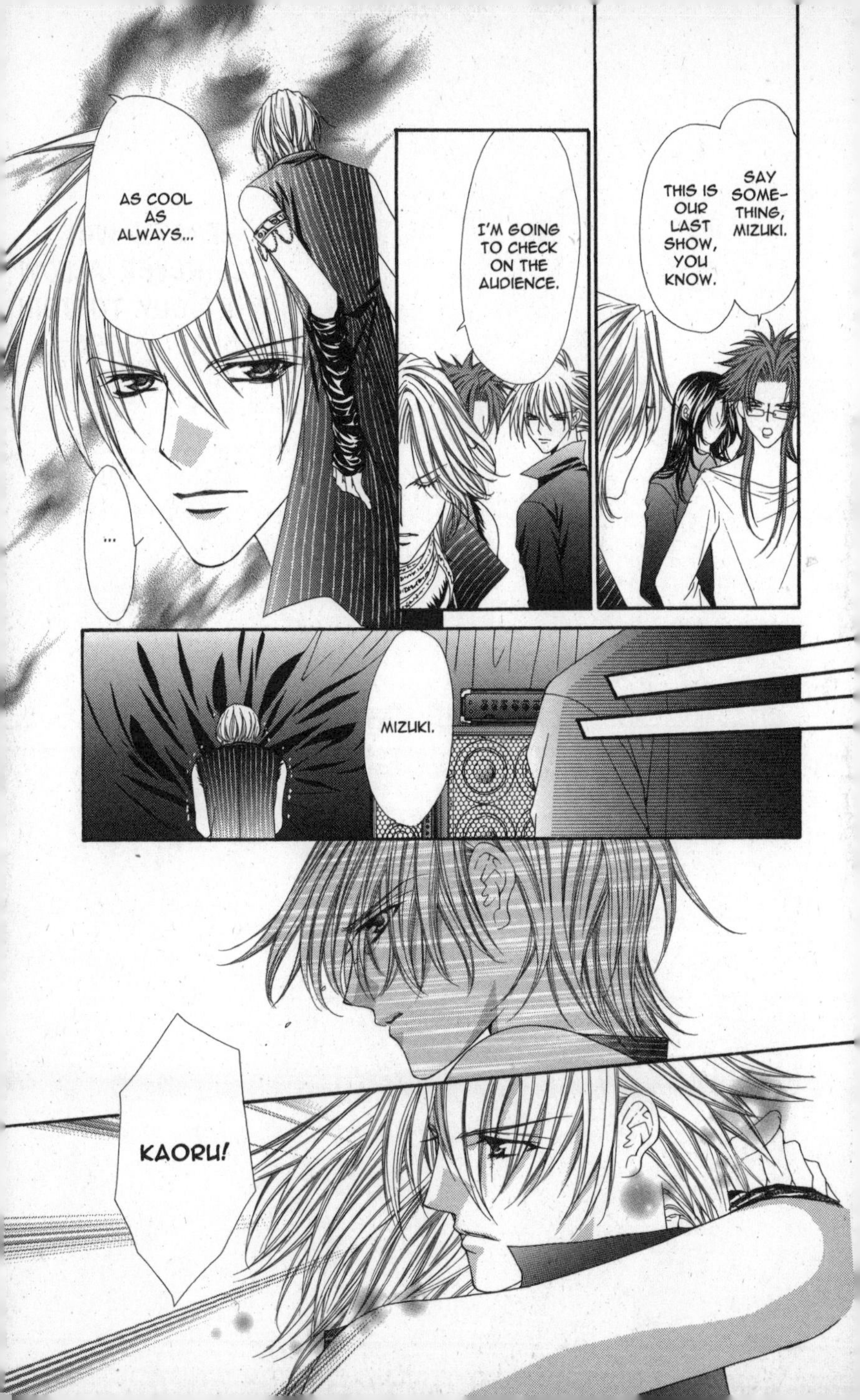
SAY SOME-THING, MIZUKI.
THIS IS OUR LAST SHOW, YOU KNOW.
I'M GOING TO CHECK ON THE AUDIENCE.
AS COOL AS ALWAYS...
...
MIZUKI.
KAORU!

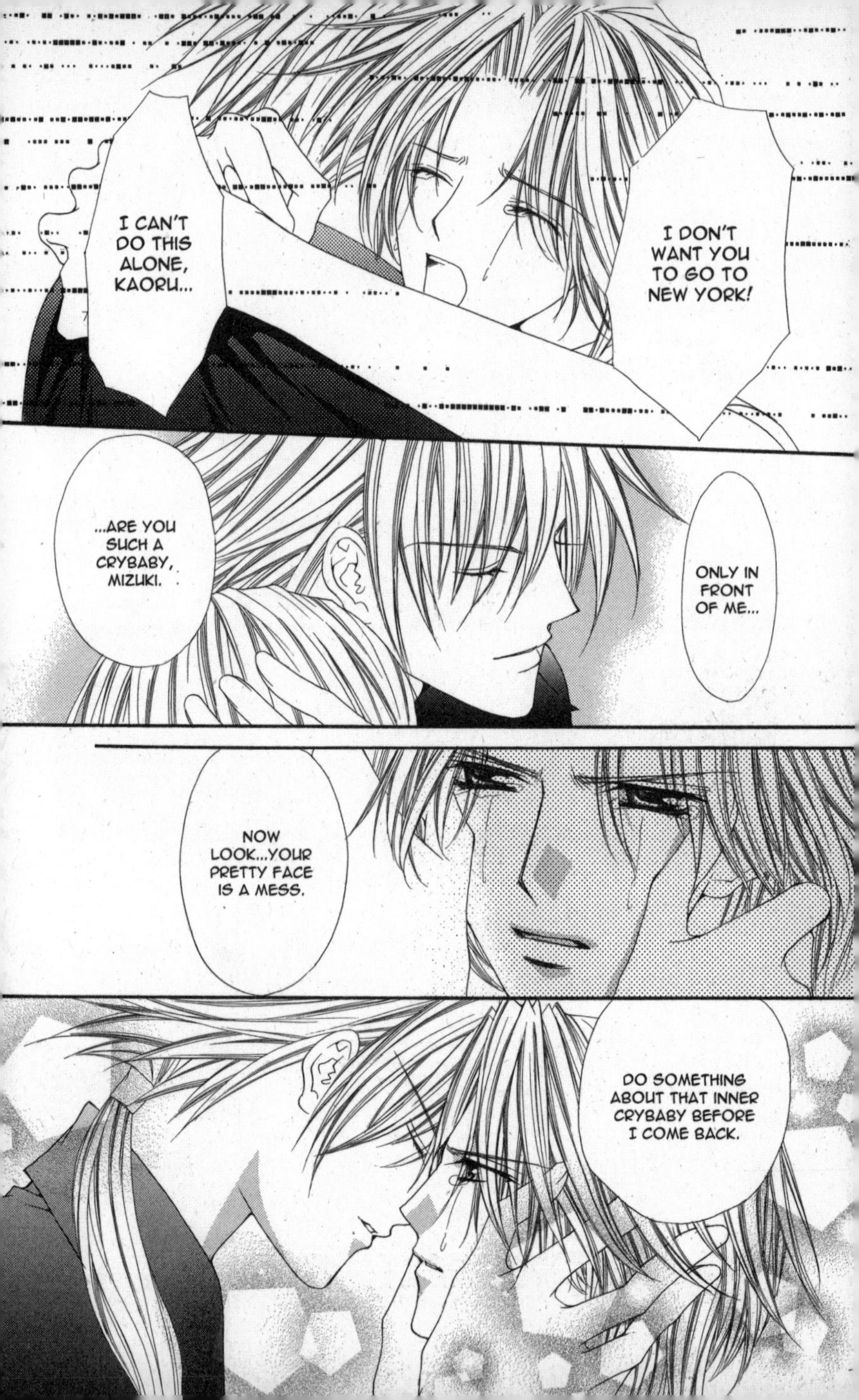
I DON'T WANT YOU TO GO TO NEW YORK!
I CAN'T DO THIS ALONE, KAORU...
ONLY IN FRONT OF ME...
...ARE YOU SUCH A CRYBABY, MIZUKI.
NOW LOOK...YOUR PRETTY FACE IS A MESS.
DO SOMETHING ABOUT THAT INNER CRYBABY BEFORE I COME BACK.

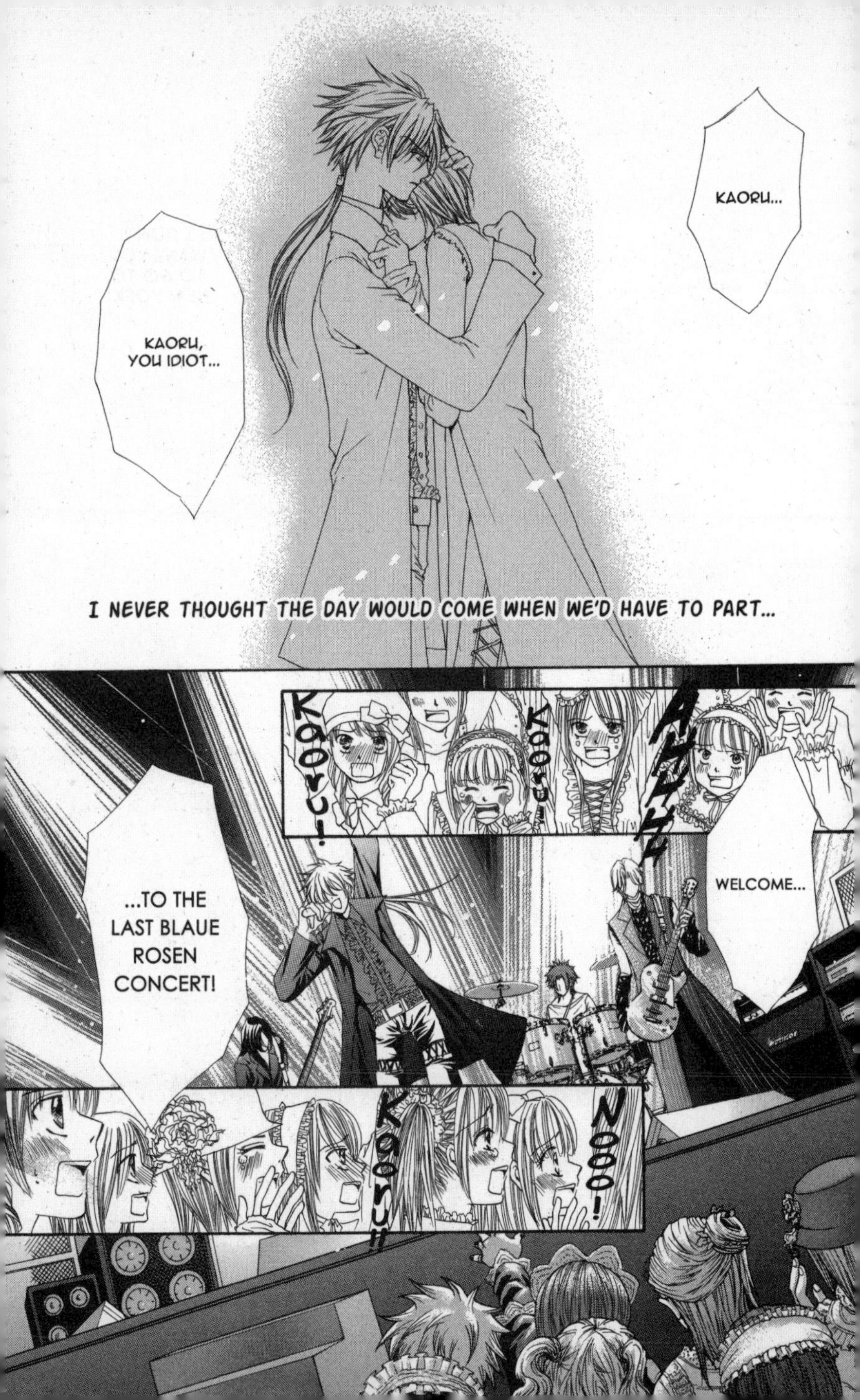
KAORU...
KAORU, YOU IDIOT...
I NEVER THOUGHT THE DAY WOULD COME WHEN WE'D HAVE TO PART...
AHHHH
Kaoru...
Kaoru!
WELCOME...
...TO THE LAST BLAUE ROSEN CONCERT!
Nooo!
Kaoru!!

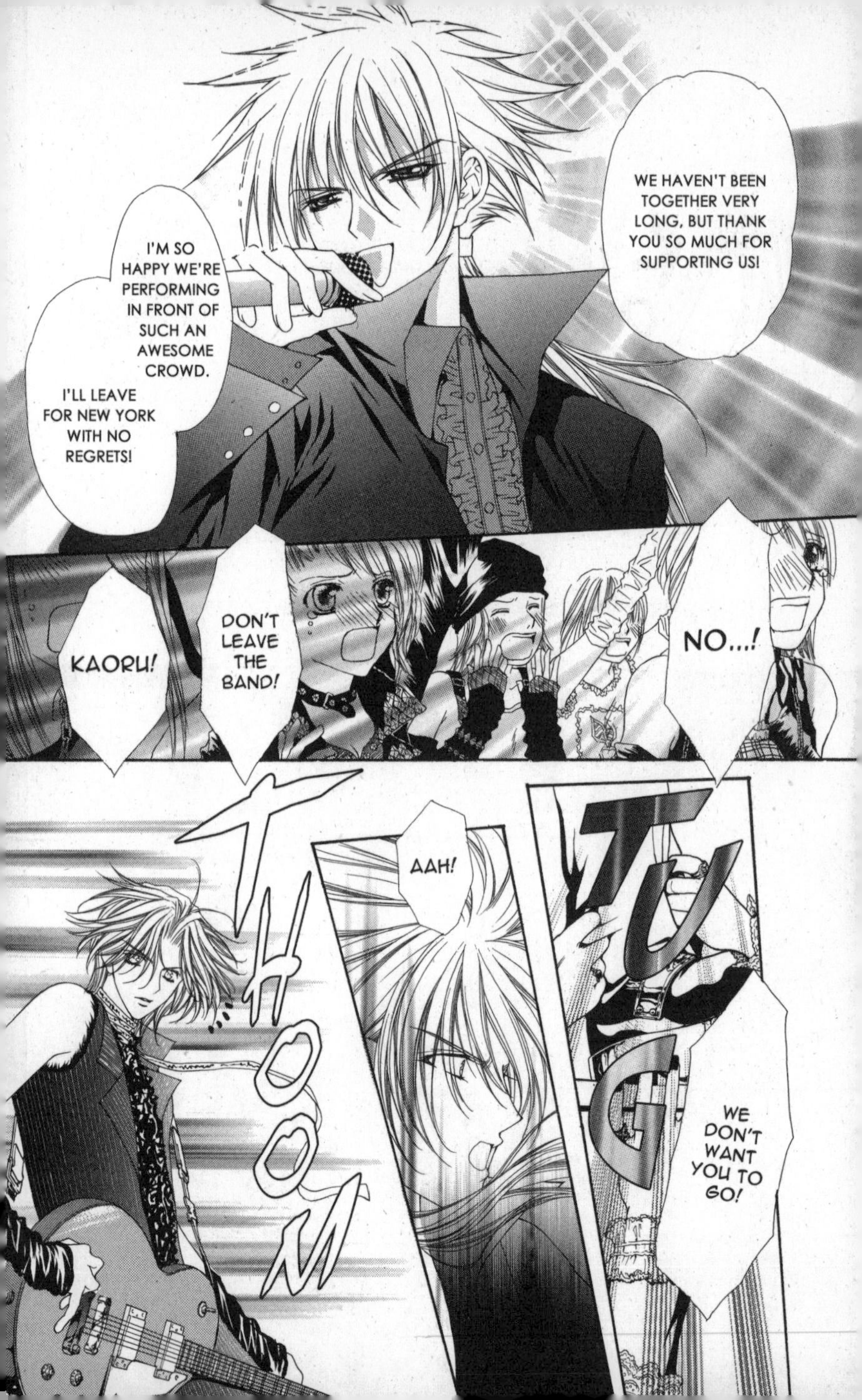
WE HAVEN'T BEEN TOGETHER VERY LONG, BUT THANK YOU SO MUCH FOR SUPPORTING US!
I'M SO HAPPY WE'RE PERFORMING IN FRONT OF SUCH AN AWESOME CROWD.
I'LL LEAVE FOR NEW YORK WITH NO REGRETS!
NO...!
DON'T LEAVE THE BAND!
KAORU!
TUG
WE DON'T WANT YOU TO GO!
AAH!
THOOM

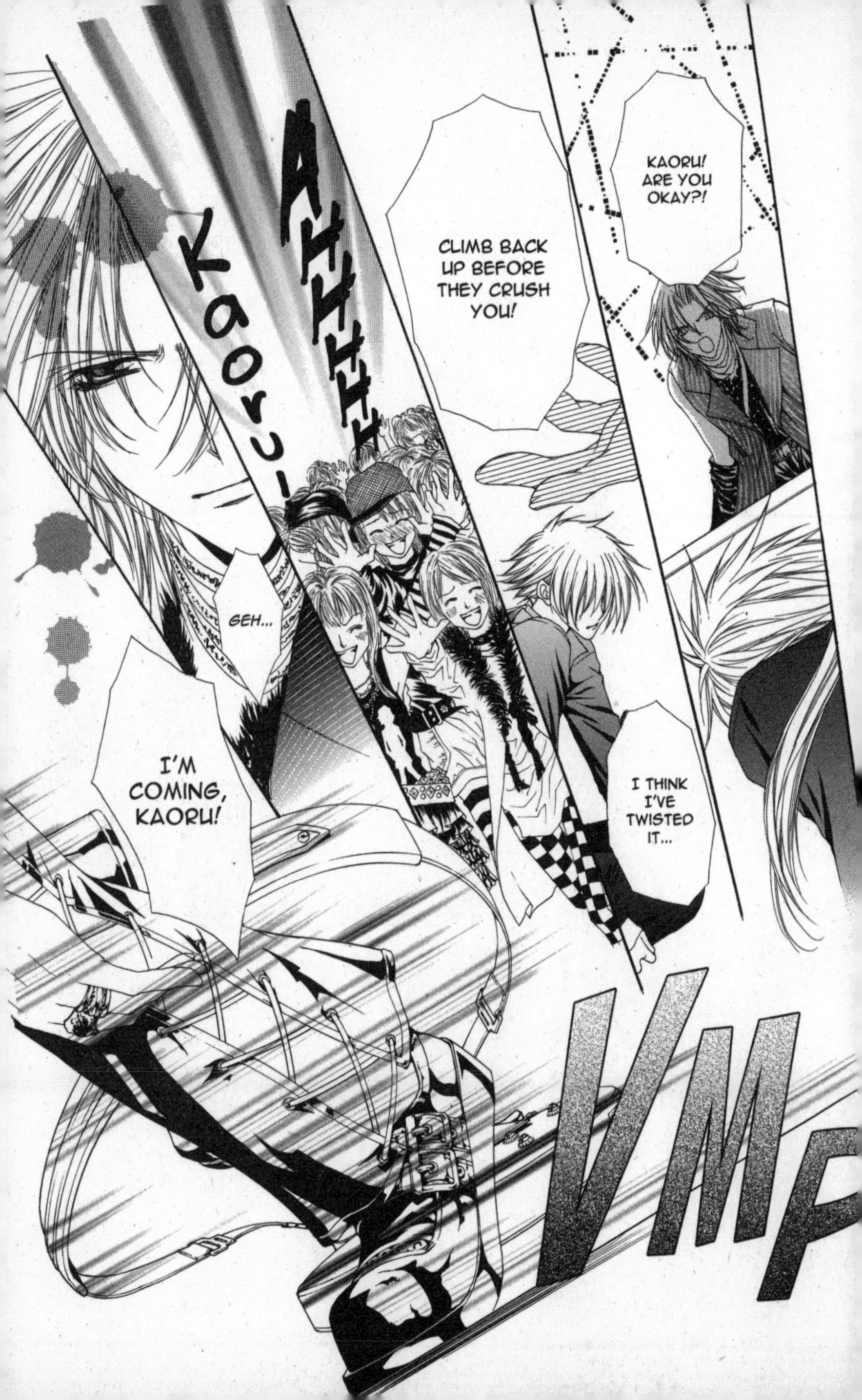
KAORU! ARE YOU OKAY?!
CLIMB BACK UP BEFORE THEY CRUSH YOU!
I THINK I'VE TWISTED IT...
AHHHHHH
Kaoru!
GEH...
I'M COMING, KAORU!
VMF

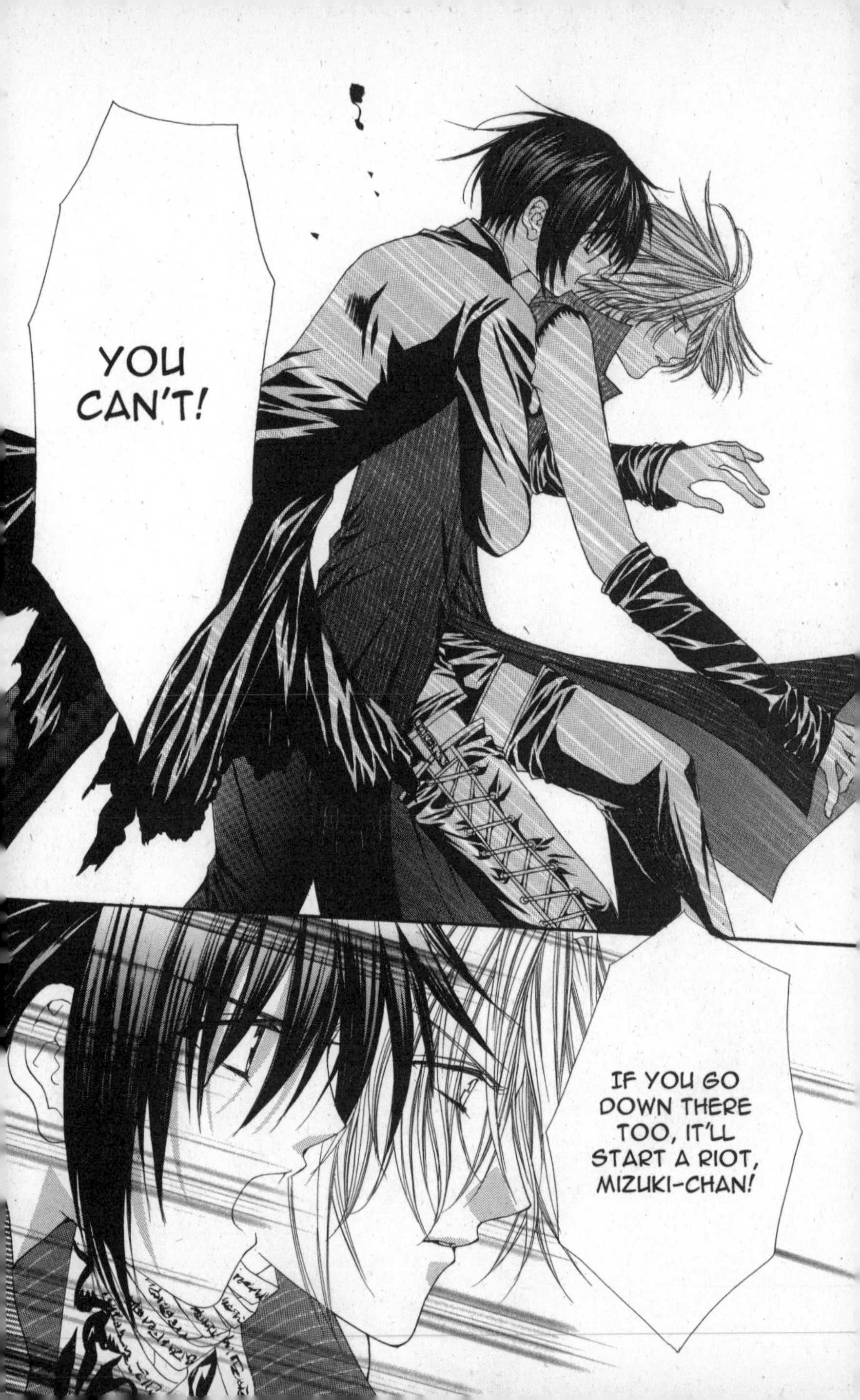
YOU CAN'T!
IF YOU GO DOWN THERE TOO, IT'LL START A RIOT, MIZUKI-CHAN!

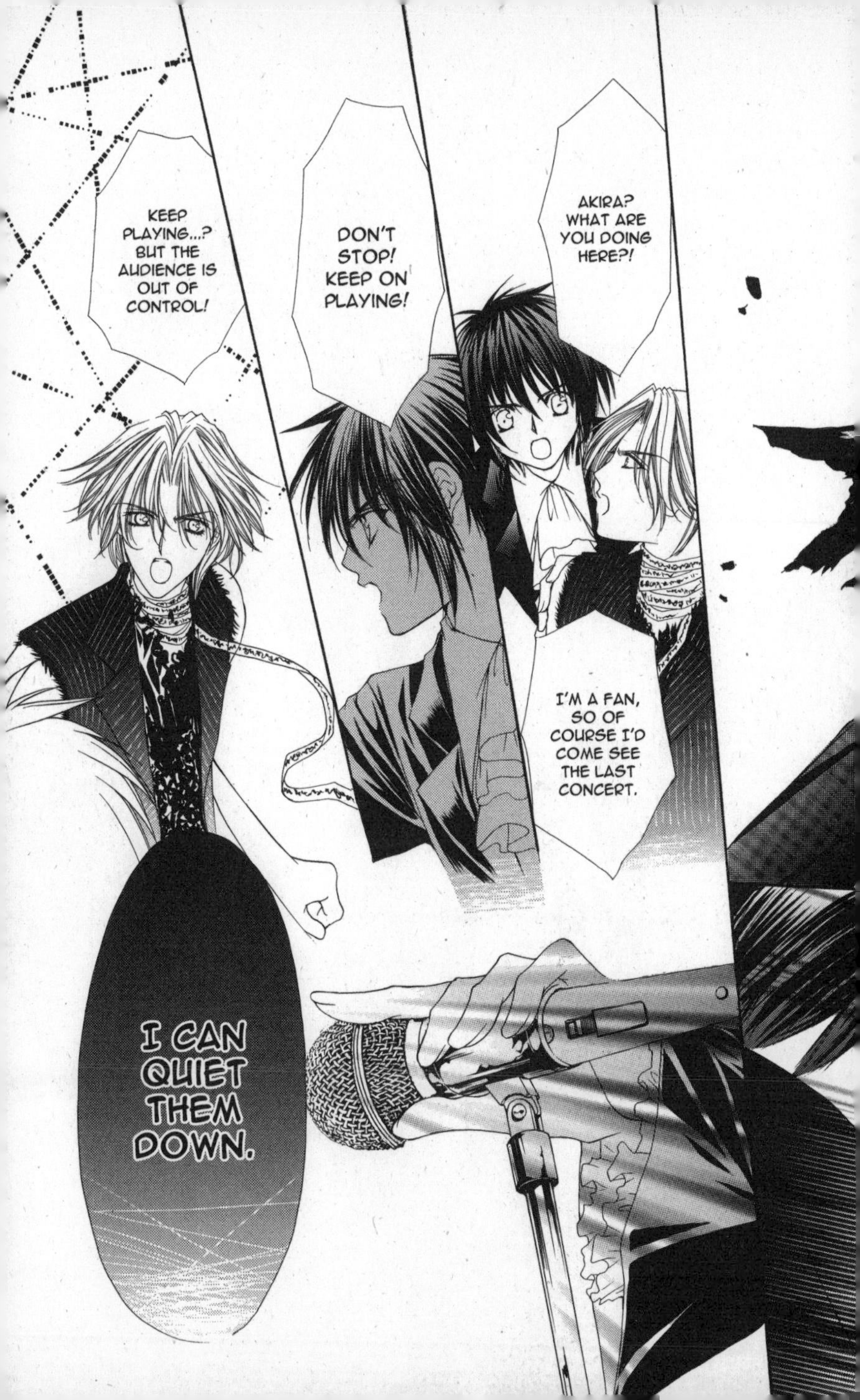
AKIRA? WHAT ARE YOU DOING HERE?!
I'M A FAN, SO OF COURSE I'D COME SEE THE LAST CONCERT.
DON'T STOP! KEEP ON PLAYING!
KEEP PLAYING...? BUT THE AUDIENCE IS OUT OF CONTROL!
I CAN QUIET THEM DOWN.

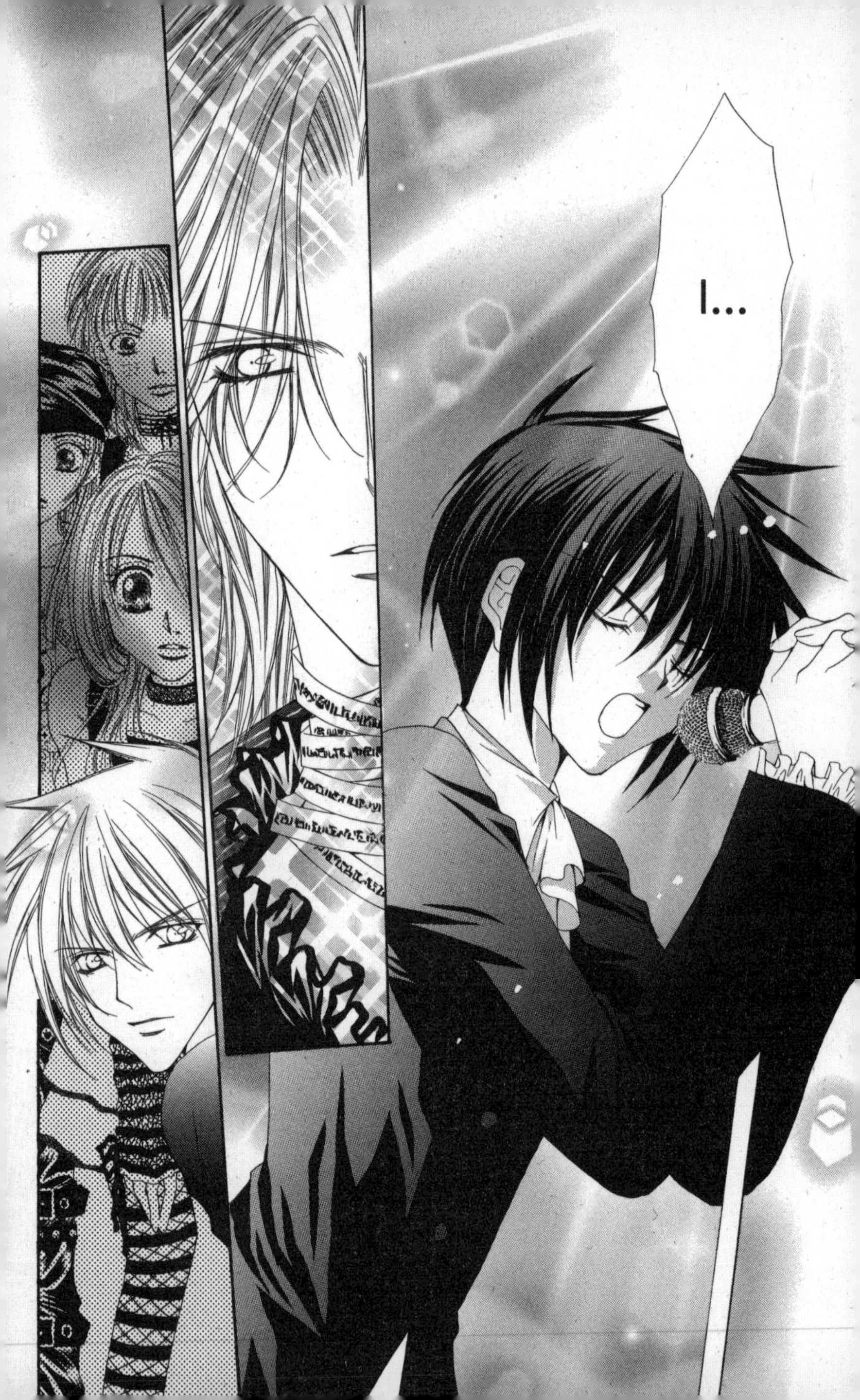
I...

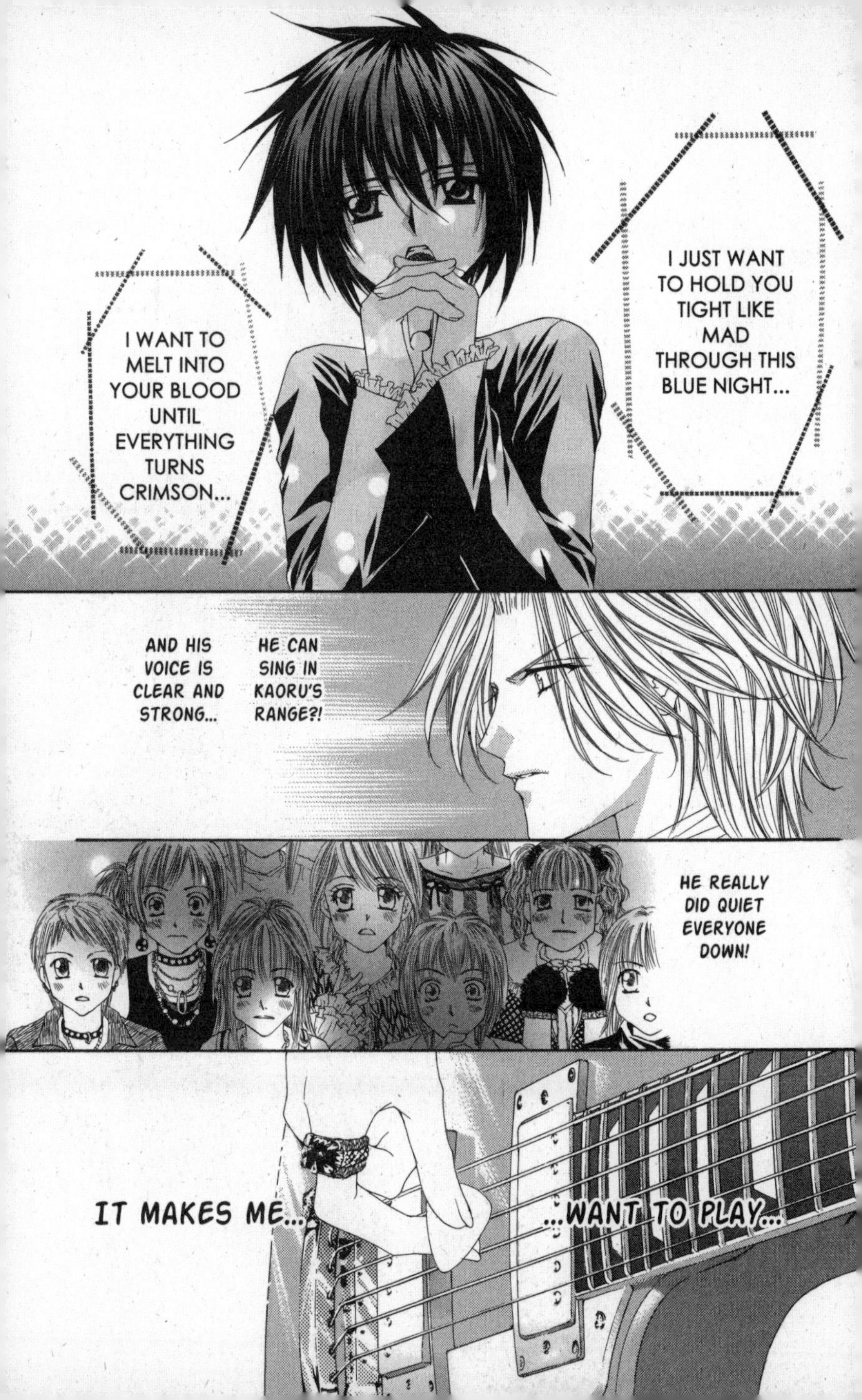
I JUST WANT TO HOLD YOU TIGHT LIKE MAD THROUGH THIS BLUE NIGHT...
I WANT TO MELT INTO YOUR BLOOD UNTIL EVERYTHING TURNS CRIMSON...
HE CAN SING IN KAORU'S RANGE?!
AND HIS VOICE IS CLEAR AND STRONG...
HE REALLY DID QUIET EVERYONE DOWN!
IT MAKES ME...
...WANT TO PLAY...

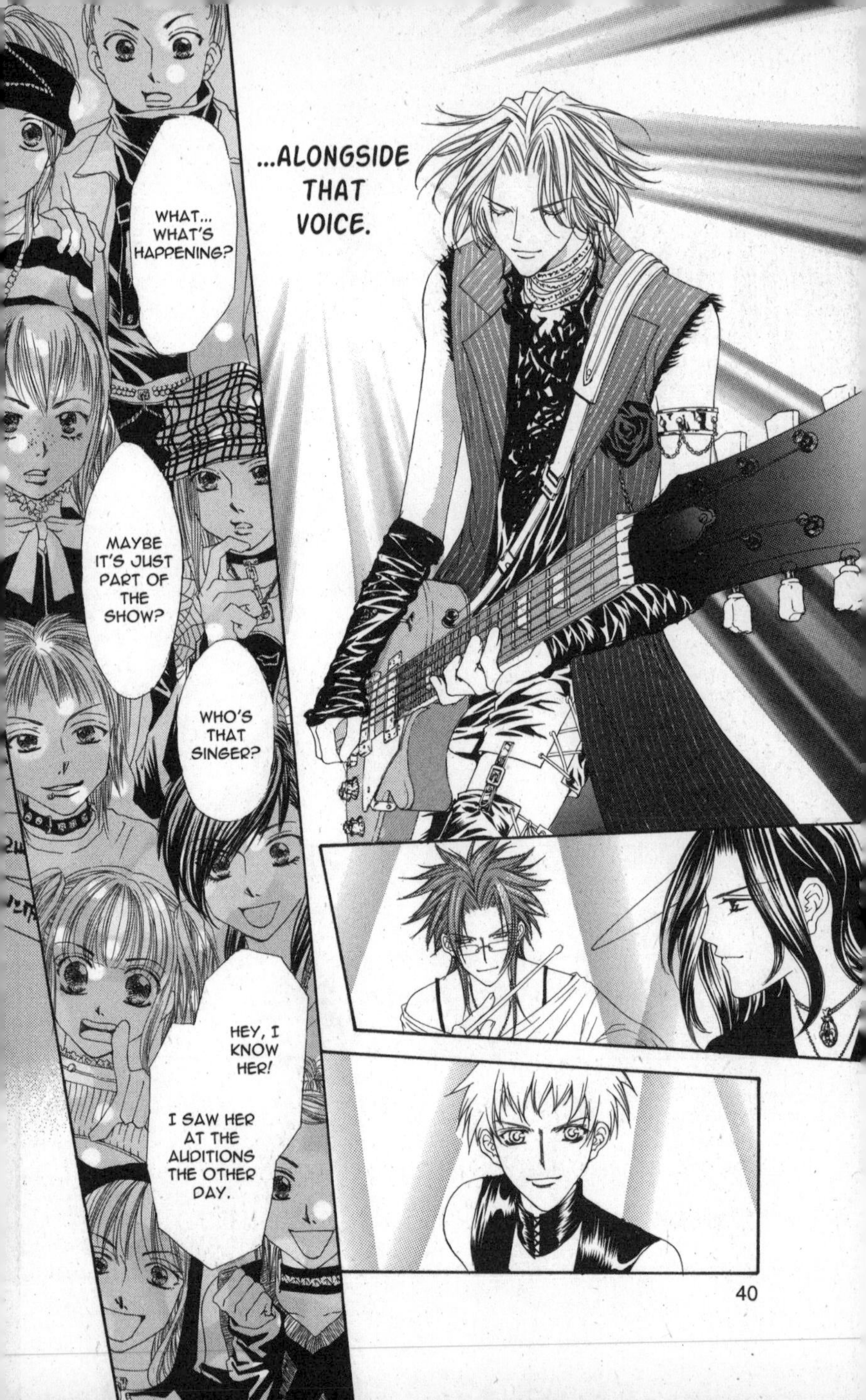
...ALONGSIDE THAT VOICE.
WHAT... WHAT'S HAPPENING?
MAYBE IT'S JUST PART OF THE SHOW?
WHO'S THAT SINGER?
HEY, I KNOW HER!
I SAW HER AT THE AUDITIONS THE OTHER DAY.

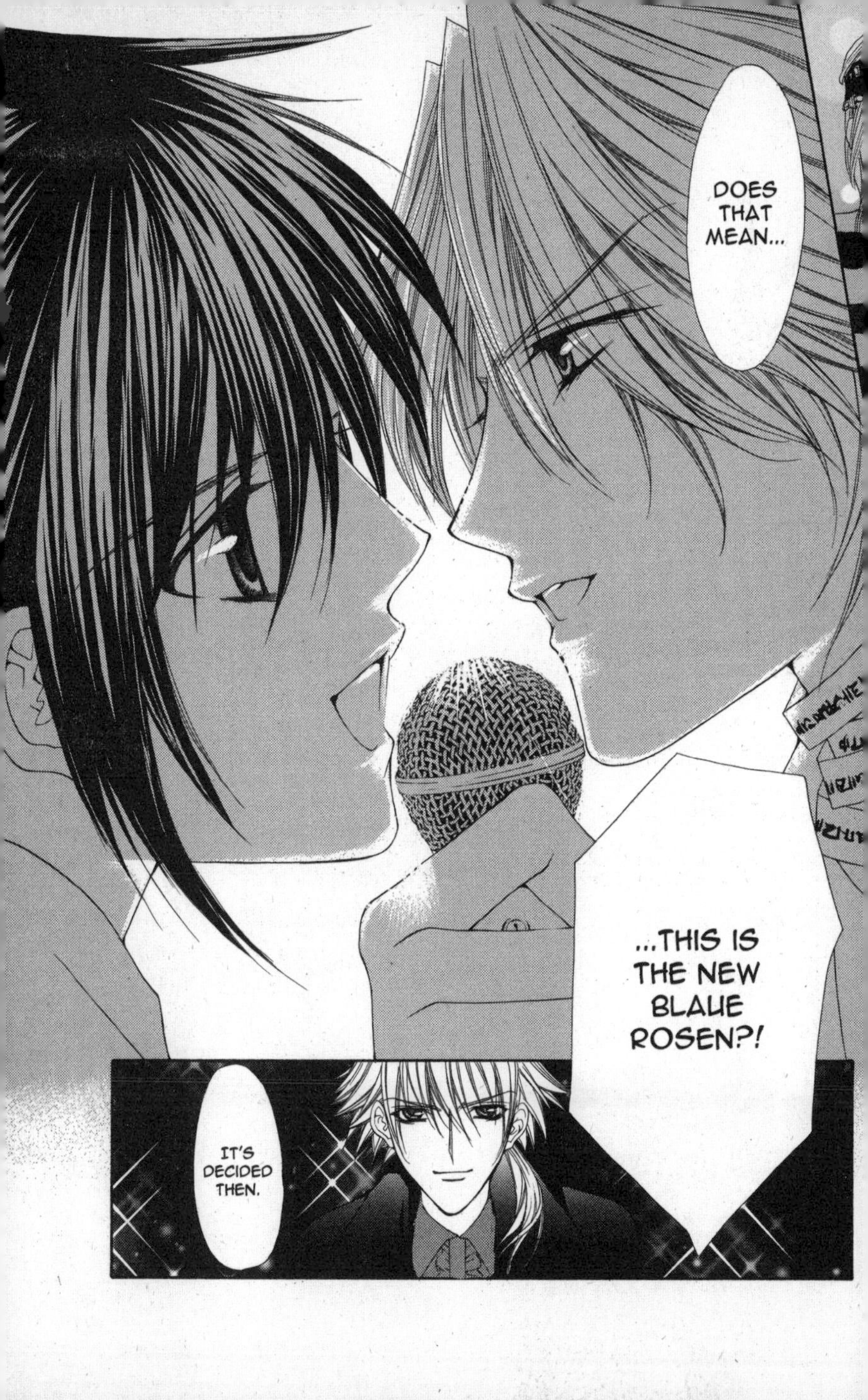
DOES THAT MEAN...
...THIS IS THE NEW BLAUE ROSEN?!
IT'S DECIDED THEN.

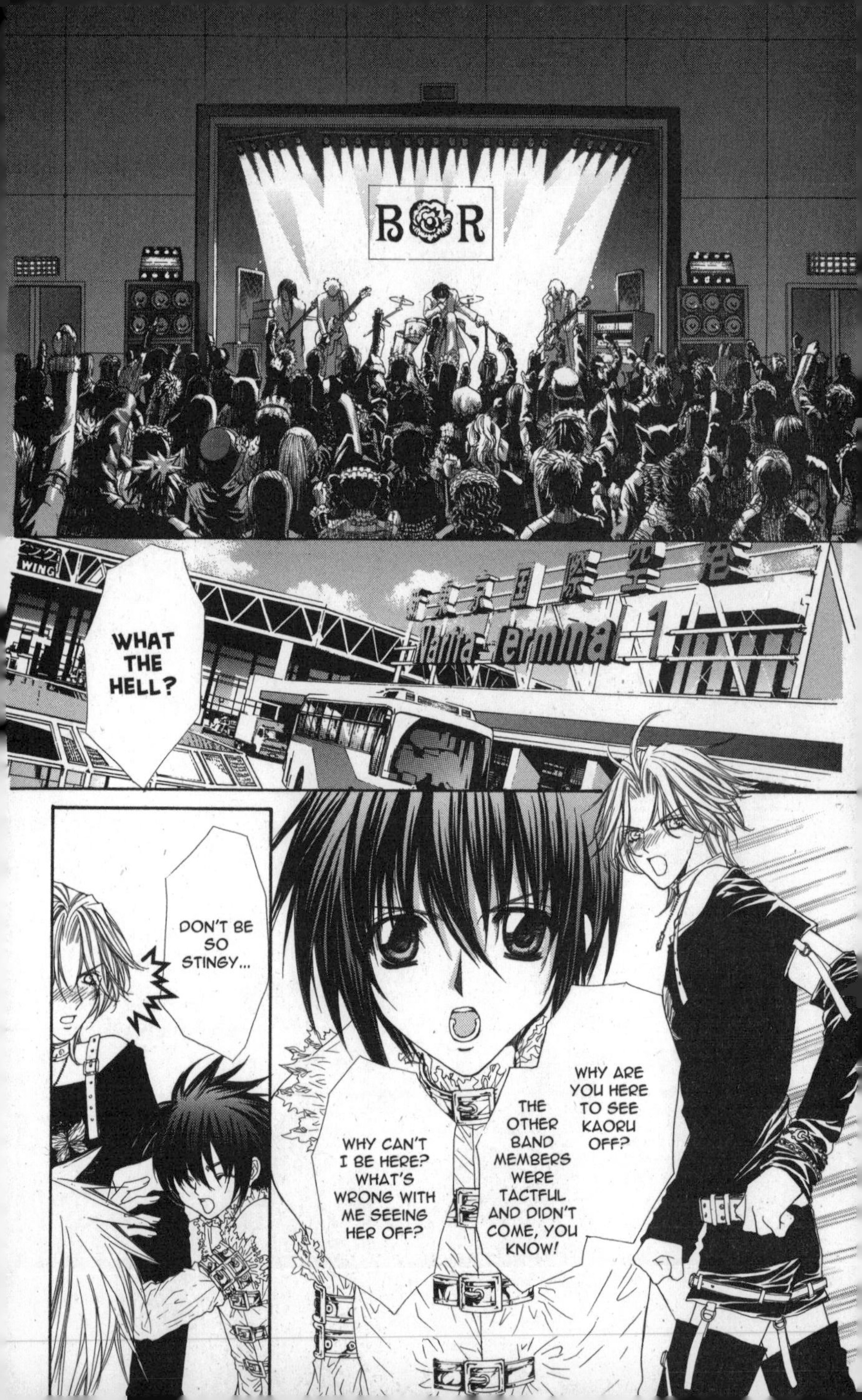
WING
WHAT THE HELL?
WHY ARE YOU HERE TO SEE KAORU OFF?
THE OTHER BAND MEMBERS WERE TACTFUL AND DIDN'T COME, YOU KNOW!
WHY CAN'T I BE HERE? WHAT'S WRONG WITH ME SEEING HER OFF?
DON'T BE SO STINGY...

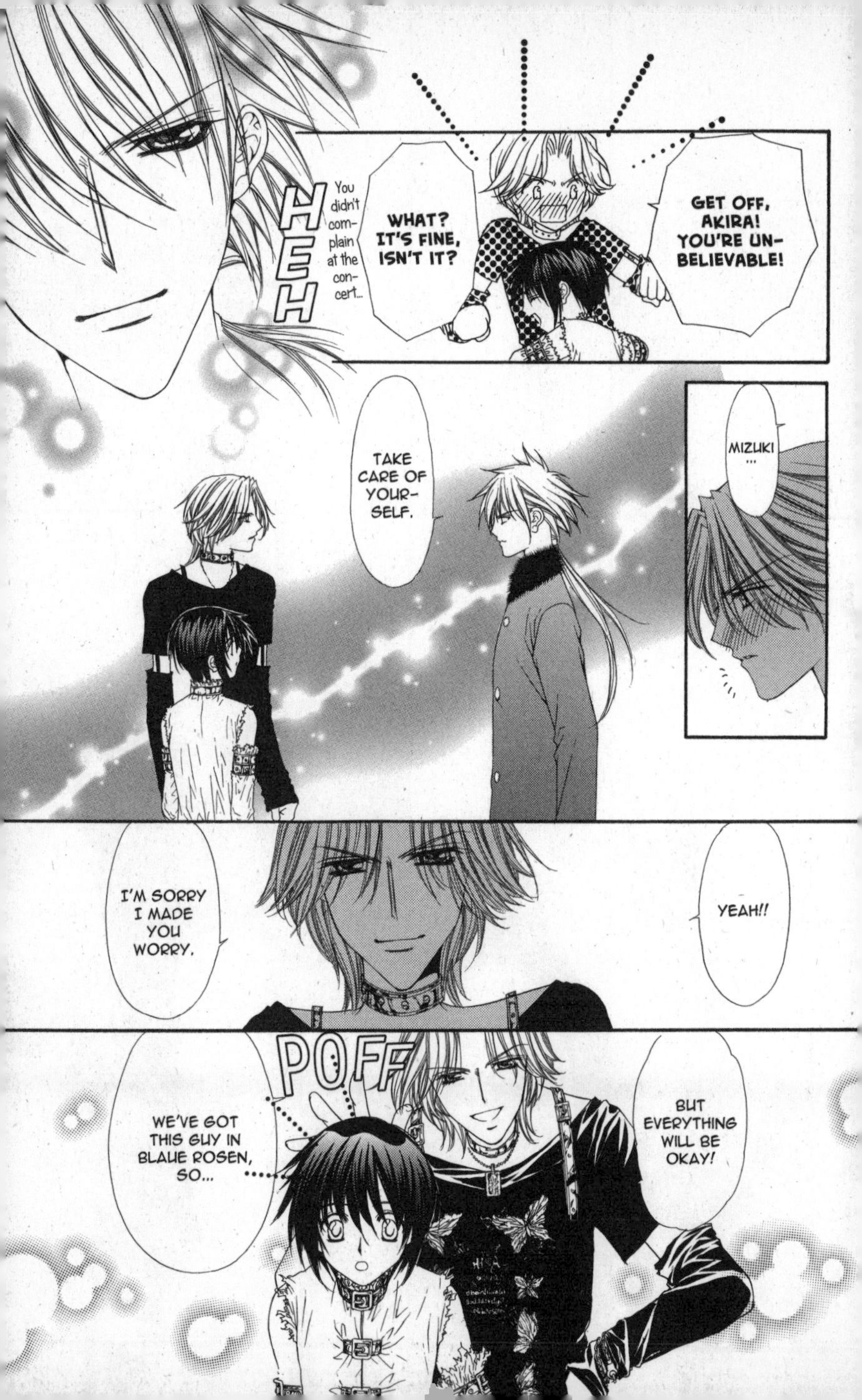
GET OFF, AKIRA! YOU'RE UN-BELIEVABLE!
WHAT? IT'S FINE, ISN'T IT?
You didn't com-plain at the con-cert...
HEH
MIZUKI ...
TAKE CARE OF YOUR-SELF.
YEAH!!
I'M SORRY I MADE YOU WORRY.
BUT EVERYTHING WILL BE OKAY!
POFF
WE'VE GOT THIS GUY IN BLAUE ROSEN, SO...

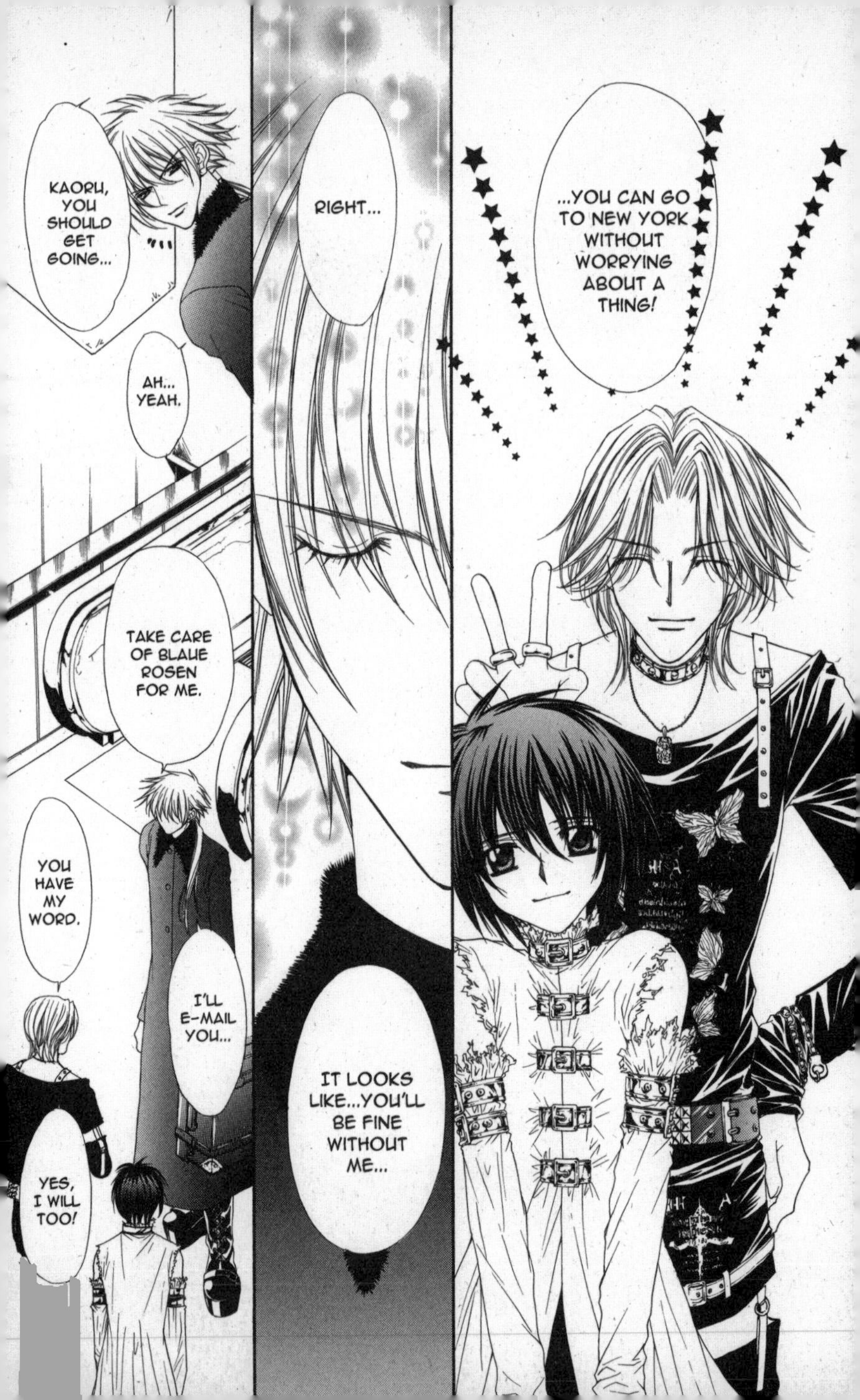
...YOU CAN GO TO NEW YORK WITHOUT WORRYING ABOUT A THING!
RIGHT...
IT LOOKS LIKE...YOU'LL BE FINE WITHOUT ME...
KAORU, YOU SHOULD GET GOING...
AH... YEAH.
TAKE CARE OF BLAUE ROSEN FOR ME.
YOU HAVE MY WORD.
I'LL E-MAIL YOU...
YES, I WILL TOO!

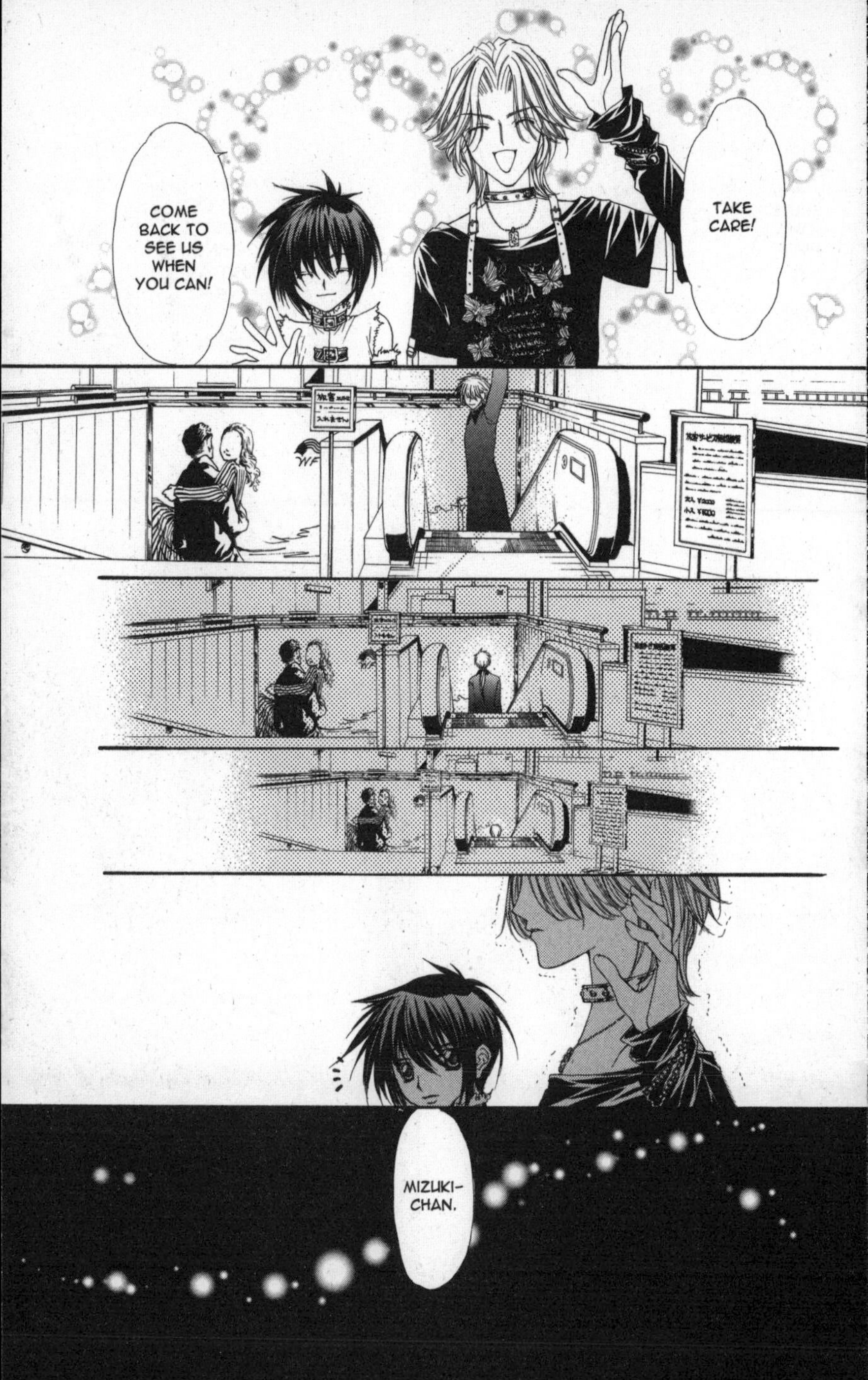
TAKE CARE!
COME BACK TO SEE US WHEN YOU CAN!
MIZUKI-CHAN.

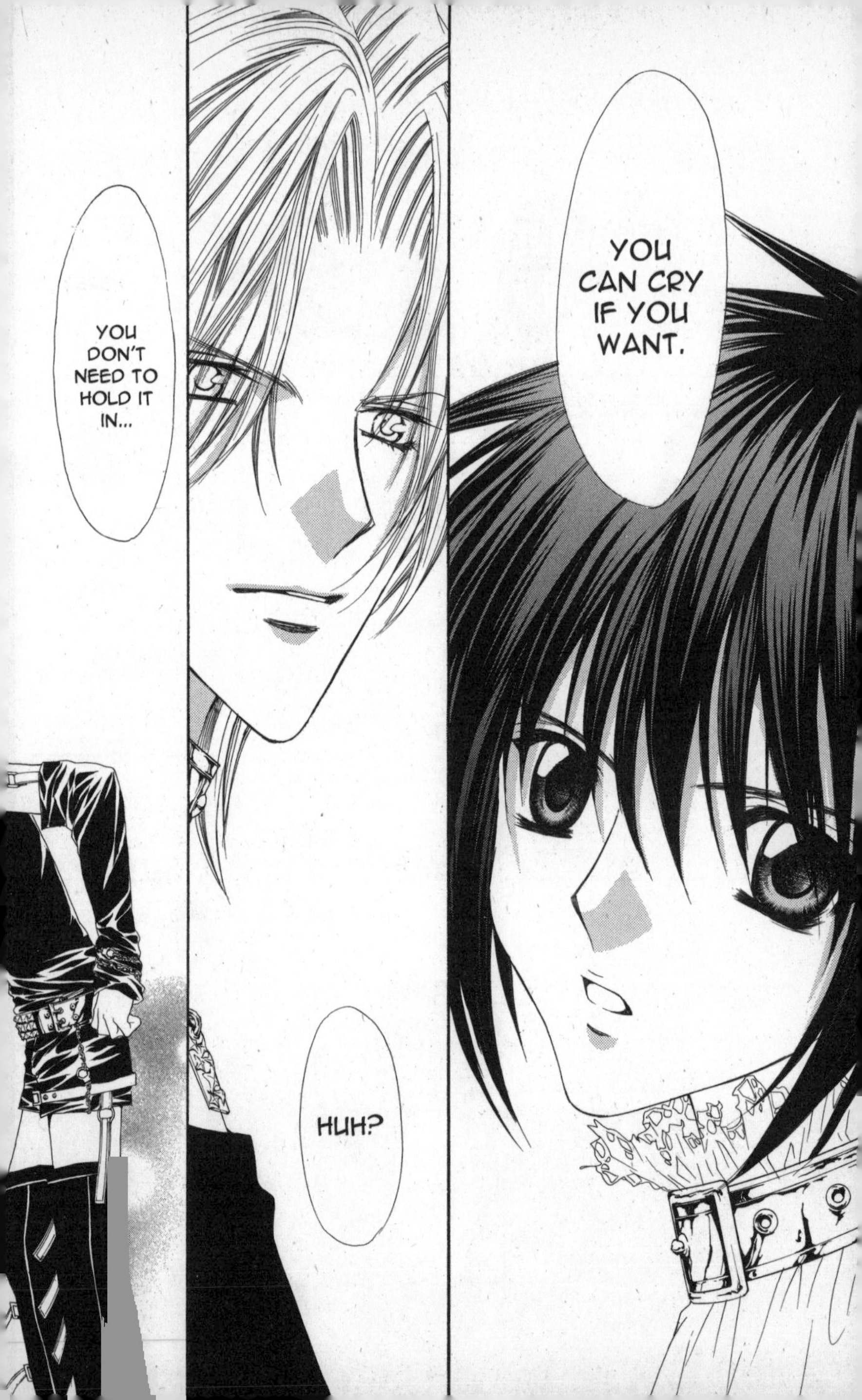
YOU CAN CRY IF YOU WANT.
HUH?
YOU DON'T NEED TO HOLD IT IN...

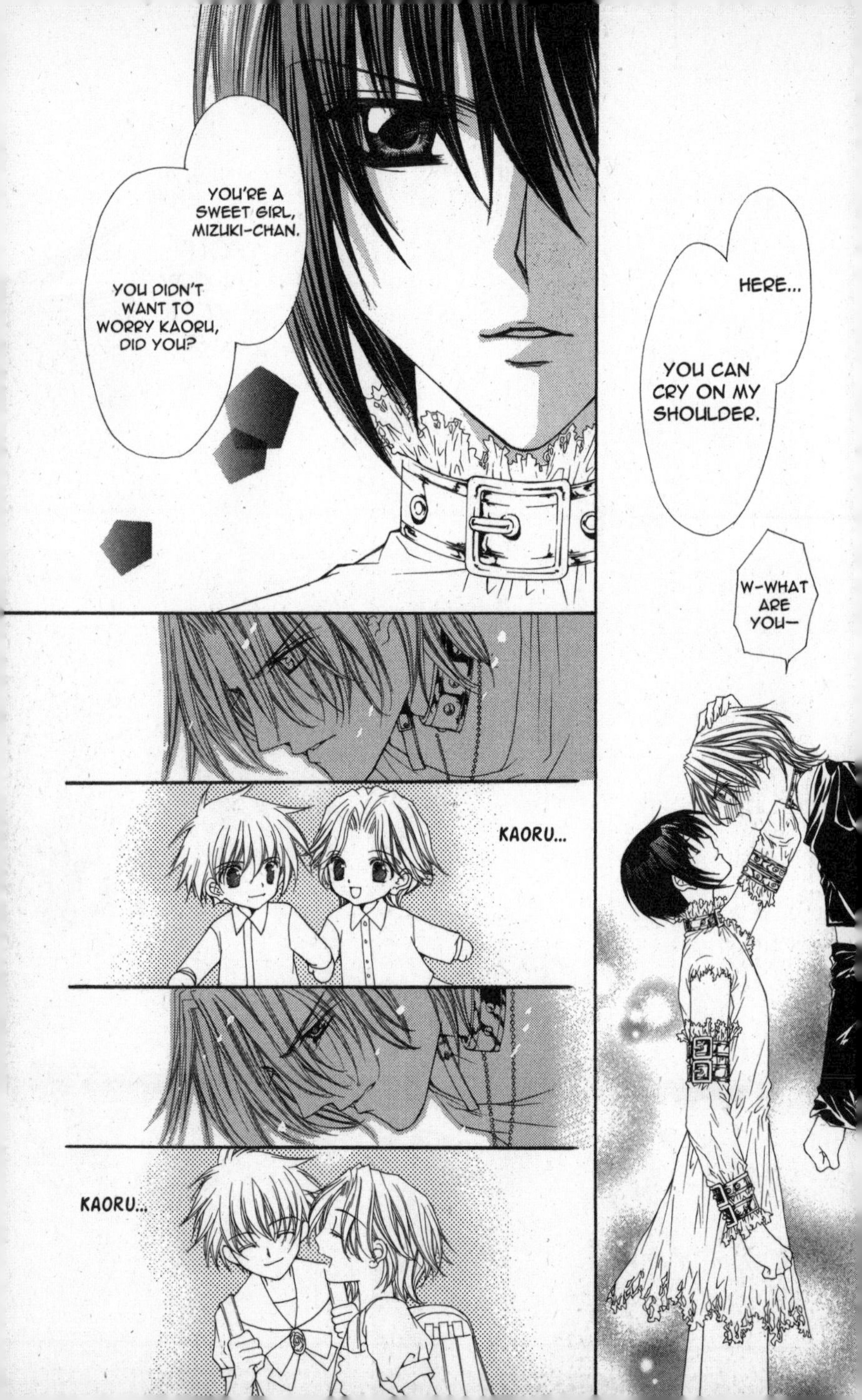
HERE...
YOU CAN CRY ON MY SHOULDER.
W-WHAT ARE YOU—
YOU'RE A SWEET GIRL, MIZUKI-CHAN.
YOU DIDN'T WANT TO WORRY KAORU, DID YOU?
KAORU...
KAORU...

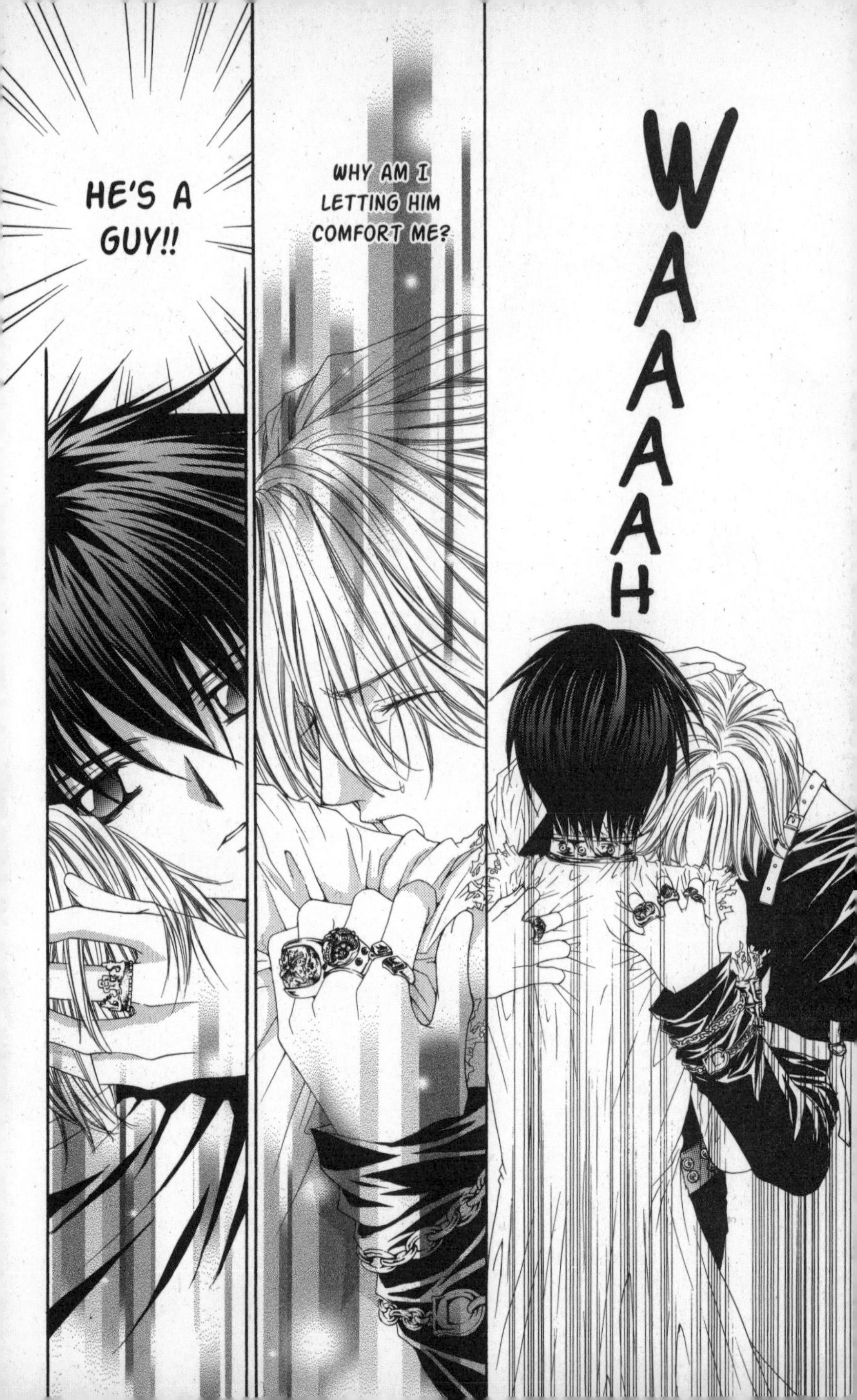
WAAAAH
WHY AM I LETTING HIM COMFORT ME?
HE'S A GUY!!

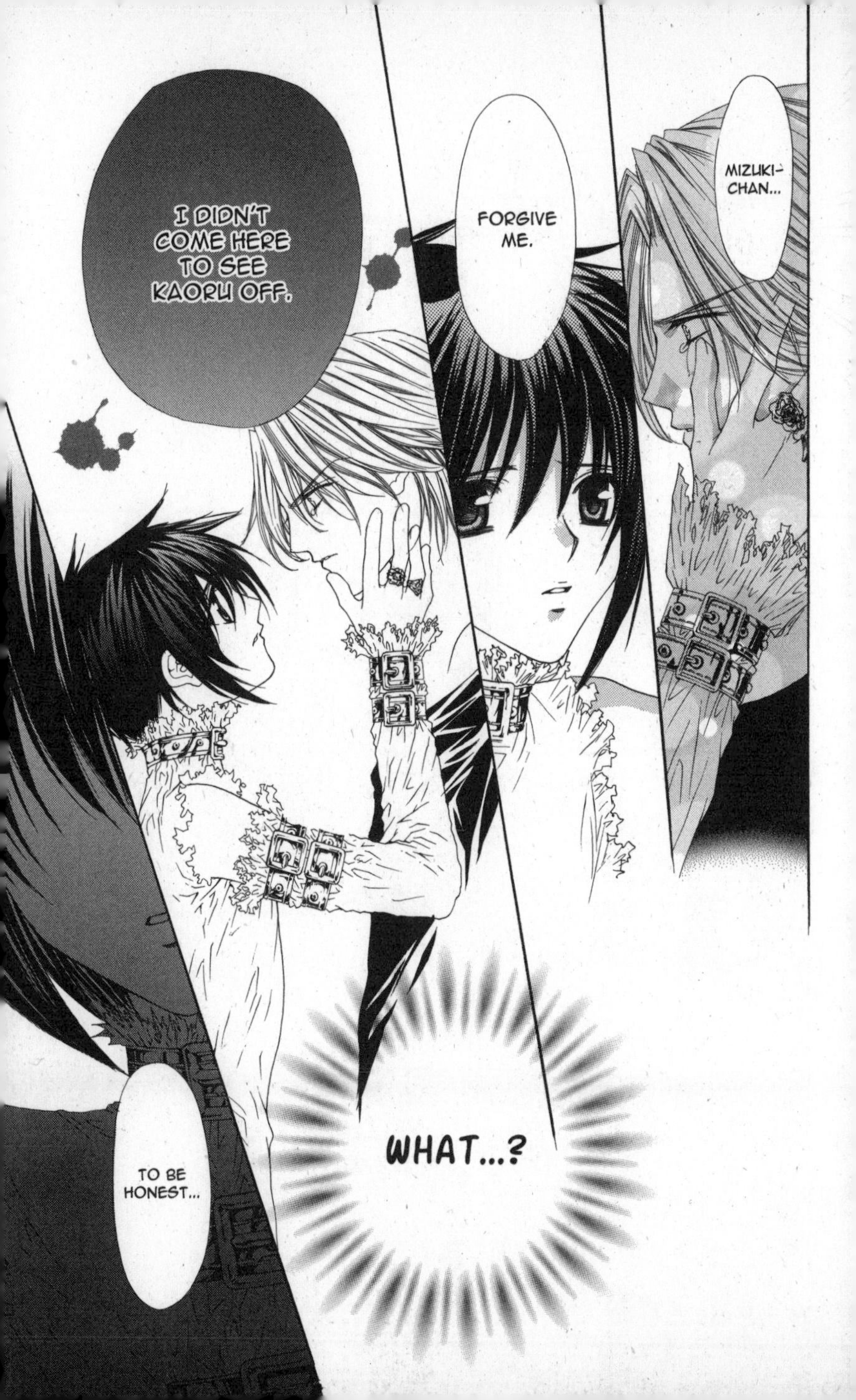
MIZUKI-CHAN...
FORGIVE ME.
I DIDN'T COME HERE TO SEE KAORU OFF.
WHAT...?
TO BE HONEST...

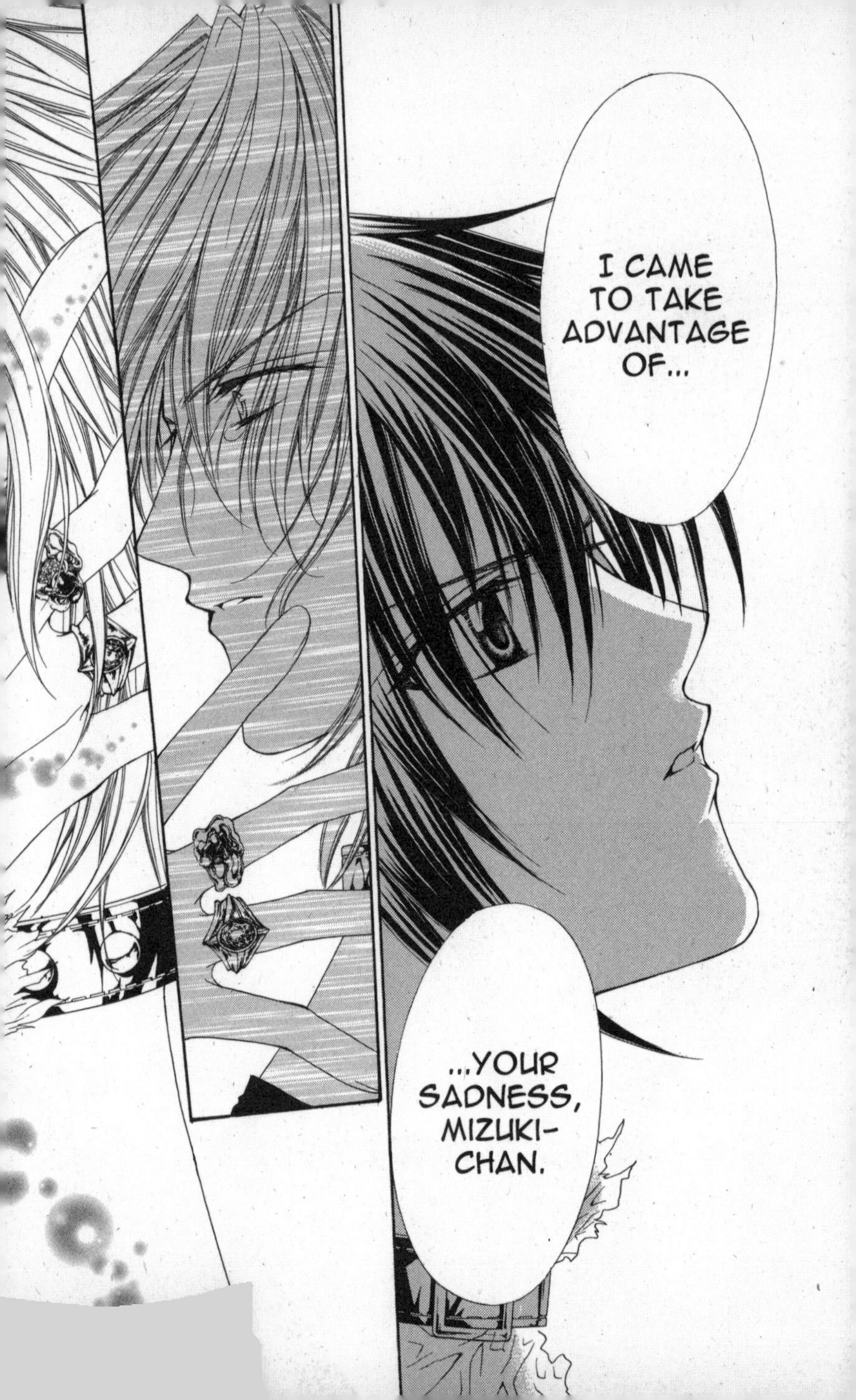
I CAME TO TAKE ADVANTAGE OF...
...YOUR SADNESS, MIZUKI-CHAN.

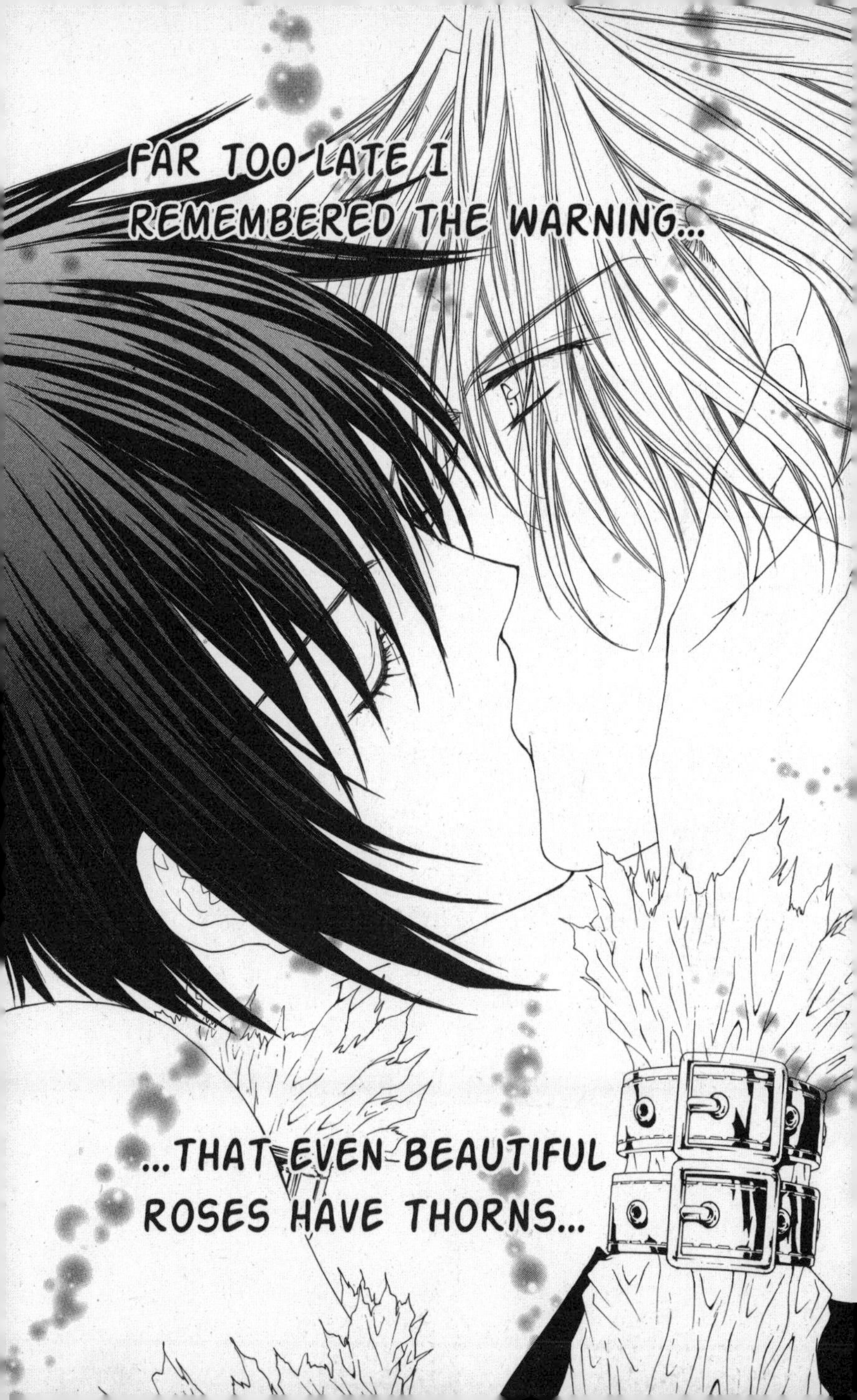
FAR TOO LATE I REMEMBERED THE WARNING...
...THAT EVEN BEAUTIFUL ROSES HAVE THORNS...

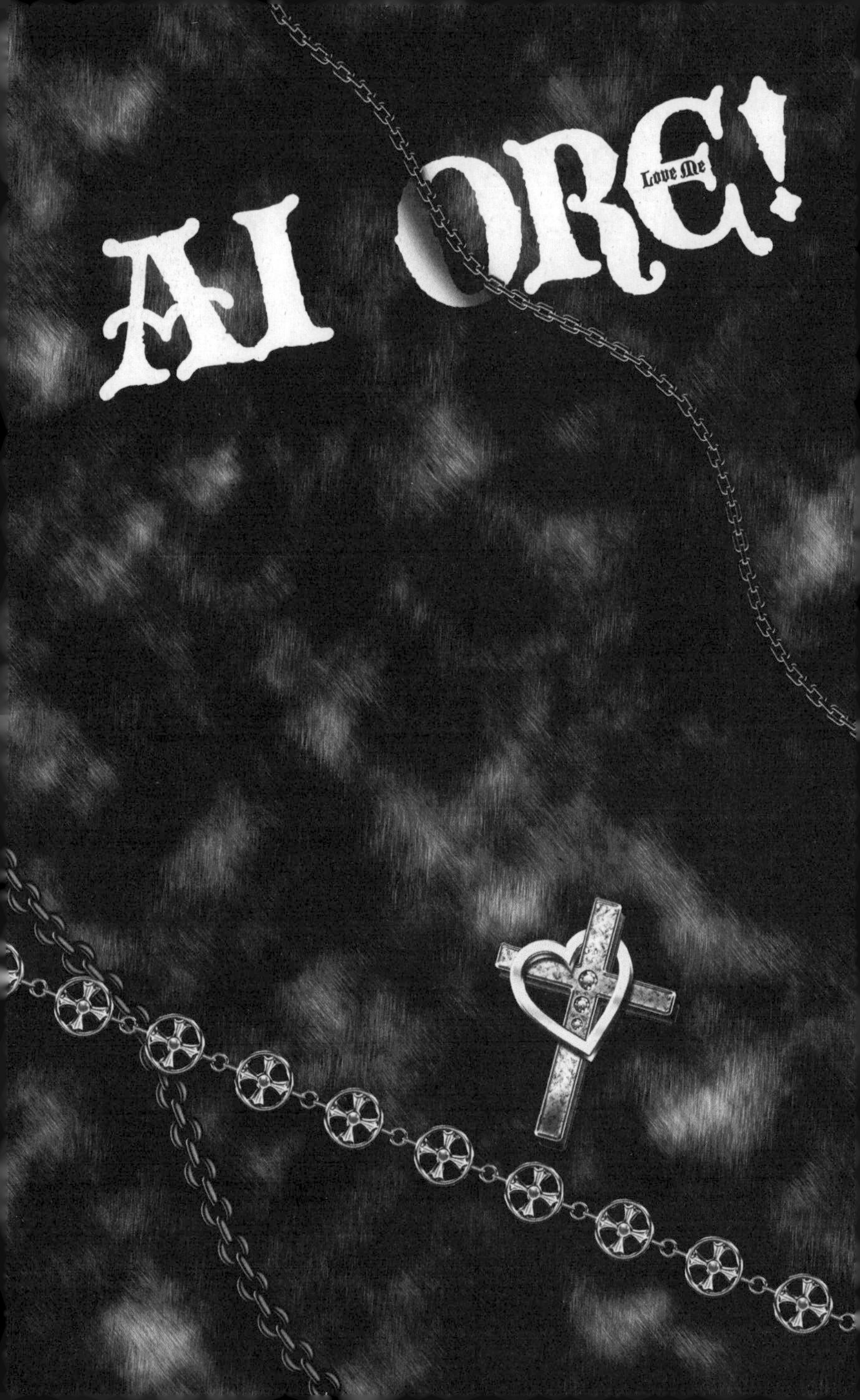
AI ORE!
Love Me

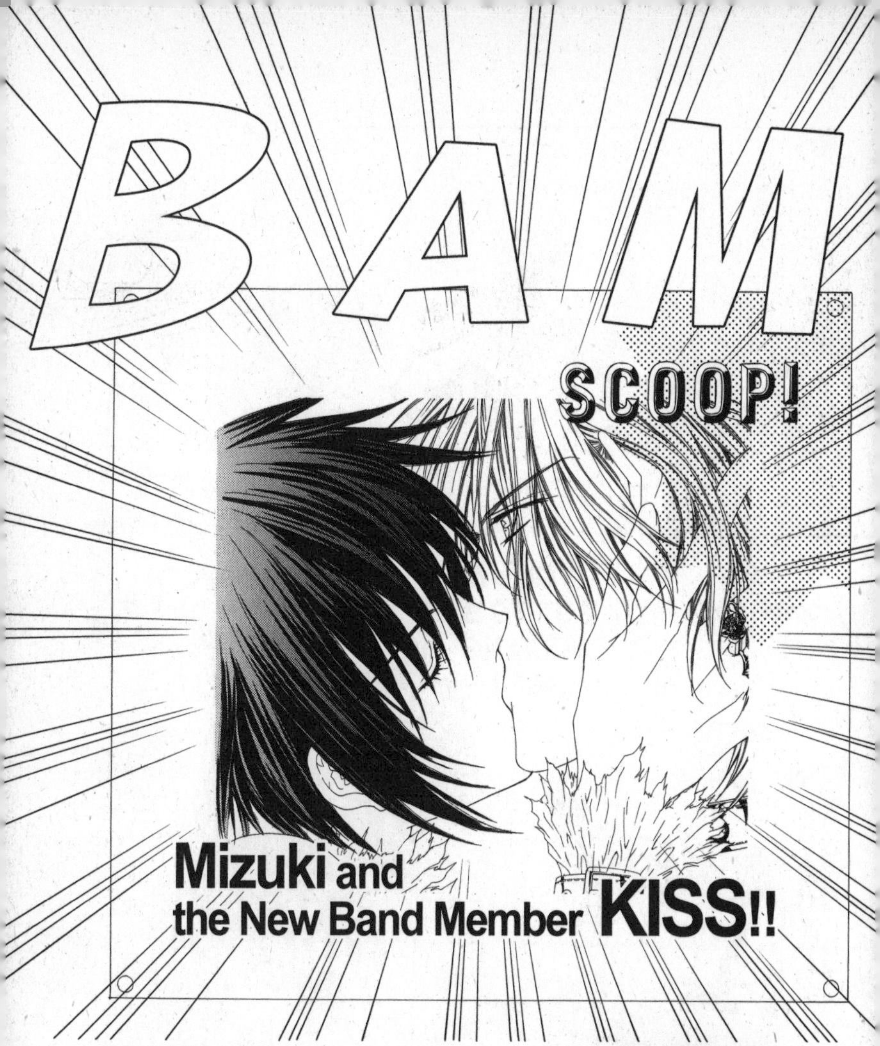
BAM
SCOOP!
Mizuki and
the New Band Member KISS!!

Akira's Q&A!!

Q1: How do you feel about being called the princess of the boys school?

A1: It's GROSS. I... I like girls...
And I hate people taking candid photos of me!!
Even my older brothers treat me as if I was their younger sister...
What exactly does everyone ultimately want to do with me, anyway?

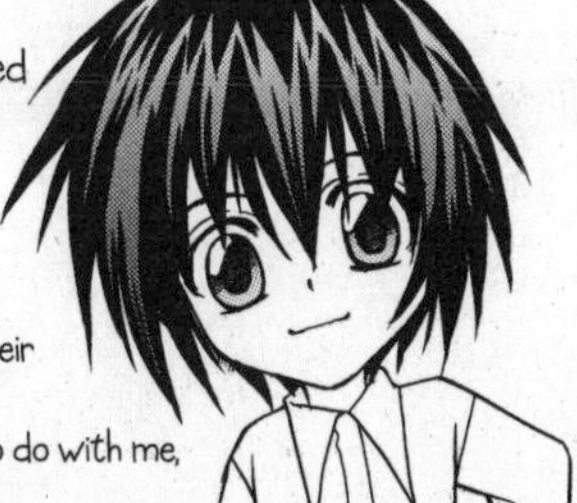

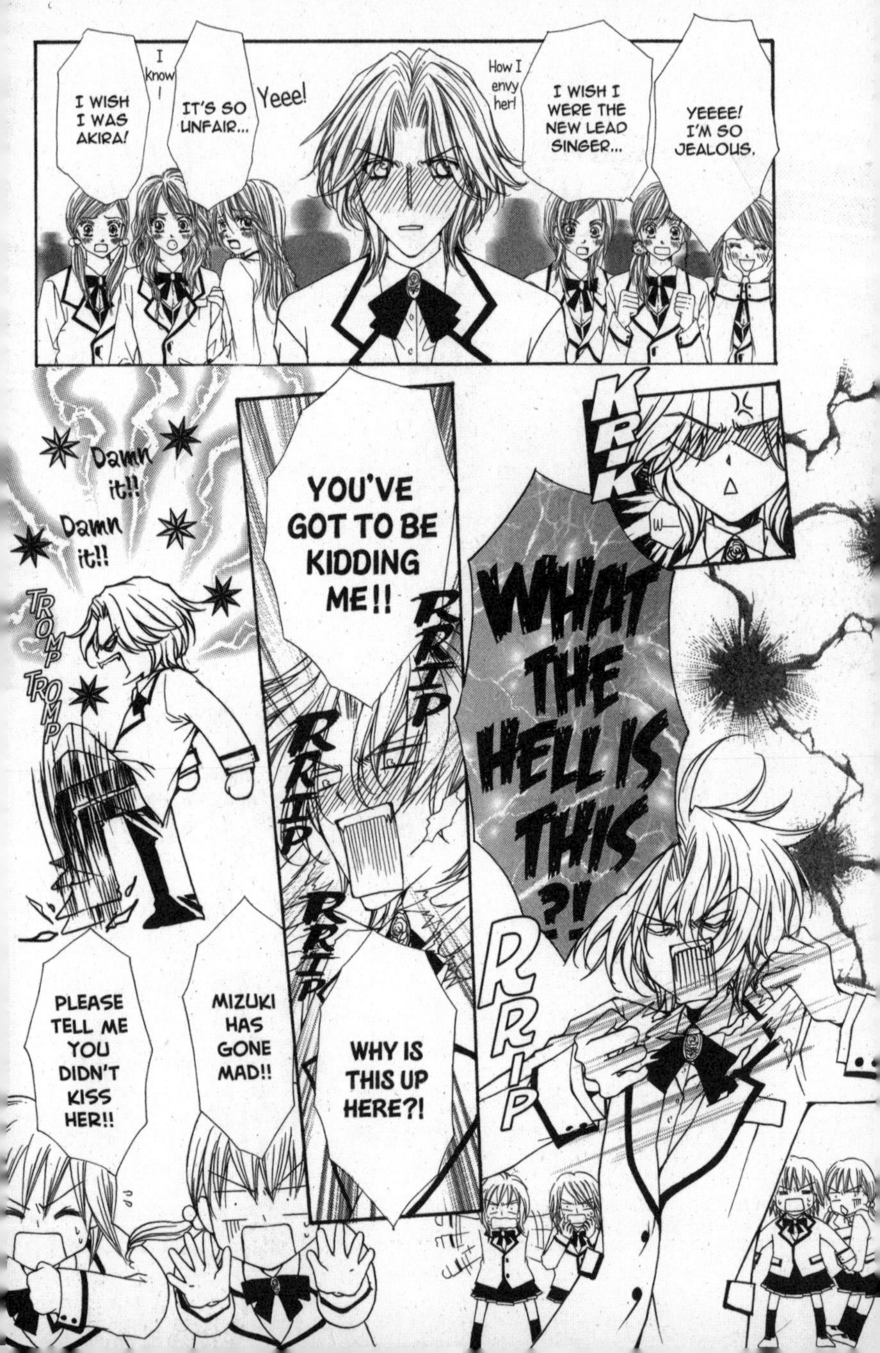
YEEEE! I'M SO JEALOUS.
I WISH I WERE THE NEW LEAD SINGER...
How I envy her!
Yeee!
IT'S SO UNFAIR...
I know!
I WISH I WAS AKIRA!
KRIK
WHAT THE HELL IS THIS?!
RRIP
YOU'VE GOT TO BE KIDDING ME!!
RRIP
RRIP
RRIP
WHY IS THIS UP HERE?!
Damn it!! Damn it!!
TROMP TROMP
MIZUKI HAS GONE MAD!!
PLEASE TELL ME YOU DIDN'T KISS HER!!

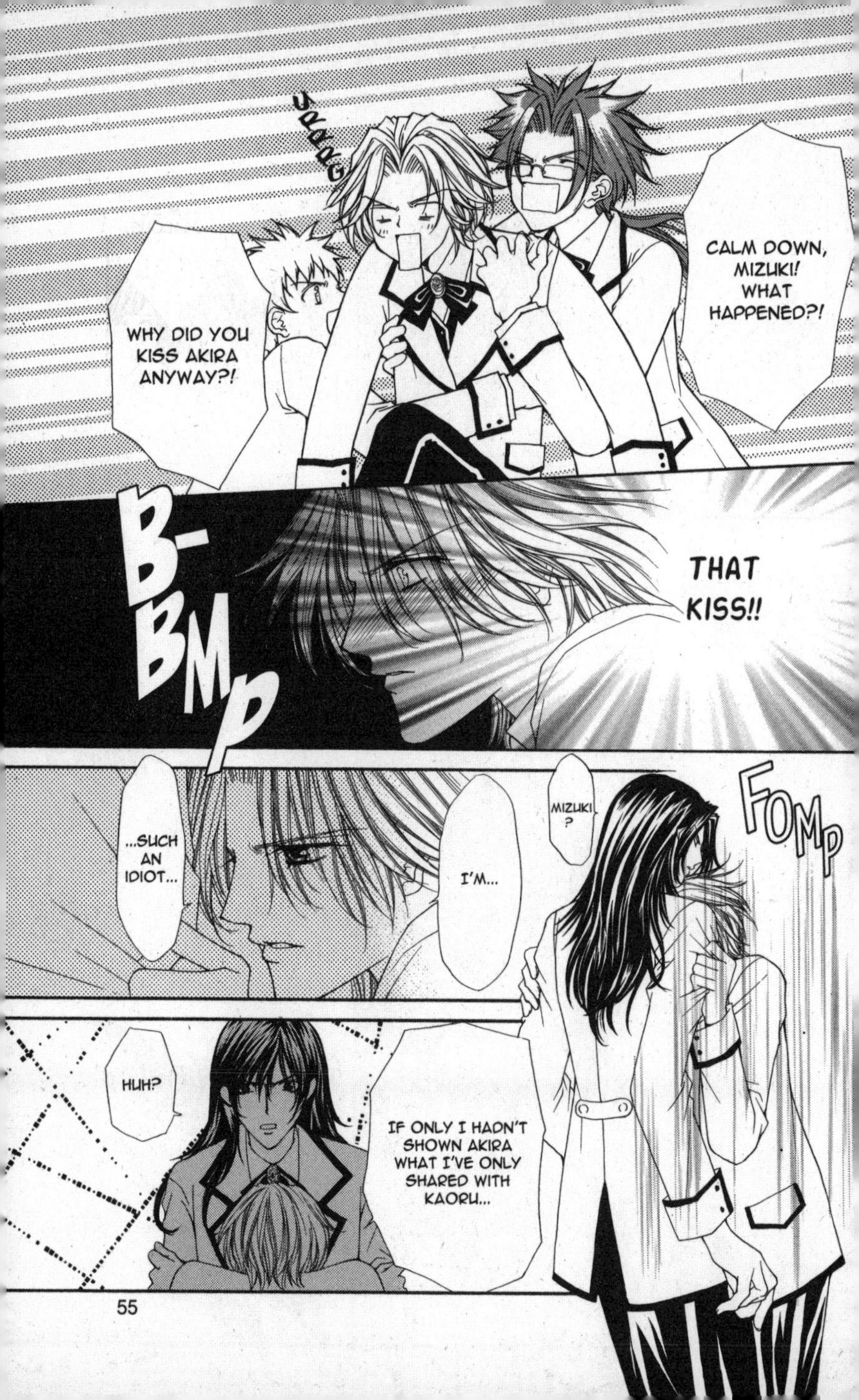
CALM DOWN, MIZUKI! WHAT HAPPENED?!
URRRG
WHY DID YOU KISS AKIRA ANYWAY?!
THAT KISS!!
B-BMP
FOMP
MIZUKI?
I'M...
...SUCH AN IDIOT...
IF ONLY I HADN'T SHOWN AKIRA WHAT I'VE ONLY SHARED WITH KAORU...
HUH?

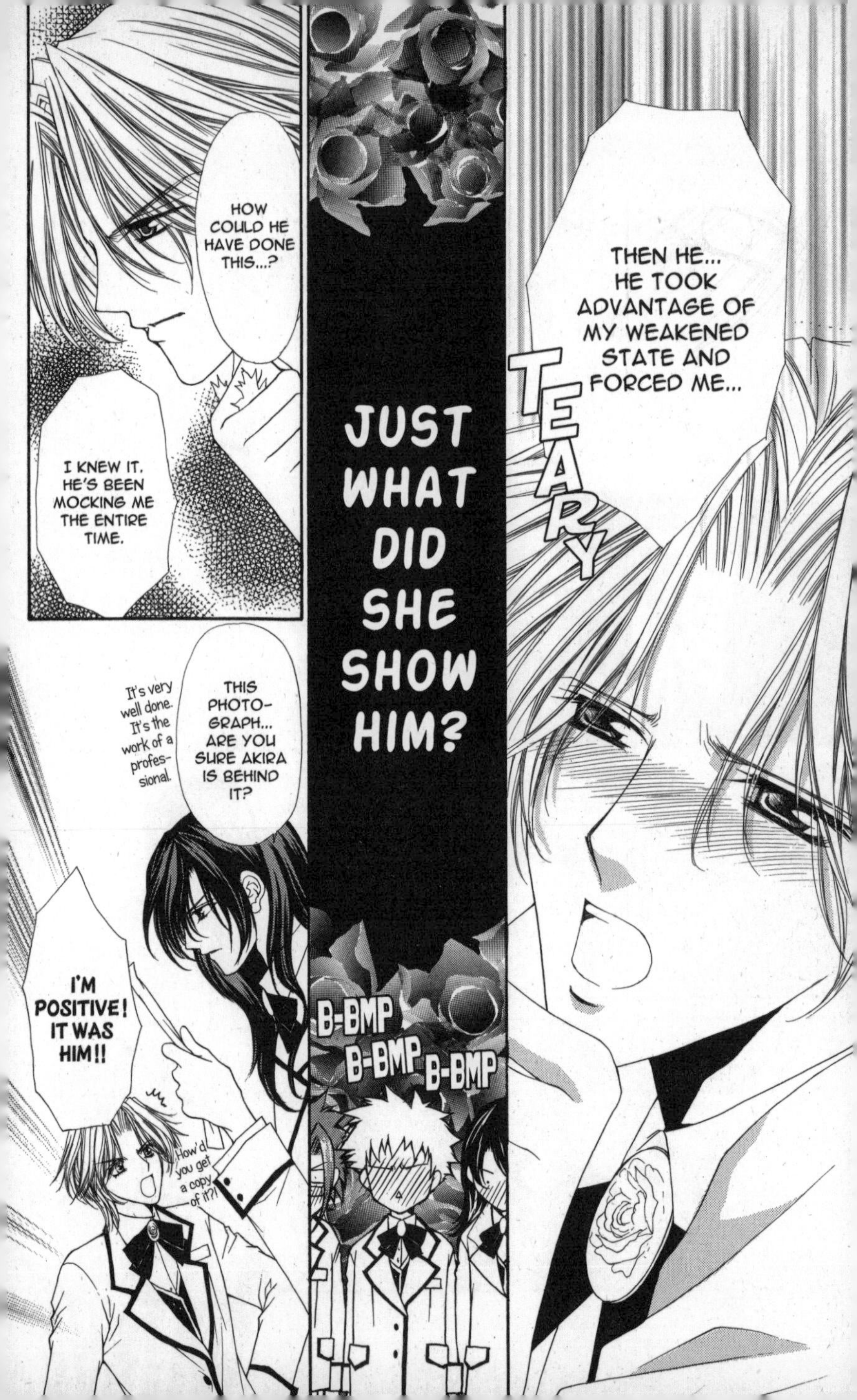
THEN HE... HE TOOK ADVANTAGE OF MY WEAKENED STATE AND FORCED ME...
TEARY
JUST WHAT DID SHE SHOW HIM?
B-BMP B-BMP B-BMP
HOW COULD HE HAVE DONE THIS...?
I KNEW IT. HE'S BEEN MOCKING ME THE ENTIRE TIME.
THIS PHOTOGRAPH... ARE YOU SURE AKIRA IS BEHIND IT?
It's very well done. It's the work of a professional.
I'M POSITIVE! IT WAS HIM!!
How'd you get a copy of it?!

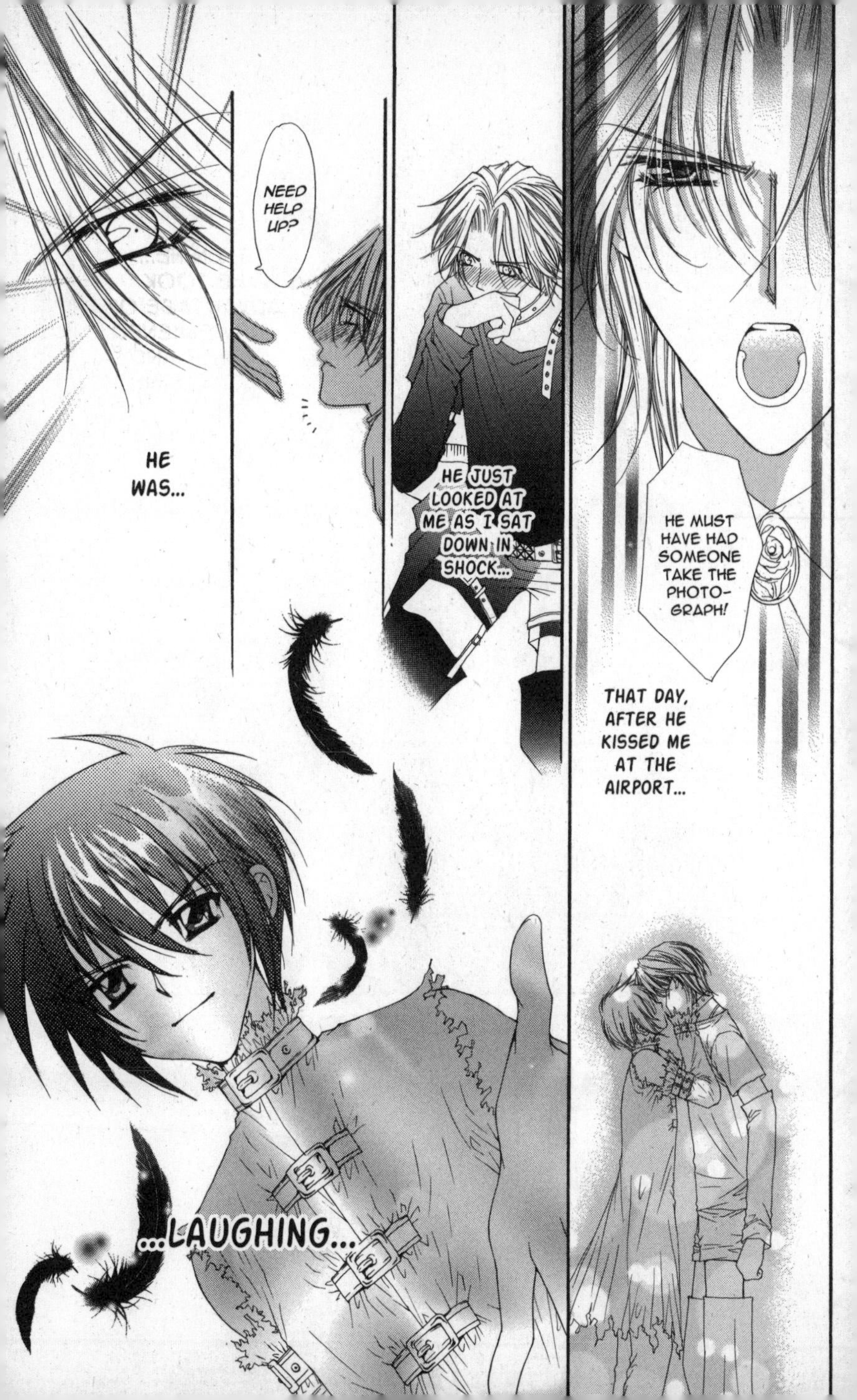
HE MUST HAVE HAD SOMEONE TAKE THE PHOTOGRAPH!
THAT DAY, AFTER HE KISSED ME AT THE AIRPORT...
NEED HELP UP?
HE JUST LOOKED AT ME AS I SAT DOWN IN SHOCK...
HE WAS...
...LAUGHING...

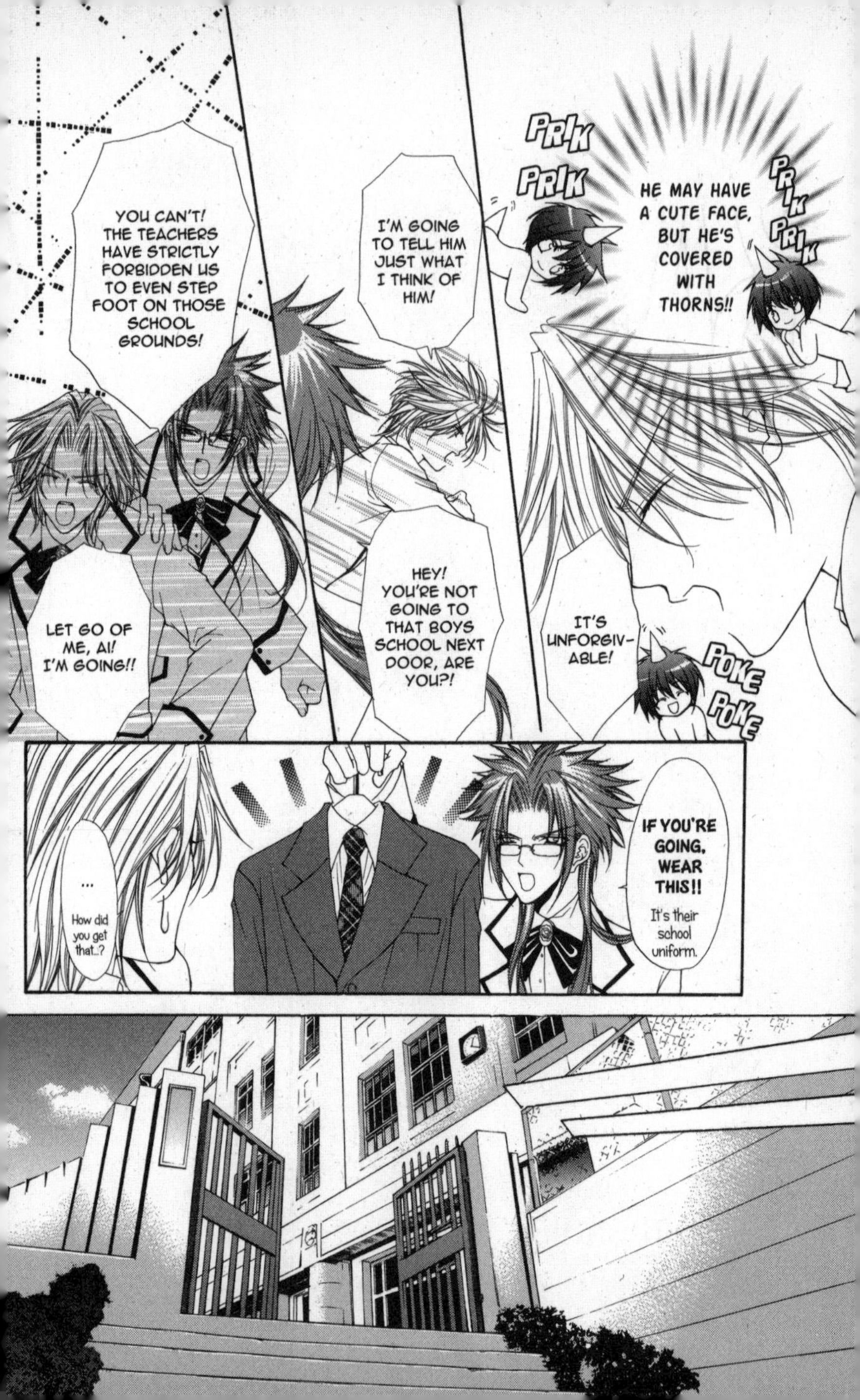
PRIK PRIK
HE MAY HAVE A CUTE FACE, BUT HE'S COVERED WITH THORNS!!
PRIK PRIK
IT'S UNFORGIV-ABLE!
POKE POKE
I'M GOING TO TELL HIM JUST WHAT I THINK OF HIM!
HEY! YOU'RE NOT GOING TO THAT BOYS SCHOOL NEXT DOOR, ARE YOU?!
YOU CAN'T! THE TEACHERS HAVE STRICTLY FORBIDDEN US TO EVEN STEP FOOT ON THOSE SCHOOL GROUNDS!
LET GO OF ME, AI! I'M GOING!!
IF YOU'RE GOING, WEAR THIS!!
It's their school uniform.
...
How did you get that...?

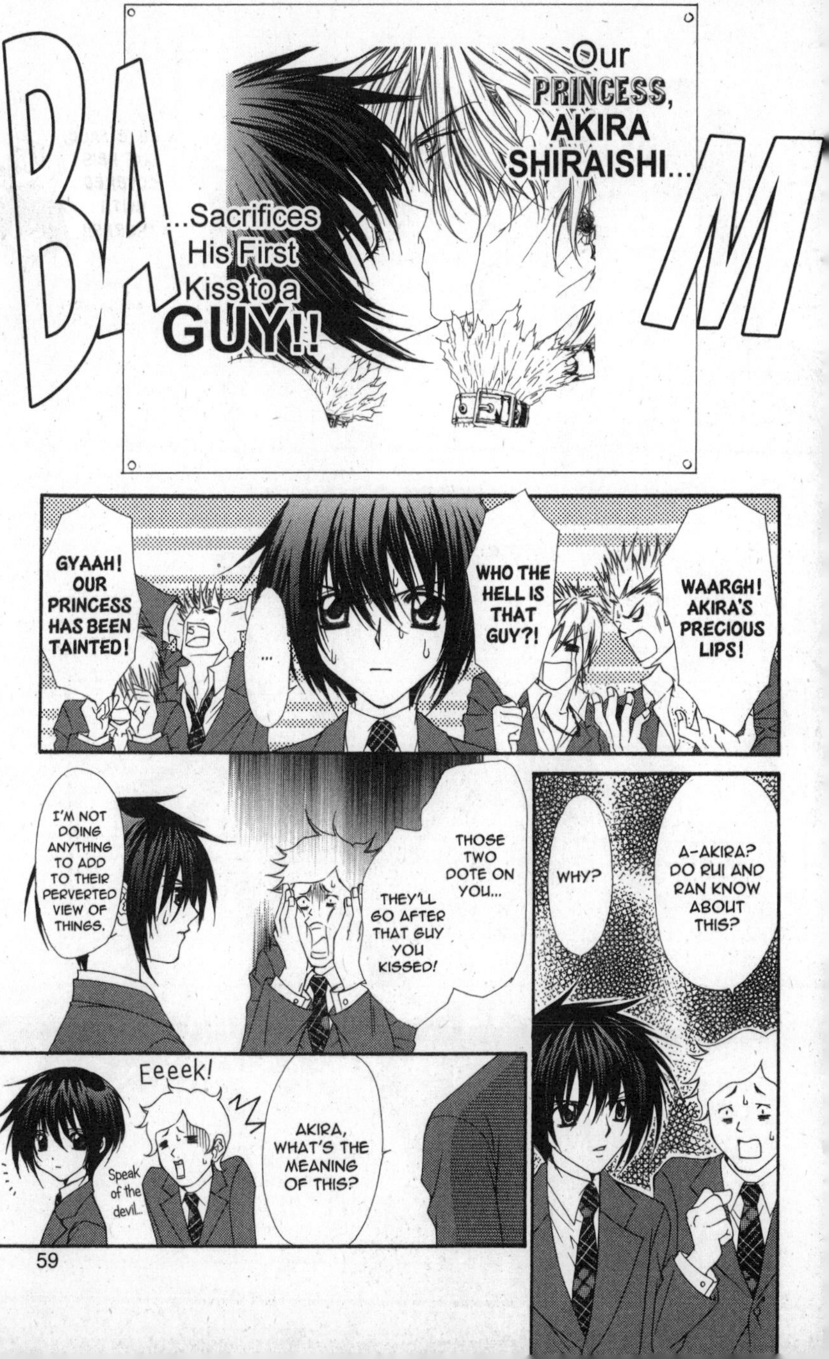
BA
Our PRINCESS, AKIRA SHIRAISHI...
...Sacrifices His First Kiss to a GUY!!
M
WAARGH! AKIRA'S PRECIOUS LIPS!
WHO THE HELL IS THAT GUY?!
...
GYAAH! OUR PRINCESS HAS BEEN TAINTED!
A-AKIRA? DO RUI AND RAN KNOW ABOUT THIS?
WHY?
THOSE TWO DOTE ON YOU...
THEY'LL GO AFTER THAT GUY YOU KISSED!
I'M NOT DOING ANYTHING TO ADD TO THEIR PERVERTED VIEW OF THINGS.
AKIRA, WHAT'S THE MEANING OF THIS?
Eeeek!
Speak of the devil...

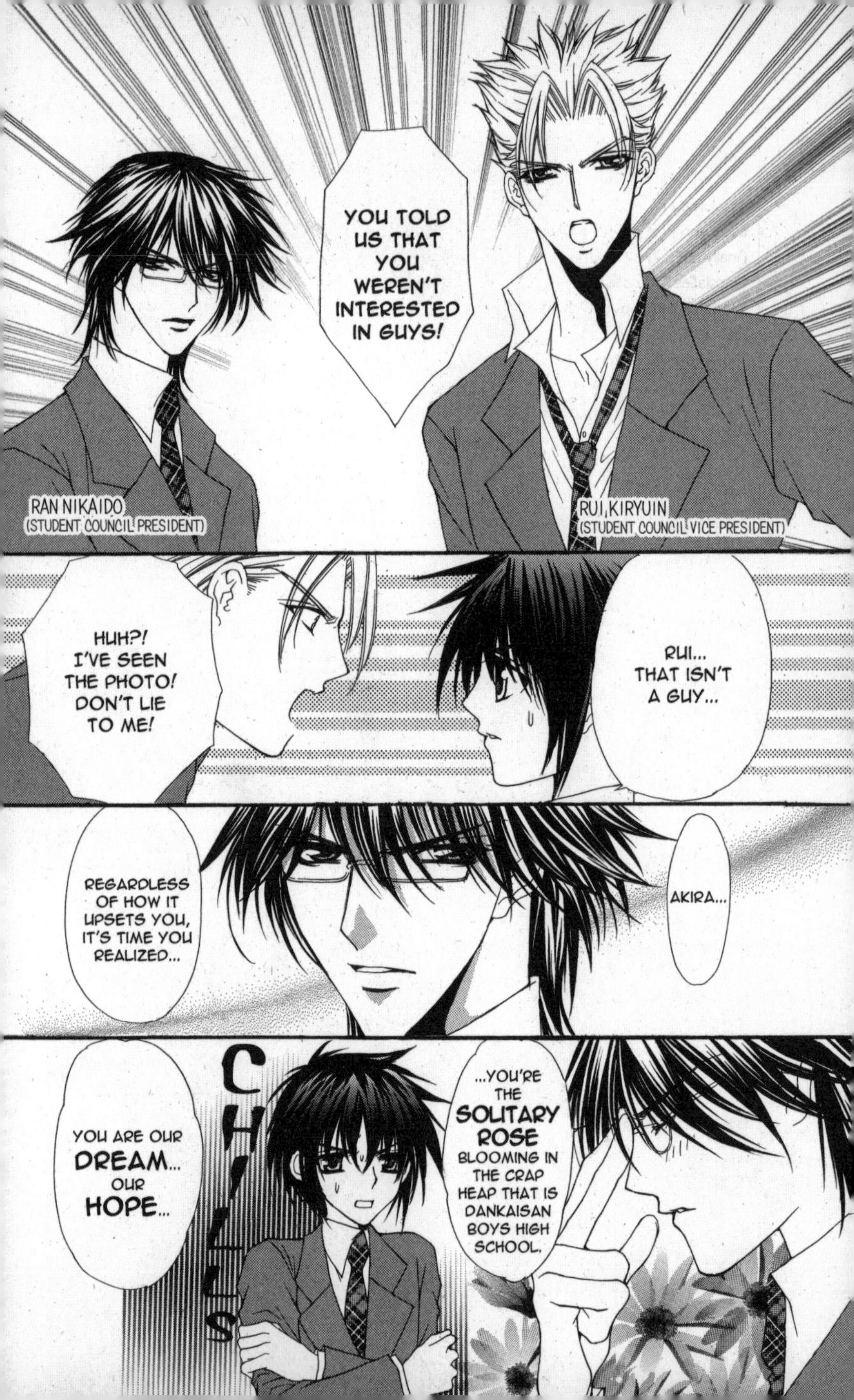
YOU TOLD US THAT YOU WEREN'T INTERESTED IN GUYS!
RUI KIRYUIN (STUDENT COUNCIL VICE PRESIDENT)
RAN NIKAIDO (STUDENT COUNCIL PRESIDENT)
RUI... THAT ISN'T A GUY...
HUH?! I'VE SEEN THE PHOTO! DON'T LIE TO ME!
AKIRA...
REGARDLESS OF HOW IT UPSETS YOU, IT'S TIME YOU REALIZED...
...YOU'RE THE **SOLITARY ROSE** BLOOMING IN THE CRAP HEAP THAT IS DANKAISAN BOYS HIGH SCHOOL.
CHILLS
YOU ARE OUR **DREAM**... OUR **HOPE**...

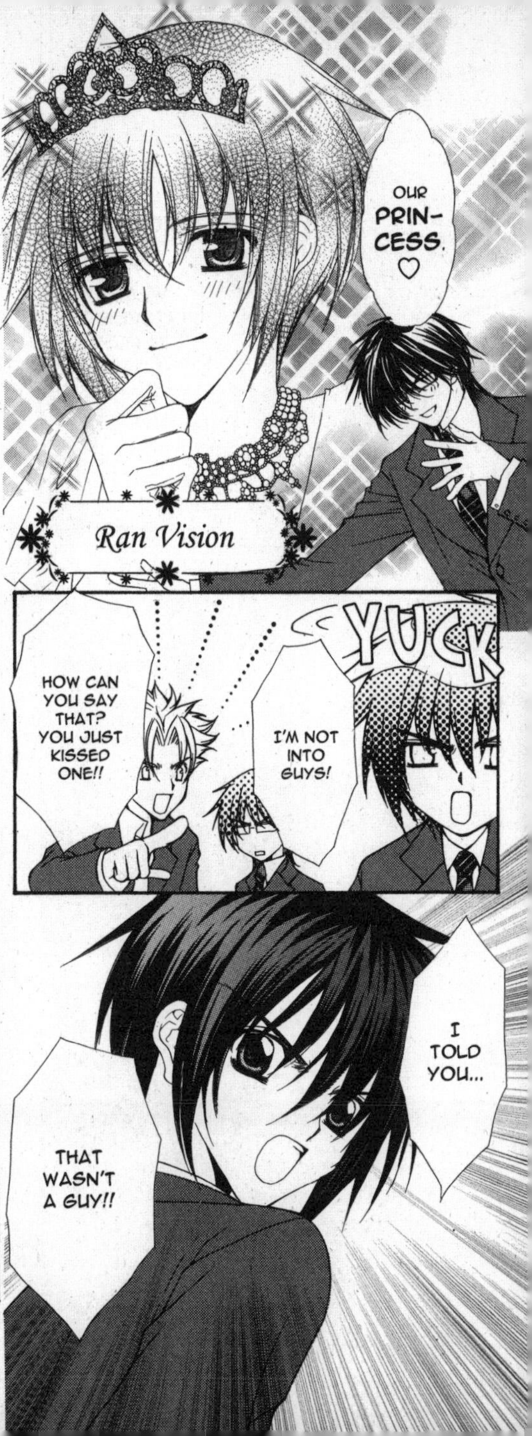
OUR PRIN-CESS. ♡
Ran Vision
YUCK
I'M NOT INTO GUYS!
HOW CAN YOU SAY THAT? YOU JUST KISSED ONE!!
I TOLD YOU...
THAT WASN'T A GUY!!

Hello!! Shinjo here.

Volume 1 of *Ai Ore!*, or *Ai o Utau yori Ore ni Oborero!* is finally out. [The full title translates as "Instead of Singing About Love, Drown Yourself in Me." –Ed.]

This work has been the second biggest challenge for me as a mangaka. By the way, my biggest challenge was completely changing the way I drew characters when I made my debut in *ShoComi* magazine. And this places second.

The male lead is not a tall guy with long, narrow eyes. Most of my fans who have supported me up to now like my male characters, but I have changed that appealing male character design and done something entirely different. I needed a lot of courage, determination, and faith to do it. I'm happy to see it come together in a book like this. This is thanks to all your support, and to the work of my current editor. Thank you very much!

To top it off, I am extremely happy to find out that many people reading this series have never read my manga before. So I am very glad I gave it a try! I'm glad I kept working on it.

I hope you all will continue to support me!

(Continues...)

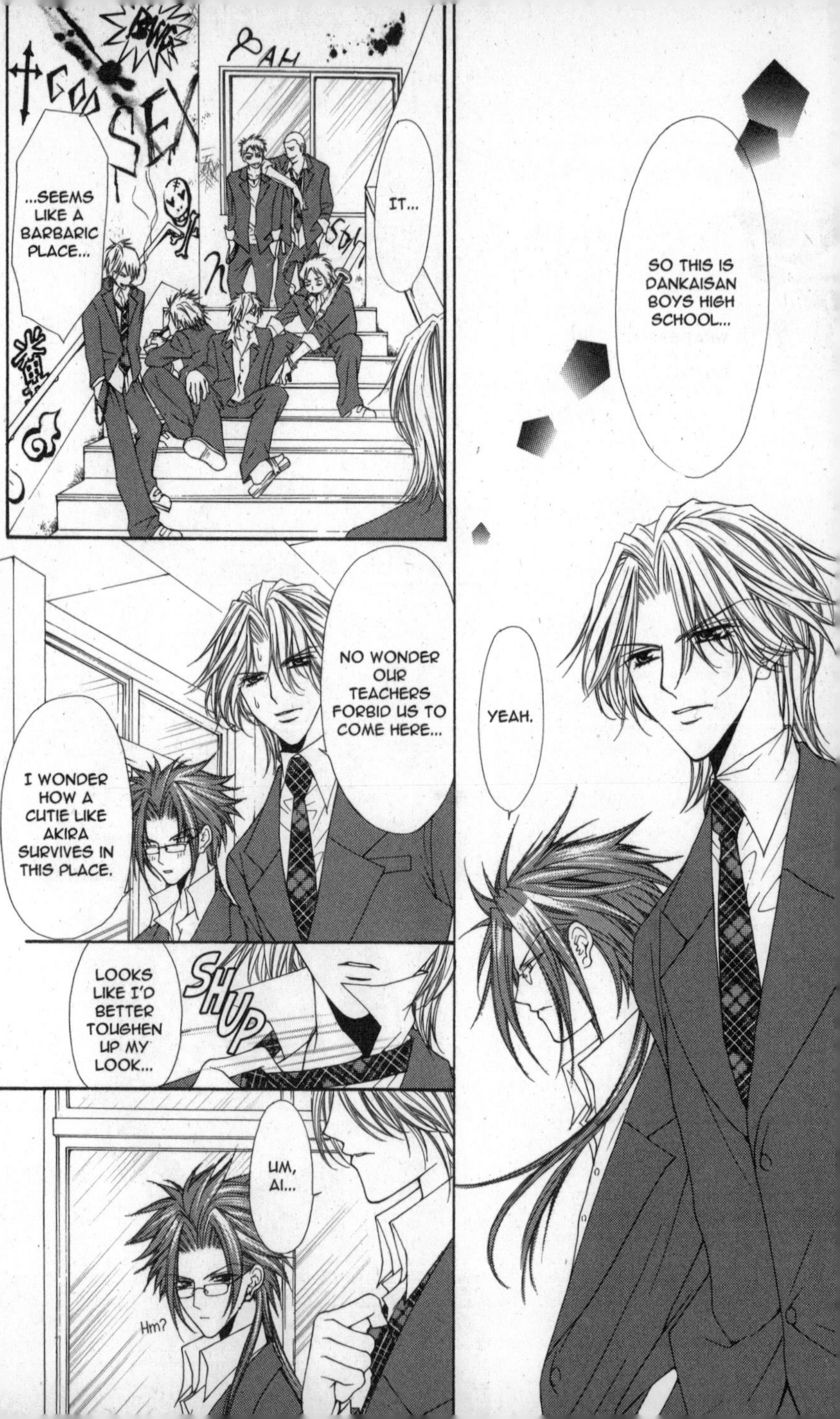
SO THIS IS DANKAISAN BOYS HIGH SCHOOL...
YEAH.
BANG
AH
GOD
SEX
IT...
...SEEMS LIKE A BARBARIC PLACE...
NO WONDER OUR TEACHERS FORBID US TO COME HERE...
I WONDER HOW A CUTIE LIKE AKIRA SURVIVES IN THIS PLACE.
SHUP
LOOKS LIKE I'D BETTER TOUGHEN UP MY LOOK...
UM, AI...
Hm?

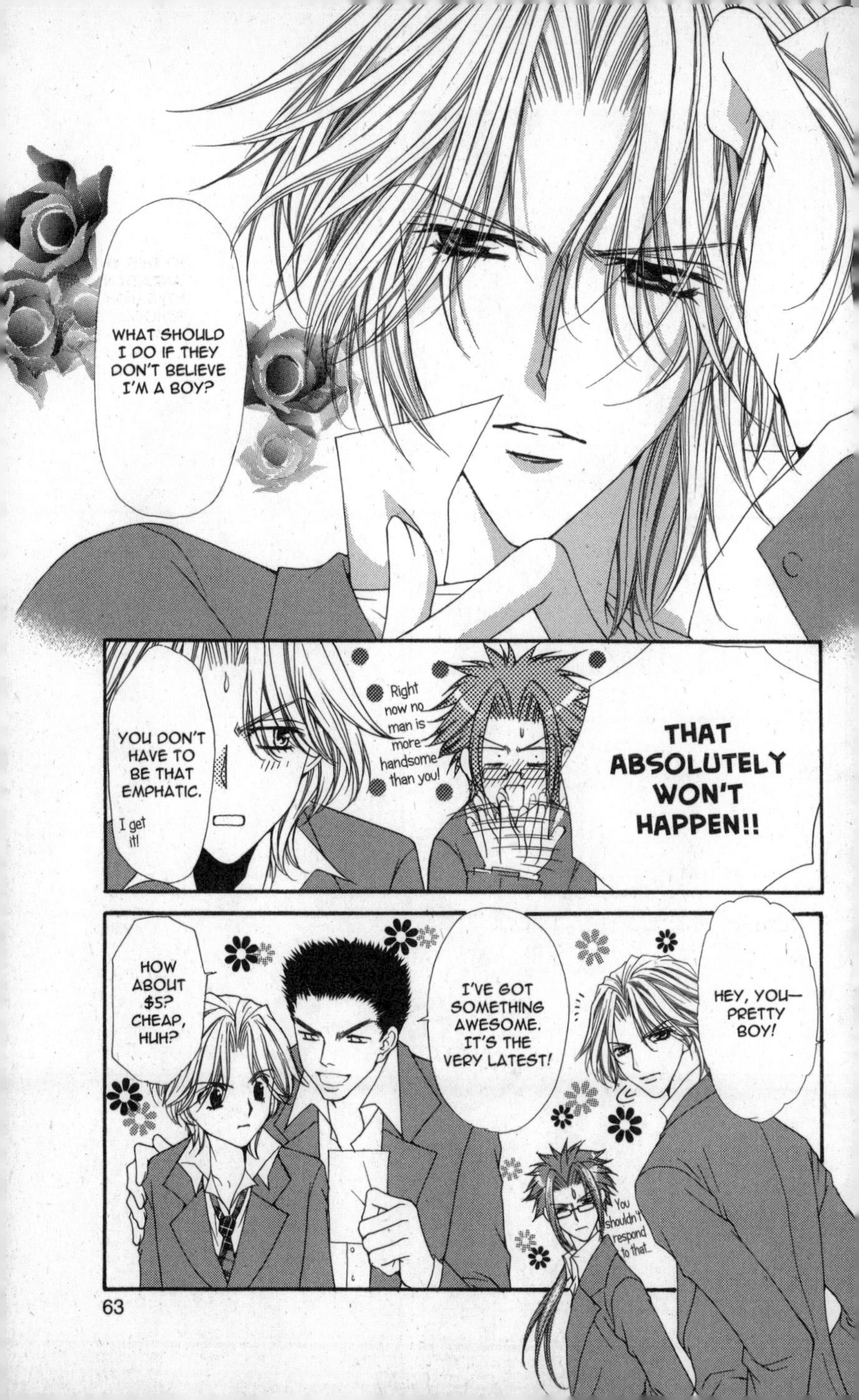
WHAT SHOULD I DO IF THEY DON'T BELIEVE I'M A BOY?
THAT ABSOLUTELY WON'T HAPPEN!!
Right now no man is more handsome than you!
YOU DON'T HAVE TO BE THAT EMPHATIC.
I get it!
HEY, YOU— PRETTY BOY!
You shouldn't respond to that...
I'VE GOT SOMETHING AWESOME. IT'S THE VERY LATEST!
HOW ABOUT $5? CHEAP, HUH?

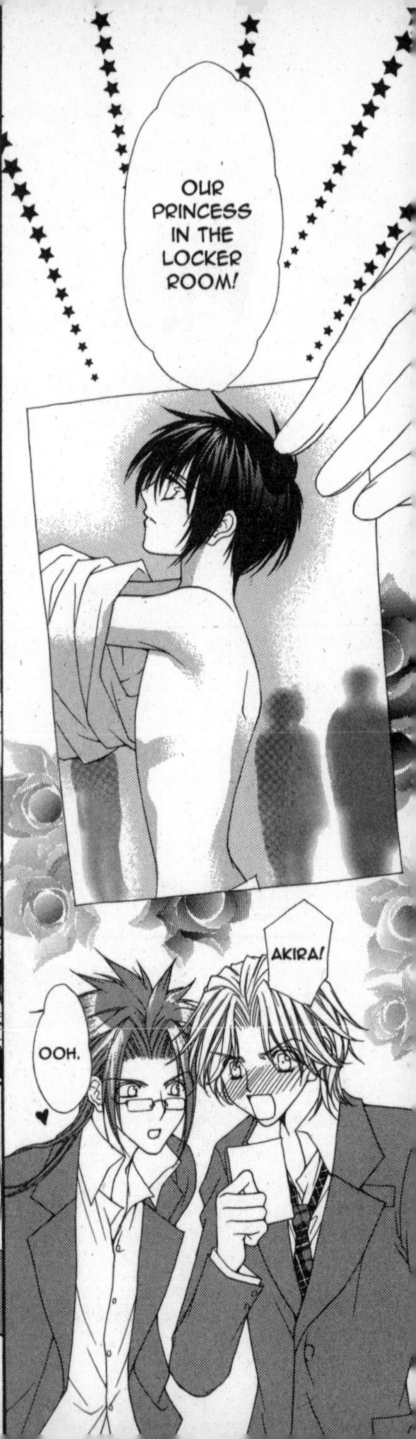
OUR PRINCESS IN THE LOCKER ROOM!
AKIRA!
OOH.
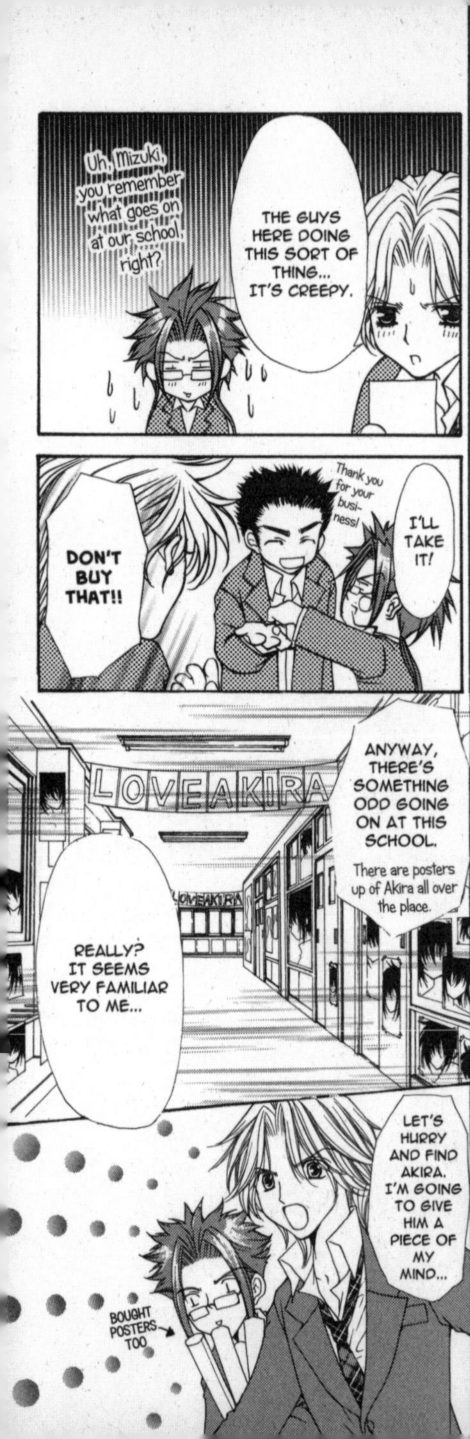
THE GUYS HERE DOING THIS SORT OF THING... IT'S CREEPY.
Uh, Mizuki, you remember what goes on at our school, right?
I'LL TAKE IT!
Thank you for your business!
DON'T BUY THAT!!
ANYWAY, THERE'S SOMETHING ODD GOING ON AT THIS SCHOOL.
There are posters up of Akira all over the place.
LOVEAKIRA
LOVEAKIRA
REALLY? IT SEEMS VERY FAMILIAR TO ME...
LET'S HURRY AND FIND AKIRA. I'M GOING TO GIVE HIM A PIECE OF MY MIND...
BOUGHT POSTERS TOO

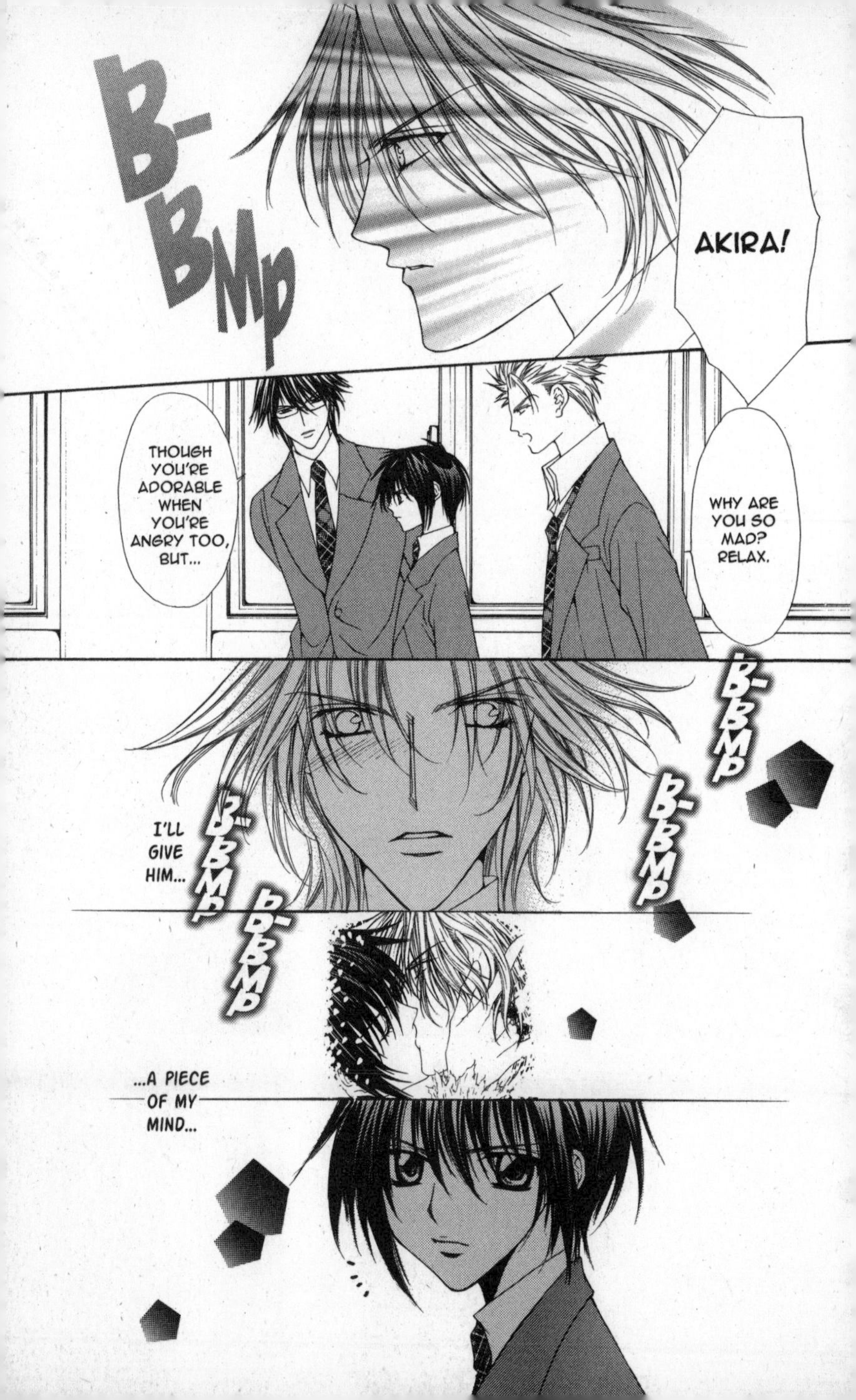
AKIRA!
B-BMP
WHY ARE YOU SO MAD? RELAX.
THOUGH YOU'RE ADORABLE WHEN YOU'RE ANGRY TOO, BUT...
B-BMP
B-BMP
I'LL GIVE HIM...
B-BMP
B-BMP
...A PIECE OF MY MIND...
...

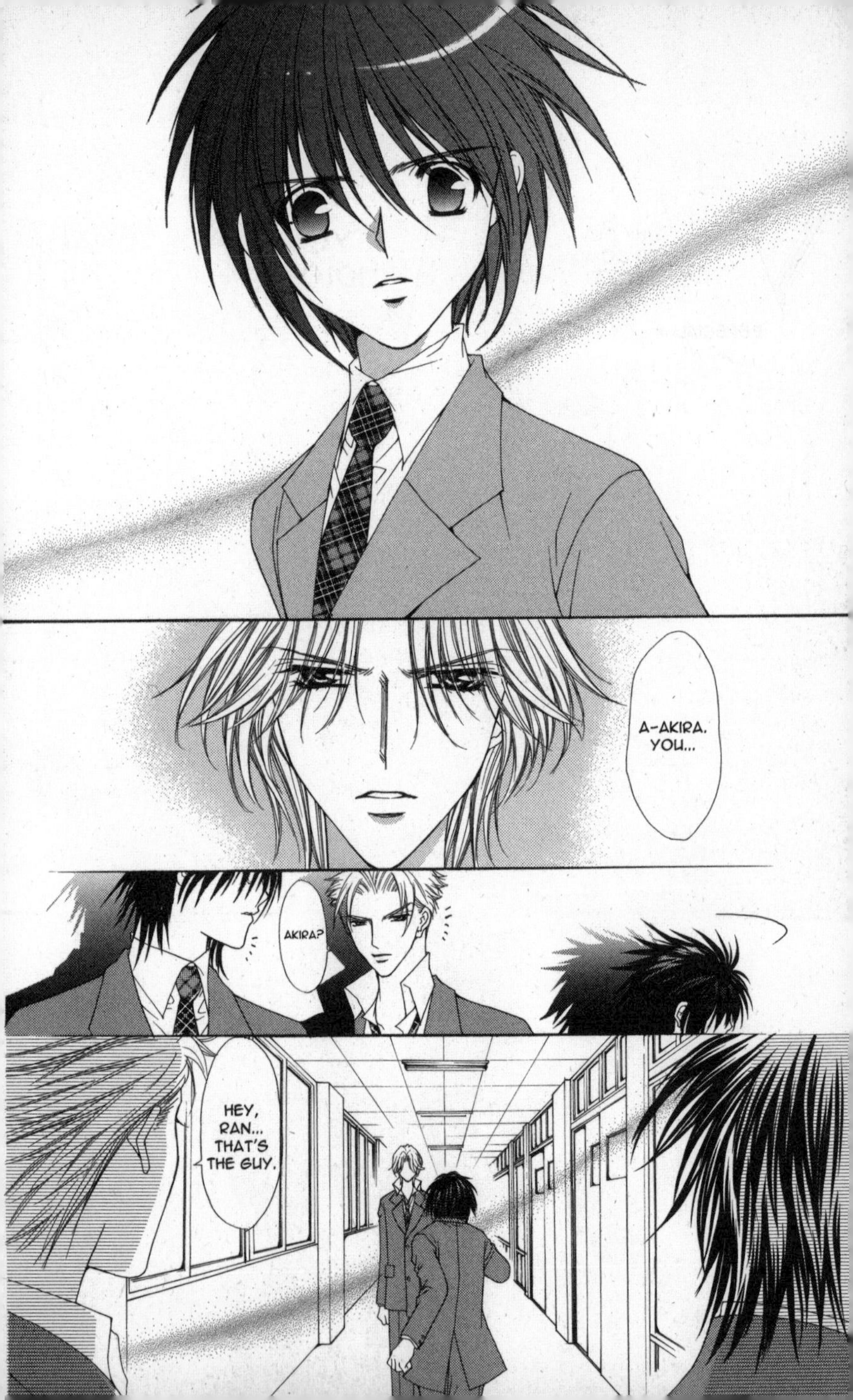
A-AKIRA. YOU...
AKIRA?
HEY, RAN... THAT'S THE GUY.

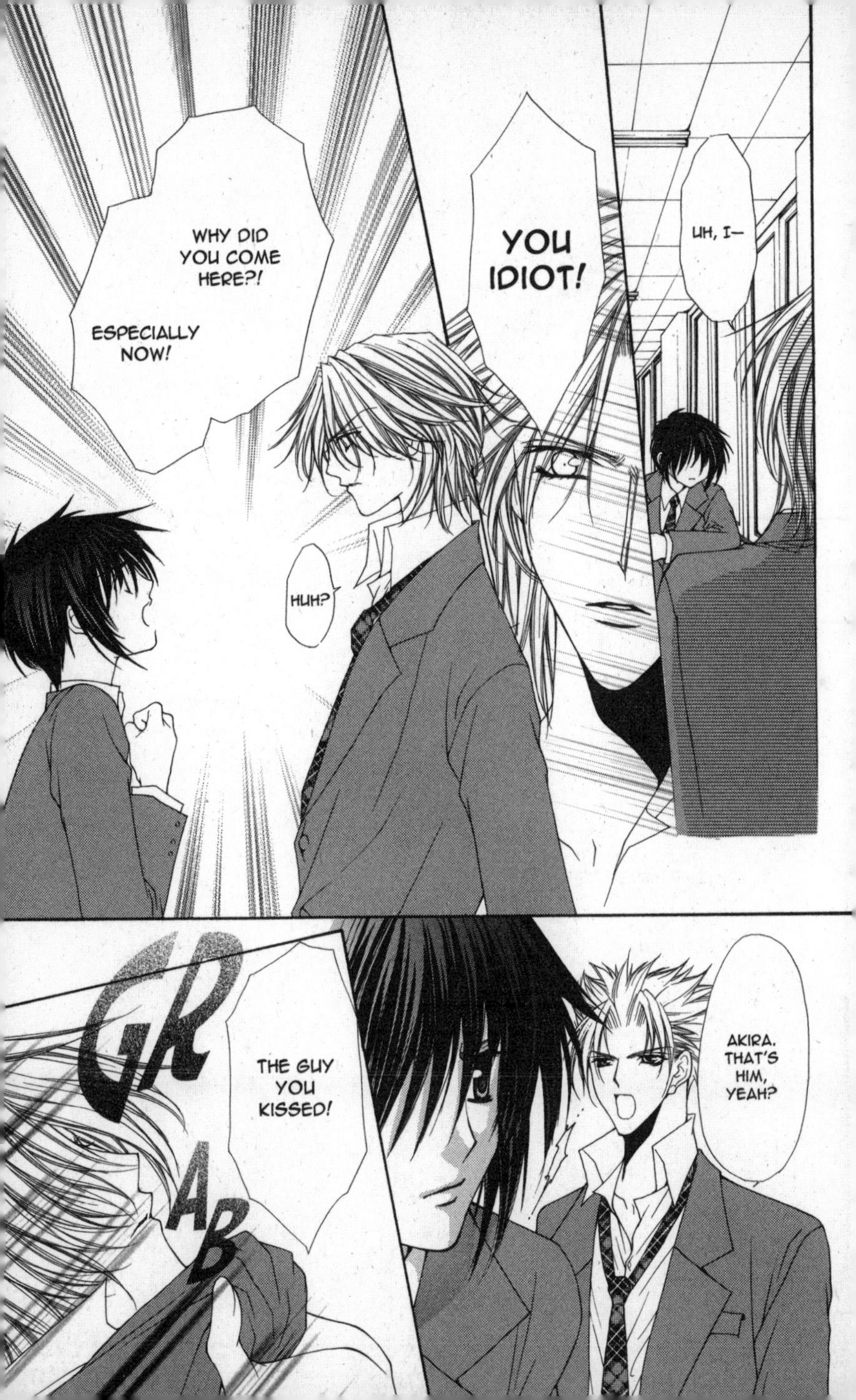
UH, I—
YOU IDIOT!
WHY DID YOU COME HERE?!
ESPECIALLY NOW!
HUH?
AKIRA. THAT'S HIM, YEAH?
GRAB
THE GUY YOU KISSED!

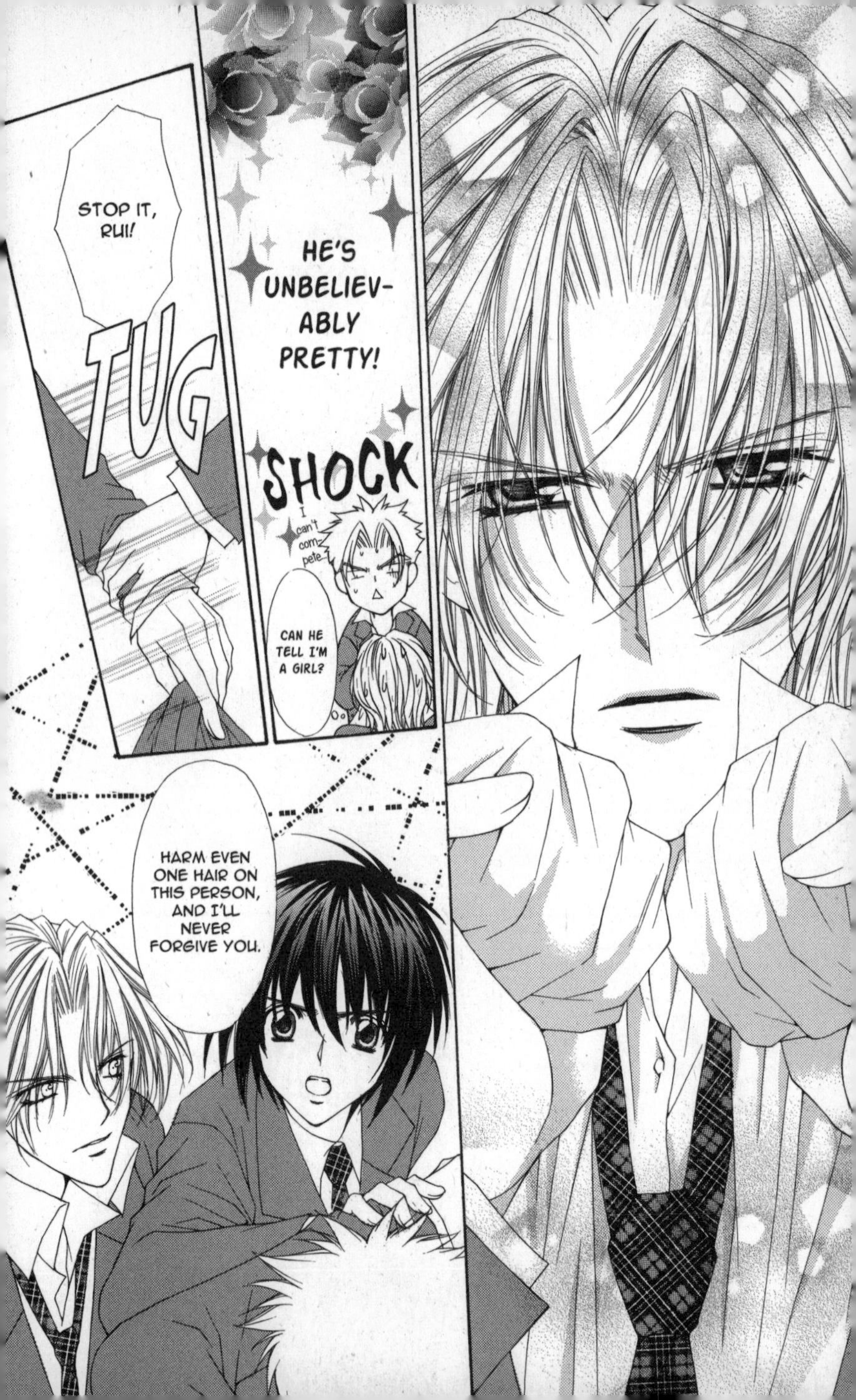
HE'S UNBELIEV-ABLY PRETTY!
SHOCK
I can't com-pete...
CAN HE TELL I'M A GIRL?
STOP IT, RUI!
TUG
HARM EVEN ONE HAIR ON THIS PERSON, AND I'LL NEVER FORGIVE YOU.

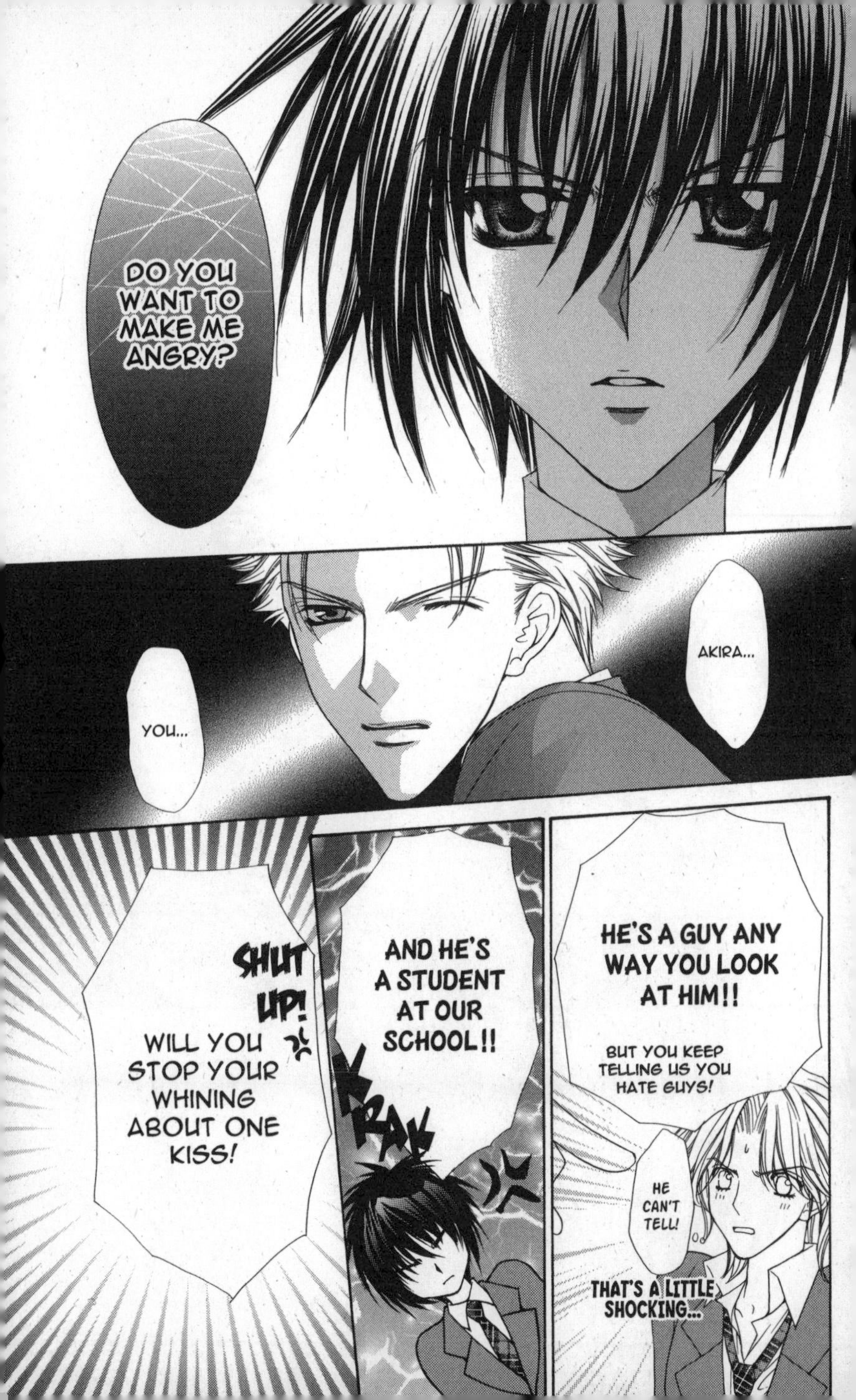
DO YOU WANT TO MAKE ME ANGRY?
AKIRA...
YOU...
HE'S A GUY ANY WAY YOU LOOK AT HIM!!
BUT YOU KEEP TELLING US YOU HATE GUYS!
HE CAN'T TELL!
THAT'S A LITTLE SHOCKING...
AND HE'S A STUDENT AT OUR SCHOOL!!
KRAK
SHUT UP!
WILL YOU STOP YOUR WHINING ABOUT ONE KISS!

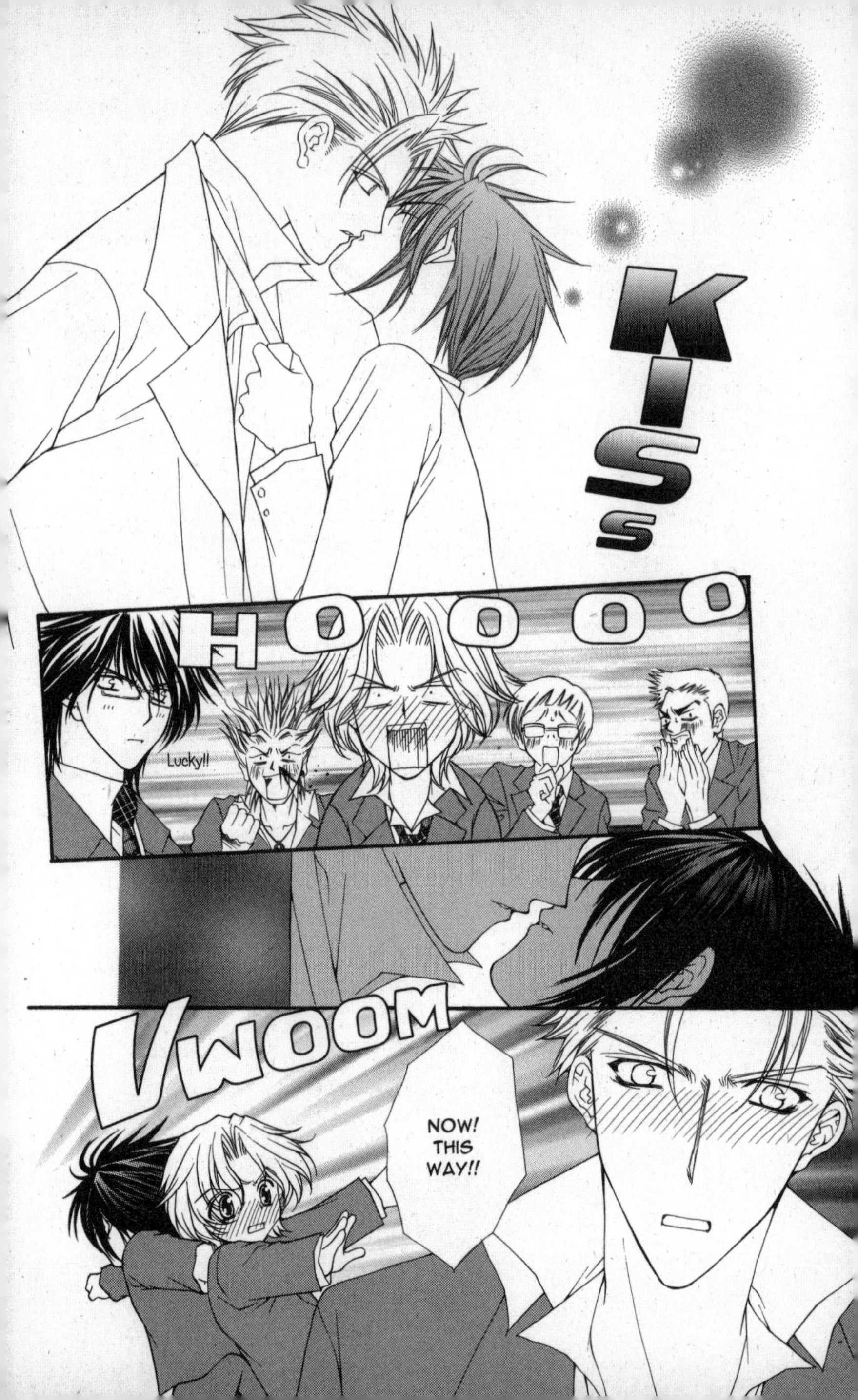
KISs
HOOOOO
Lucky!!
VWOOM
NOW! THIS WAY!!

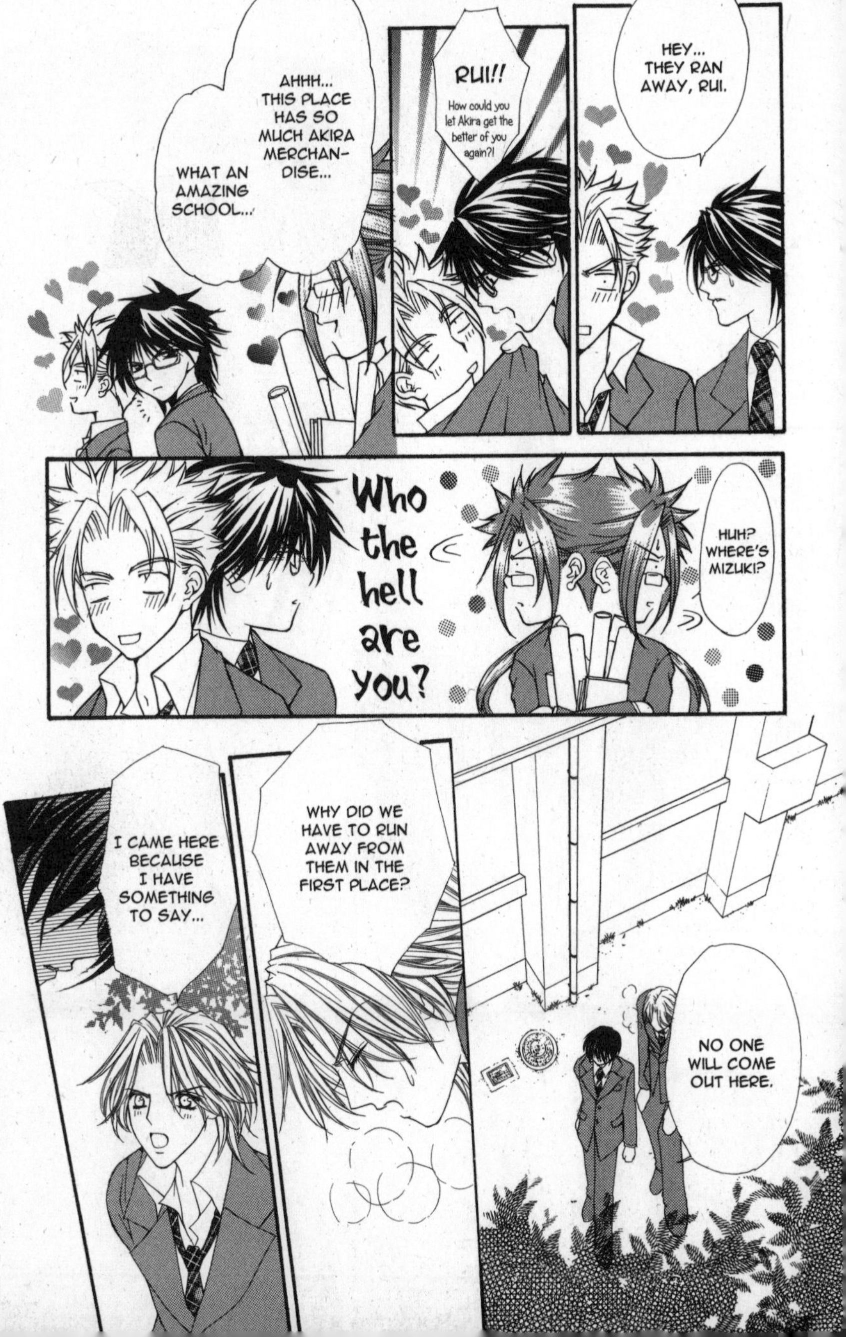
HEY... THEY RAN AWAY, RUI.
RUI!!
How could you let Akira get the better of you again?!
AHHH... THIS PLACE HAS SO MUCH AKIRA MERCHANDISE...
WHAT AN AMAZING SCHOOL...!
HUH? WHERE'S MIZUKI?
Who the hell are you?
NO ONE WILL COME OUT HERE.
WHY DID WE HAVE TO RUN AWAY FROM THEM IN THE FIRST PLACE?
I CAME HERE BECAUSE I HAVE SOMETHING TO SAY...

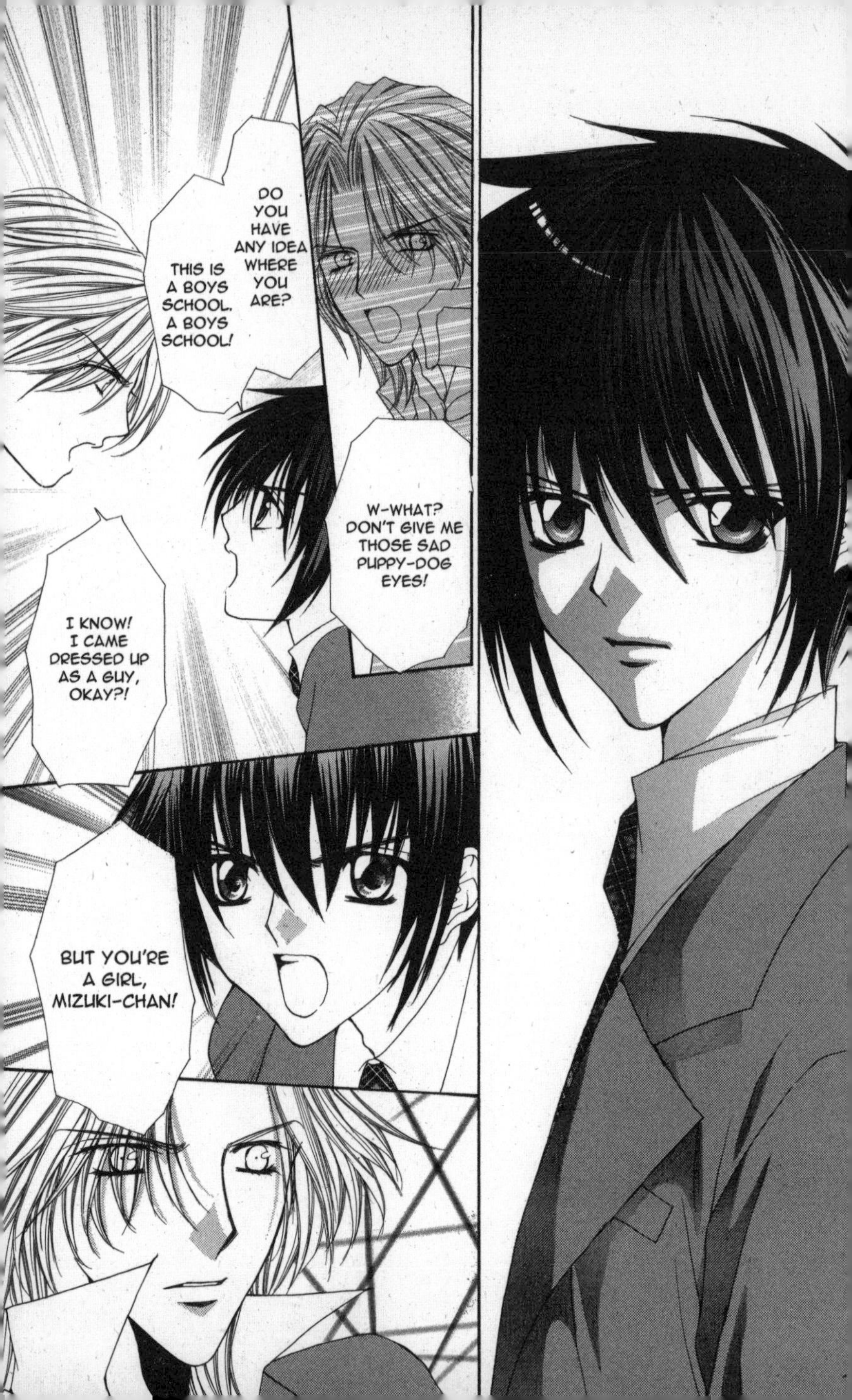
DO YOU HAVE ANY IDEA WHERE YOU ARE?
THIS IS A BOYS SCHOOL. A BOYS SCHOOL!
W-WHAT? DON'T GIVE ME THOSE SAD PUPPY-DOG EYES!
I KNOW! I CAME DRESSED UP AS A GUY, OKAY?!
BUT YOU'RE A GIRL, MIZUKI-CHAN!

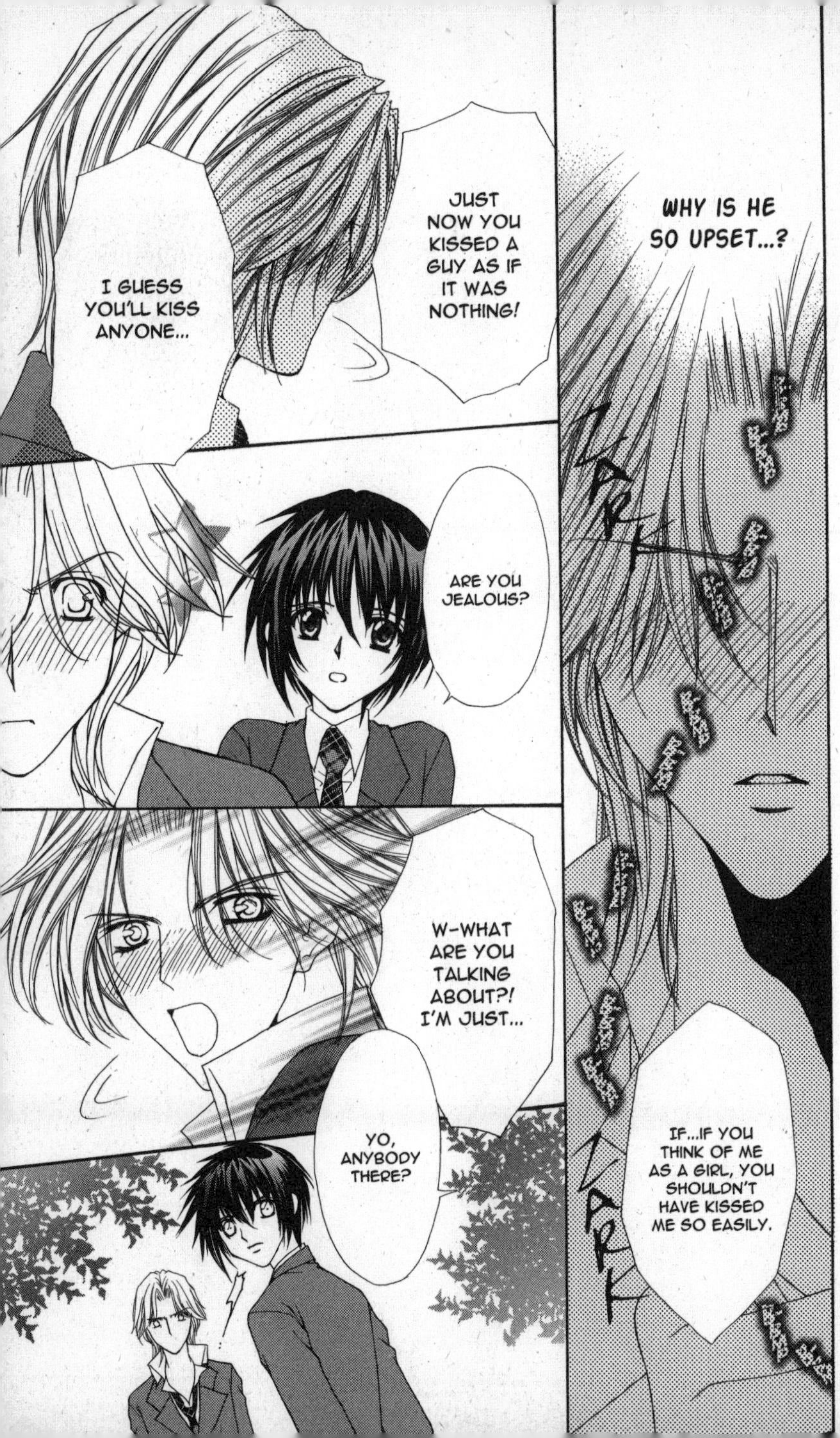
WHY IS HE SO UPSET...?
ZARK
IF...IF YOU THINK OF ME AS A GIRL, YOU SHOULDN'T HAVE KISSED ME SO EASILY.
JUST NOW YOU KISSED A GUY AS IF IT WAS NOTHING!
I GUESS YOU'LL KISS ANYONE...
ARE YOU JEALOUS?
W-WHAT ARE YOU TALKING ABOUT?! I'M JUST...
YO, ANYBODY THERE?

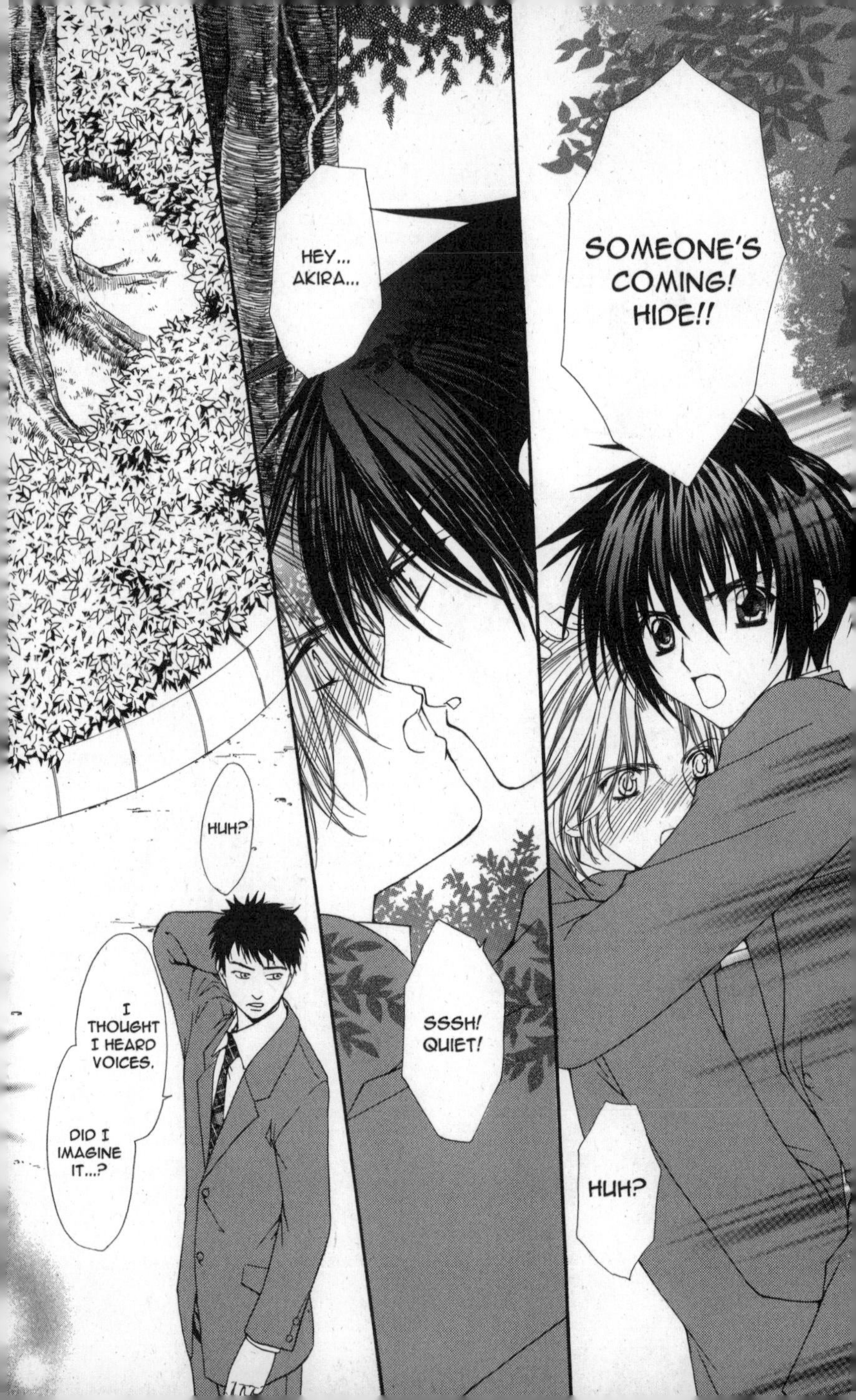
SOMEONE'S COMING! HIDE!!
HUH?
HEY... AKIRA...
SSSH! QUIET!
HUH?
I THOUGHT I HEARD VOICES.
DID I IMAGINE IT...?

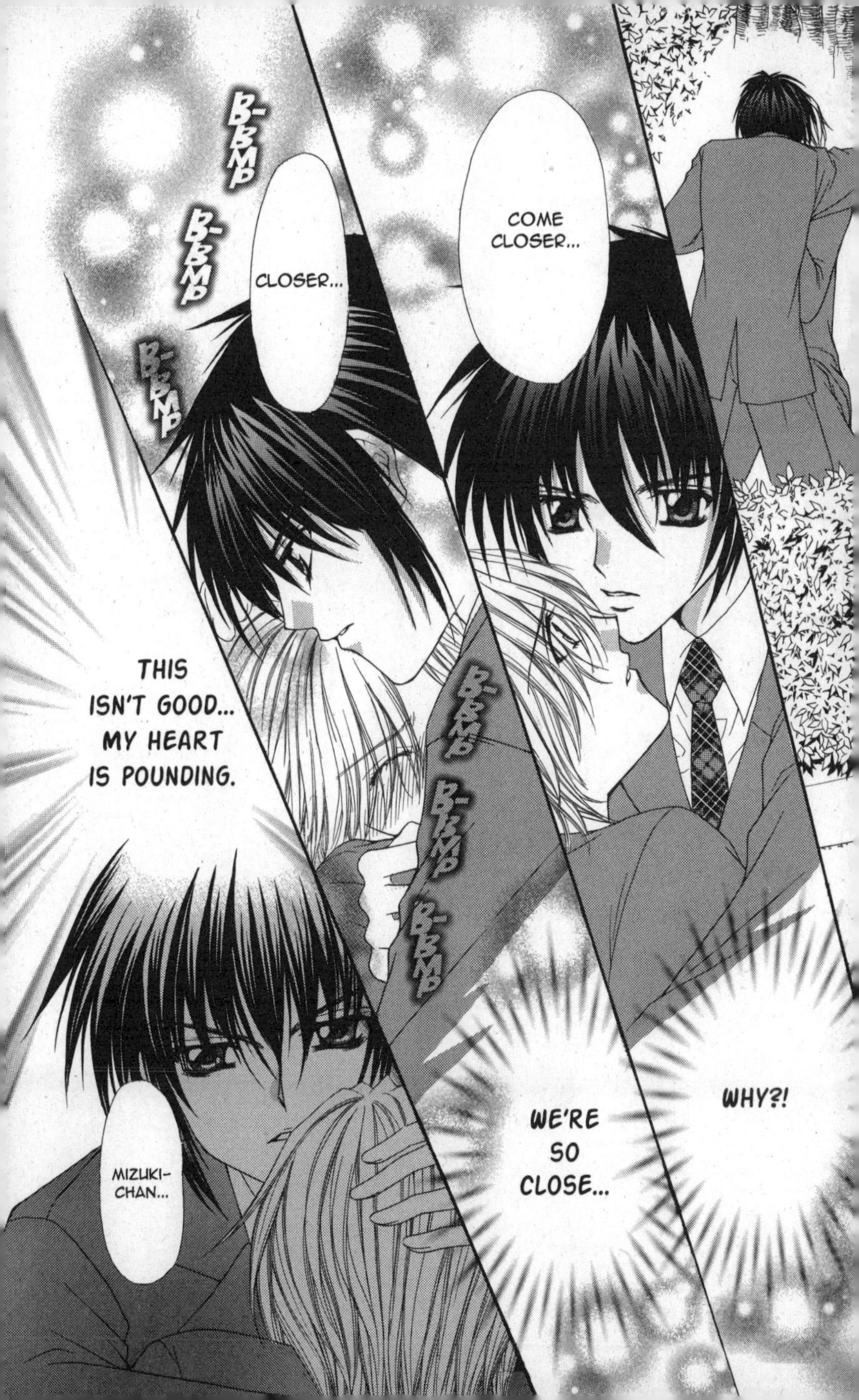
COME CLOSER...
B-BMP B-BMP B-BMP
WHY?!
WE'RE SO CLOSE...
CLOSER...
B-BMP B-BMP B-BMP
THIS ISN'T GOOD... MY HEART IS POUNDING.
MIZUKI-CHAN...

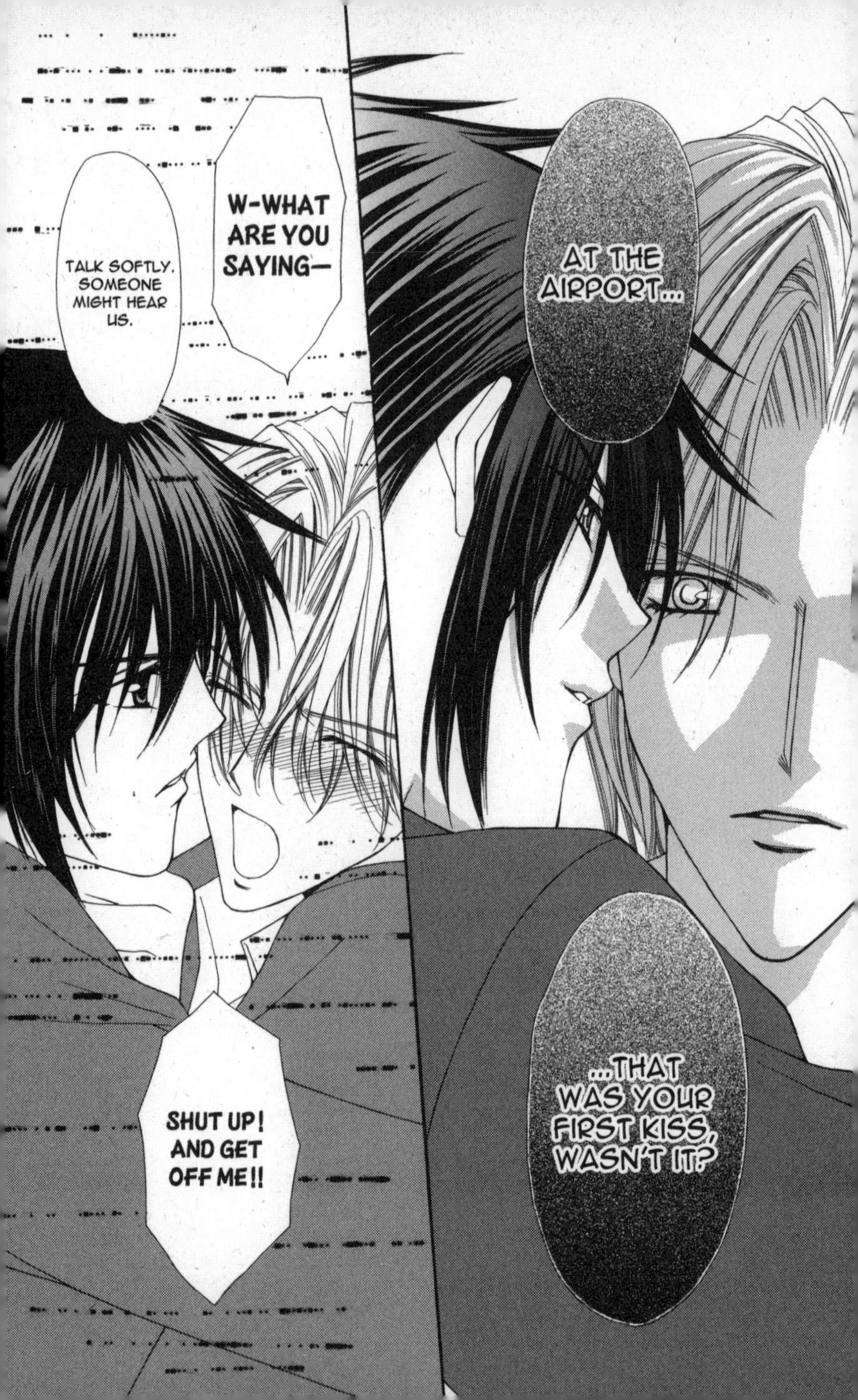
AT THE AIRPORT...
...THAT WAS YOUR FIRST KISS, WASN'T IT?
W-WHAT ARE YOU SAYING—
TALK SOFTLY. SOMEONE MIGHT HEAR US.
SHUT UP! AND GET OFF ME!!

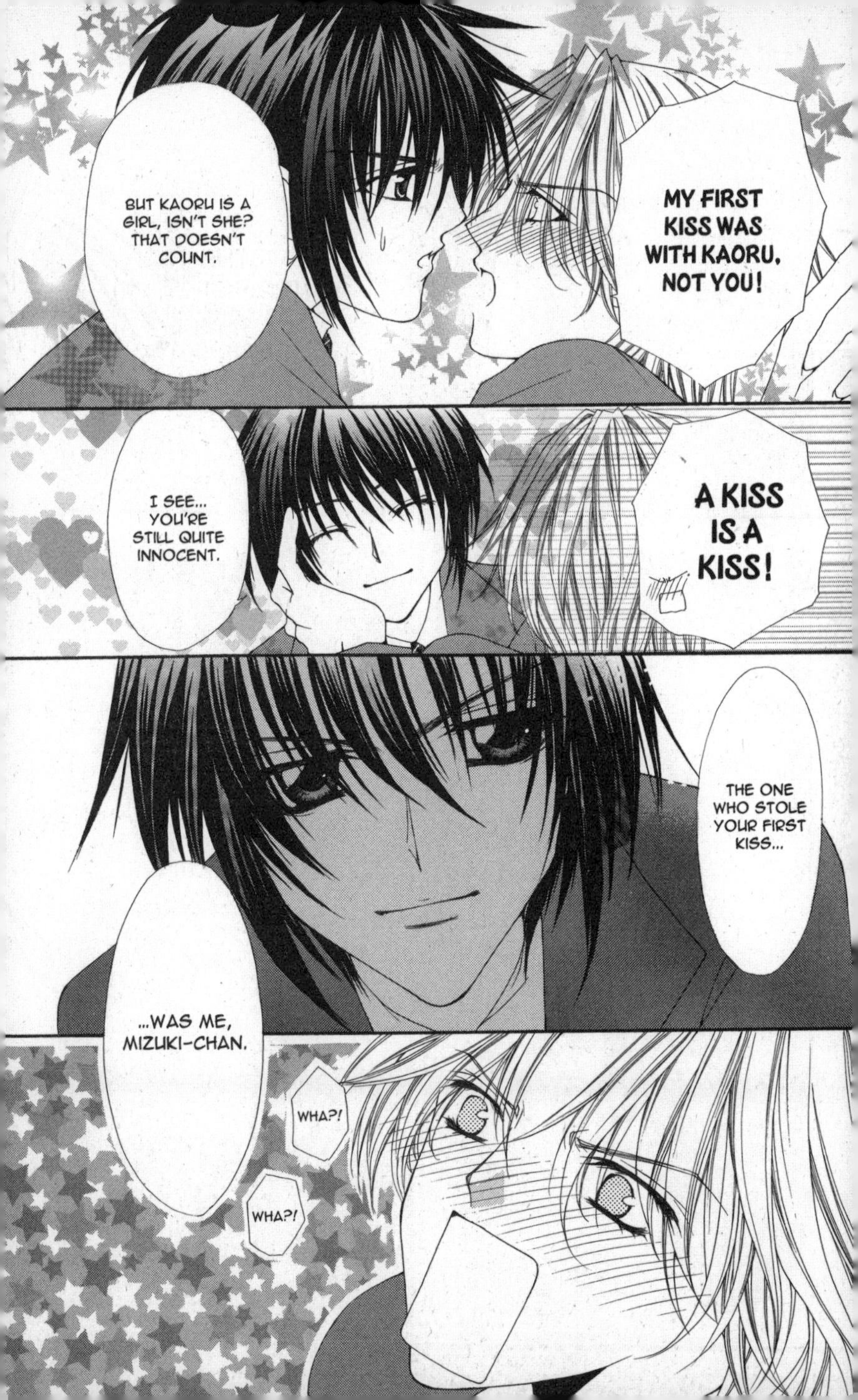
MY FIRST KISS WAS WITH KAORU, NOT YOU!
BUT KAORU IS A GIRL, ISN'T SHE? THAT DOESN'T COUNT.
A KISS IS A KISS!
I SEE... YOU'RE STILL QUITE INNOCENT.
THE ONE WHO STOLE YOUR FIRST KISS...
...WAS ME, MIZUKI-CHAN.
WHA?!
WHA?!

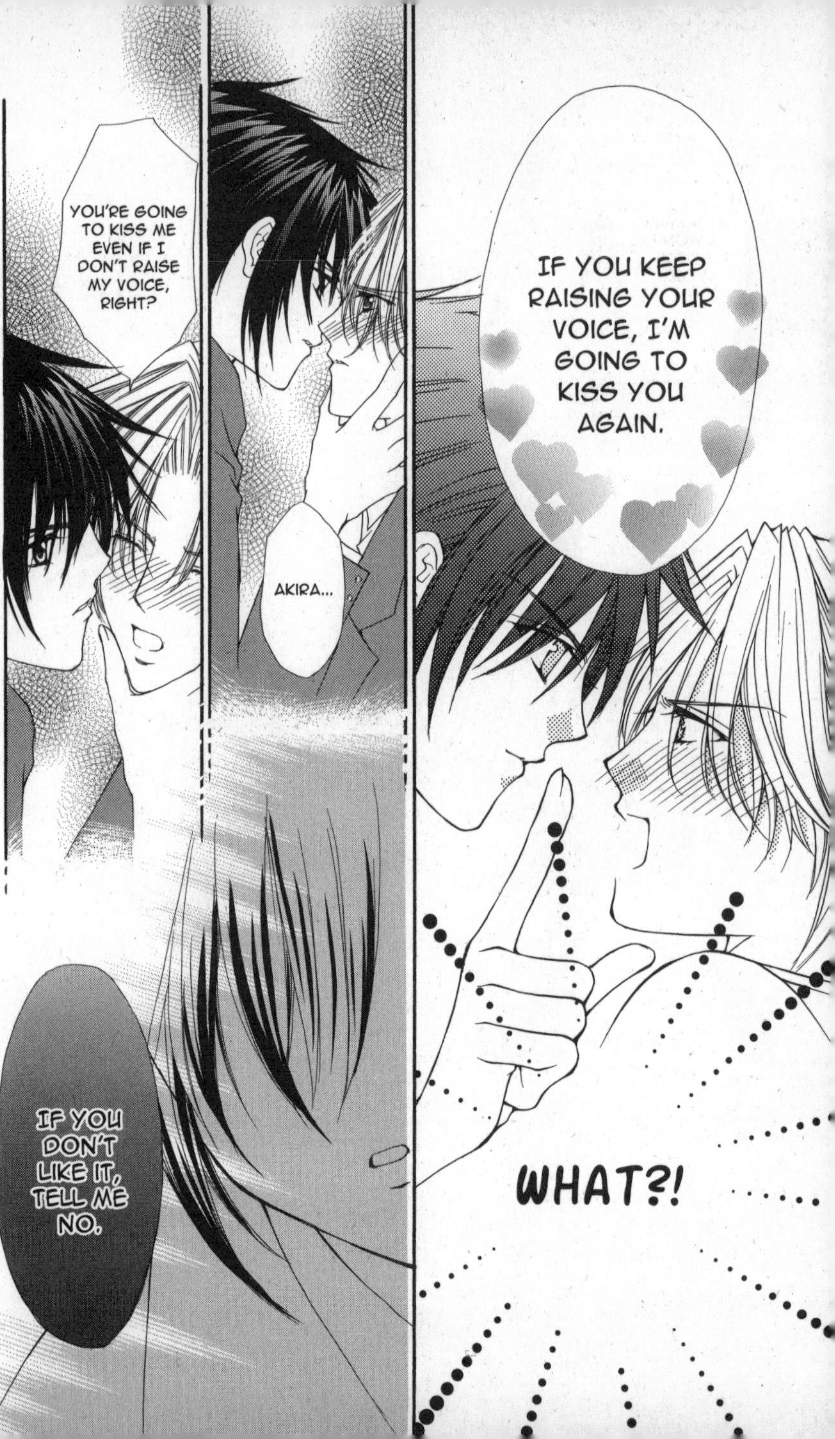
IF YOU KEEP RAISING YOUR VOICE, I'M GOING TO KISS YOU AGAIN.
WHAT?!
AKIRA...
YOU'RE GOING TO KISS ME EVEN IF I DON'T RAISE MY VOICE, RIGHT?
IF YOU DON'T LIKE IT, TELL ME NO.

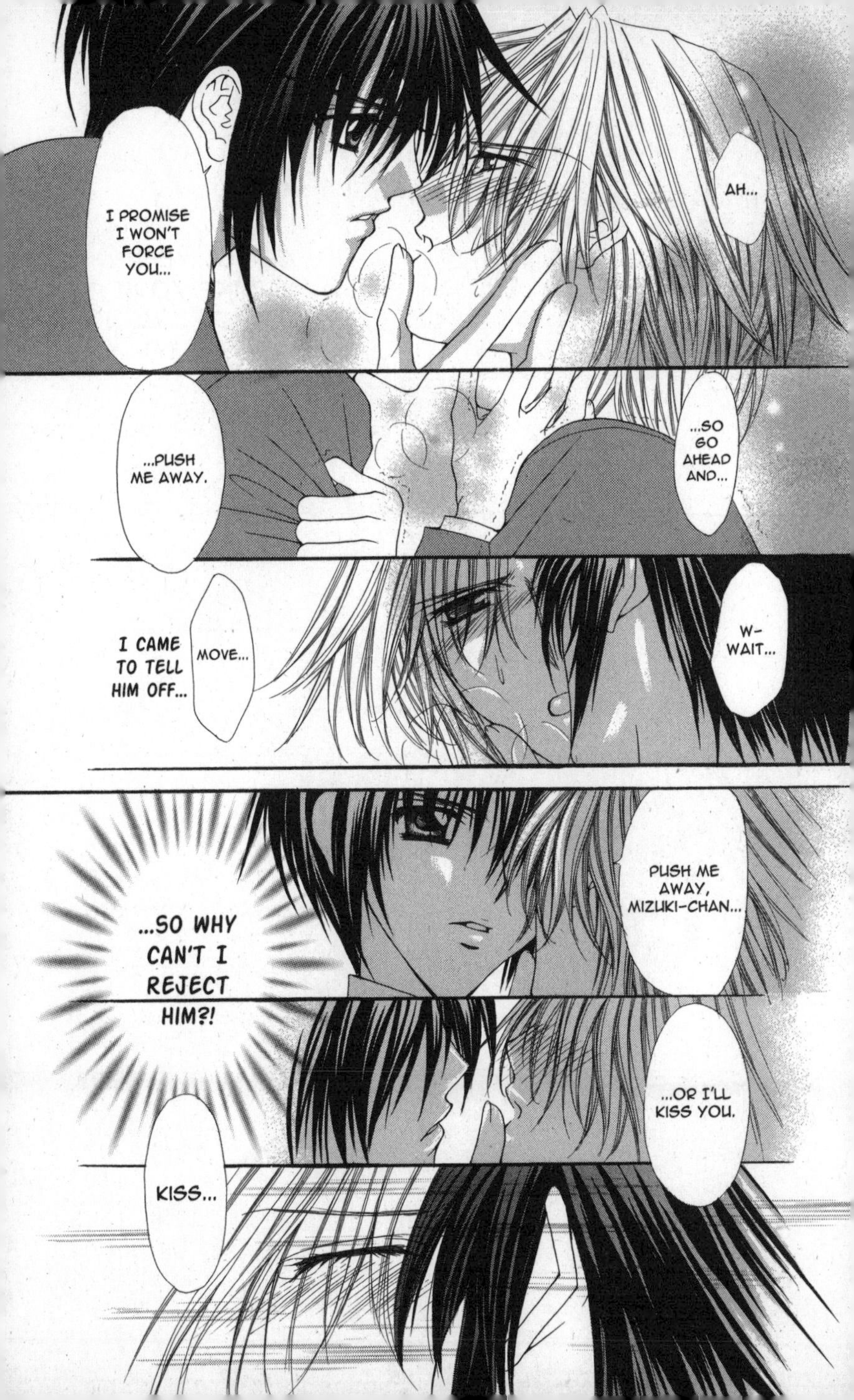
AH...
I PROMISE I WON'T FORCE YOU...
...SO GO AHEAD AND...
...PUSH ME AWAY.
W-WAIT...
MOVE...
I CAME TO TELL HIM OFF...
PUSH ME AWAY, MIZUKI-CHAN...
...SO WHY CAN'T I REJECT HIM?!
...OR I'LL KISS YOU.
KISS...

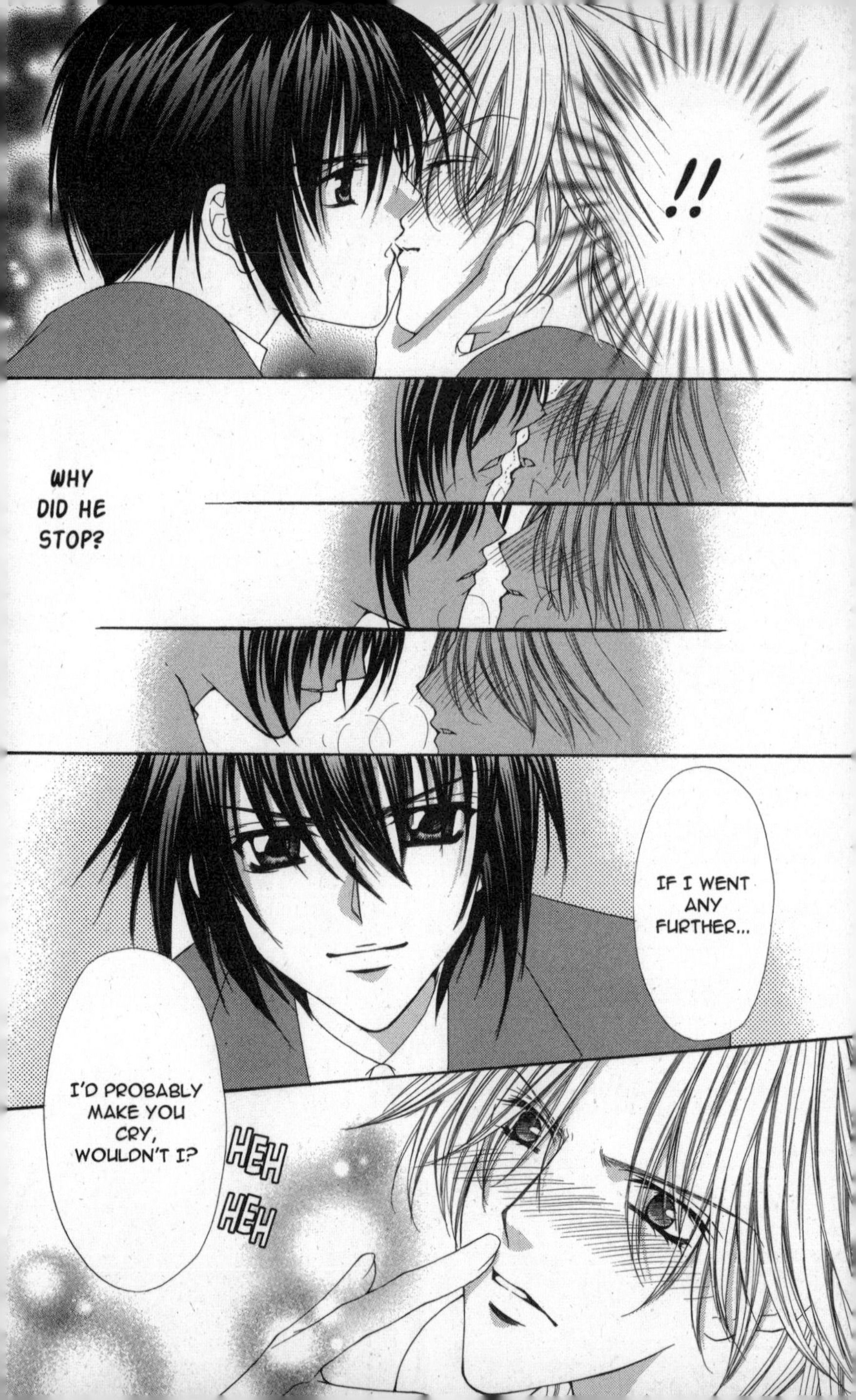
!!
WHY DID HE STOP?
IF I WENT ANY FURTHER...
I'D PROBABLY MAKE YOU CRY, WOULDN'T I?
HEH HEH

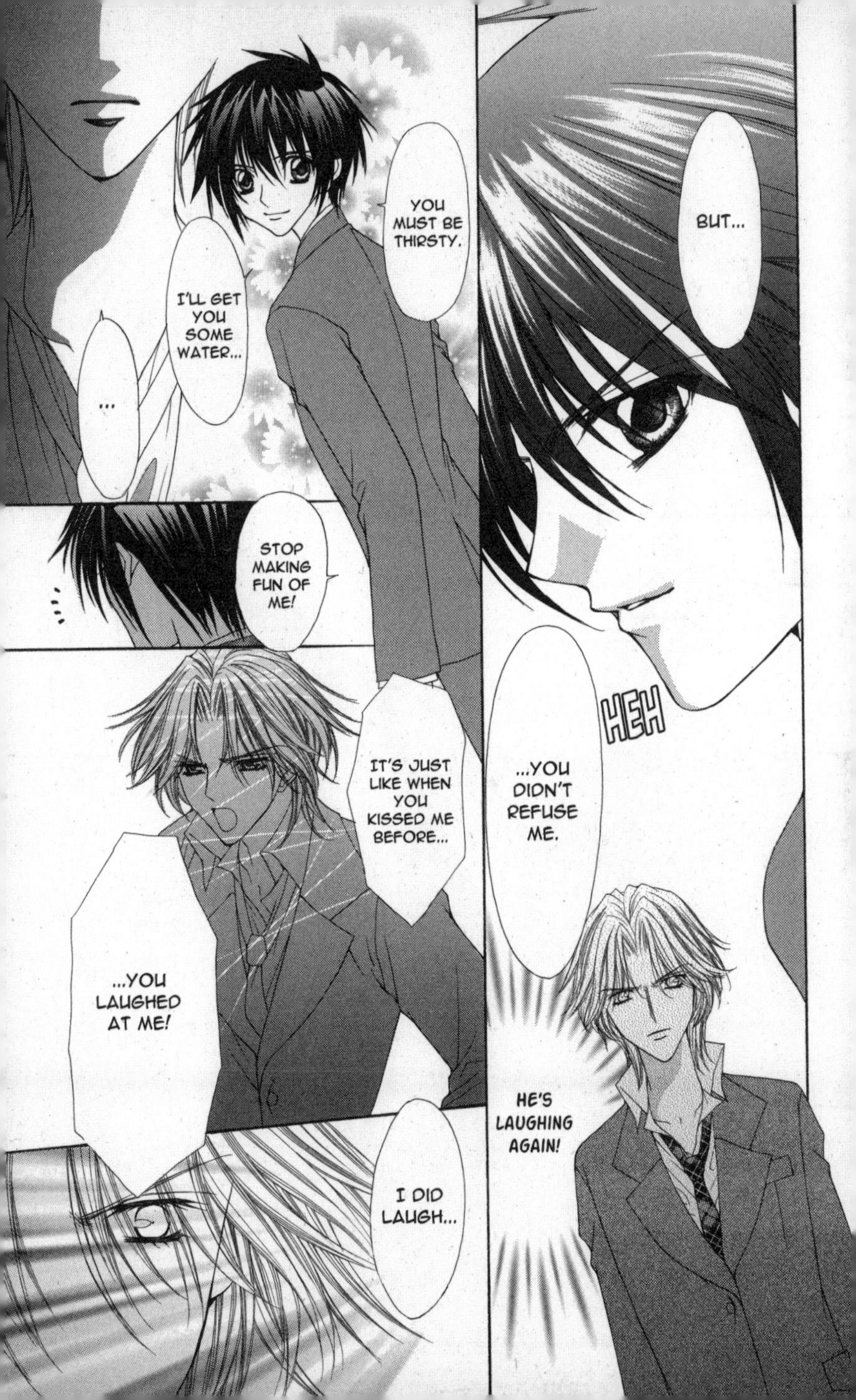
YOU MUST BE THIRSTY.
I'LL GET YOU SOME WATER...
...
STOP MAKING FUN OF ME!
IT'S JUST LIKE WHEN YOU KISSED ME BEFORE...
...YOU LAUGHED AT ME!
I DID LAUGH...
BUT...
HEH
...YOU DIDN'T REFUSE ME.
HE'S LAUGHING AGAIN!

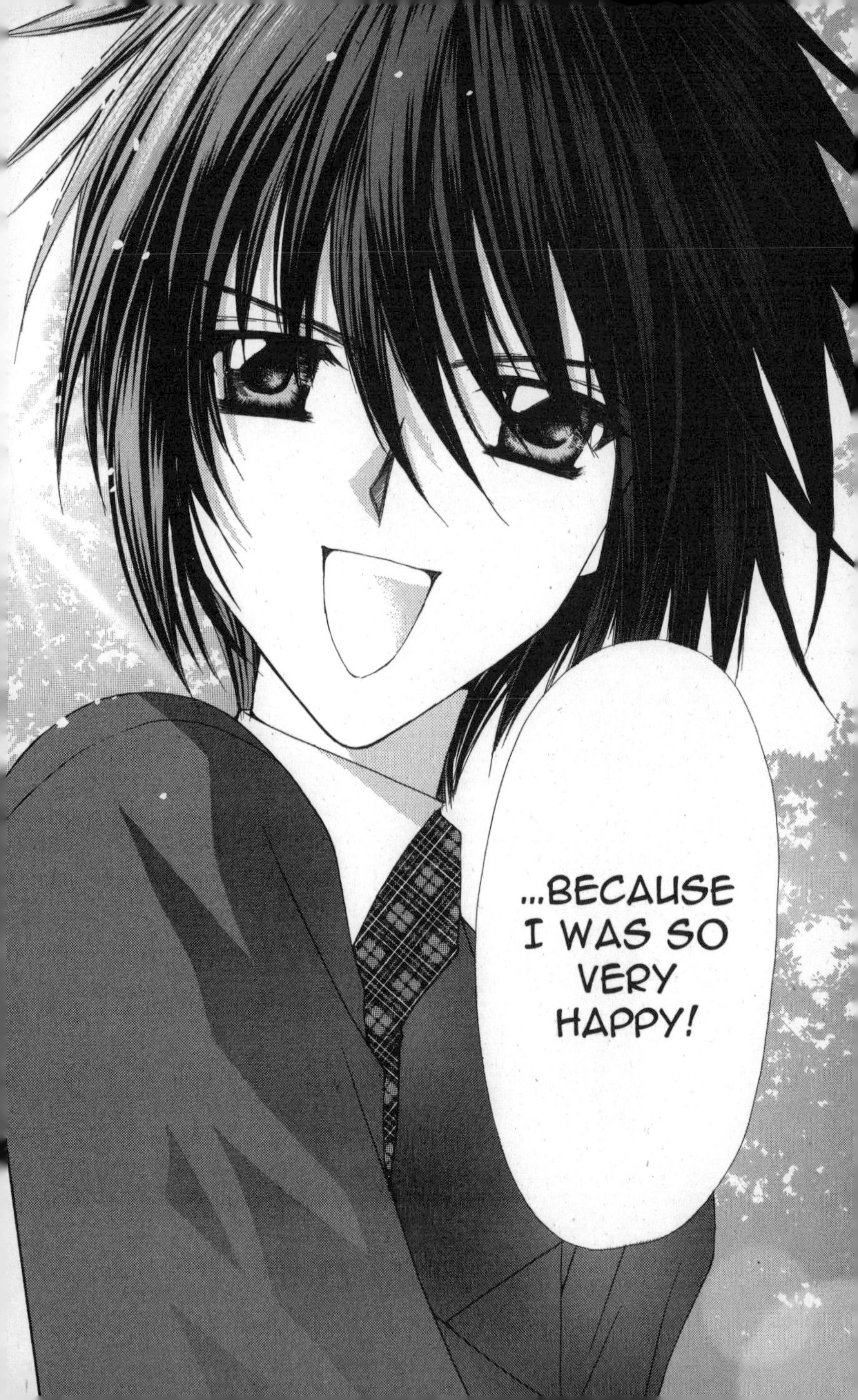
...BECAUSE I WAS SO VERY HAPPY!

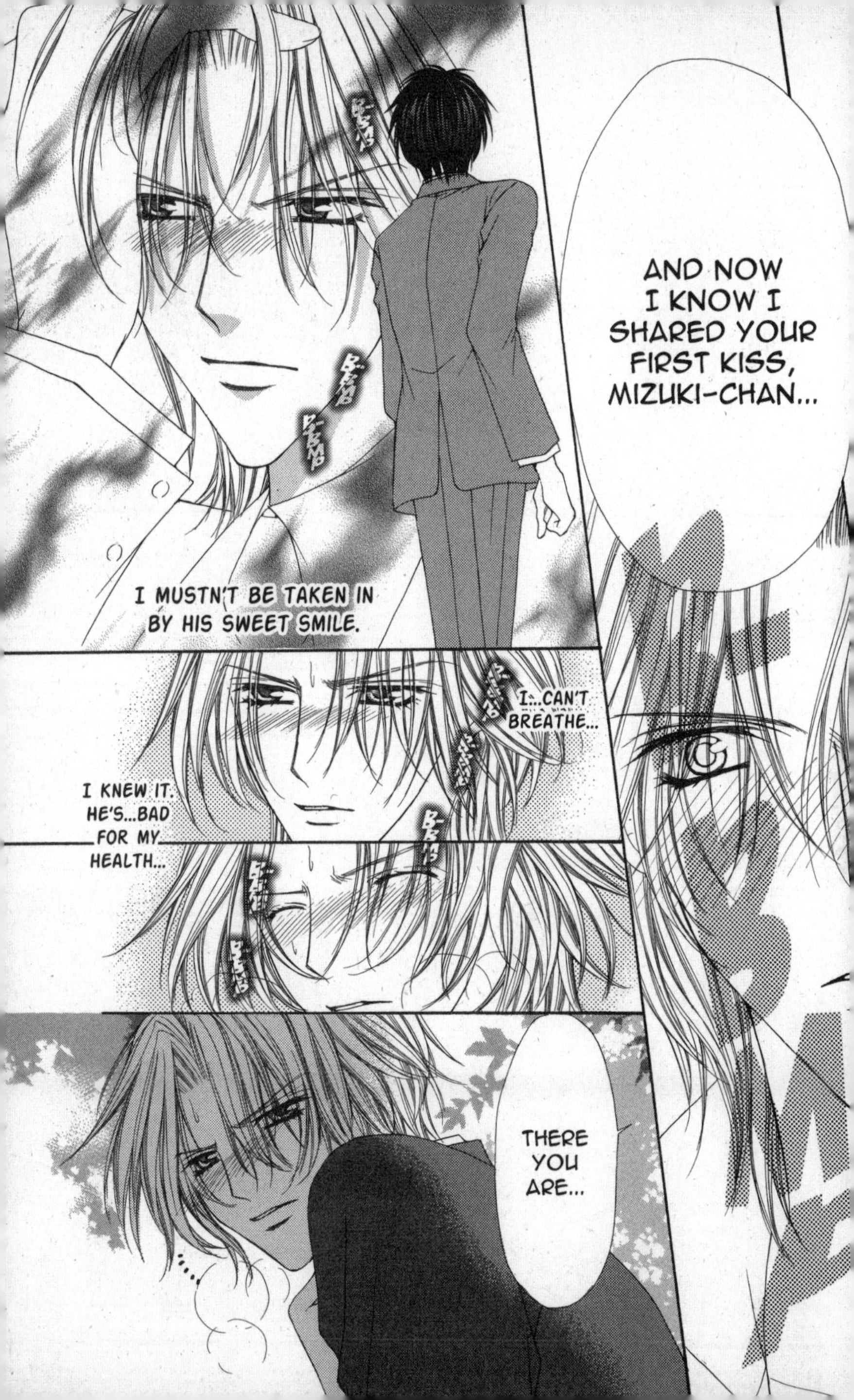
AND NOW I KNOW I SHARED YOUR FIRST KISS, MIZUKI-CHAN...
I MUSTN'T BE TAKEN IN BY HIS SWEET SMILE.
I...CAN'T BREATHE...
I KNEW IT. HE'S...BAD FOR MY HEALTH...
THERE YOU ARE...
...

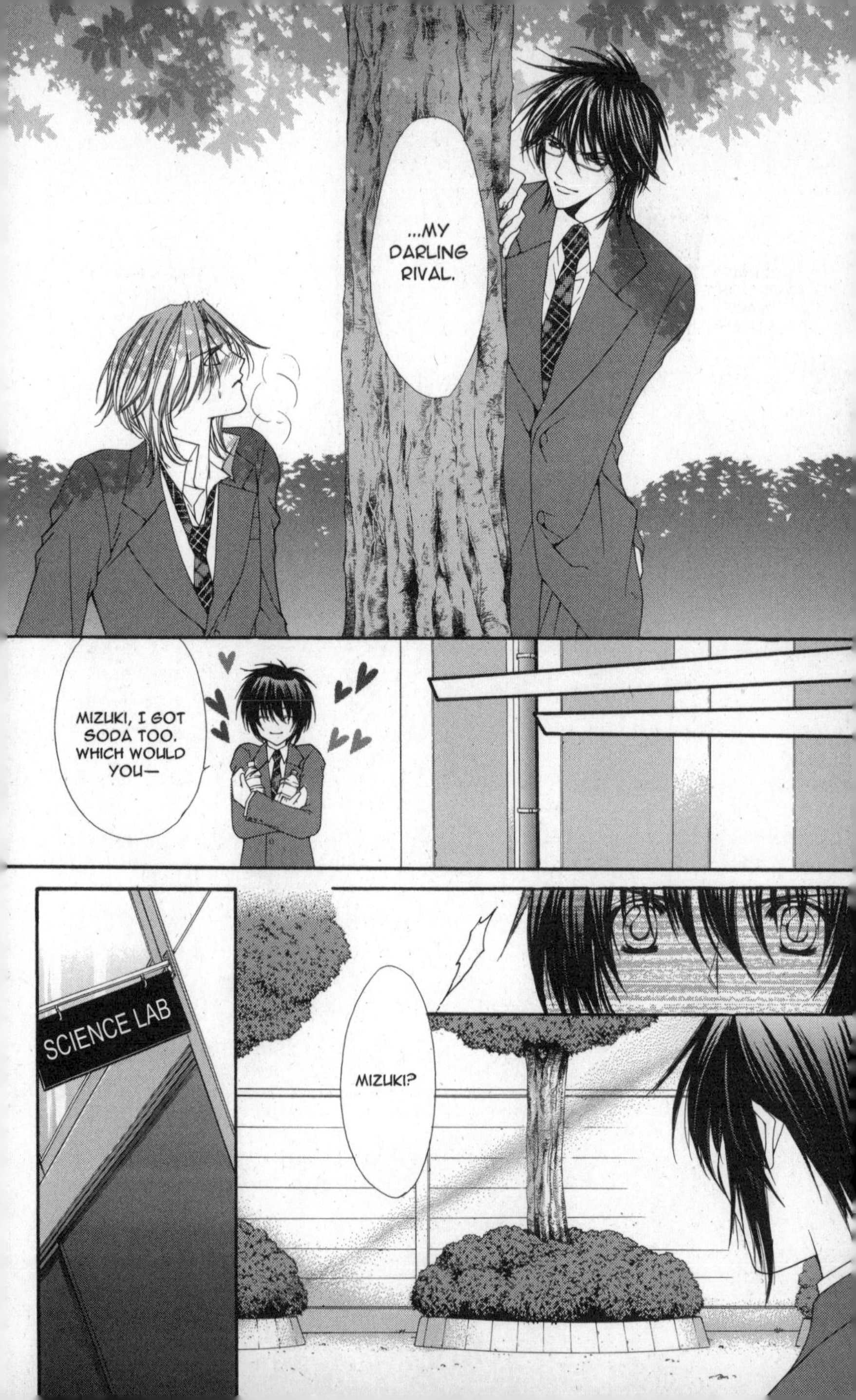
...MY DARLING RIVAL.
MIZUKI, I GOT SODA TOO. WHICH WOULD YOU—
MIZUKI?
SCIENCE LAB

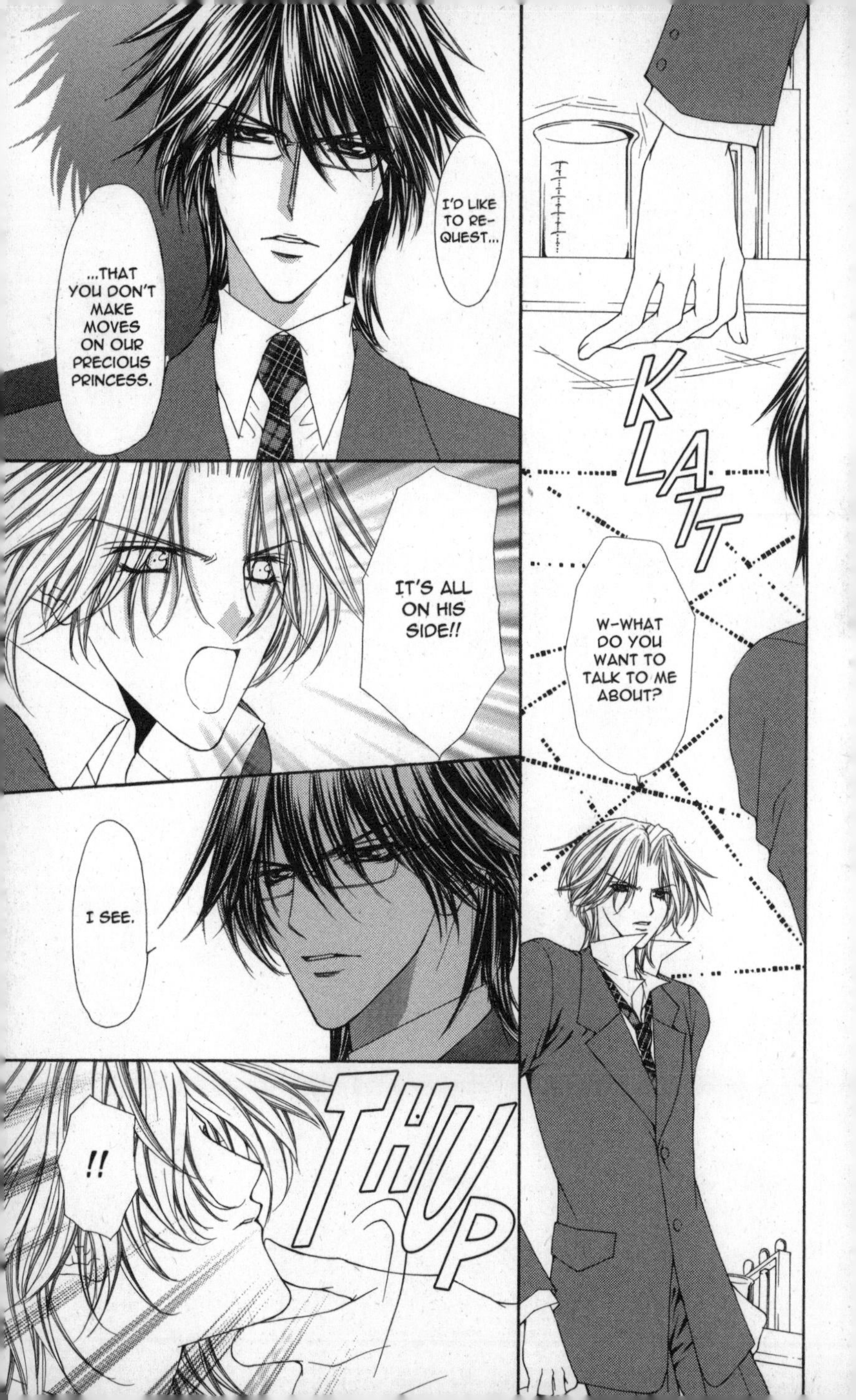
KLATT
W-WHAT DO YOU WANT TO TALK TO ME ABOUT?
I'D LIKE TO RE-QUEST...
...THAT YOU DON'T MAKE MOVES ON OUR PRECIOUS PRINCESS.
IT'S ALL ON HIS SIDE!!
I SEE.
THUP
!!

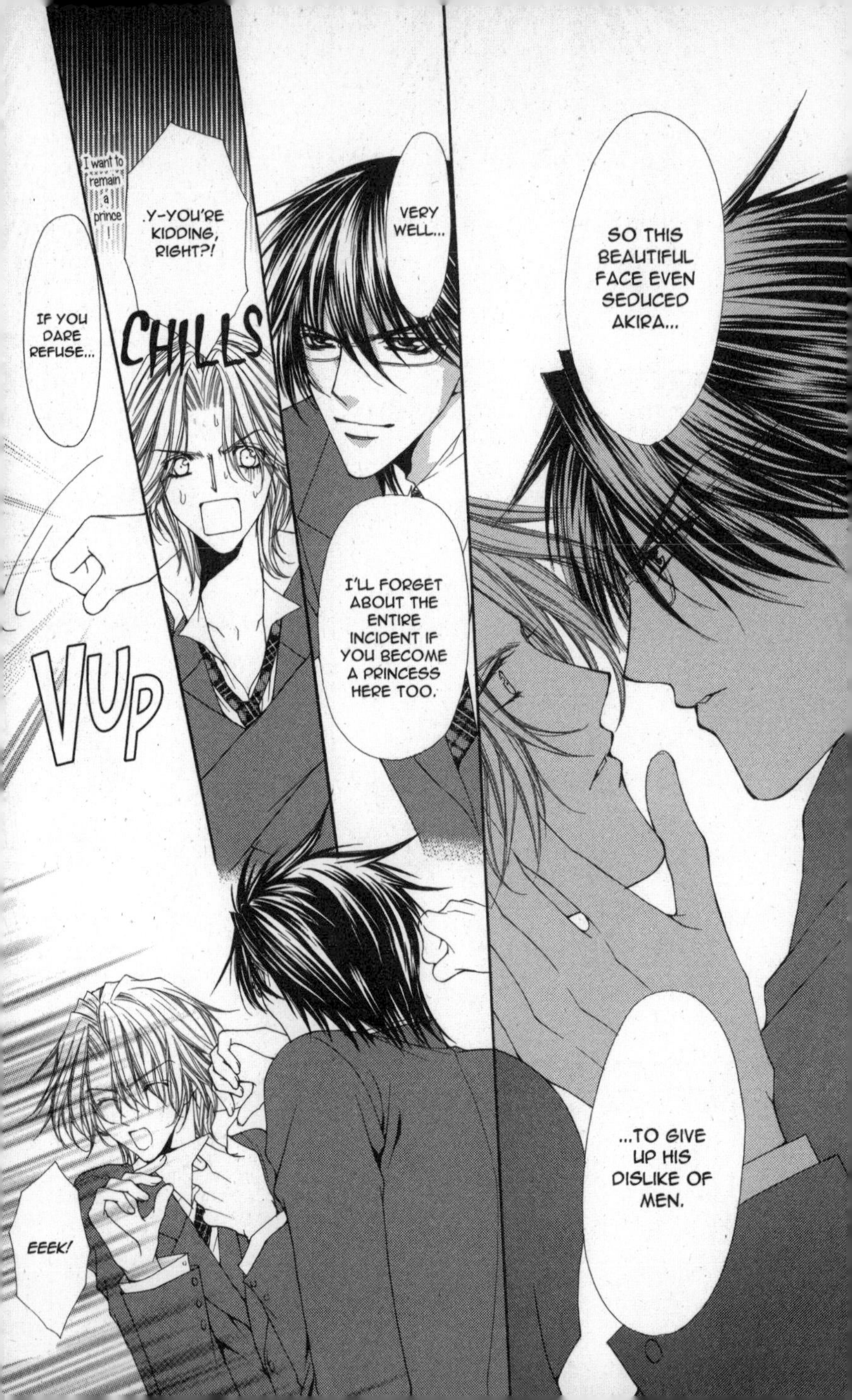

SO THIS BEAUTIFUL FACE EVEN SEDUCED AKIRA...
...TO GIVE UP HIS DISLIKE OF MEN.
VERY WELL...
I'LL FORGET ABOUT THE ENTIRE INCIDENT IF YOU BECOME A PRINCESS HERE TOO.
Y-YOU'RE KIDDING, RIGHT?!
CHILLS
I want to remain a prince!
IF YOU DARE REFUSE...
VUP
EEEK!

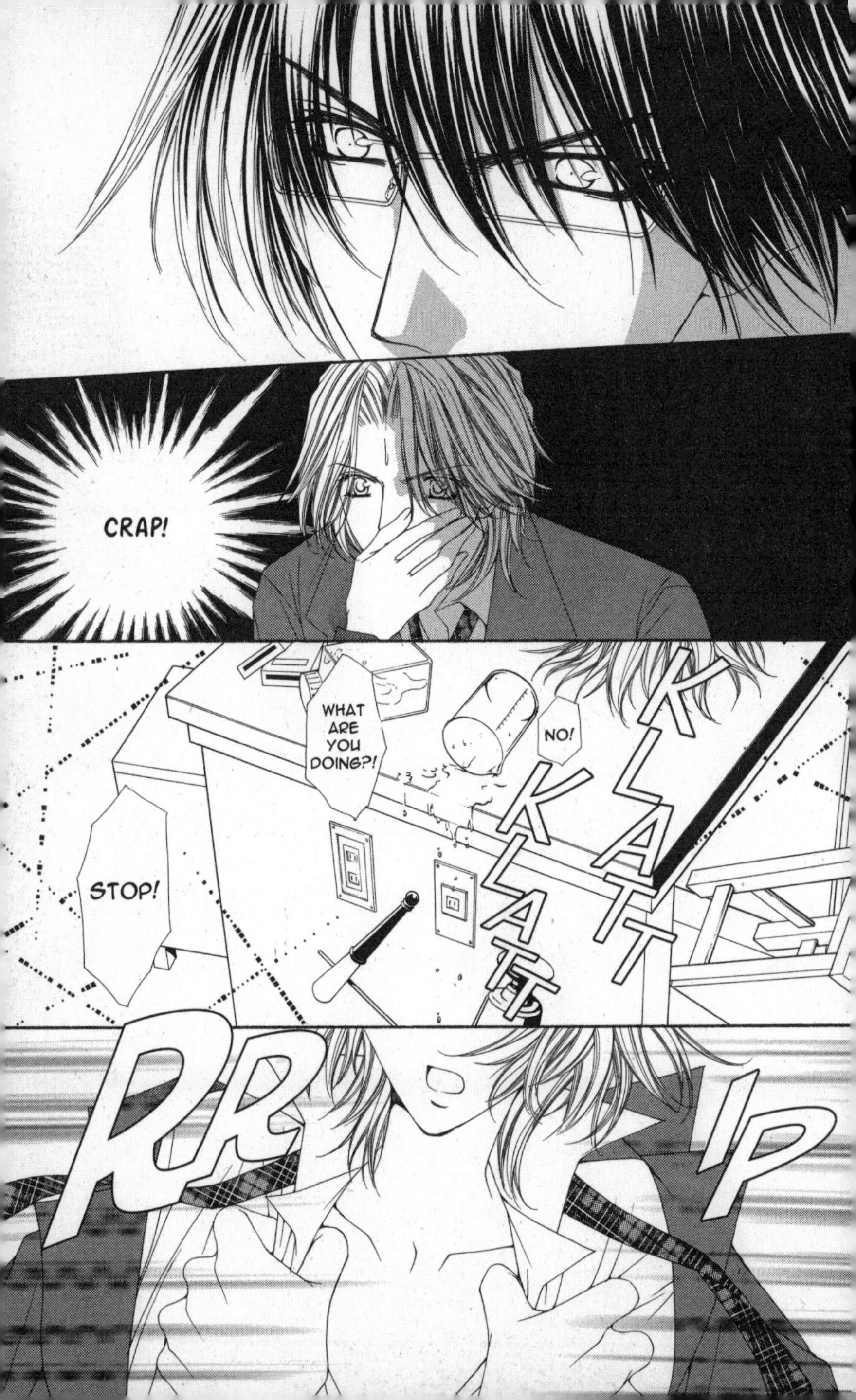
CRAP!
KLATT KLATT
NO!
WHAT ARE YOU DOING?!
STOP!
RRRIP

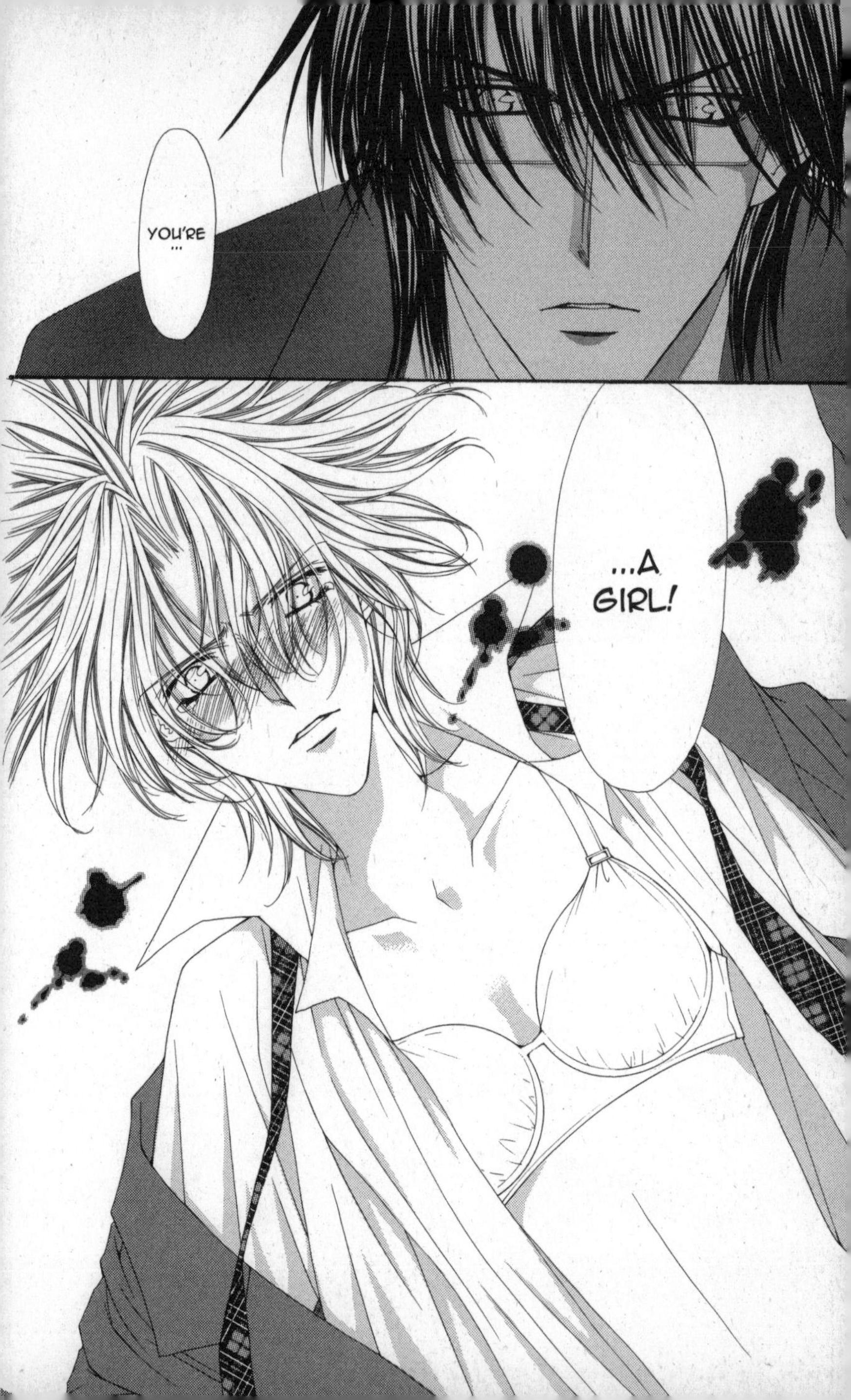
YOU'RE ...
...A GIRL!

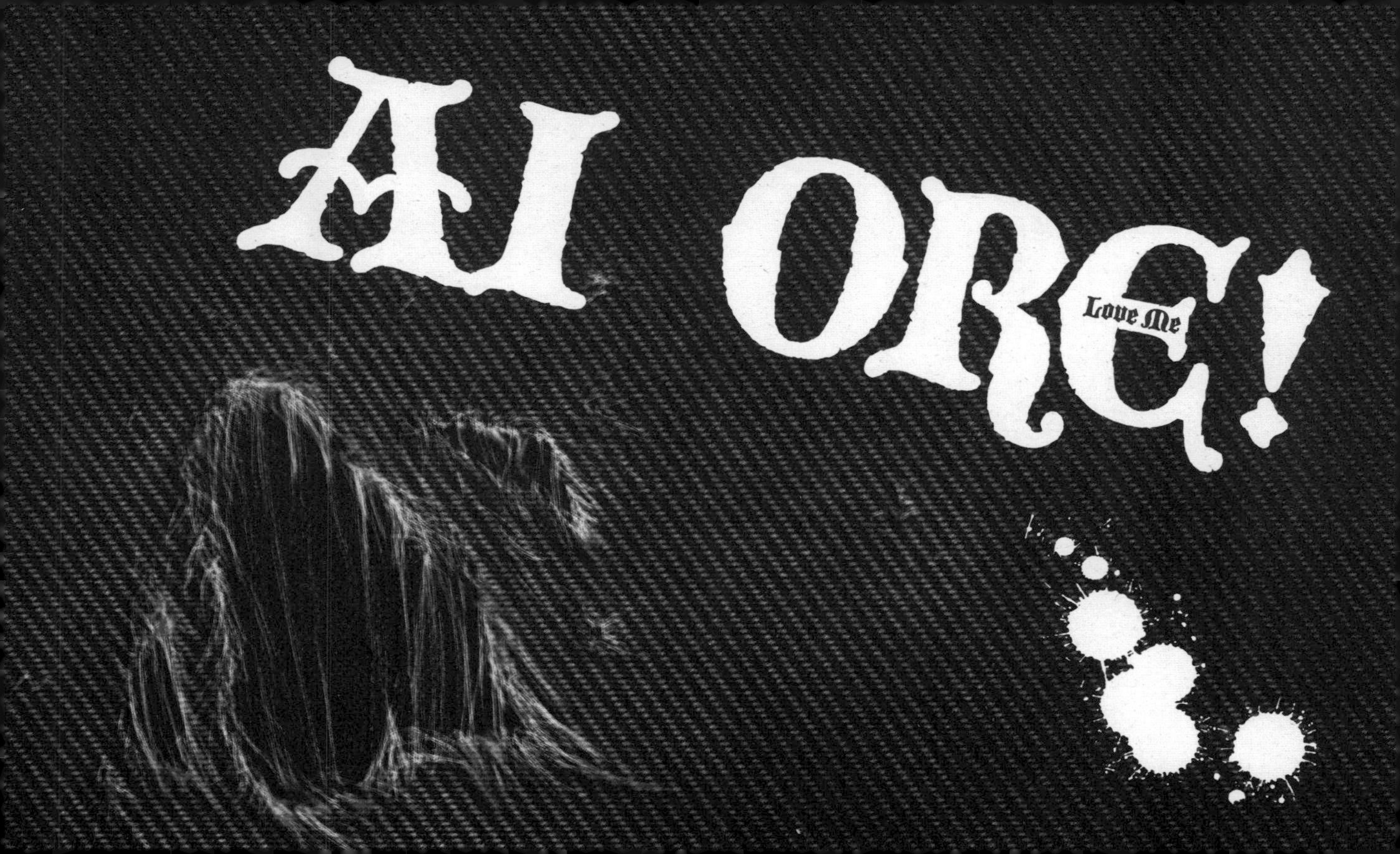
AI ORE!
Love Me

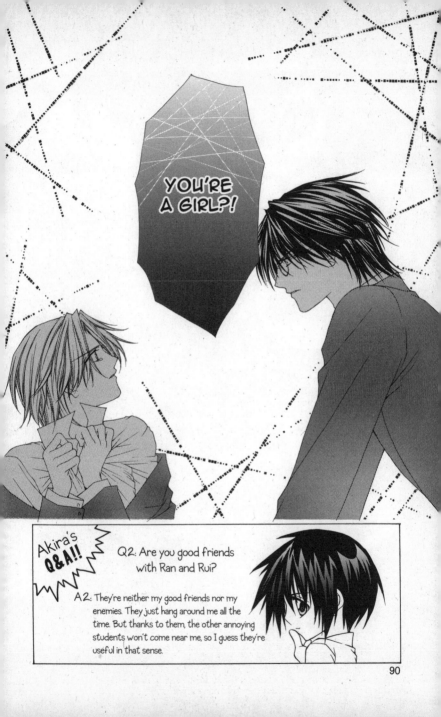

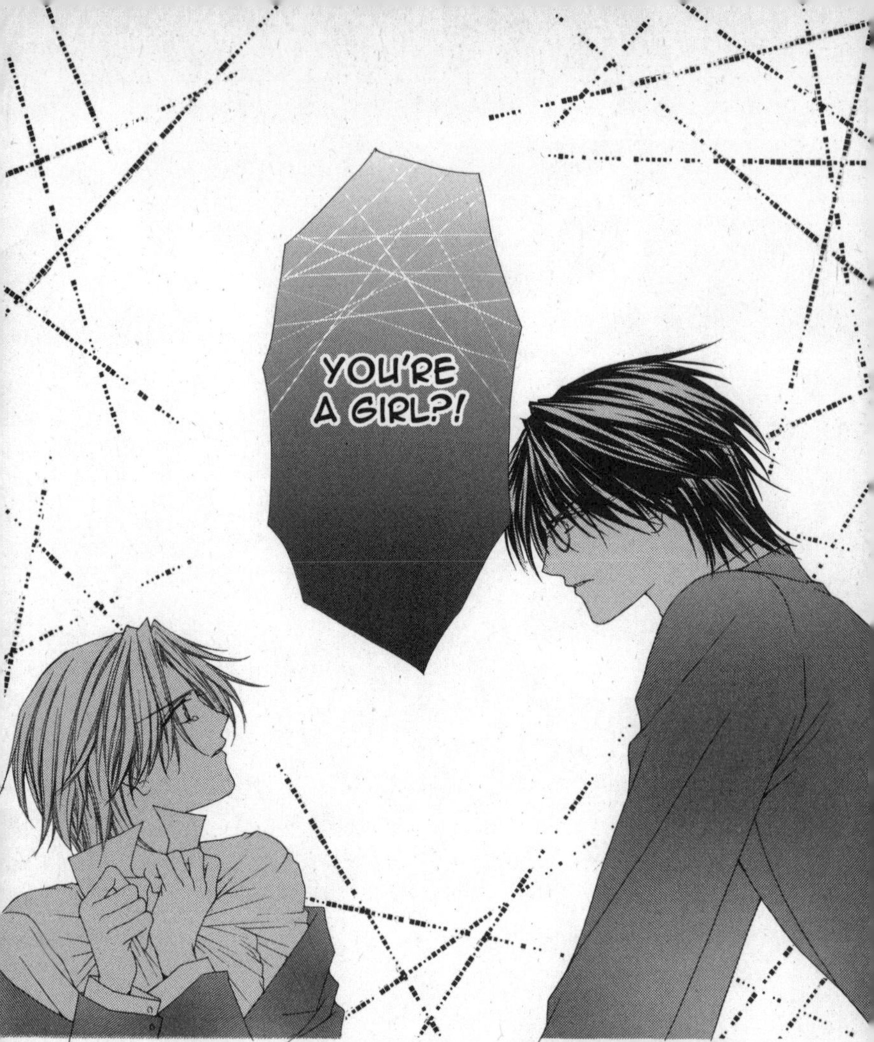
YOU'RE A GIRL?!

Akira's Q&A!!

Q2: Are you good friends with Ran and Rui?

A2: They're neither my good friends nor my enemies. They just hang around me all the time. But thanks to them, the other annoying students won't come near me, so I guess they're useful in that sense.

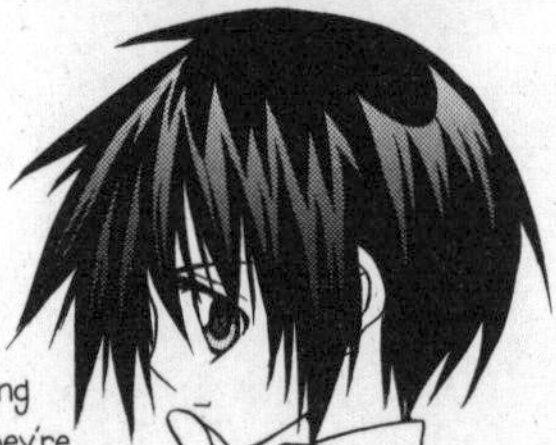

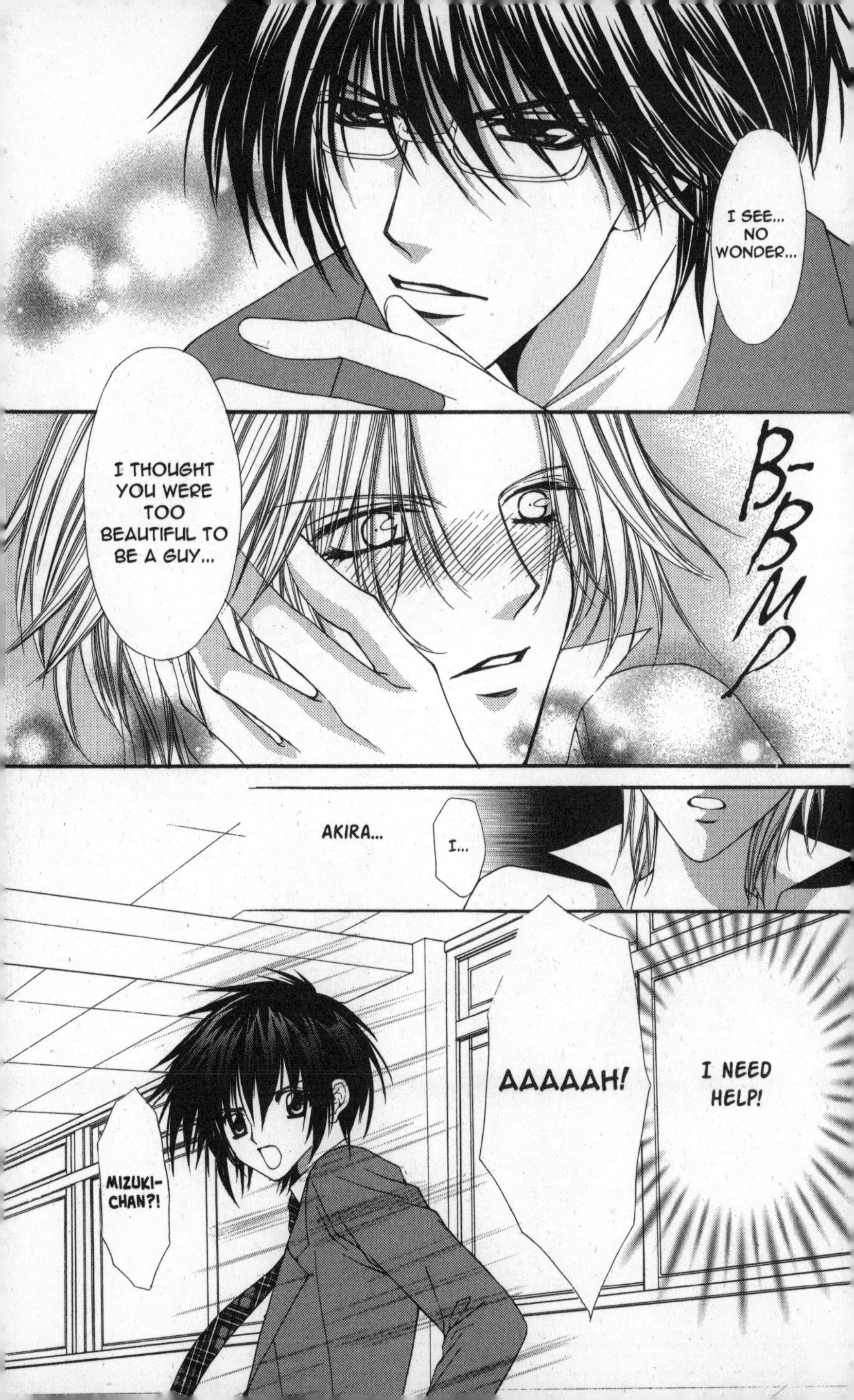
I SEE... NO WONDER...
I THOUGHT YOU WERE TOO BEAUTIFUL TO BE A GUY...
B-BUMP!
I...
AKIRA...
I NEED HELP!
AAAAAH!
MIZUKI-CHAN?!

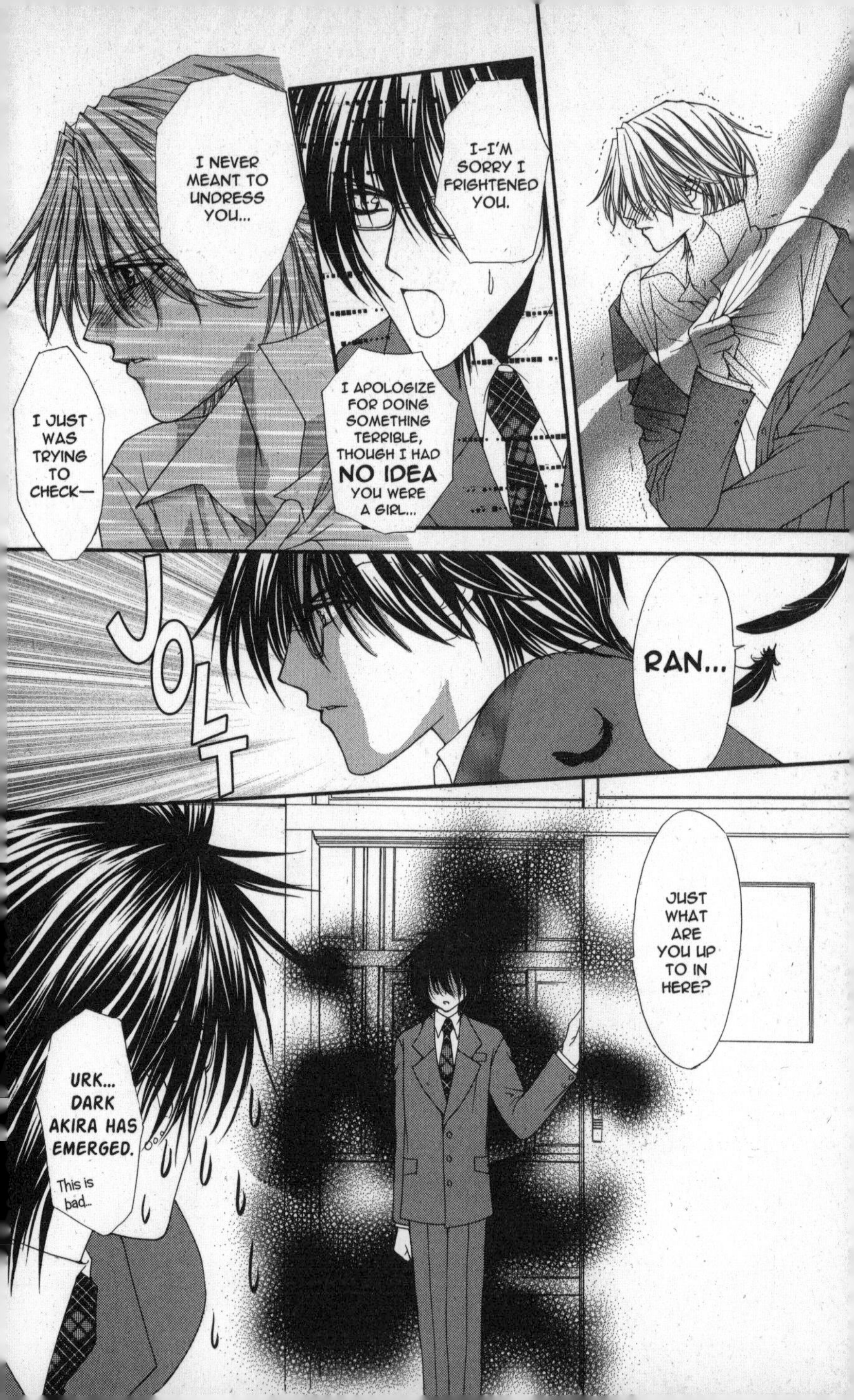
I-I'M SORRY I FRIGHTENED YOU.
I APOLOGIZE FOR DOING SOMETHING TERRIBLE, THOUGH I HAD NO IDEA YOU WERE A GIRL...
I NEVER MEANT TO UNDRESS YOU...
I JUST WAS TRYING TO CHECK—
RAN...
JOLT
JUST WHAT ARE YOU UP TO IN HERE?
URK... DARK AKIRA HAS EMERGED.
This is bad...

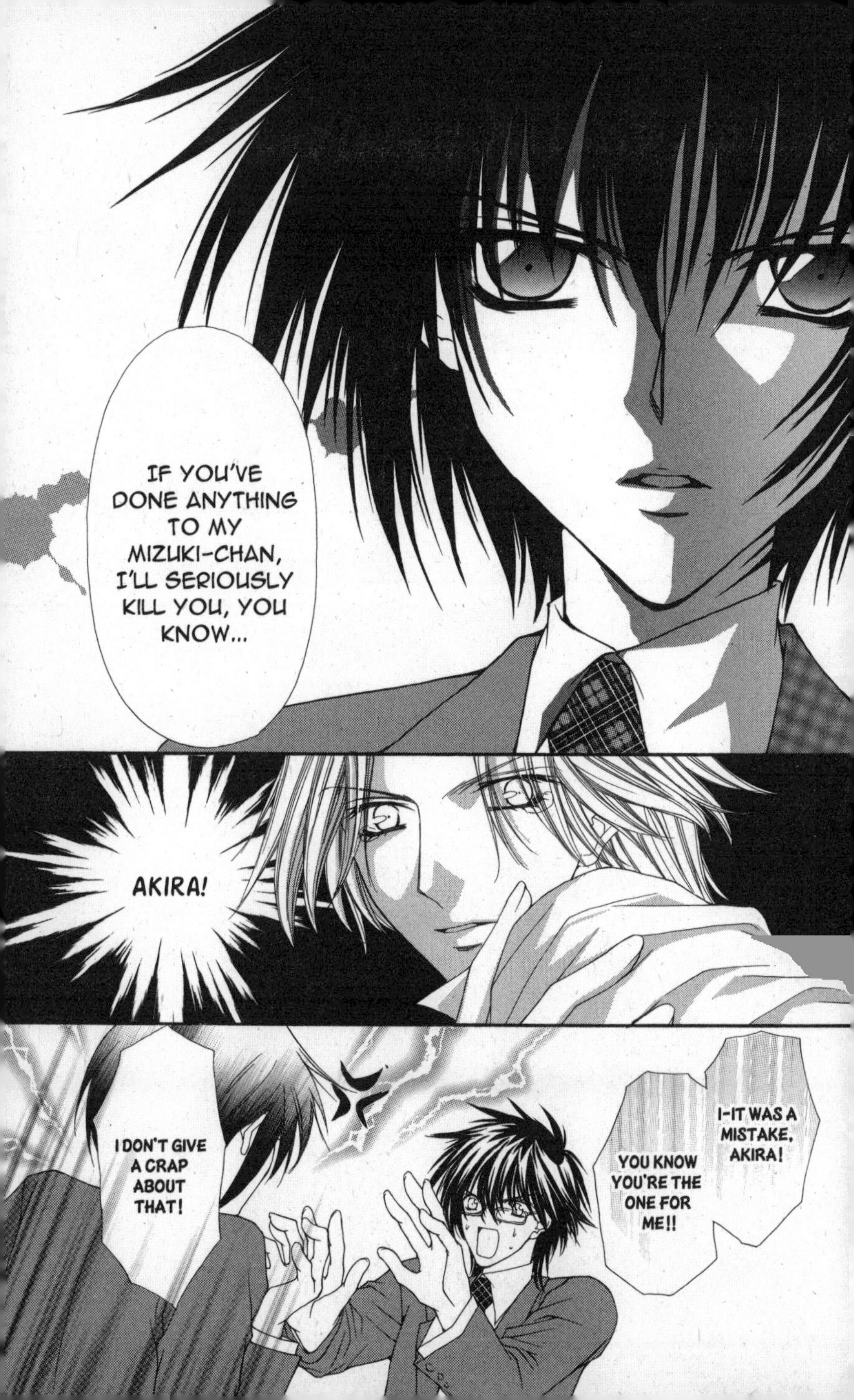
IF YOU'VE DONE ANYTHING TO MY MIZUKI-CHAN, I'LL SERIOUSLY KILL YOU, YOU KNOW...
AKIRA!
I-IT WAS A MISTAKE, AKIRA!
YOU KNOW YOU'RE THE ONE FOR ME!!
I DON'T GIVE A CRAP ABOUT THAT!

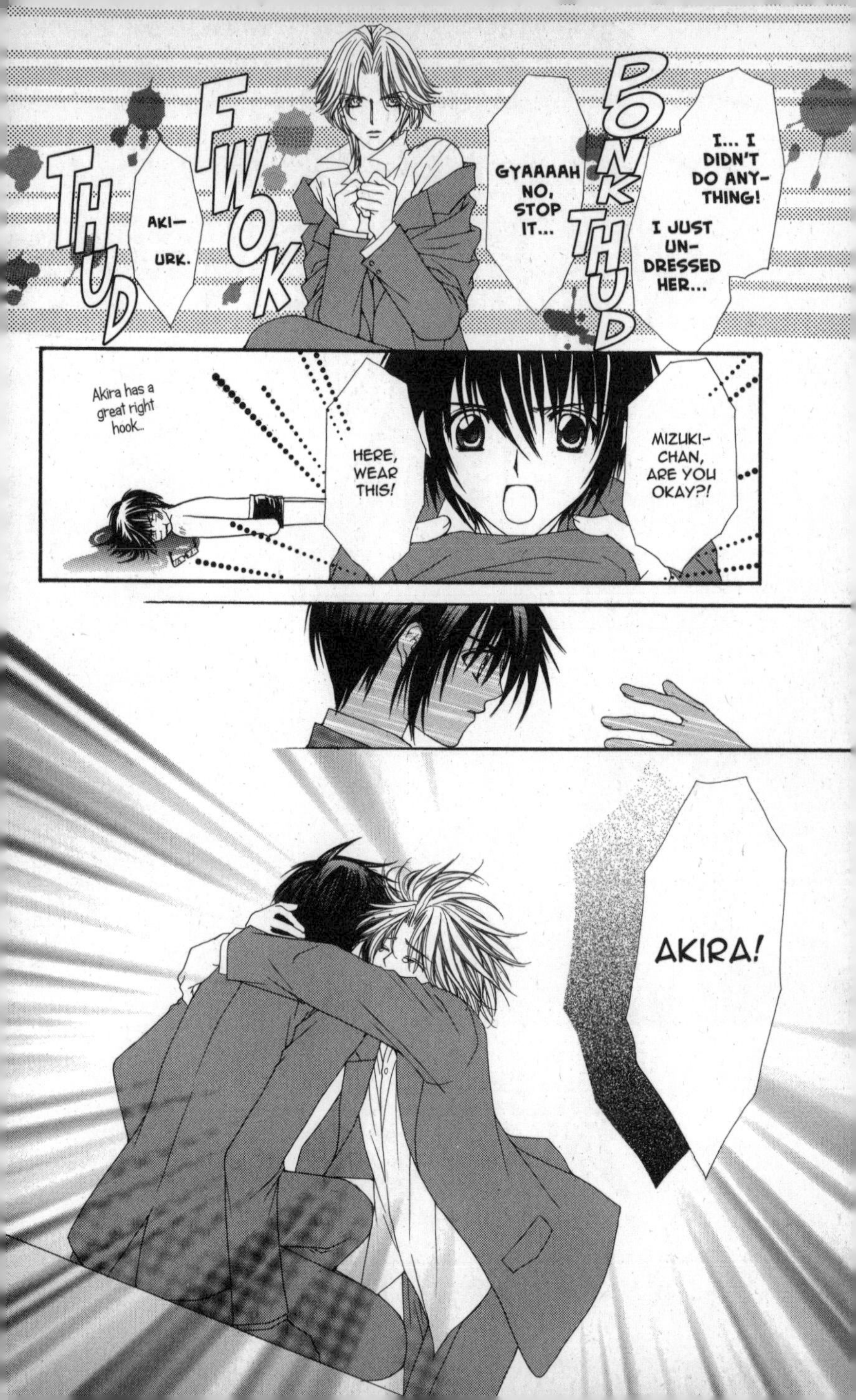
I... I DIDN'T DO ANYTHING!
I JUST UNDRESSED HER...
THUD
BONK
GYAAAAH NO, STOP IT...
FWOK
AKI— URK.
THUD
MIZUKI-CHAN, ARE YOU OKAY?!
HERE, WEAR THIS!
Akira has a great right hook...
AKIRA!

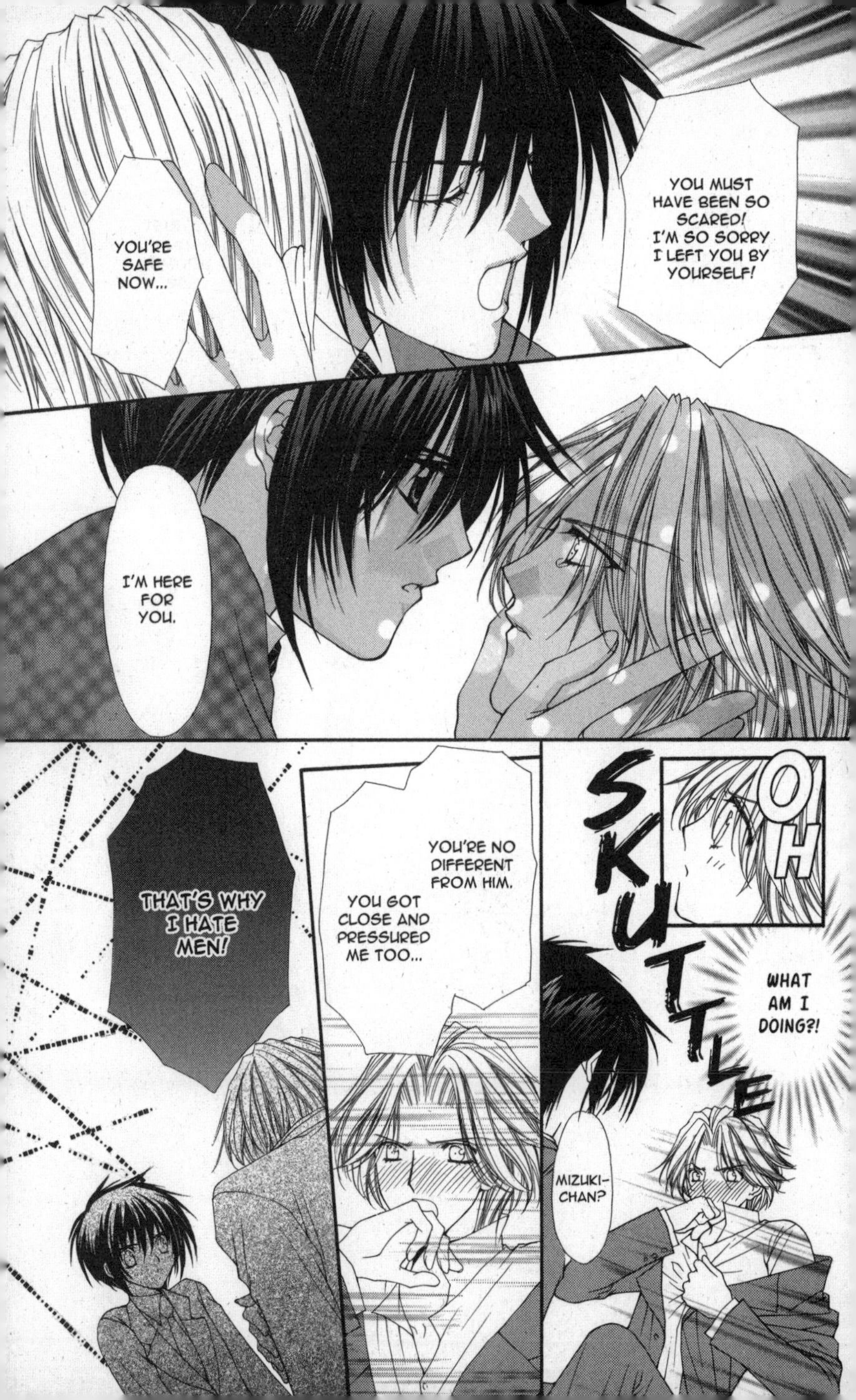
YOU MUST HAVE BEEN SO SCARED! I'M SO SORRY I LEFT YOU BY YOURSELF!
YOU'RE SAFE NOW...
I'M HERE FOR YOU.
OH
SKUTTLE
WHAT AM I DOING?!
MIZUKI-CHAN?
YOU'RE NO DIFFERENT FROM HIM.
YOU GOT CLOSE AND PRESSURED ME TOO...
THAT'S WHY I HATE MEN!

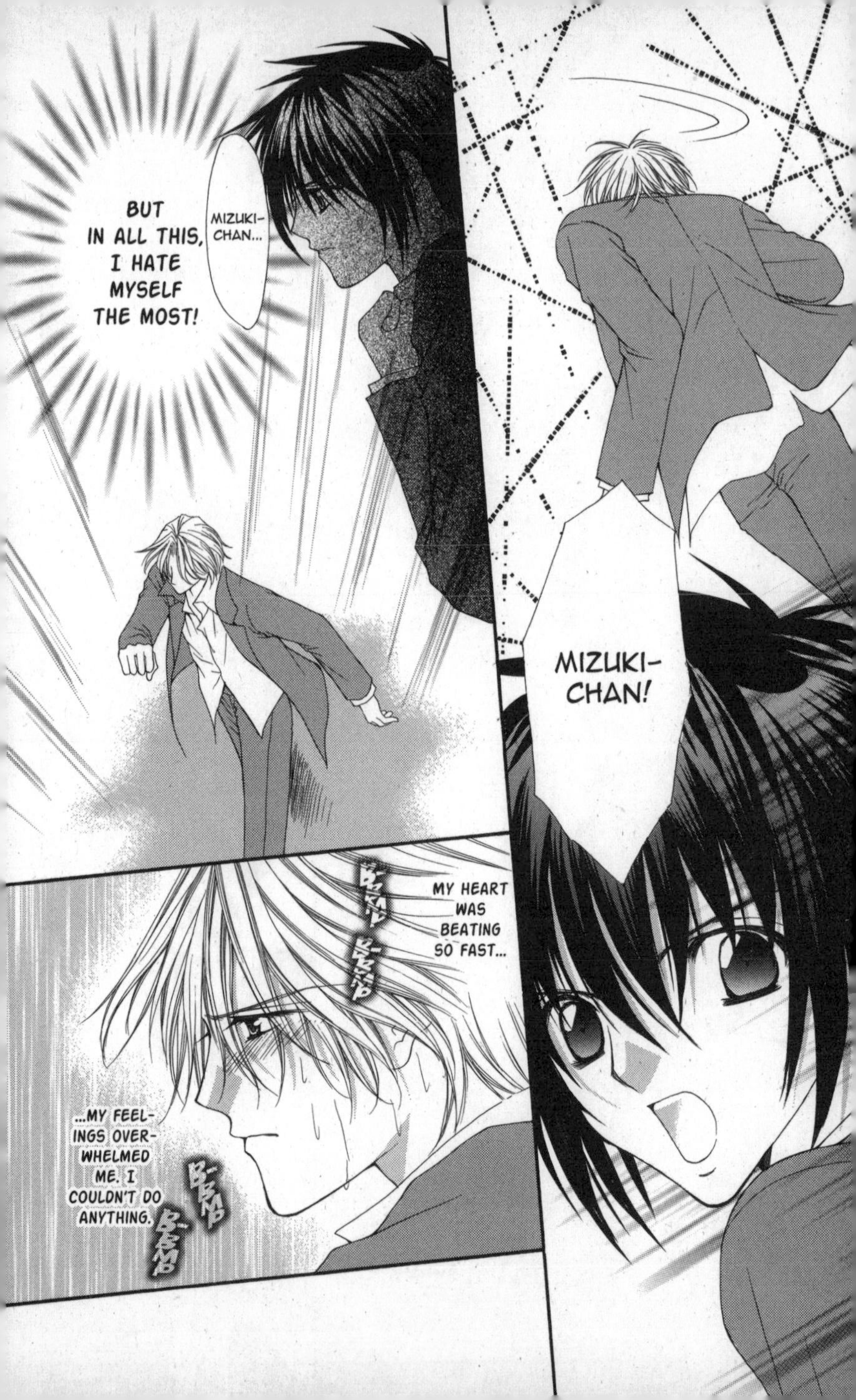
MIZUKI-CHAN!
MIZUKI-CHAN...
BUT IN ALL THIS, I HATE MYSELF THE MOST!
MY HEART WAS BEATING SO FAST...
B-BMP B-BMP
...MY FEELINGS OVERWHELMED ME. I COULDN'T DO ANYTHING.

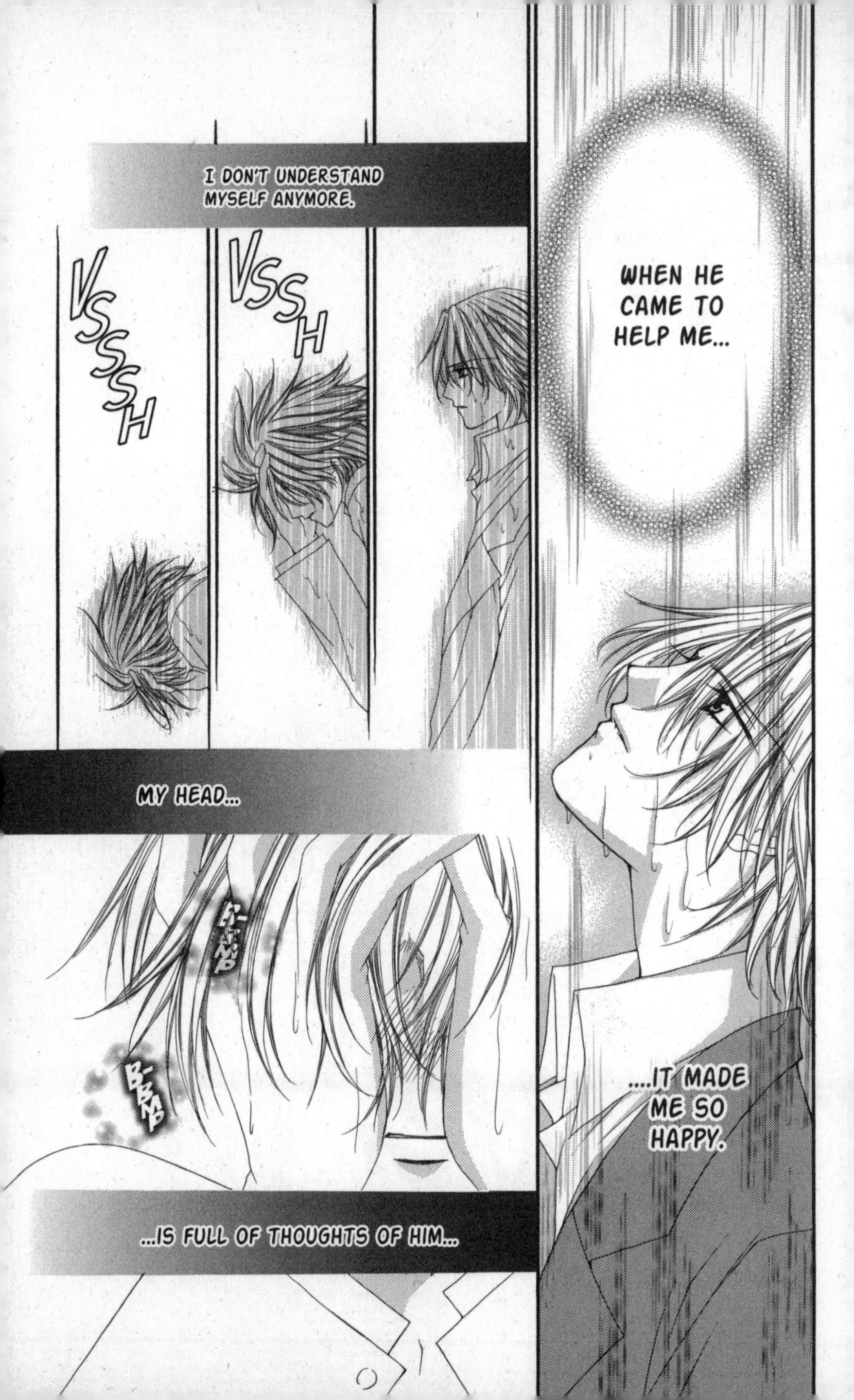
WHEN HE CAME TO HELP ME...
....IT MADE ME SO HAPPY.
I DON'T UNDERSTAND MYSELF ANYMORE.
VSSH
VSSSH
MY HEAD...
B-BMP
B-BMP
...IS FULL OF THOUGHTS OF HIM...

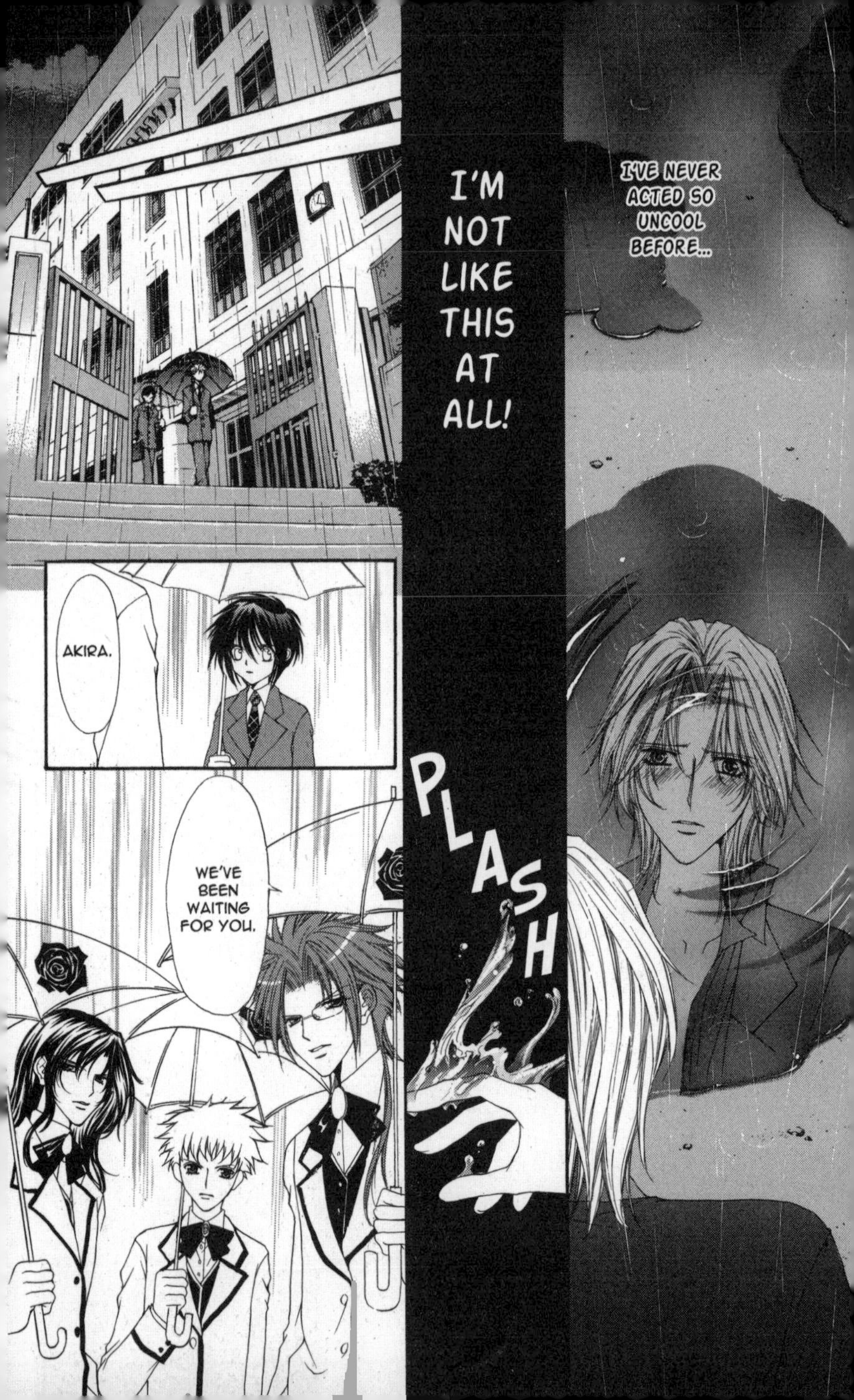
I'VE NEVER ACTED SO UNCOOL BEFORE...
I'M NOT LIKE THIS AT ALL!
PLASH
AKIRA.
WE'VE BEEN WAITING FOR YOU.

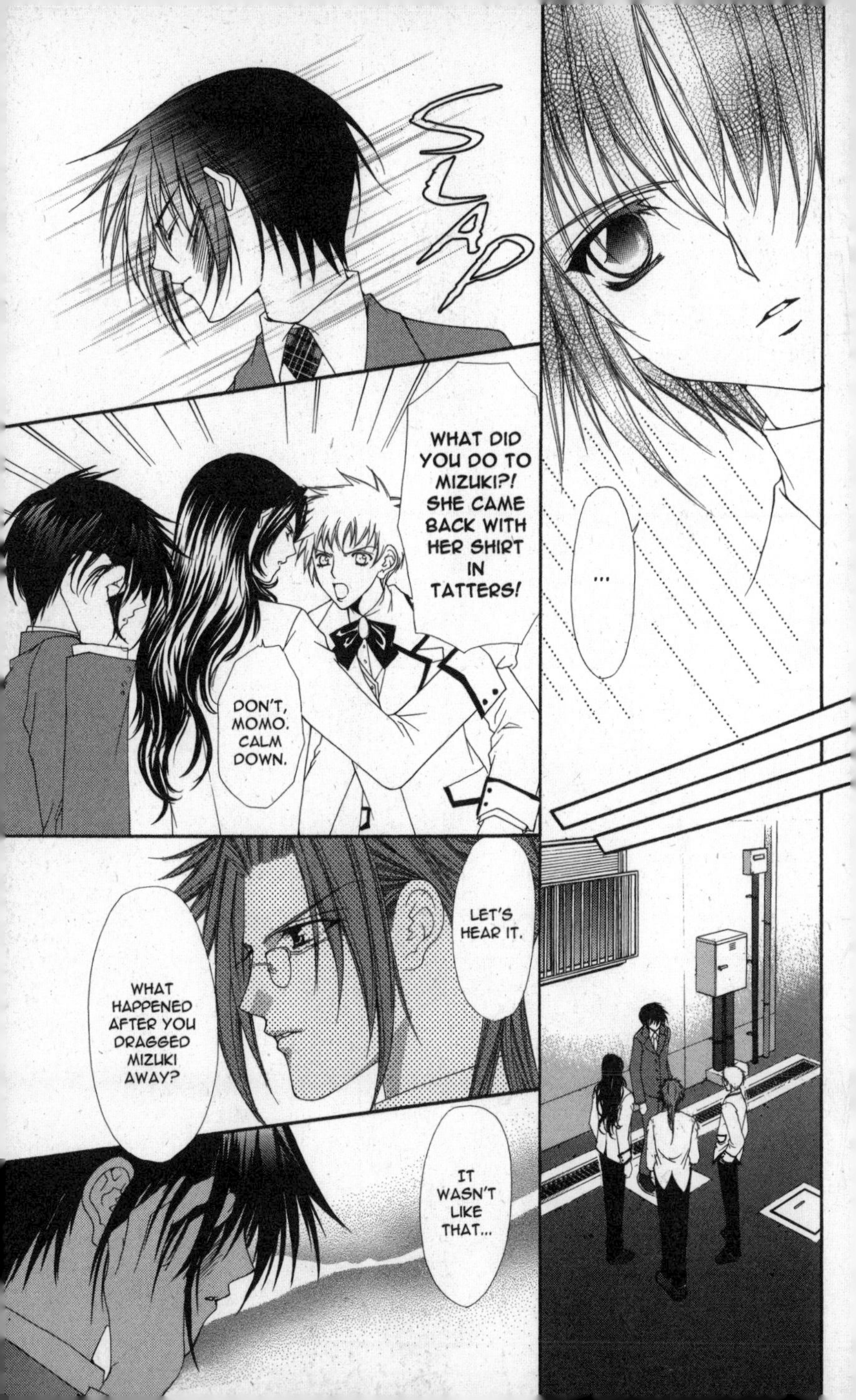
...
SLAP
WHAT DID YOU DO TO MIZUKI?! SHE CAME BACK WITH HER SHIRT IN TATTERS!
DON'T, MOMO. CALM DOWN.
LET'S HEAR IT.
WHAT HAPPENED AFTER YOU DRAGGED MIZUKI AWAY?
IT WASN'T LIKE THAT...

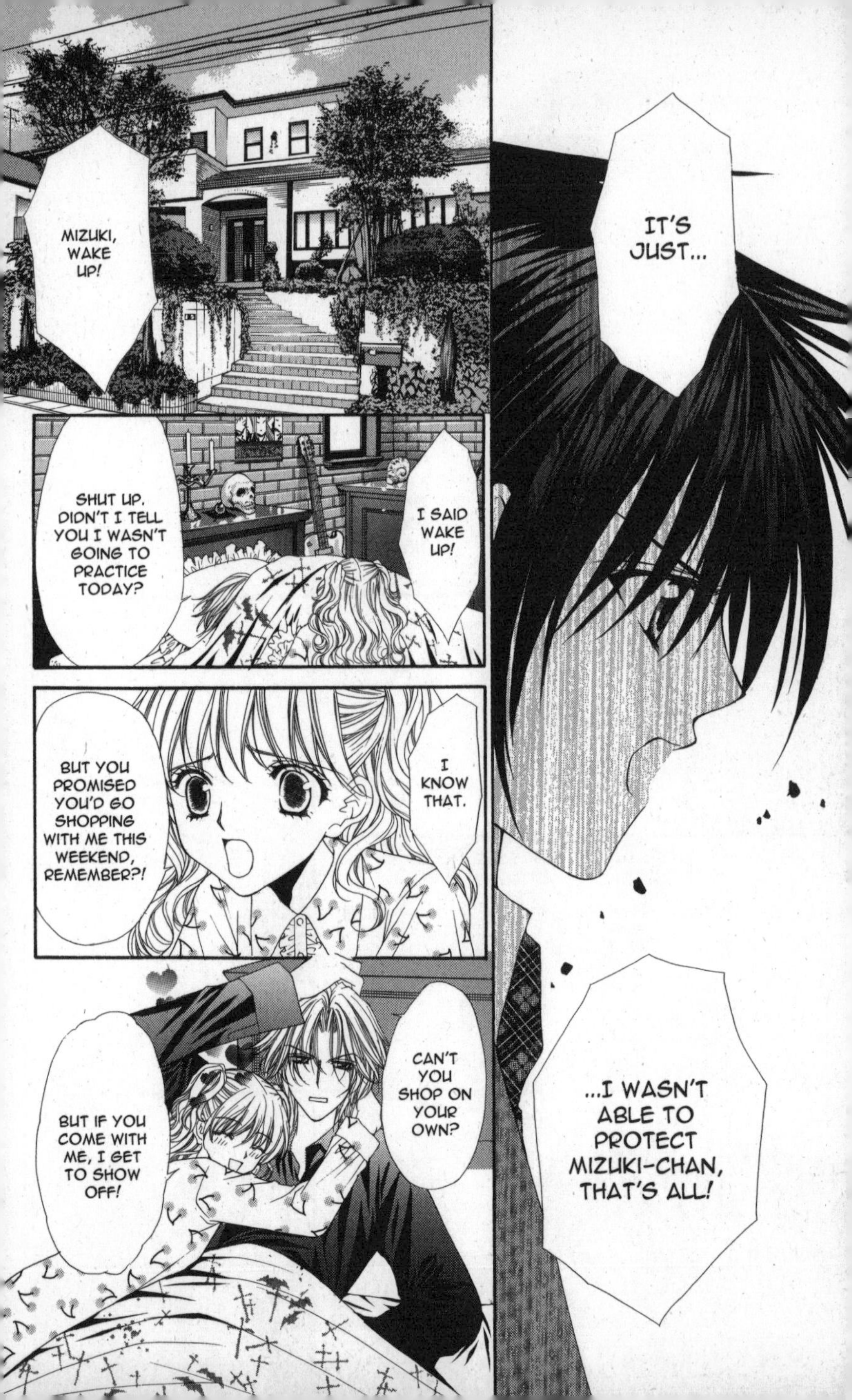
IT'S JUST...
...I WASN'T ABLE TO PROTECT MIZUKI-CHAN, THAT'S ALL!
MIZUKI, WAKE UP!
I SAID WAKE UP!
SHUT UP. DIDN'T I TELL YOU I WASN'T GOING TO PRACTICE TODAY?
I KNOW THAT.
BUT YOU PROMISED YOU'D GO SHOPPING WITH ME THIS WEEKEND, REMEMBER?!
CAN'T YOU SHOP ON YOUR OWN?
BUT IF YOU COME WITH ME, I GET TO SHOW OFF!

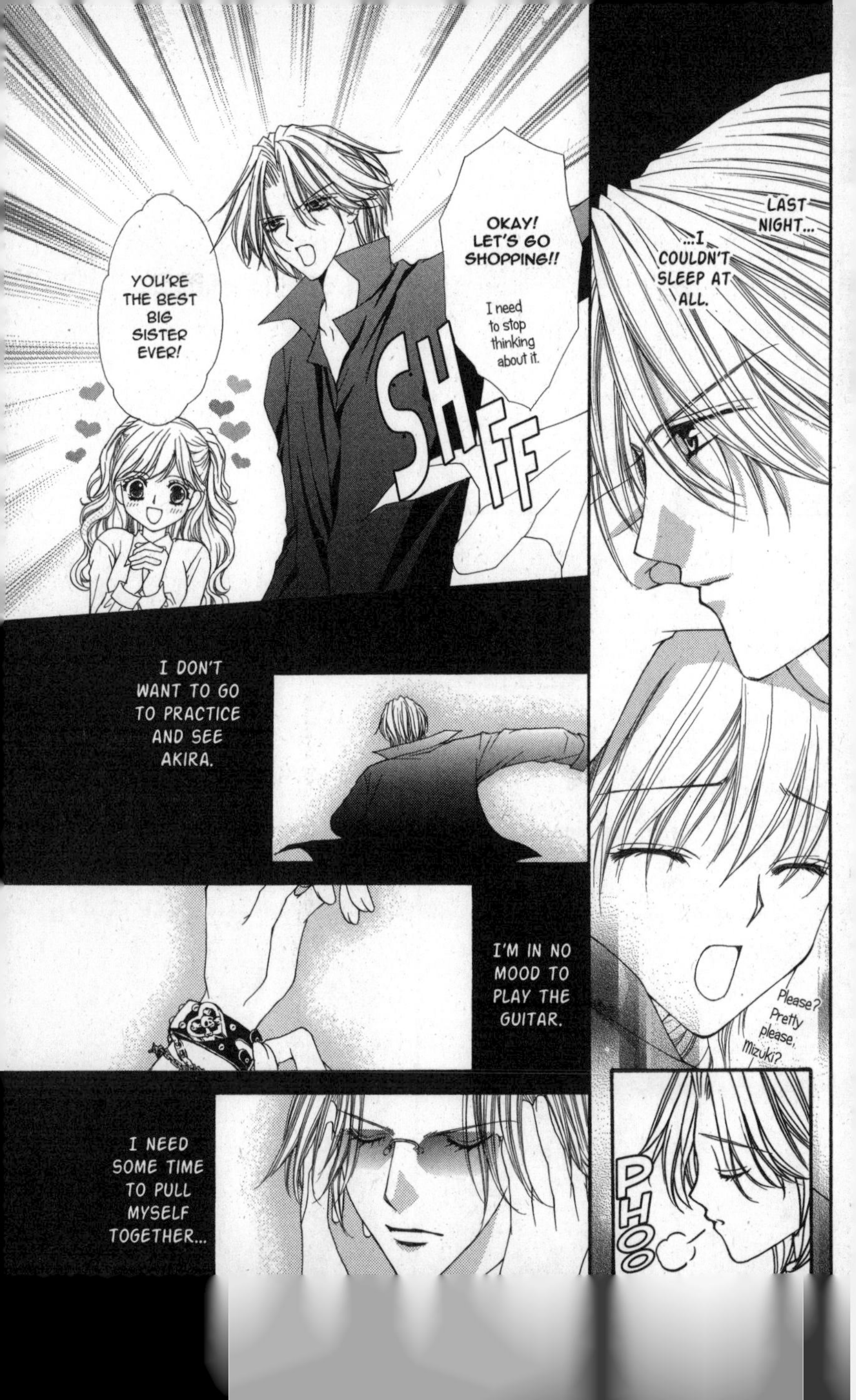
LAST NIGHT...
...I COULDN'T SLEEP AT ALL.
Please? Pretty please, Mizuki?
PHOO
OKAY! LET'S GO SHOPPING!!
I need to stop thinking about it.
SHFF
YOU'RE THE BEST BIG SISTER EVER!
I DON'T WANT TO GO TO PRACTICE AND SEE AKIRA.
I'M IN NO MOOD TO PLAY THE GUITAR.
I NEED SOME TIME TO PULL MYSELF TOGETHER...

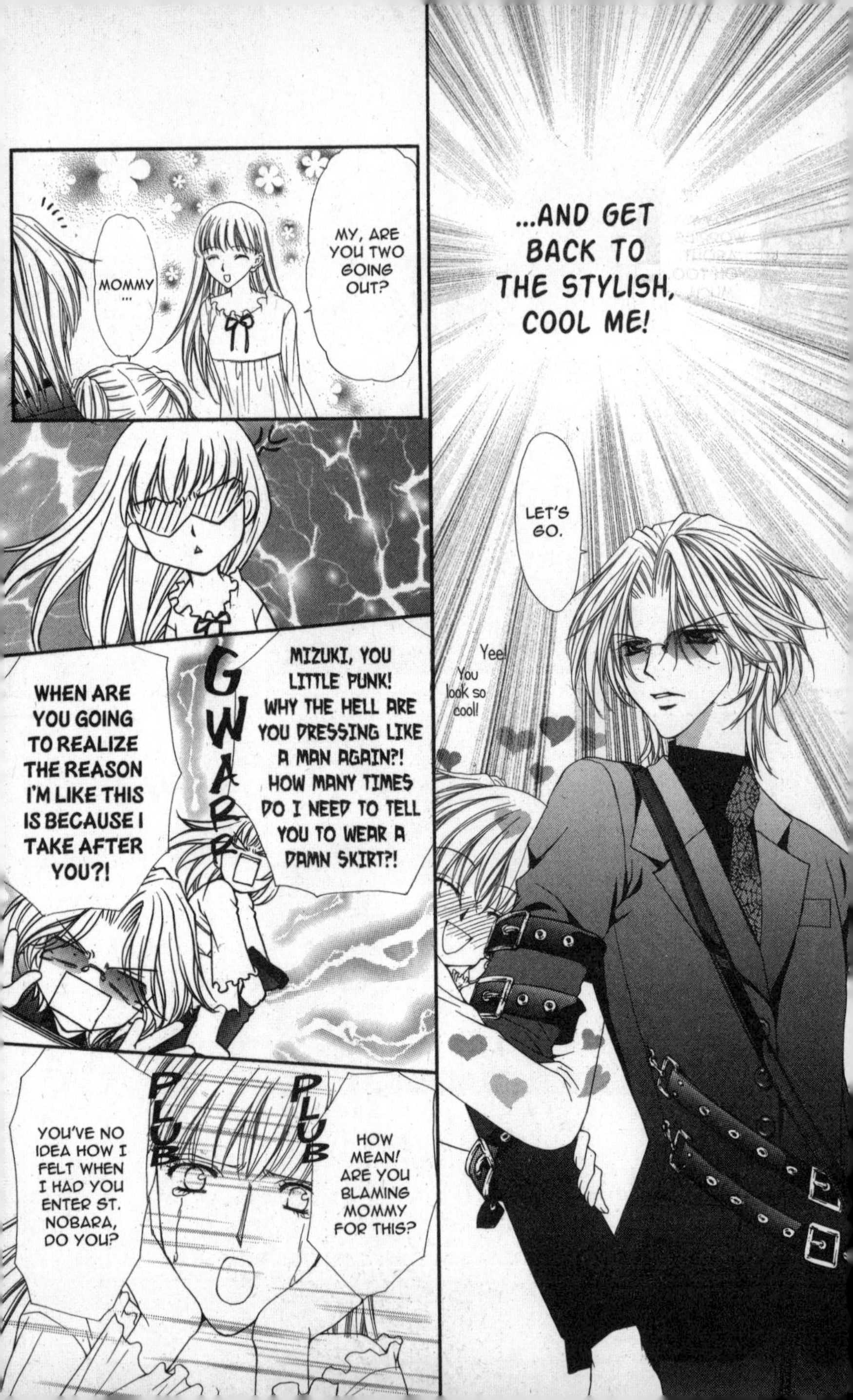
...AND GET BACK TO THE STYLISH, COOL ME!
LET'S GO.
Yee! You look so cool!
MY, ARE YOU TWO GOING OUT?
MOMMY ...
MIZUKI, YOU LITTLE PUNK! WHY THE HELL ARE YOU DRESSING LIKE A MAN AGAIN?! HOW MANY TIMES DO I NEED TO TELL YOU TO WEAR A DAMN SKIRT?!
GWARR
WHEN ARE YOU GOING TO REALIZE THE REASON I'M LIKE THIS IS BECAUSE I TAKE AFTER YOU?!
HOW MEAN! ARE YOU BLAMING MOMMY FOR THIS?
PLUB
PLUB
YOU'VE NO IDEA HOW I FELT WHEN I HAD YOU ENTER ST. NOBARA, DO YOU?

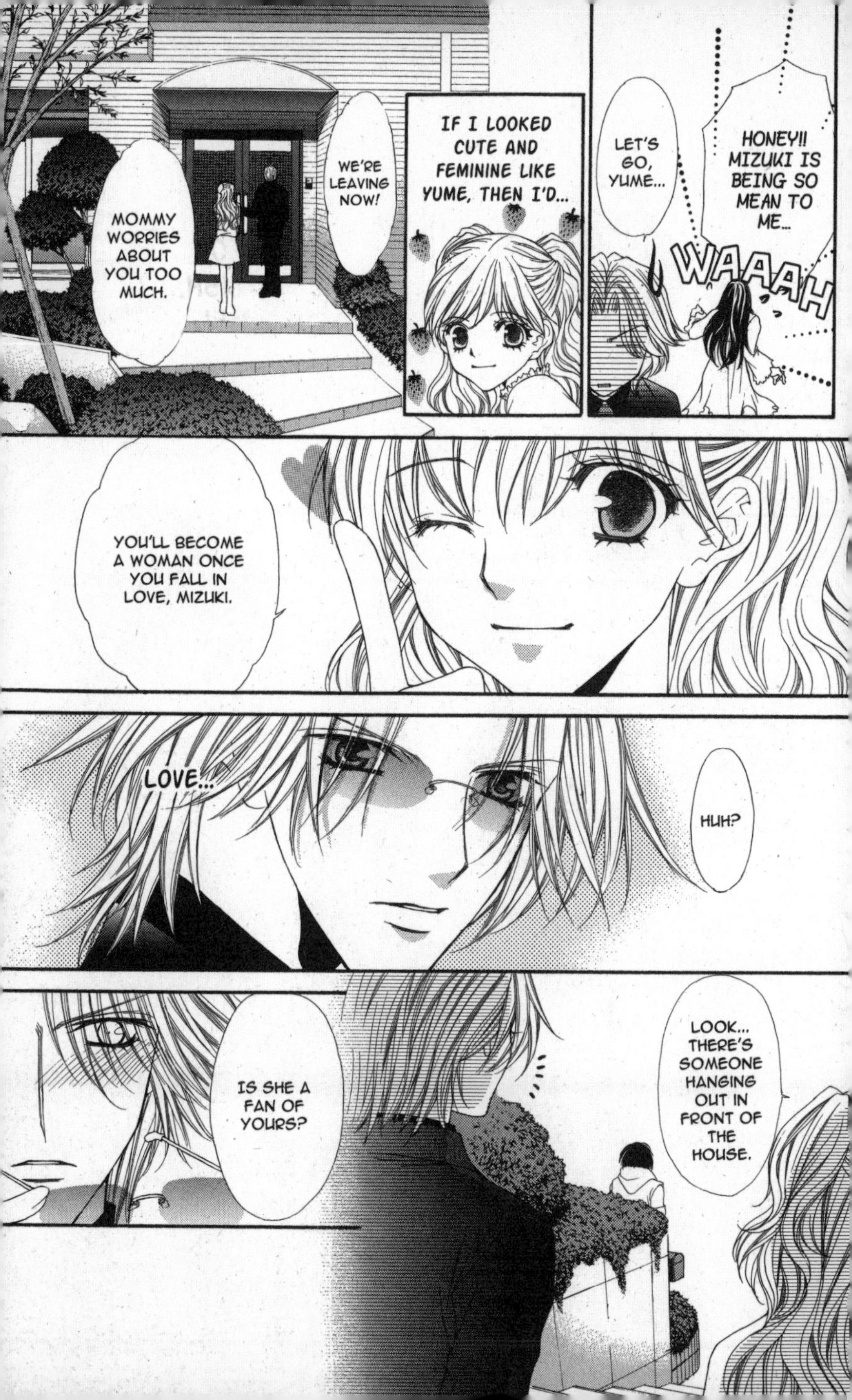
HONEY!! MIZUKI IS BEING SO MEAN TO ME...
WAAAAH
LET'S GO, YUME...
IF I LOOKED CUTE AND FEMININE LIKE YUME, THEN I'D...
WE'RE LEAVING NOW!
MOMMY WORRIES ABOUT YOU TOO MUCH.
YOU'LL BECOME A WOMAN ONCE YOU FALL IN LOVE, MIZUKI.
LOVE...
HUH?
LOOK... THERE'S SOMEONE HANGING OUT IN FRONT OF THE HOUSE.
IS SHE A FAN OF YOURS?

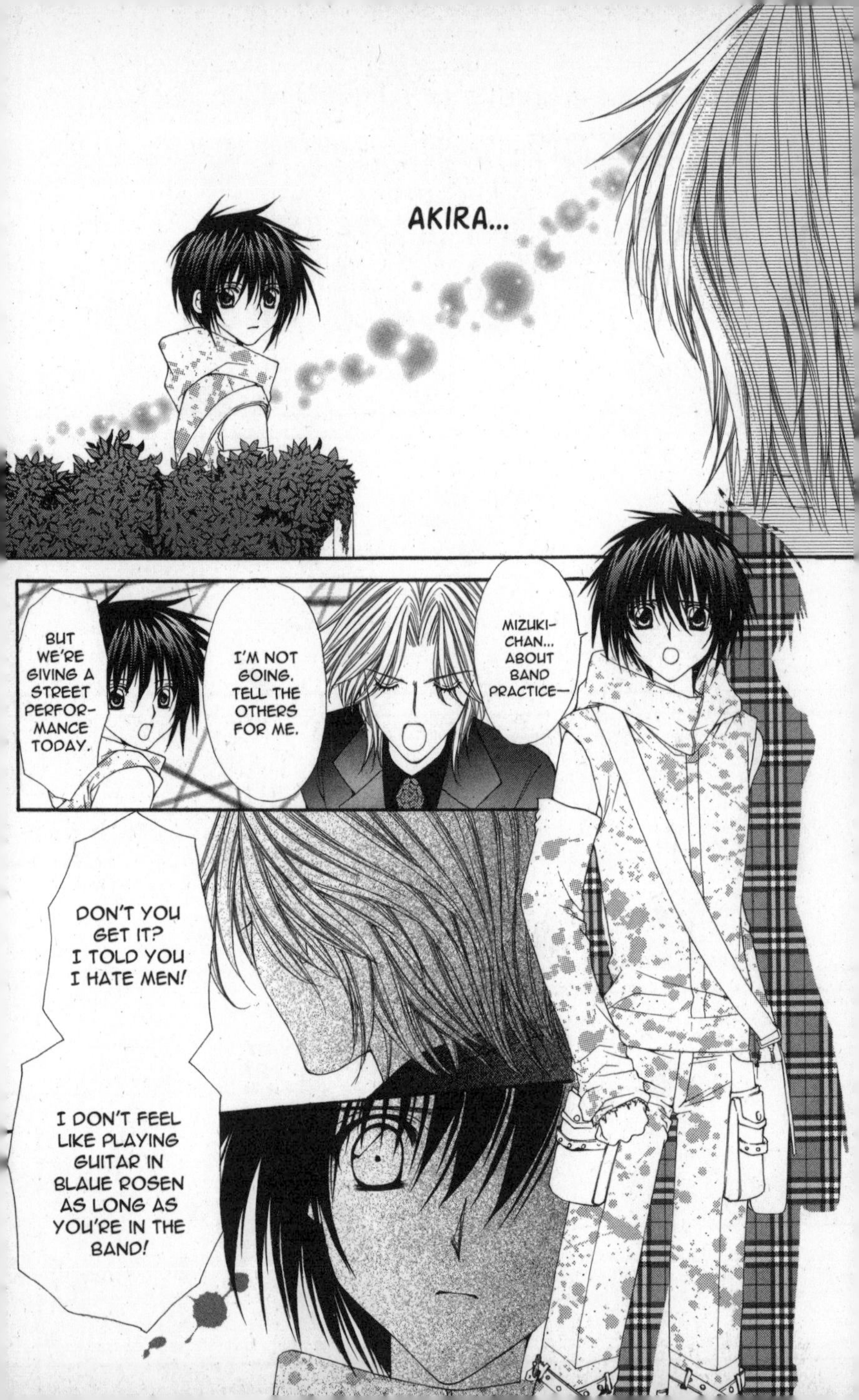
AKIRA...
MIZUKI-CHAN... ABOUT BAND PRACTICE—
I'M NOT GOING. TELL THE OTHERS FOR ME.
BUT WE'RE GIVING A STREET PERFORMANCE TODAY.
DON'T YOU GET IT? I TOLD YOU I HATE MEN!
I DON'T FEEL LIKE PLAYING GUITAR IN BLAUE ROSEN AS LONG AS YOU'RE IN THE BAND!

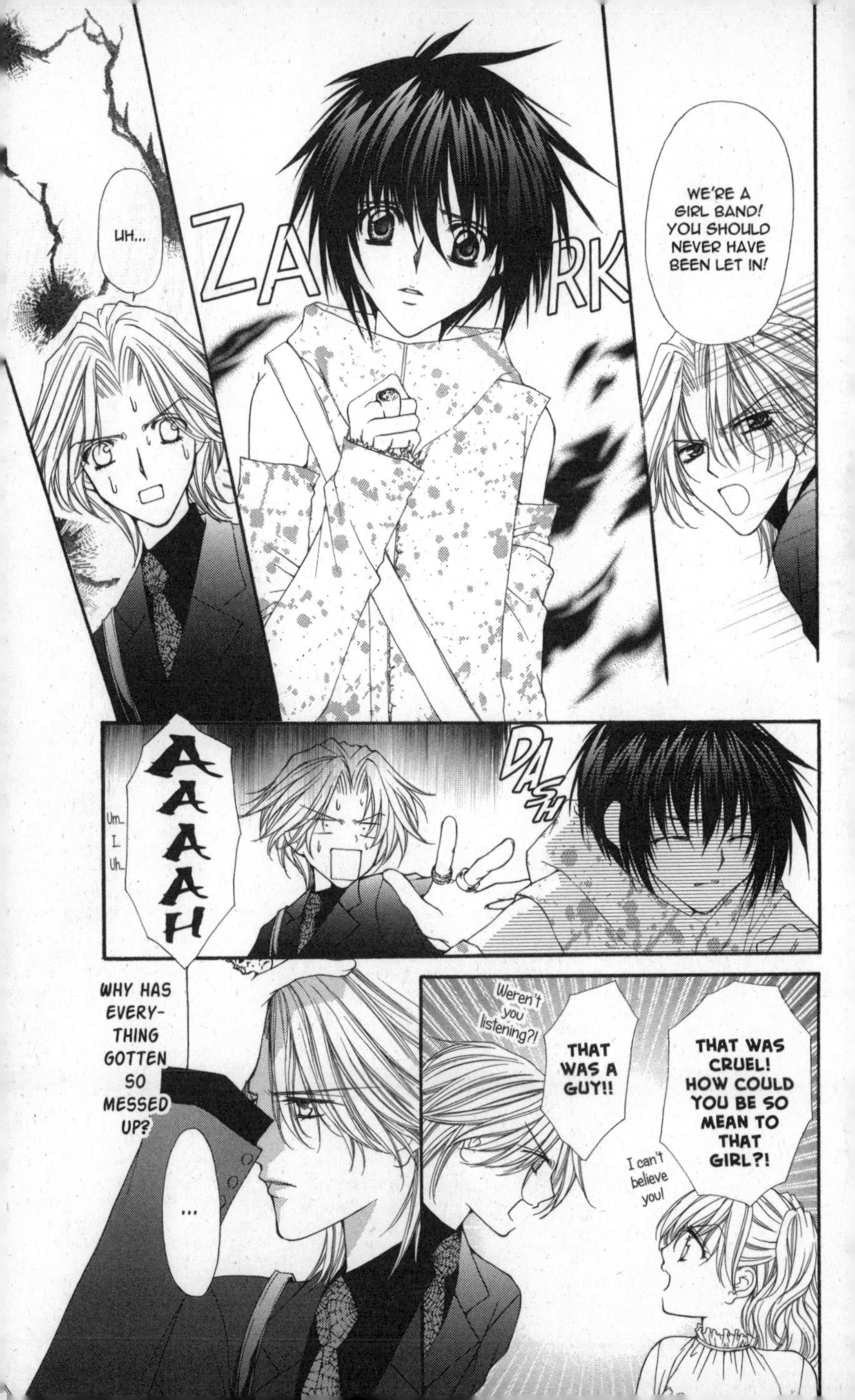
WE'RE A GIRL BAND! YOU SHOULD NEVER HAVE BEEN LET IN!
ZA RK
UH...
DASH
AAAAH
Um... I... Uh...
THAT WAS CRUEL! HOW COULD YOU BE SO MEAN TO THAT GIRL?!
I can't believe you!
Weren't you listening?!
THAT WAS A GUY!!
WHY HAS EVERY-THING GOTTEN SO MESSED UP?
...

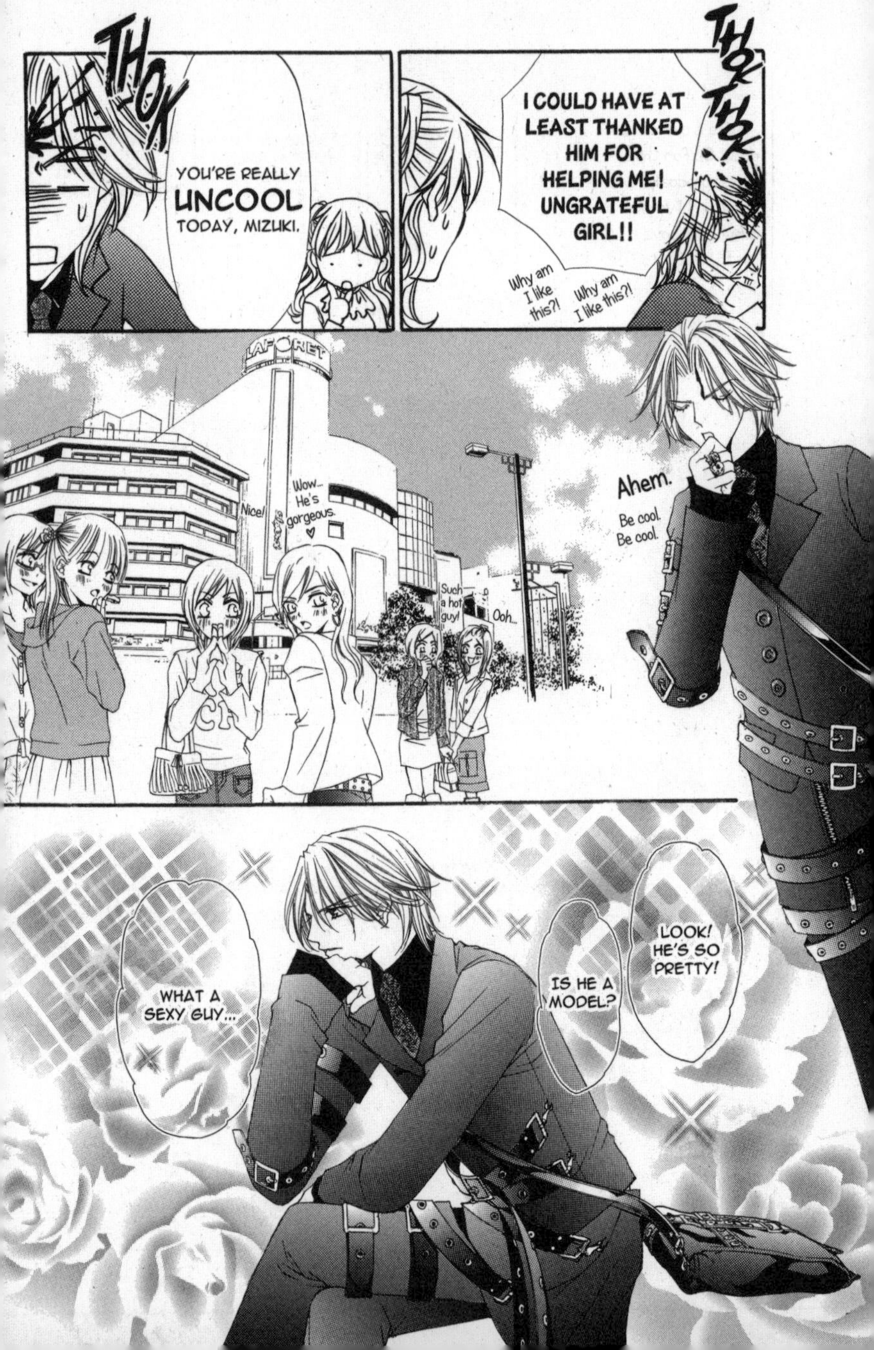
THOK THOK
I COULD HAVE AT LEAST THANKED HIM FOR HELPING ME! UNGRATEFUL GIRL!!
Why am I like this?!
Why am I like this?!
THOK
YOU'RE REALLY UNCOOL TODAY, MIZUKI.
Ahem.
Be cool. Be cool.
LAFORET
Such a hot guy!
Ooh...
Wow... He's gorgeous.
Nice!
LOOK! HE'S SO PRETTY!
IS HE A MODEL?
WHAT A SEXY GUY...

About Akira

Akira is extremely fun to draw. So fun that I feel all my stress gradually fade away as I draw him! I've always loved to draw cute boys, so it's satisfying to be able to finally draw one!

Although he looks cute, he's not altogether too different on the inside from my other male characters. Though I think he's stronger mentally than Gin in *Love Celeb*. He's the strongest character ever.

I'm really surprised to see Akira has more devotees than ever. More so than even Sakuya, I think. I'm so pleased about it. The best thing is that my assistants and staff are very fond of him too. We always come up with random stories about Akira, as well as Rui and Ran, and shout "Moe...!" together. (laugh)

As for Akira, we're thinking about creating some goods at my official website, so please check it out:

http://www.mayutan.com

He is a male character unlike any of my past characters, but I'm doing my best to make him look cool in every chapter!!

And cute every now and then...

I hope Akira grows to become a character who all my fans—as well as the people who just happened to pick this up—will love...

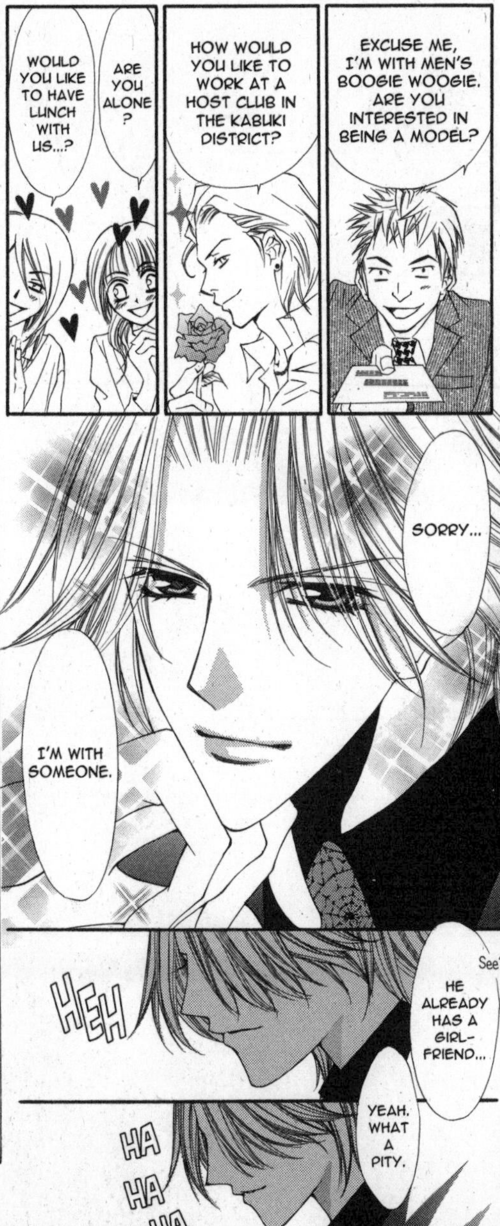
EXCUSE ME, I'M WITH MEN'S BOOGIE WOOGIE. ARE YOU INTERESTED IN BEING A MODEL?
HOW WOULD YOU LIKE TO WORK AT A HOST CLUB IN THE KABUKI DISTRICT?
ARE YOU ALONE?
WOULD YOU LIKE TO HAVE LUNCH WITH US...?
SORRY...
I'M WITH SOMEONE.
See?!
HE ALREADY HAS A GIRL-FRIEND...
HEH
YEAH. WHAT A PITY.
HA HA HA

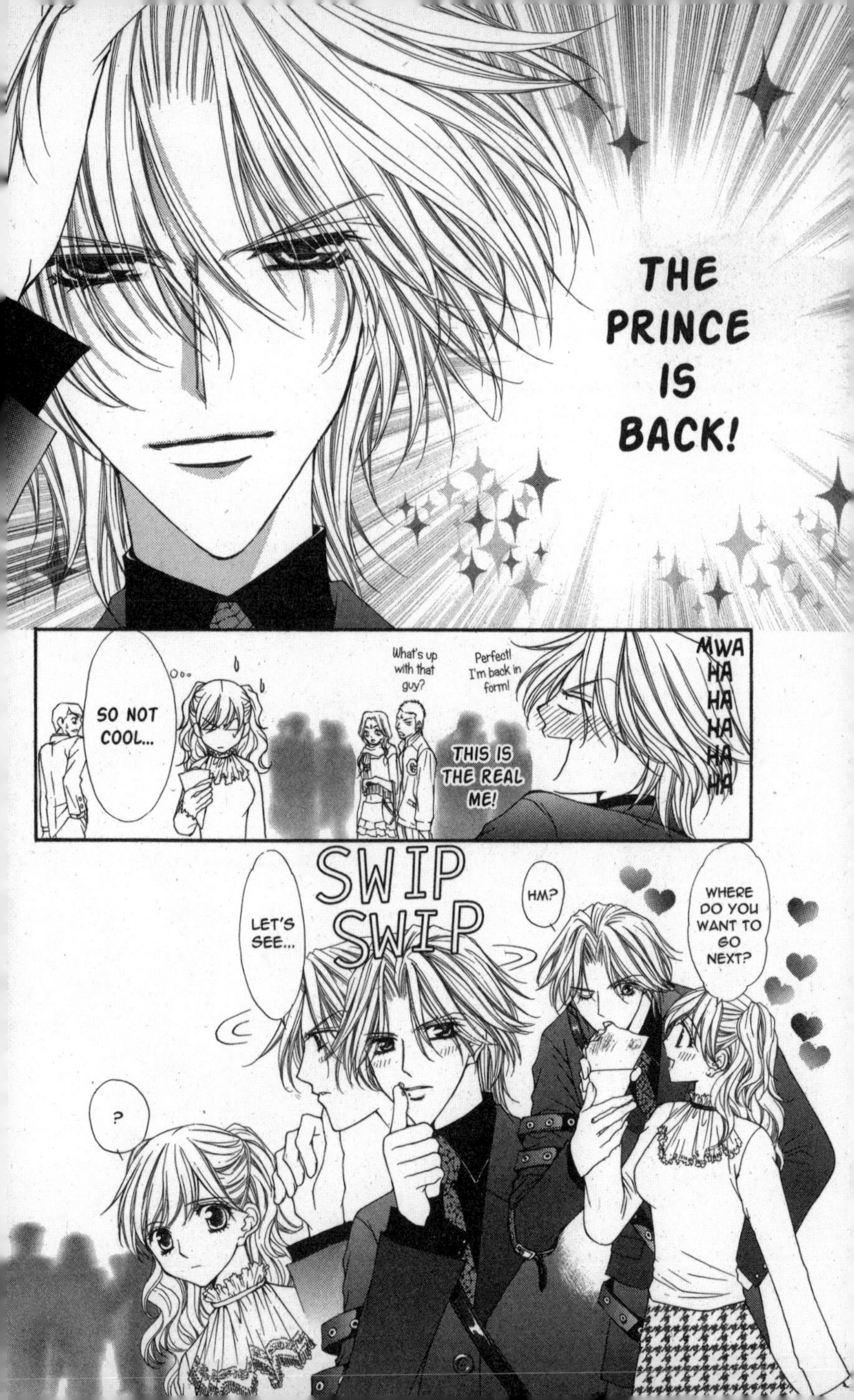
THE PRINCE IS BACK!
MWA HA HA HA HA HA
Perfect! I'm back in form!
THIS IS THE REAL ME!
What's up with that guy?
SO NOT COOL...
WHERE DO YOU WANT TO GO NEXT?
HM?
SWIP SWIP
LET'S SEE...
?

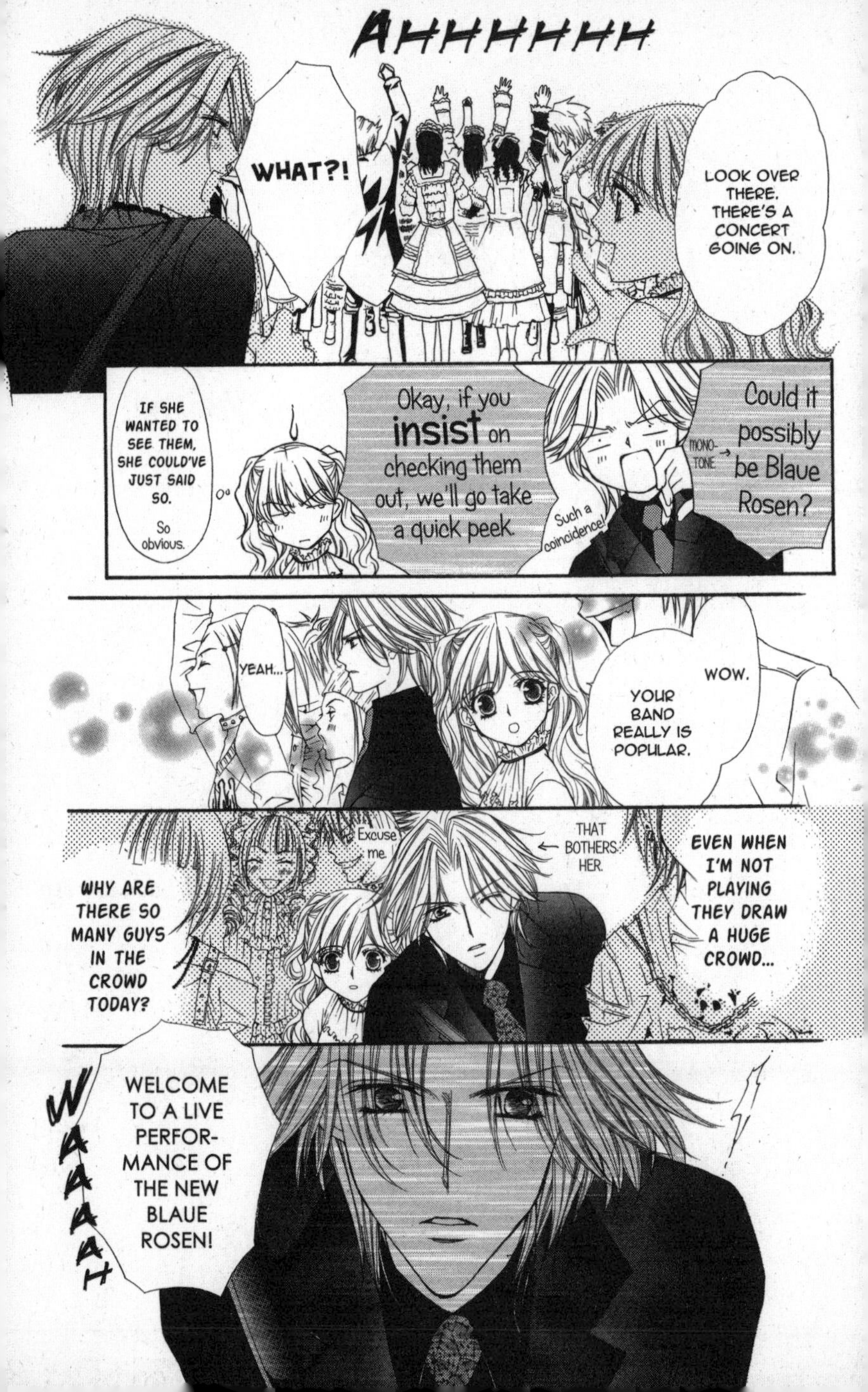
LOOK OVER THERE. THERE'S A CONCERT GOING ON.
AHHHHHHH
WHAT?!
Could it possibly be Blaue Rosen?
MONO-TONE
Such a coincidence!
Okay, if you insist on checking them out, we'll go take a quick peek.
IF SHE WANTED TO SEE THEM, SHE COULD'VE JUST SAID SO.
So obvious.
WOW. YOUR BAND REALLY IS POPULAR.
YEAH...
EVEN WHEN I'M NOT PLAYING THEY DRAW A HUGE CROWD...
THAT BOTHERS HER.
Excuse me.
WHY ARE THERE SO MANY GUYS IN THE CROWD TODAY?
WELCOME TO A LIVE PERFORMANCE OF THE NEW BLAUE ROSEN!
WAAAAAH

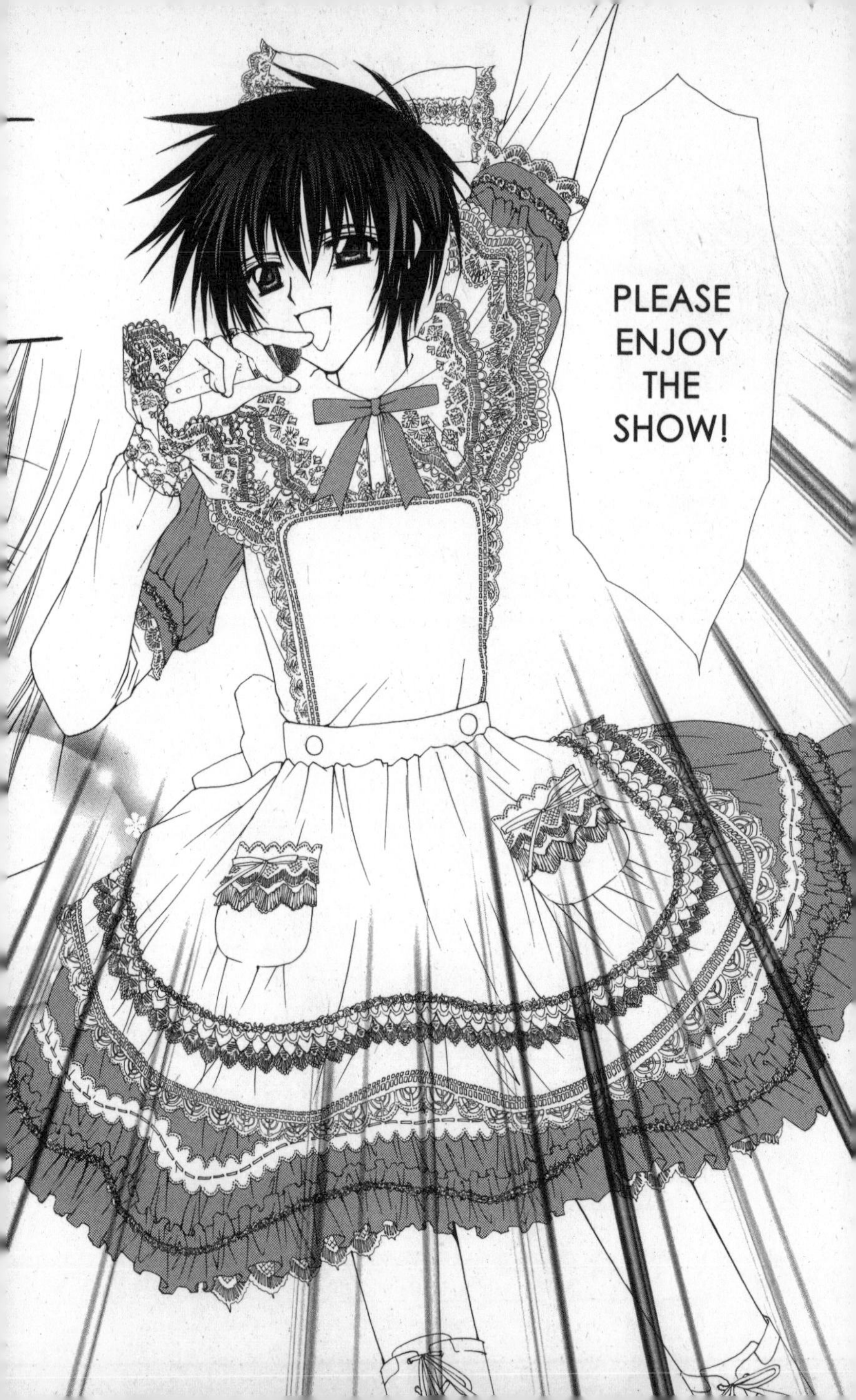
PLEASE ENJOY THE SHOW!

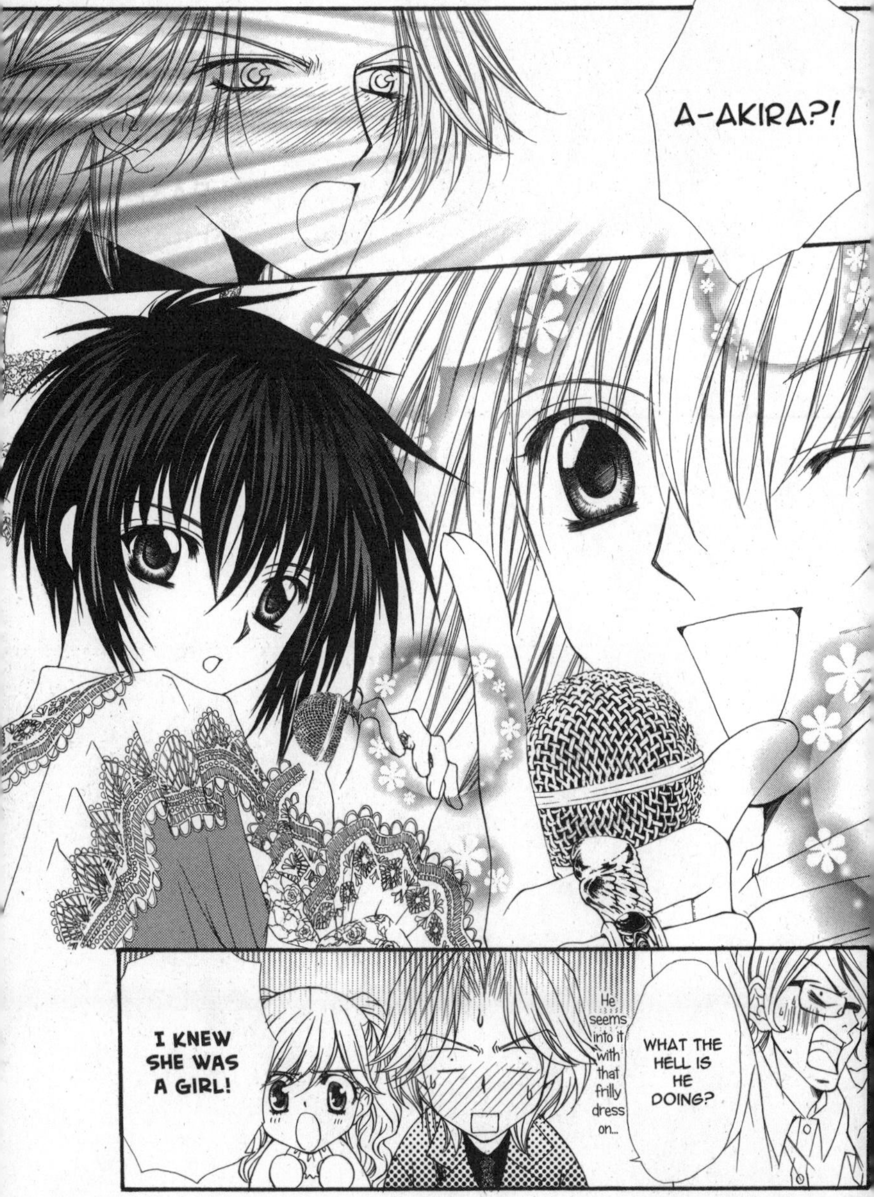
A-AKIRA?!
WHAT THE HELL IS HE DOING?
He seems into it with that frilly dress on...
I KNEW SHE WAS A GIRL!

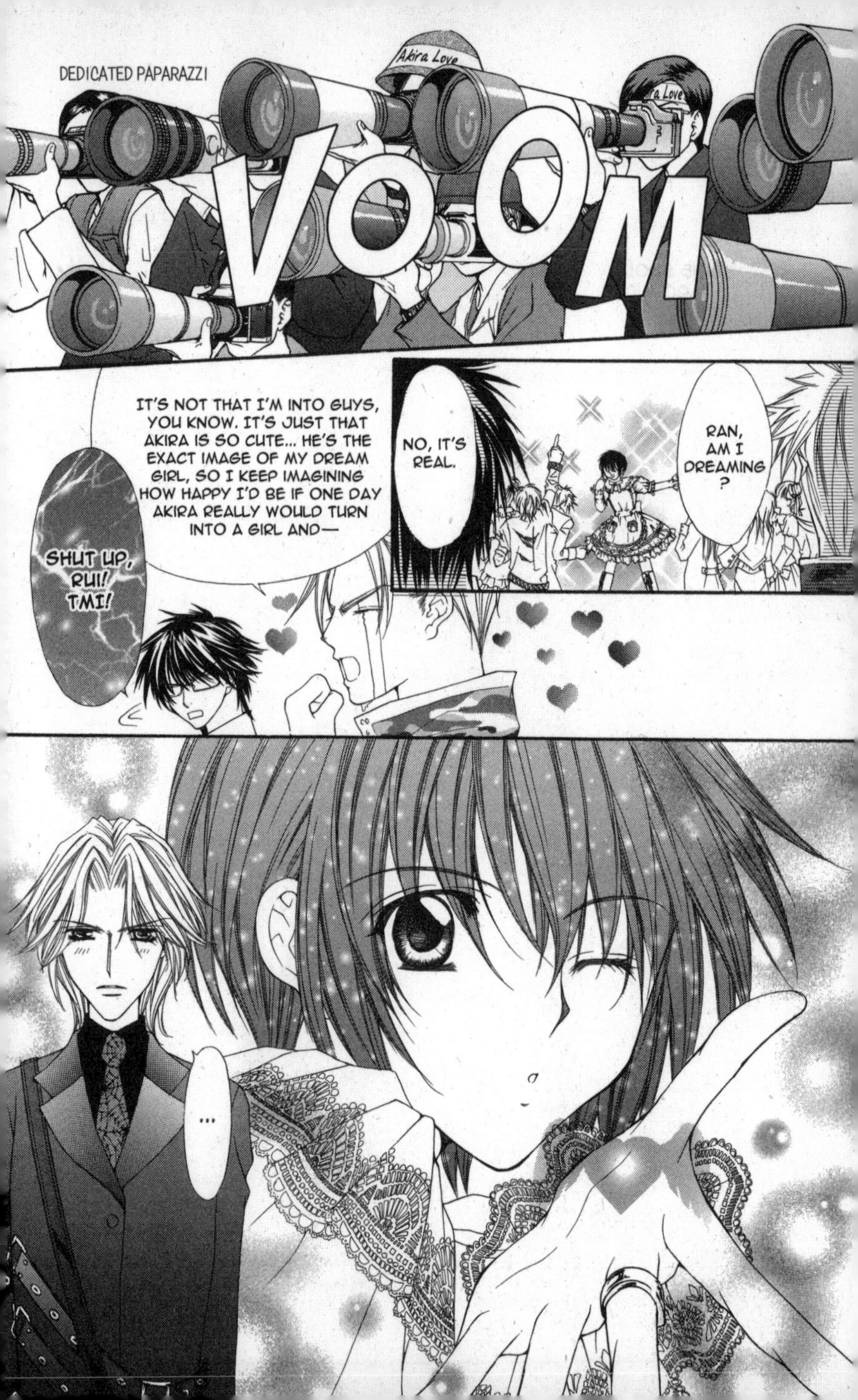
DEDICATED PAPARAZZI
Akira Love
VOOM
RAN, AM I DREAMING?
NO, IT'S REAL.
IT'S NOT THAT I'M INTO GUYS, YOU KNOW. IT'S JUST THAT AKIRA IS SO CUTE... HE'S THE EXACT IMAGE OF MY DREAM GIRL, SO I KEEP IMAGINING HOW HAPPY I'D BE IF ONE DAY AKIRA REALLY WOULD TURN INTO A GIRL AND—
SHUT UP, RUI! TMI!
...

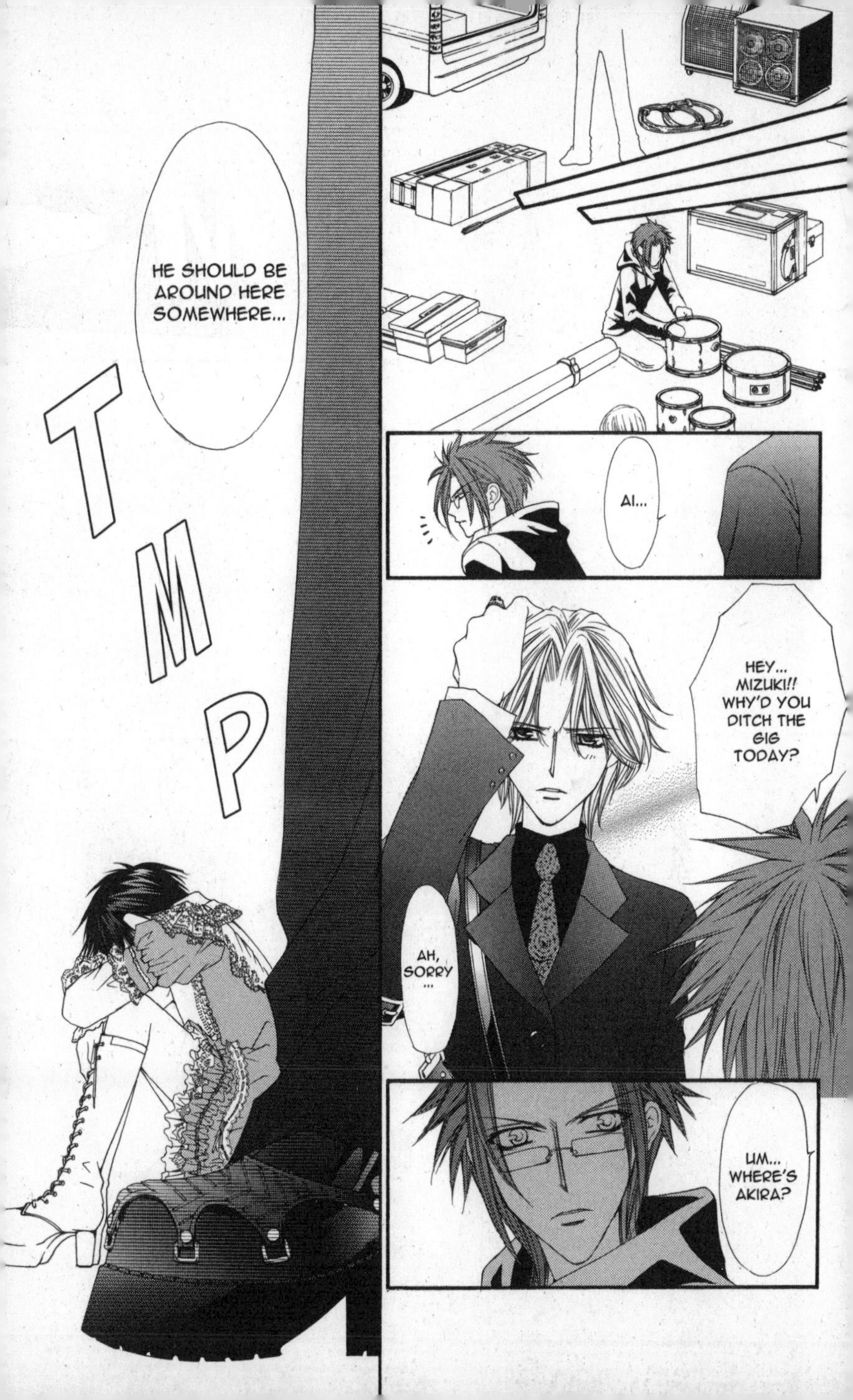
AI...
HEY... MIZUKI!! WHY'D YOU DITCH THE GIG TODAY?
AH, SORRY ...
UM... WHERE'S AKIRA?
HE SHOULD BE AROUND HERE SOMEWHERE...
TMP

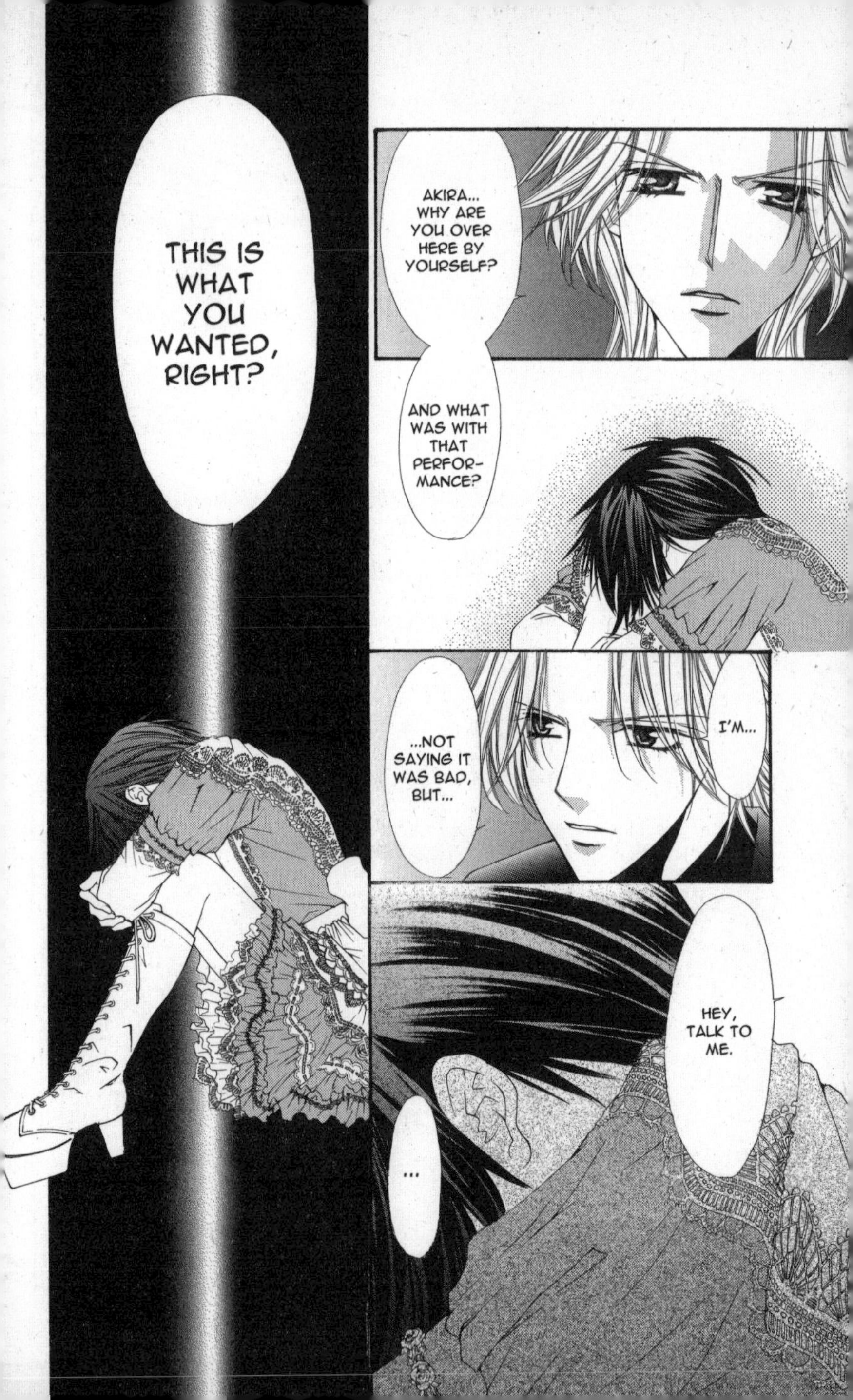
AKIRA... WHY ARE YOU OVER HERE BY YOURSELF?
AND WHAT WAS WITH THAT PERFORMANCE?
I'M...
...NOT SAYING IT WAS BAD, BUT...
HEY, TALK TO ME.
...
THIS IS WHAT YOU WANTED, RIGHT?

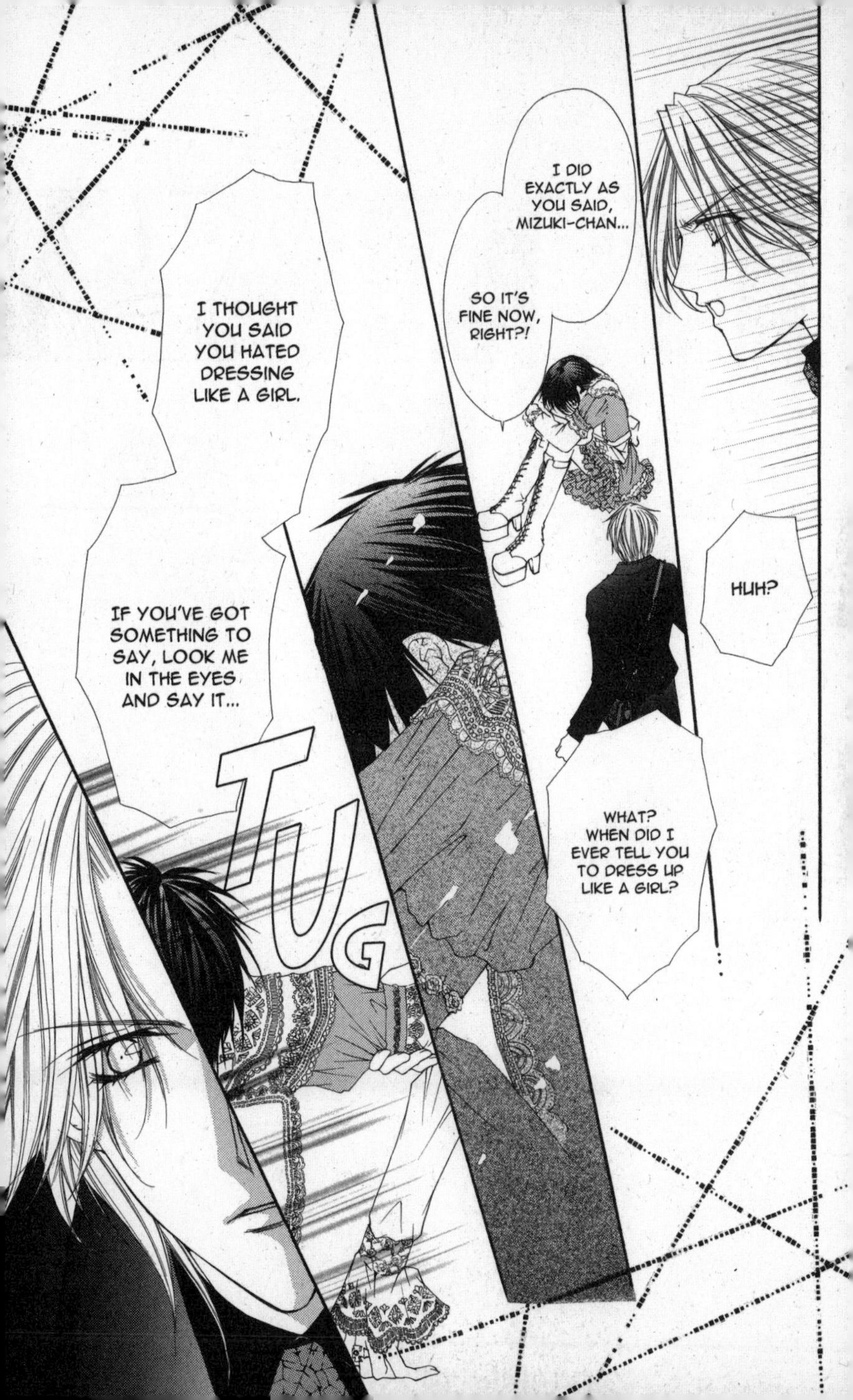
HUH?
I DID EXACTLY AS YOU SAID, MIZUKI-CHAN...
SO IT'S FINE NOW, RIGHT?!
WHAT? WHEN DID I EVER TELL YOU TO DRESS UP LIKE A GIRL?
TUG
I THOUGHT YOU SAID YOU HATED DRESSING LIKE A GIRL.
IF YOU'VE GOT SOMETHING TO SAY, LOOK ME IN THE EYES AND SAY IT...

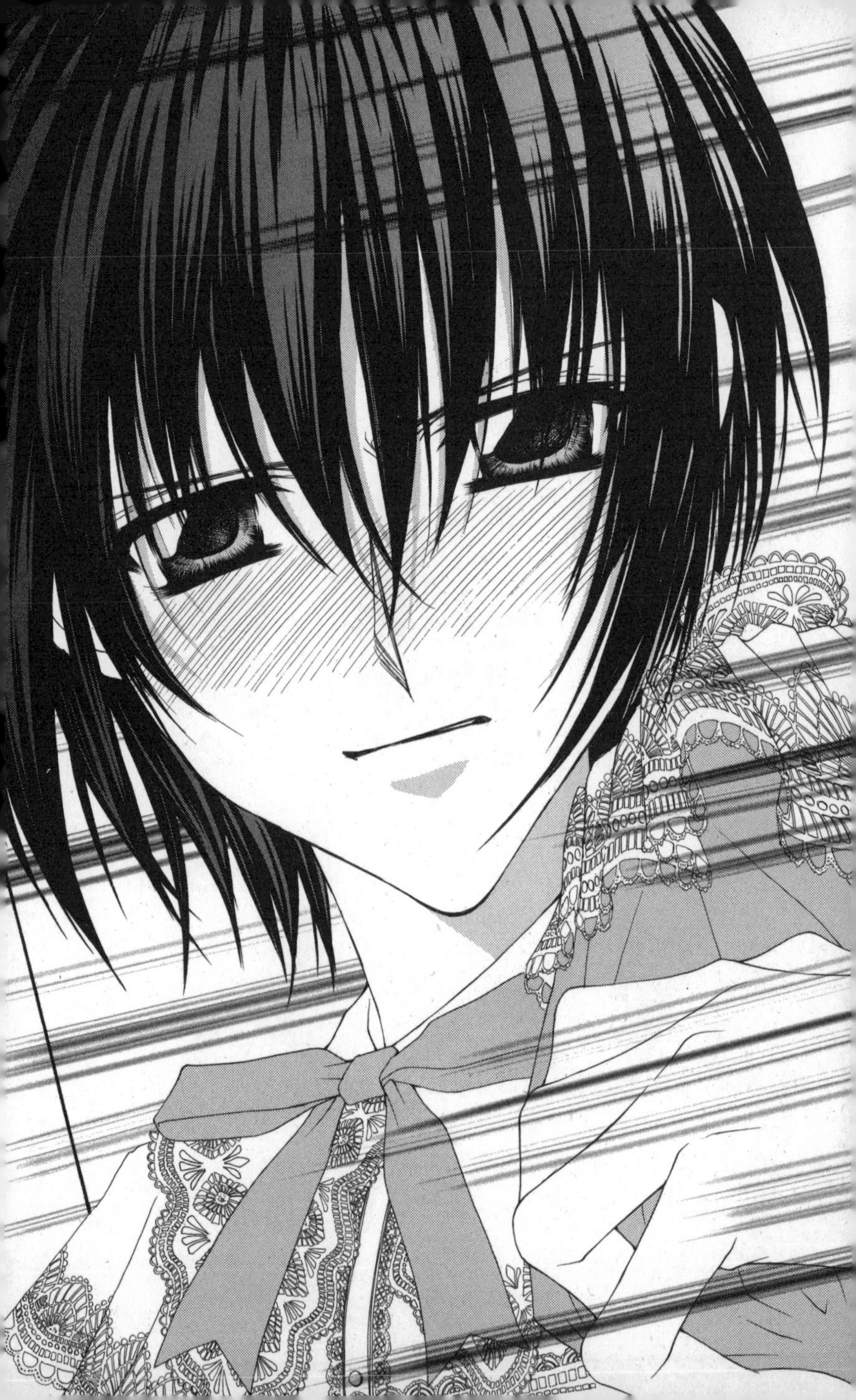

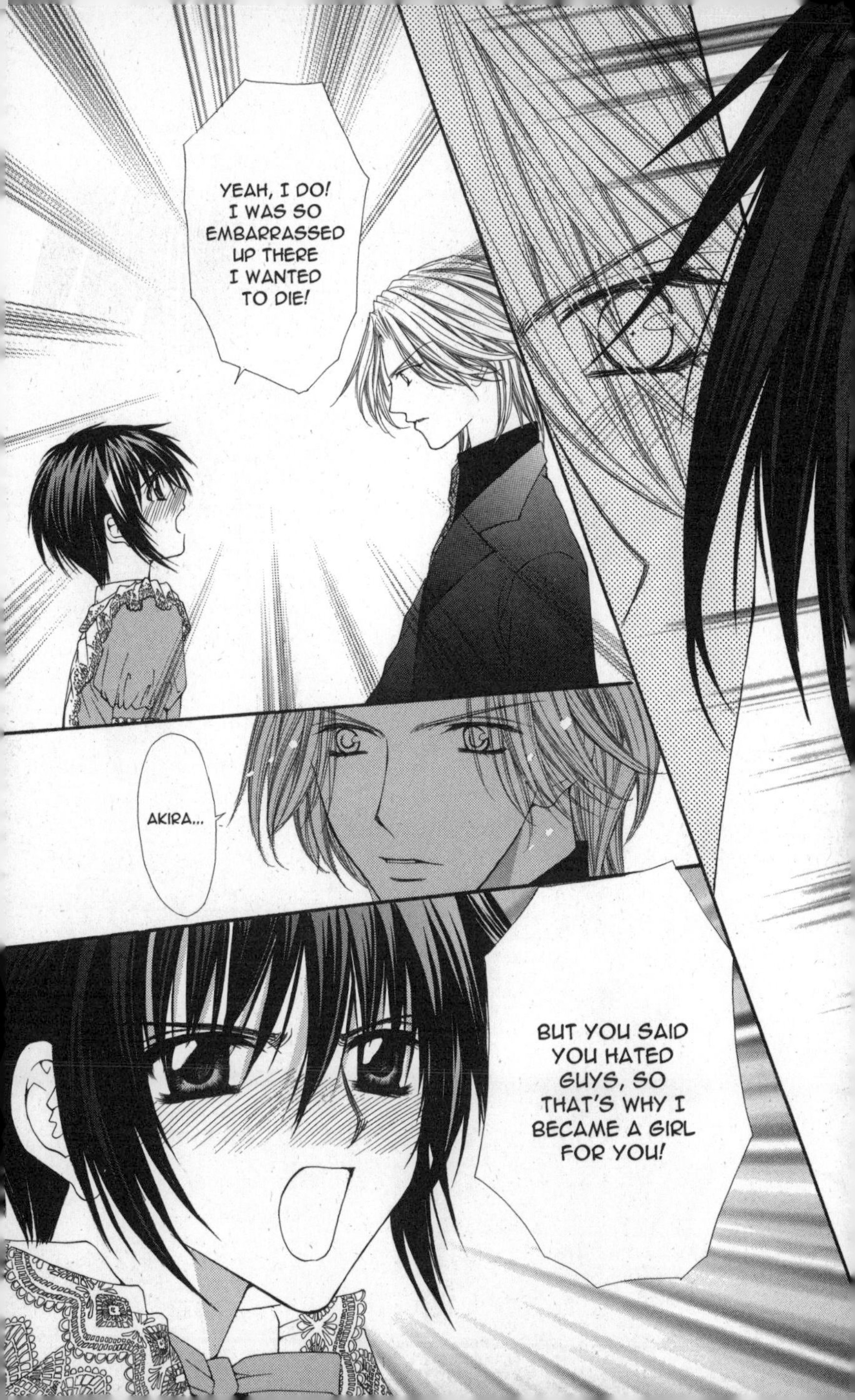
YEAH, I DO! I WAS SO EMBARRASSED UP THERE I WANTED TO DIE!
AKIRA...
BUT YOU SAID YOU HATED GUYS, SO THAT'S WHY I BECAME A GIRL FOR YOU!

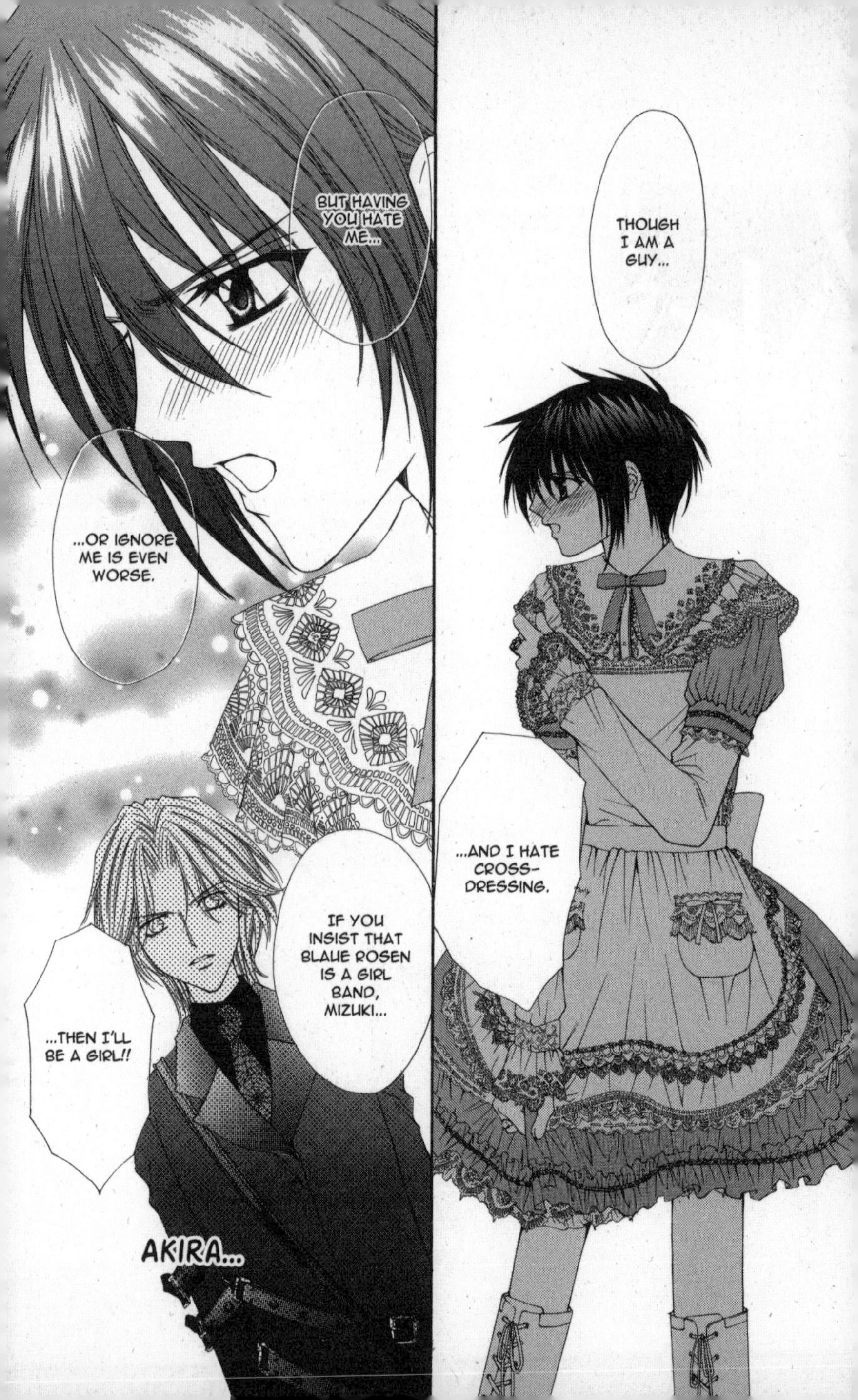
THOUGH I AM A GUY...
...AND I HATE CROSS-DRESSING.
BUT HAVING YOU HATE ME...
...OR IGNORE ME IS EVEN WORSE.
IF YOU INSIST THAT BLAUE ROSEN IS A GIRL BAND, MIZUKI...
...THEN I'LL BE A GIRL!!
AKIRA...

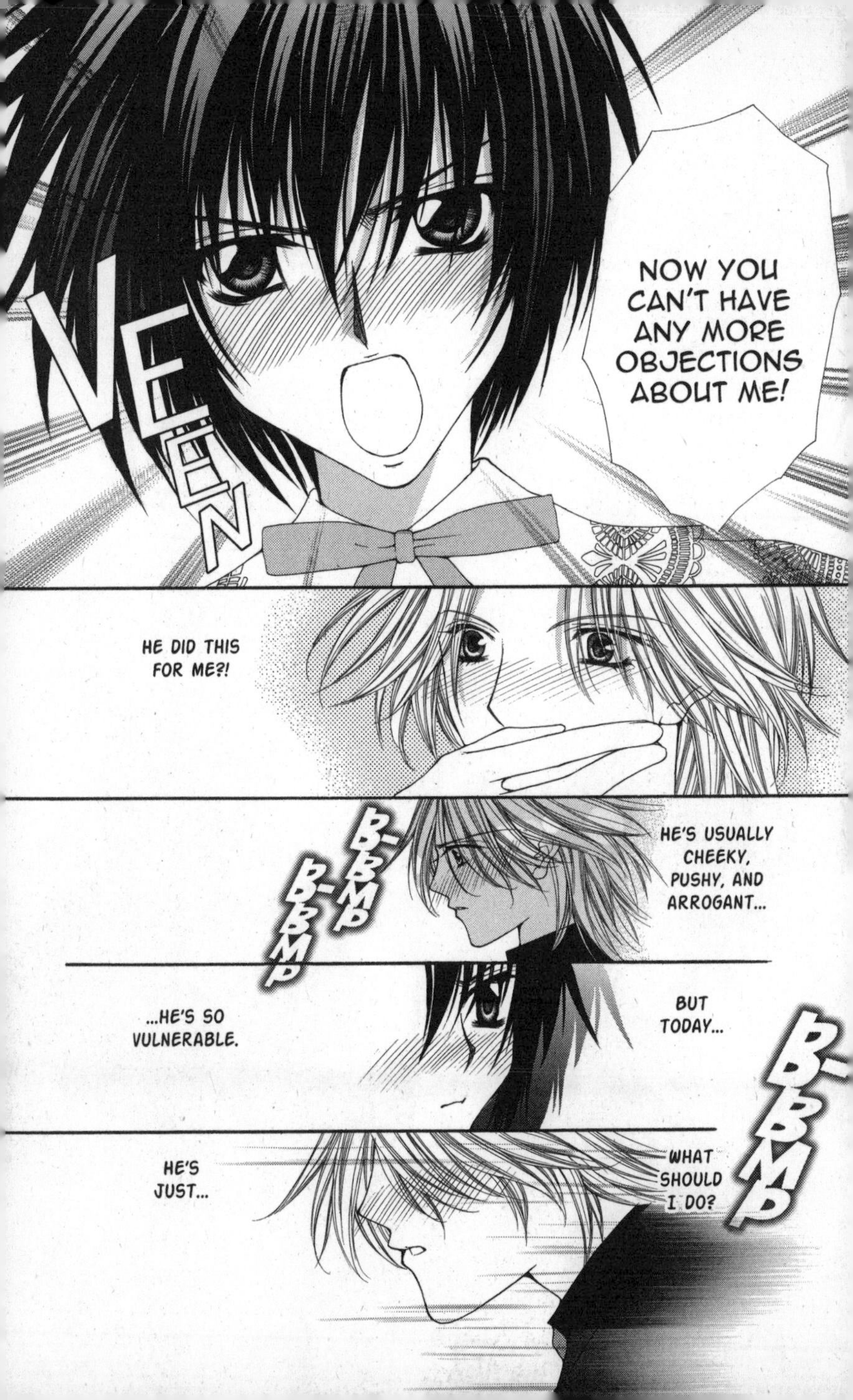
NOW YOU CAN'T HAVE ANY MORE OBJECTIONS ABOUT ME!
VEEEN
HE DID THIS FOR ME?!
HE'S USUALLY CHEEKY, PUSHY, AND ARROGANT...
B-BMP
B-BMP
BUT TODAY...
...HE'S SO VULNERABLE.
B-BMP
WHAT SHOULD I DO?
HE'S JUST...

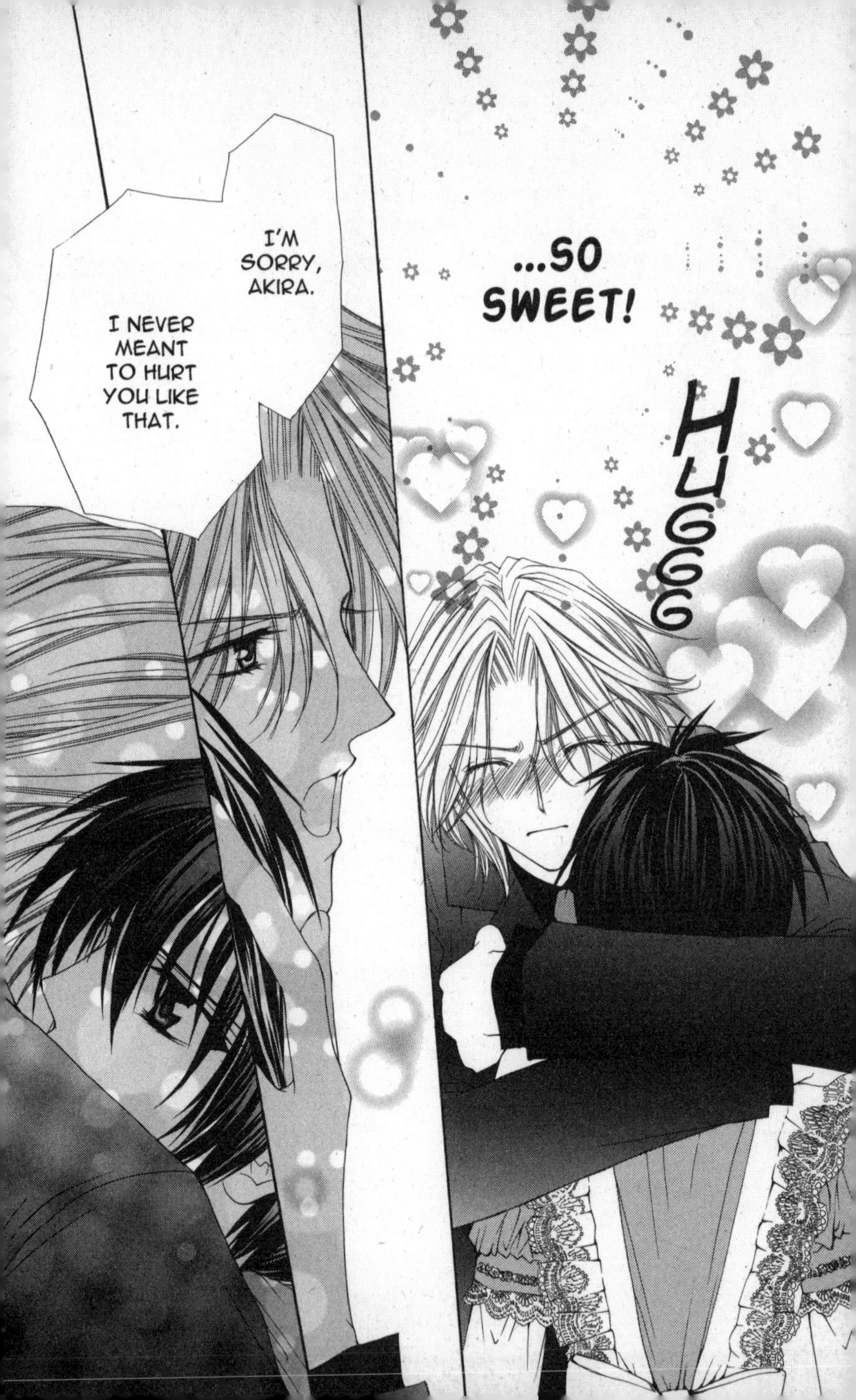
...SO SWEET!
HUGGG
I'M SORRY, AKIRA.
I NEVER MEANT TO HURT YOU LIKE THAT.

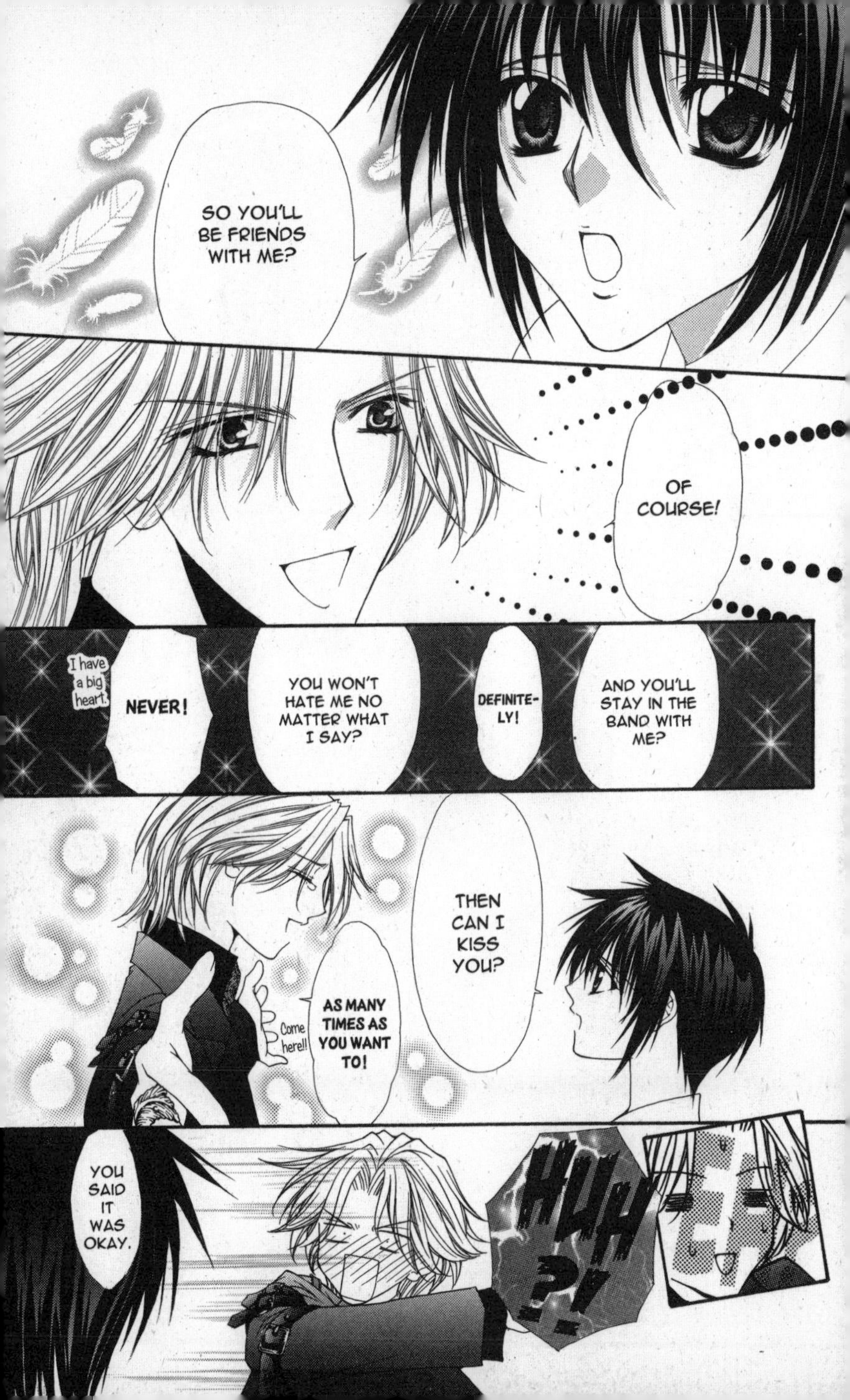
SO YOU'LL BE FRIENDS WITH ME?
OF COURSE!
AND YOU'LL STAY IN THE BAND WITH ME?
DEFINITE-LY!
YOU WON'T HATE ME NO MATTER WHAT I SAY?
NEVER!
I have a big heart.
THEN CAN I KISS YOU?
AS MANY TIMES AS YOU WANT TO!
Come here!!
HUH?!
YOU SAID IT WAS OKAY.

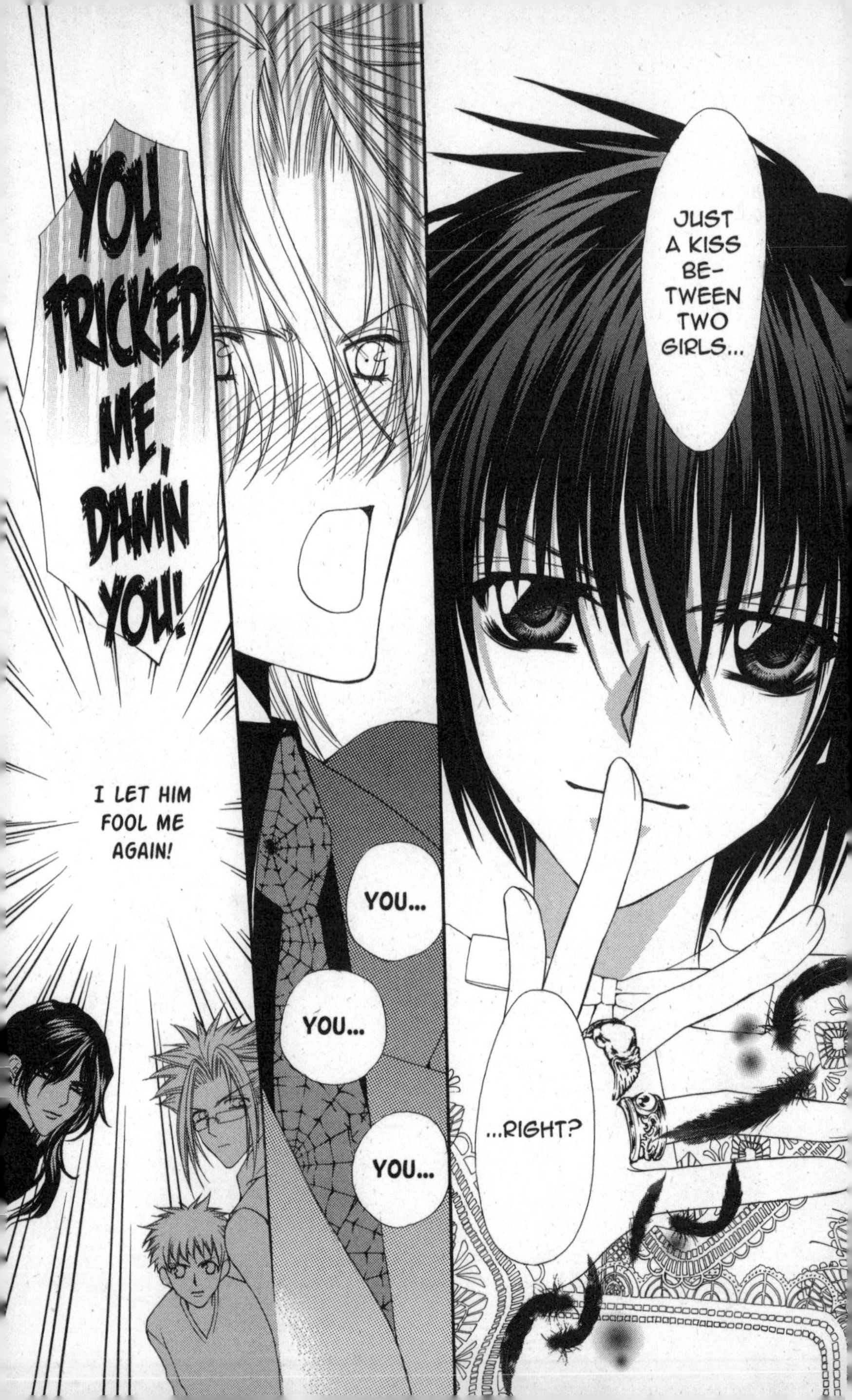
JUST A KISS BE-TWEEN TWO GIRLS...
...RIGHT?
YOU...
YOU...
YOU...
YOU TRICKED ME, DAMN YOU!
I LET HIM FOOL ME AGAIN!

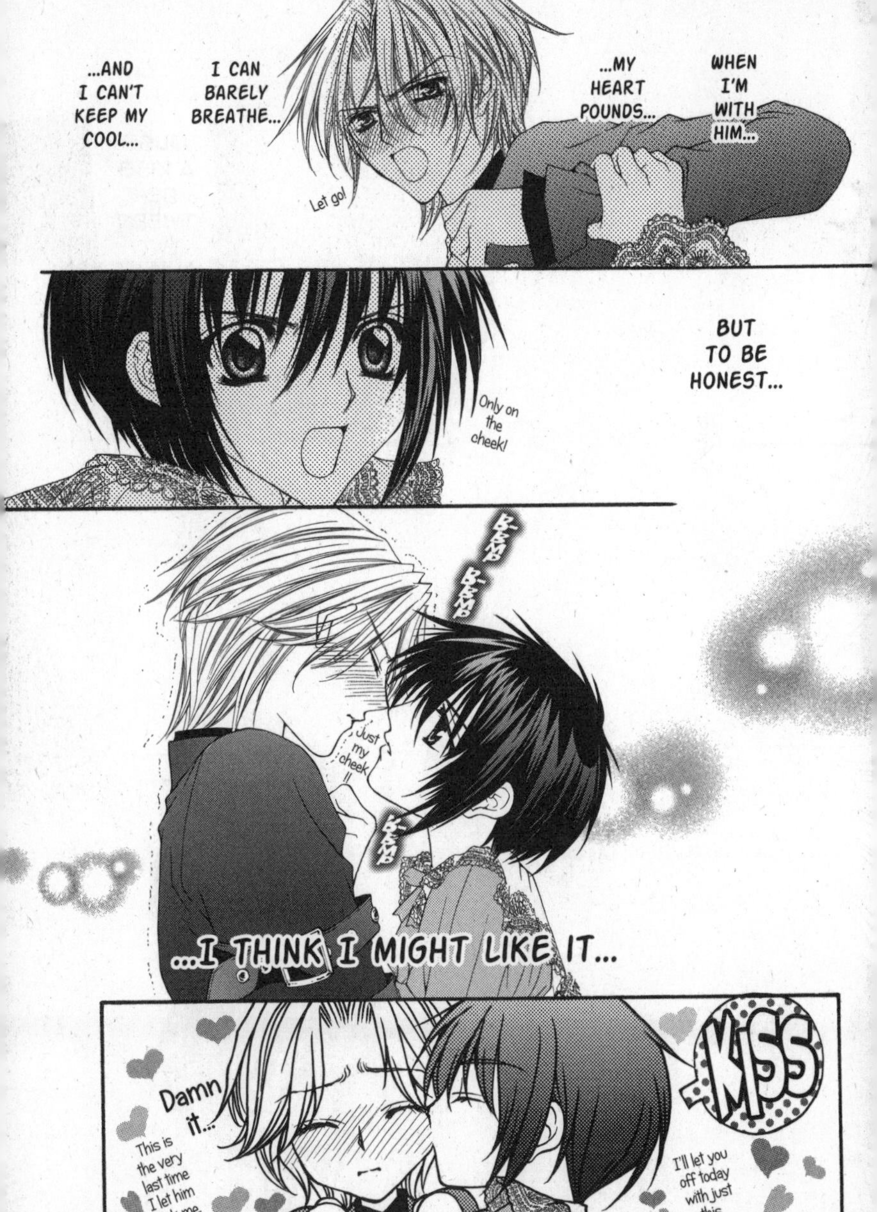
WHEN I'M WITH HIM...
...MY HEART POUNDS...
Let go!
I CAN BARELY BREATHE...
...AND I CAN'T KEEP MY COOL...
BUT TO BE HONEST...
Only on the cheek!
B-BMP B-BMP
Just my cheek!!
B-BMP
...I THINK I MIGHT LIKE IT...
KISS
I'll let you off today with just this.
Damn it...
This is the very last time I let him trick me.

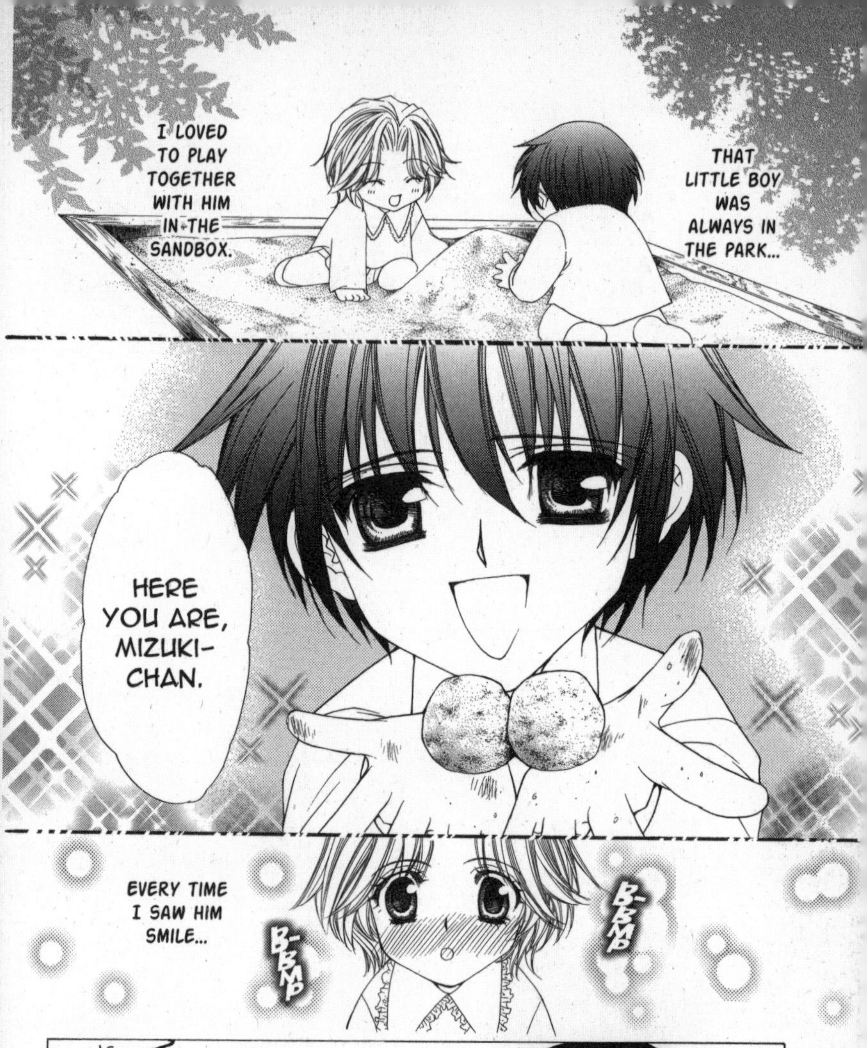
THAT LITTLE BOY WAS ALWAYS IN THE PARK...
I LOVED TO PLAY TOGETHER WITH HIM IN THE SANDBOX.
HERE YOU ARE, MIZUKI-CHAN.
B-BMP
EVERY TIME I SAW HIM SMILE...
B-BMP

Akira's Q&A!!

Q3: Of course we want to know!
Akira, are you a virgin?

A3: That's a secret!! A secret...!!
But I will say I am good at making out...
How's that?

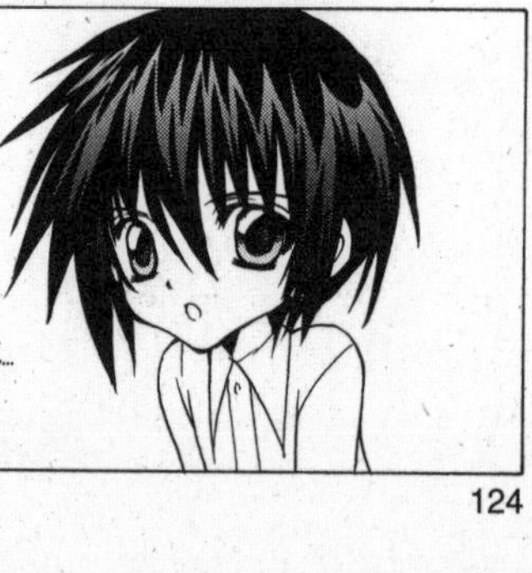

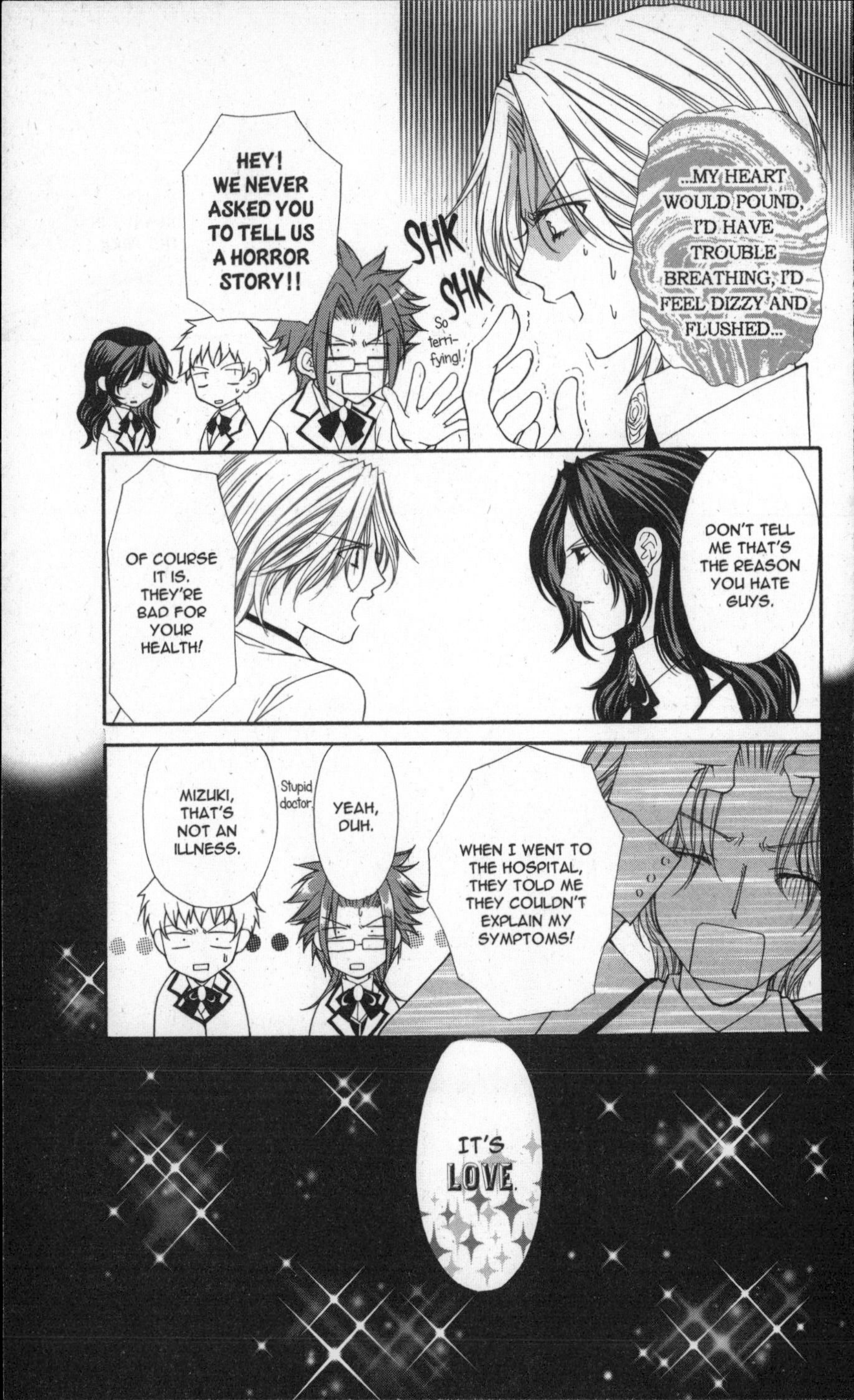
...MY HEART WOULD POUND, I'D HAVE TROUBLE BREATHING, I'D FEEL DIZZY AND FLUSHED...
SHK SHK
So terri-fying!
HEY! WE NEVER ASKED YOU TO TELL US A HORROR STORY!!
DON'T TELL ME THAT'S THE REASON YOU HATE GUYS.
OF COURSE IT IS. THEY'RE BAD FOR YOUR HEALTH!
WHEN I WENT TO THE HOSPITAL, THEY TOLD ME THEY COULDN'T EXPLAIN MY SYMPTOMS!
YEAH, DUH.
Stupid doctor.
MIZUKI, THAT'S NOT AN ILLNESS.
IT'S LOVE.

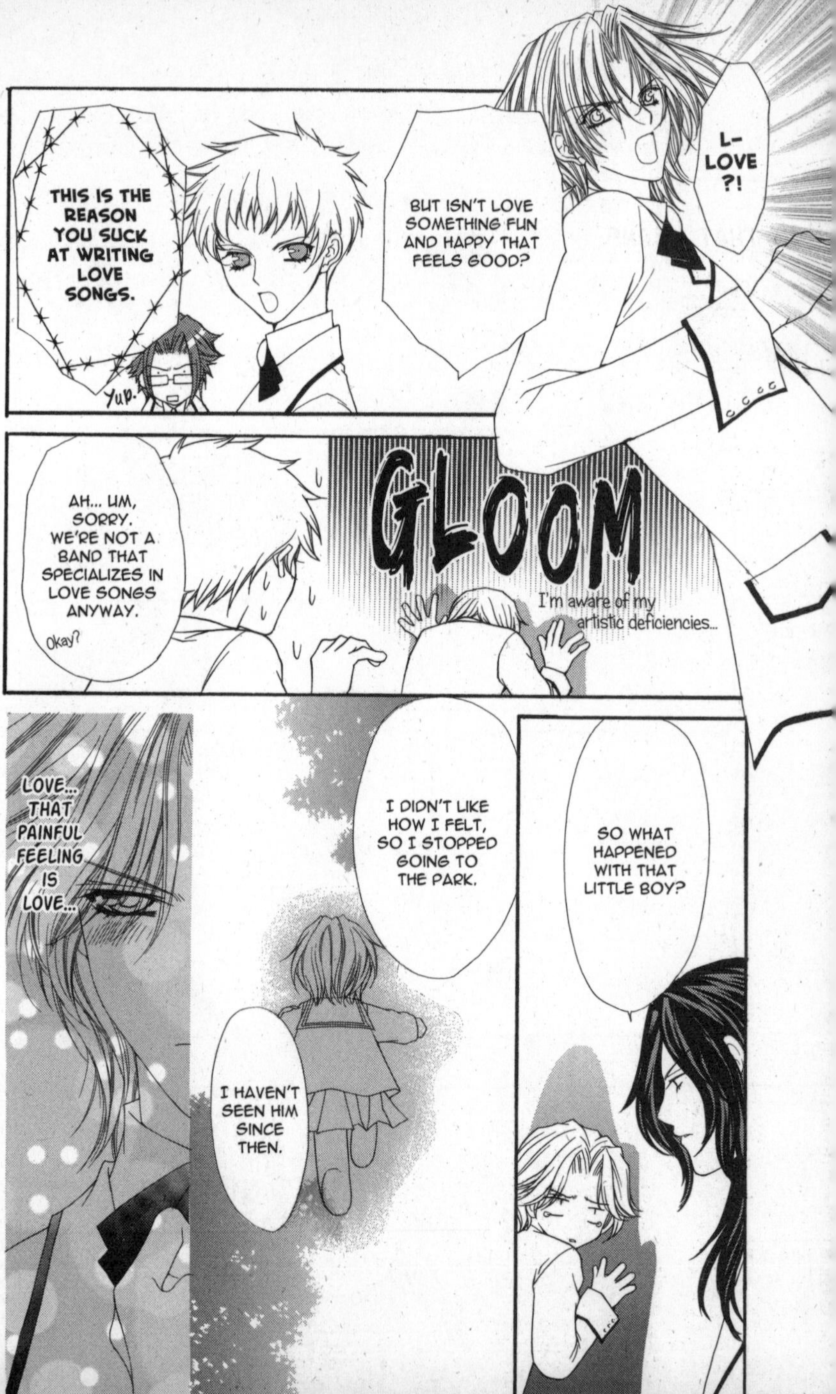
L-LOVE?!
BUT ISN'T LOVE SOMETHING FUN AND HAPPY THAT FEELS GOOD?
THIS IS THE REASON YOU SUCK AT WRITING LOVE SONGS.
Yup.
GLOOM
I'm aware of my artistic deficiencies...
AH... UM, SORRY. WE'RE NOT A BAND THAT SPECIALIZES IN LOVE SONGS ANYWAY.
Okay?
SO WHAT HAPPENED WITH THAT LITTLE BOY?
I DIDN'T LIKE HOW I FELT, SO I STOPPED GOING TO THE PARK.
I HAVEN'T SEEN HIM SINCE THEN.
LOVE... THAT PAINFUL FEELING IS LOVE...

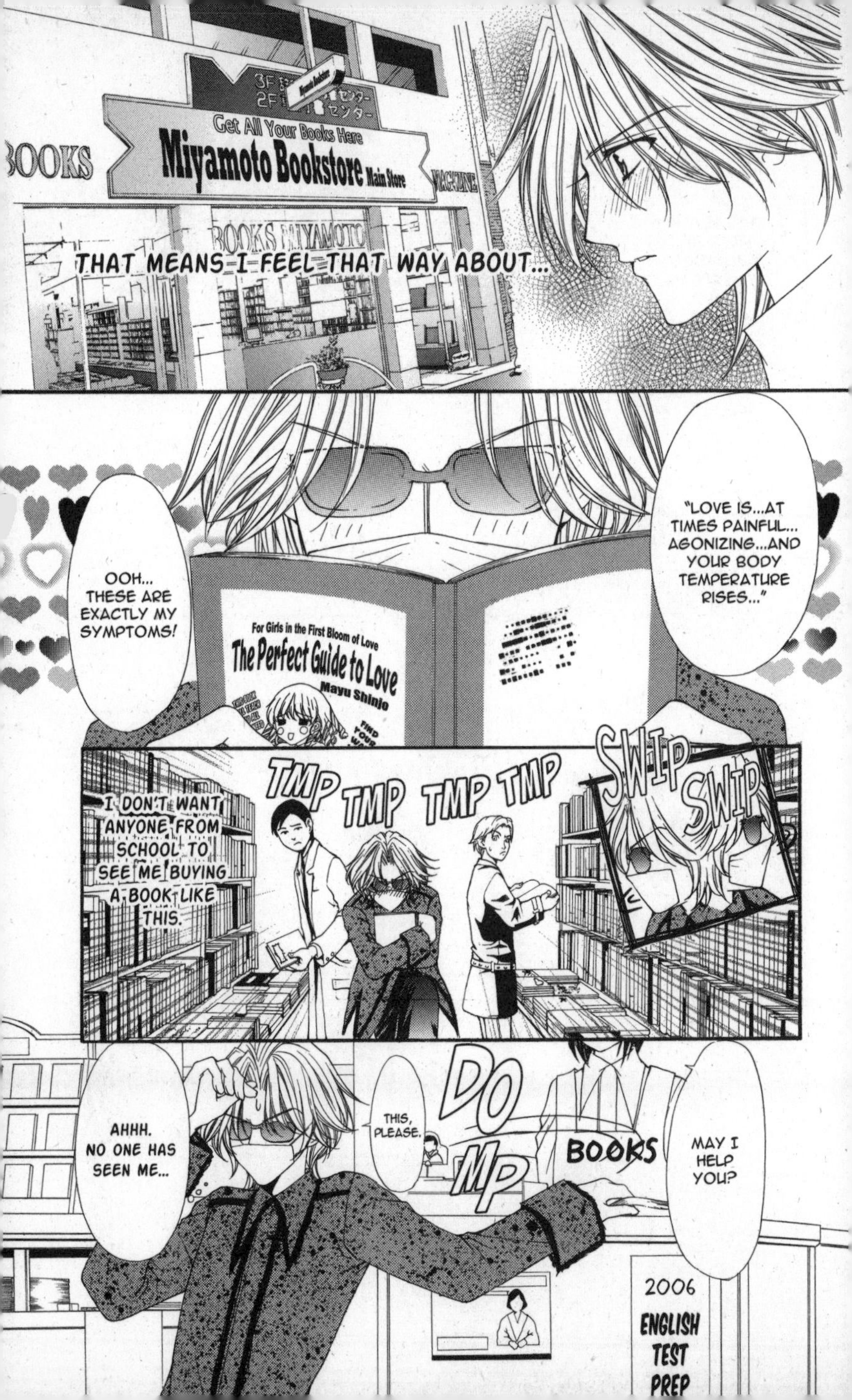

Get All Your Books Here
Miyamoto Bookstore Main Store
BOOKS
MAGAZINE
BOOKS MIYAMOTO
THAT MEANS I FEEL THAT WAY ABOUT...
"LOVE IS...AT TIMES PAINFUL... AGONIZING...AND YOUR BODY TEMPERATURE RISES..."
OOH... THESE ARE EXACTLY MY SYMPTOMS!
For Girls in the First Bloom of Love
The Perfect Guide to Love
Mayu Shinjo
SWIP SWIP
TMP TMP TMP TMP
I DON'T WANT ANYONE FROM SCHOOL TO SEE ME BUYING A BOOK LIKE THIS.
MAY I HELP YOU?
2006 ENGLISH TEST PREP
BOOKS
DOMP
THIS, PLEASE.
AHHH. NO ONE HAS SEEN ME...

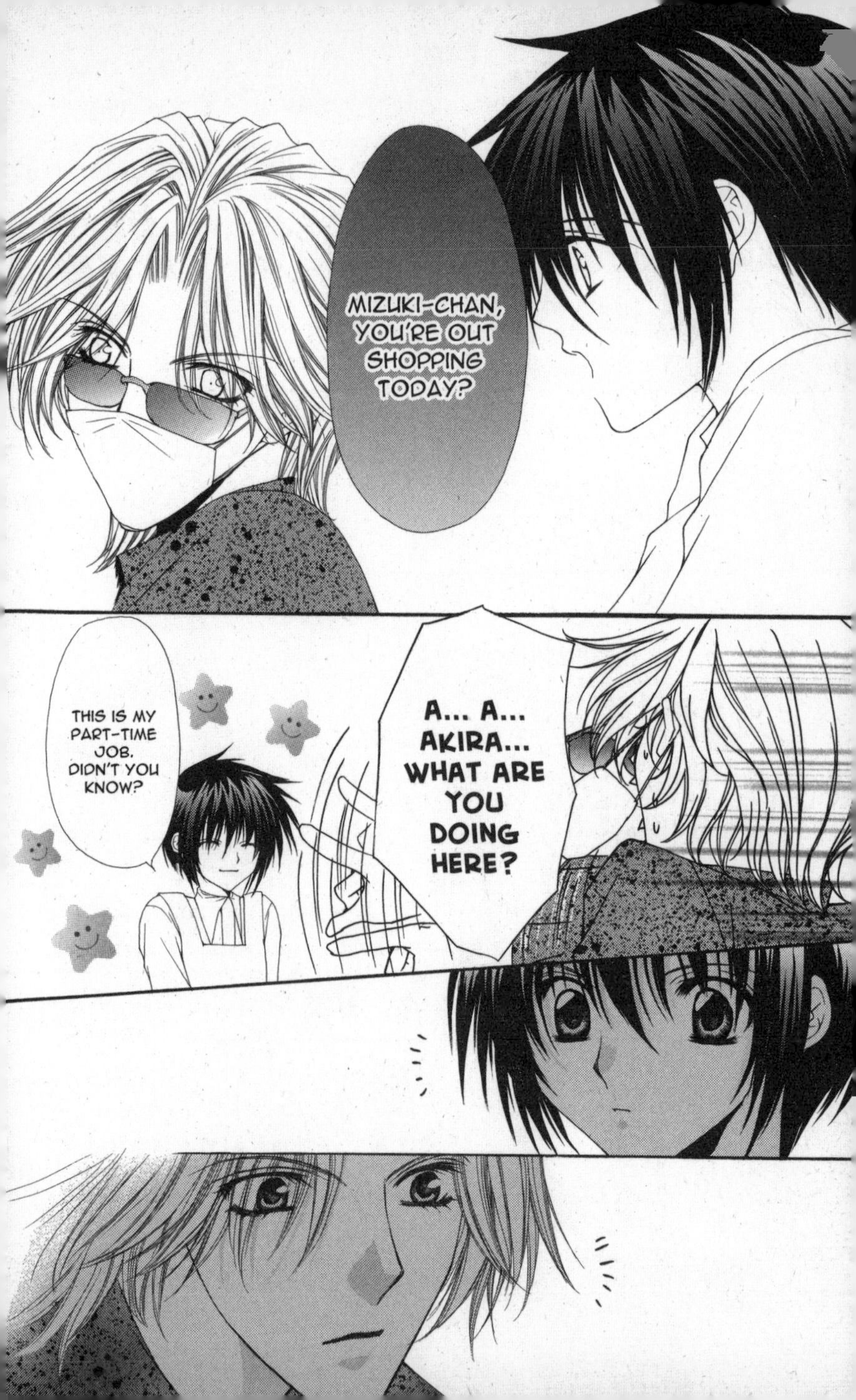
MIZUKI-CHAN, YOU'RE OUT SHOPPING TODAY?
A... A... AKIRA... WHAT ARE YOU DOING HERE?
THIS IS MY PART-TIME JOB. DIDN'T YOU KNOW?

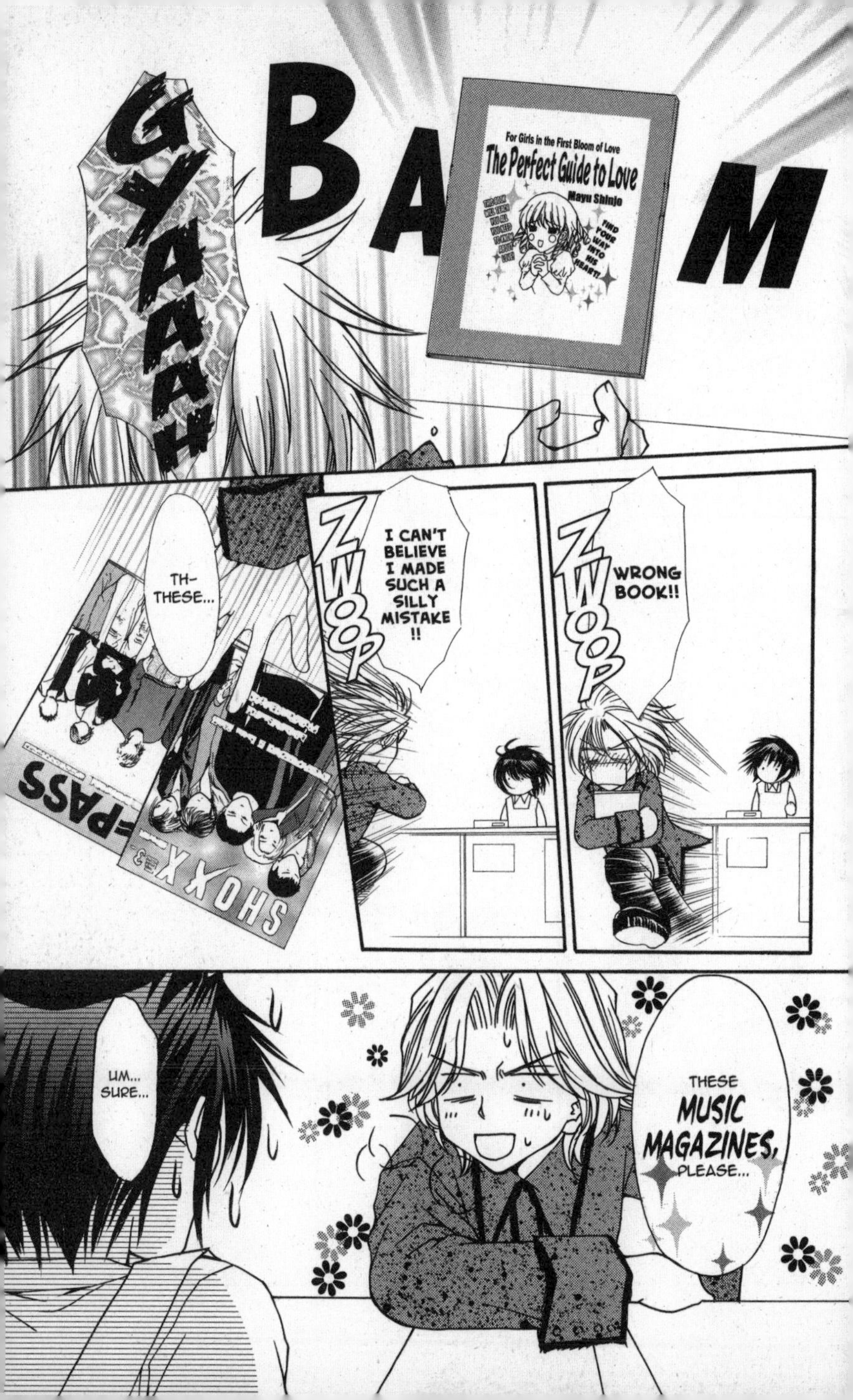
BAM
For Girls in the First Bloom of Love
The Perfect Guide to Love
Mayu Shinjo
THIS BOOK WILL TEACH YOU ALL YOU NEED TO KNOW ABOUT LOVE!
FIND YOUR WAY INTO HIS HEART!?
GYAAAH
WRONG BOOK!!
ZWOOP
I CAN'T BELIEVE I MADE SUCH A SILLY MISTAKE!!
ZWOOP
TH-THESE...
THESE MUSIC MAGAZINES, PLEASE...
UM... SURE...

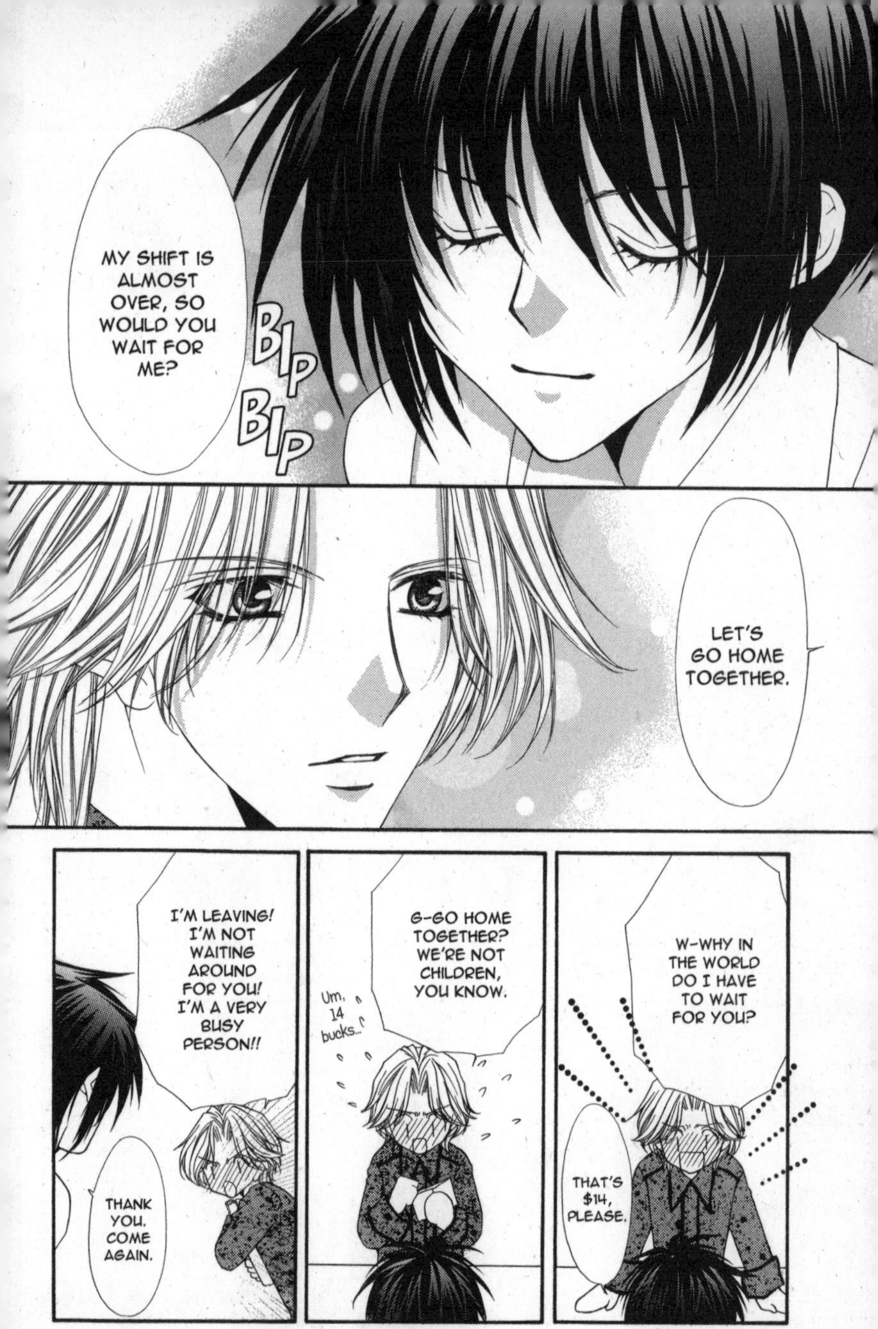
MY SHIFT IS ALMOST OVER, SO WOULD YOU WAIT FOR ME?
BIP BIP
LET'S GO HOME TOGETHER.
W-WHY IN THE WORLD DO I HAVE TO WAIT FOR YOU?
THAT'S $14, PLEASE.
G-GO HOME TOGETHER? WE'RE NOT CHILDREN, YOU KNOW.
Um, 14 bucks...
I'M LEAVING! I'M NOT WAITING AROUND FOR YOU! I'M A VERY BUSY PERSON!!
THANK YOU. COME AGAIN.

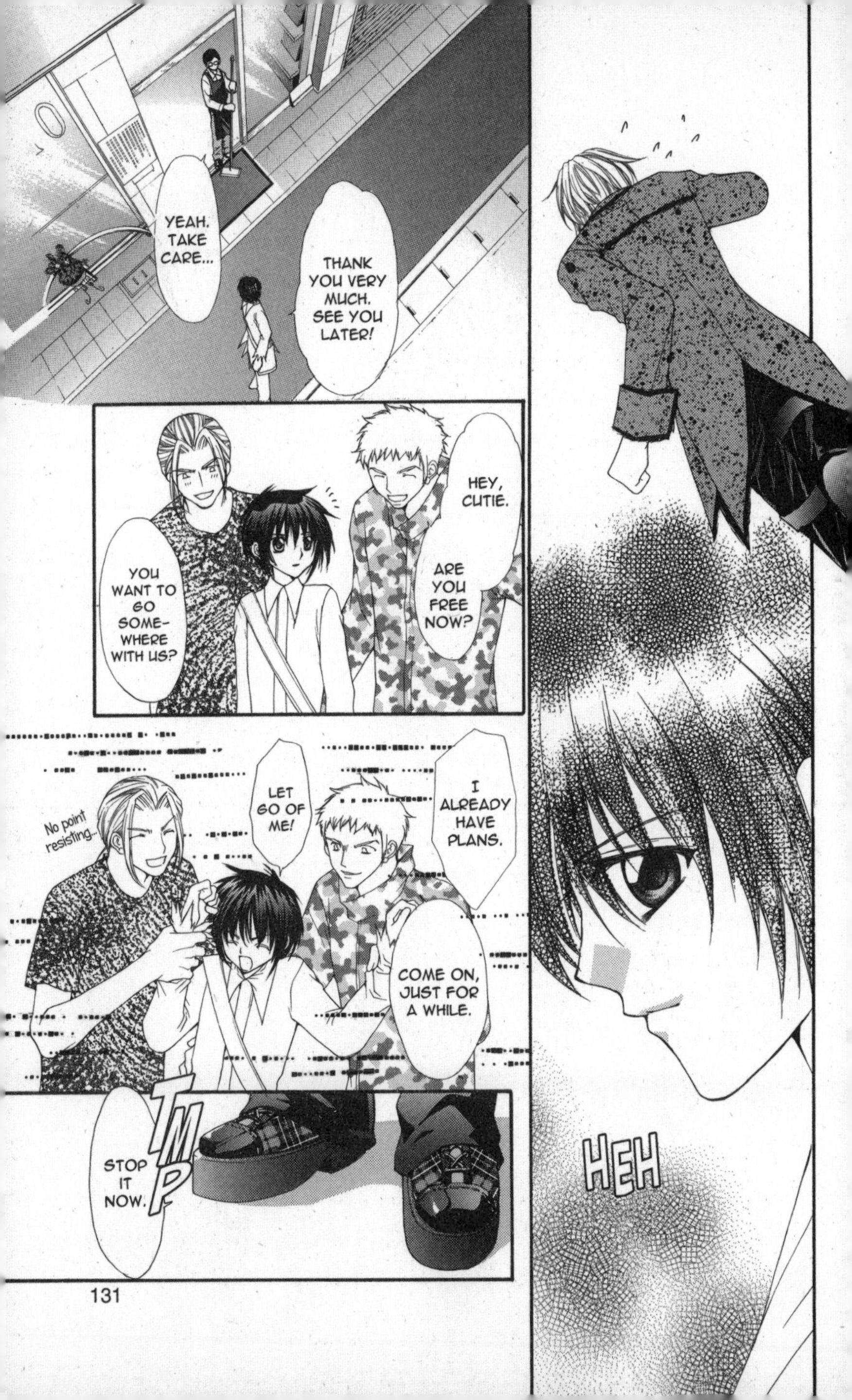
HEH
THANK YOU VERY MUCH. SEE YOU LATER!
YEAH. TAKE CARE...
HEY, CUTIE.
ARE YOU FREE NOW?
YOU WANT TO GO SOME-WHERE WITH US?
I ALREADY HAVE PLANS.
LET GO OF ME!
No point resisting...
COME ON, JUST FOR A WHILE.
TMP
STOP IT NOW.

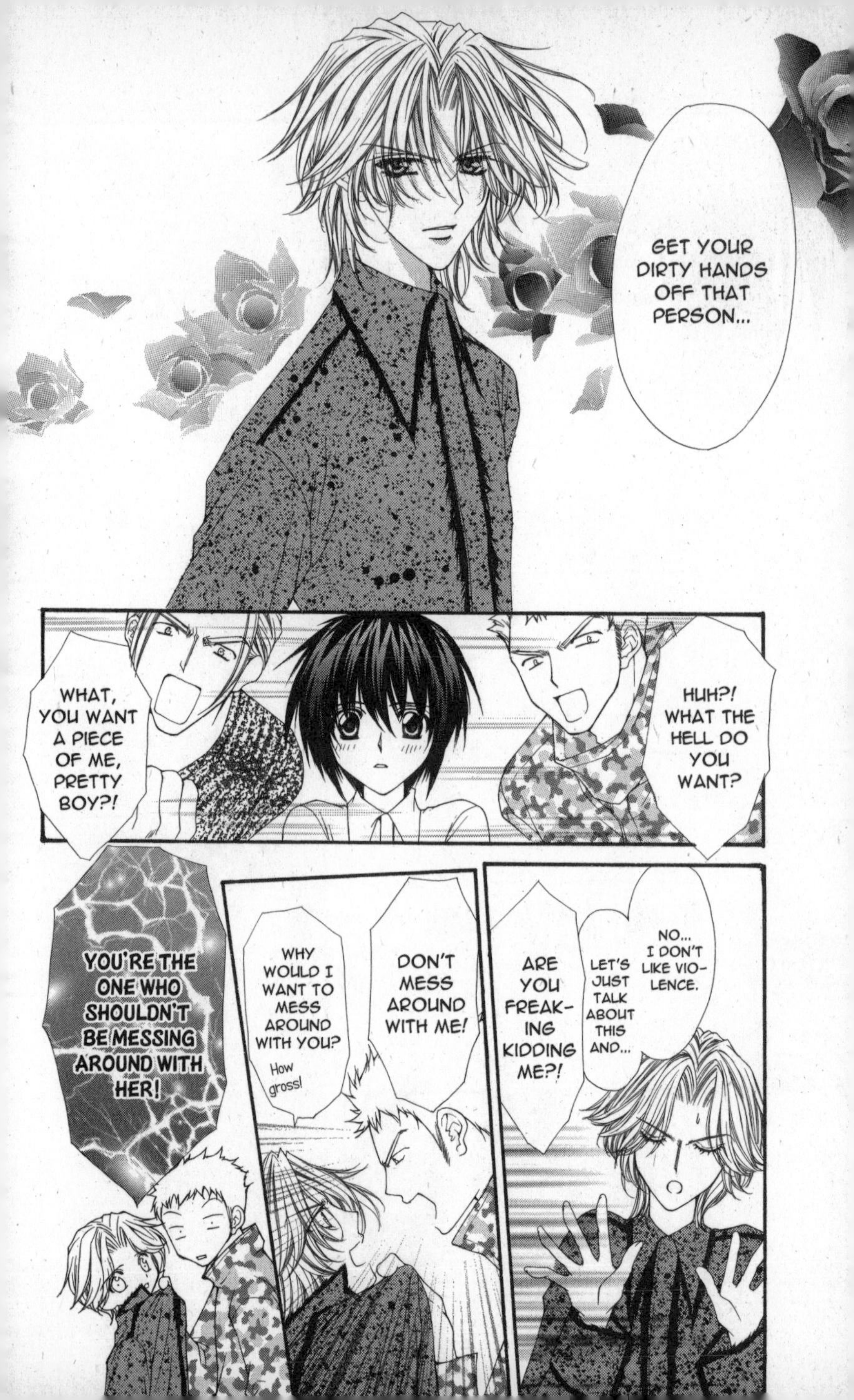
GET YOUR DIRTY HANDS OFF THAT PERSON...
HUH?! WHAT THE HELL DO YOU WANT?
WHAT, YOU WANT A PIECE OF ME, PRETTY BOY?!
NO... I DON'T LIKE VIO-LENCE.
LET'S JUST TALK ABOUT THIS AND...
ARE YOU FREAK-ING KIDDING ME?!
DON'T MESS AROUND WITH ME!
WHY WOULD I WANT TO MESS AROUND WITH YOU?
How gross!
YOU'RE THE ONE WHO SHOULDN'T BE MESSING AROUND WITH HER!

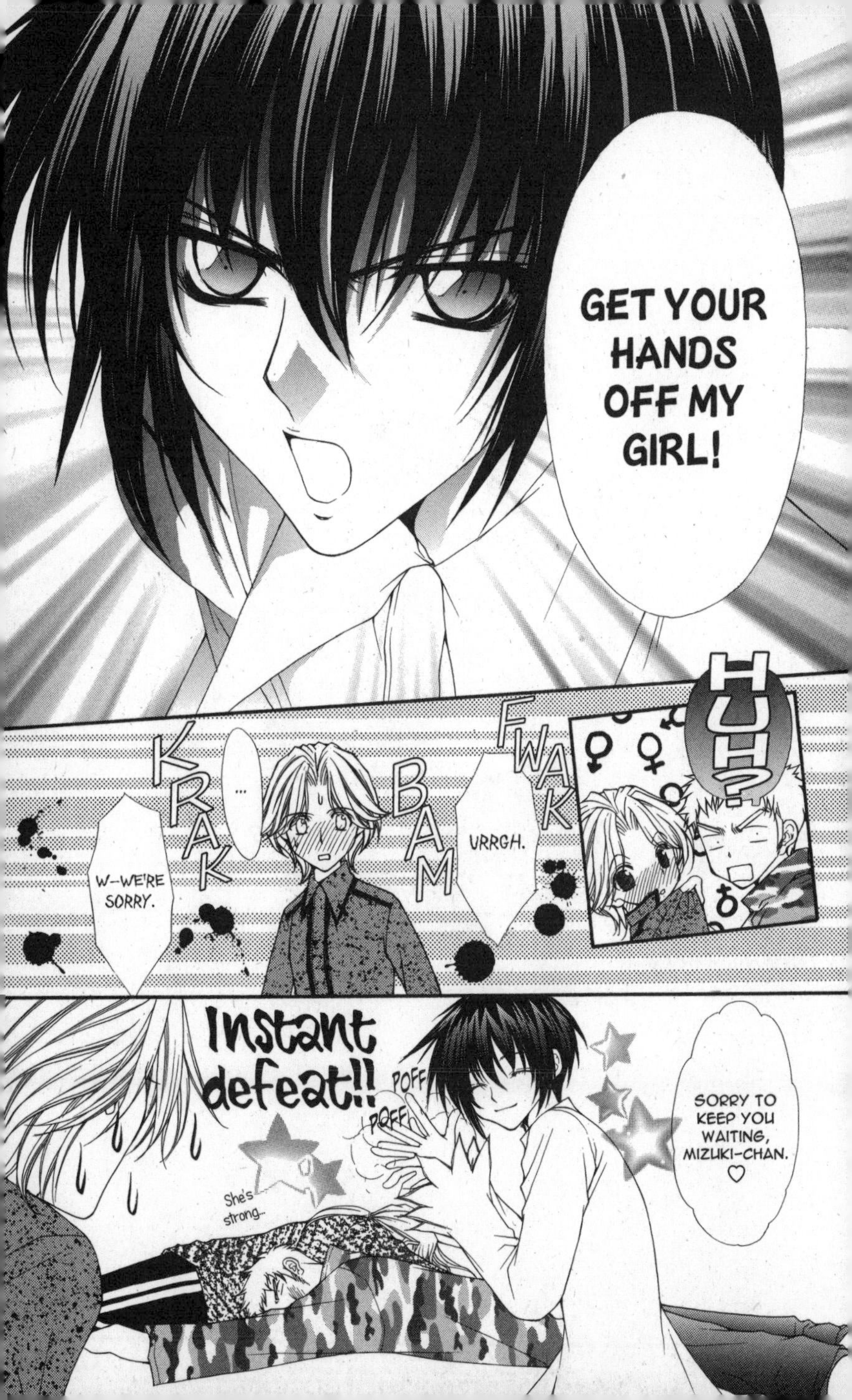
GET YOUR HANDS OFF MY GIRL!
HUH?
FWAK
URRGH.
BAM
...
KRAK
W-WE'RE SORRY.
SORRY TO KEEP YOU WAITING, MIZUKI-CHAN. ♡
POFF
POFF
Instant defeat!!
She's strong...

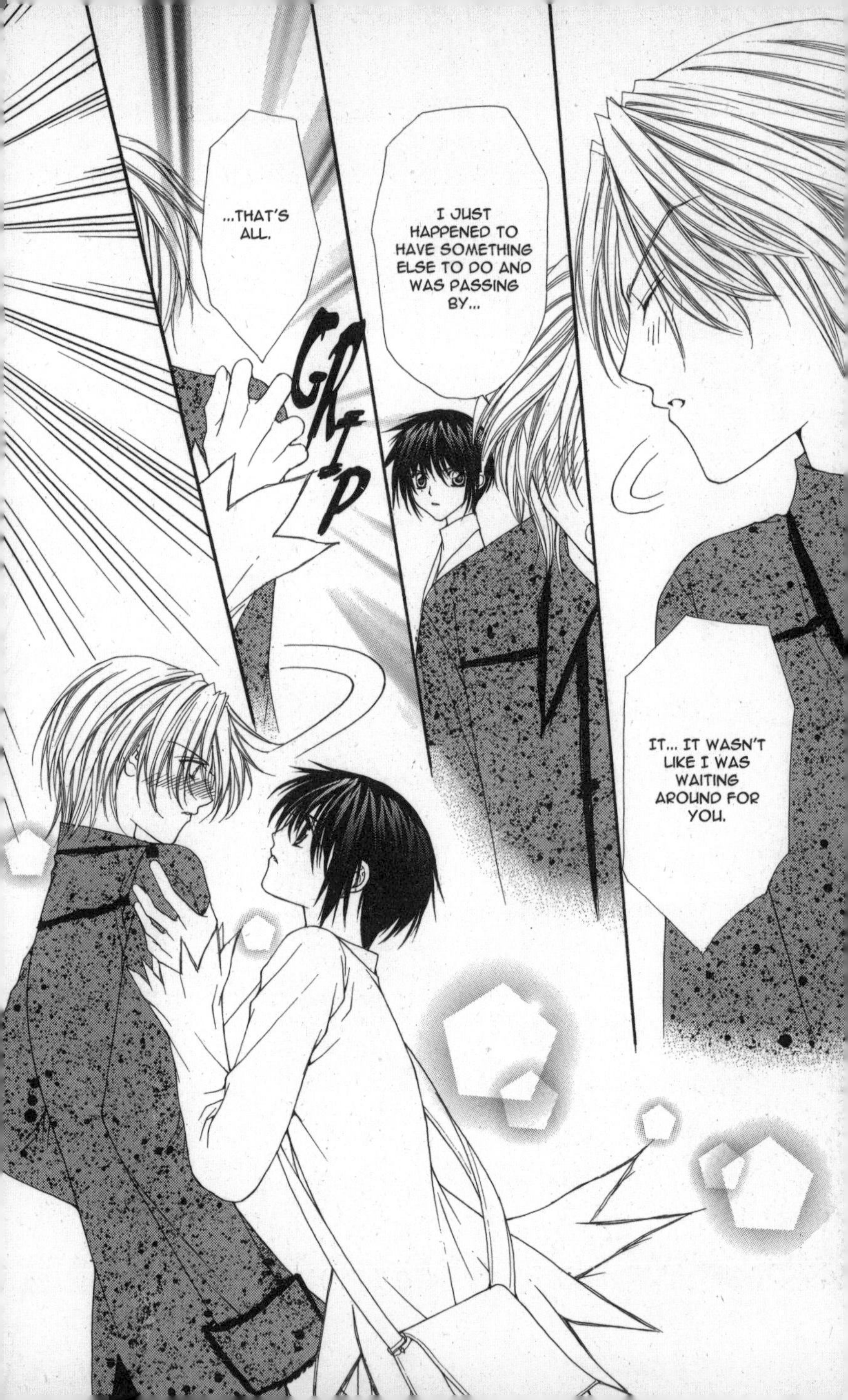
IT... IT WASN'T LIKE I WAS WAITING AROUND FOR YOU.
I JUST HAPPENED TO HAVE SOMETHING ELSE TO DO AND WAS PASSING BY...
...THAT'S ALL.
GRIP

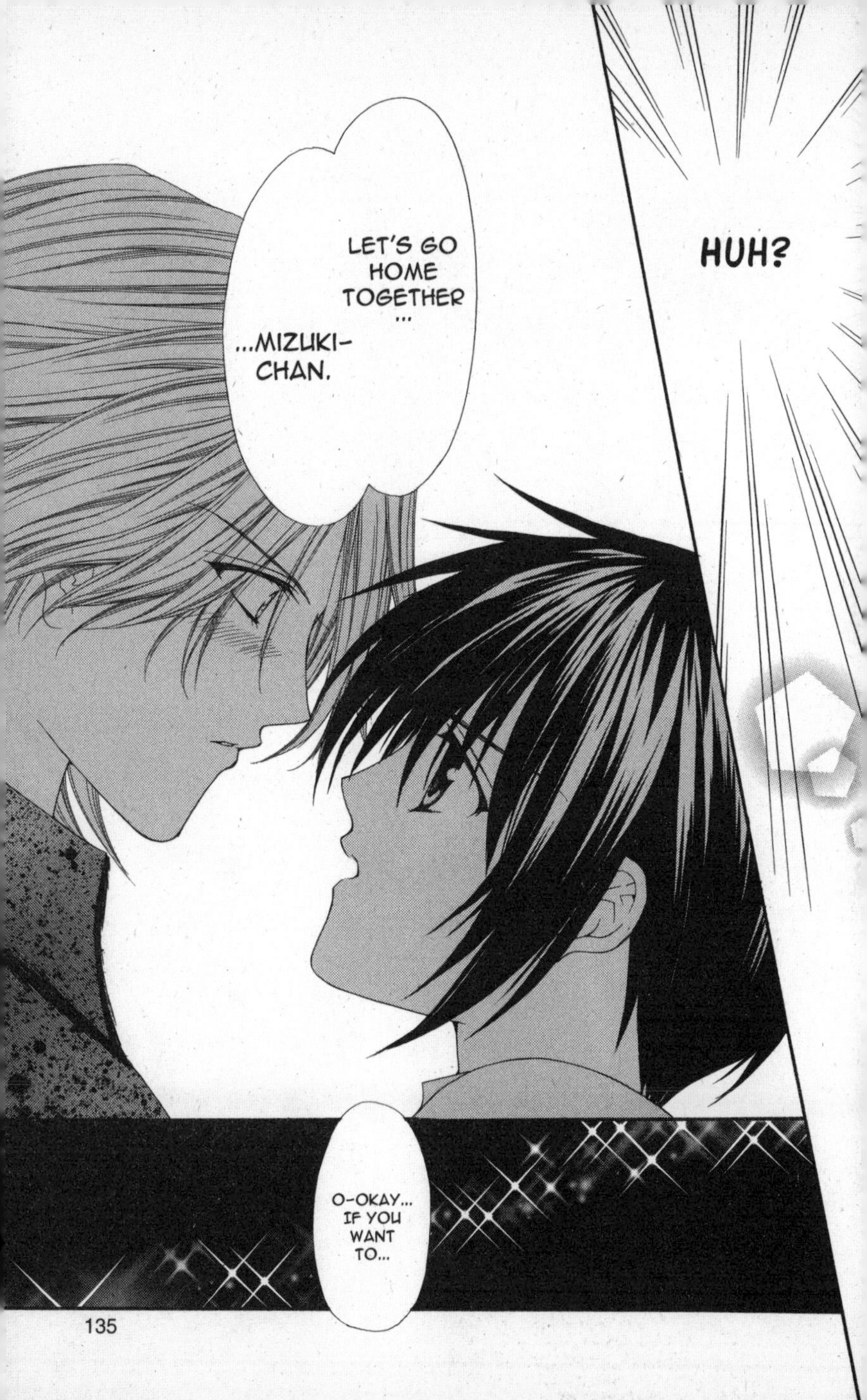
HUH?
LET'S GO HOME TOGETHER ... ...MIZUKI-CHAN.
O-OKAY... IF YOU WANT TO...

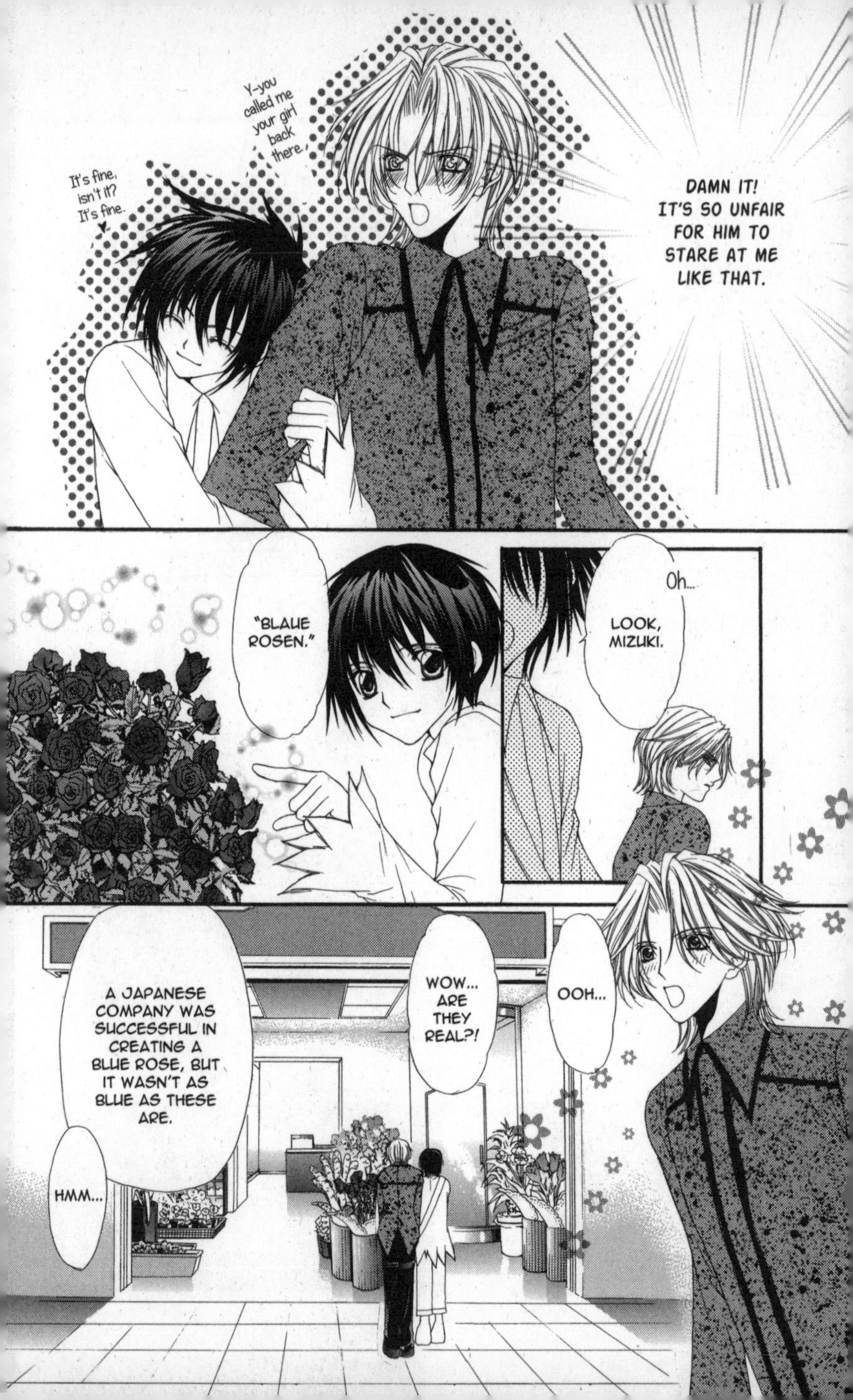
DAMN IT! IT'S SO UNFAIR FOR HIM TO STARE AT ME LIKE THAT.
Y-you called me your girl back there.
It's fine, isn't it? It's fine.
Oh...
LOOK, MIZUKI.
"BLAUE ROSEN."
OOH...
WOW... ARE THEY REAL?!
A JAPANESE COMPANY WAS SUCCESSFUL IN CREATING A BLUE ROSE, BUT IT WASN'T AS BLUE AS THESE ARE.
HMM...

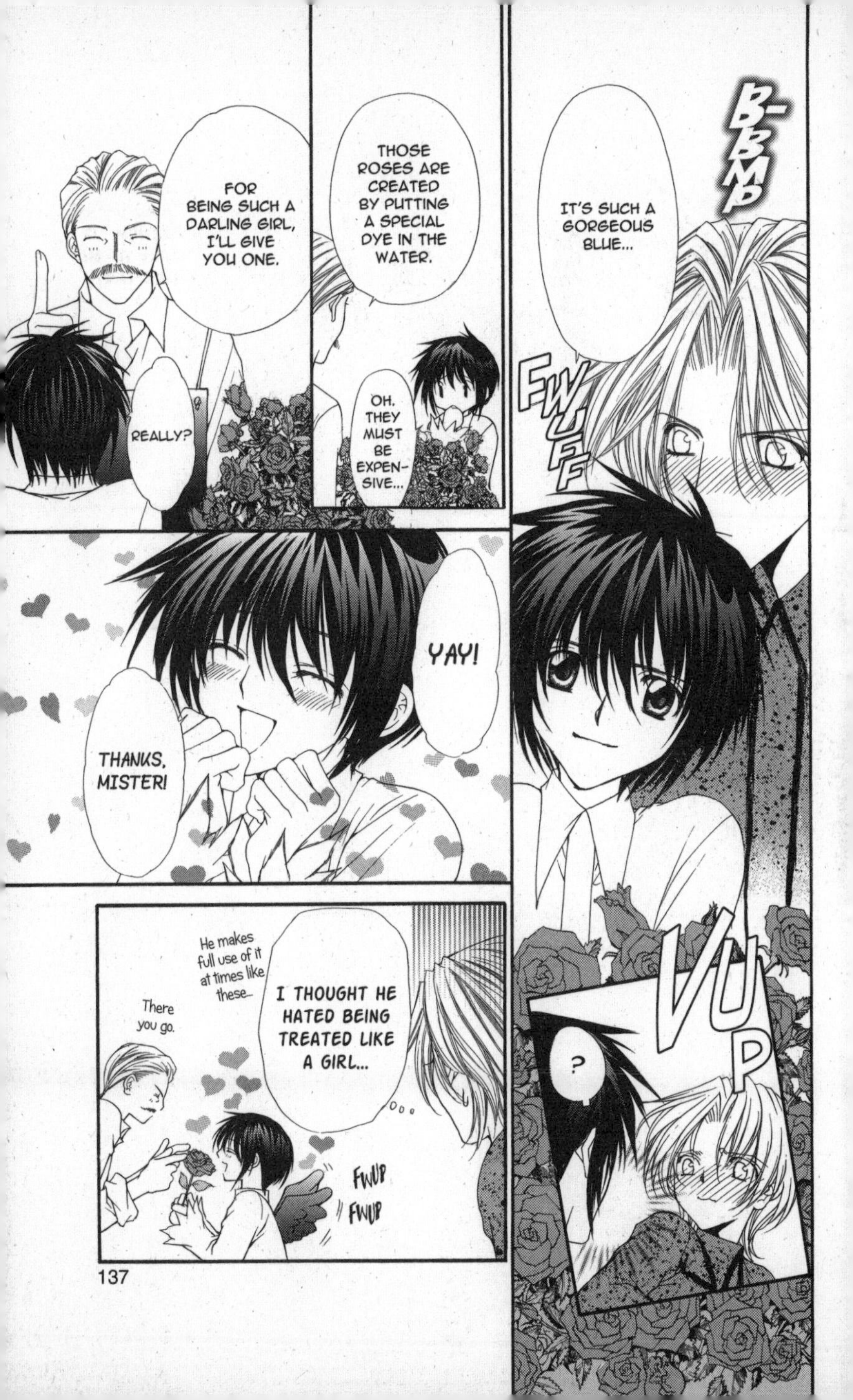
B-BMP
IT'S SUCH A GORGEOUS BLUE...
FWUFF
VUP
?
THOSE ROSES ARE CREATED BY PUTTING A SPECIAL DYE IN THE WATER.
OH. THEY MUST BE EXPENSIVE...
FOR BEING SUCH A DARLING GIRL, I'LL GIVE YOU ONE.
REALLY?
YAY!
THANKS, MISTER!
I THOUGHT HE HATED BEING TREATED LIKE A GIRL...
He makes full use of it at times like these...
There you go.
FWUP
FWUP

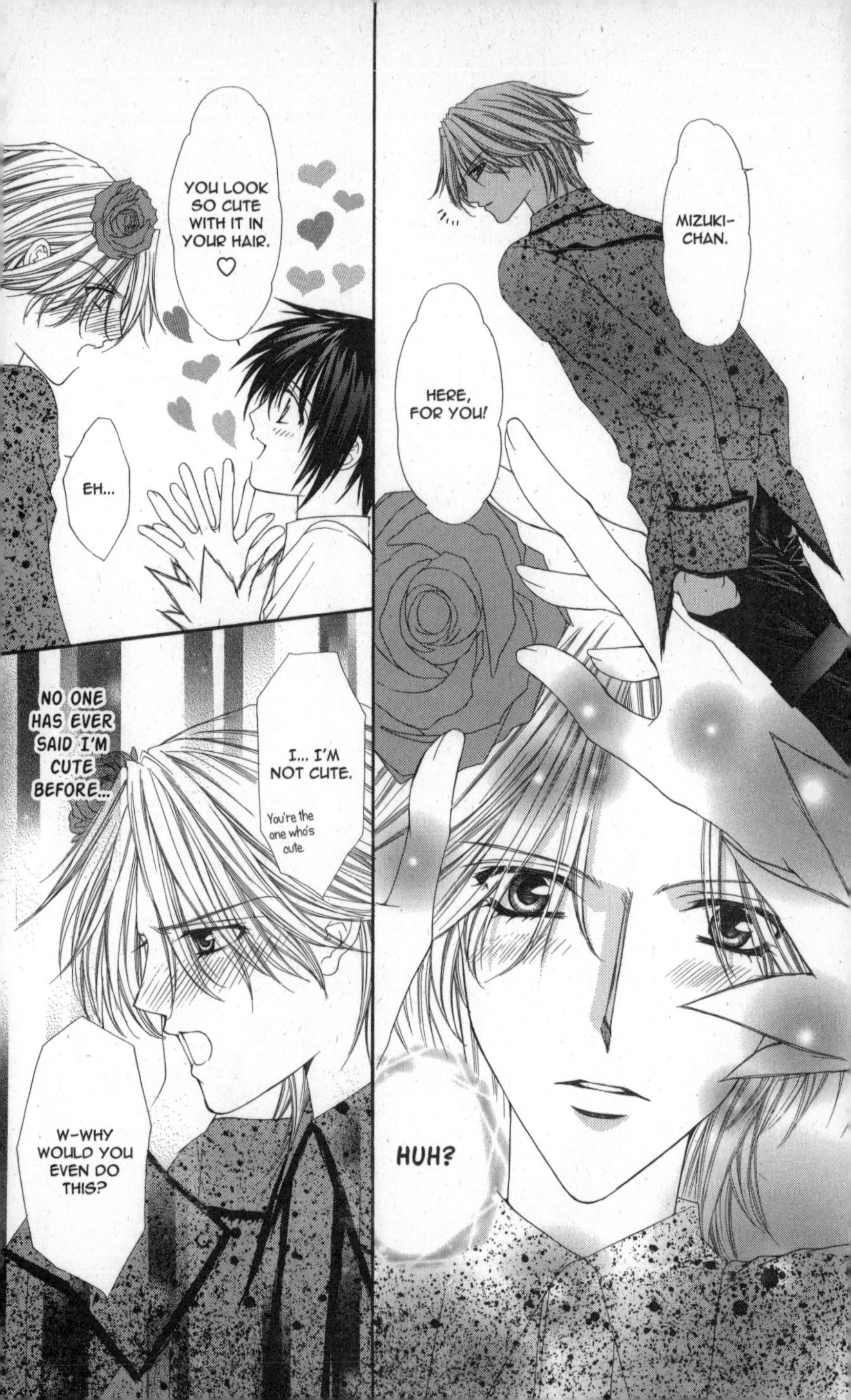
MIZUKI-CHAN.
HERE, FOR YOU!
HUH?
YOU LOOK SO CUTE WITH IT IN YOUR HAIR. ♡
EH...
I... I'M NOT CUTE.
You're the one who's cute.
NO ONE HAS EVER SAID I'M CUTE BEFORE...
W-WHY WOULD YOU EVEN DO THIS?

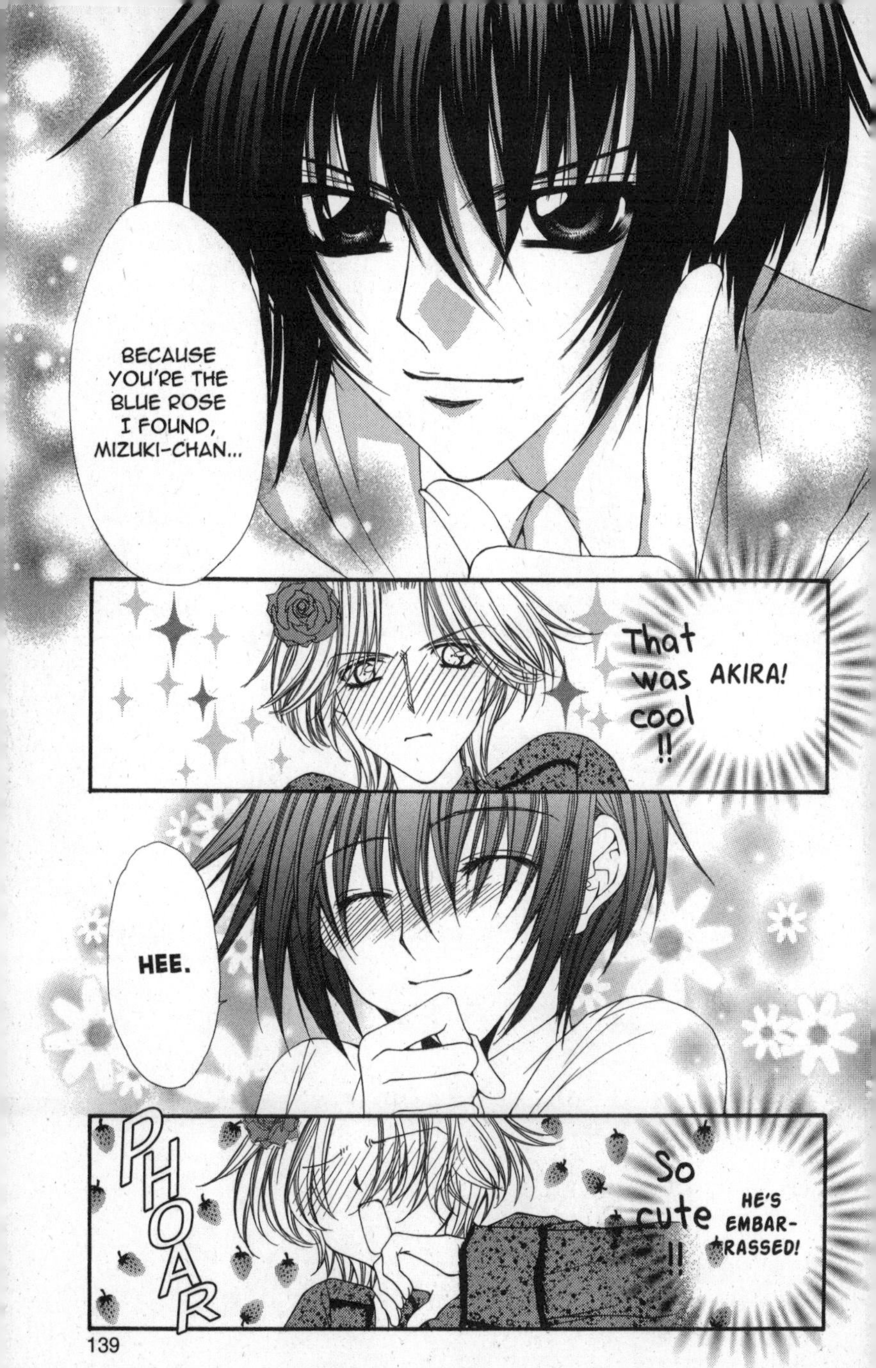
BECAUSE YOU'RE THE BLUE ROSE I FOUND, MIZUKI-CHAN...
AKIRA!
That was cool!!
HEE.
HE'S EMBAR-RASSED!
So cute!!
PHOAR

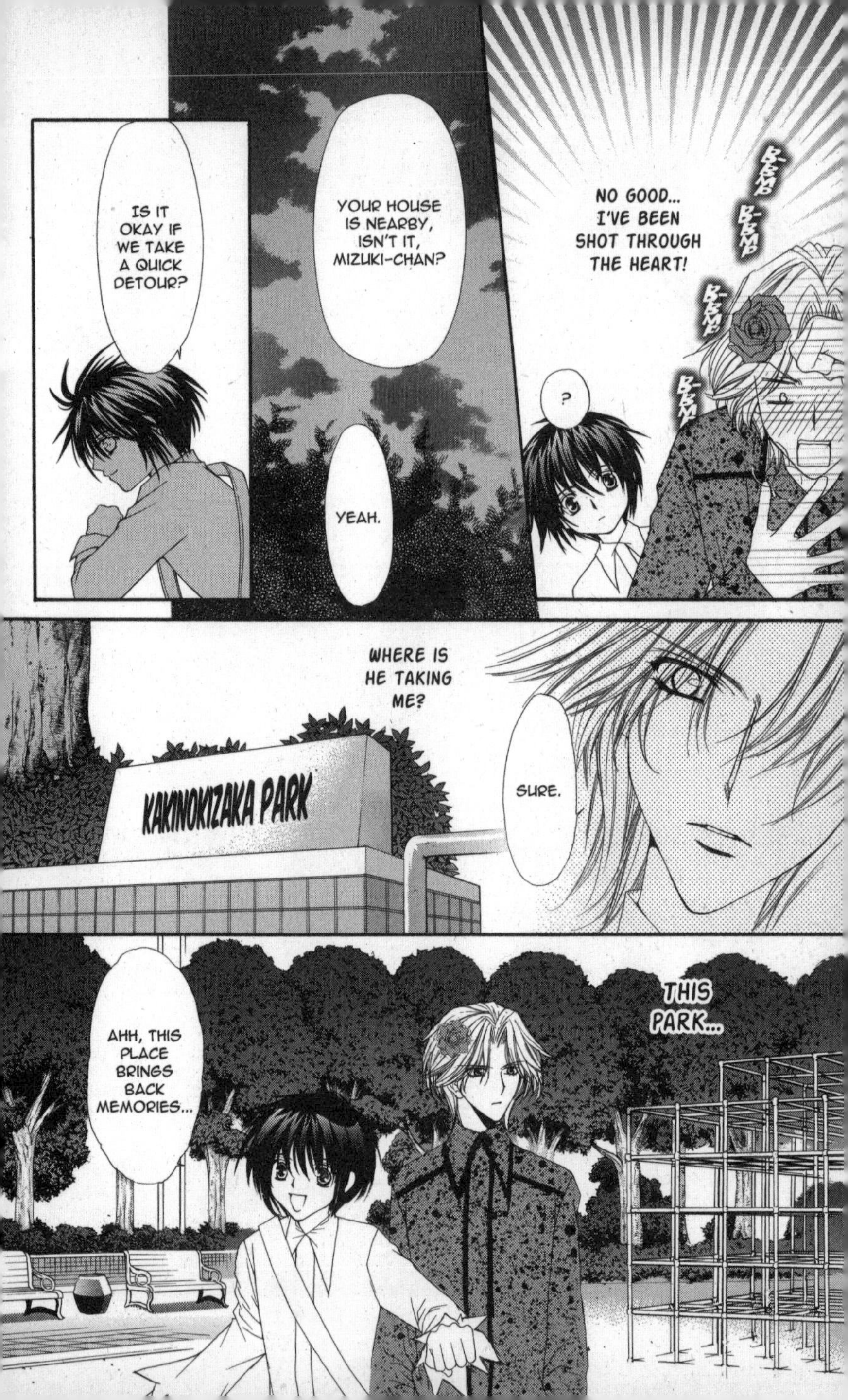

B-BMP
B-BMP
B-BMP
B-BMP
NO GOOD... I'VE BEEN SHOT THROUGH THE HEART!
?
YOUR HOUSE IS NEARBY, ISN'T IT, MIZUKI-CHAN?
YEAH.
IS IT OKAY IF WE TAKE A QUICK DETOUR?
WHERE IS HE TAKING ME?
SURE.
KAKINOKIZAKA PARK
THIS PARK...
AHH, THIS PLACE BRINGS BACK MEMORIES...

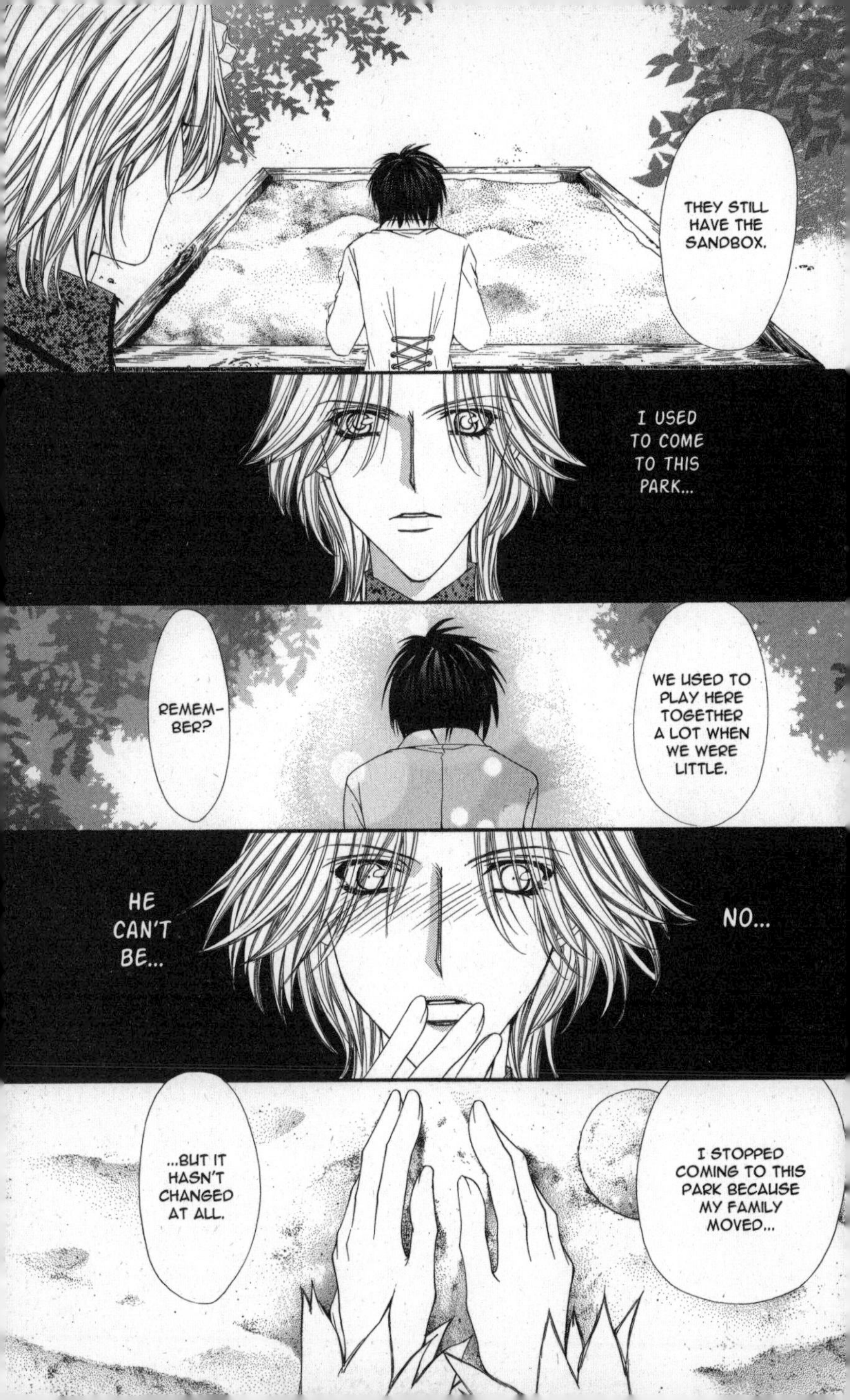
THEY STILL HAVE THE SANDBOX.
I USED TO COME TO THIS PARK...
WE USED TO PLAY HERE TOGETHER A LOT WHEN WE WERE LITTLE.
REMEMBER?
NO...
HE CAN'T BE...
I STOPPED COMING TO THIS PARK BECAUSE MY FAMILY MOVED...
...BUT IT HASN'T CHANGED AT ALL.

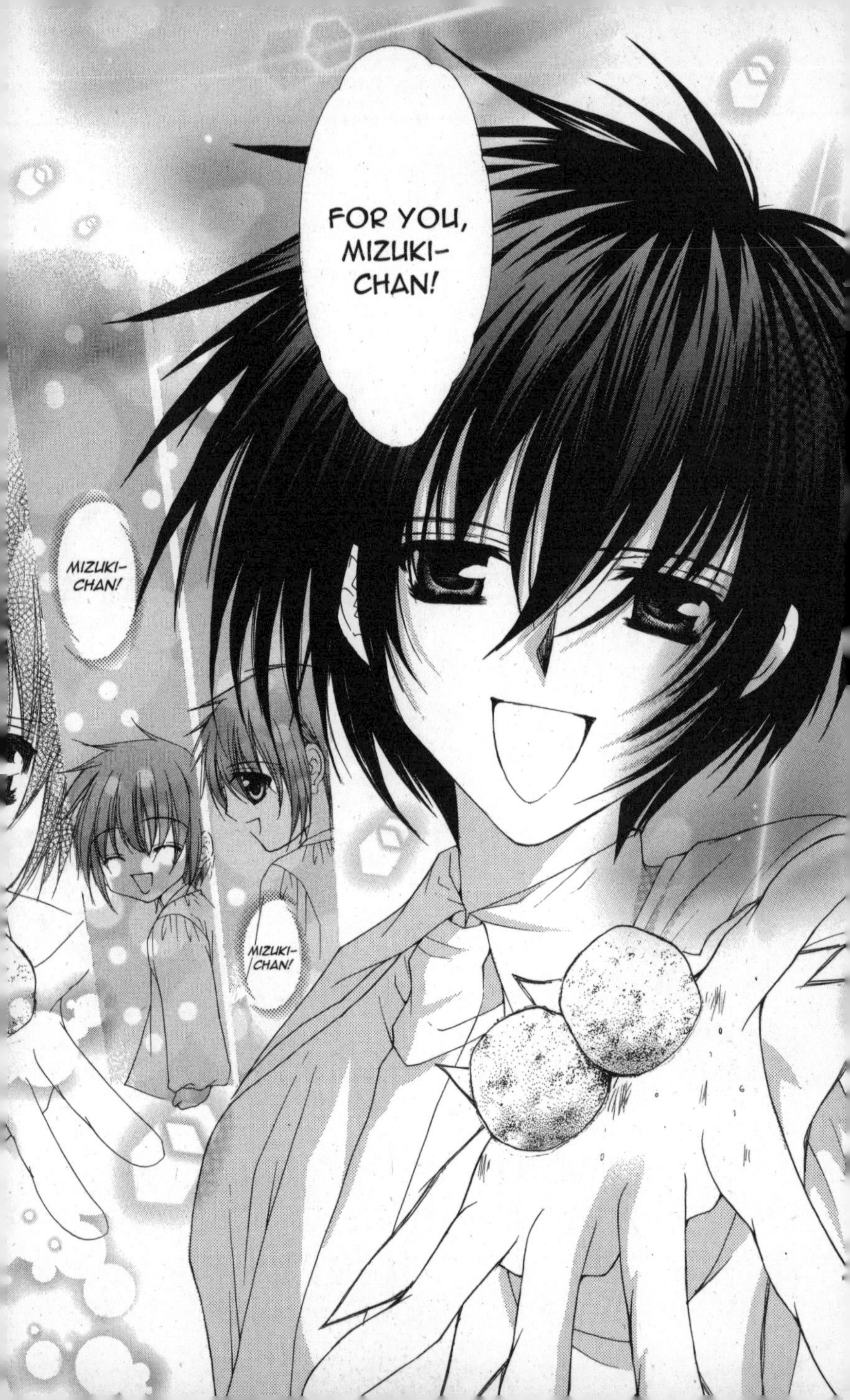
FOR YOU, MIZUKI-CHAN!
MIZUKI-CHAN!
MIZUKI-CHAN!

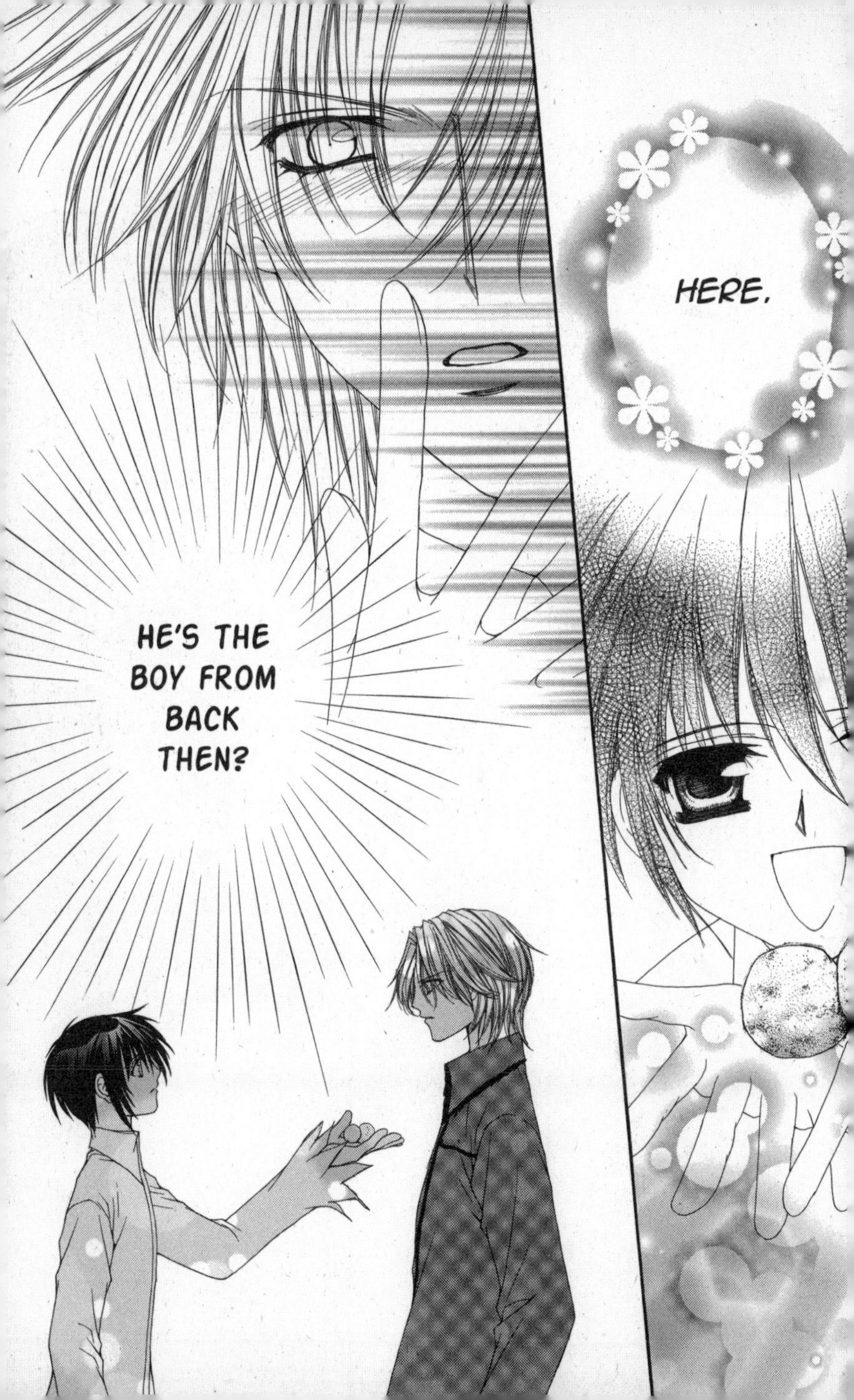
HERE.
HE'S THE BOY FROM BACK THEN?

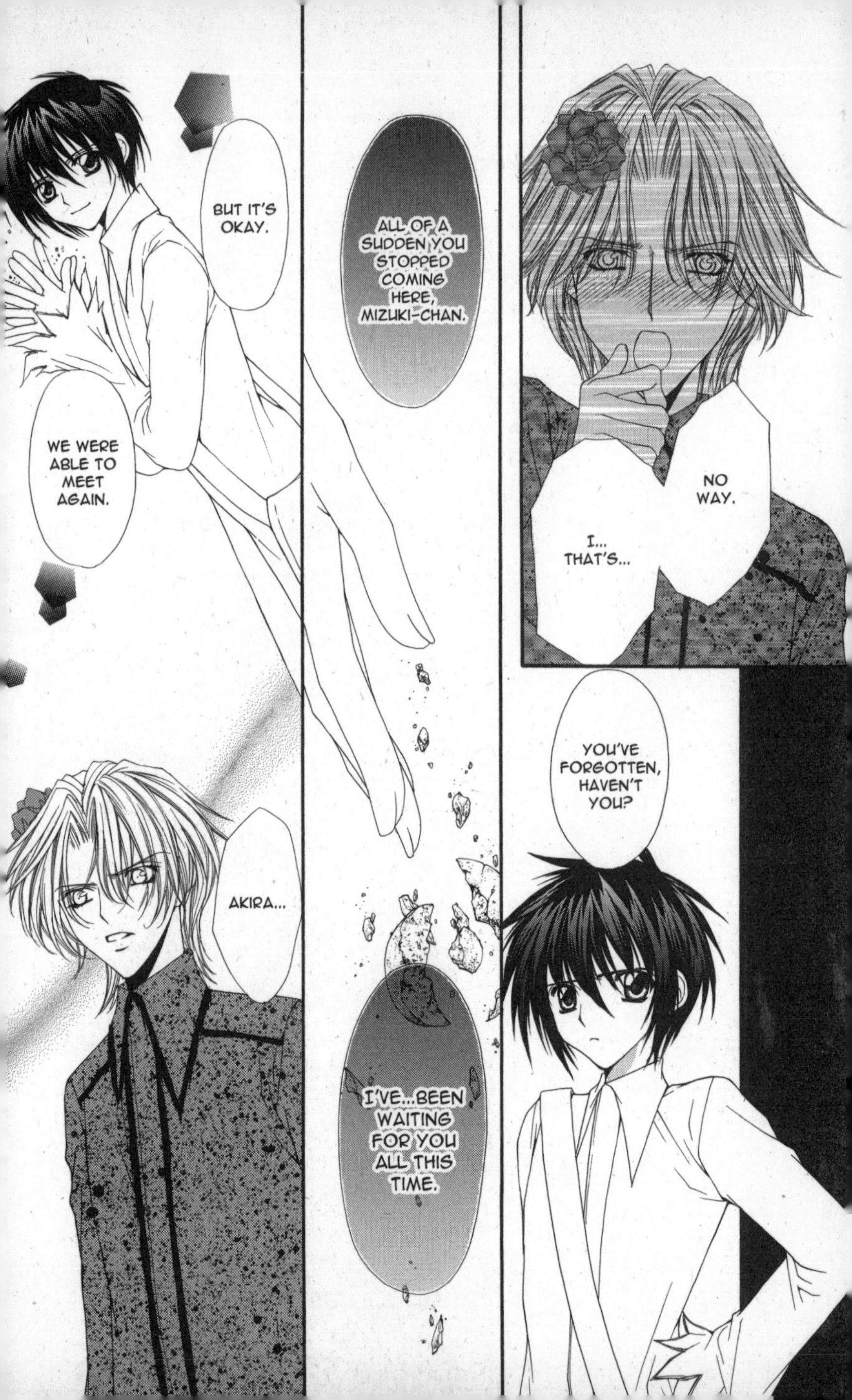
NO WAY.
I... THAT'S...
YOU'VE FORGOTTEN, HAVEN'T YOU?
ALL OF A SUDDEN YOU STOPPED COMING HERE, MIZUKI-CHAN.
I'VE...BEEN WAITING FOR YOU ALL THIS TIME.
BUT IT'S OKAY.
WE WERE ABLE TO MEET AGAIN.
AKIRA...

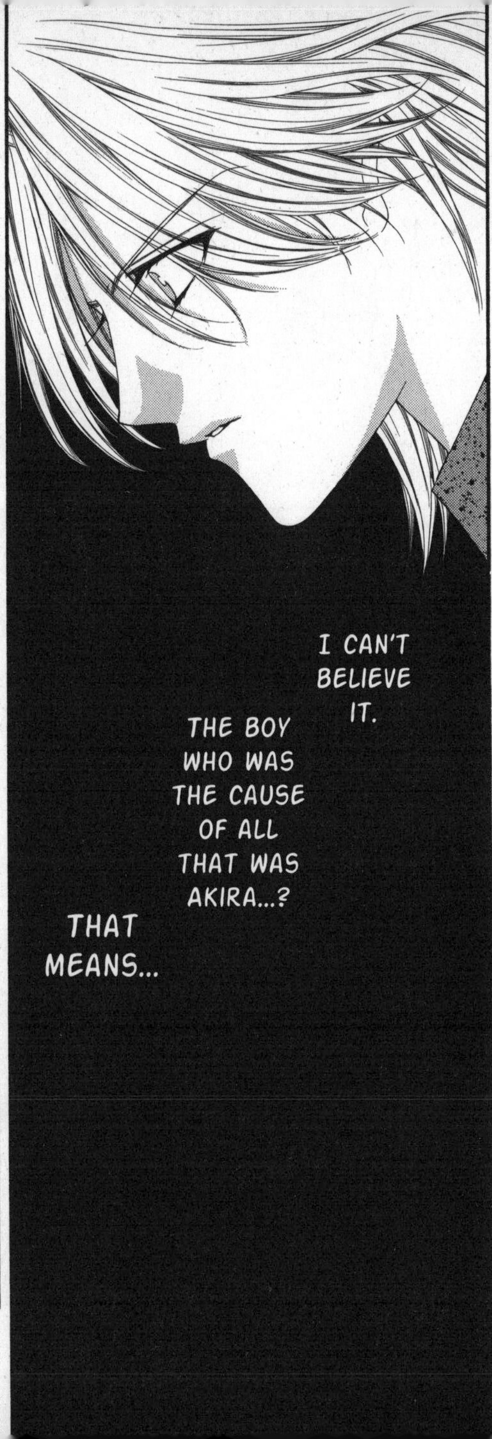
I CAN'T BELIEVE IT.
THE BOY WHO WAS THE CAUSE OF ALL THAT WAS AKIRA...?
THAT MEANS...

About Mizuki

She was a tough one!! An extremely difficult character to create. She's the prince of an all-girls school who doesn't know what love is. I wanted to draw an unbelievably cool girl. The kind of girl who'd look good no matter what she was doing, with great looks and a great physique! She has that *tsundere* (standoffish at first but softens once she gets to know you) characteristic.

I didn't go to a girls school, but we used to borrow a boy's school uniform and have a cool-looking girl wear it while she'd pose with her arm around our shoulders for photos.

Boyish girls are attractive, aren't they?

Mizuki is a character I wanted girls to find attractive.

Actually, there is a model for Mizuki. But if I said, "It's this person!!" I have a feeling that the fans would kill me, so I'm going to keep it a secret. The model is male, by the way.

As the creator, I want Mizuki to become cooler and much, much prettier than she is now. So much so that she'll rival Akira's popularity...

Mizuki is a very difficult character to draw, but she may be the most popular female character of all my series. I'm really happy about that!

Mizuki will continue to be the greatest tsundere girl around. I hope you'll support her to the end.

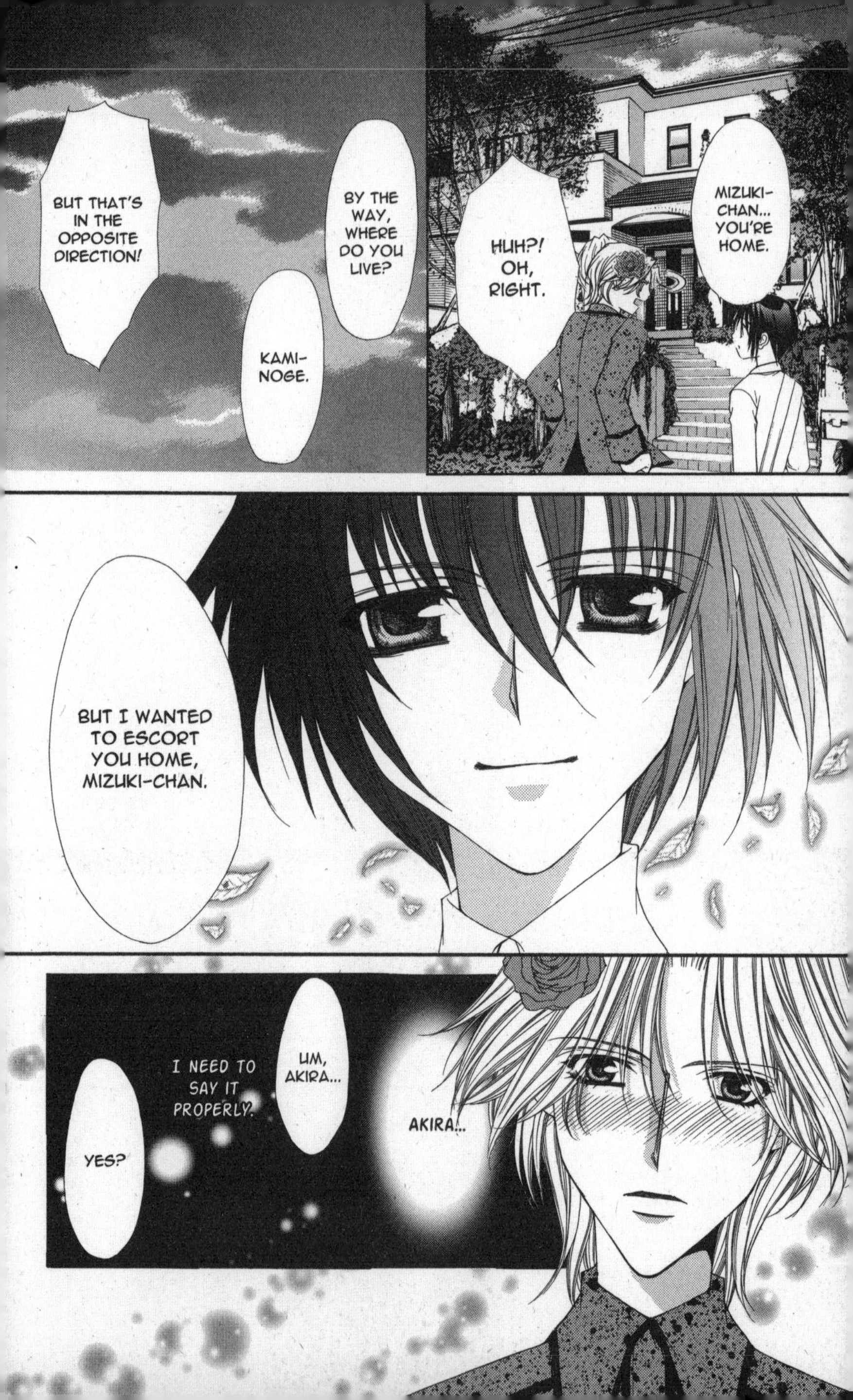
MIZUKI-CHAN... YOU'RE HOME.
HUH?! OH, RIGHT.
BY THE WAY, WHERE DO YOU LIVE?
KAMI-NOGE.
BUT THAT'S IN THE OPPOSITE DIRECTION!
BUT I WANTED TO ESCORT YOU HOME, MIZUKI-CHAN.
AKIRA...
UM, AKIRA...
I NEED TO SAY IT PROPERLY.
YES?

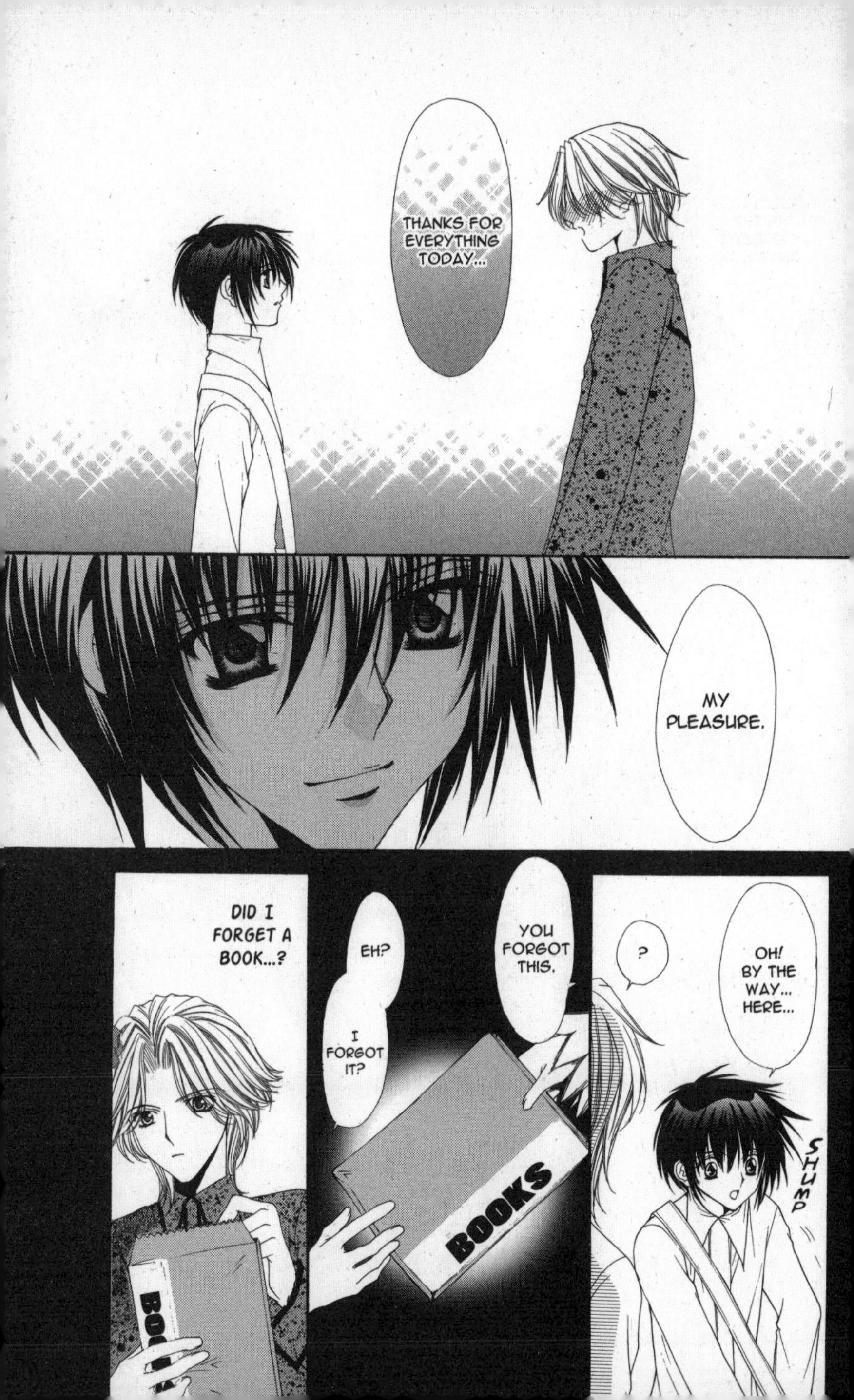
THANKS FOR EVERYTHING TODAY...
MY PLEASURE.
OH! BY THE WAY... HERE...
?
SHUMP
YOU FORGOT THIS.
EH?
I FORGOT IT?
BOOKS
DID I FORGET A BOOK...?

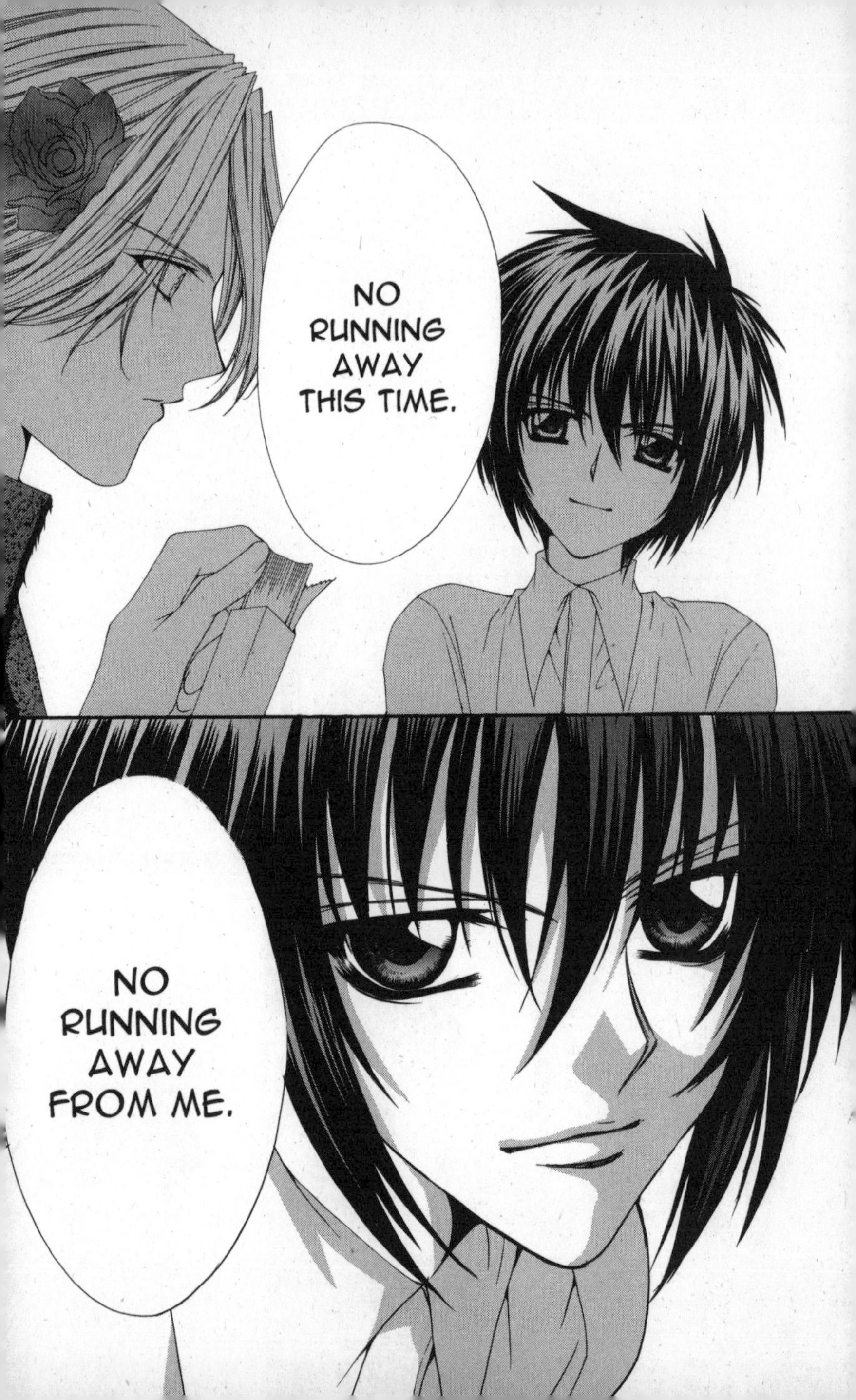
NO RUNNING AWAY THIS TIME.
NO RUNNING AWAY FROM ME.

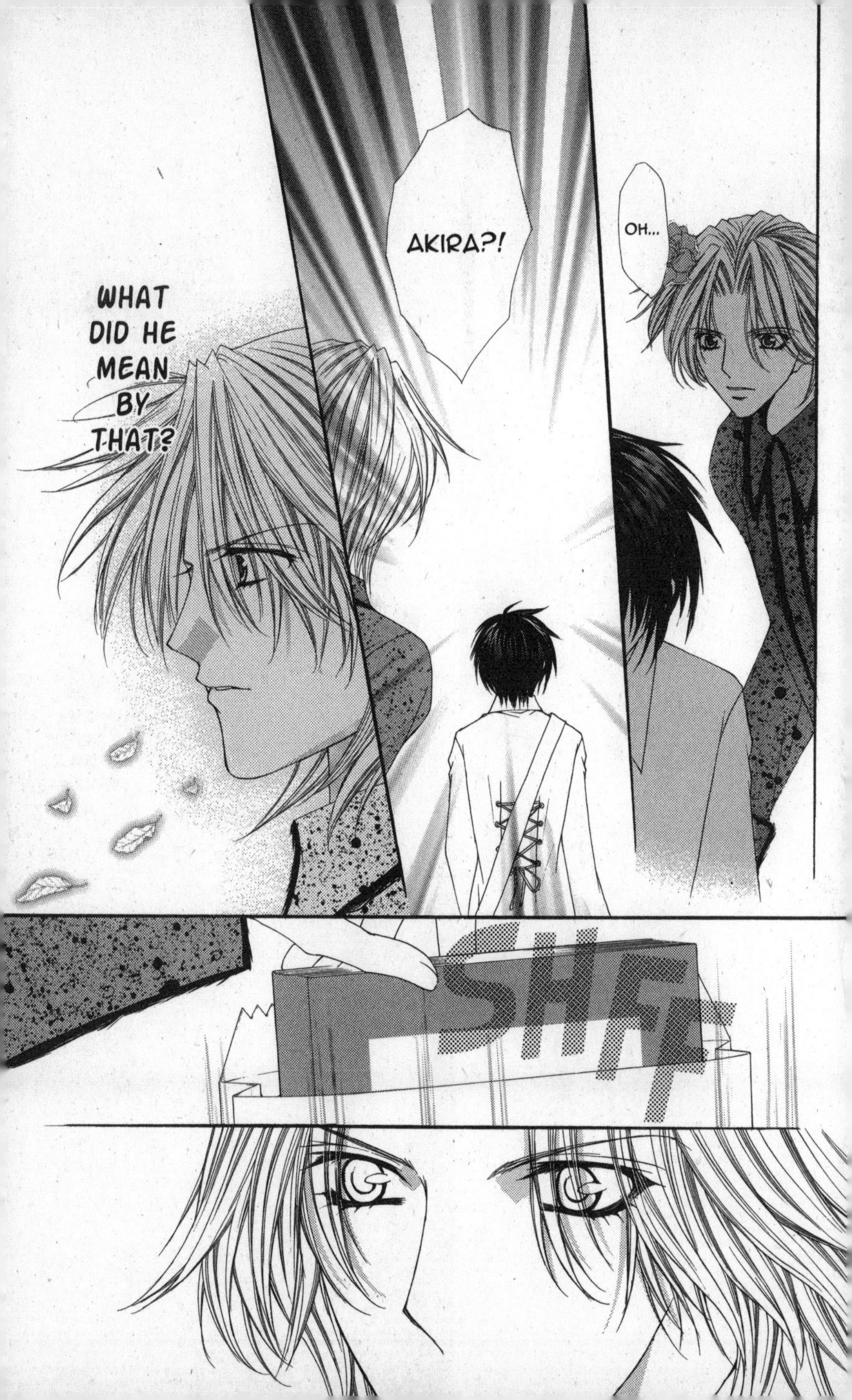
OH...
AKIRA?!
WHAT DID HE MEAN BY THAT?
SHF

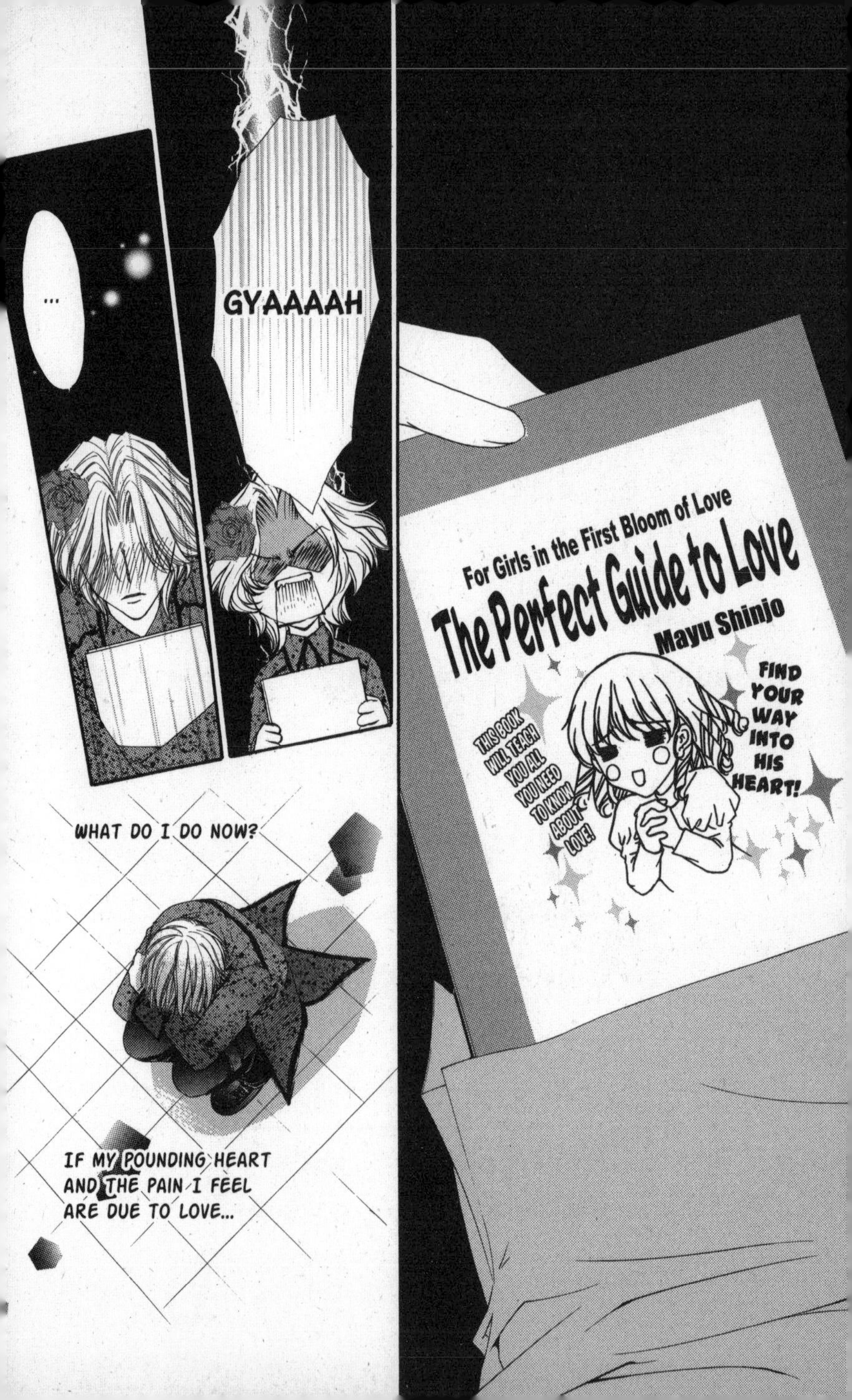
For Girls in the First Bloom of Love
The Perfect Guide to Love
Mayu Shinjo
FIND YOUR WAY INTO HIS HEART!
THIS BOOK WILL TEACH YOU ALL YOU NEED TO KNOW ABOUT LOVE!
GYAAAAH
...
WHAT DO I DO NOW?
IF MY POUNDING HEART AND THE PAIN I FEEL ARE DUE TO LOVE...

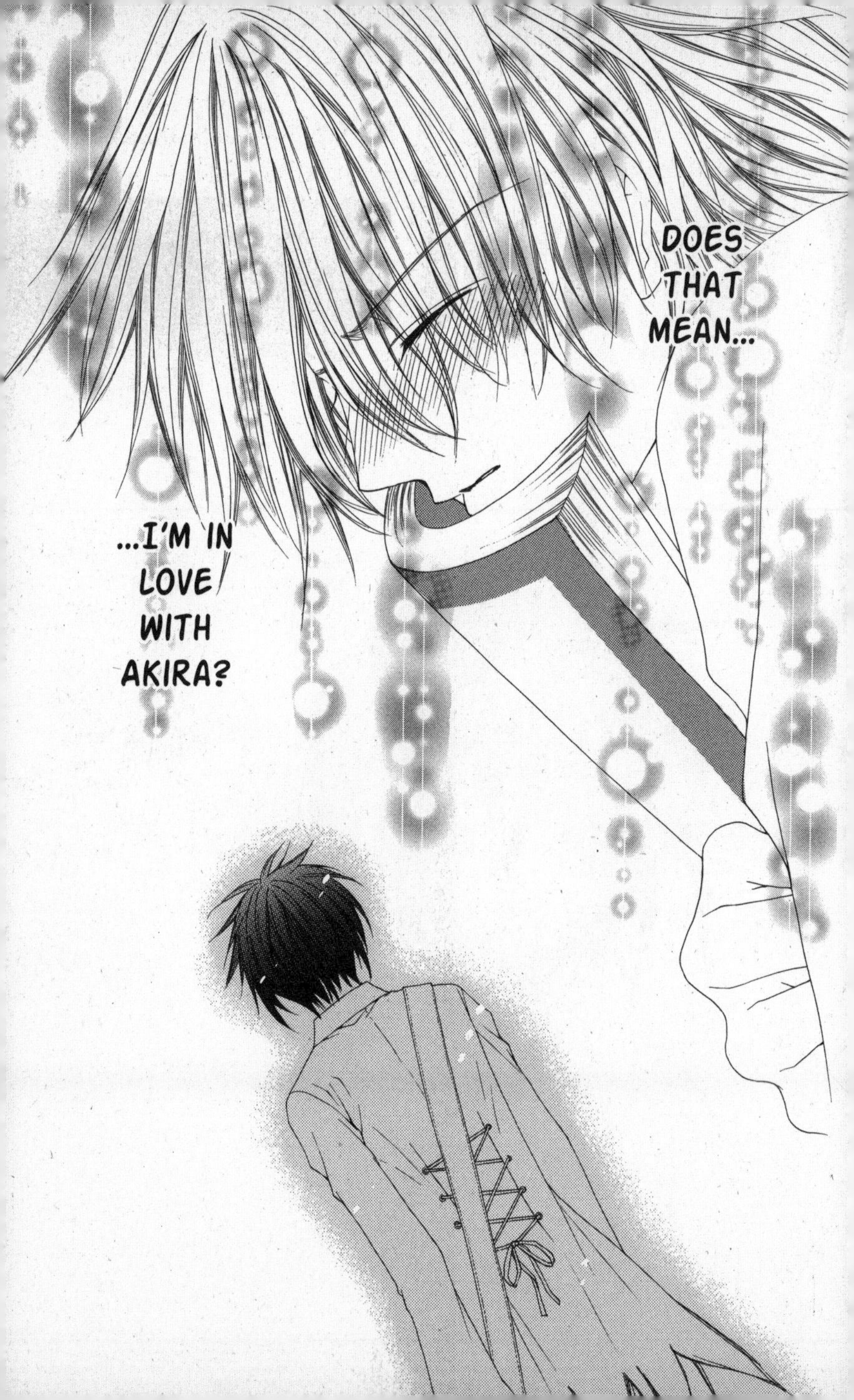
DOES THAT MEAN...
...I'M IN LOVE WITH AKIRA?

Akira Shiraishi

First-year at Dankaisan High School

Age: 16

Height: 5'3"

Weight: 95 lbs

Birthday: August 15, Leo

Blood Type: B

Address: Setagaya-ku, Tokyo

Family: Father, mother, three older brothers

Hobby: Martial Arts

Skills: Karate 3rd-Dan, Qigong/Chinese
martial arts

Good point: Kind to girls

Bad point: Selfish

Favorite food: Anything sweet, candies

Least favorite food: Milk

The type of girl he likes: A pretty girl

The brand of clothes he often wears: h. naoto

Favorite sport: Long-distance track

Favorite quote: "If it won't sing, kill the cuckoo."

Favorite subject: Music

Least favorite subject: Reading Comprehension

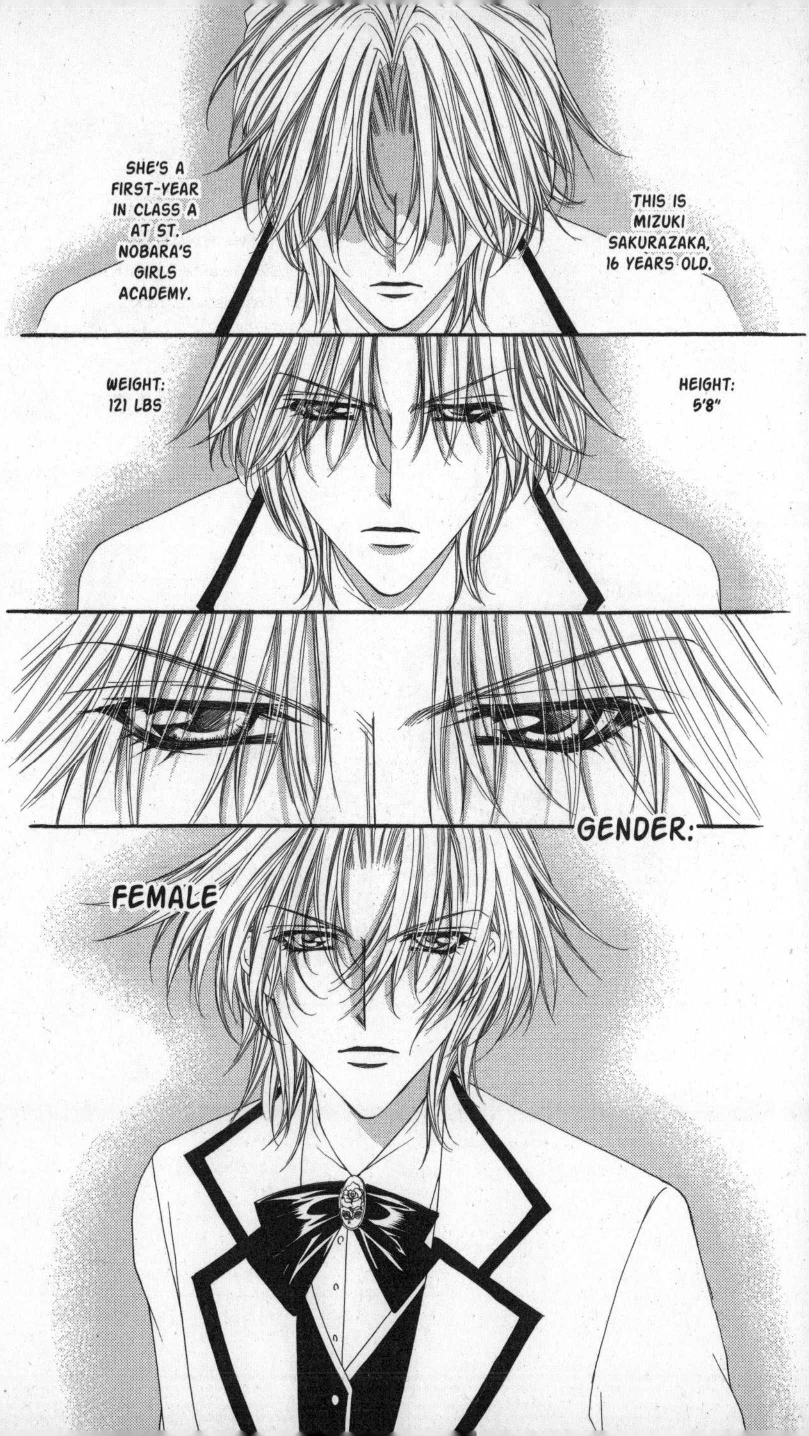
THIS IS MIZUKI SAKURAZAKA, 16 YEARS OLD.
SHE'S A FIRST-YEAR IN CLASS A AT ST. NOBARA'S GIRLS ACADEMY.
HEIGHT: 5'8"
WEIGHT: 121 LBS
GENDER:
FEMALE

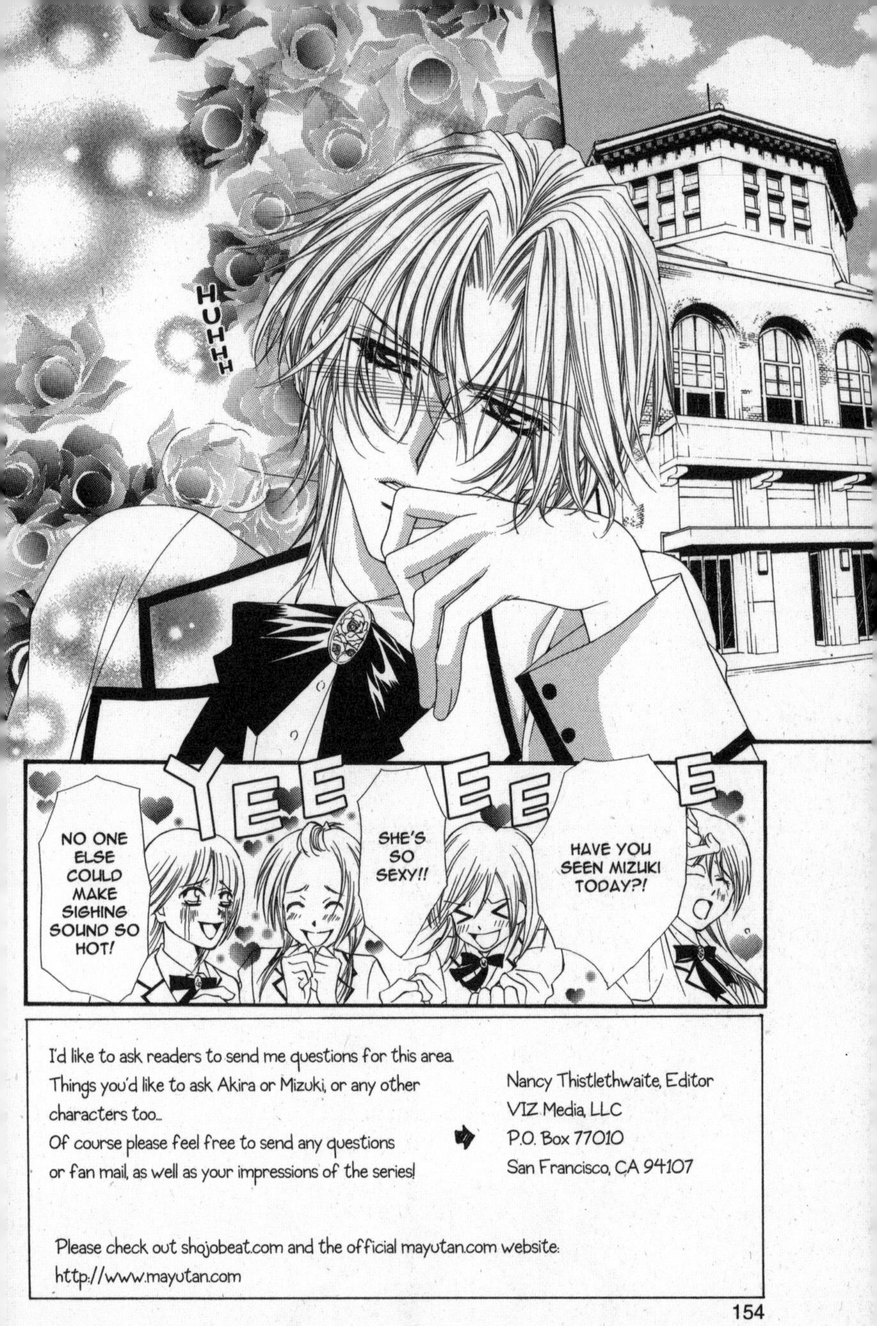
HUHHH
YEEEEE
HAVE YOU SEEN MIZUKI TODAY?!
SHE'S SO SEXY!!
NO ONE ELSE COULD MAKE SIGHING SOUND SO HOT!

I'd like to ask readers to send me questions for this area.
Things you'd like to ask Akira or Mizuki, or any other characters too...
Of course please feel free to send any questions or fan mail, as well as your impressions of the series!

Nancy Thistlethwaite, Editor
VIZ Media, LLC
P.O. Box 77010
San Francisco, CA 94107

Please check out shojobeat.com and the official mayutan.com website:
http://www.mayutan.com

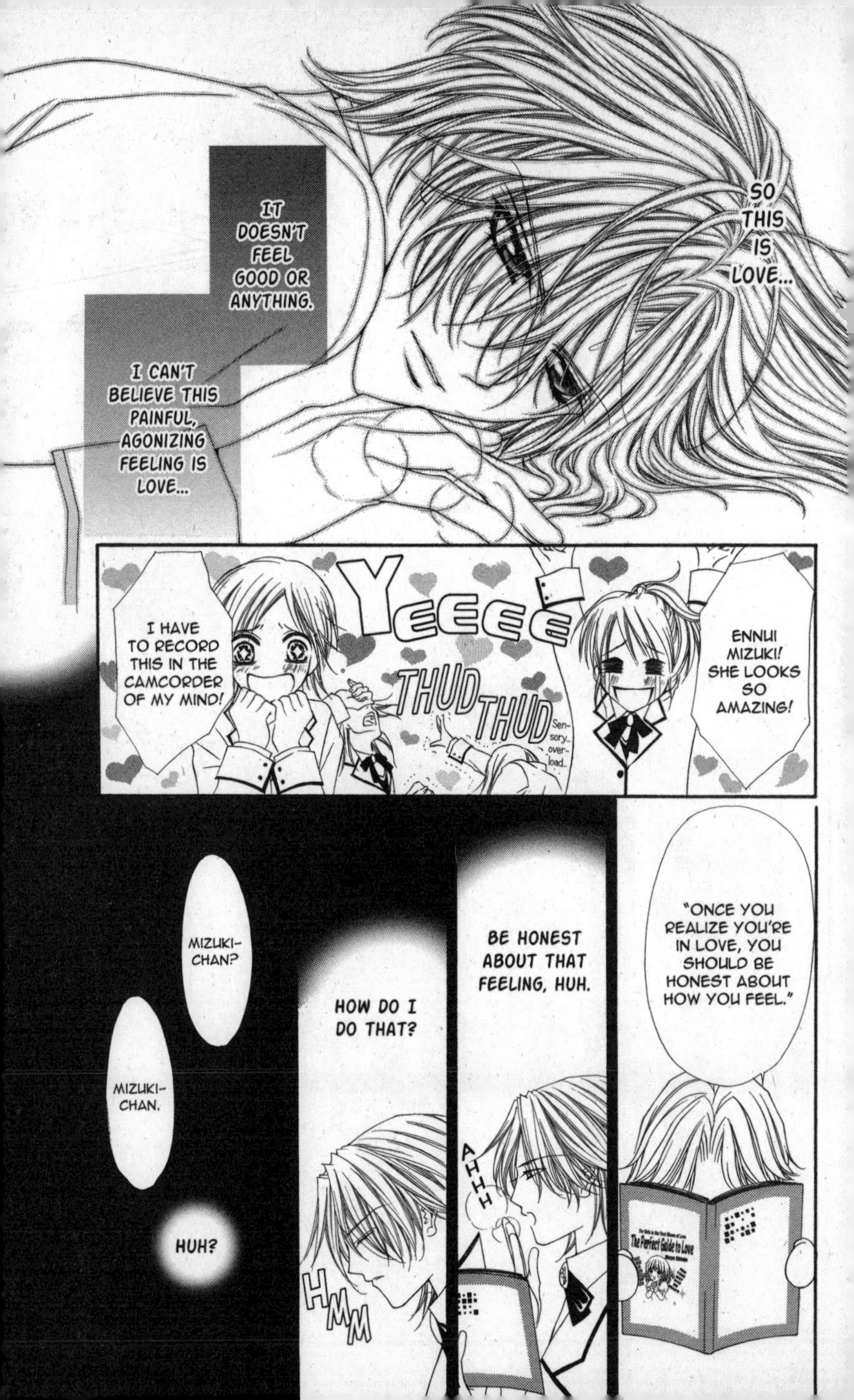
SO THIS IS LOVE...
IT DOESN'T FEEL GOOD OR ANYTHING.
I CAN'T BELIEVE THIS PAINFUL, AGONIZING FEELING IS LOVE...
ENNUI MIZUKI! SHE LOOKS SO AMAZING!
YEEEE
I HAVE TO RECORD THIS IN THE CAMCORDER OF MY MIND!
THUD THUD
Sensory... over-load...
"ONCE YOU REALIZE YOU'RE IN LOVE, YOU SHOULD BE HONEST ABOUT HOW YOU FEEL."
The Perfect Guide to Love
BE HONEST ABOUT THAT FEELING, HUH.
AHHH
HOW DO I DO THAT?
MIZUKI-CHAN?
MIZUKI-CHAN.
HUH?
HMM

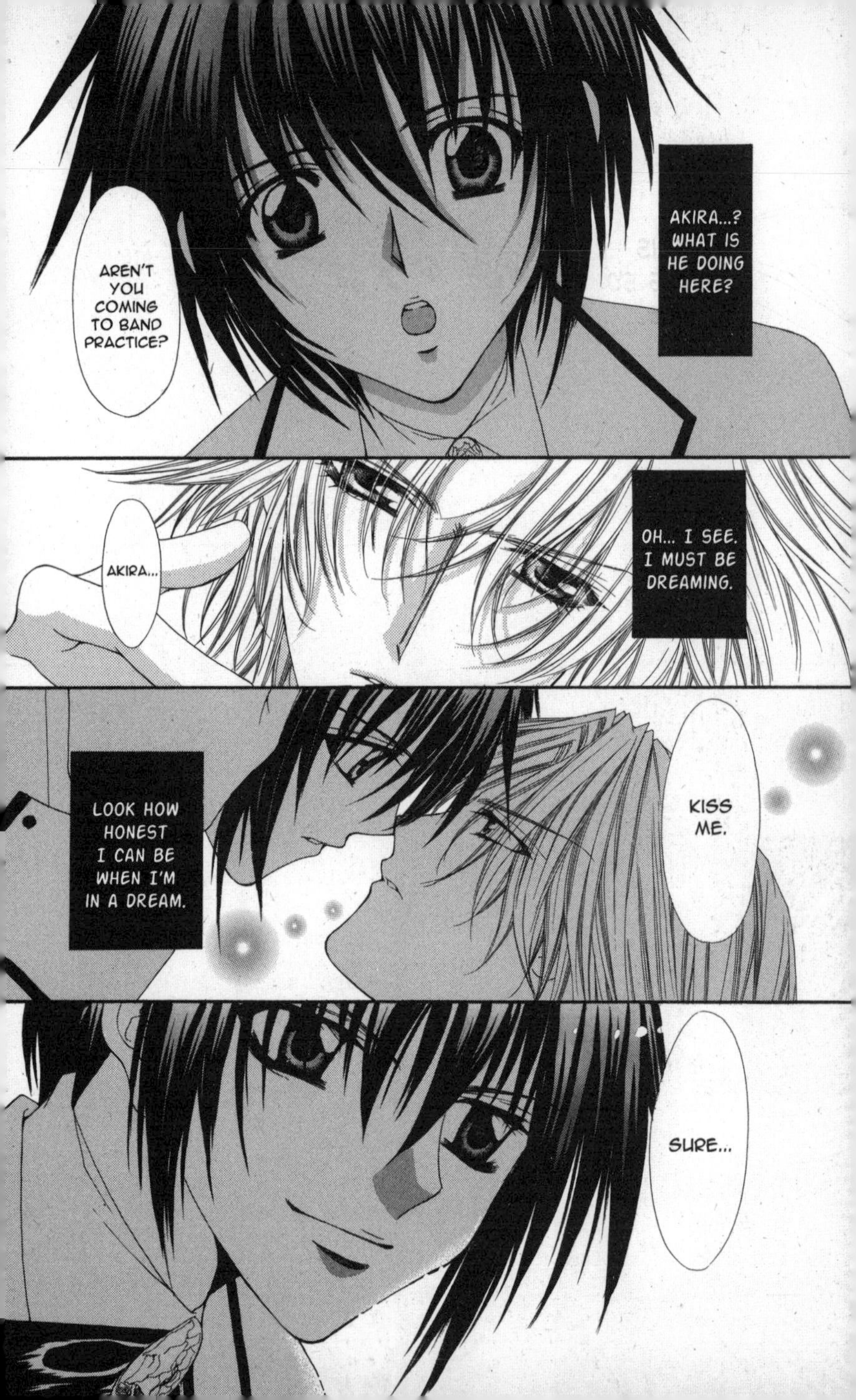
AKIRA...? WHAT IS HE DOING HERE?
AREN'T YOU COMING TO BAND PRACTICE?
OH... I SEE. I MUST BE DREAMING.
AKIRA...
KISS ME.
LOOK HOW HONEST I CAN BE WHEN I'M IN A DREAM.
SURE...

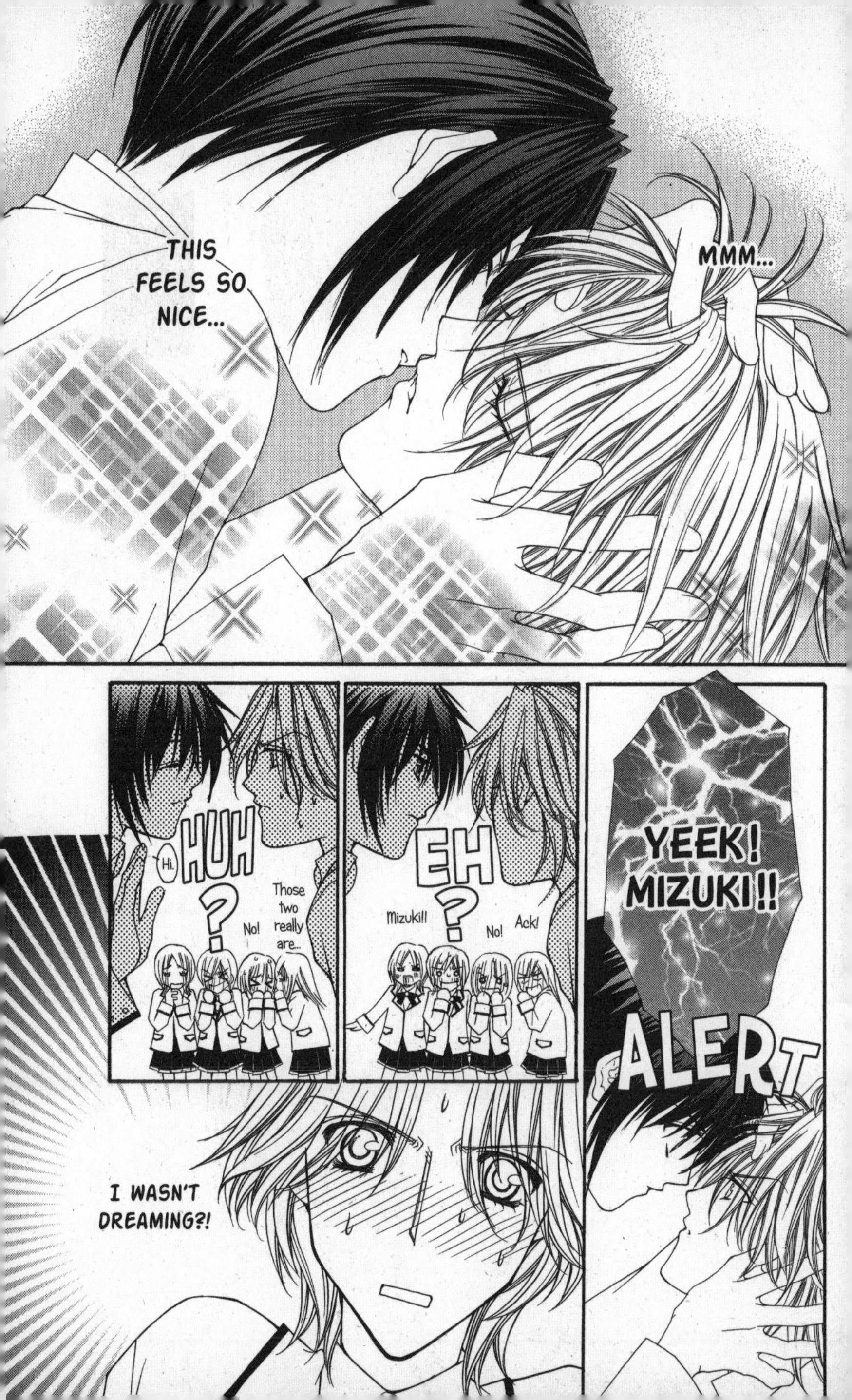
MMM...
THIS FEELS SO NICE...
YEEK! MIZUKI!!
ALERT
EH?
Ack!
No!
Mizuki!!
HUH?
Those two really are...
No!
Hi.
I WASN'T DREAMING?!

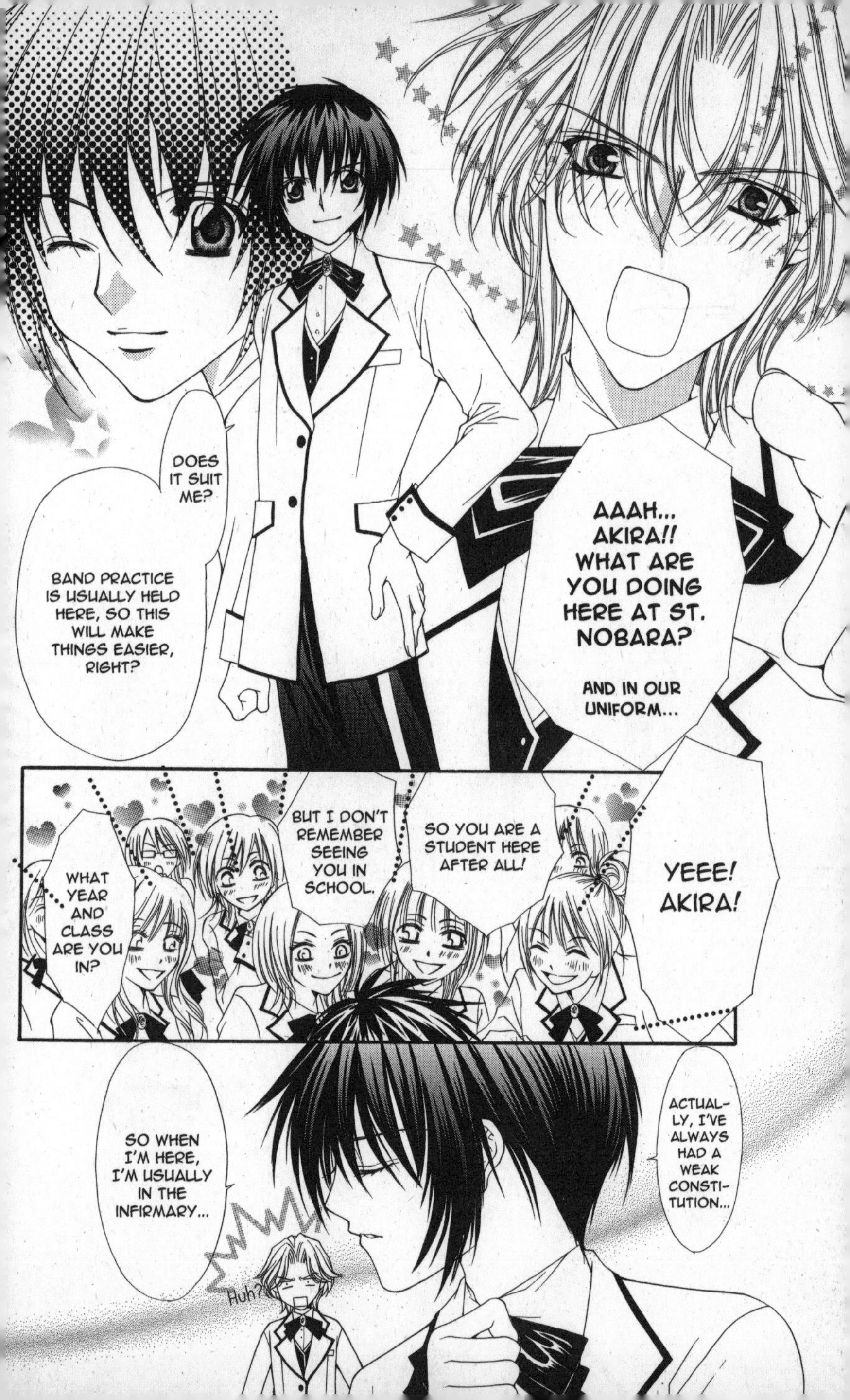

AAAH... AKIRA!! WHAT ARE YOU DOING HERE AT ST. NOBARA?
AND IN OUR UNIFORM...
DOES IT SUIT ME?
BAND PRACTICE IS USUALLY HELD HERE, SO THIS WILL MAKE THINGS EASIER, RIGHT?
YEEE! AKIRA!
SO YOU ARE A STUDENT HERE AFTER ALL!
BUT I DON'T REMEMBER SEEING YOU IN SCHOOL.
WHAT YEAR AND CLASS ARE YOU IN?
ACTUAL-LY, I'VE ALWAYS HAD A WEAK CONSTI-TUTION...
SO WHEN I'M HERE, I'M USUALLY IN THE INFIRMARY...
Huh?

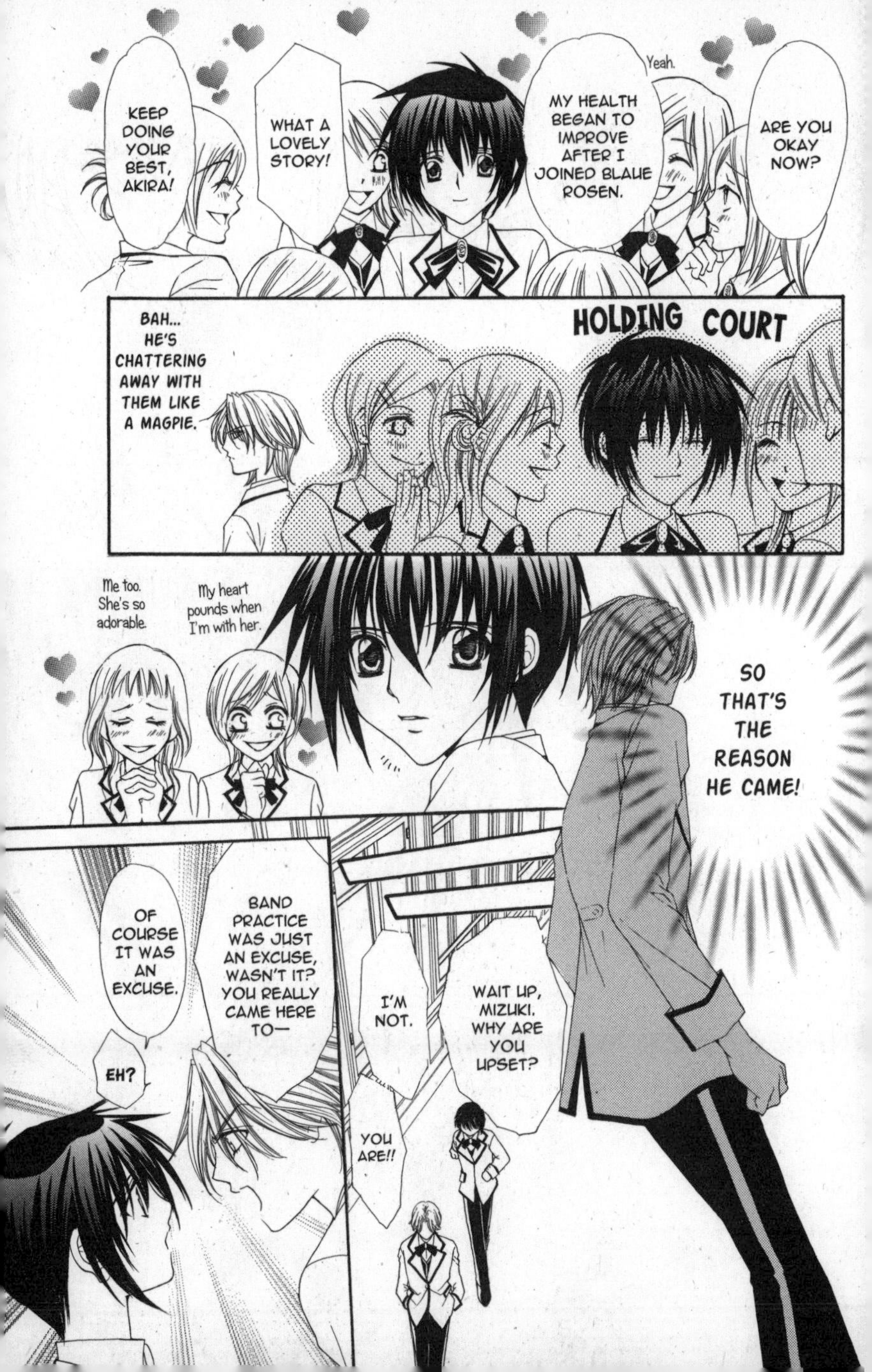
ARE YOU OKAY NOW?
Yeah.
MY HEALTH BEGAN TO IMPROVE AFTER I JOINED BLAUE ROSEN.
WHAT A LOVELY STORY!
KEEP DOING YOUR BEST, AKIRA!
HOLDING COURT
BAH... HE'S CHATTERING AWAY WITH THEM LIKE A MAGPIE.
SO THAT'S THE REASON HE CAME!
My heart pounds when I'm with her.
Me too. She's so adorable.
WAIT UP, MIZUKI. WHY ARE YOU UPSET?
I'M NOT.
YOU ARE!!
BAND PRACTICE WAS JUST AN EXCUSE, WASN'T IT? YOU REALLY CAME HERE TO—
EH?
OF COURSE IT WAS AN EXCUSE.

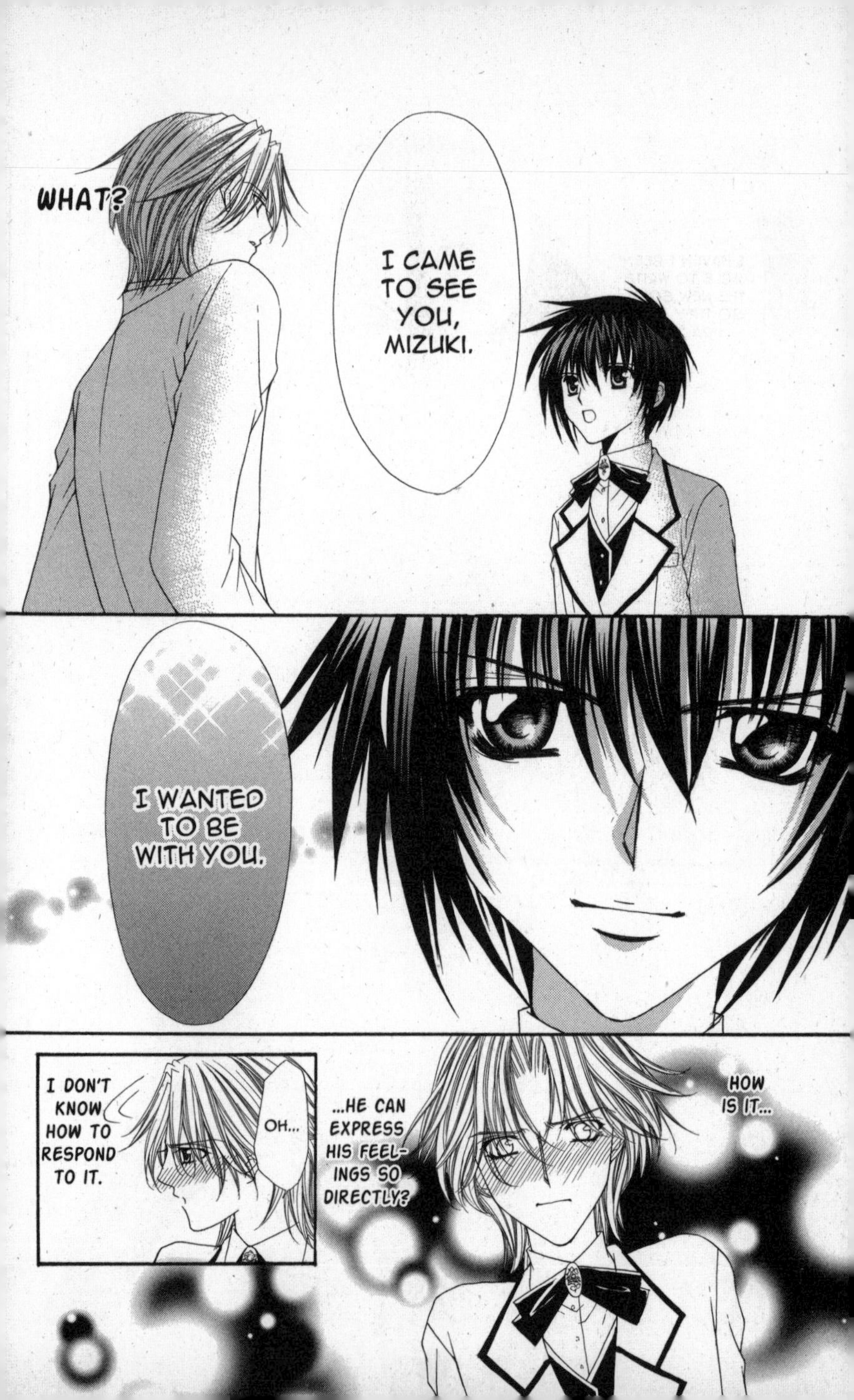
I CAME TO SEE YOU, MIZUKI.
WHAT?
I WANTED TO BE WITH YOU.
HOW IS IT...
...HE CAN EXPRESS HIS FEEL-INGS SO DIRECTLY?
OH...
I DON'T KNOW HOW TO RESPOND TO IT.

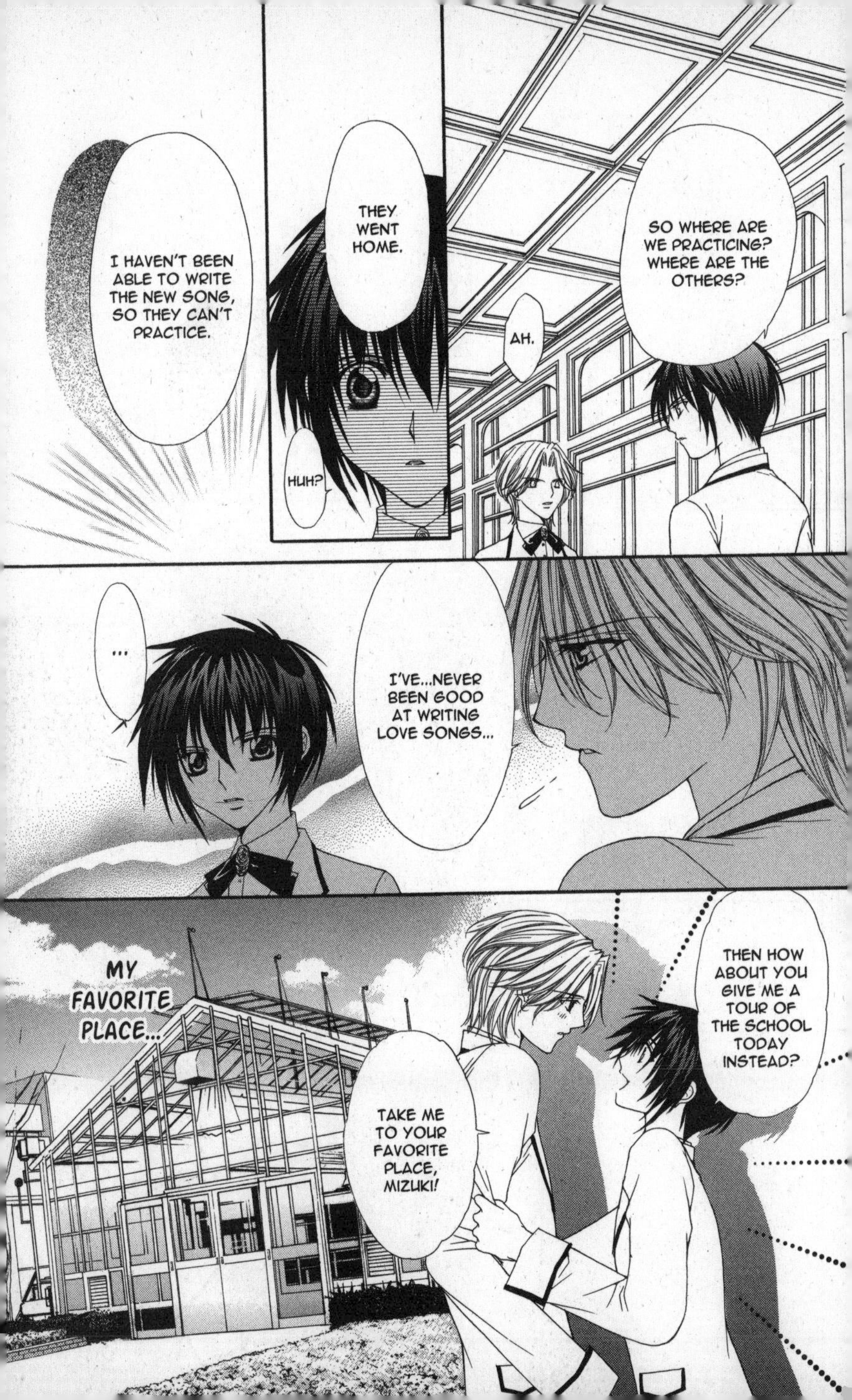
SO WHERE ARE WE PRACTICING? WHERE ARE THE OTHERS?
AH.
THEY WENT HOME.
HUH?
I HAVEN'T BEEN ABLE TO WRITE THE NEW SONG, SO THEY CAN'T PRACTICE.
I'VE...NEVER BEEN GOOD AT WRITING LOVE SONGS...
...
THEN HOW ABOUT YOU GIVE ME A TOUR OF THE SCHOOL TODAY INSTEAD?
TAKE ME TO YOUR FAVORITE PLACE, MIZUKI!
MY FAVORITE PLACE...

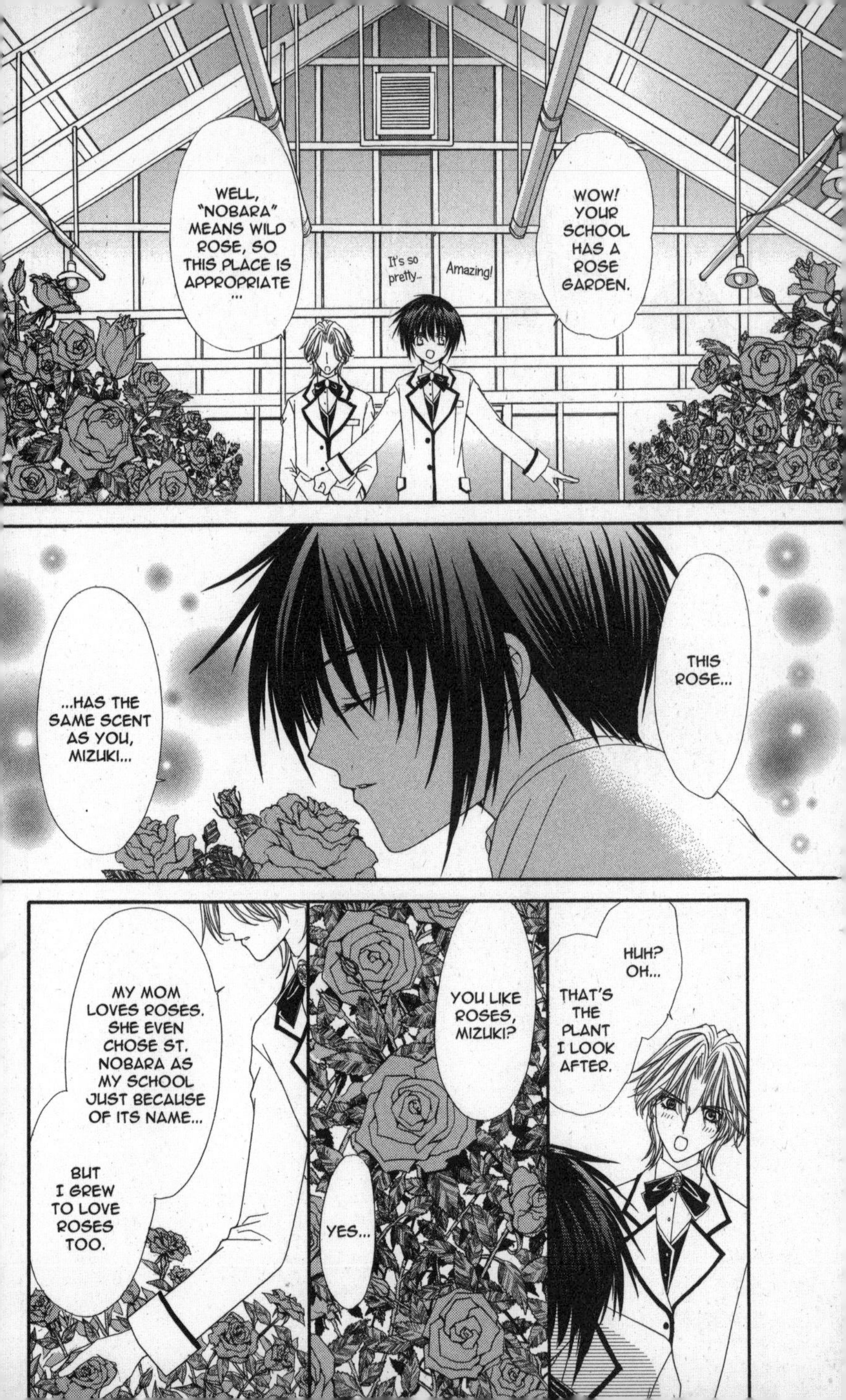
WOW! YOUR SCHOOL HAS A ROSE GARDEN.
Amazing!
It's so pretty...
WELL, "NOBARA" MEANS WILD ROSE, SO THIS PLACE IS APPROPRIATE...
THIS ROSE...
...HAS THE SAME SCENT AS YOU, MIZUKI...
HUH? OH...
THAT'S THE PLANT I LOOK AFTER.
YOU LIKE ROSES, MIZUKI?
YES...
MY MOM LOVES ROSES. SHE EVEN CHOSE ST. NOBARA AS MY SCHOOL JUST BECAUSE OF ITS NAME...
BUT I GREW TO LOVE ROSES TOO.

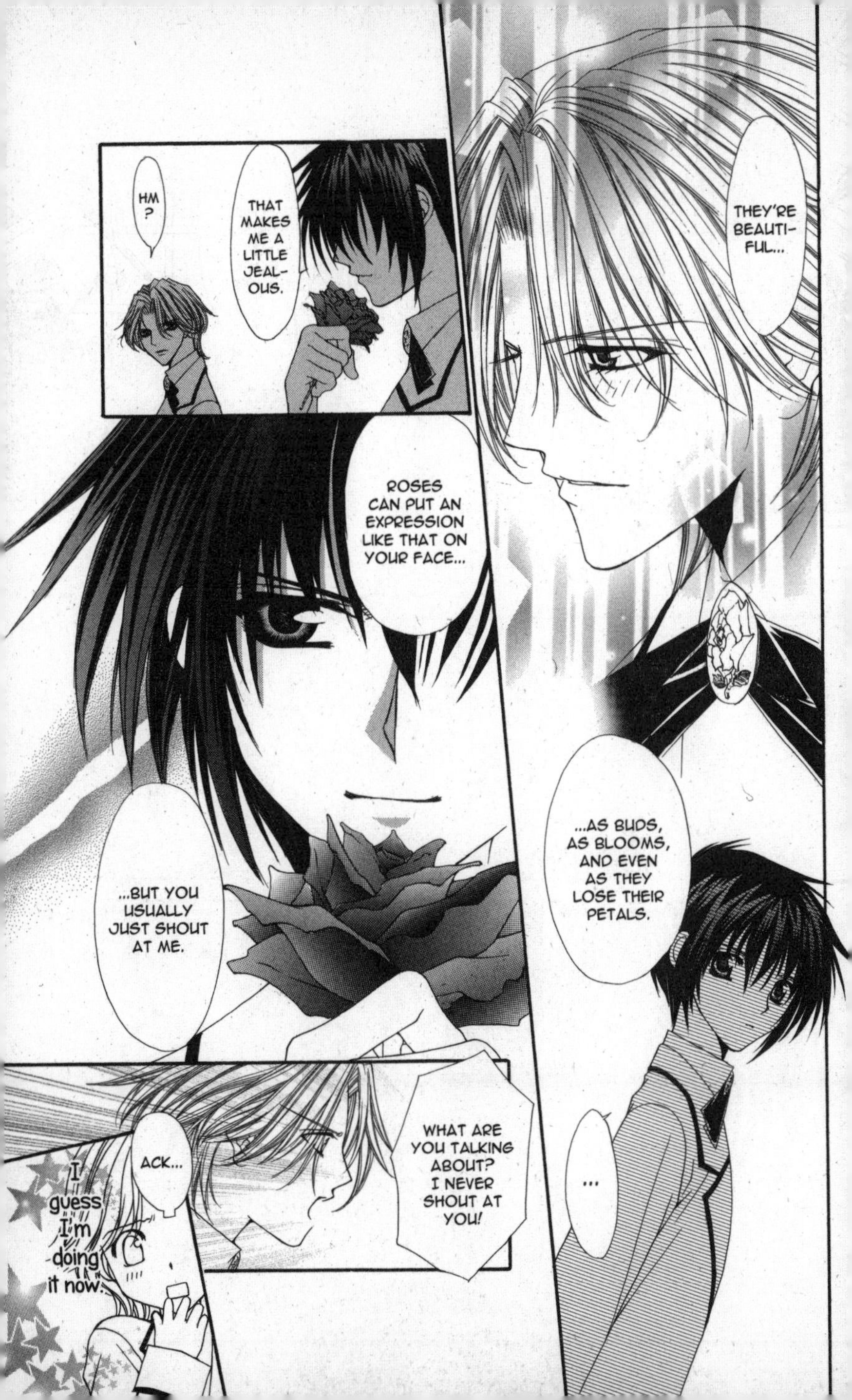
THEY'RE BEAUTIFUL...
...AS BUDS, AS BLOOMS, AND EVEN AS THEY LOSE THEIR PETALS.
...
THAT MAKES ME A LITTLE JEALOUS.
HM?
ROSES CAN PUT AN EXPRESSION LIKE THAT ON YOUR FACE...
...BUT YOU USUALLY JUST SHOUT AT ME.
WHAT ARE YOU TALKING ABOUT? I NEVER SHOUT AT YOU!
ACK...
I guess I'm doing it now.

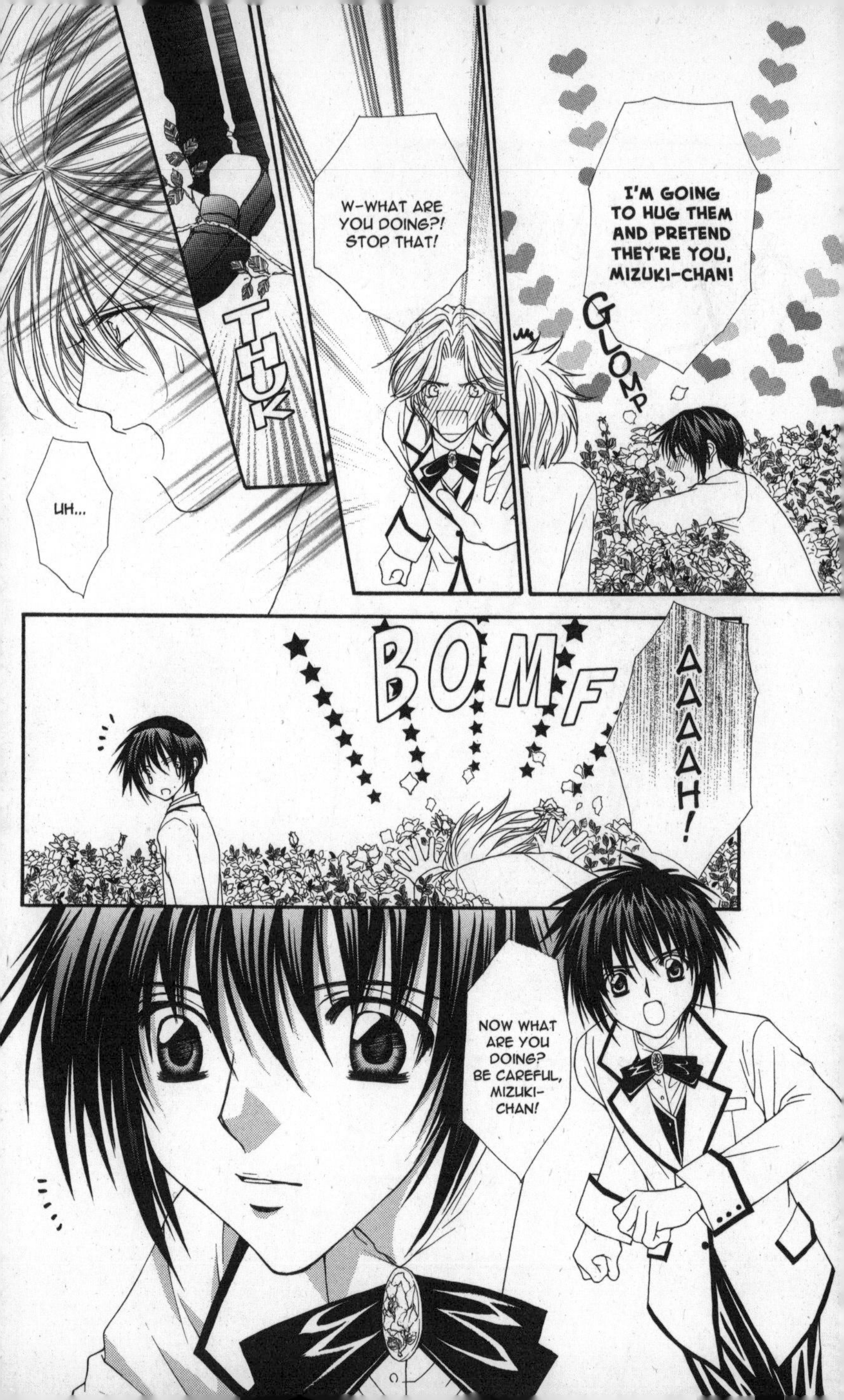
I'M GOING TO HUG THEM AND PRETEND THEY'RE YOU, MIZUKI-CHAN!
GLOMP
W-WHAT ARE YOU DOING?! STOP THAT!
THUK
UH...
AAAAAH!
BOMF
NOW WHAT ARE YOU DOING? BE CAREFUL, MIZUKI-CHAN!

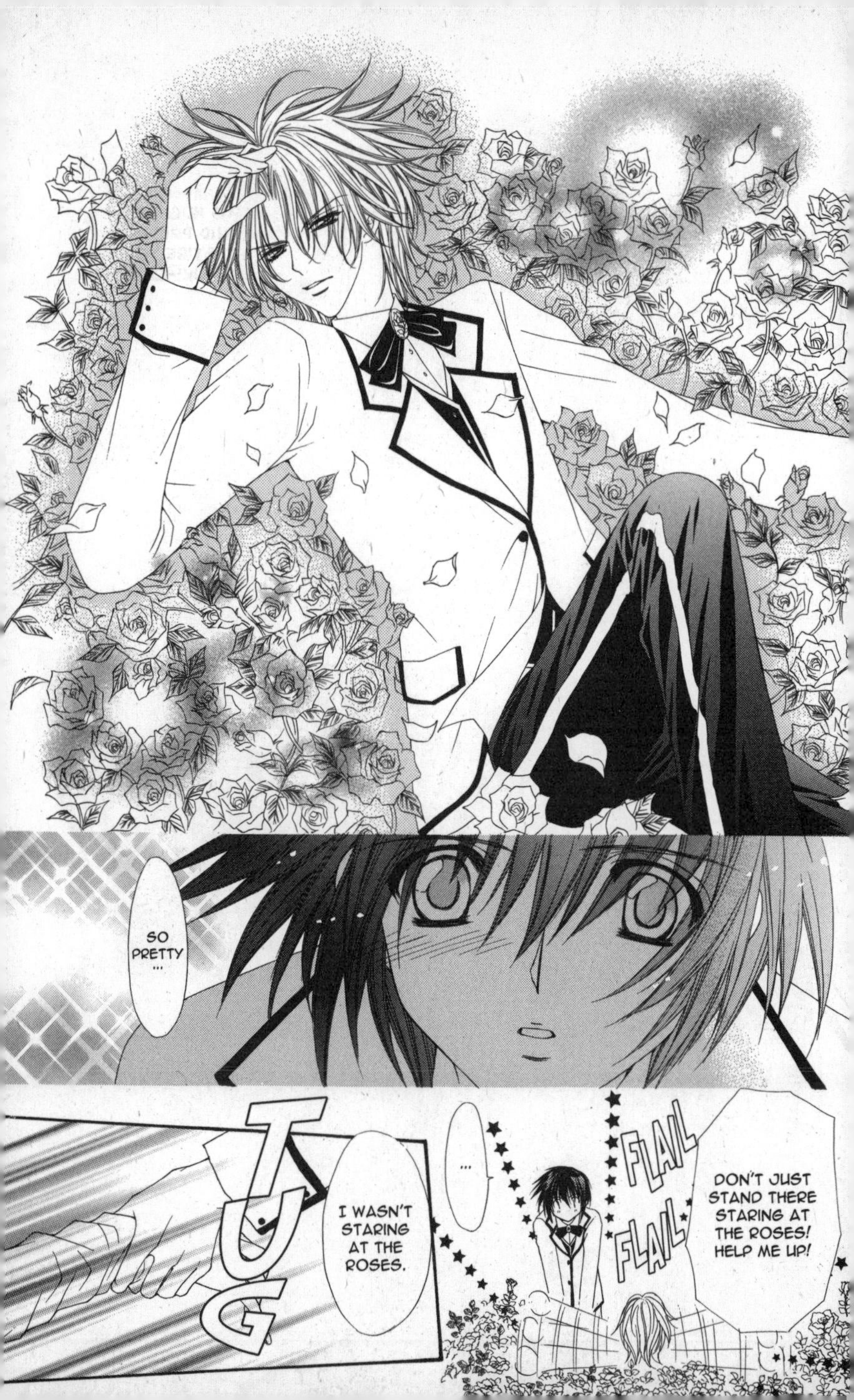
SO PRETTY ...
DON'T JUST STAND THERE STARING AT THE ROSES! HELP ME UP!
FLAIL
FLAIL
...
I WASN'T STARING AT THE ROSES.
TUG

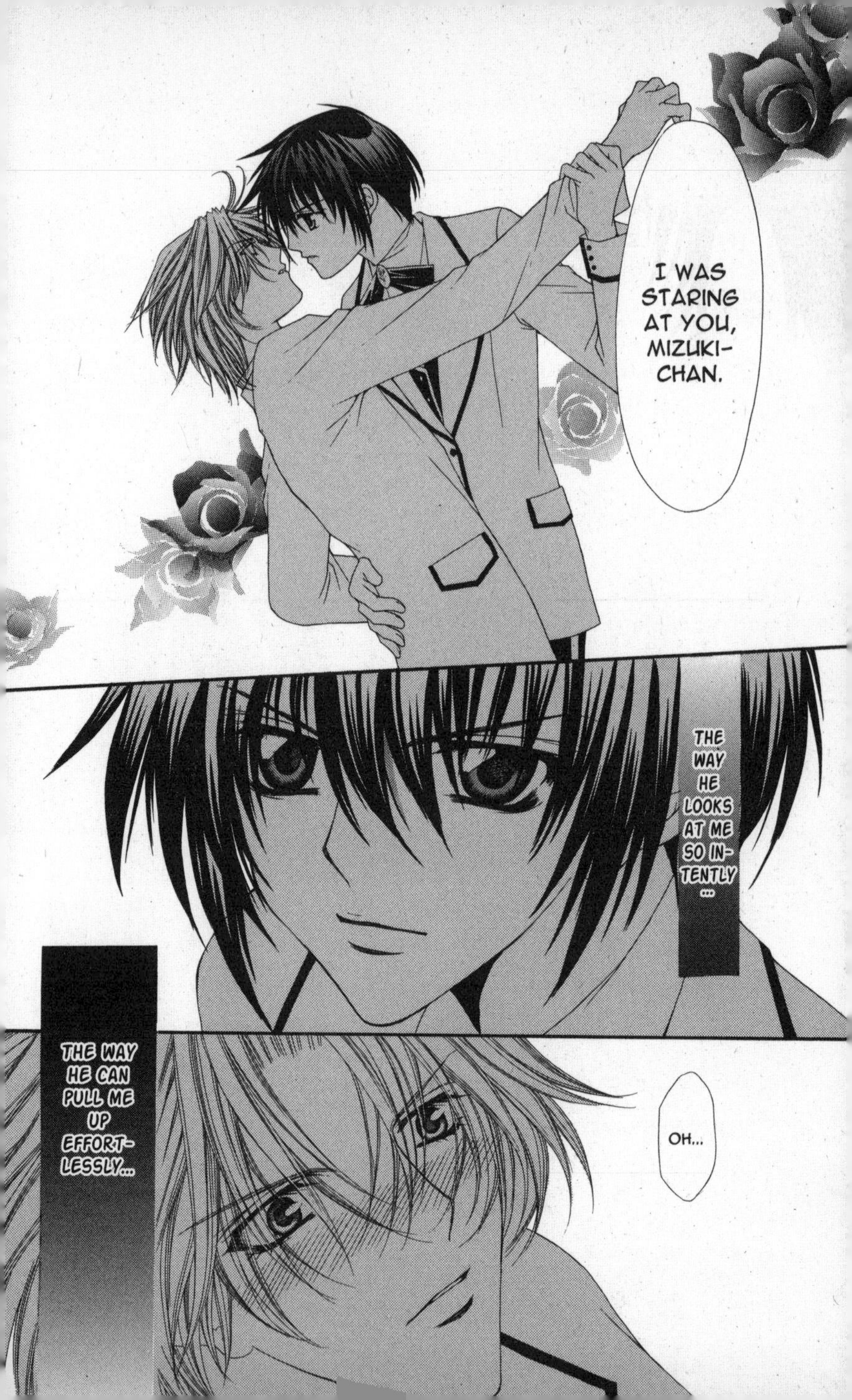
I WAS STARING AT YOU, MIZUKI-CHAN.
THE WAY HE LOOKS AT ME SO IN-TENTLY...
OH...
THE WAY HE CAN PULL ME UP EFFORT-LESSLY...

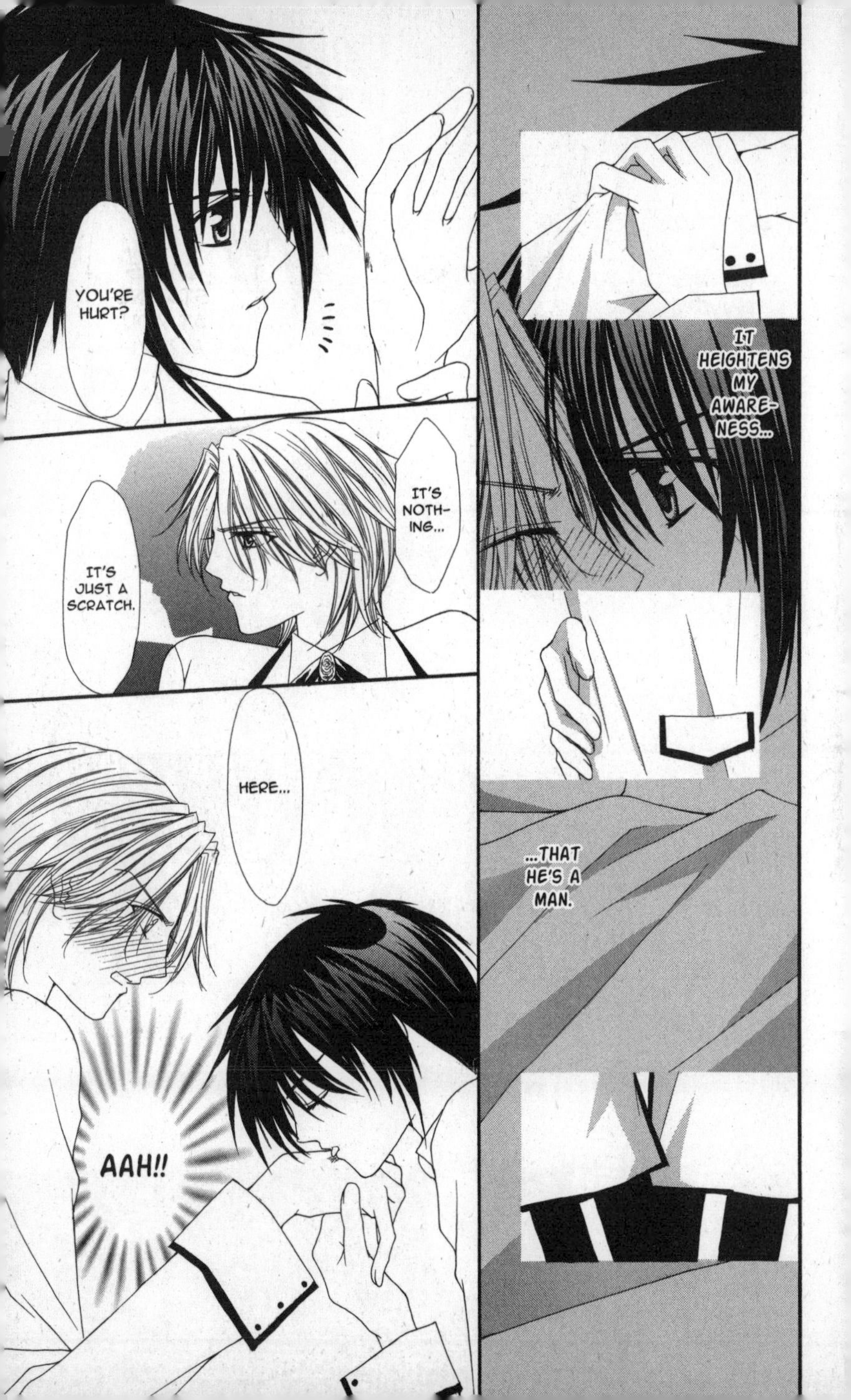

IT HEIGHTENS MY AWARE- NESS...
...THAT HE'S A MAN.
YOU'RE HURT?
IT'S NOTH- ING...
IT'S JUST A SCRATCH.
HERE...
AAH!!

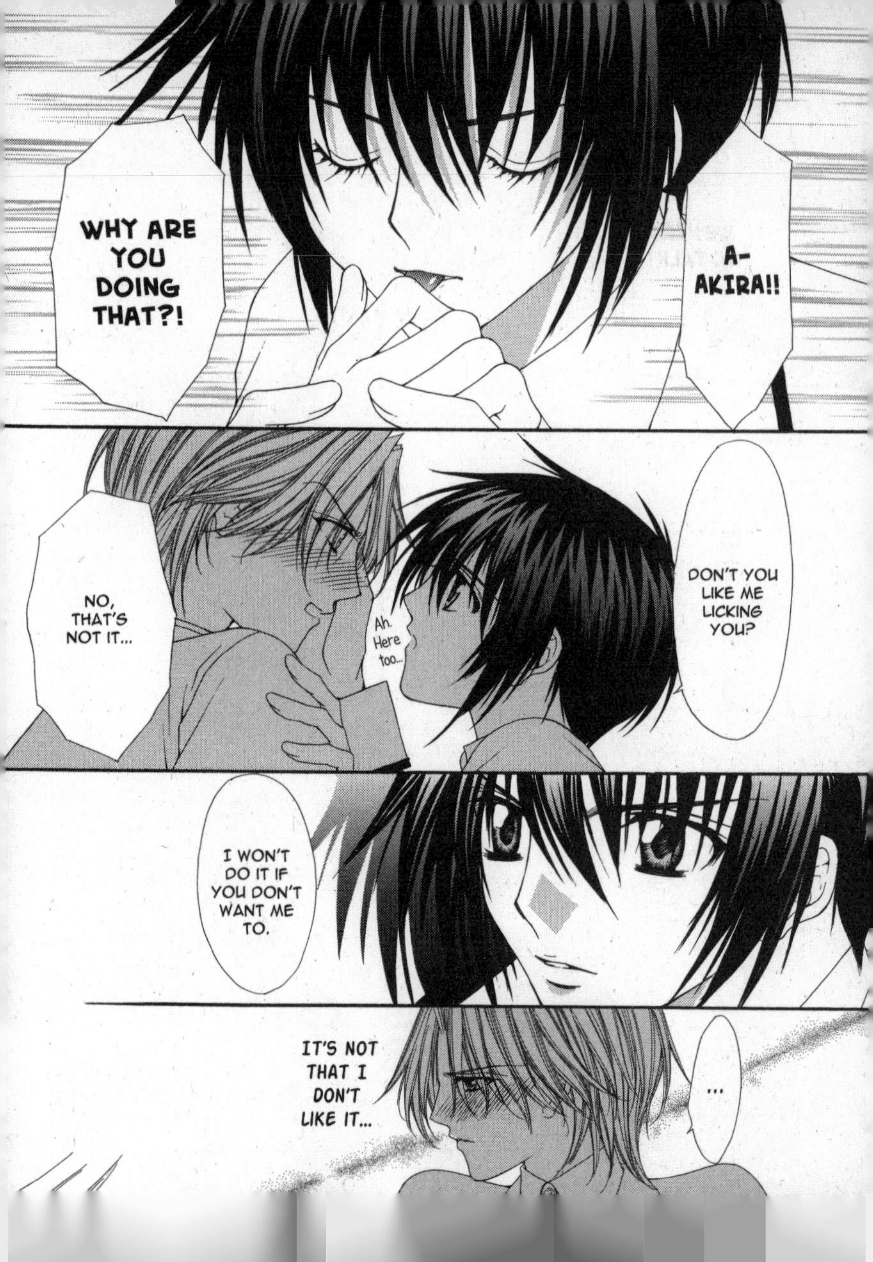
A- AKIRA!!
WHY ARE YOU DOING THAT?!
DON'T YOU LIKE ME LICKING YOU?
Ah. Here too...
NO, THAT'S NOT IT...
I WON'T DO IT IF YOU DON'T WANT ME TO.
...
IT'S NOT THAT I DON'T LIKE IT...

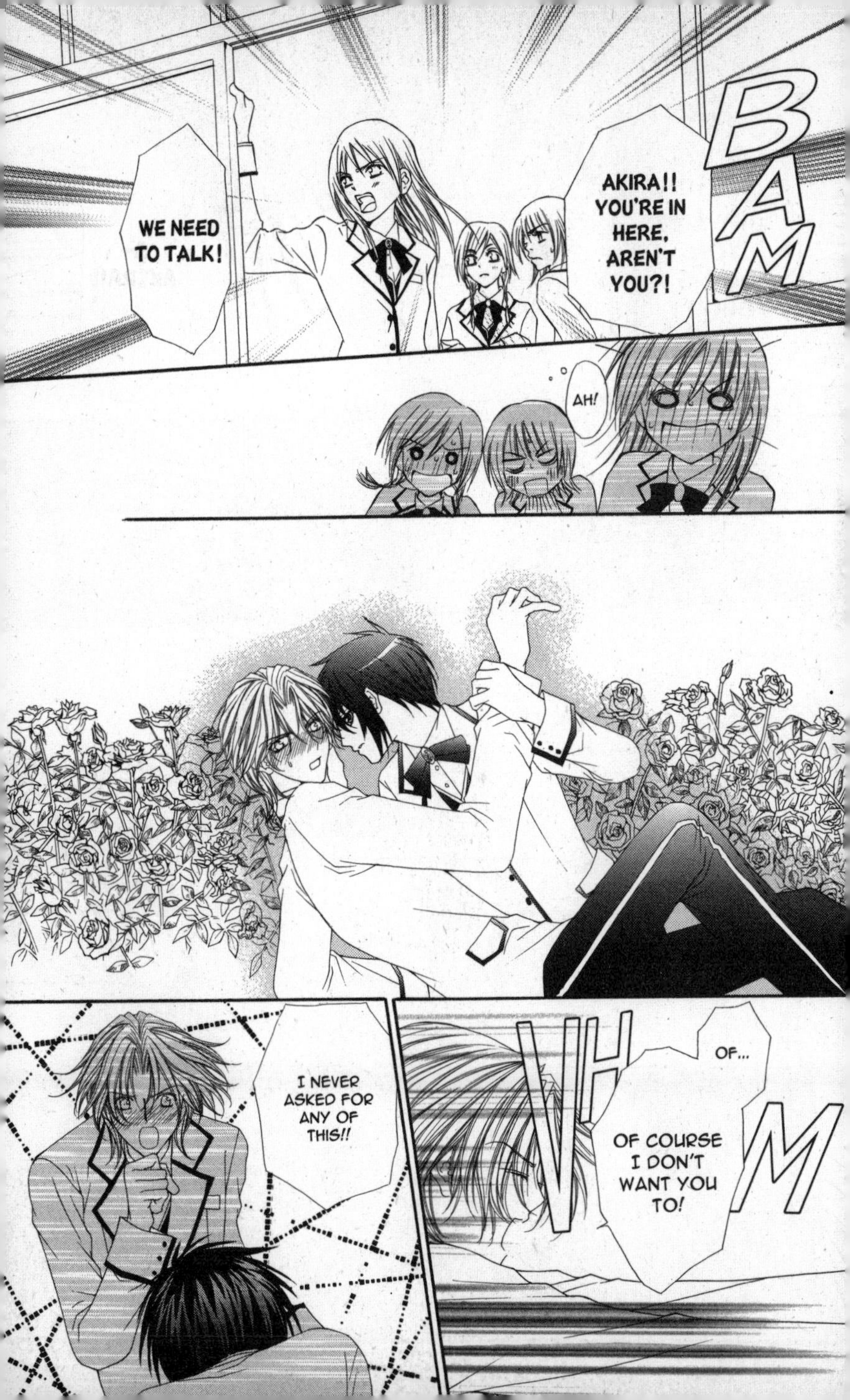
BAM
AKIRA!! YOU'RE IN HERE, AREN'T YOU?!
WE NEED TO TALK!
AH!
OF...
OF COURSE I DON'T WANT YOU TO!
WHM
I NEVER ASKED FOR ANY OF THIS!!

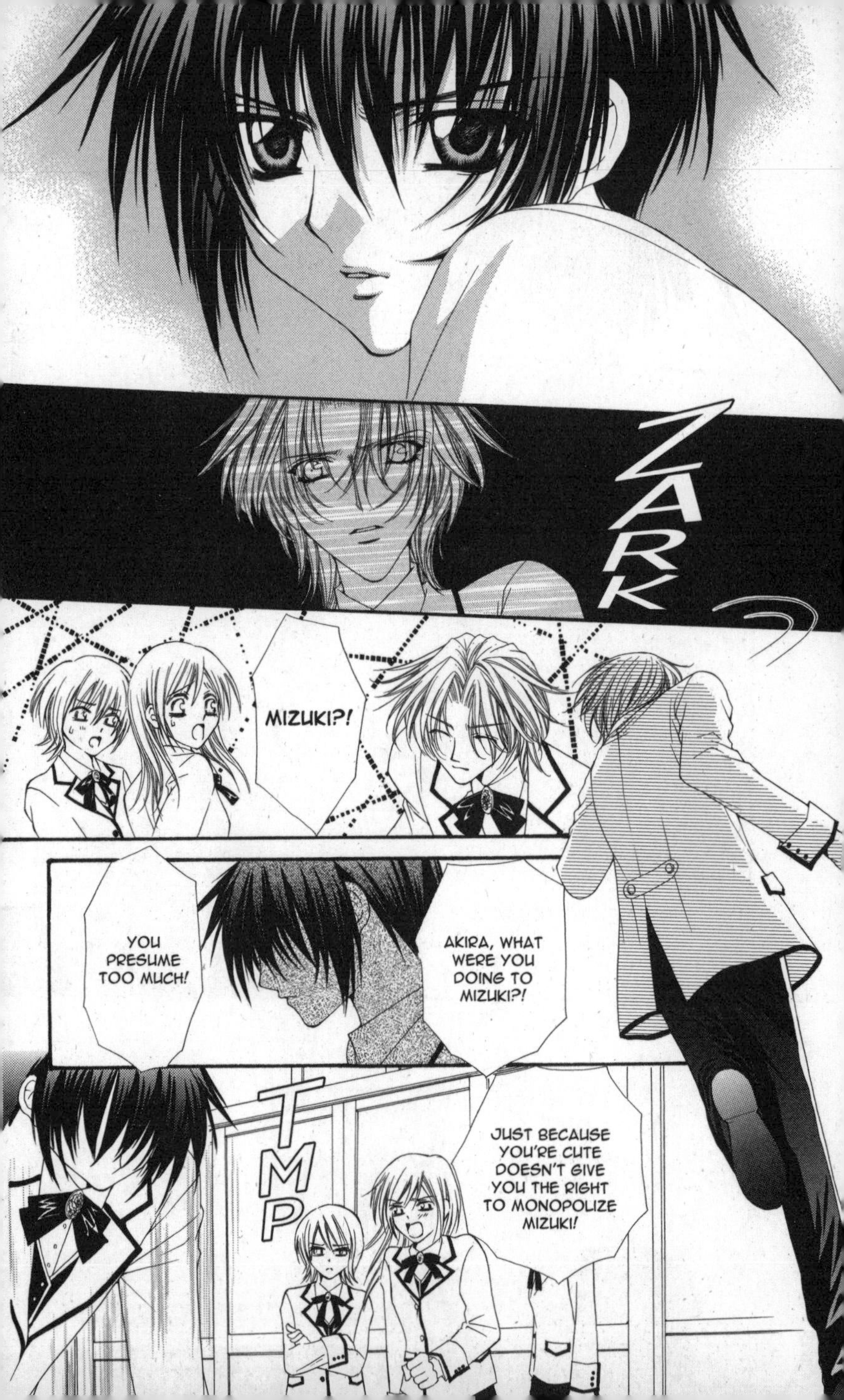
ZARK
MIZUKI?!
AKIRA, WHAT WERE YOU DOING TO MIZUKI?!
YOU PRESUME TOO MUCH!
JUST BECAUSE YOU'RE CUTE DOESN'T GIVE YOU THE RIGHT TO MONOPOLIZE MIZUKI!
TMP

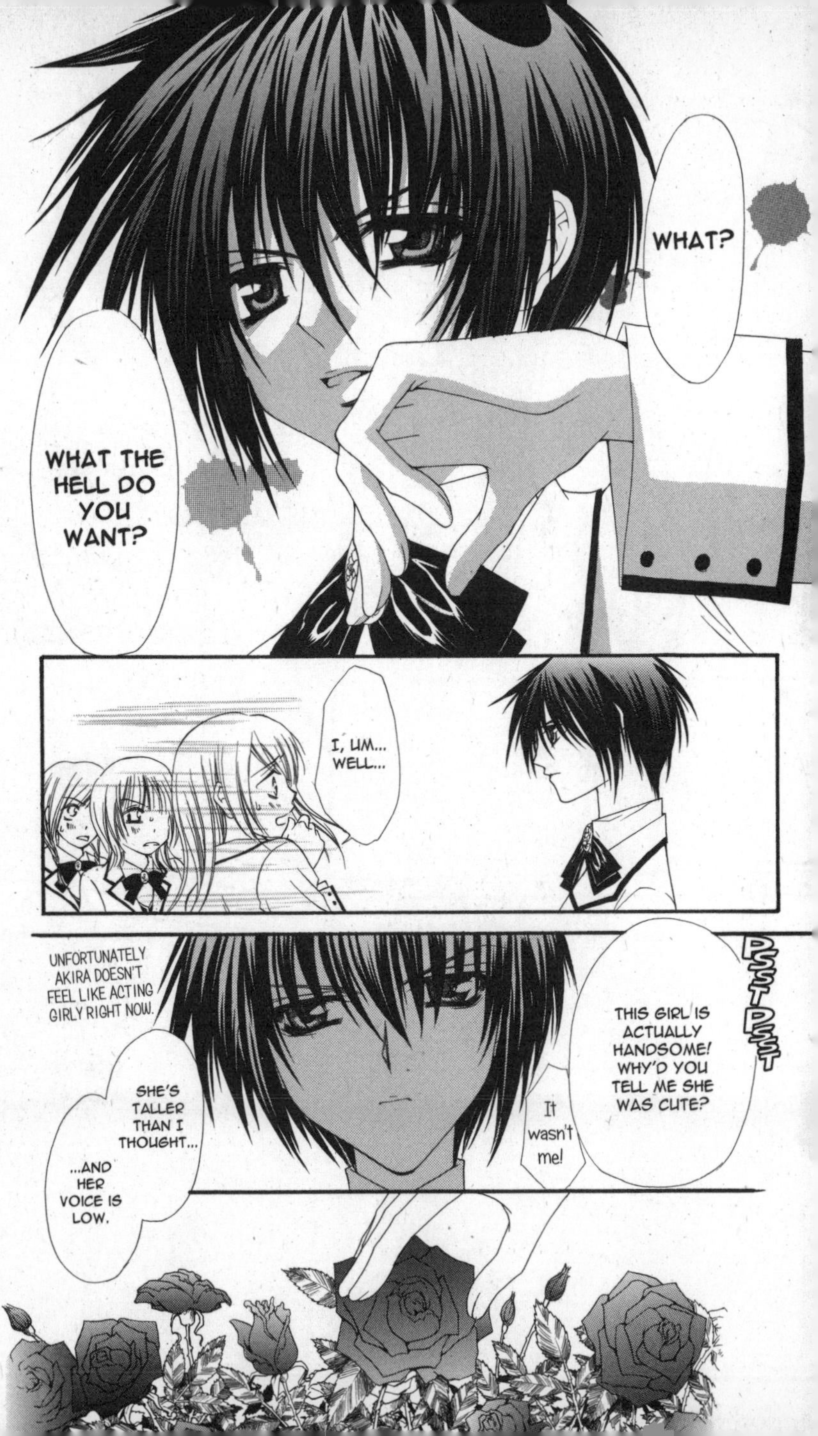
WHAT?
WHAT THE HELL DO YOU WANT?
I, UM... WELL...
PSST PSST
THIS GIRL IS ACTUALLY HANDSOME! WHY'D YOU TELL ME SHE WAS CUTE?
It wasn't me!
SHE'S TALLER THAN I THOUGHT...
...AND HER VOICE IS LOW.
UNFORTUNATELY AKIRA DOESN'T FEEL LIKE ACTING GIRLY RIGHT NOW.

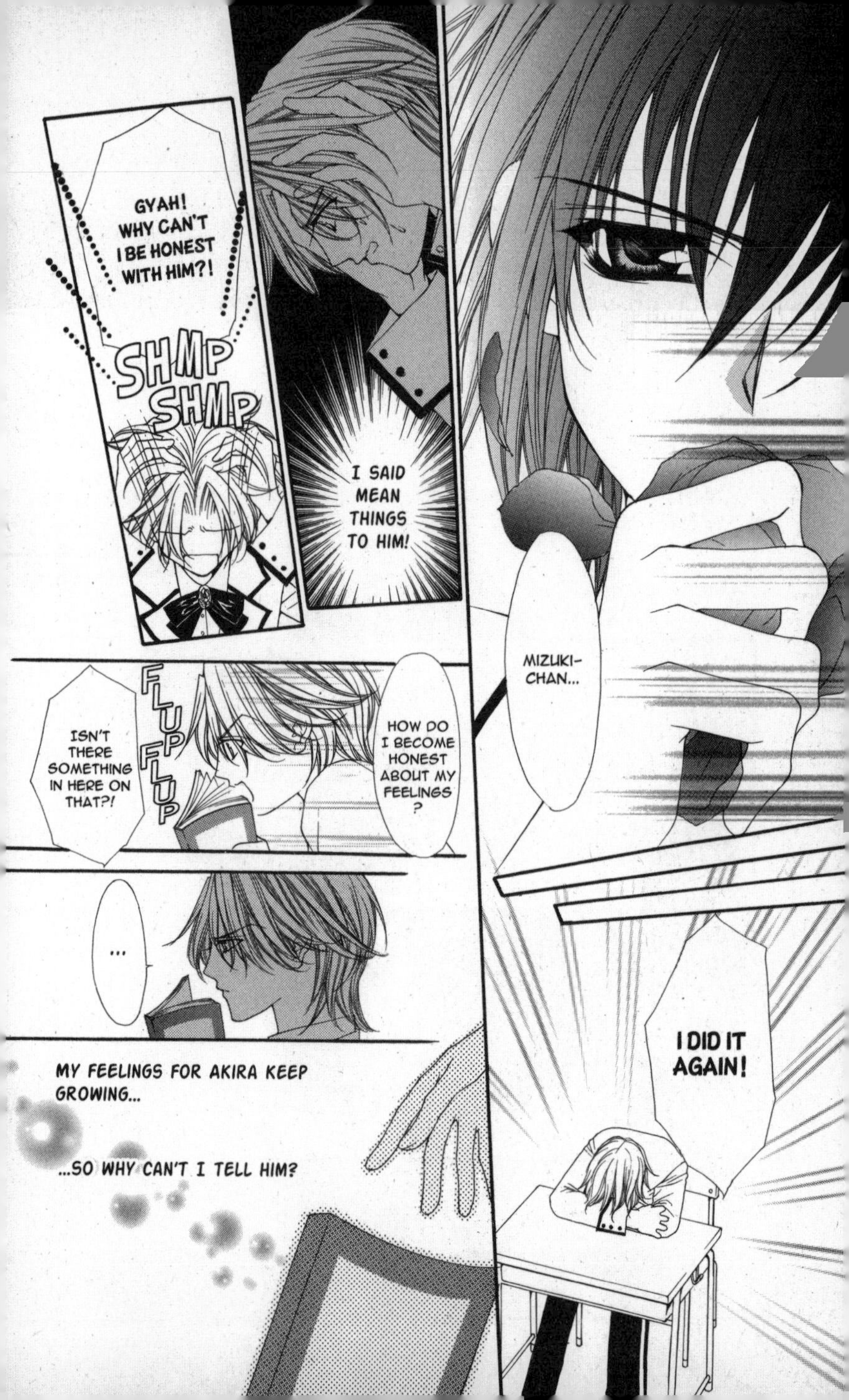
MIZUKI-CHAN...
I DID IT AGAIN!
I SAID MEAN THINGS TO HIM!
GYAH! WHY CAN'T I BE HONEST WITH HIM?!
SHMP SHMP
HOW DO I BECOME HONEST ABOUT MY FEELINGS?
ISN'T THERE SOMETHING IN HERE ON THAT?!
FLUP FLUP
...
MY FEELINGS FOR AKIRA KEEP GROWING...
...SO WHY CAN'T I TELL HIM?

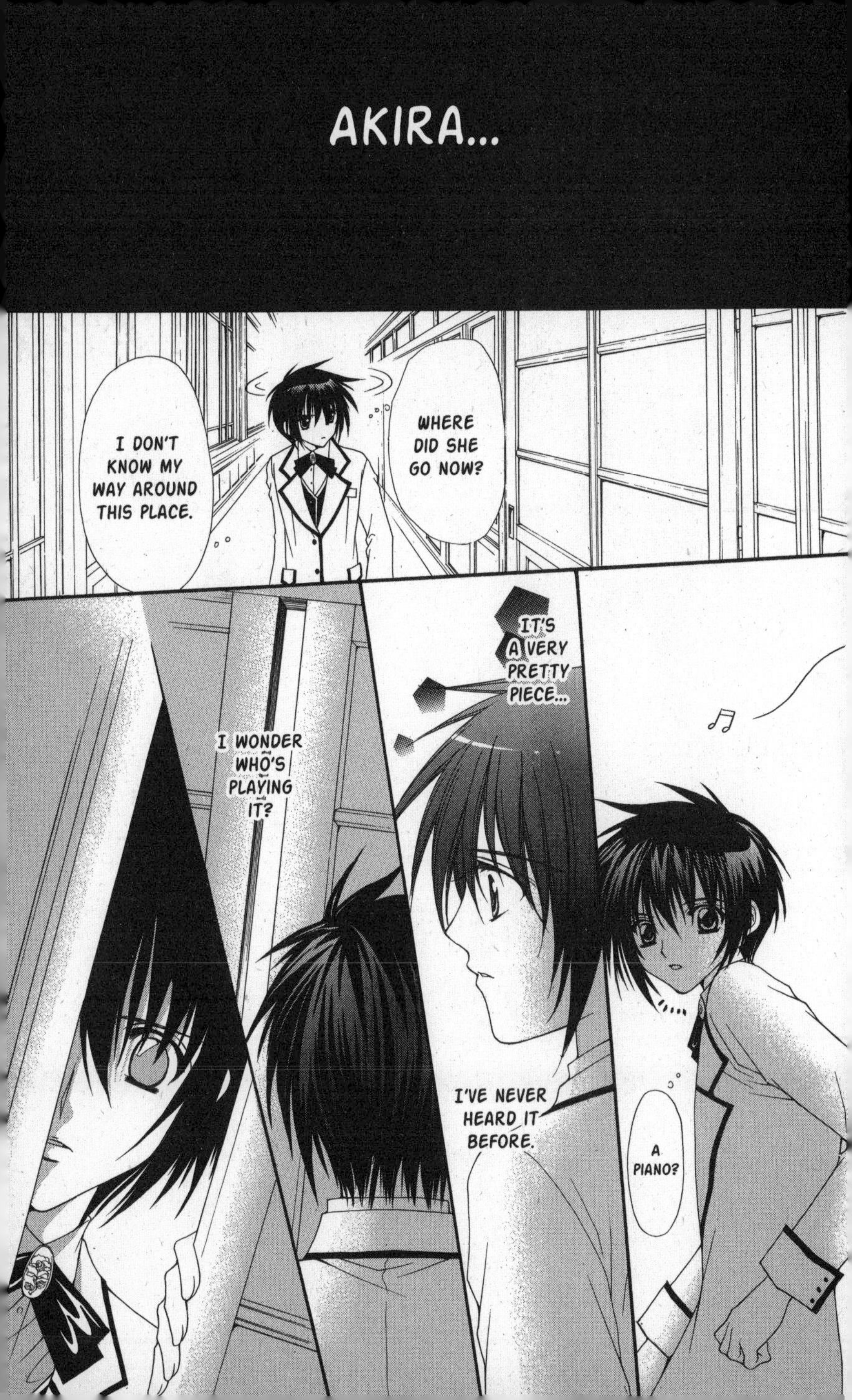
AKIRA...
WHERE DID SHE GO NOW?
I DON'T KNOW MY WAY AROUND THIS PLACE.
A PIANO?
IT'S A VERY PRETTY PIECE...
I'VE NEVER HEARD IT BEFORE.
I WONDER WHO'S PLAYING IT?

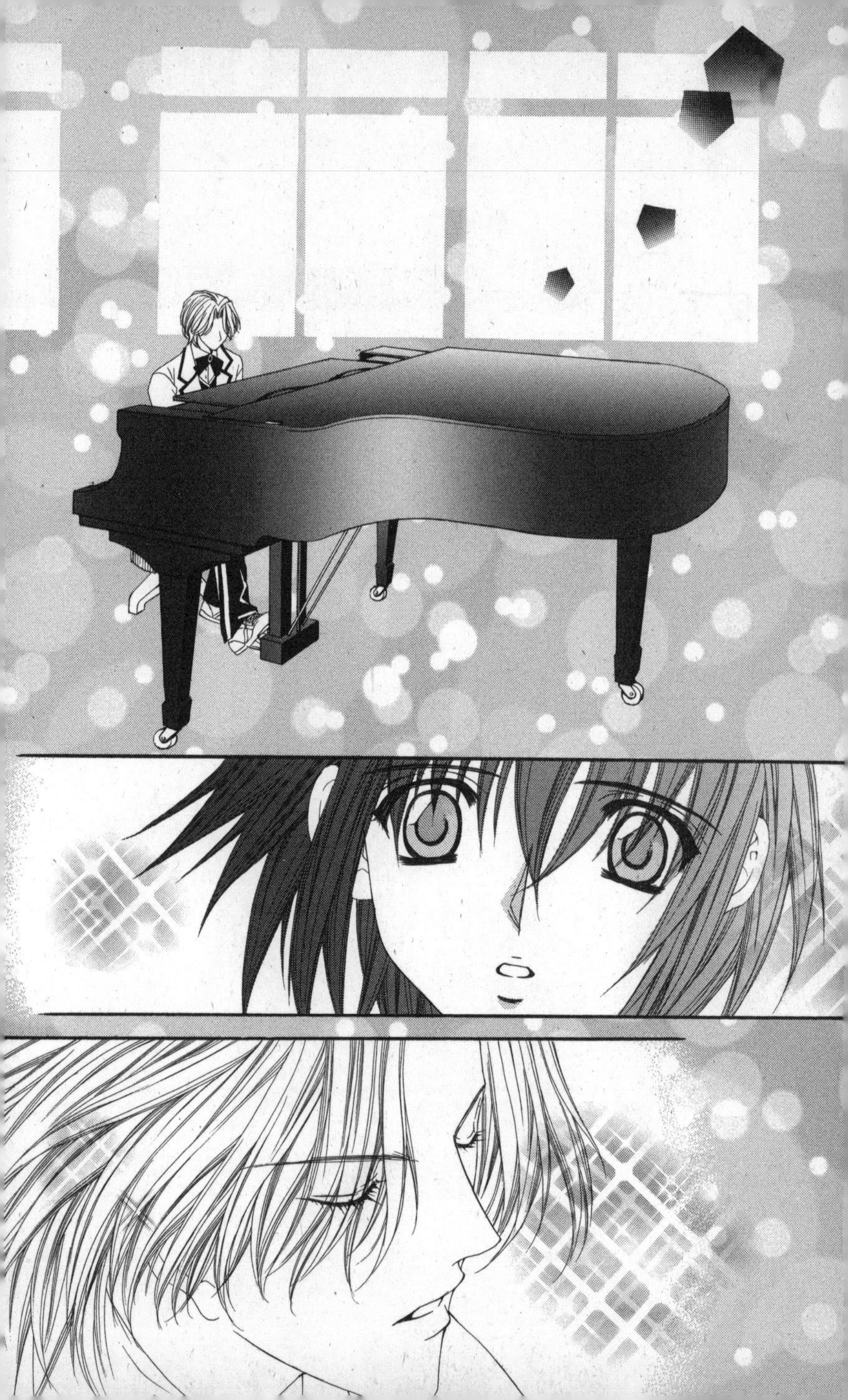

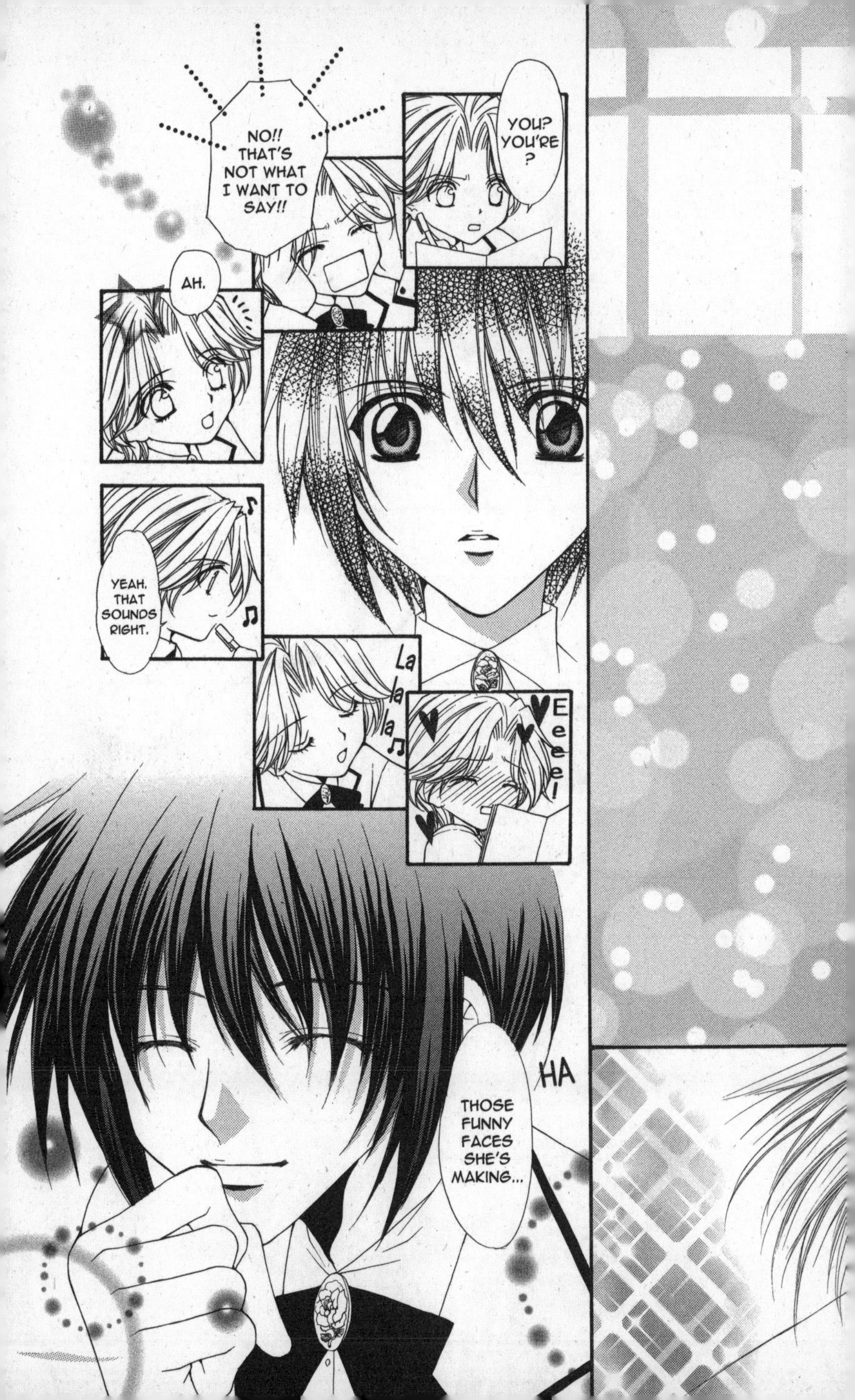
YOU? YOU'RE ?
NO!! THAT'S NOT WHAT I WANT TO SAY!!
AH.
YEAH. THAT SOUNDS RIGHT.
La la la
Eeee!
HA
THOSE FUNNY FACES SHE'S MAKING...

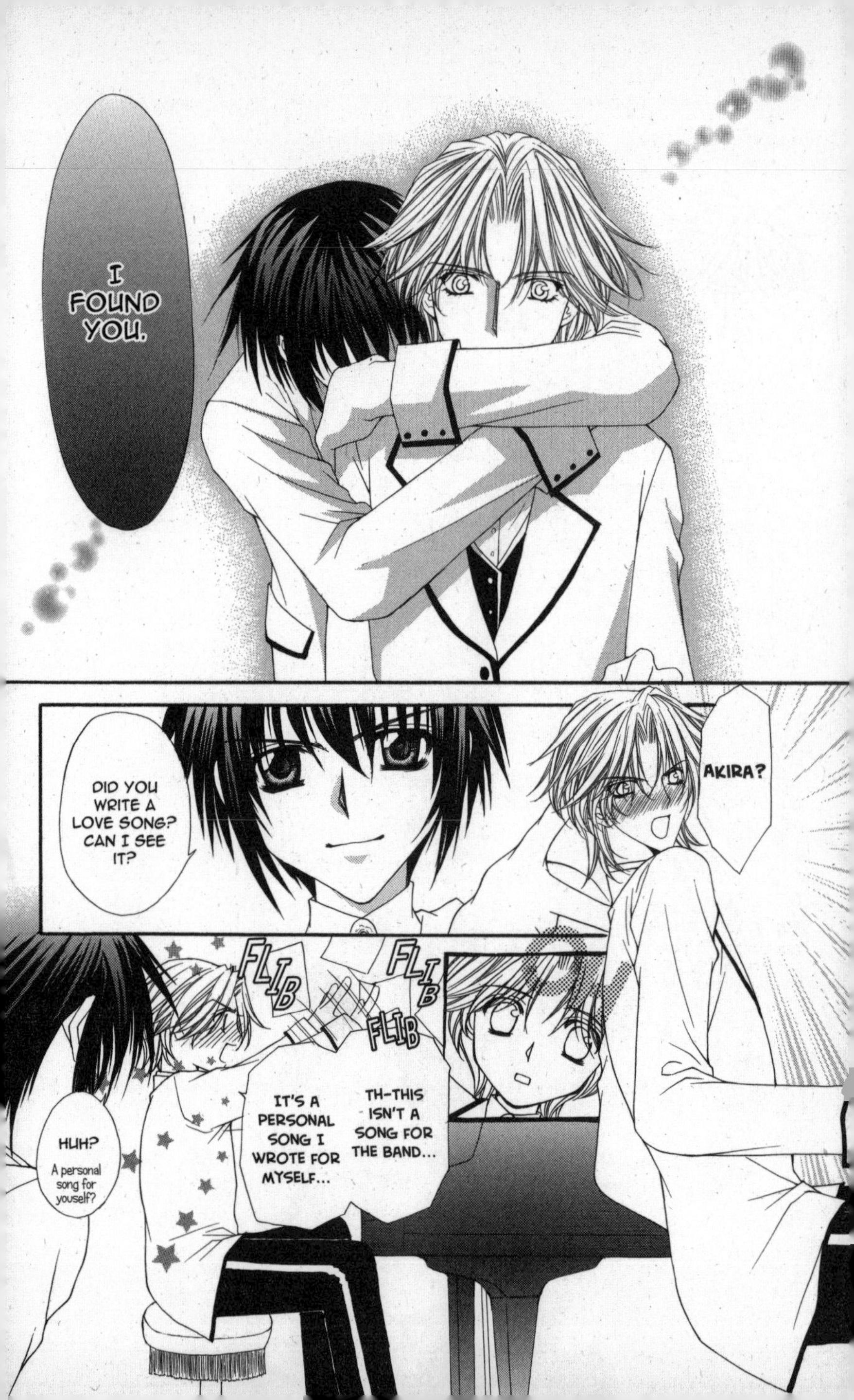
I FOUND YOU.
AKIRA?
DID YOU WRITE A LOVE SONG? CAN I SEE IT?
FLIB
FLIB
FLIB
TH-THIS ISN'T A SONG FOR THE BAND...
IT'S A PERSONAL SONG I WROTE FOR MYSELF...
HUH?
A personal song for youself?

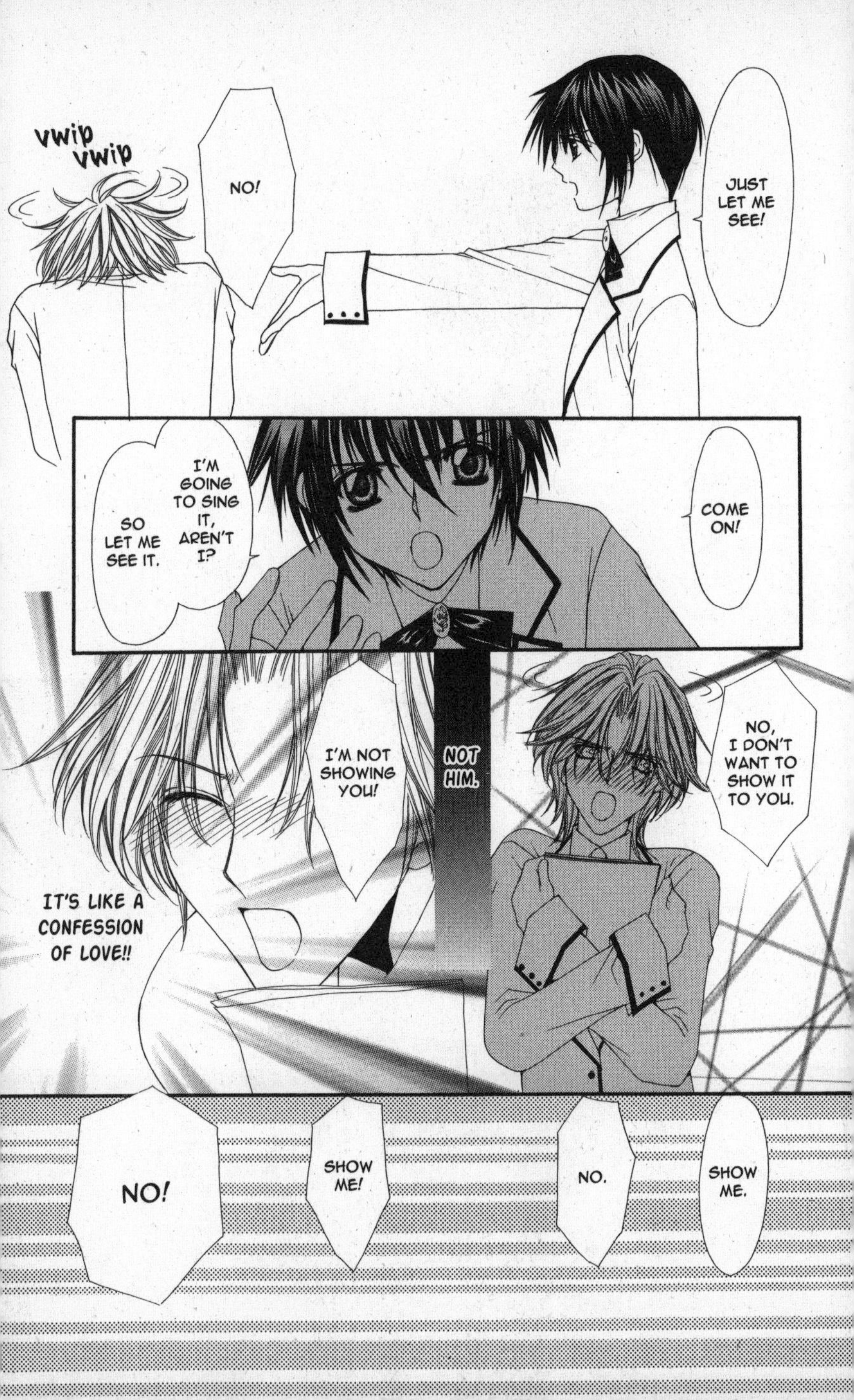
JUST LET ME SEE!
NO!
VWIP VWIP
COME ON!
I'M GOING TO SING IT, AREN'T I?
SO LET ME SEE IT.
NO, I DON'T WANT TO SHOW IT TO YOU.
NOT HIM.
I'M NOT SHOWING YOU!
IT'S LIKE A CONFESSION OF LOVE!!
SHOW ME.
NO.
SHOW ME!
NO!

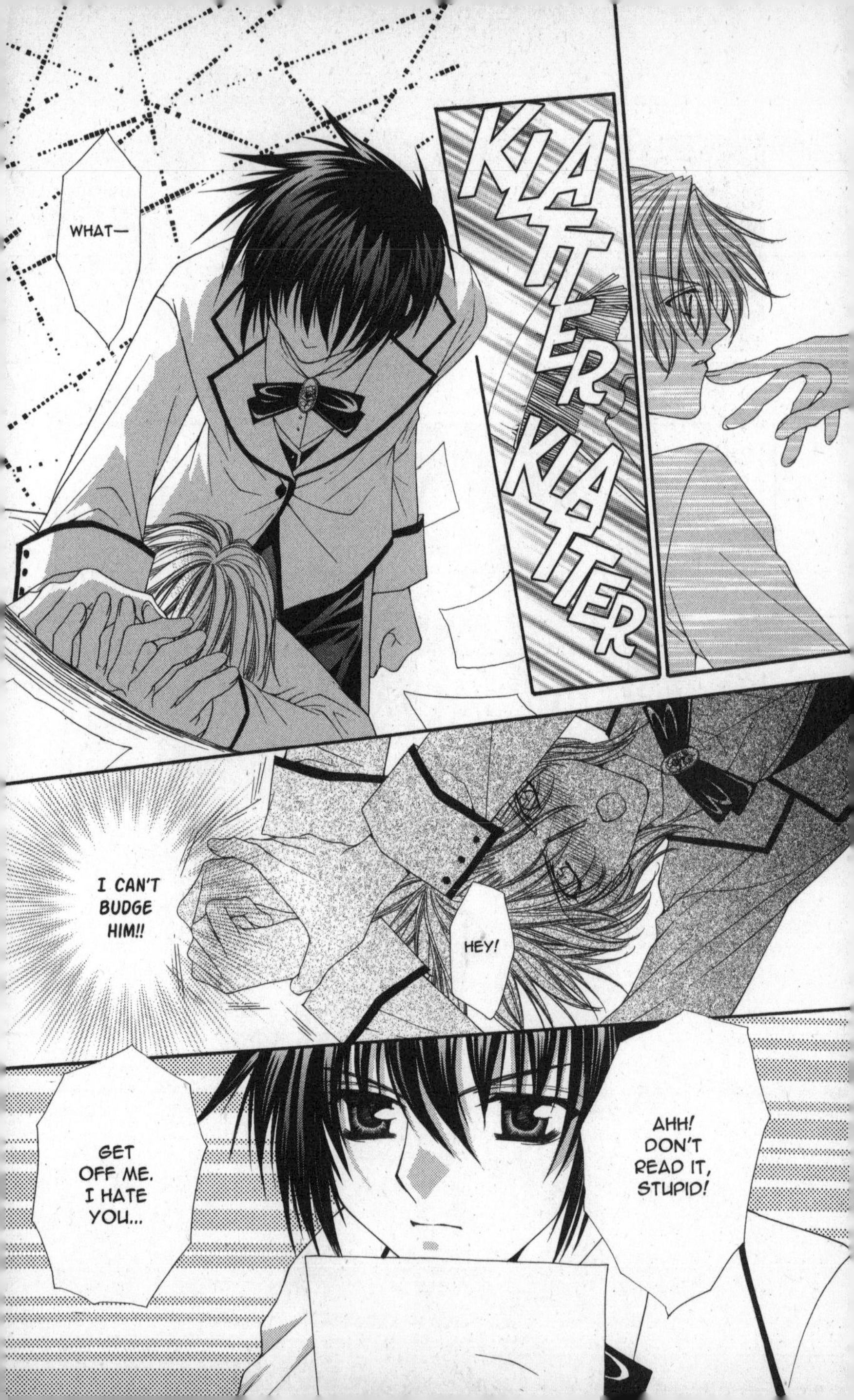
KLATTER
KLATTER
WHAT—
HEY!
I CAN'T BUDGE HIM!!
AHH! DON'T READ IT, STUPID!
GET OFF ME. I HATE YOU...

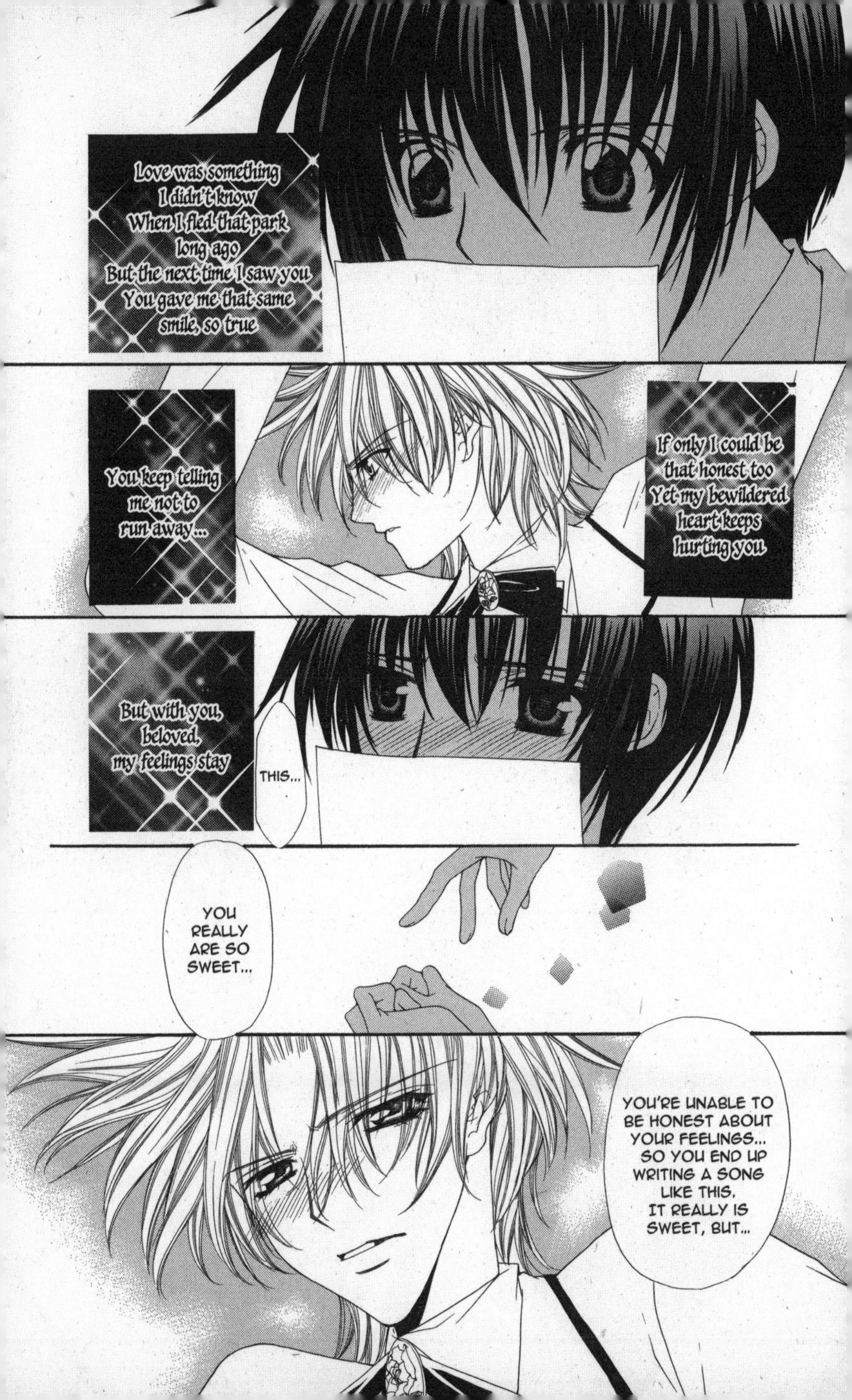
Love was something I didn't know When I fled that park long ago But the next time I saw you You gave me that same smile, so true
If only I could be that honest too Yet my bewildered heart keeps hurting you
You keep telling me not to run away...
THIS...
But with you, beloved, my feelings stay
YOU REALLY ARE SO SWEET...
YOU'RE UNABLE TO BE HONEST ABOUT YOUR FEELINGS... SO YOU END UP WRITING A SONG LIKE THIS. IT REALLY IS SWEET, BUT...

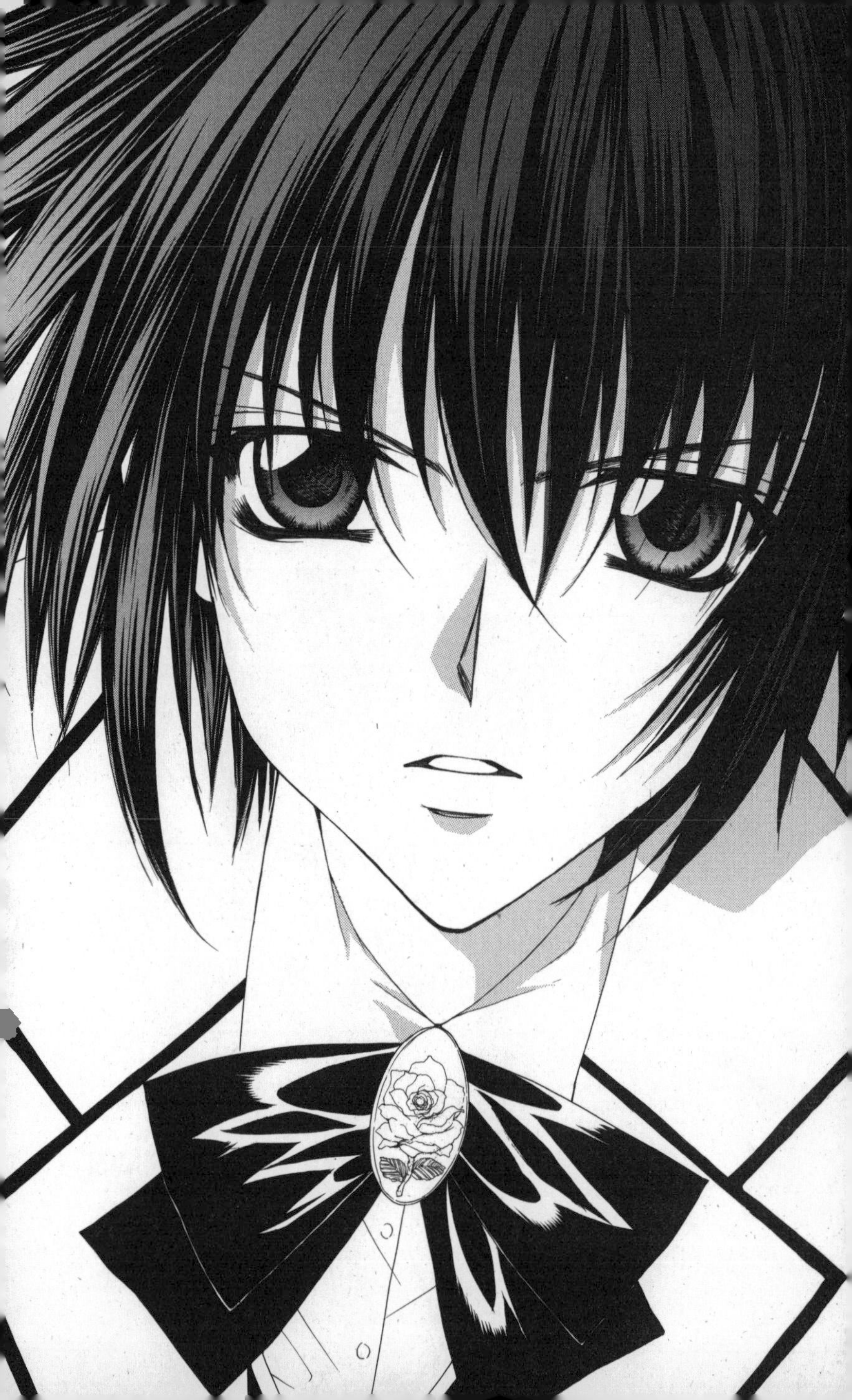

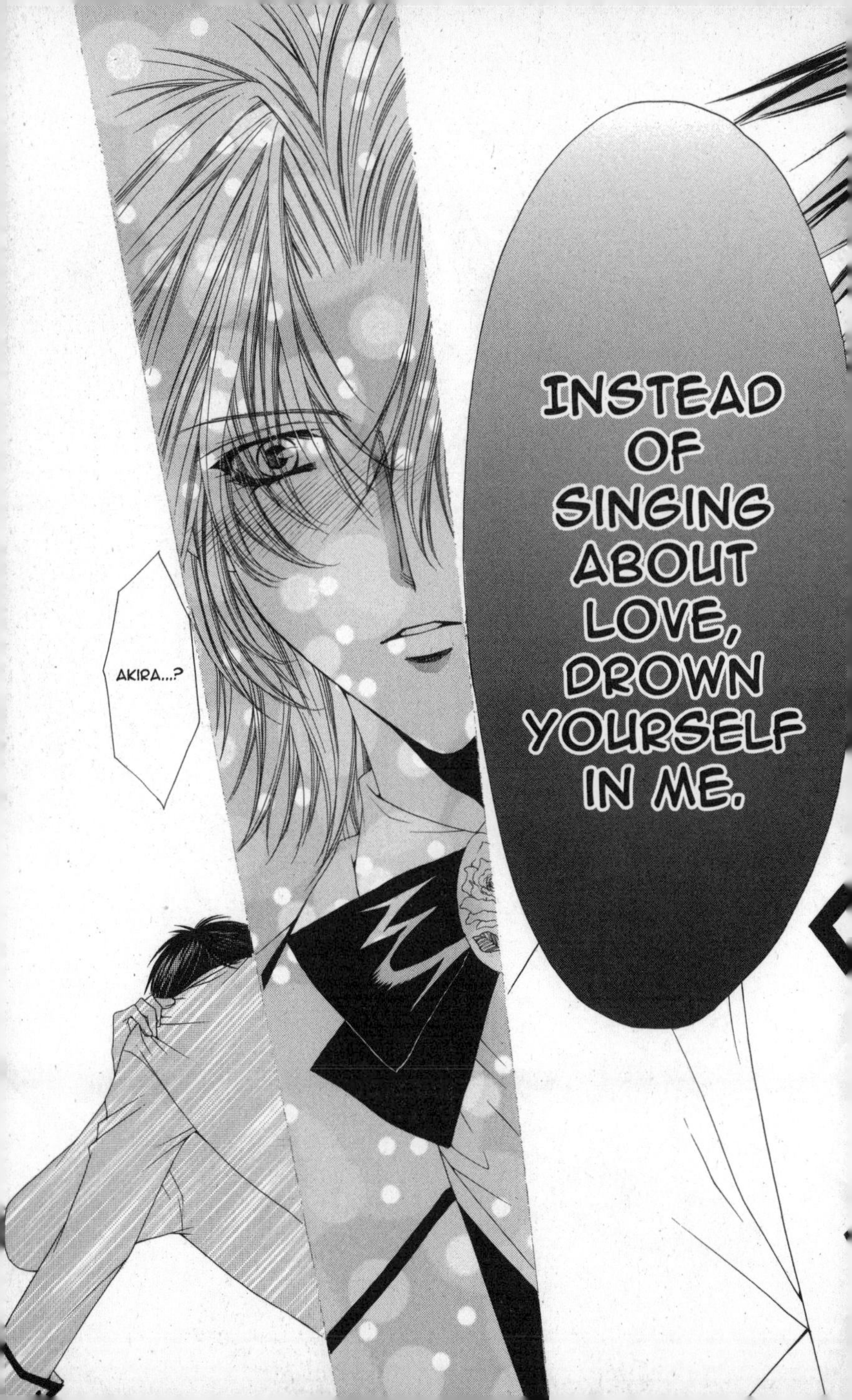
INSTEAD OF SINGING ABOUT LOVE, DROWN YOURSELF IN ME.
AKIRA...?

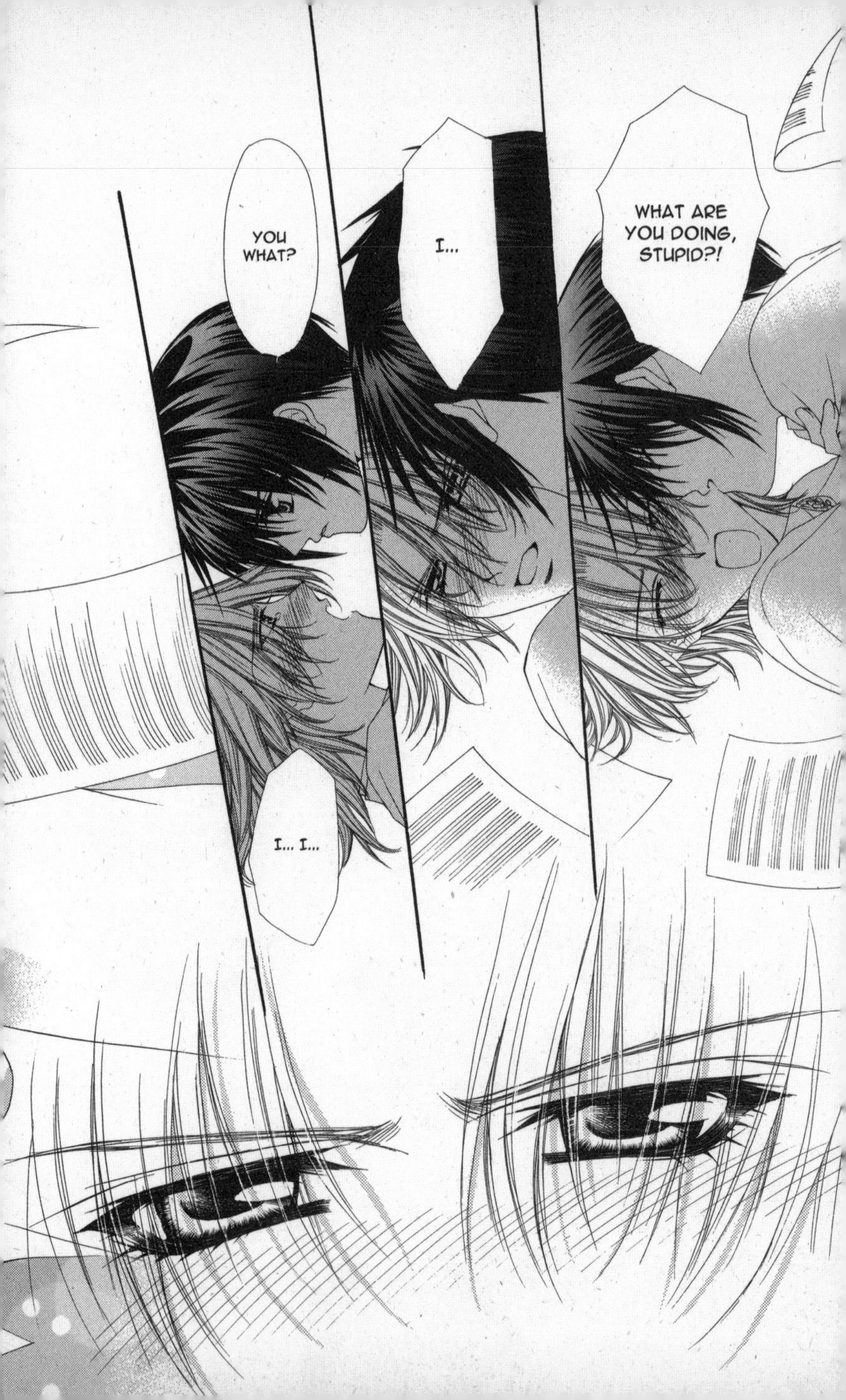
WHAT ARE YOU DOING, STUPID?!
I...
YOU WHAT?
I... I...

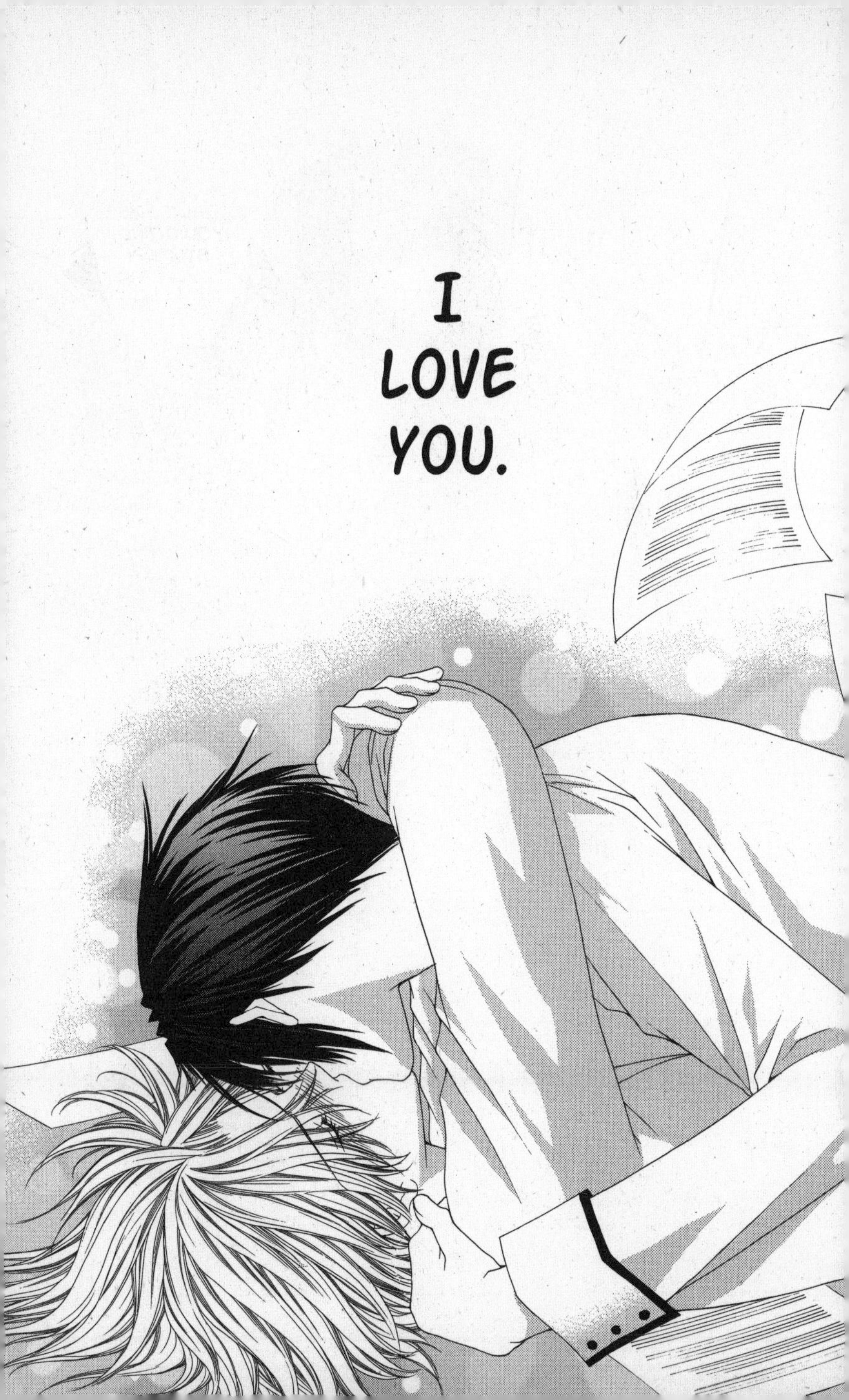
I LOVE YOU.

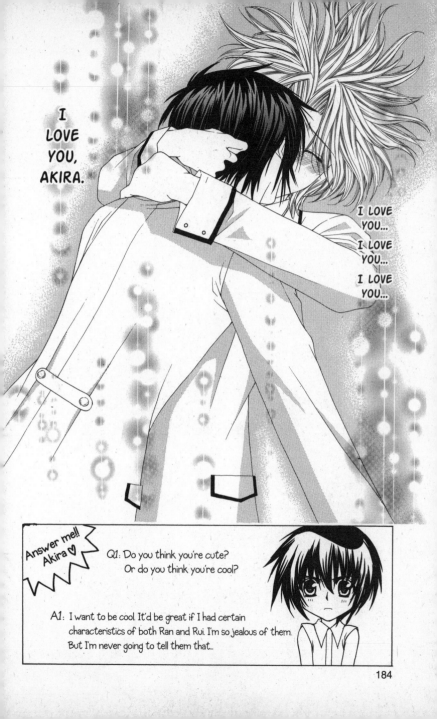

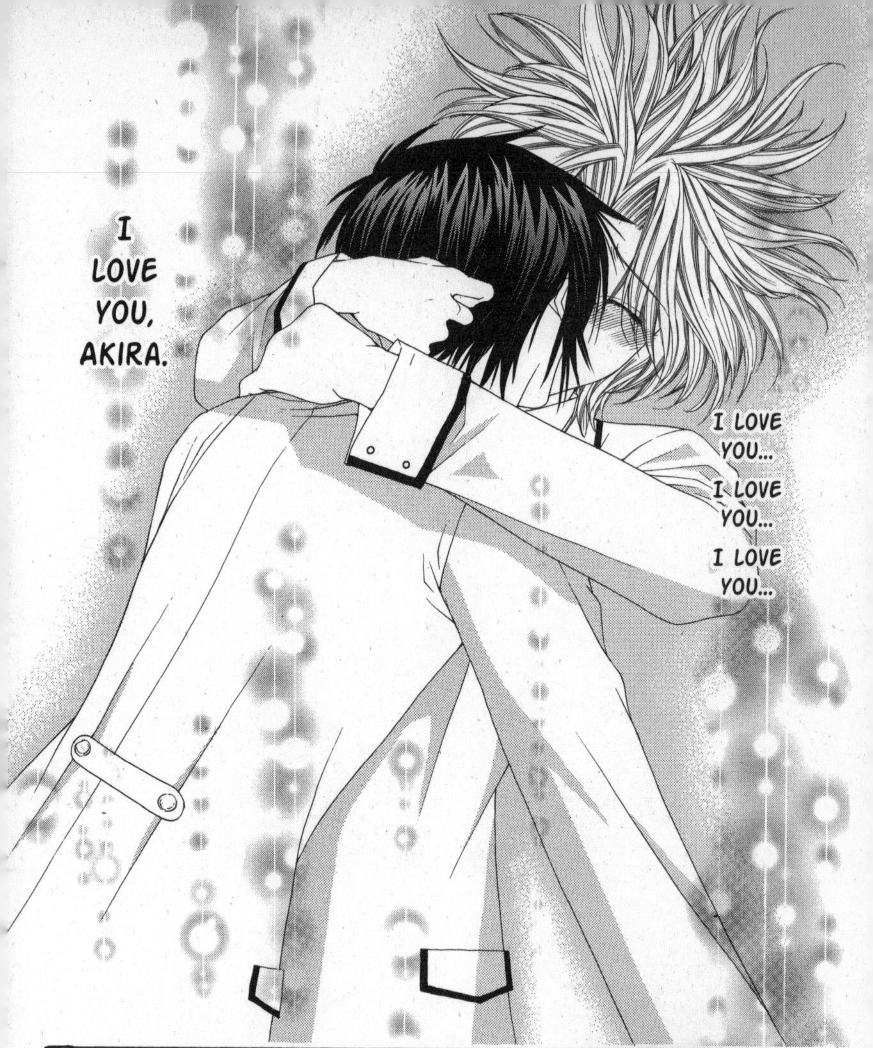
I LOVE YOU, AKIRA.
I LOVE YOU...
I LOVE YOU...
I LOVE YOU...

Answer me!! Akira ♡

Q1: Do you think you're cute?
Or do you think you're cool?

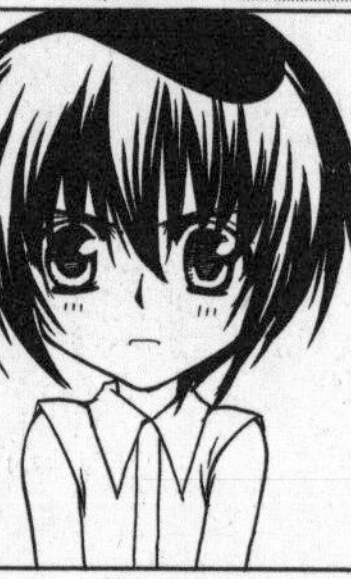

A1: I want to be cool. It'd be great if I had certain characteristics of both Ran and Rui. I'm so jealous of them. But I'm never going to tell them that...

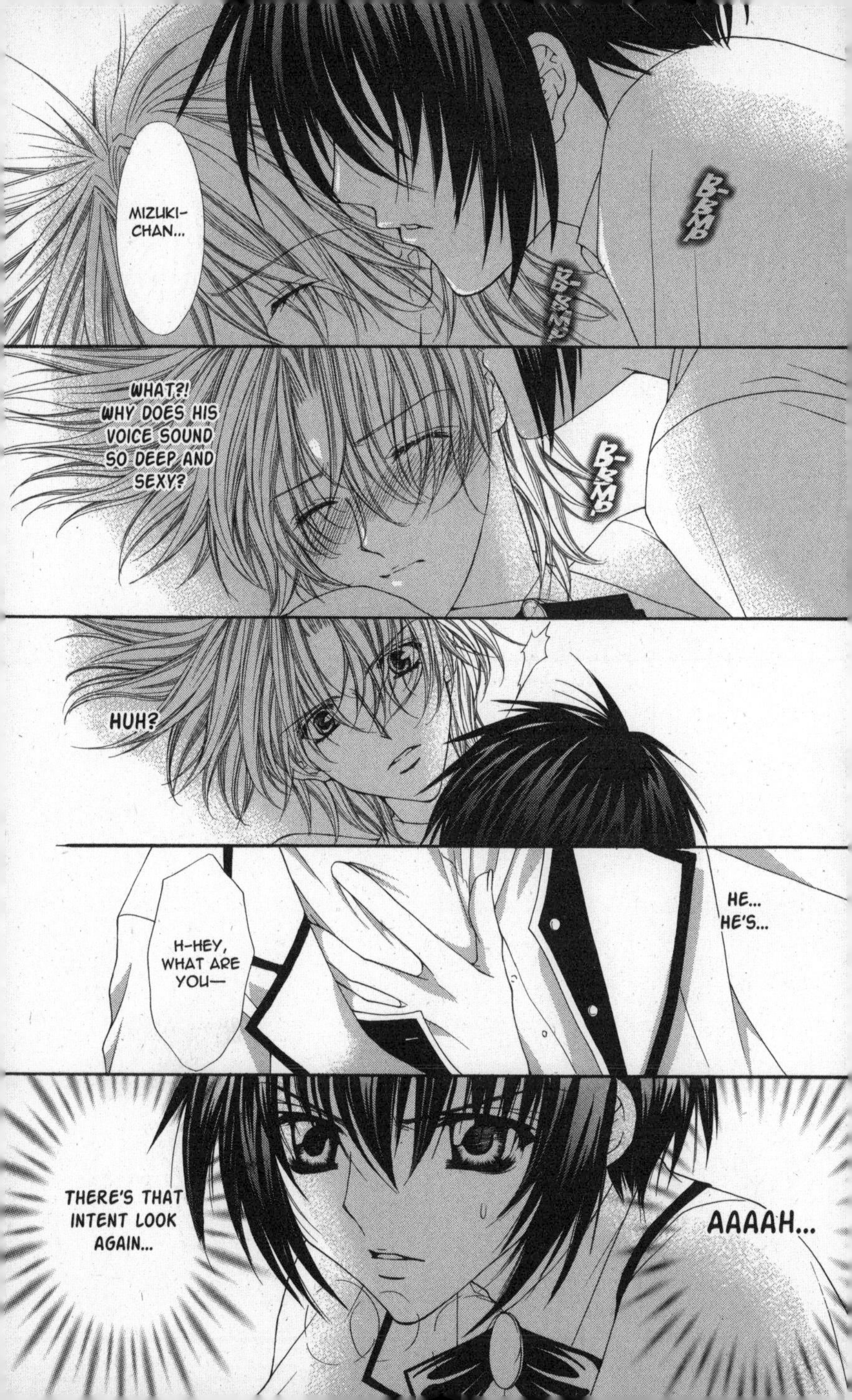
B-BMP
B-BMP
MIZUKI-CHAN...
B-BMP
WHAT?! WHY DOES HIS VOICE SOUND SO DEEP AND SEXY?
HUH?
HE... HE'S...
H-HEY, WHAT ARE YOU—
AAAAH...
THERE'S THAT INTENT LOOK AGAIN...

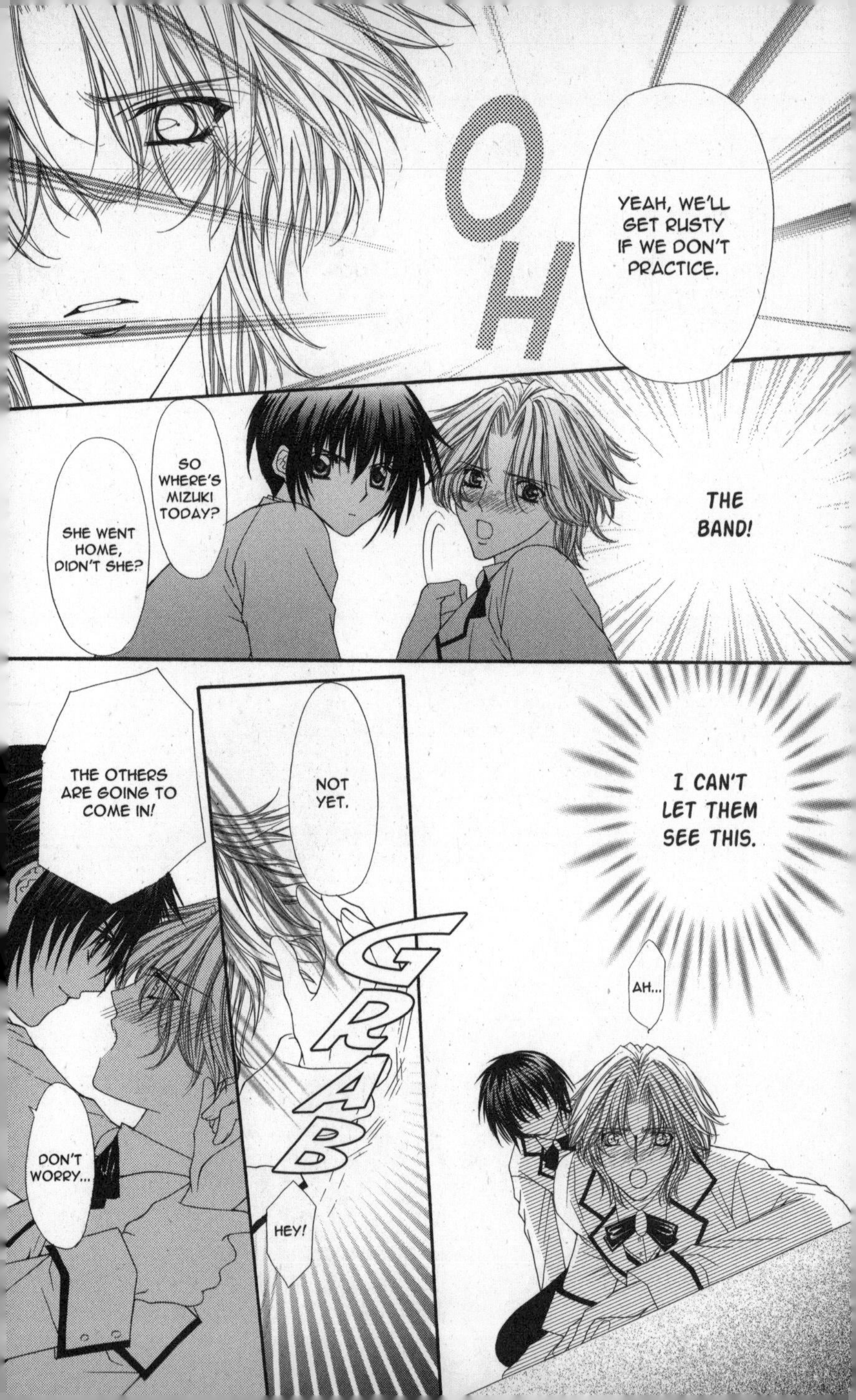
YEAH, WE'LL GET RUSTY IF WE DON'T PRACTICE.
OH
THE BAND!
SO WHERE'S MIZUKI TODAY?
SHE WENT HOME, DIDN'T SHE?
I CAN'T LET THEM SEE THIS.
AH...
NOT YET.
GRAB
HEY!
THE OTHERS ARE GOING TO COME IN!
DON'T WORRY...

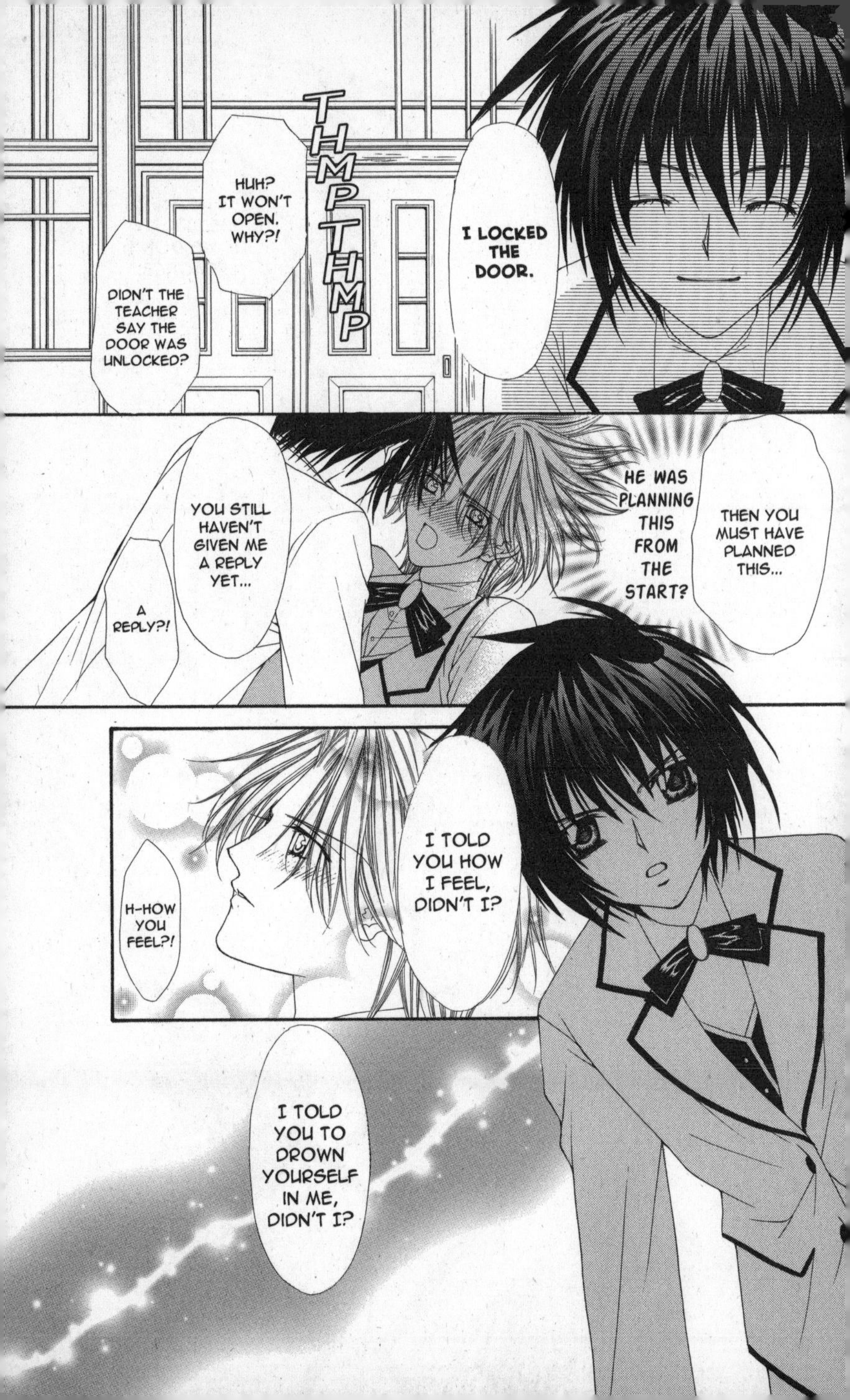
THMP THMP
HUH? IT WON'T OPEN. WHY?!
DIDN'T THE TEACHER SAY THE DOOR WAS UNLOCKED?
I LOCKED THE DOOR.
THEN YOU MUST HAVE PLANNED THIS...
HE WAS PLANNING THIS FROM THE START?
YOU STILL HAVEN'T GIVEN ME A REPLY YET...
A REPLY?!
I TOLD YOU HOW I FEEL, DIDN'T I?
H-HOW YOU FEEL?!
I TOLD YOU TO DROWN YOURSELF IN ME, DIDN'T I?

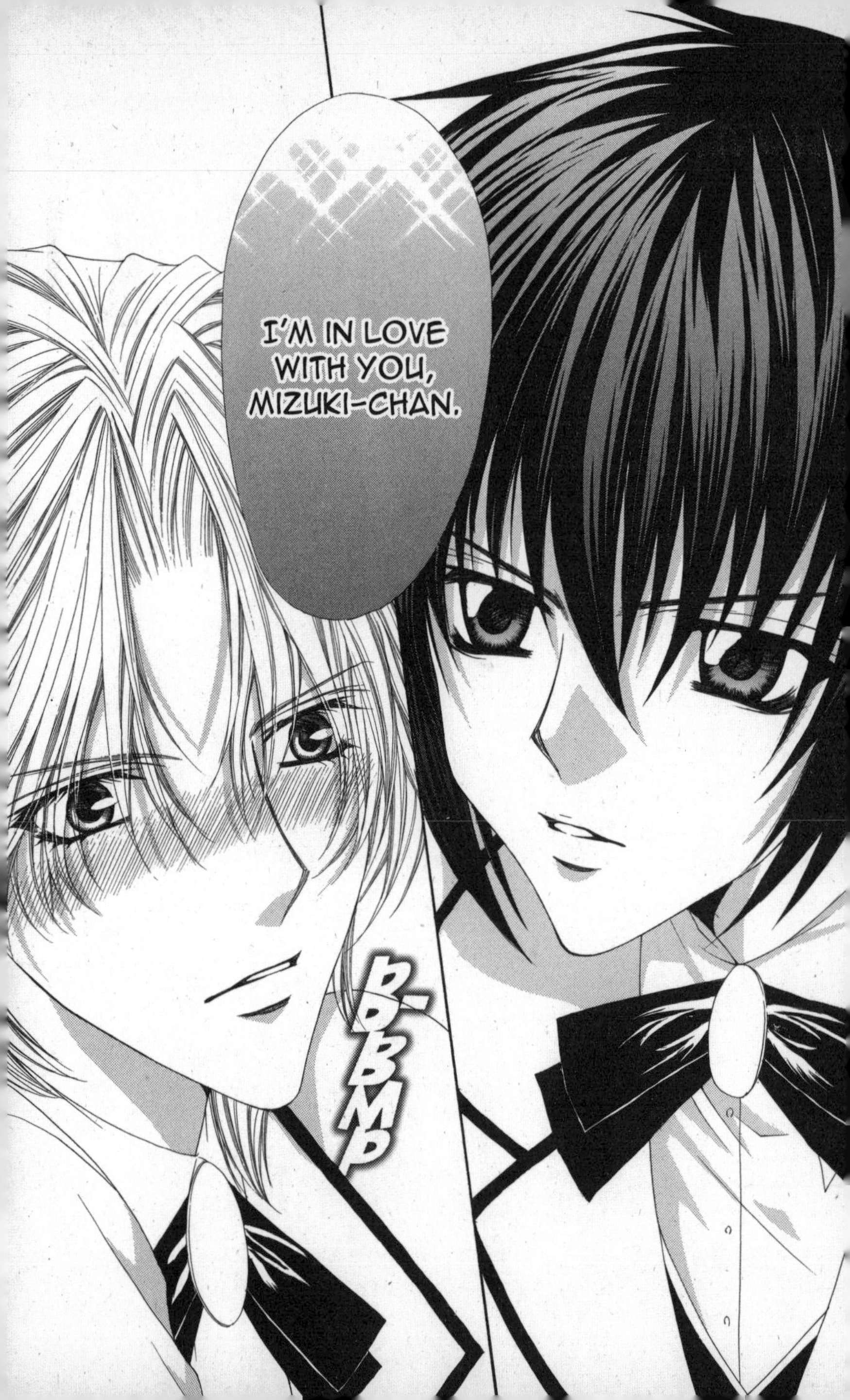
I'M IN LOVE WITH YOU, MIZUKI-CHAN.
B-BUMP

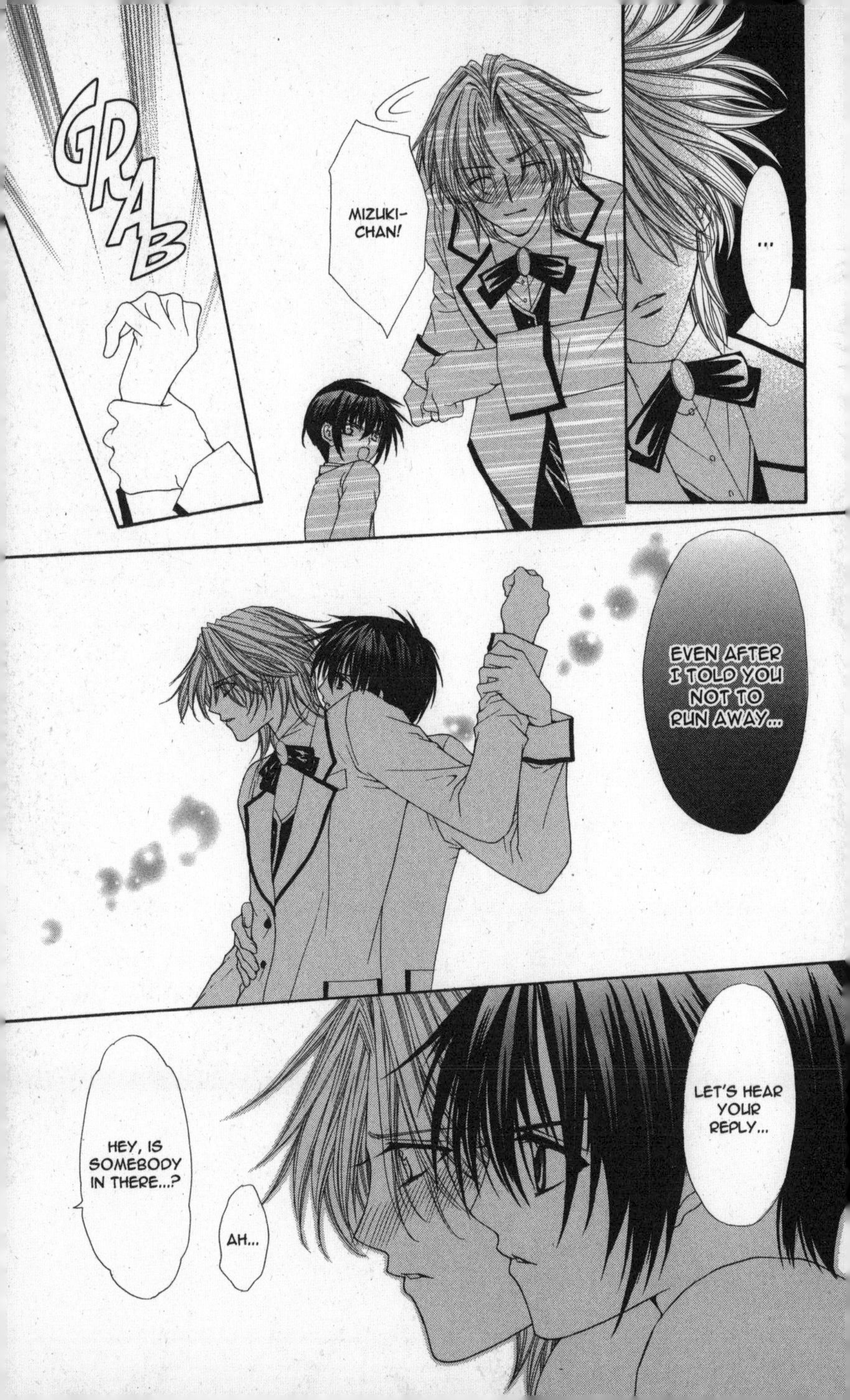
...
MIZUKI-CHAN!
GRAB
EVEN AFTER I TOLD YOU NOT TO RUN AWAY...
LET'S HEAR YOUR REPLY...
AH...
HEY, IS SOMEBODY IN THERE...?

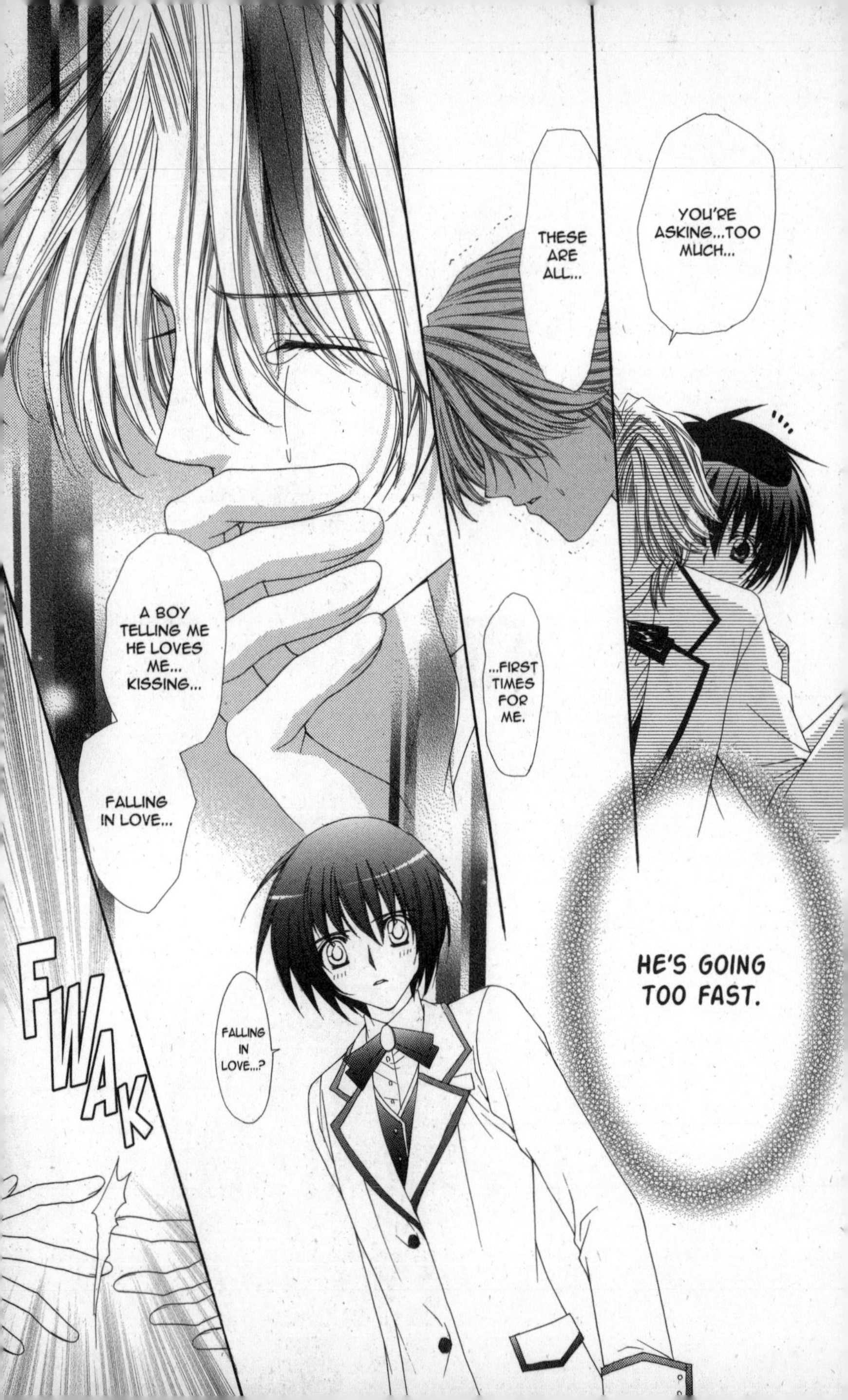
YOU'RE ASKING...TOO MUCH...
....
THESE ARE ALL...
...FIRST TIMES FOR ME.
A BOY TELLING ME HE LOVES ME... KISSING...
FALLING IN LOVE...
HE'S GOING TOO FAST.
FALLING IN LOVE...?
FWAK

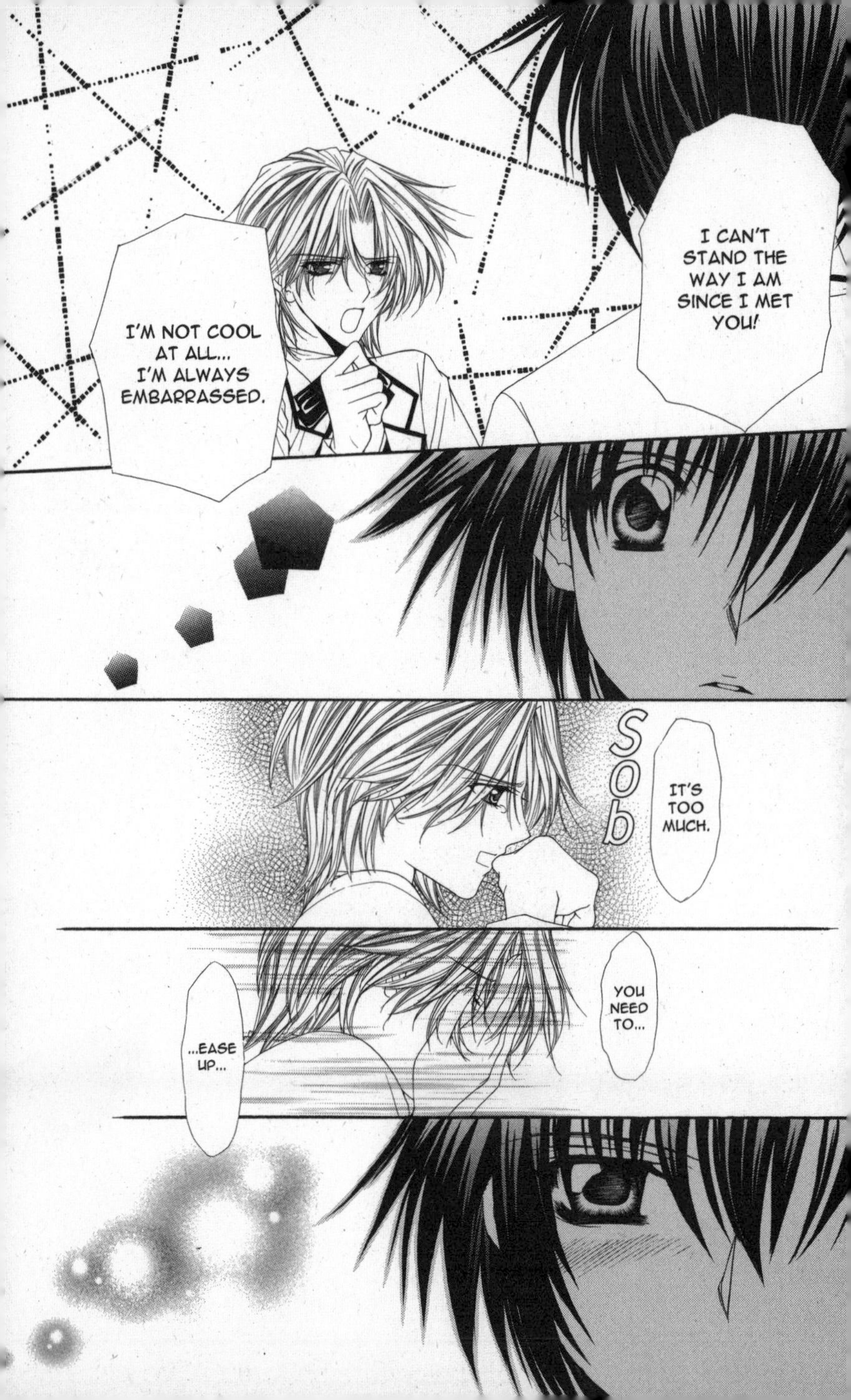
I CAN'T STAND THE WAY I AM SINCE I MET YOU!
I'M NOT COOL AT ALL... I'M ALWAYS EMBARRASSED.
SOB
IT'S TOO MUCH.
YOU NEED TO...
...EASE UP...

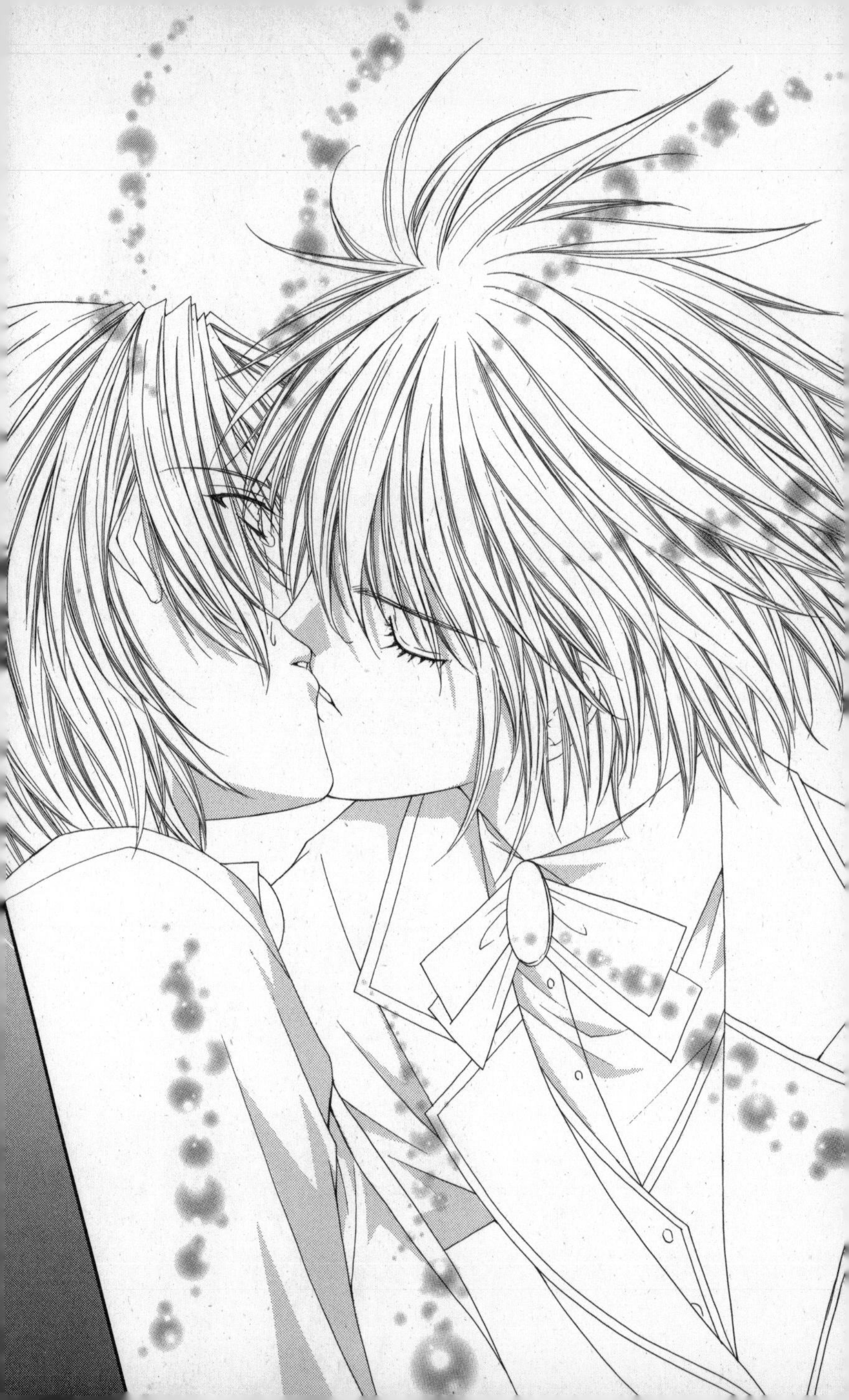

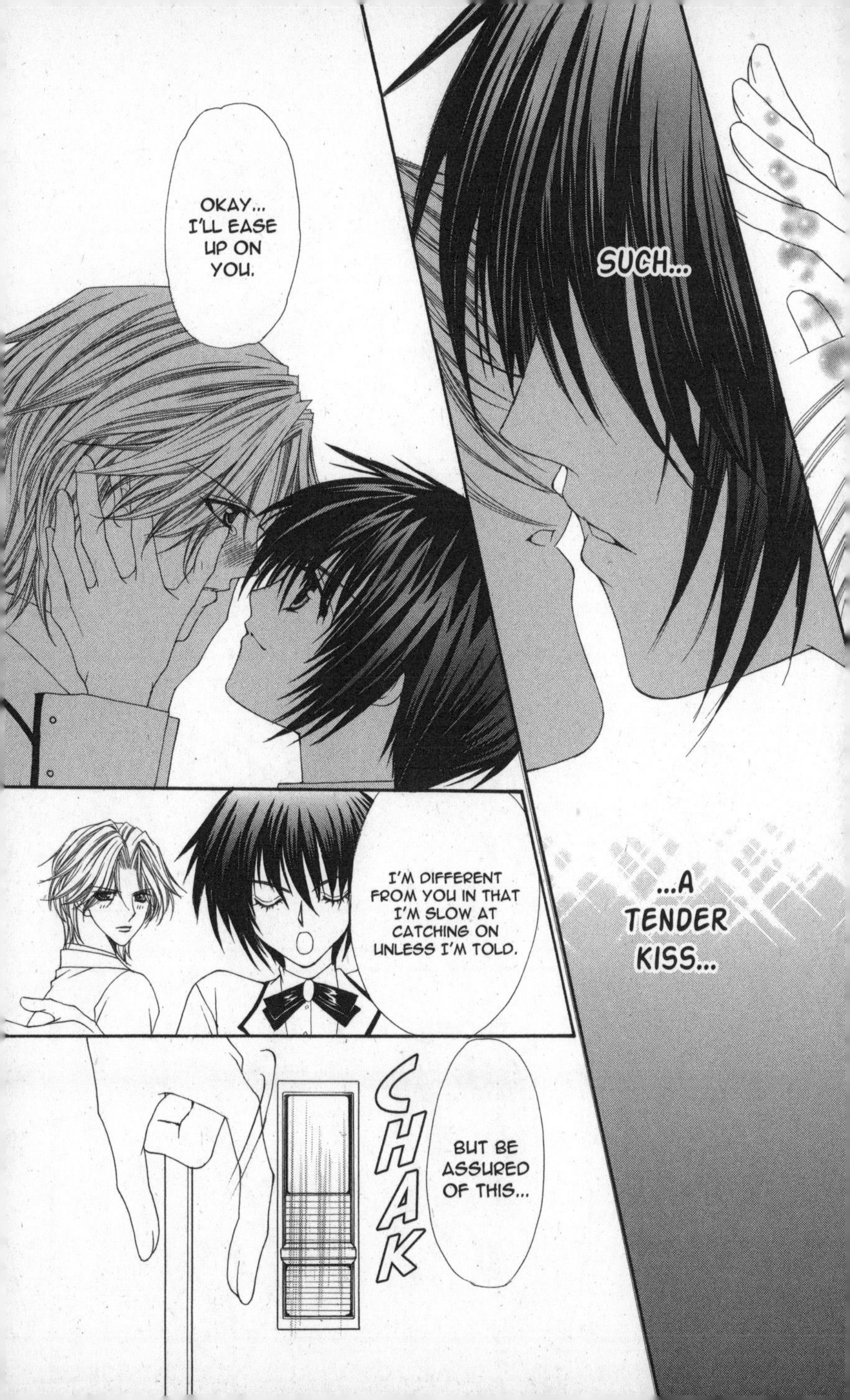
SUCH...
...A TENDER KISS...
OKAY... I'LL EASE UP ON YOU.
I'M DIFFERENT FROM YOU IN THAT I'M SLOW AT CATCHING ON UNLESS I'M TOLD.
BUT BE ASSURED OF THIS...
CHAK

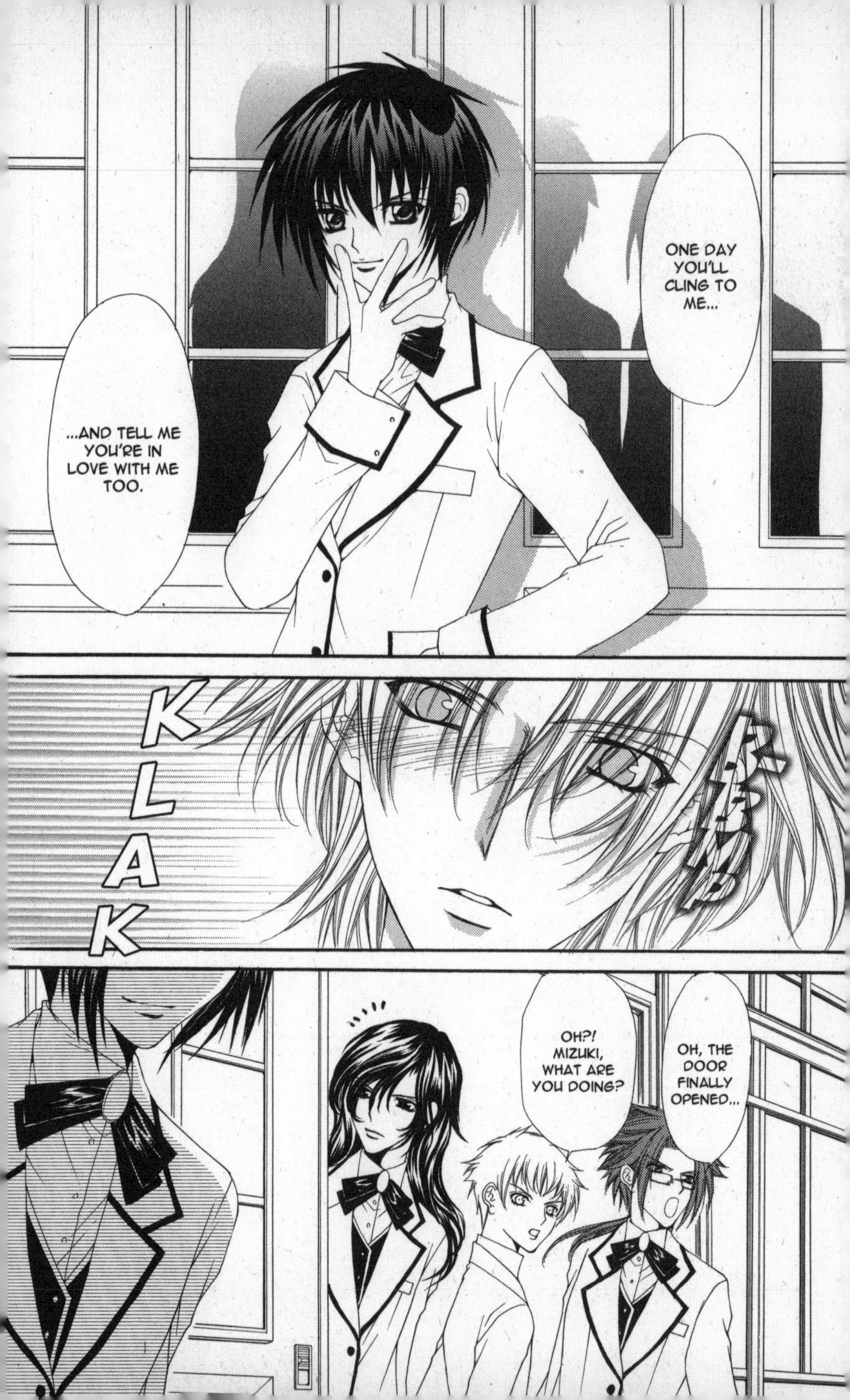
ONE DAY YOU'LL CLING TO ME...
...AND TELL ME YOU'RE IN LOVE WITH ME TOO.
KLAK
OH, THE DOOR FINALLY OPENED...
OH?! MIZUKI, WHAT ARE YOU DOING?

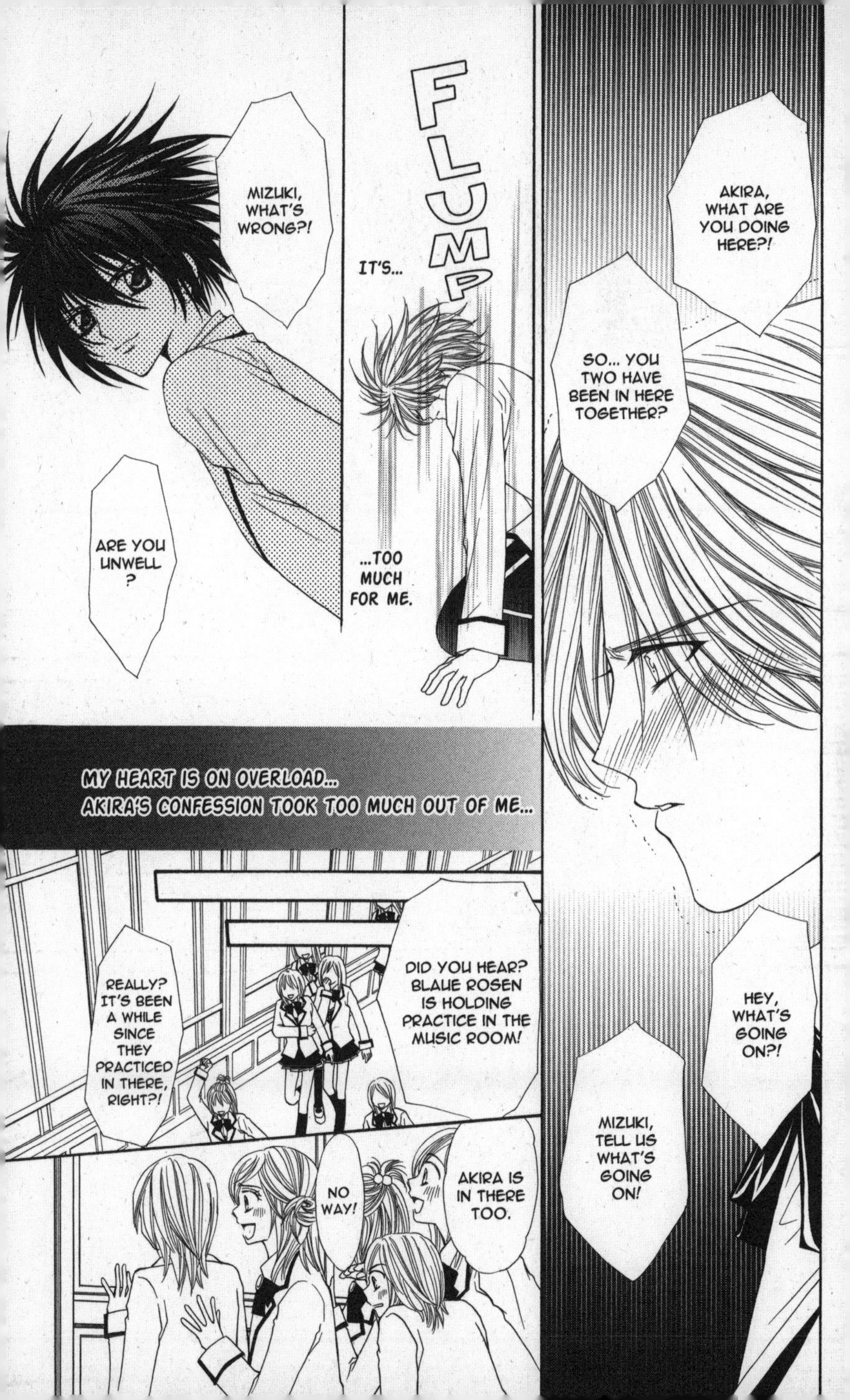

AKIRA, WHAT ARE YOU DOING HERE?!
SO... YOU TWO HAVE BEEN IN HERE TOGETHER?
HEY, WHAT'S GOING ON?!
MIZUKI, TELL US WHAT'S GOING ON!
FLUMP
IT'S...
...TOO MUCH FOR ME.
MIZUKI, WHAT'S WRONG?!
ARE YOU UNWELL?
MY HEART IS ON OVERLOAD...
AKIRA'S CONFESSION TOOK TOO MUCH OUT OF ME...
DID YOU HEAR? BLAUE ROSEN IS HOLDING PRACTICE IN THE MUSIC ROOM!
REALLY? IT'S BEEN A WHILE SINCE THEY PRACTICED IN THERE, RIGHT?!
AKIRA IS IN THERE TOO.
NO WAY!

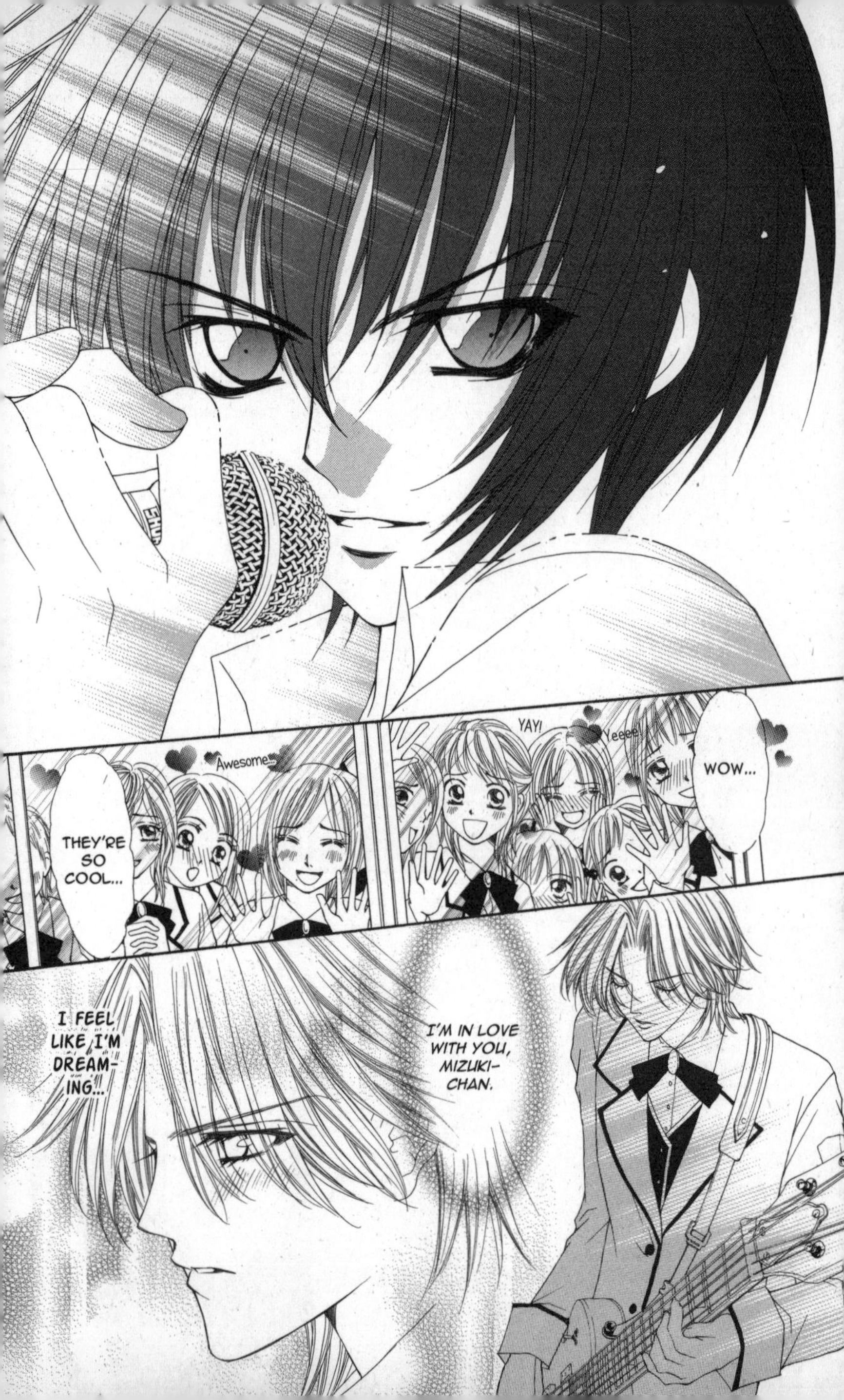
WOW...
Yeeee!
YAY!
Awesome...
THEY'RE SO COOL...
I'M IN LOVE WITH YOU, MIZUKI-CHAN.
I FEEL LIKE I'M DREAMING...

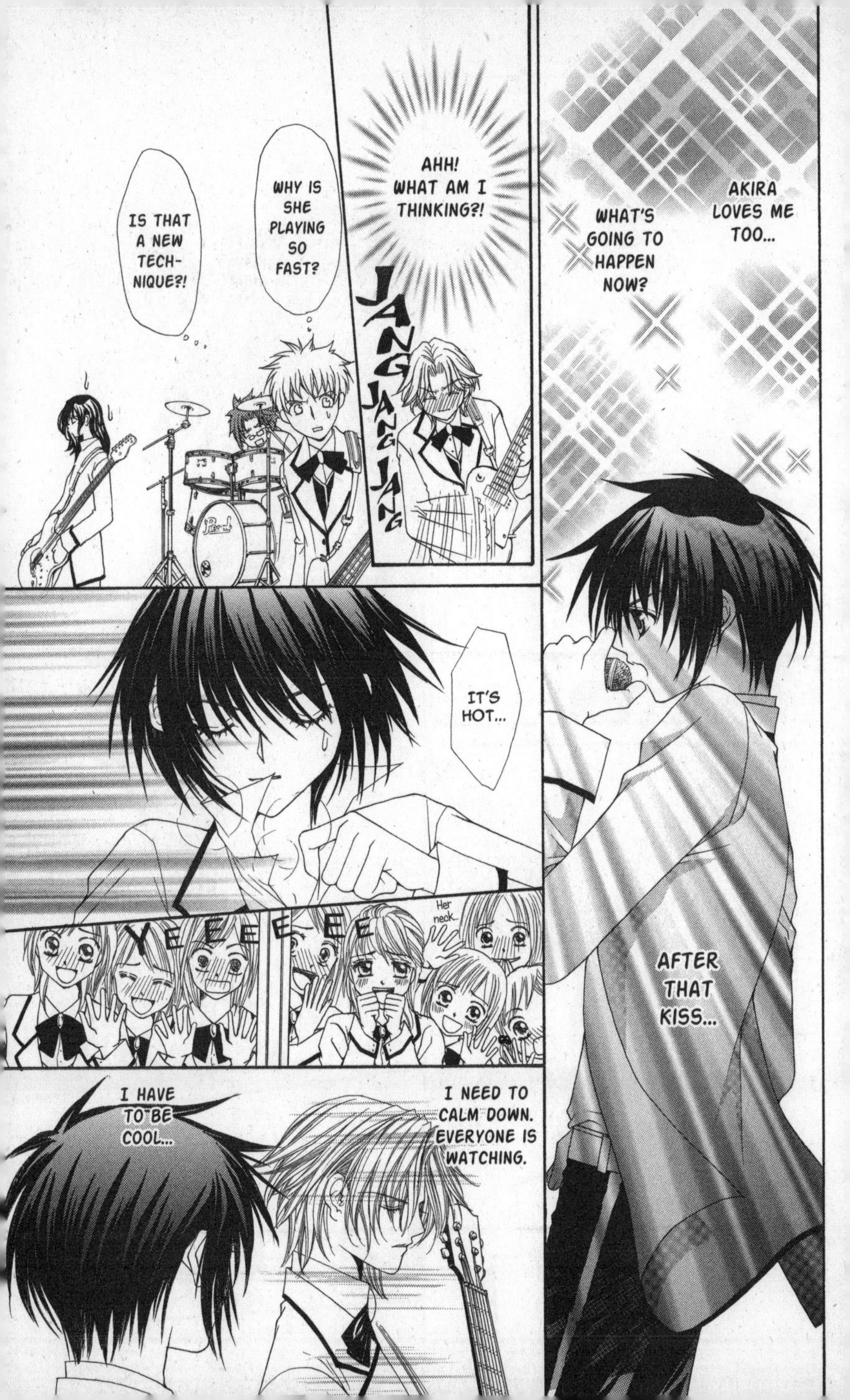
AKIRA LOVES ME TOO...
WHAT'S GOING TO HAPPEN NOW?
AFTER THAT KISS...
AHH! WHAT AM I THINKING?!
JANG JANG JANG
WHY IS SHE PLAYING SO FAST?
IS THAT A NEW TECH-NIQUE?!
IT'S HOT...
Her neck..
YEEEEEE
I NEED TO CALM DOWN. EVERYONE IS WATCHING.
I HAVE TO BE COOL...

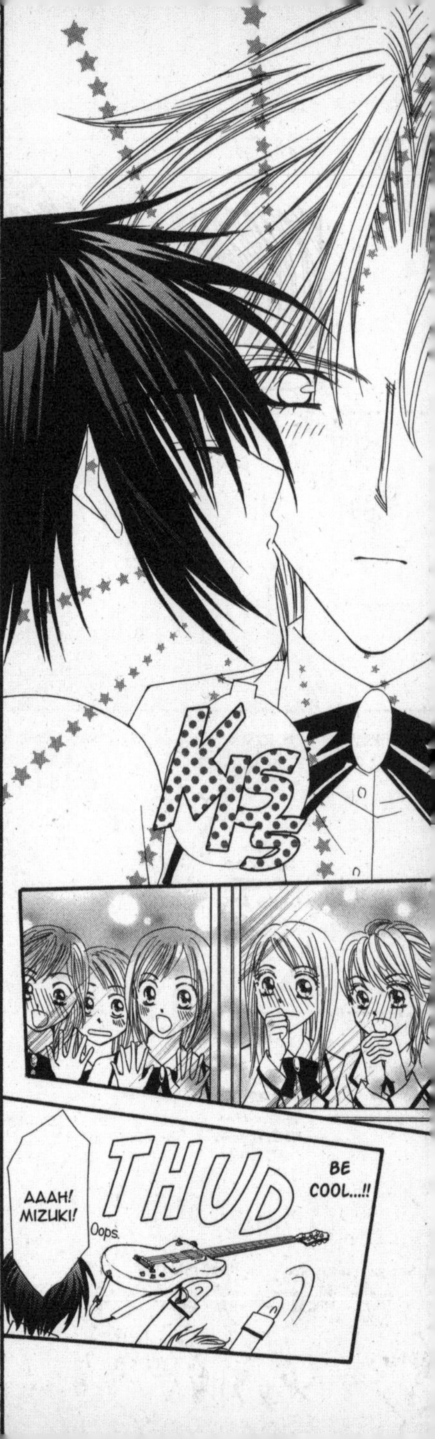
KISS
BE COOL...!!
THUD
AAAH! MIZUKI!
Oops.
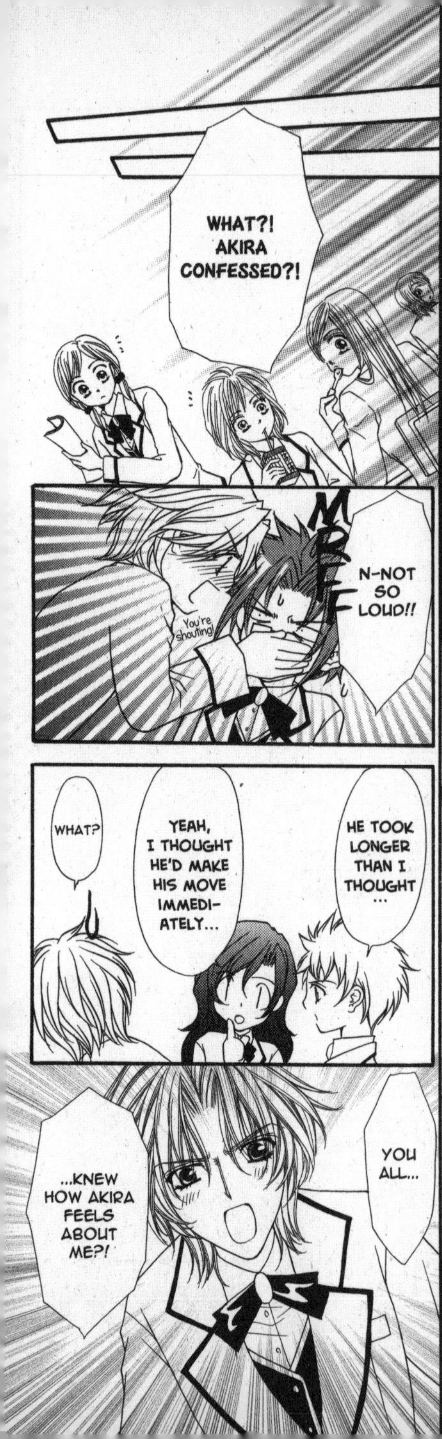
WHAT?! AKIRA CONFESSED?!
N-NOT SO LOUD!!
MRFF
You're shouting!
HE TOOK LONGER THAN I THOUGHT...
YEAH, I THOUGHT HE'D MAKE HIS MOVE IMMEDI-ATELY...
WHAT?
YOU ALL...
...KNEW HOW AKIRA FEELS ABOUT ME?!

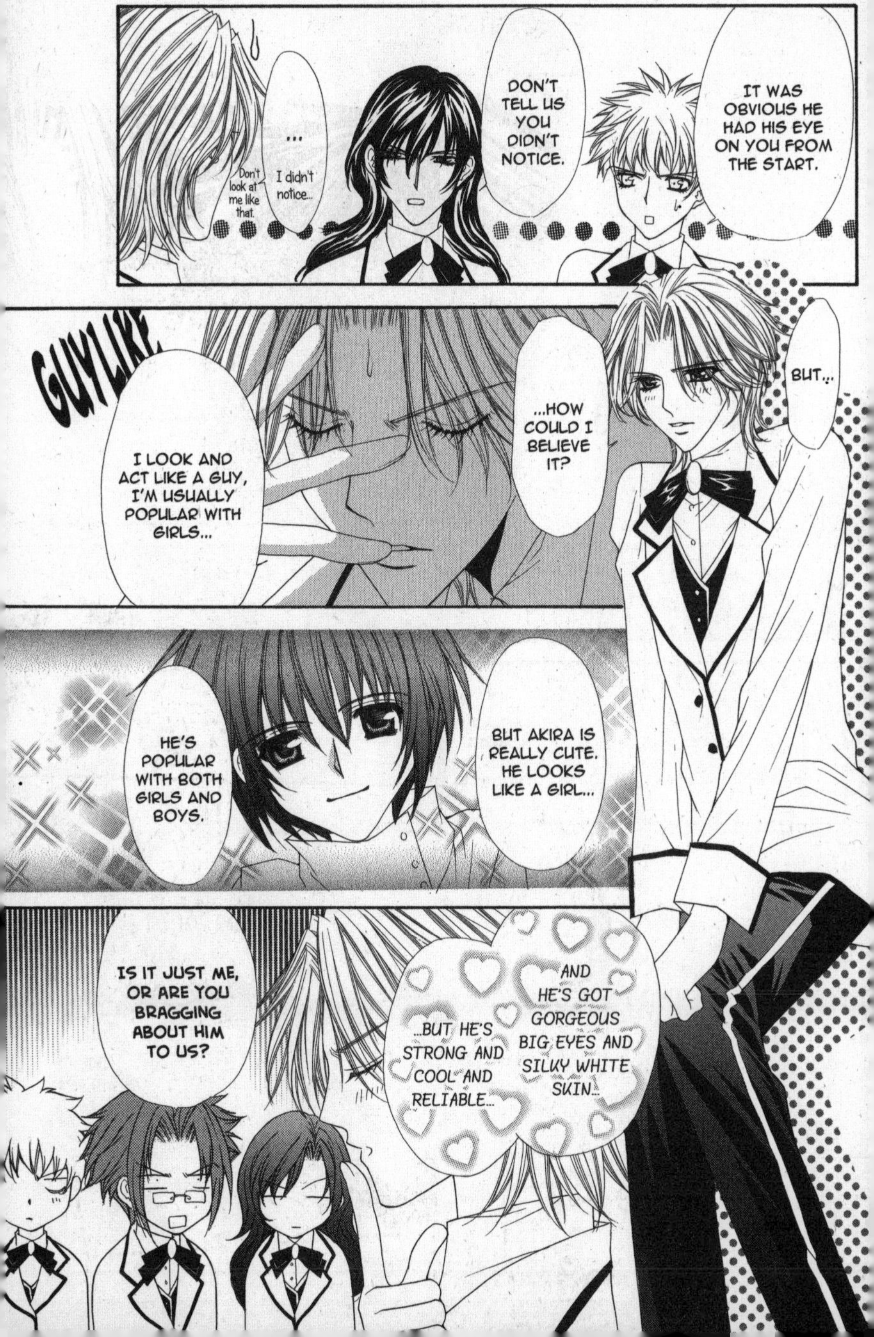
IT WAS OBVIOUS HE HAD HIS EYE ON YOU FROM THE START.
DON'T TELL US YOU DIDN'T NOTICE.
...
I didn't notice...
Don't look at me like that.
BUT...
...HOW COULD I BELIEVE IT?
GUYLIKE
I LOOK AND ACT LIKE A GUY, I'M USUALLY POPULAR WITH GIRLS...
BUT AKIRA IS REALLY CUTE. HE LOOKS LIKE A GIRL...
HE'S POPULAR WITH BOTH GIRLS AND BOYS.
AND HE'S GOT GORGEOUS BIG EYES AND SILKY WHITE SKIN...
...BUT HE'S STRONG AND COOL AND RELIABLE...
IS IT JUST ME, OR ARE YOU BRAGGING ABOUT HIM TO US?

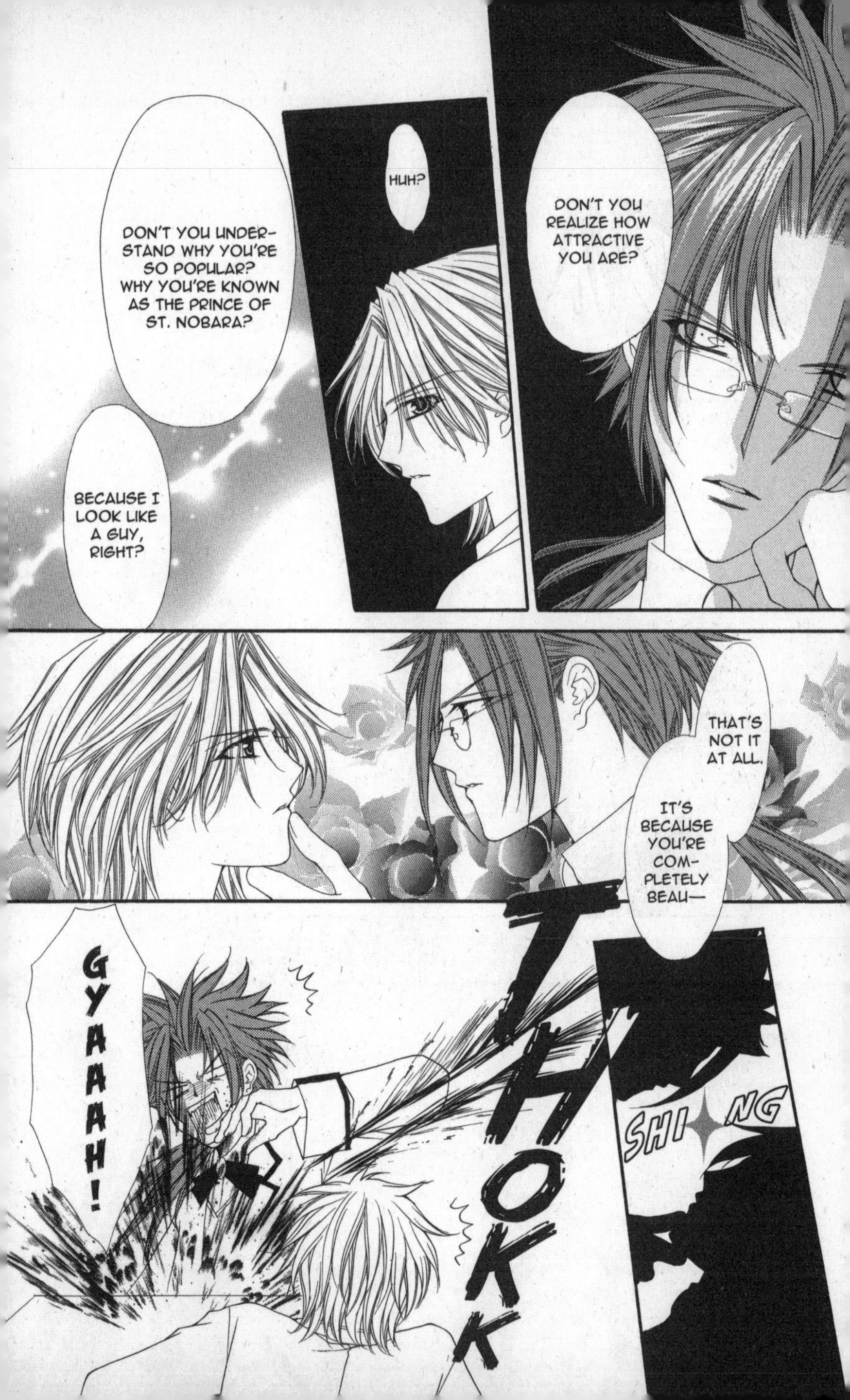
DON'T YOU REALIZE HOW ATTRACTIVE YOU ARE?
HUH?
DON'T YOU UNDER-STAND WHY YOU'RE SO POPULAR? WHY YOU'RE KNOWN AS THE PRINCE OF ST. NOBARA?
BECAUSE I LOOK LIKE A GUY, RIGHT?
THAT'S NOT IT AT ALL.
IT'S BECAUSE YOU'RE COM-PLETELY BEAU—
SHING
THOKK
GYAAAAH!

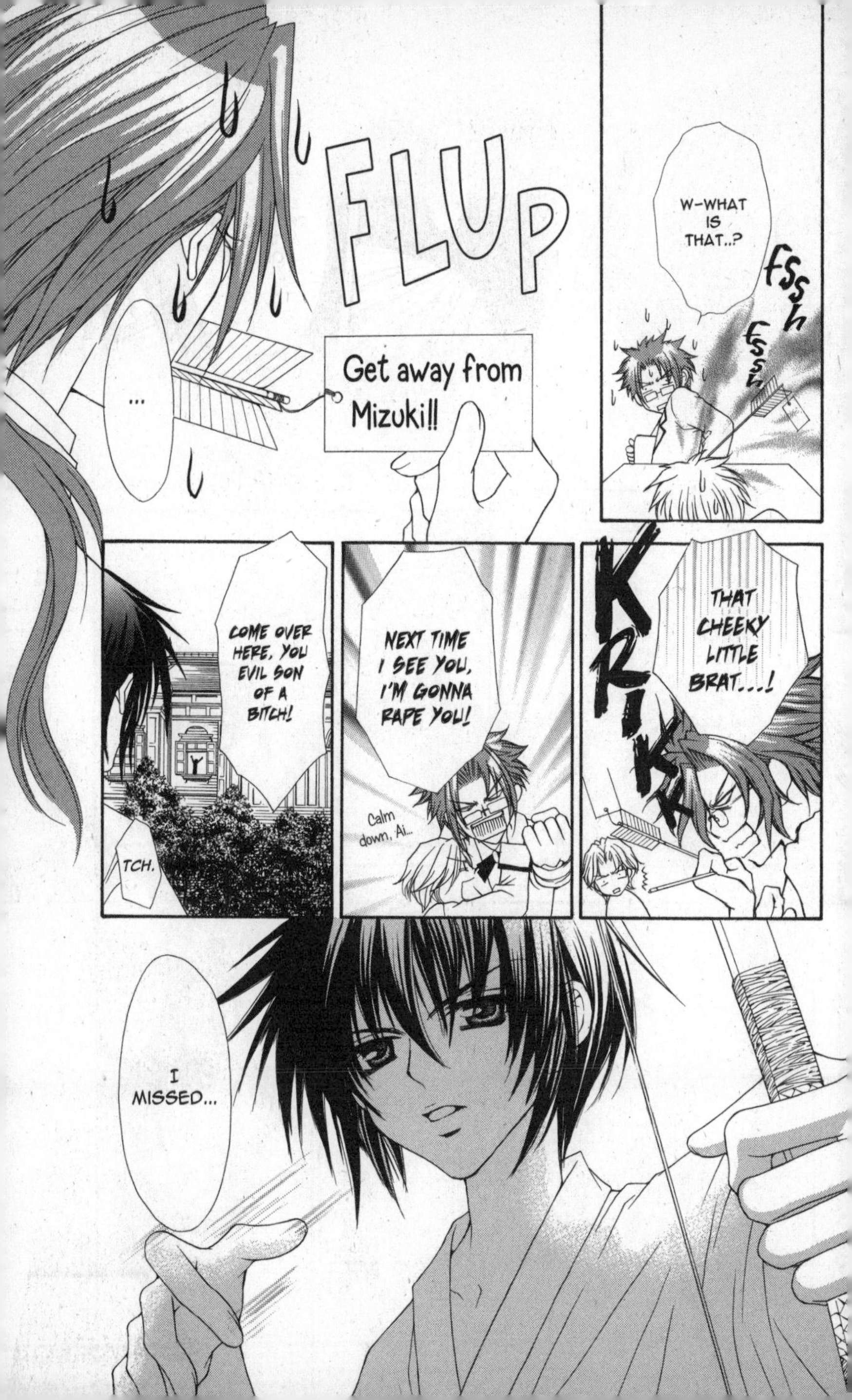
W-WHAT IS THAT..?
FSSH
FSSH
FLUP
...
Get away from Mizuki!!
KRIKK
THAT CHEEKY LITTLE BRAT...!
NEXT TIME I SEE YOU, I'M GONNA RAPE YOU!
Calm down, Ai...
COME OVER HERE, YOU EVIL SON OF A BITCH!
TCH.
I MISSED...

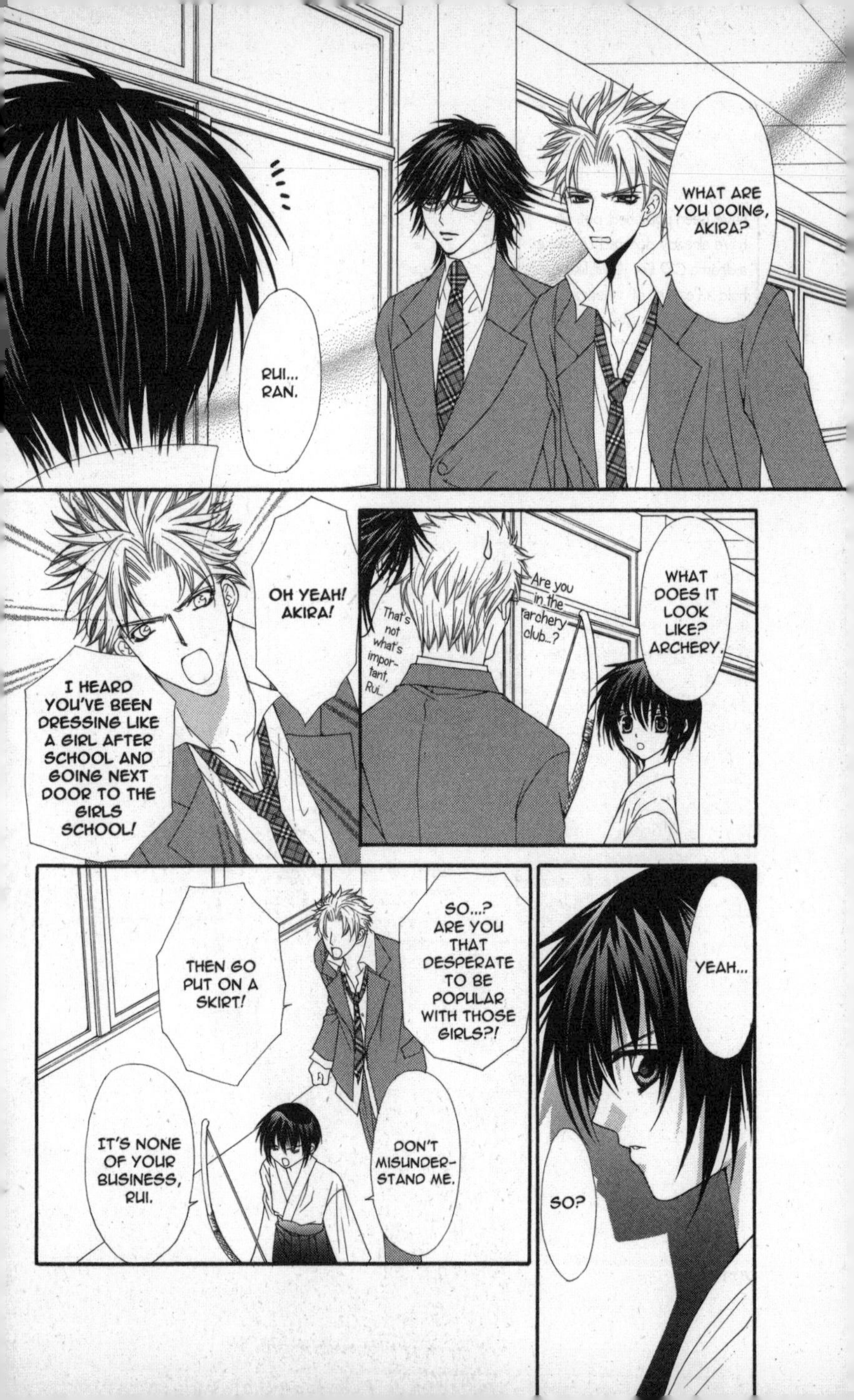
WHAT ARE YOU DOING, AKIRA?
RUI... RAN.
WHAT DOES IT LOOK LIKE? ARCHERY.
Are you in the archery club...?
That's not what's important, Rui...
OH YEAH! AKIRA!
I HEARD YOU'VE BEEN DRESSING LIKE A GIRL AFTER SCHOOL AND GOING NEXT DOOR TO THE GIRLS SCHOOL!
YEAH...
SO?
SO...? ARE YOU THAT DESPERATE TO BE POPULAR WITH THOSE GIRLS?!
THEN GO PUT ON A SKIRT!
DON'T MISUNDERSTAND ME.
IT'S NONE OF YOUR BUSINESS, RUI.

Hello!! It's Mayu Shinjo!

Only two volumes of *Ai Ore!* have been published, but we have already decided to make a drama CD for it. I'd like to hold a festival of celebration in this manga for it!! I've written about the details on another page, so please take a look at that. This drama CD has been created by a wonderful group of voice actors—but first I'd like to write a **report on the dubbing!!**

Tokyo, on a certain day... The dubbing for the *Ai Ore!* drama CD was held.

I got there early and waited for the voice actors to appear. The first person to arrive was Mitsuki Saiga, who is playing Mizuki. For a moment... I thought a handsome guy had appeared. But she's a woman! She's tall and has a very low voice. If I passed her by in town, I'd definitely think she was a man! She was a real, live Mizuki! The other famous voice actors appeared after that... And he was among them!! Soichiro Hoshi plays the role of Akira!! H-he's so cute!! (BAM)

His voice is cute too...

Together with Saiga-san they made a real Mizuki and Akira pair. Wow...

They seemed to know each other well, and the dubbing got off to a good start.

And now for the actual dubbing process...

(Continues)

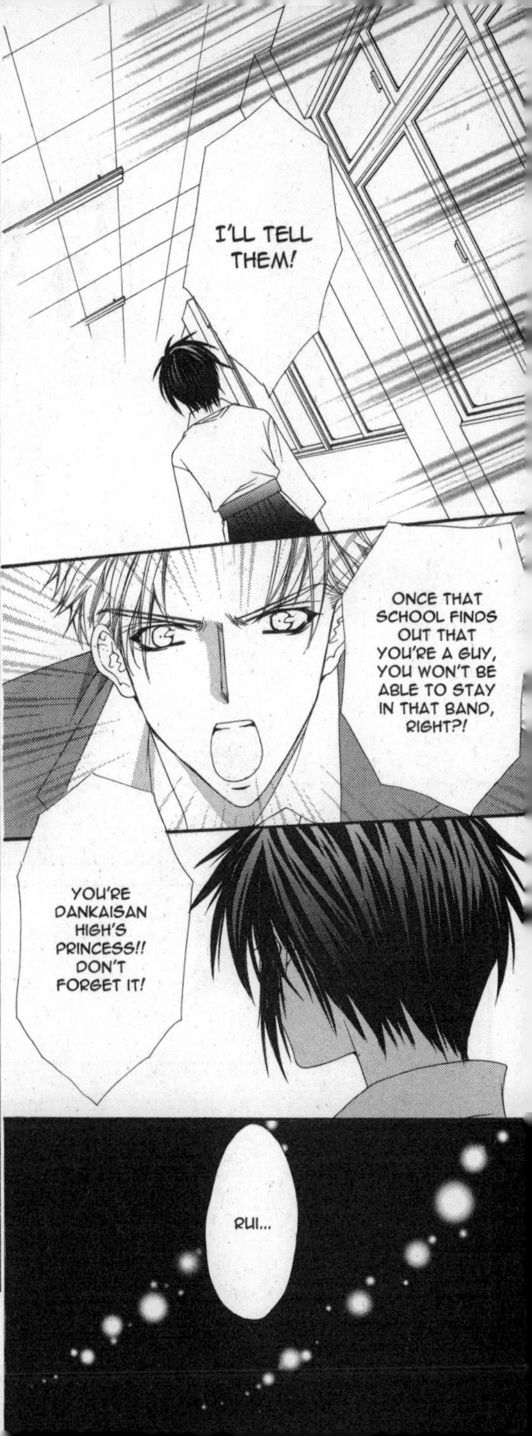
I'LL TELL THEM!
ONCE THAT SCHOOL FINDS OUT THAT YOU'RE A GUY, YOU WON'T BE ABLE TO STAY IN THAT BAND, RIGHT?!
YOU'RE DANKAISAN HIGH'S PRINCESS!! DON'T FORGET IT!
RUI...

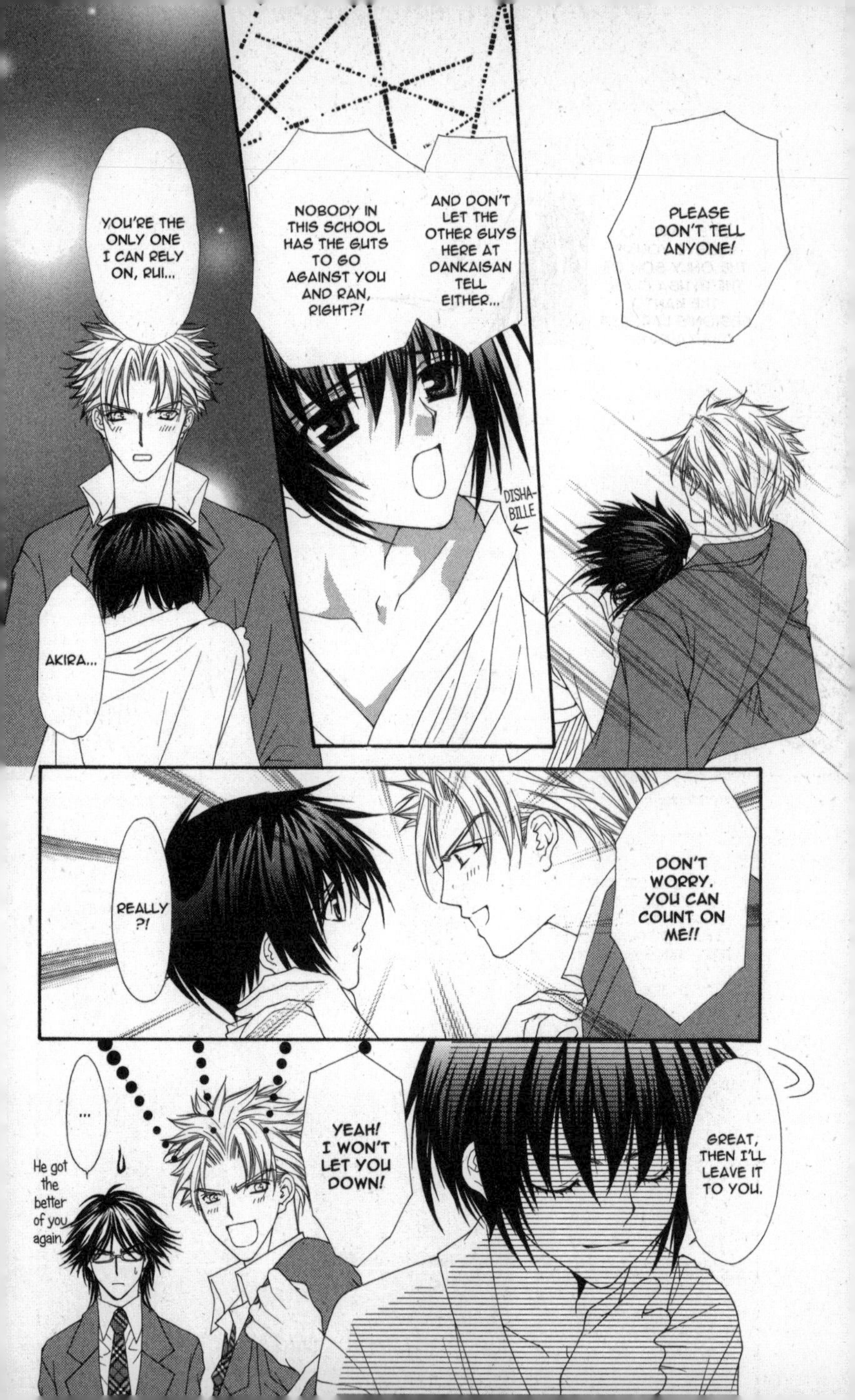
PLEASE DON'T TELL ANYONE!
AND DON'T LET THE OTHER GUYS HERE AT DANKAISAN TELL EITHER...
NOBODY IN THIS SCHOOL HAS THE GUTS TO GO AGAINST YOU AND RAN, RIGHT?!
DISHA-BILLE
YOU'RE THE ONLY ONE I CAN RELY ON, RUI...
AKIRA...
DON'T WORRY. YOU CAN COUNT ON ME!!
REALLY?!
GREAT, THEN I'LL LEAVE IT TO YOU.
YEAH! I WON'T LET YOU DOWN!
...
He got the better of you again.

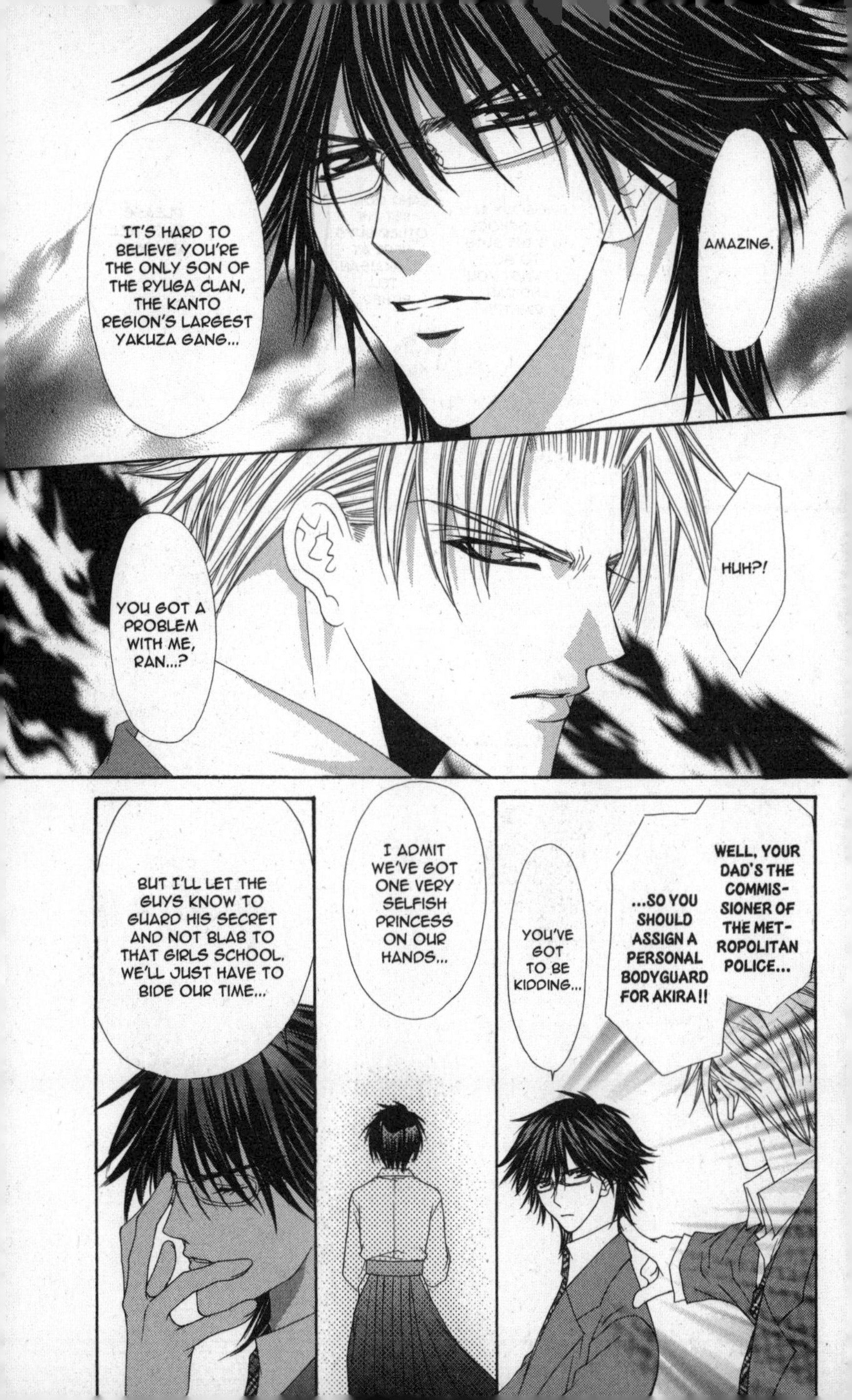
AMAZING.
IT'S HARD TO BELIEVE YOU'RE THE ONLY SON OF THE RYUGA CLAN, THE KANTO REGION'S LARGEST YAKUZA GANG...
HUH?!
YOU GOT A PROBLEM WITH ME, RAN...?
WELL, YOUR DAD'S THE COMMISSIONER OF THE METROPOLITAN POLICE...
...SO YOU SHOULD ASSIGN A PERSONAL BODYGUARD FOR AKIRA!!
YOU'VE GOT TO BE KIDDING...
I ADMIT WE'VE GOT ONE VERY SELFISH PRINCESS ON OUR HANDS...
BUT I'LL LET THE GUYS KNOW TO GUARD HIS SECRET AND NOT BLAB TO THAT GIRLS SCHOOL. WE'LL JUST HAVE TO BIDE OUR TIME...

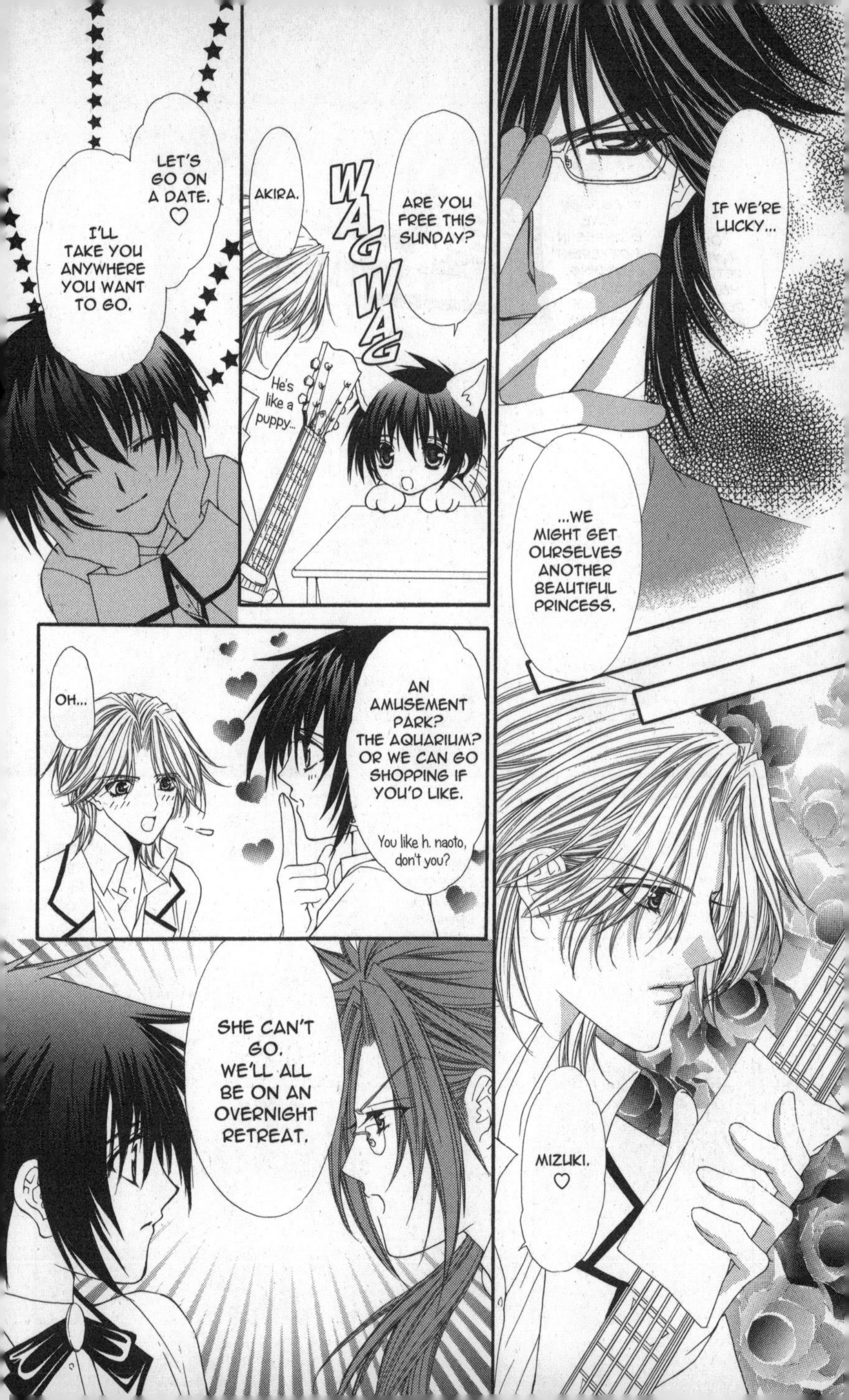
IF WE'RE LUCKY...
...WE MIGHT GET OURSELVES ANOTHER BEAUTIFUL PRINCESS.
MIZUKI. ♡
ARE YOU FREE THIS SUNDAY?
AKIRA.
WAG WAG
He's like a puppy...
LET'S GO ON A DATE. ♡
I'LL TAKE YOU ANYWHERE YOU WANT TO GO.
AN AMUSEMENT PARK? THE AQUARIUM? OR WE CAN GO SHOPPING IF YOU'D LIKE.
You like h. naoto, don't you?
OH...
SHE CAN'T GO. WE'LL ALL BE ON AN OVERNIGHT RETREAT.

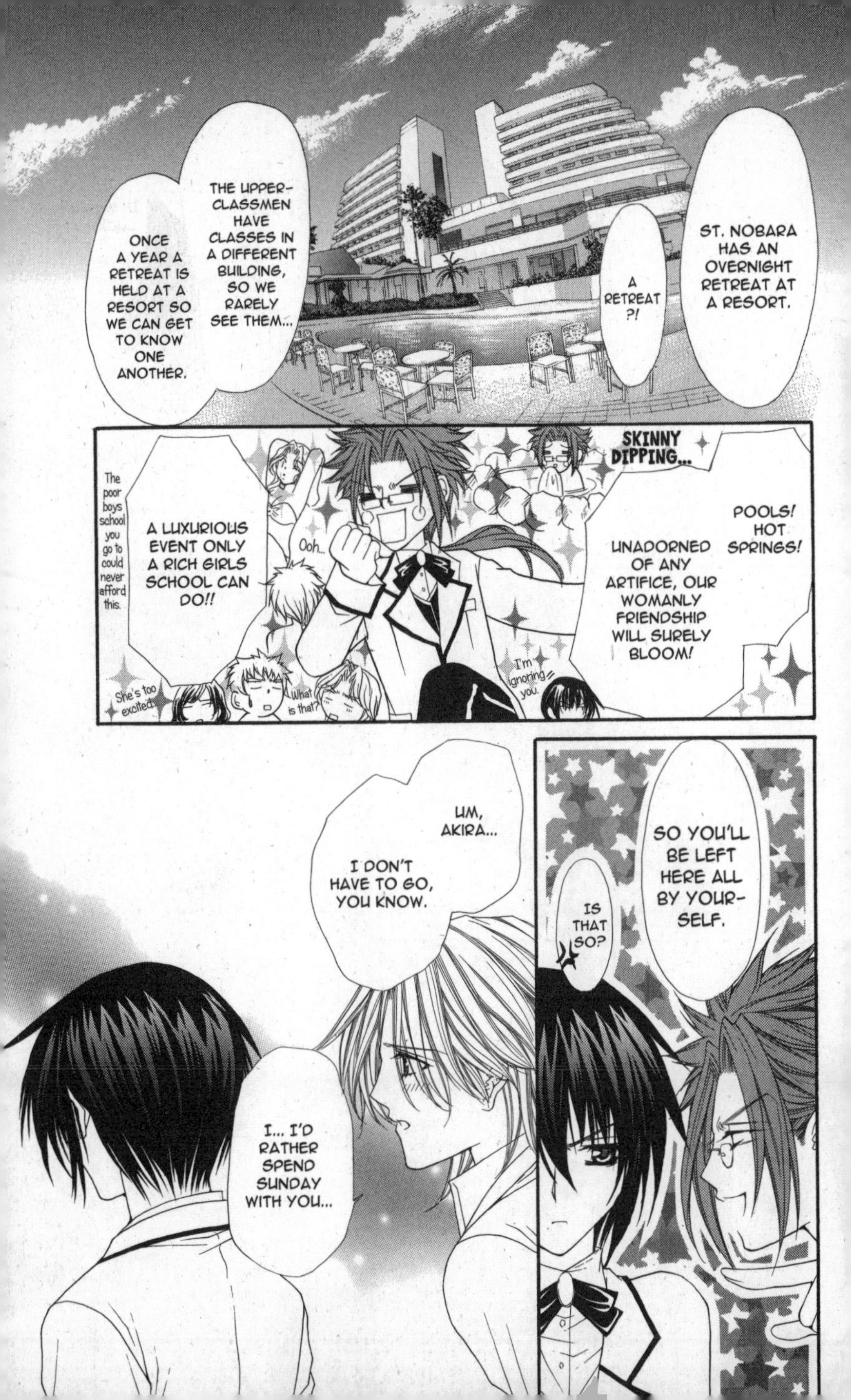
ST. NOBARA HAS AN OVERNIGHT RETREAT AT A RESORT.
A RETREAT?!
THE UPPER-CLASSMEN HAVE CLASSES IN A DIFFERENT BUILDING, SO WE RARELY SEE THEM...
ONCE A YEAR A RETREAT IS HELD AT A RESORT SO WE CAN GET TO KNOW ONE ANOTHER.
SKINNY DIPPING...
POOLS! HOT SPRINGS!
UNADORNED OF ANY ARTIFICE, OUR WOMANLY FRIENDSHIP WILL SURELY BLOOM!
I'm ignoring you.
A LUXURIOUS EVENT ONLY A RICH GIRLS SCHOOL CAN DO!!
Ooh...
The poor boys school you go to could never afford this.
What is that?
She's too excited.
SO YOU'LL BE LEFT HERE ALL BY YOUR-SELF.
IS THAT SO?
UM, AKIRA...
I DON'T HAVE TO GO, YOU KNOW.
I... I'D RATHER SPEND SUNDAY WITH YOU...

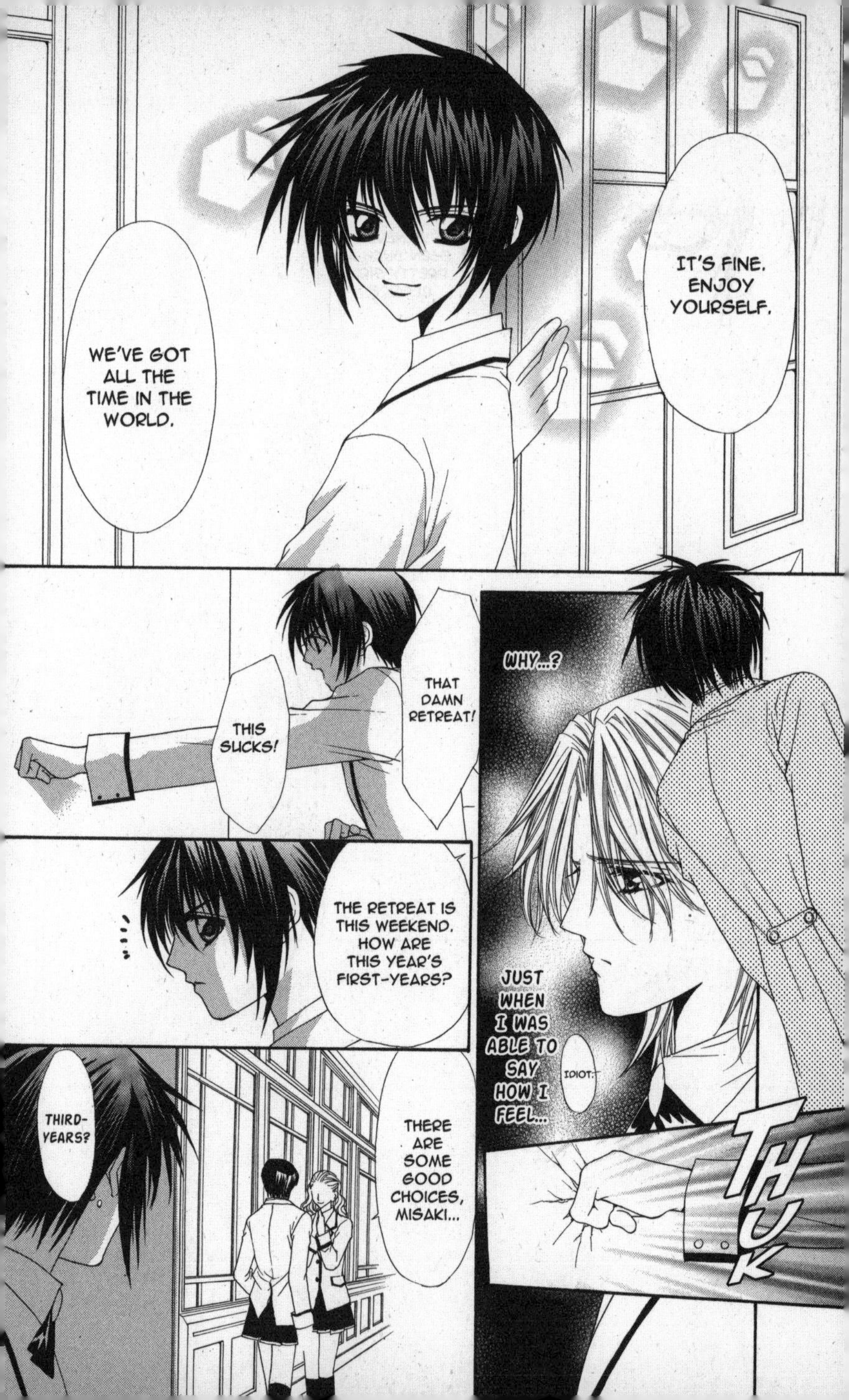
IT'S FINE. ENJOY YOURSELF.
WE'VE GOT ALL THE TIME IN THE WORLD.
WHY...?
JUST WHEN I WAS ABLE TO SAY HOW I FEEL...
IDIOT.
THUK
THAT DAMN RETREAT!
THIS SUCKS!
THE RETREAT IS THIS WEEKEND. HOW ARE THIS YEAR'S FIRST-YEARS?
...
THERE ARE SOME GOOD CHOICES, MISAKI...
THIRD-YEARS?

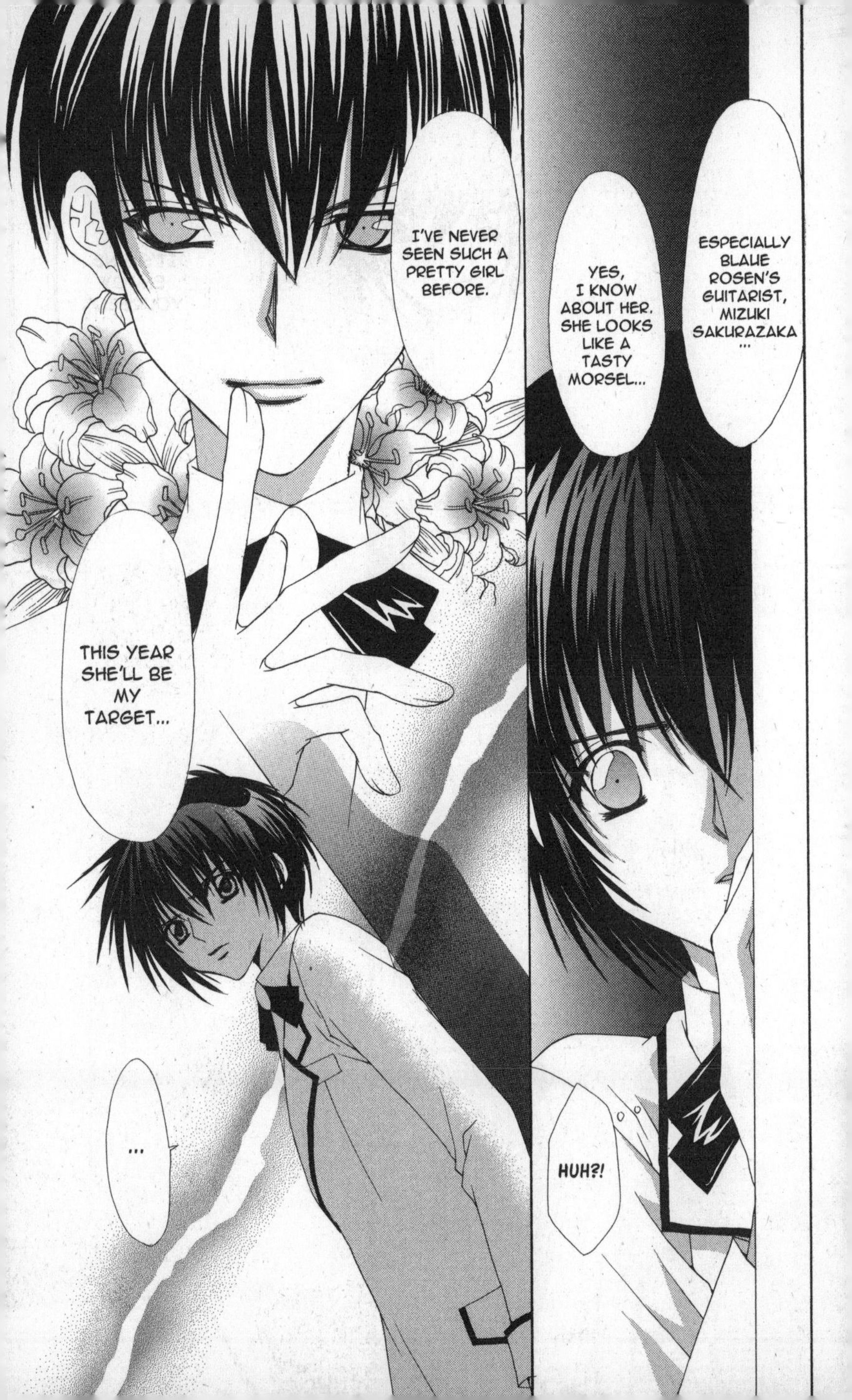
ESPECIALLY BLAUE ROSEN'S GUITARIST, MIZUKI SAKURAZAKA...
YES, I KNOW ABOUT HER. SHE LOOKS LIKE A TASTY MORSEL...
HUH?!
I'VE NEVER SEEN SUCH A PRETTY GIRL BEFORE.
THIS YEAR SHE'LL BE MY TARGET...
...

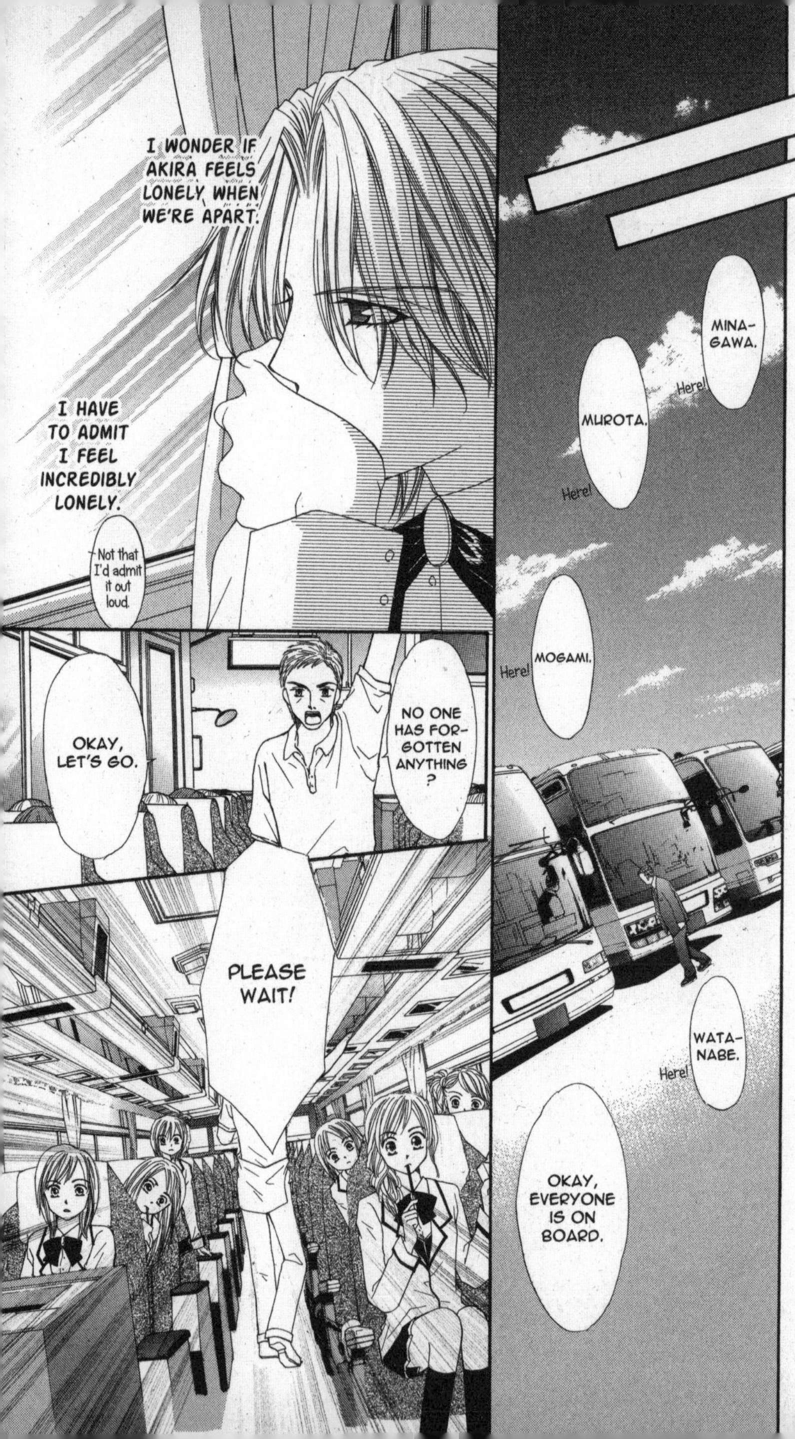
MINA-GAWA.
Here!
MUROTA.
Here!
MOGAMI.
Here!
WATA-NABE.
Here!
OKAY, EVERYONE IS ON BOARD.
I WONDER IF AKIRA FEELS LONELY WHEN WE'RE APART.
I HAVE TO ADMIT I FEEL INCREDIBLY LONELY.
Not that I'd admit it out loud.
NO ONE HAS FOR-GOTTEN ANYTHING?
OKAY, LET'S GO.
PLEASE WAIT!

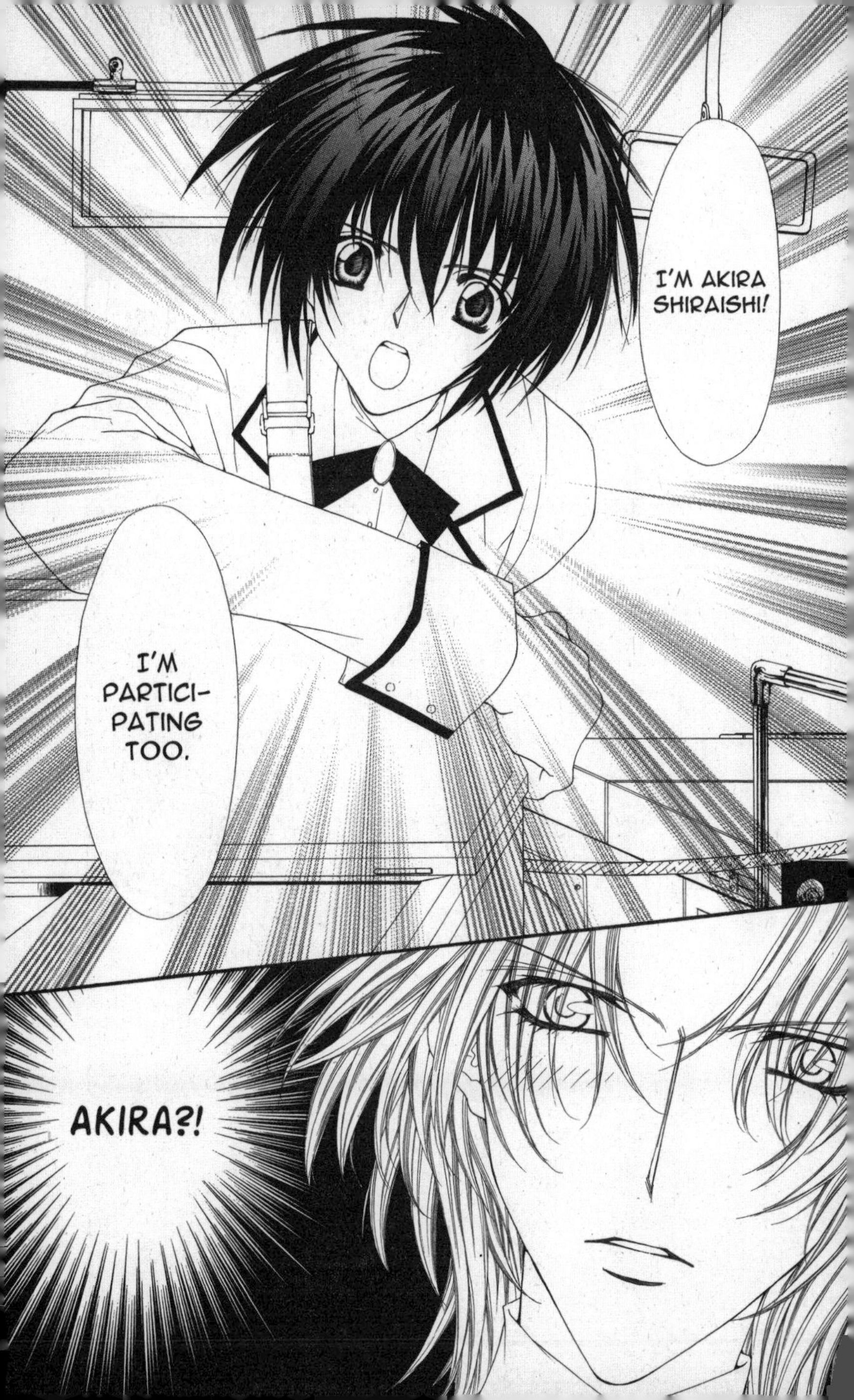
I'M AKIRA SHIRAISHI!
I'M PARTICI-PATING TOO.
AKIRA?!

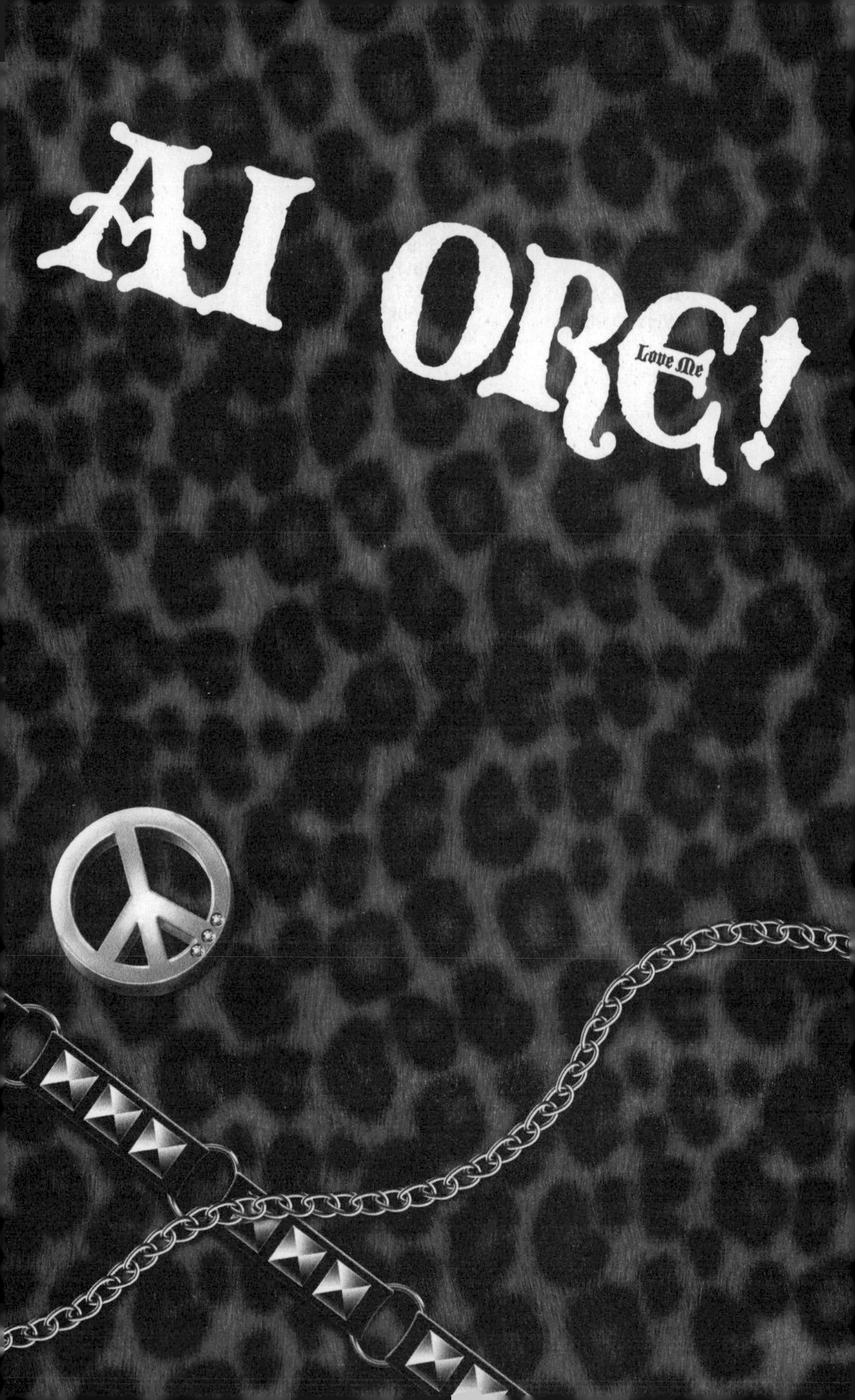
AI ORE!
Love Me

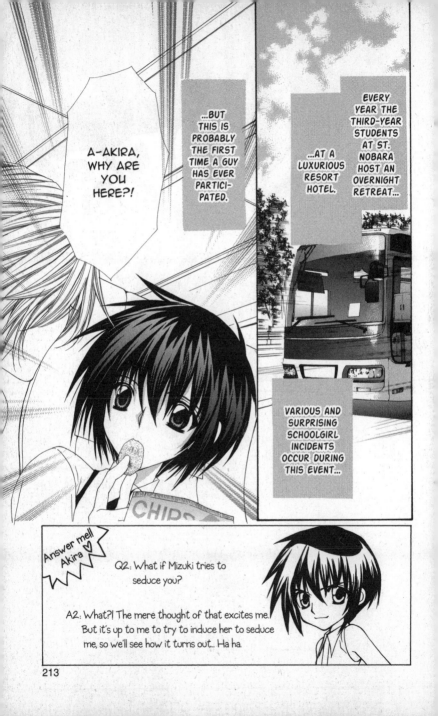

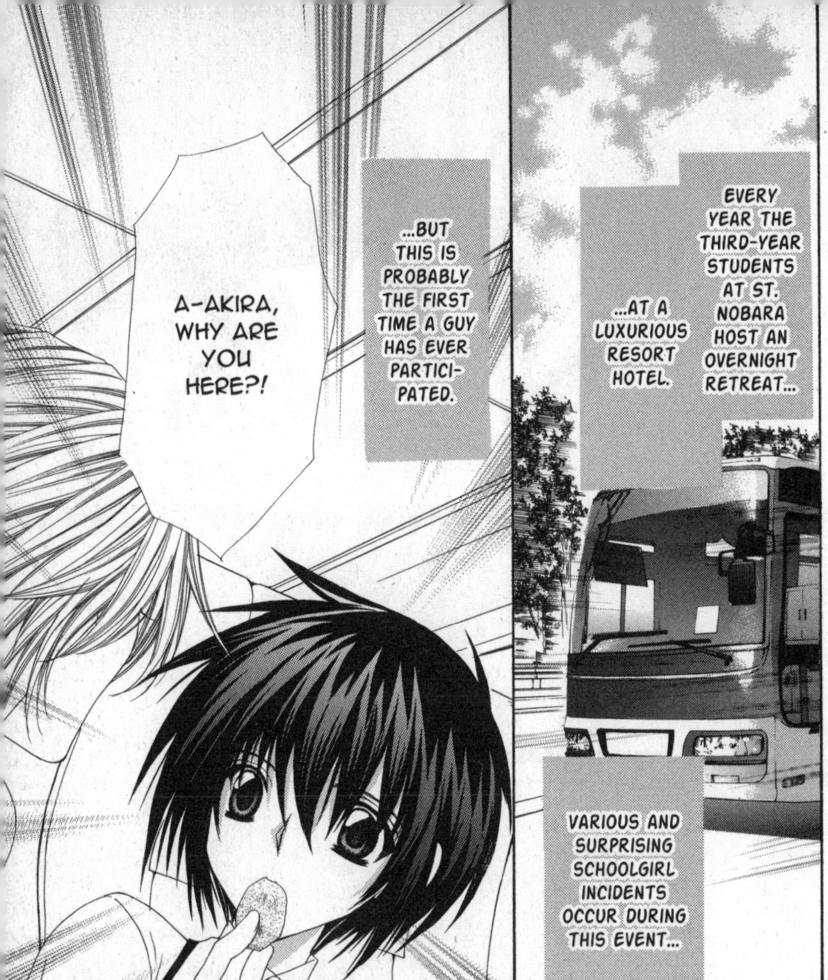
EVERY YEAR THE THIRD-YEAR STUDENTS AT ST. NOBARA HOST AN OVERNIGHT RETREAT...
...AT A LUXURIOUS RESORT HOTEL.
VARIOUS AND SURPRISING SCHOOLGIRL INCIDENTS OCCUR DURING THIS EVENT...
...BUT THIS IS PROBABLY THE FIRST TIME A GUY HAS EVER PARTICIPATED.
A-AKIRA, WHY ARE YOU HERE?!

Answer me!! Akira ♡

Q2: What if Mizuki tries to seduce you?

A2: What?! The mere thought of that excites me. But it's up to me to try to induce her to seduce me, so we'll see how it turns out... Ha ha.

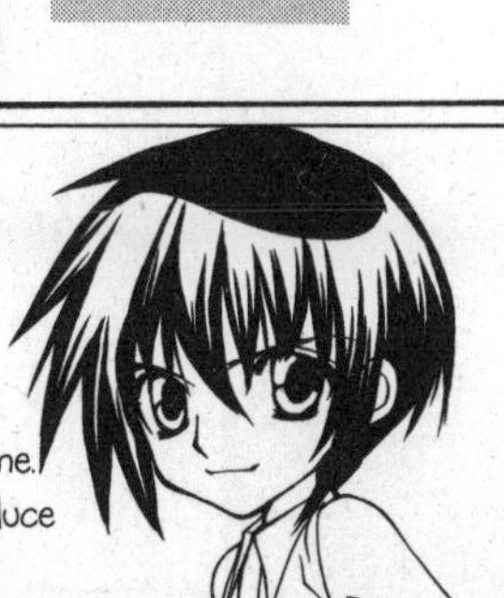

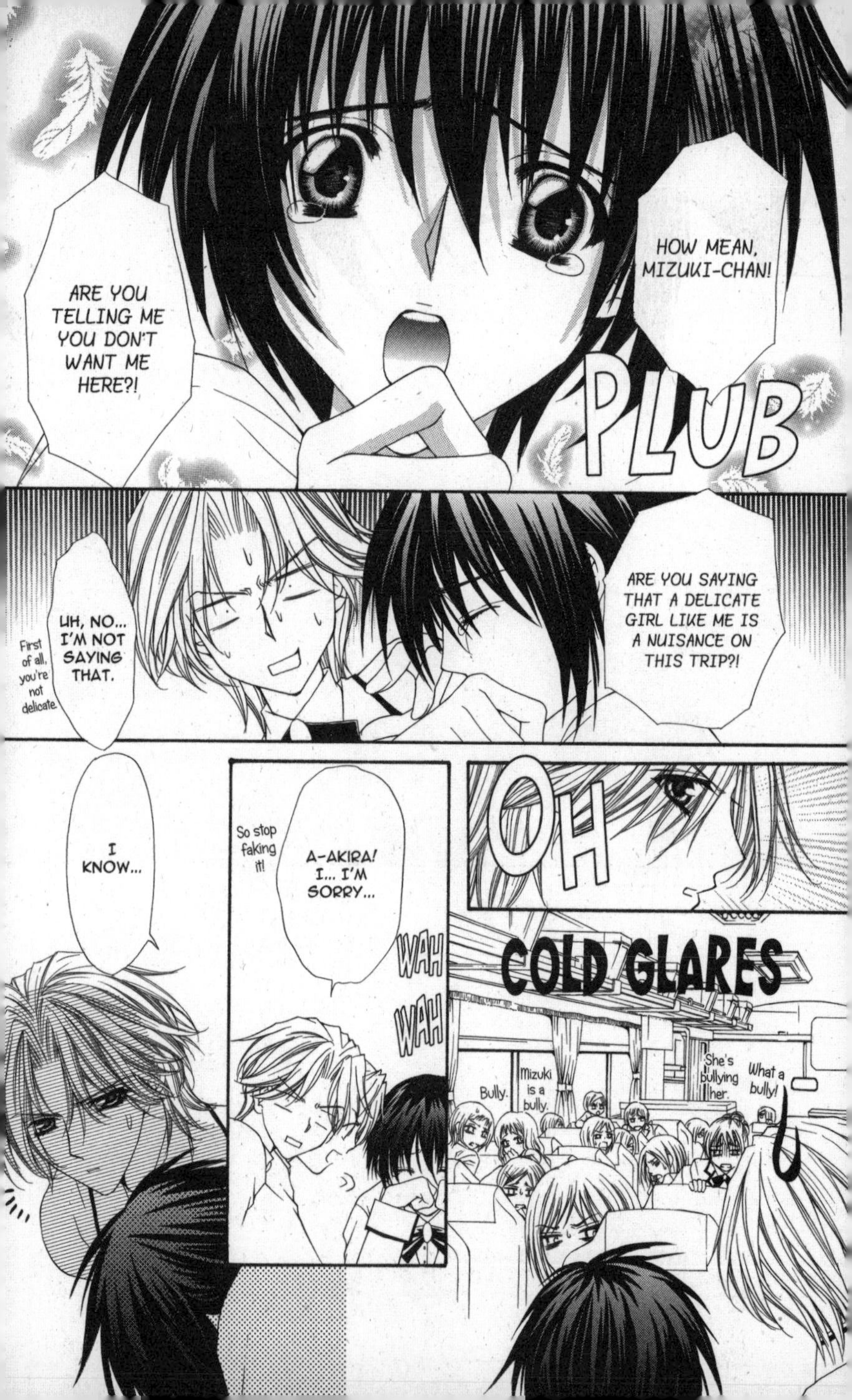
HOW MEAN, MIZUKI-CHAN!
ARE YOU TELLING ME YOU DON'T WANT ME HERE?!
PLUB
ARE YOU SAYING THAT A DELICATE GIRL LIKE ME IS A NUISANCE ON THIS TRIP?!
UH, NO... I'M NOT SAYING THAT.
First of all, you're not delicate.
OH
COLD GLARES
What a bully!
She's bullying her.
Mizuki is a bully.
Bully.
A-AKIRA! I... I'M SORRY...
So stop faking it!
WAH
WAH
I KNOW...

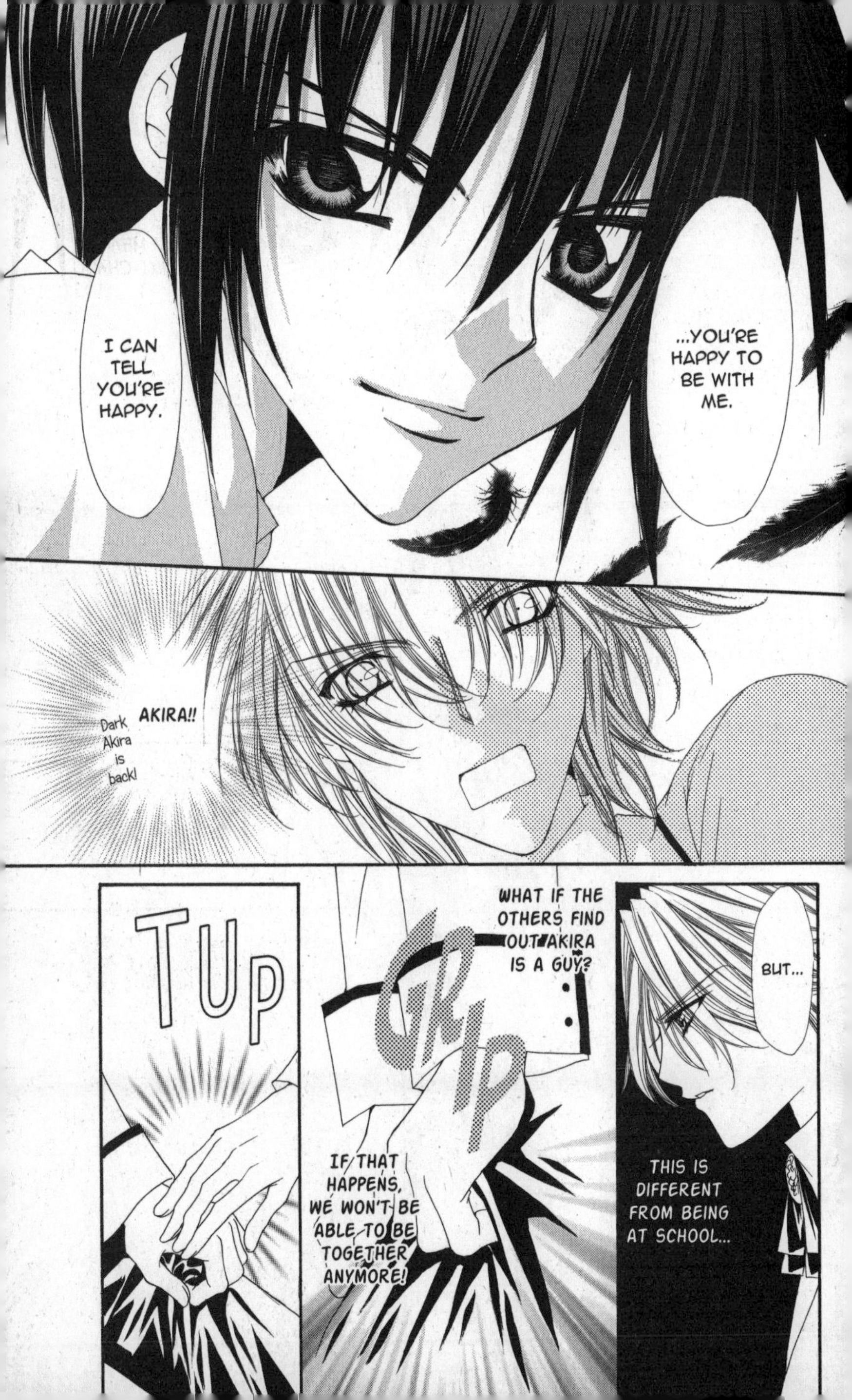
...YOU'RE HAPPY TO BE WITH ME.
I CAN TELL YOU'RE HAPPY.
AKIRA!!
Dark Akira is back!
BUT...
THIS IS DIFFERENT FROM BEING AT SCHOOL...
WHAT IF THE OTHERS FIND OUT AKIRA IS A GUY?
GRIP
IF THAT HAPPENS, WE WON'T BE ABLE TO BE TOGETHER ANYMORE!
TUP

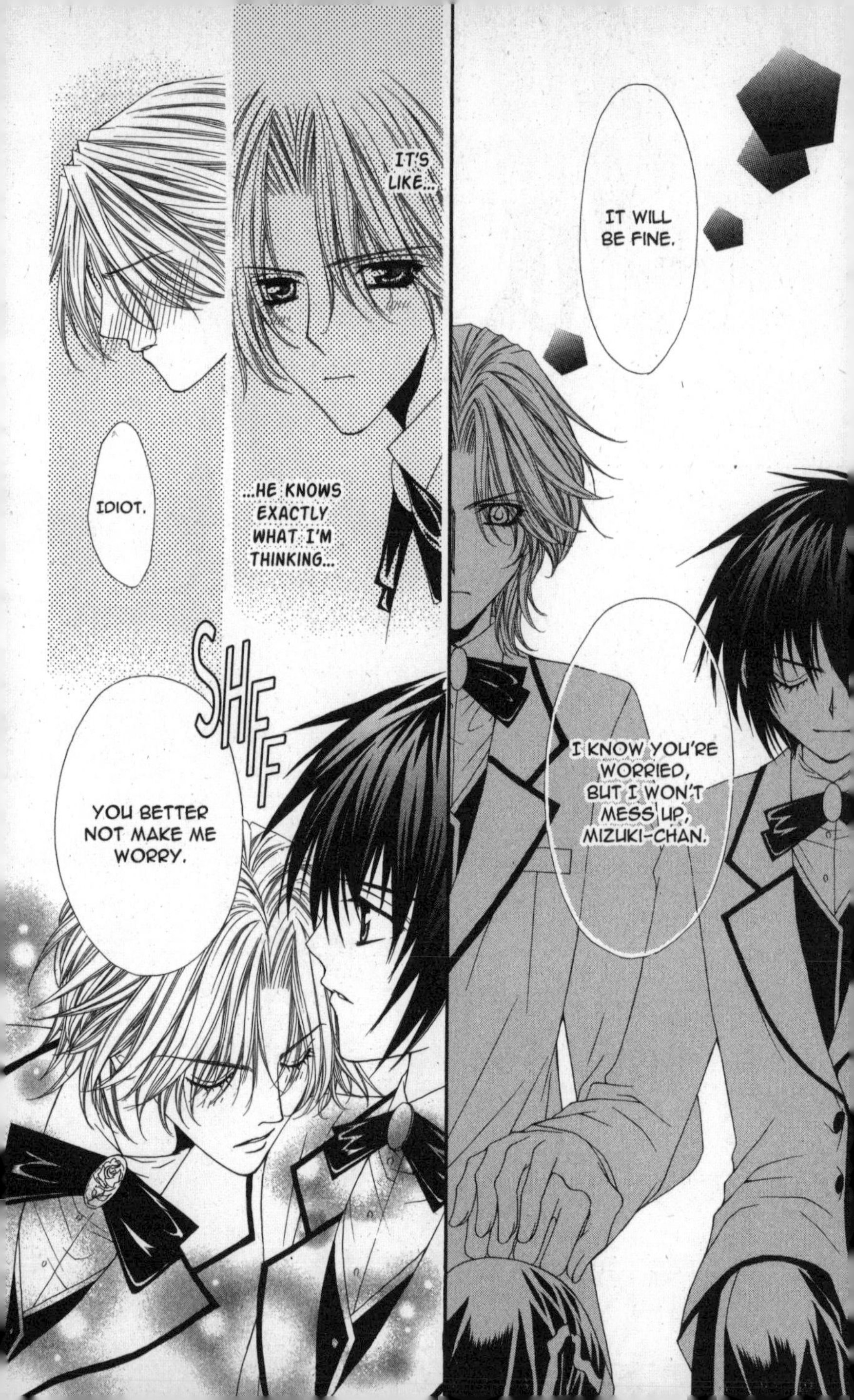
IT WILL BE FINE.
I KNOW YOU'RE WORRIED, BUT I WON'T MESS UP, MIZUKI-CHAN.
IT'S LIKE...
...HE KNOWS EXACTLY WHAT I'M THINKING...
IDIOT.
SHFF
YOU BETTER NOT MAKE ME WORRY.

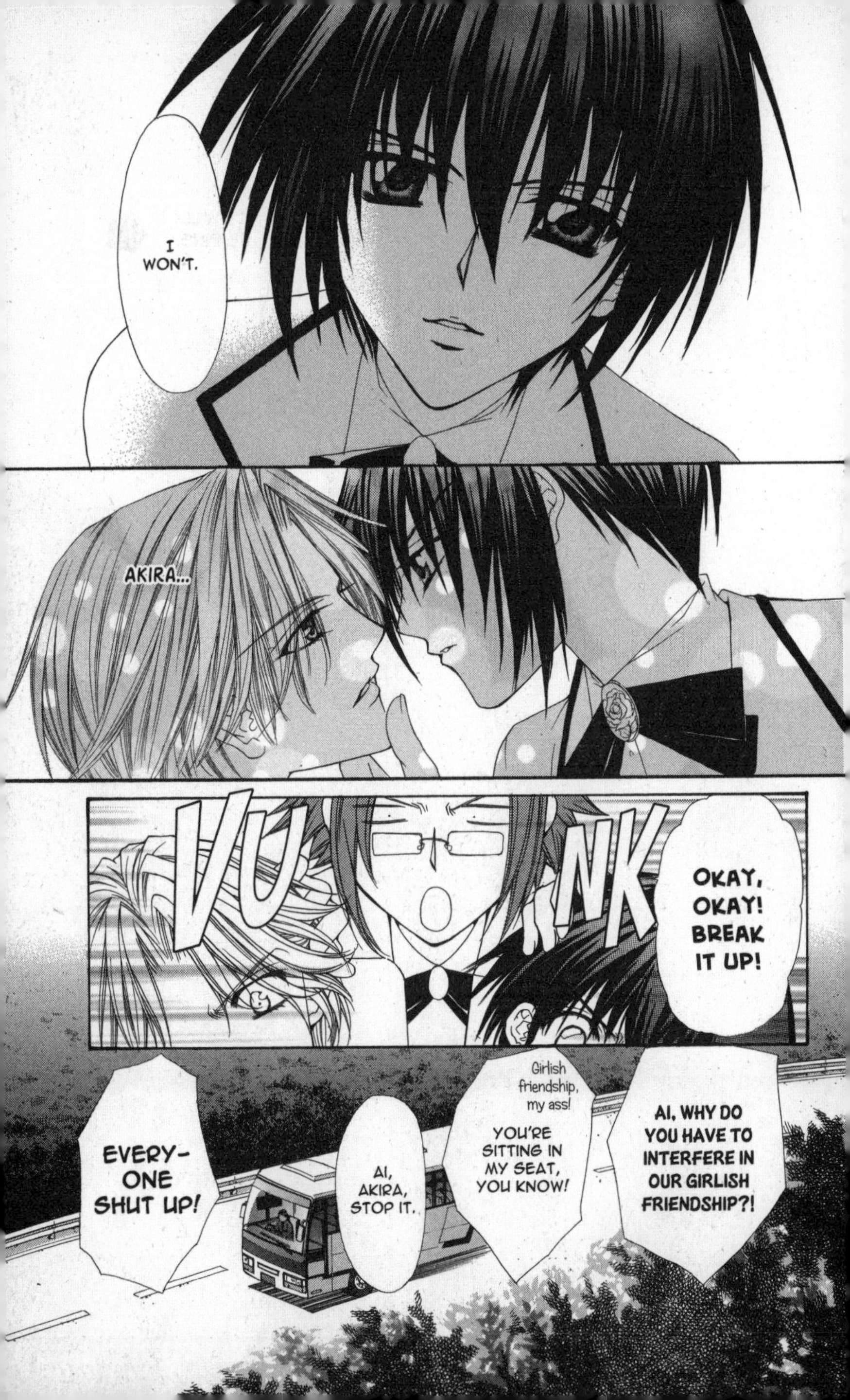
I WON'T.
AKIRA...
OKAY, OKAY! BREAK IT UP!
VUNK
AI, WHY DO YOU HAVE TO INTERFERE IN OUR GIRLISH FRIENDSHIP?!
Girlish friendship, my ass!
YOU'RE SITTING IN MY SEAT, YOU KNOW!
AI, AKIRA, STOP IT.
EVERY-ONE SHUT UP!

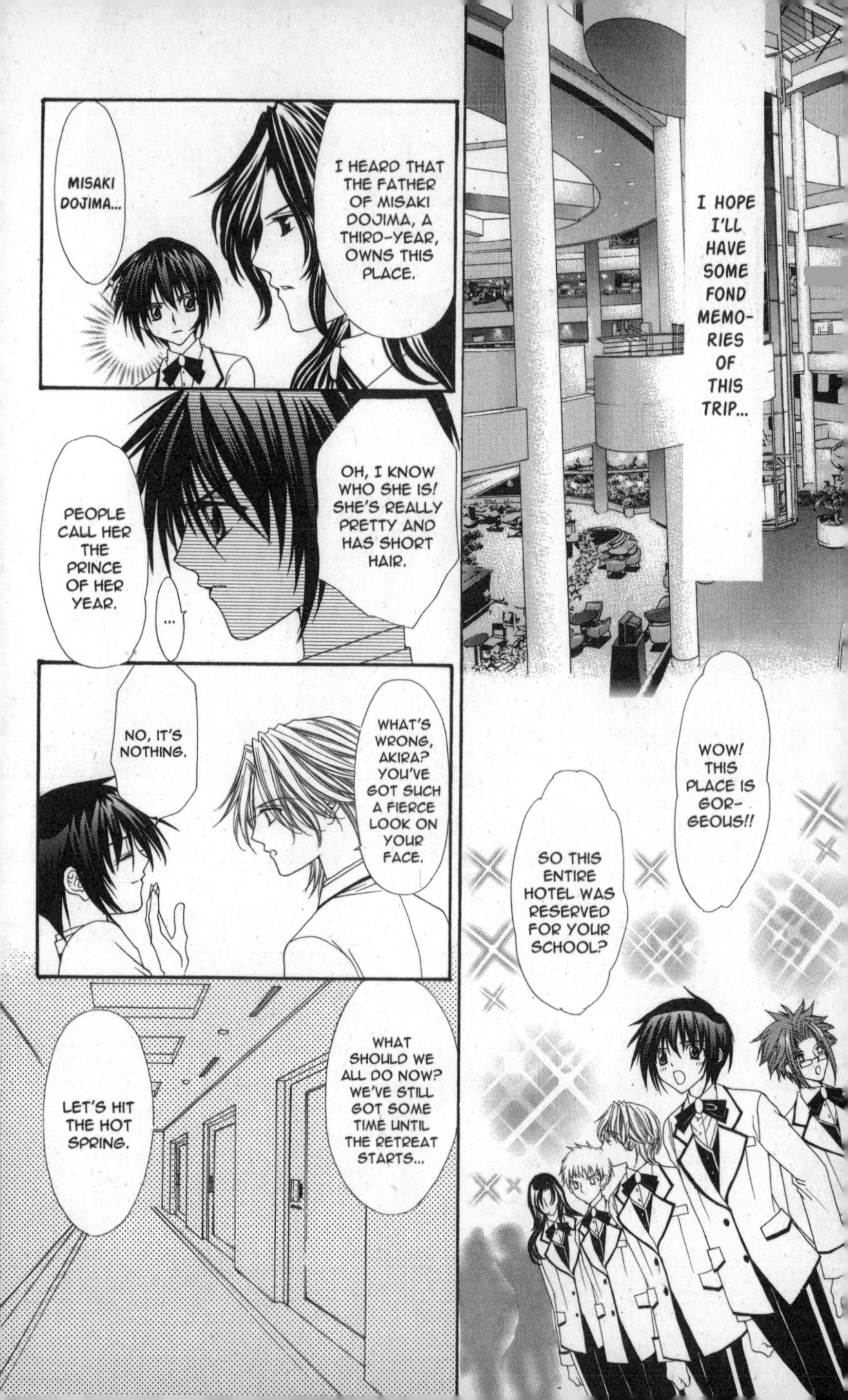
I HOPE I'LL HAVE SOME FOND MEMO-RIES OF THIS TRIP...
WOW! THIS PLACE IS GOR-GEOUS!!
SO THIS ENTIRE HOTEL WAS RESERVED FOR YOUR SCHOOL?
I HEARD THAT THE FATHER OF MISAKI DOJIMA, A THIRD-YEAR, OWNS THIS PLACE.
MISAKI DOJIMA...
OH, I KNOW WHO SHE IS! SHE'S REALLY PRETTY AND HAS SHORT HAIR.
PEOPLE CALL HER THE PRINCE OF HER YEAR.
...
WHAT'S WRONG, AKIRA? YOU'VE GOT SUCH A FIERCE LOOK ON YOUR FACE.
NO, IT'S NOTHING.
WHAT SHOULD WE ALL DO NOW? WE'VE STILL GOT SOME TIME UNTIL THE RETREAT STARTS...
LET'S HIT THE HOT SPRING.

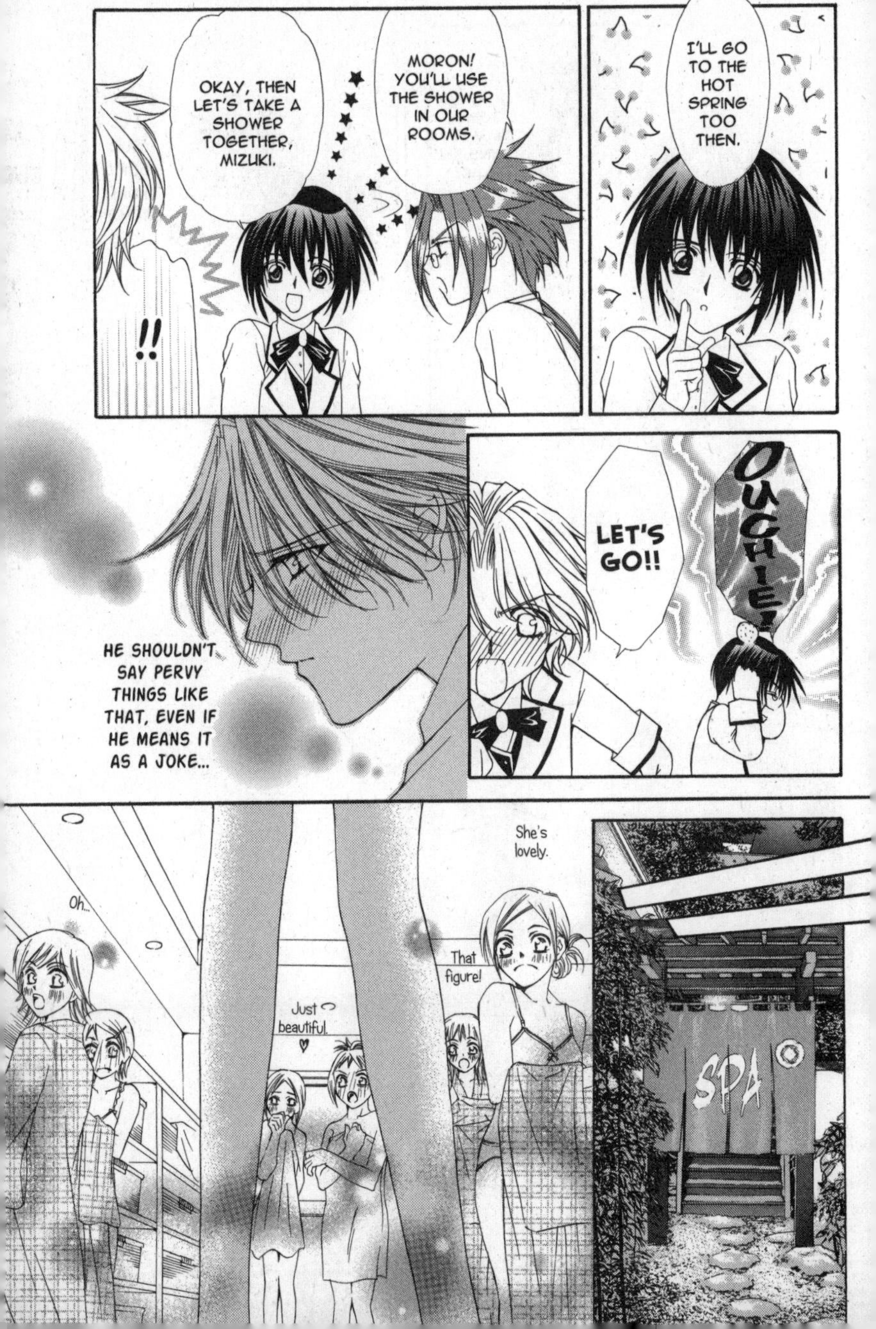

I'LL GO TO THE HOT SPRING TOO THEN.
MORON! YOU'LL USE THE SHOWER IN OUR ROOMS.
OKAY, THEN LET'S TAKE A SHOWER TOGETHER, MIZUKI.
!!
OUCHIE!
LET'S GO!!
HE SHOULDN'T SAY PERVY THINGS LIKE THAT, EVEN IF HE MEANS IT AS A JOKE...
SPA
She's lovely.
That figure!
Just beautiful.
Oh...

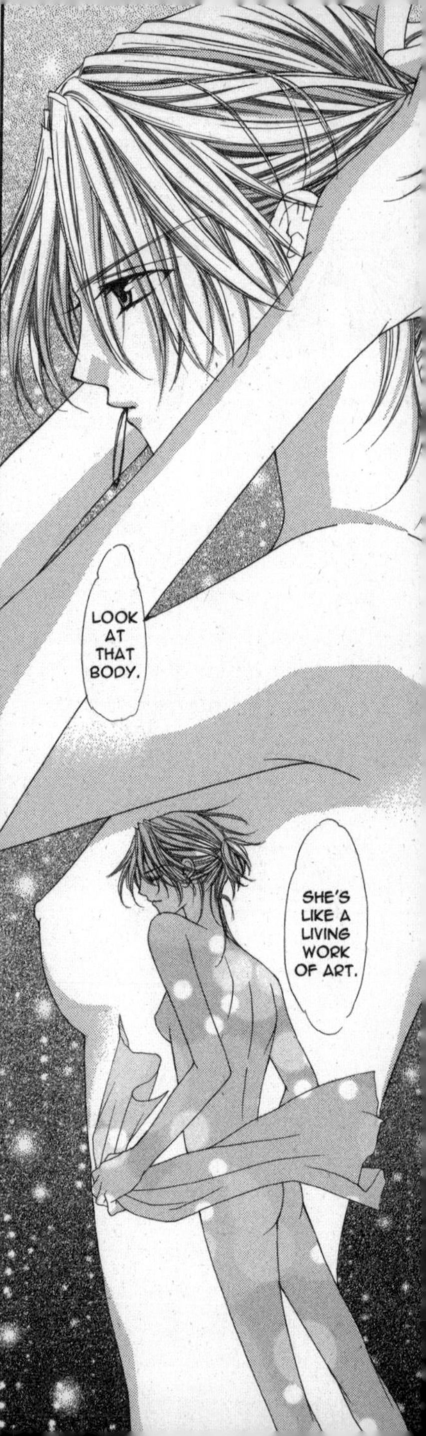
LOOK AT THAT BODY.
SHE'S LIKE A LIVING WORK OF ART.

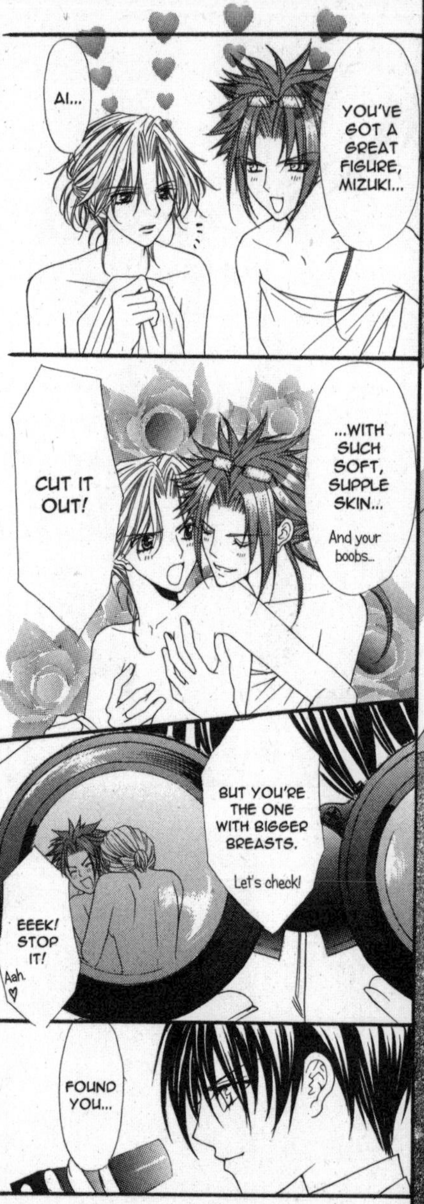
YOU'VE GOT A GREAT FIGURE, MIZUKI...
AI...
...WITH SUCH SOFT, SUPPLE SKIN...
And your boobs...
CUT IT OUT!
BUT YOU'RE THE ONE WITH BIGGER BREASTS.
Let's check!
EEEK! STOP IT!
Aah. ♥
FOUND YOU...

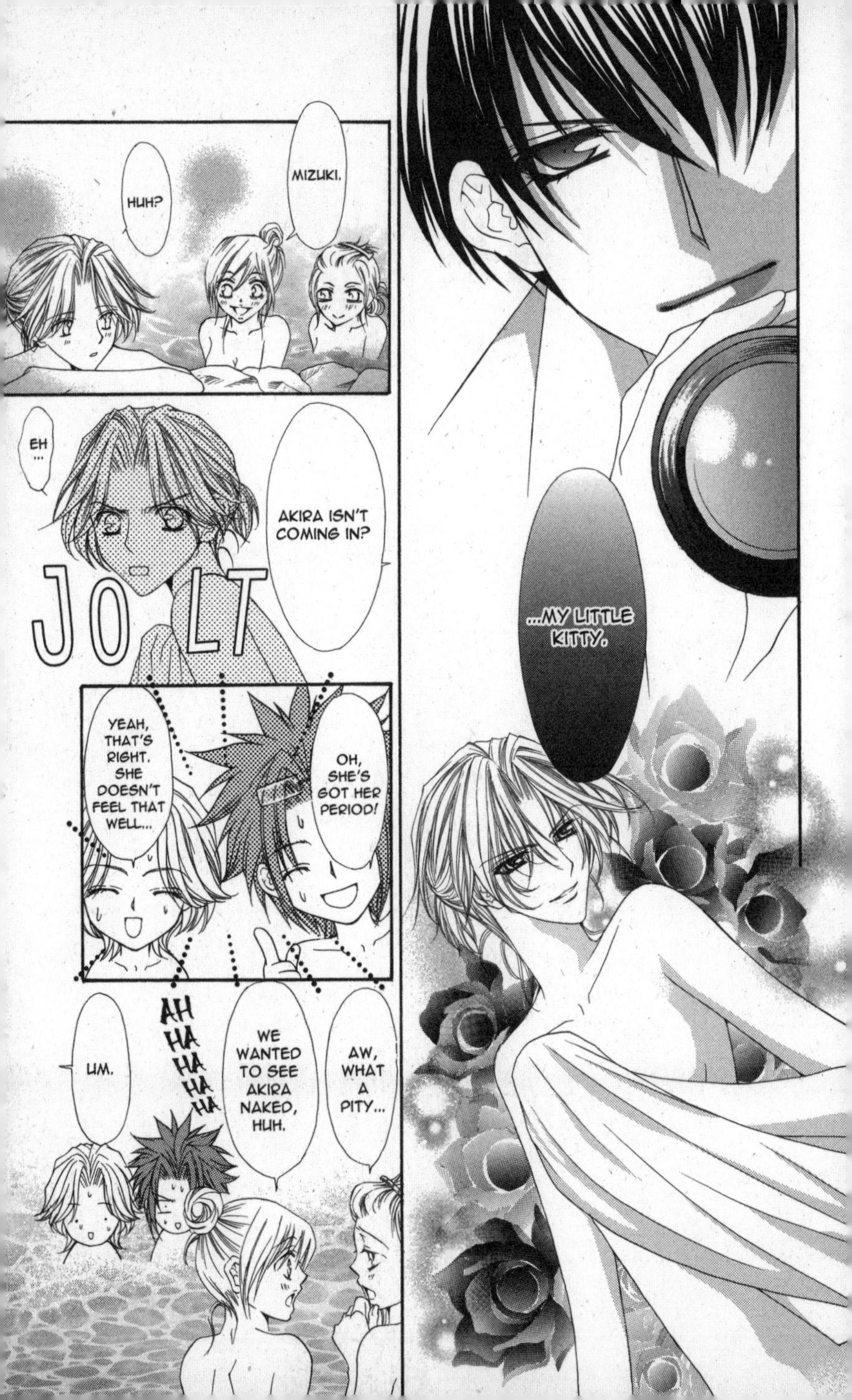
...MY LITTLE KITTY.
MIZUKI.
HUH?
AKIRA ISN'T COMING IN?
EH...
JOLT
OH, SHE'S GOT HER PERIOD!
YEAH, THAT'S RIGHT. SHE DOESN'T FEEL THAT WELL...
AW, WHAT A PITY...
WE WANTED TO SEE AKIRA NAKED, HUH.
AH HA HA HA HA
UM.

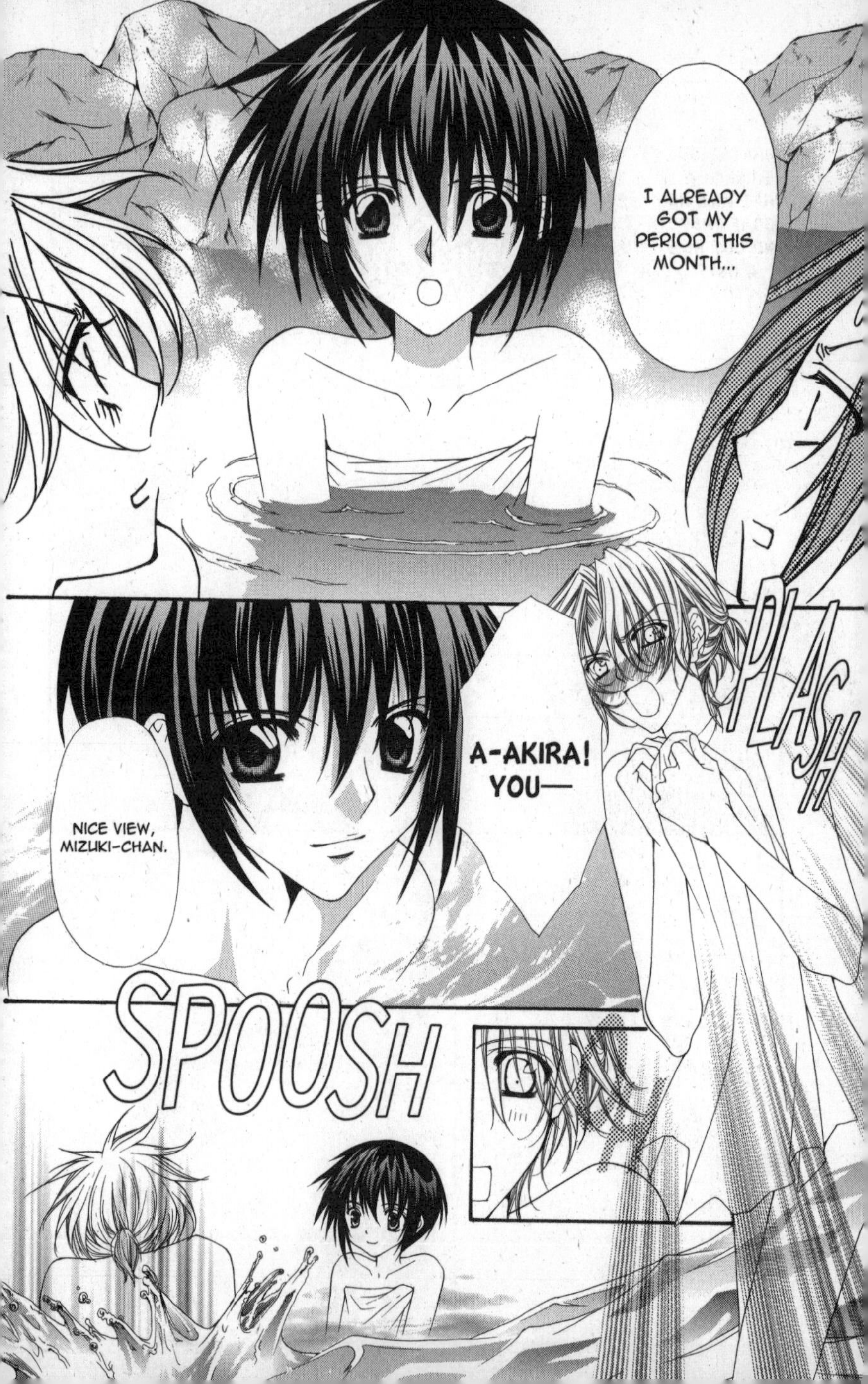
I ALREADY GOT MY PERIOD THIS MONTH...
PLASH
A-AKIRA! YOU—
NICE VIEW, MIZUKI-CHAN.
SPOOSH

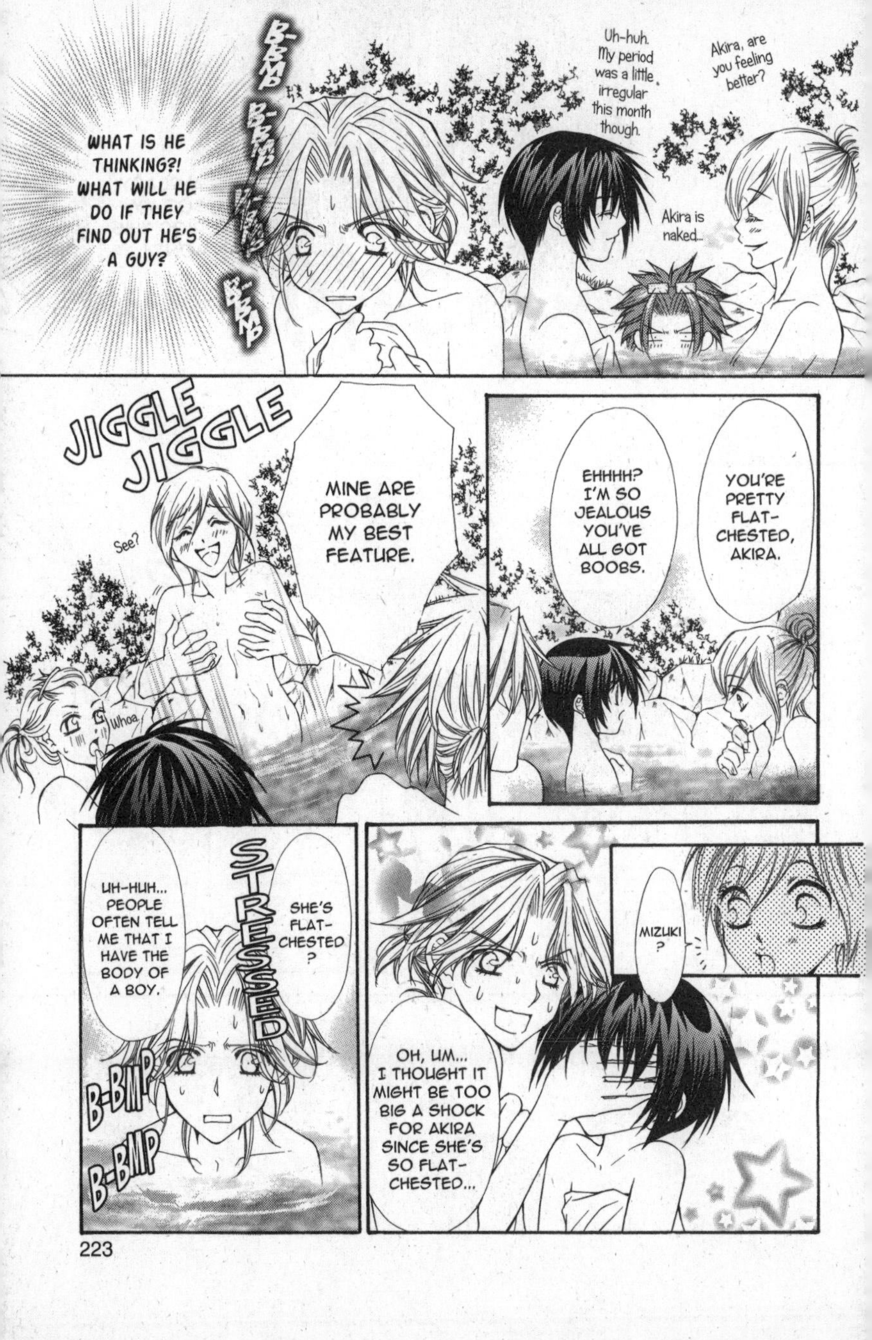
Akira, are you feeling better?
Uh-huh. My period was a little irregular this month though.
Akira is naked...
B-BMP B-BMP
B-BMP
WHAT IS HE THINKING?! WHAT WILL HE DO IF THEY FIND OUT HE'S A GUY?
YOU'RE PRETTY FLAT-CHESTED, AKIRA.
EHHHH? I'M SO JEALOUS YOU'VE ALL GOT BOOBS.
MINE ARE PROBABLY MY BEST FEATURE.
JIGGLE JIGGLE
See?
Whoa.
MIZUKI?
OH, UM... I THOUGHT IT MIGHT BE TOO BIG A SHOCK FOR AKIRA SINCE SHE'S SO FLAT-CHESTED...
SHE'S FLAT-CHESTED?
STRESSED
UH-HUH... PEOPLE OFTEN TELL ME THAT I HAVE THE BODY OF A BOY.
B-BMP
B-BMP

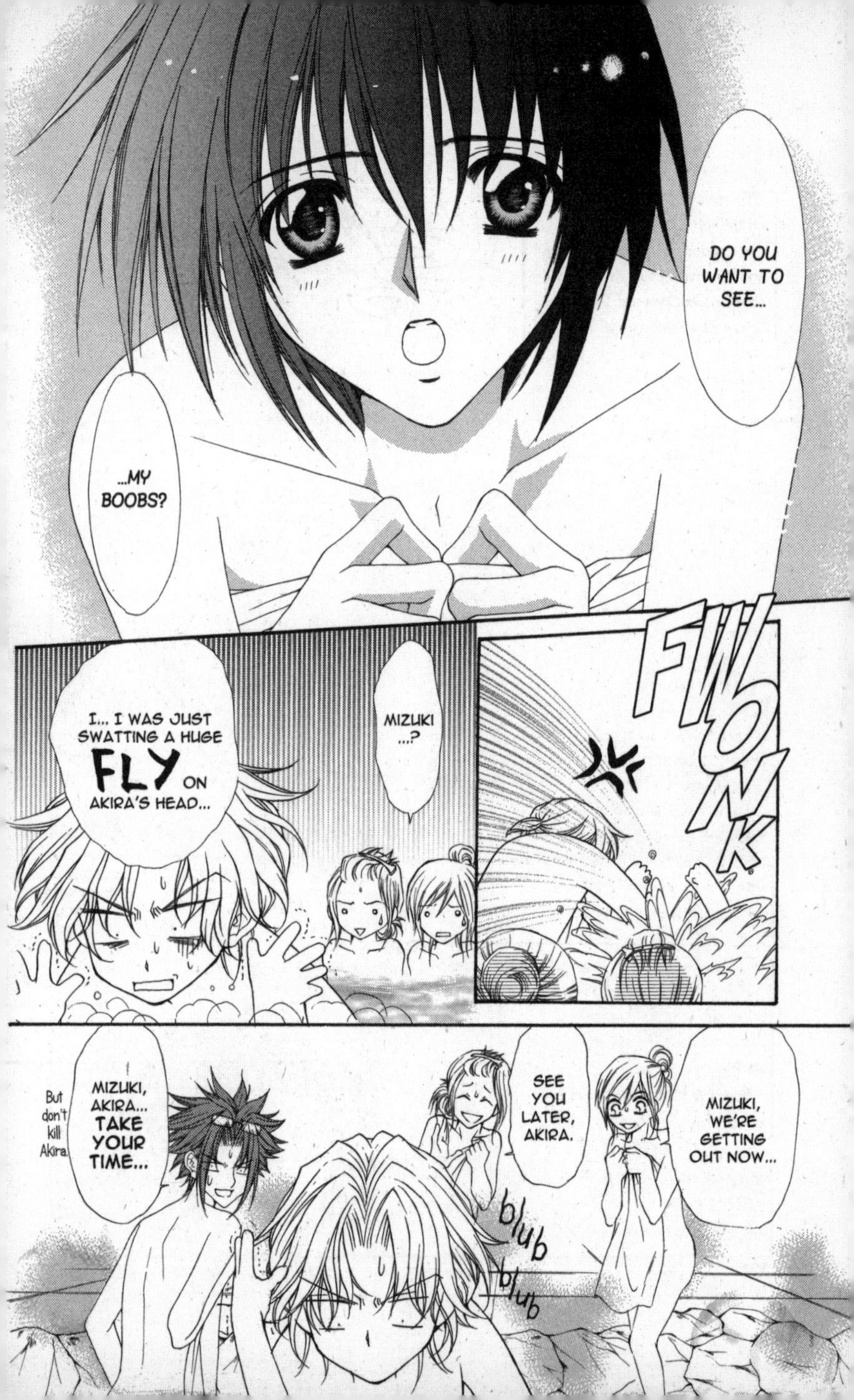
DO YOU WANT TO SEE...
...MY BOOBS?
FWONK
MIZUKI ...?
I... I WAS JUST SWATTING A HUGE FLY ON AKIRA'S HEAD...
MIZUKI, WE'RE GETTING OUT NOW...
SEE YOU LATER, AKIRA.
blub blub
MIZUKI, AKIRA... TAKE YOUR TIME...
But don't kill Akira.

And so it started—the dubbing of *Ai Ore!*

The drama CD story is based on the retreat in this volume.

We added many parts with Rui and Ran that I could never write about in *ShoComi*, and I was able to create a lovely story!! The voice actors will act their parts...

First up: Akira!

He's so cute!!

Wha...?! What, what?! What is this cute voice?! It is what you call a moe voice! (pant, pant) I really thought I was going to die from the cuteness. After all, people mistake Akira for a girl. Hoshi-san has to talk in a cutesy voice, but it seemed that he needed to give it some umph to do that. And just before the cue to start recording, he'd always "Uh... uh-hum"—give a little cough.

And that was so cute because he looked like he was trying so hard!!

The director of audiography told me, "Hoshi probably uses a lot of energy to talk in a cute voice..." but when I asked Hoshi-san himself later on, he smiled and said, "I don't have any trouble talking in a cute voice. It's just that...there are so many embarrassing lines and I'm really... embarrassed..." Then he'd fidget a bit...

Aw, he looks so cute when he's embarrassed!! I want to embarrass him even more now and—

Self-regulation...

Maybe I have a sadistic side...

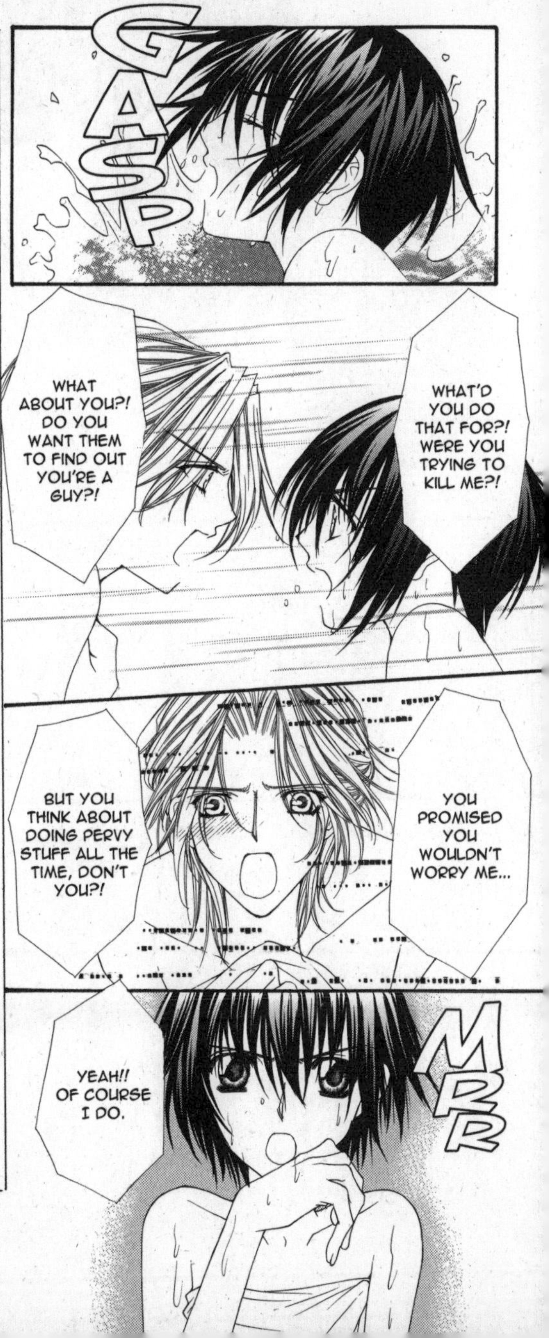
GASP
WHAT'D YOU DO THAT FOR?! WERE YOU TRYING TO KILL ME?!
WHAT ABOUT YOU?! DO YOU WANT THEM TO FIND OUT YOU'RE A GUY?!
YOU PROMISED YOU WOULDN'T WORRY ME...
BUT YOU THINK ABOUT DOING PERVY STUFF ALL THE TIME, DON'T YOU?!
MRR
YEAH!! OF COURSE I DO.

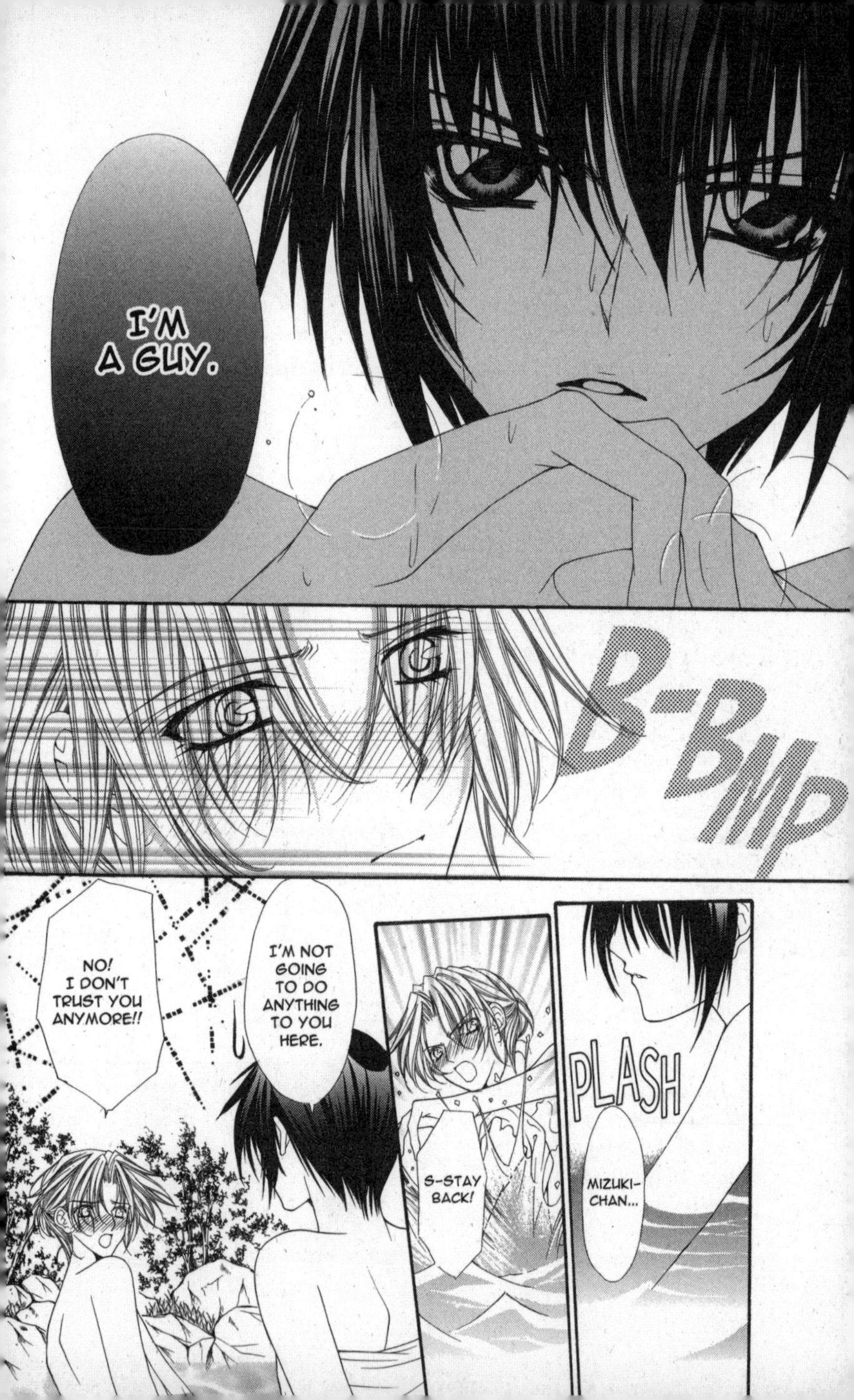
I'M A GUY.
B-BMP
PLASH
MIZUKI-CHAN...
S-STAY BACK!
I'M NOT GOING TO DO ANYTHING TO YOU HERE.
NO! I DON'T TRUST YOU ANYMORE!!

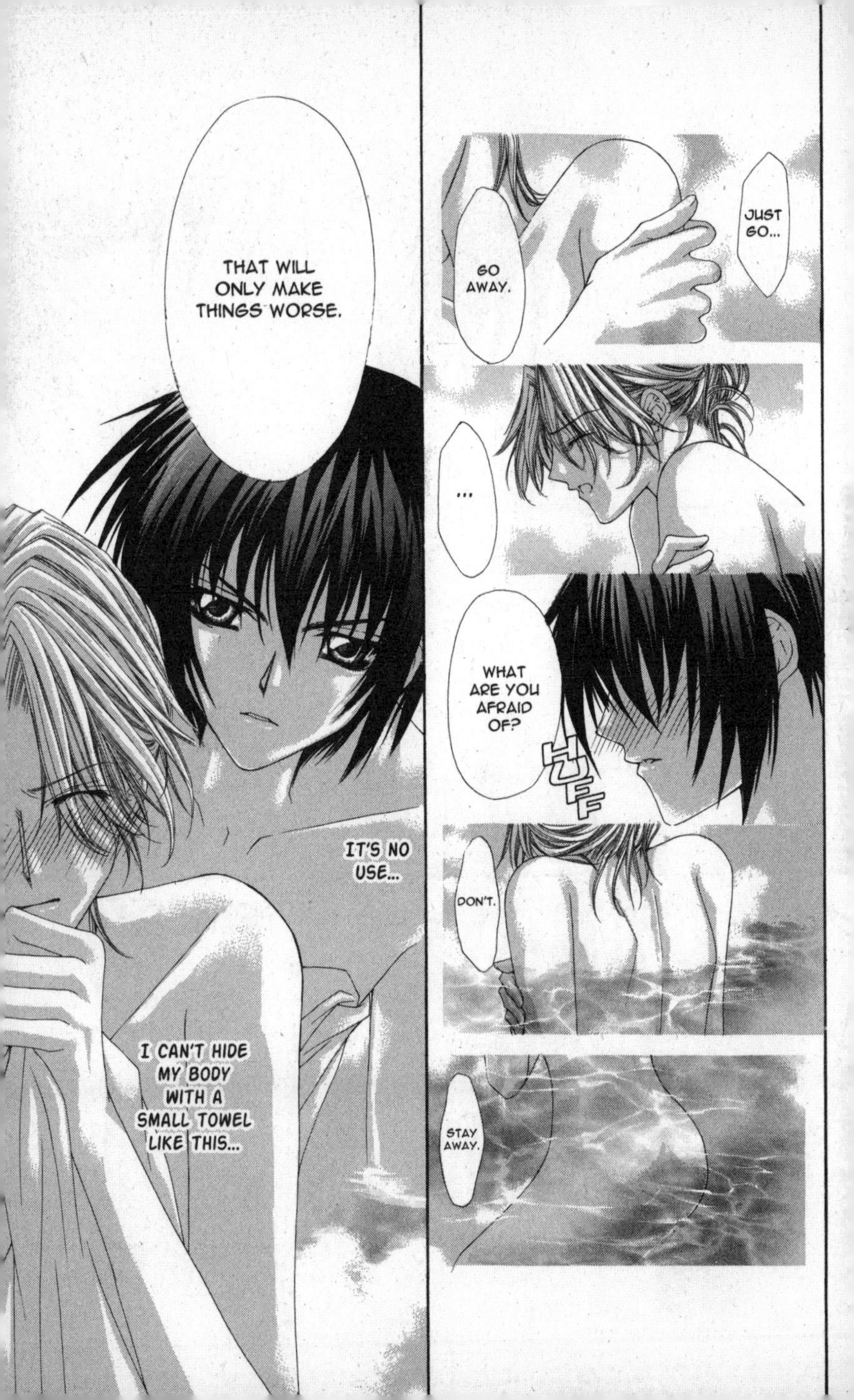
JUST GO...
GO AWAY.
...
WHAT ARE YOU AFRAID OF?
HUFF
DON'T.
STAY AWAY.
THAT WILL ONLY MAKE THINGS WORSE.
IT'S NO USE...
I CAN'T HIDE MY BODY WITH A SMALL TOWEL LIKE THIS...

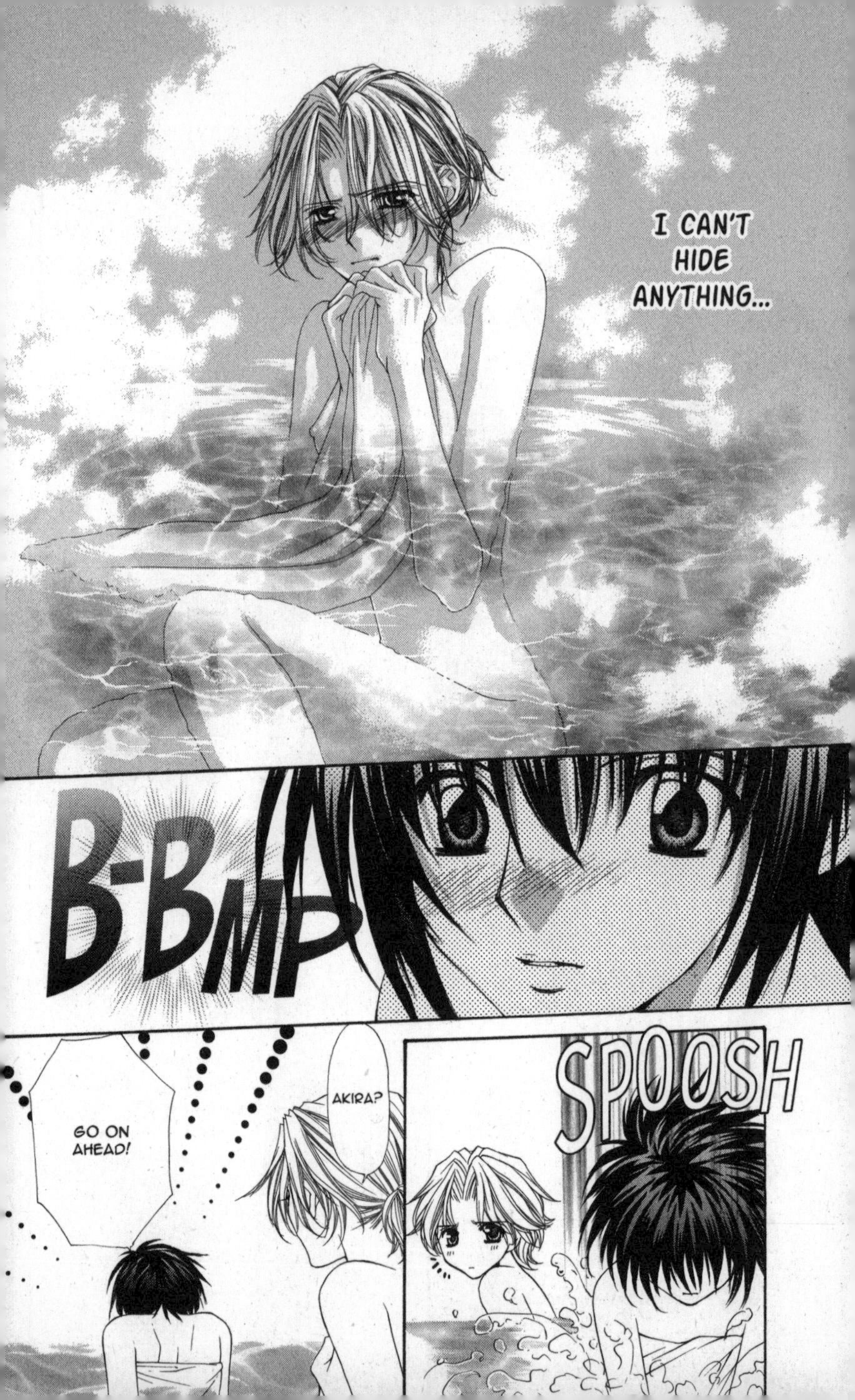
I CAN'T HIDE ANYTHING...
B-BMP
SPOOSH
AKIRA?
GO ON AHEAD!

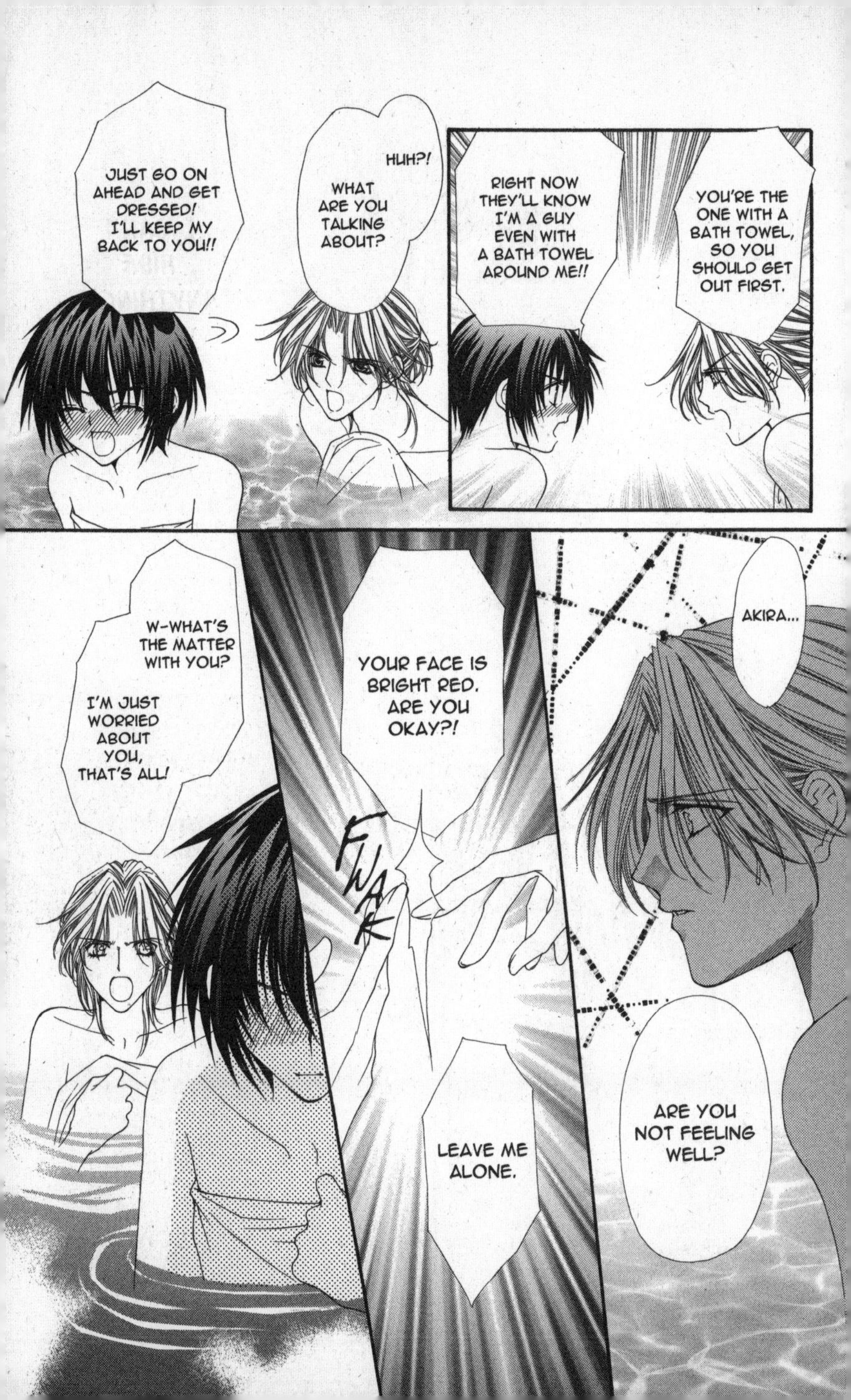
YOU'RE THE ONE WITH A BATH TOWEL, SO YOU SHOULD GET OUT FIRST.
RIGHT NOW THEY'LL KNOW I'M A GUY EVEN WITH A BATH TOWEL AROUND ME!!
HUH?!
WHAT ARE YOU TALKING ABOUT?
JUST GO ON AHEAD AND GET DRESSED! I'LL KEEP MY BACK TO YOU!!
AKIRA...
ARE YOU NOT FEELING WELL?
YOUR FACE IS BRIGHT RED. ARE YOU OKAY?!
FWAK
LEAVE ME ALONE.
W-WHAT'S THE MATTER WITH YOU?
I'M JUST WORRIED ABOUT YOU, THAT'S ALL!

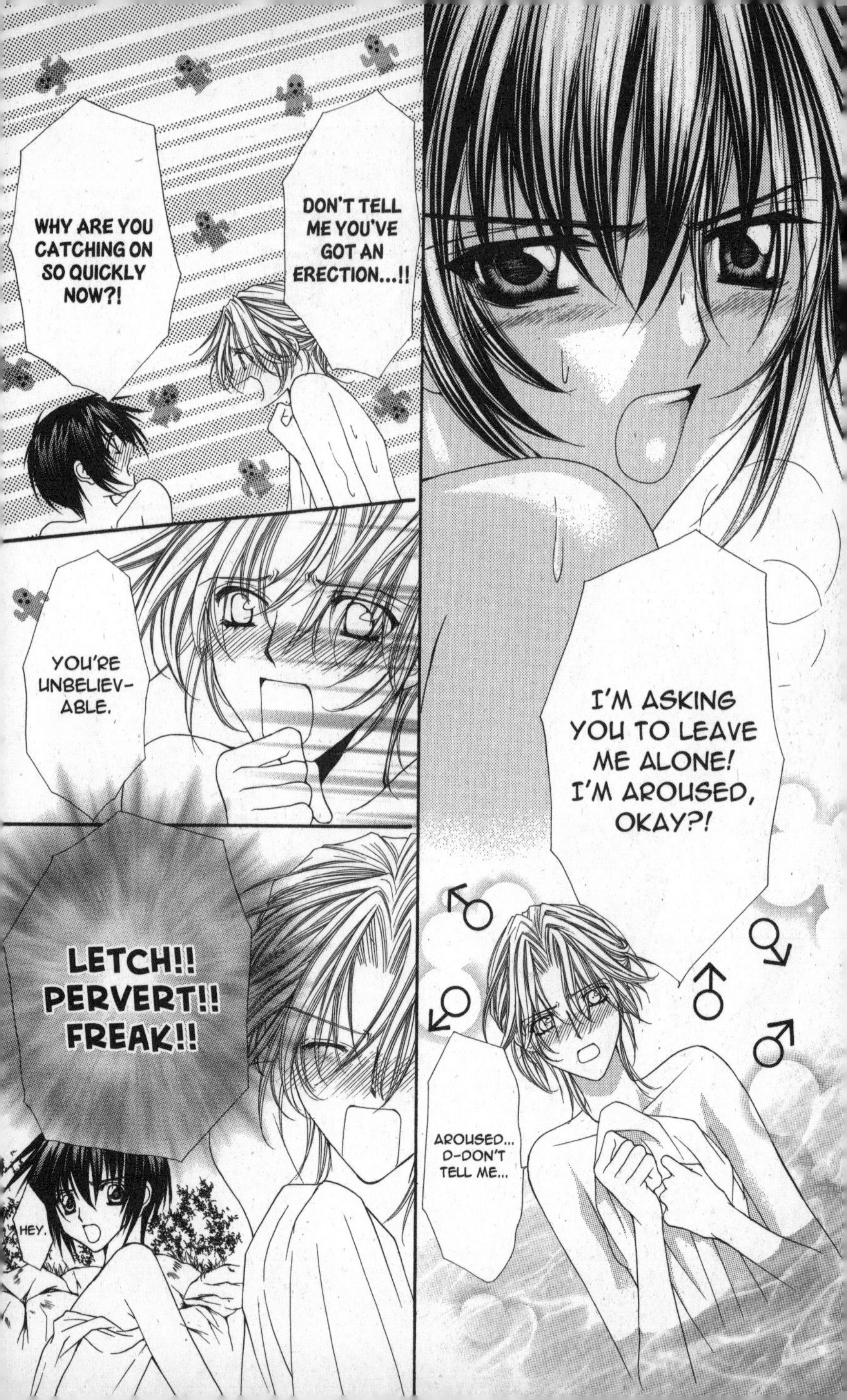
I'M ASKING YOU TO LEAVE ME ALONE! I'M AROUSED, OKAY?!
AROUSED... D-DON'T TELL ME...
DON'T TELL ME YOU'VE GOT AN ERECTION...!!
WHY ARE YOU CATCHING ON SO QUICKLY NOW?!
YOU'RE UNBELIEV-ABLE.
LETCH!! PERVERT!! FREAK!!
HEY.

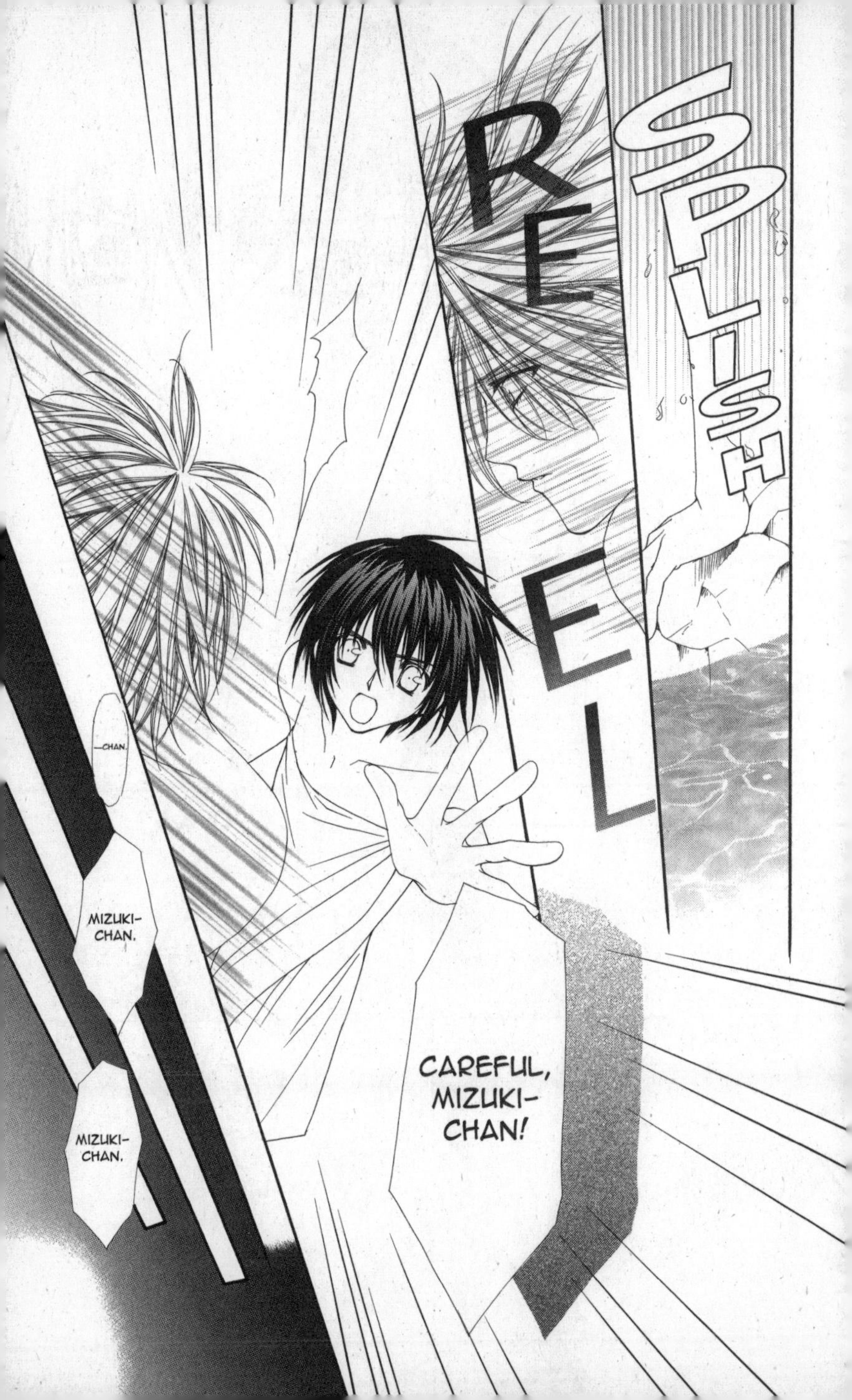
SPLISH
REEL
CAREFUL, MIZUKI-CHAN!
—CHAN.
MIZUKI-CHAN.
MIZUKI-CHAN.

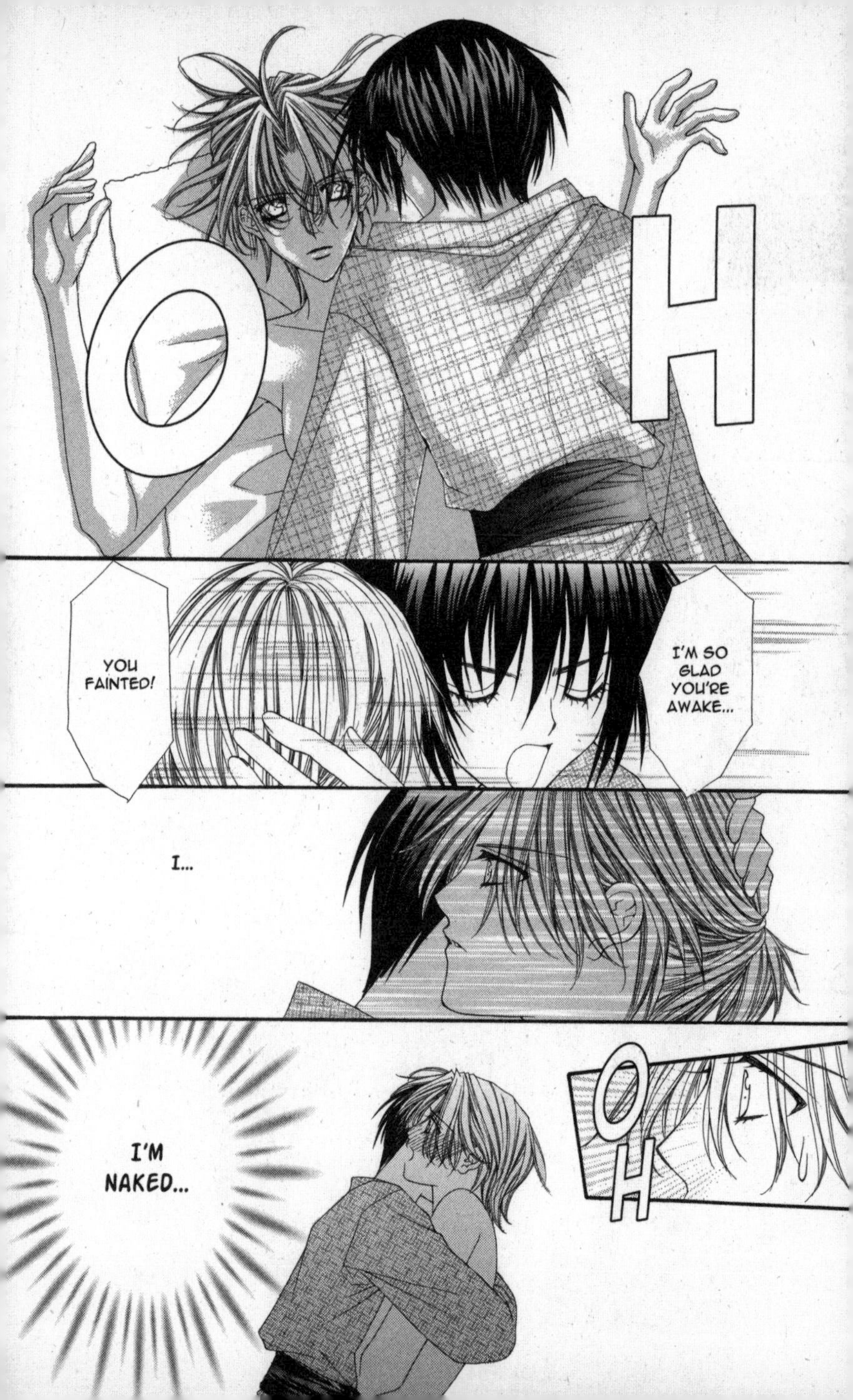
OH
I'M SO GLAD YOU'RE AWAKE...
YOU FAINTED!
I...
OH
I'M NAKED...

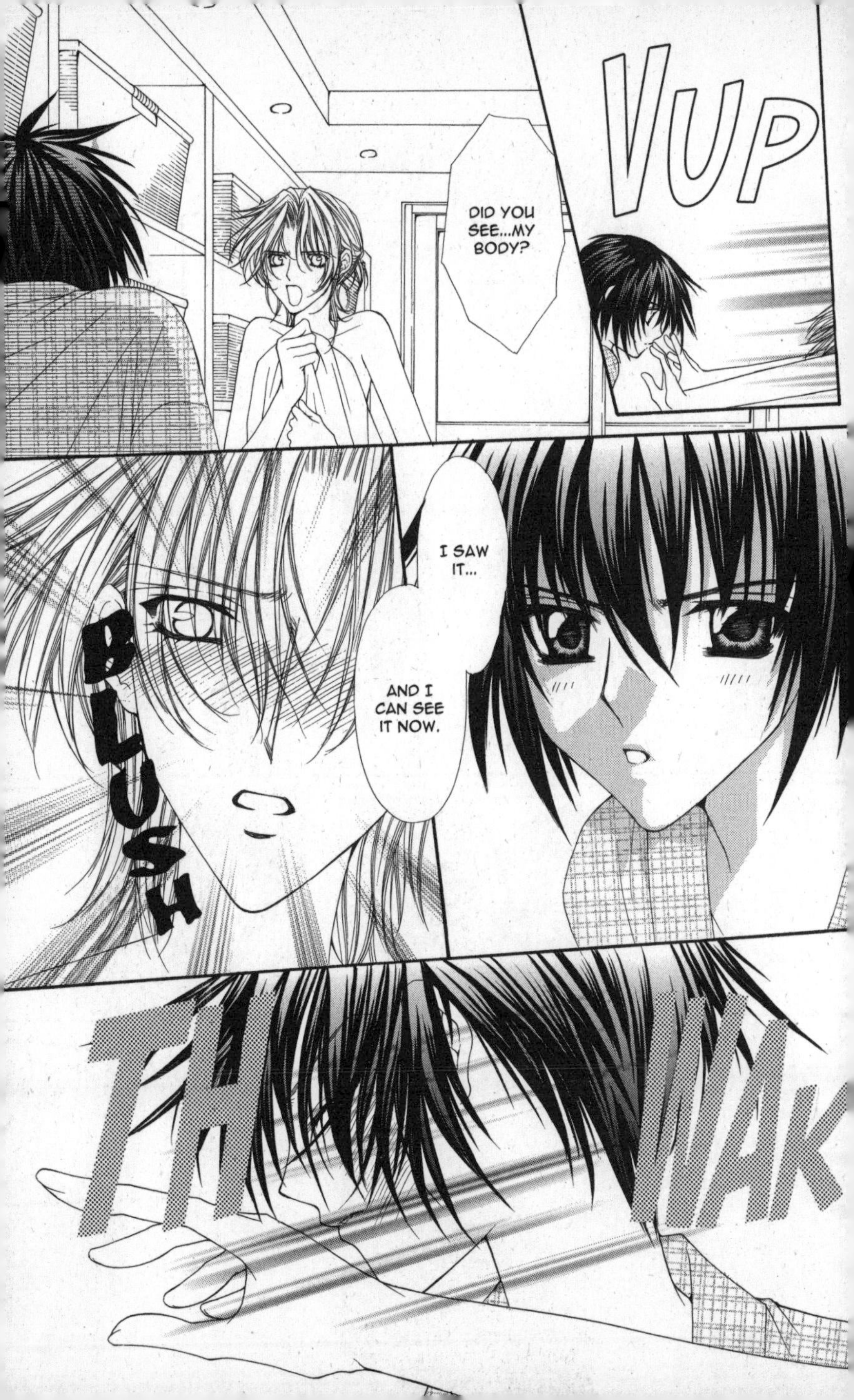
VUP
DID YOU SEE...MY BODY?
I SAW IT...
AND I CAN SEE IT NOW.
BLUSH
THWAK

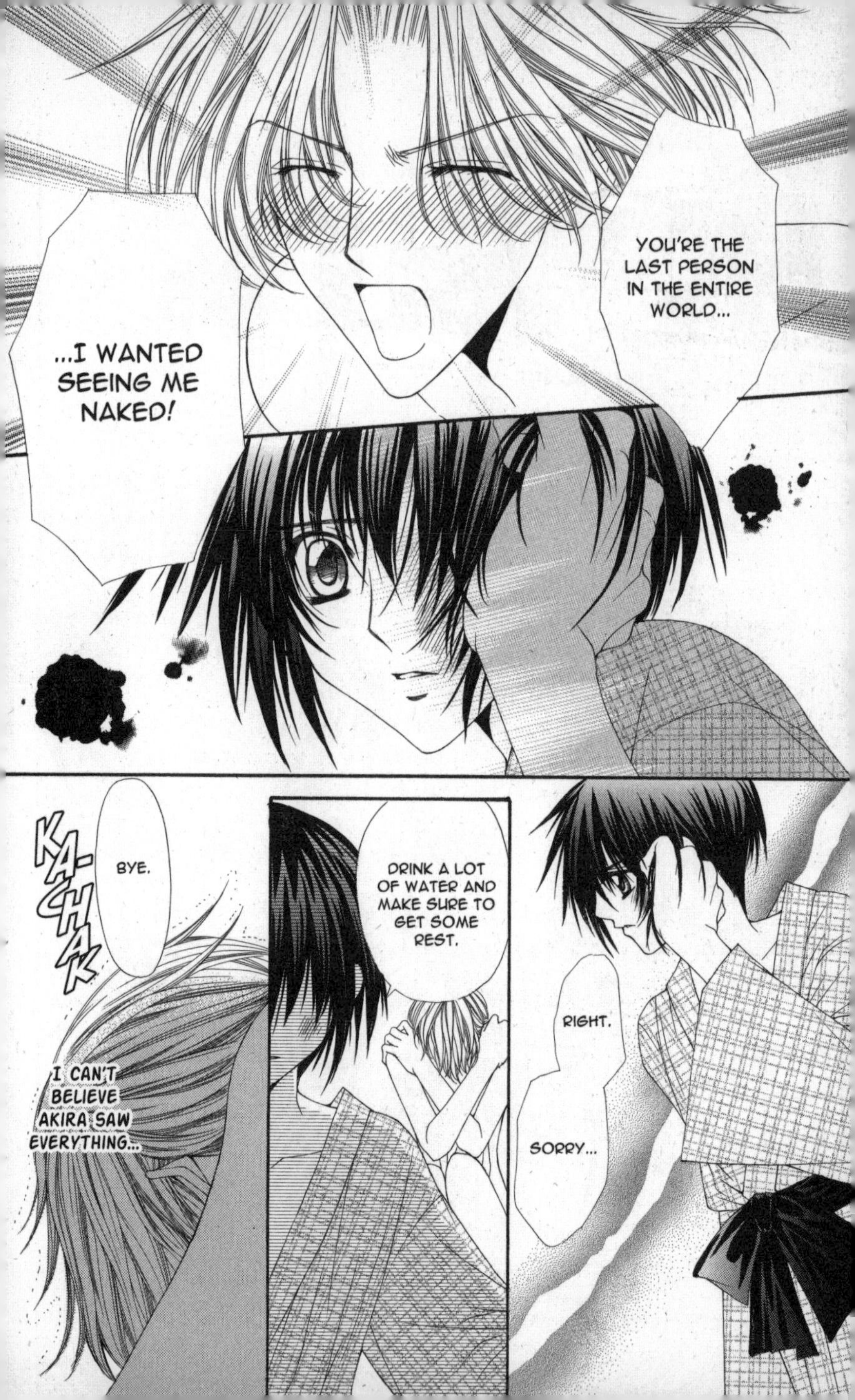

YOU'RE THE LAST PERSON IN THE ENTIRE WORLD...
...I WANTED SEEING ME NAKED!
RIGHT.
SORRY...
DRINK A LOT OF WATER AND MAKE SURE TO GET SOME REST.
BYE.
KA-CHAK
I CAN'T BELIEVE AKIRA SAW EVERYTHING...

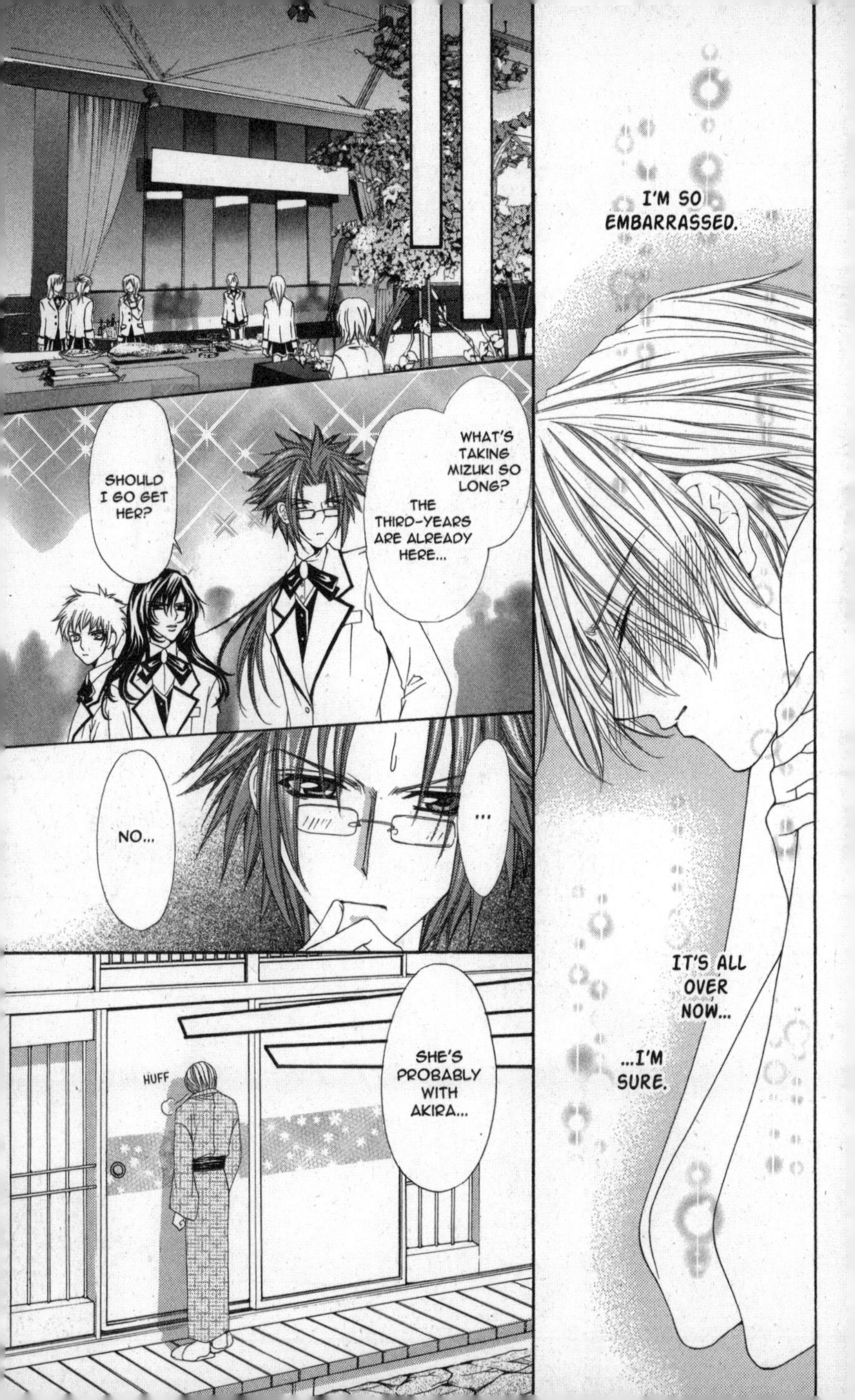
I'M SO EMBARRASSED.
IT'S ALL OVER NOW...
...I'M SURE.
WHAT'S TAKING MIZUKI SO LONG?
THE THIRD-YEARS ARE ALREADY HERE...
SHOULD I GO GET HER?
...
NO...
SHE'S PROBABLY WITH AKIRA...
HUFF

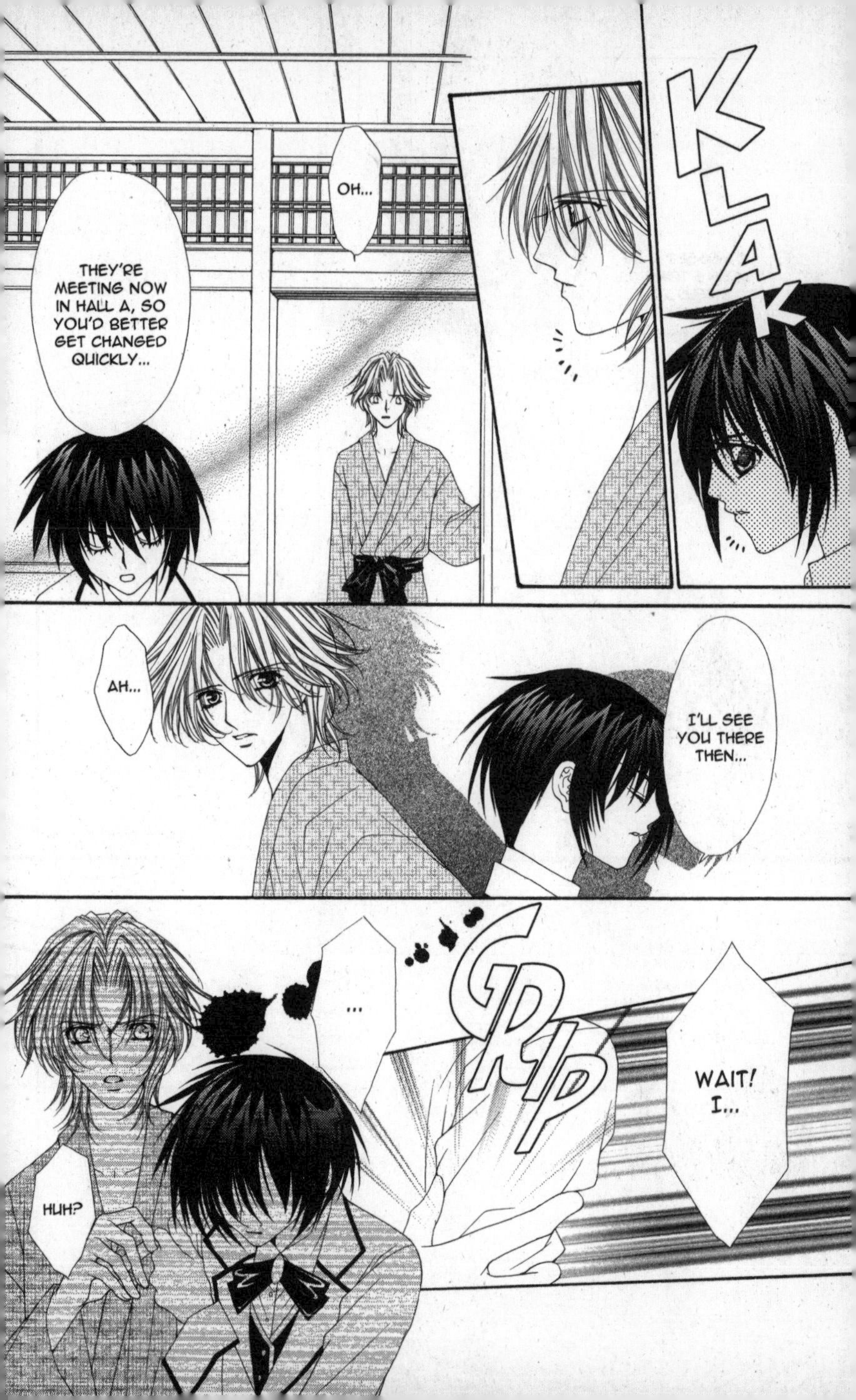
KLAK
OH...
THEY'RE MEETING NOW IN HALL A, SO YOU'D BETTER GET CHANGED QUICKLY...
I'LL SEE YOU THERE THEN...
AH...
WAIT! I...
GRIP
...
HUH?

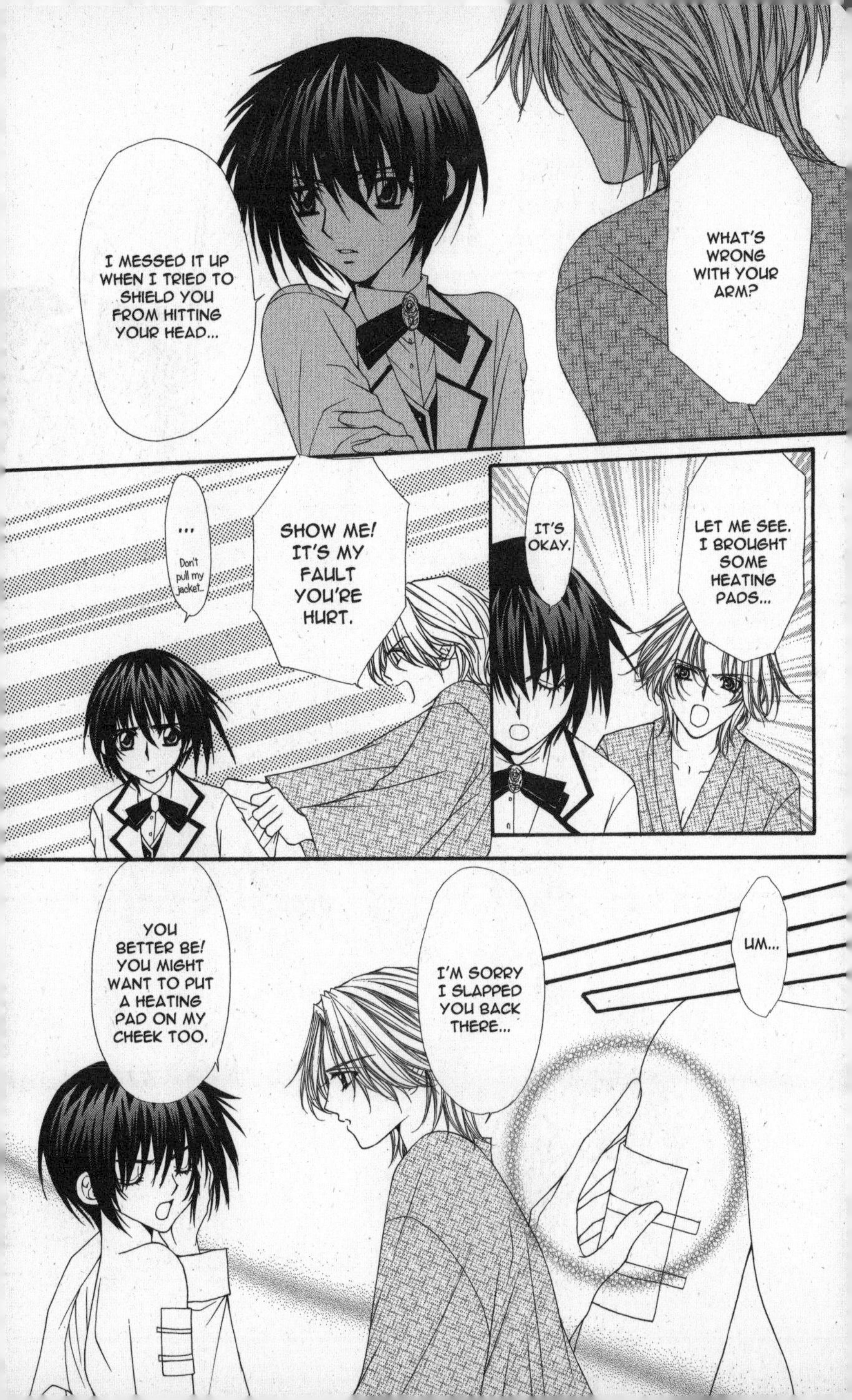
WHAT'S WRONG WITH YOUR ARM?
I MESSED IT UP WHEN I TRIED TO SHIELD YOU FROM HITTING YOUR HEAD...
LET ME SEE. I BROUGHT SOME HEATING PADS...
IT'S OKAY.
SHOW ME! IT'S MY FAULT YOU'RE HURT.
...
Don't pull my jacket...
UM...
I'M SORRY I SLAPPED YOU BACK THERE...
YOU BETTER BE! YOU MIGHT WANT TO PUT A HEATING PAD ON MY CHEEK TOO.

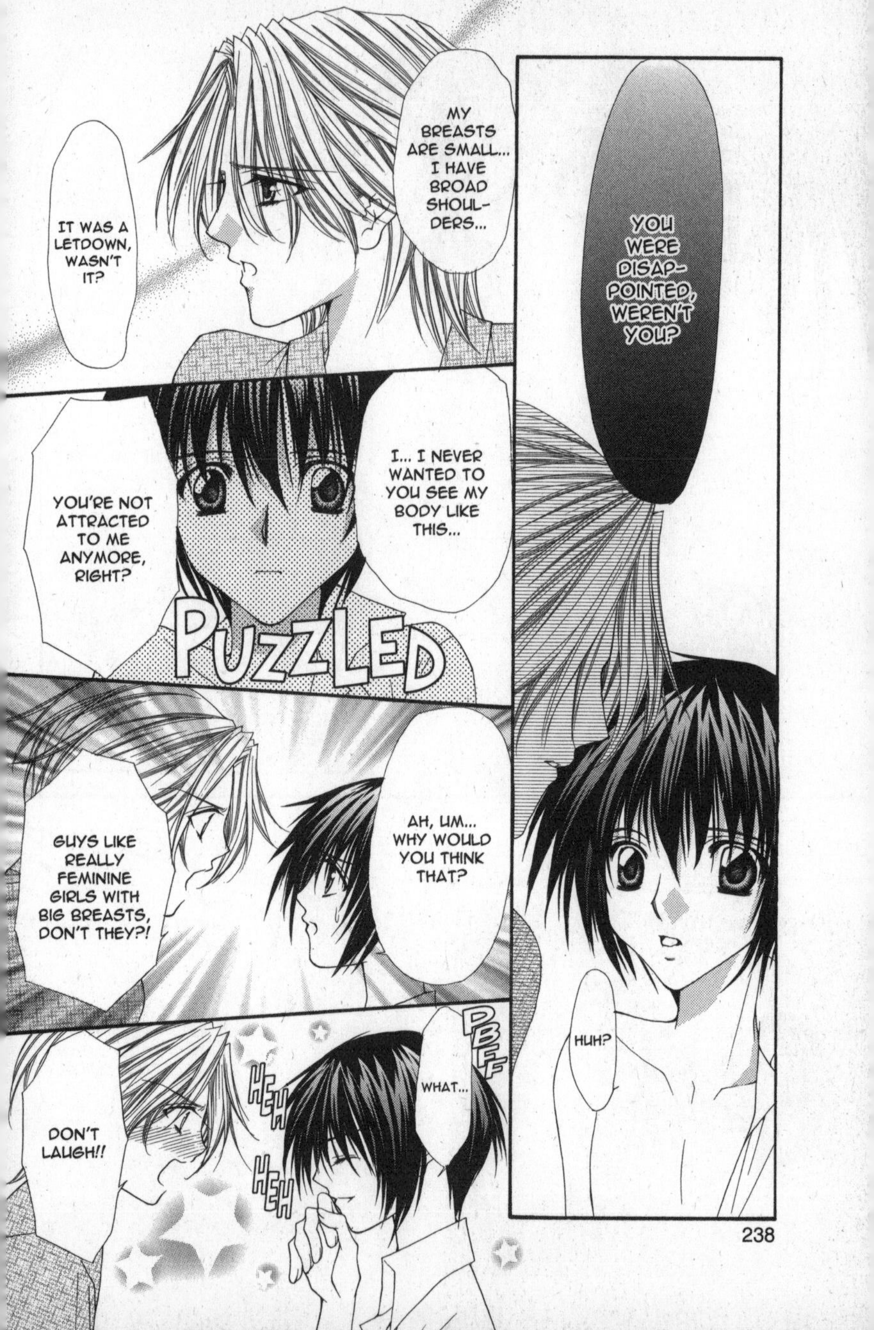
YOU WERE DISAPPOINTED, WEREN'T YOU?
HUH?
MY BREASTS ARE SMALL... I HAVE BROAD SHOULDERS...
IT WAS A LETDOWN, WASN'T IT?
I... I NEVER WANTED TO YOU SEE MY BODY LIKE THIS...
YOU'RE NOT ATTRACTED TO ME ANYMORE, RIGHT?
PUZZLED
AH, UM... WHY WOULD YOU THINK THAT?
GUYS LIKE REALLY FEMININE GIRLS WITH BIG BREASTS, DON'T THEY?!
PBFF
WHAT...
HEH
HEH
DON'T LAUGH!!

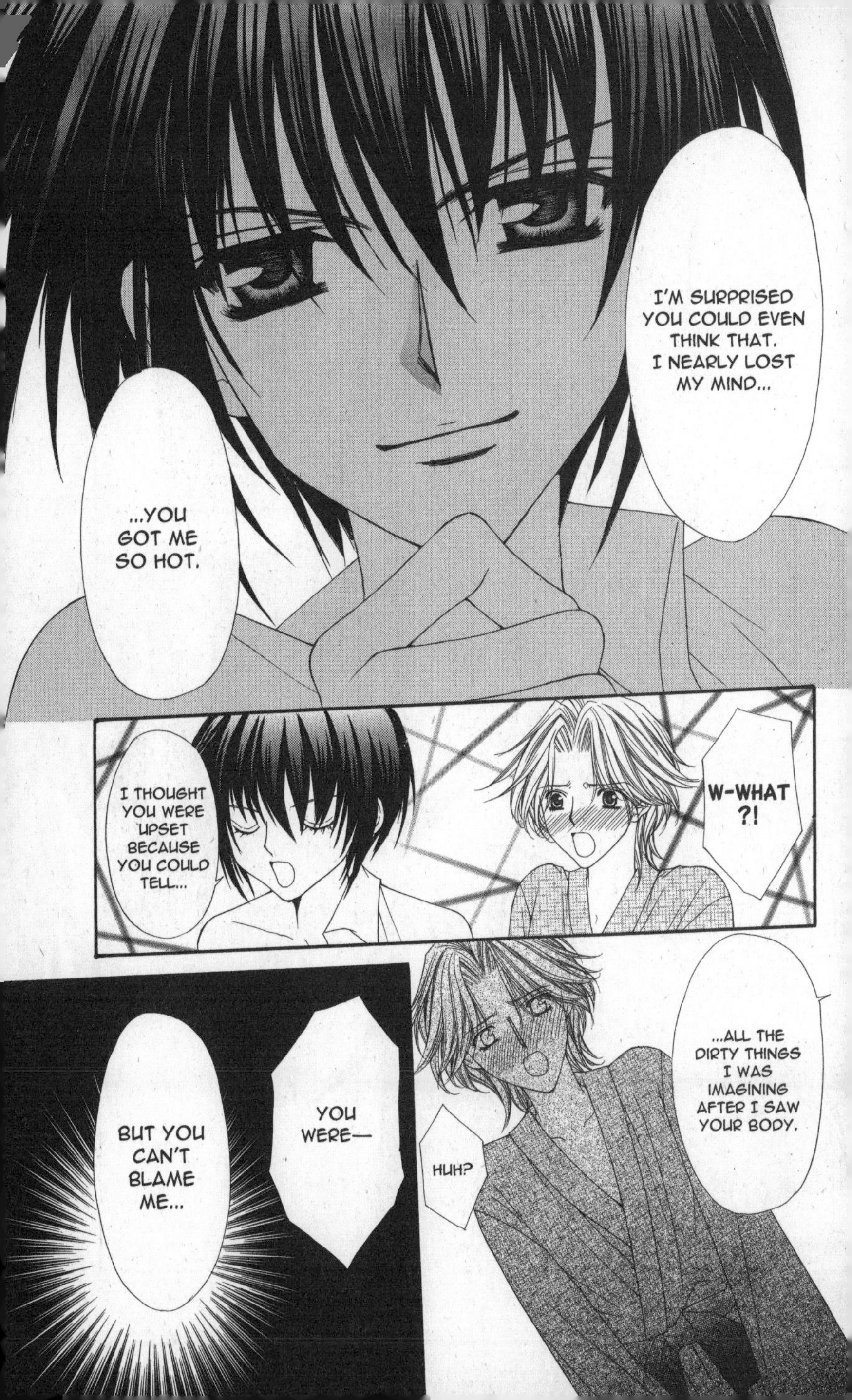
I'M SURPRISED YOU COULD EVEN THINK THAT. I NEARLY LOST MY MIND...
...YOU GOT ME SO HOT.
W-WHAT ?!
I THOUGHT YOU WERE UPSET BECAUSE YOU COULD TELL...
...ALL THE DIRTY THINGS I WAS IMAGINING AFTER I SAW YOUR BODY.
HUH?
YOU WERE—
BUT YOU CAN'T BLAME ME...

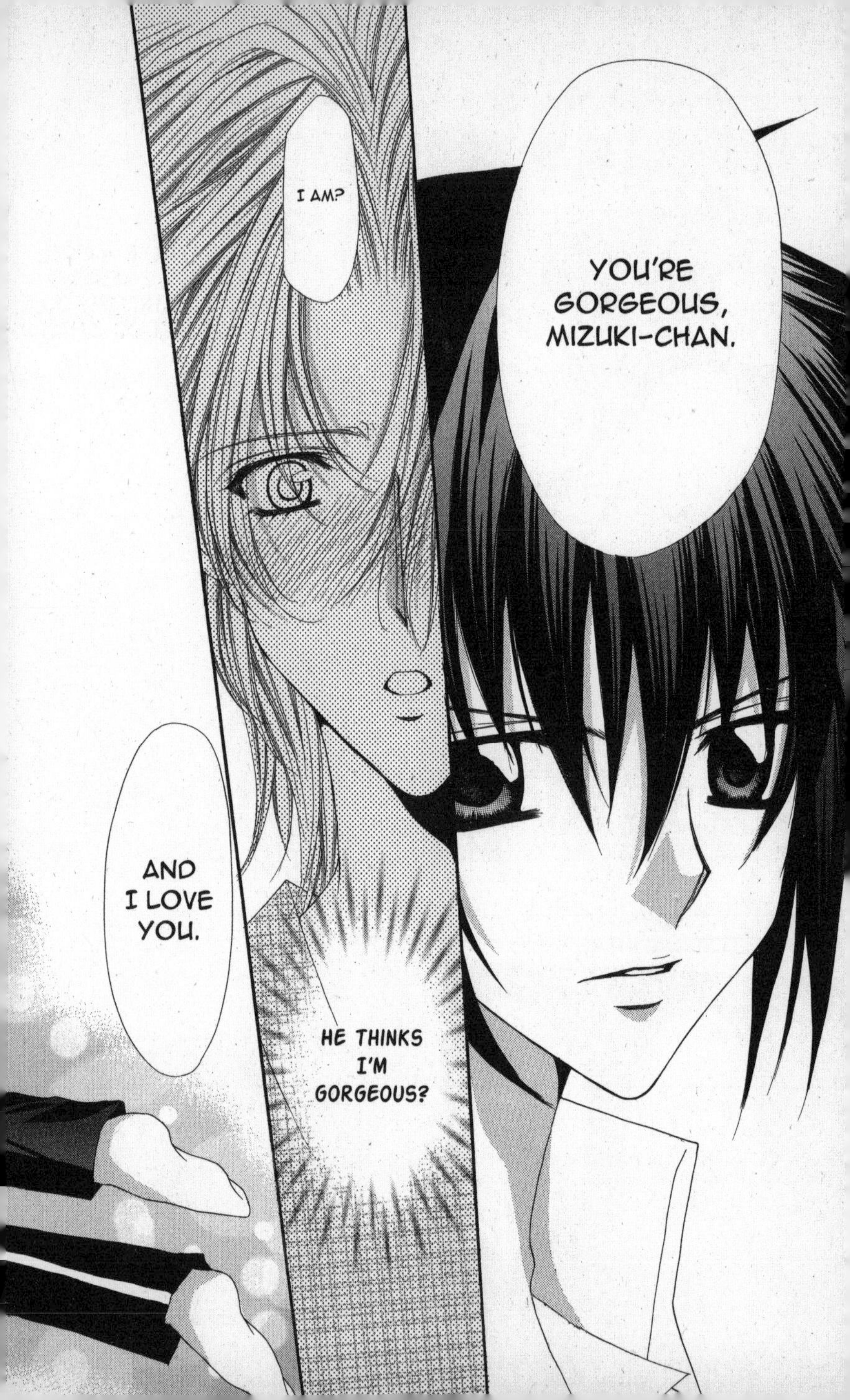
YOU'RE GORGEOUS, MIZUKI-CHAN.
I AM?
HE THINKS I'M GORGEOUS?
AND I LOVE YOU.

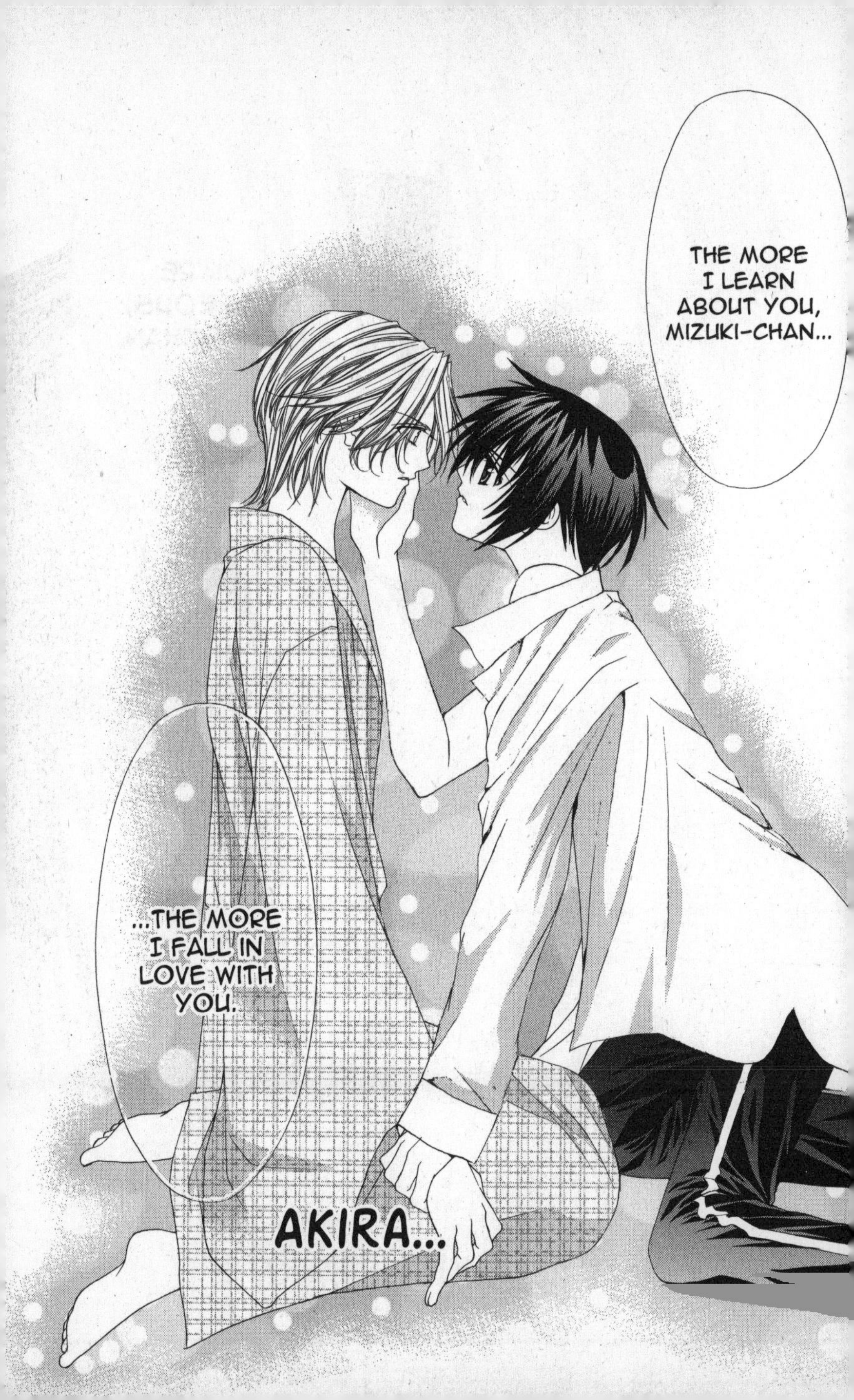
THE MORE I LEARN ABOUT YOU, MIZUKI-CHAN...
...THE MORE I FALL IN LOVE WITH YOU.
AKIRA...

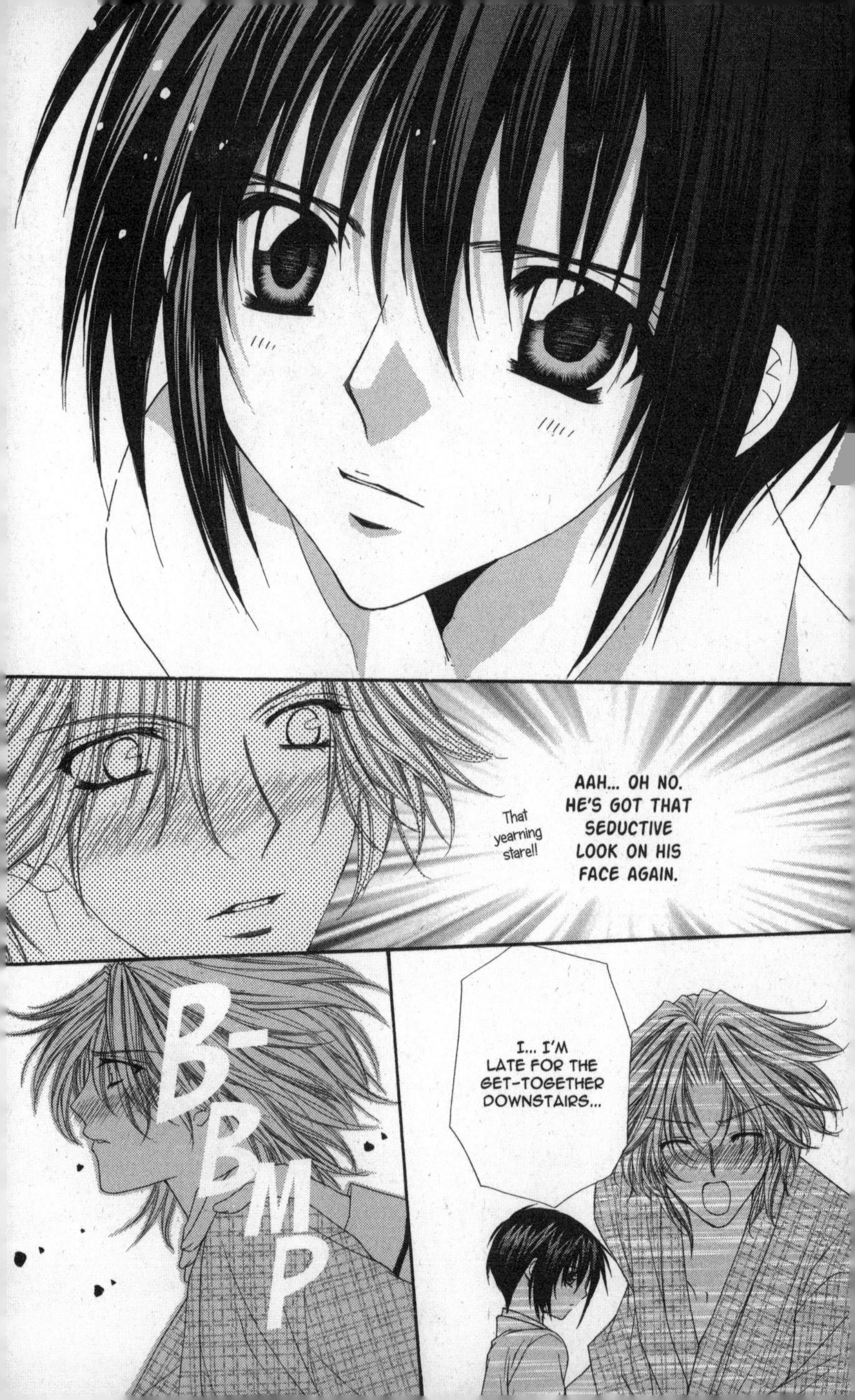
AAH... OH NO. HE'S GOT THAT SEDUCTIVE LOOK ON HIS FACE AGAIN.
That yearning stare!!
I... I'M LATE FOR THE GET-TOGETHER DOWNSTAIRS...
B-BMP

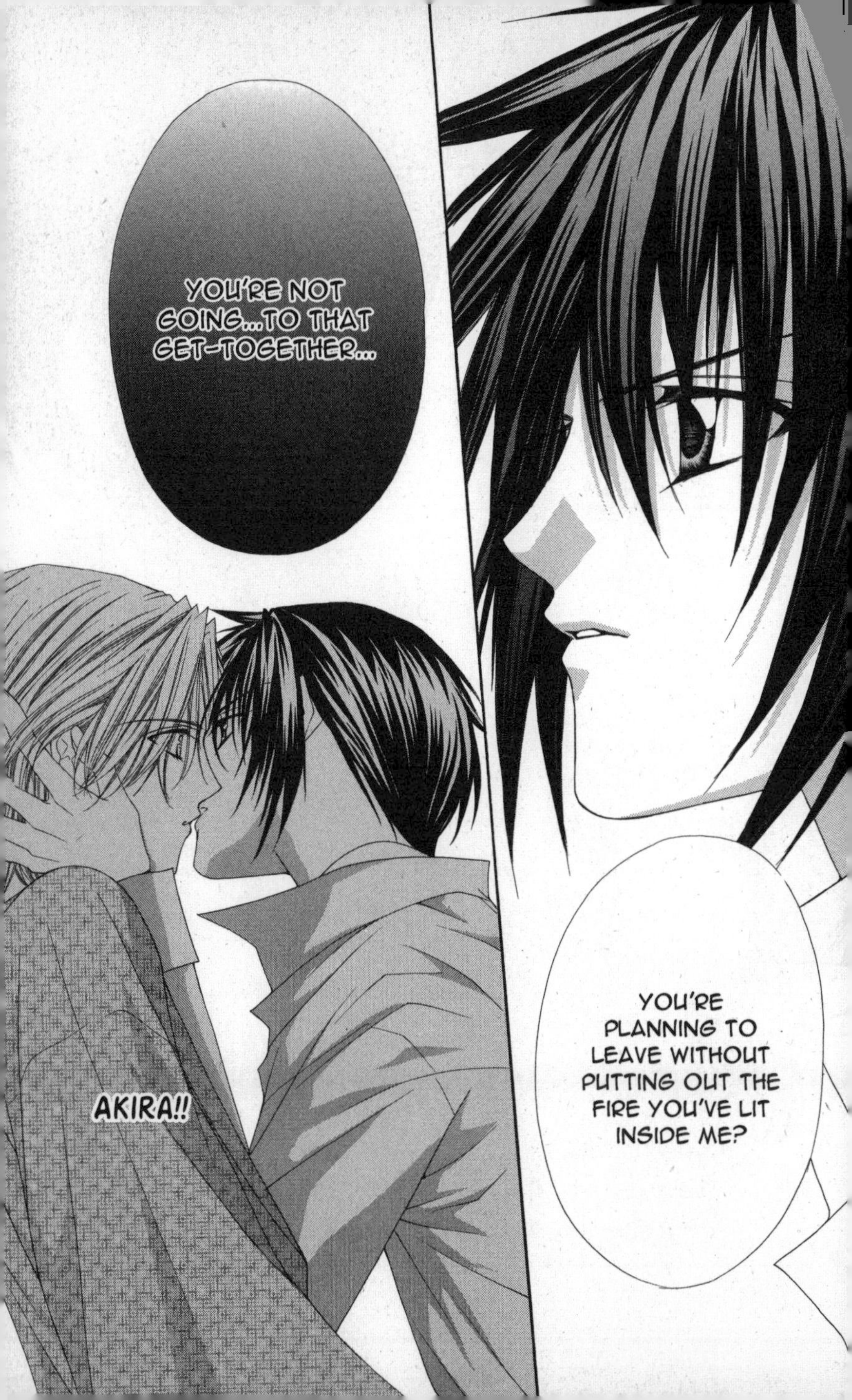
YOU'RE PLANNING TO LEAVE WITHOUT PUTTING OUT THE FIRE YOU'VE LIT INSIDE ME?
YOU'RE NOT GOING...TO THAT GET-TOGETHER...
AKIRA!!

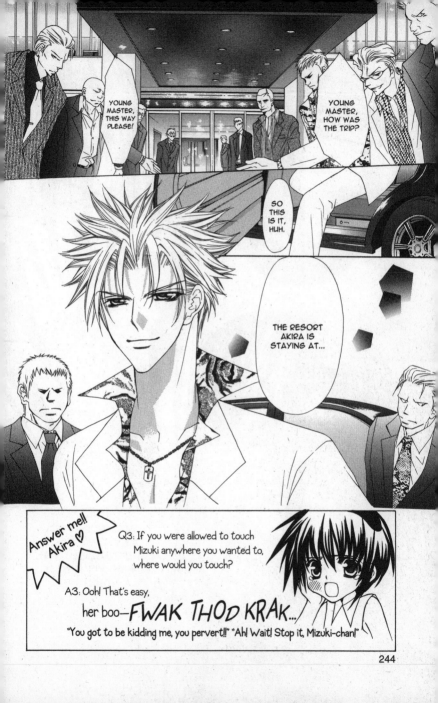

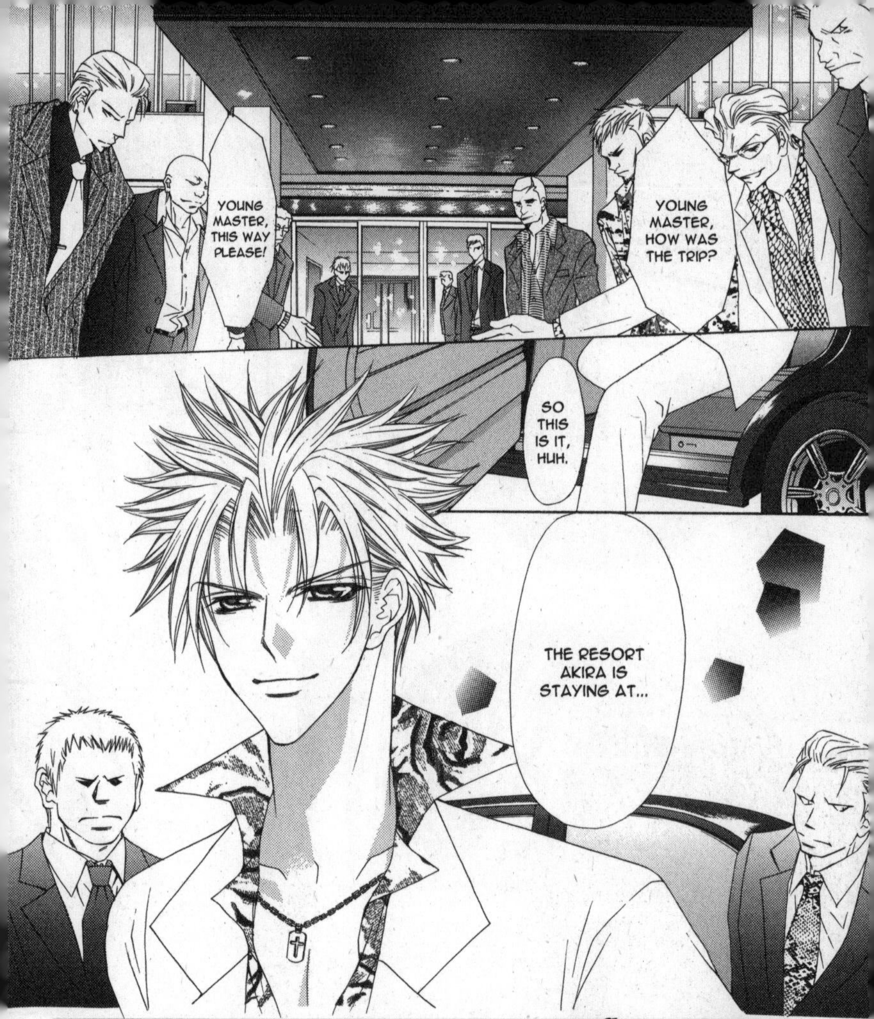
YOUNG MASTER, HOW WAS THE TRIP?
YOUNG MASTER, THIS WAY PLEASE!
SO THIS IS IT, HUH.
THE RESORT AKIRA IS STAYING AT...

Answer me!! Akira ♡

Q3: If you were allowed to touch Mizuki anywhere you wanted to, where would you touch?

A3: Ooh! That's easy, her boo–**FWAK THOD KRAK...**

"You got to be kidding me, you pervert!!" "Ah! Wait! Stop it, Mizuki-chan!"

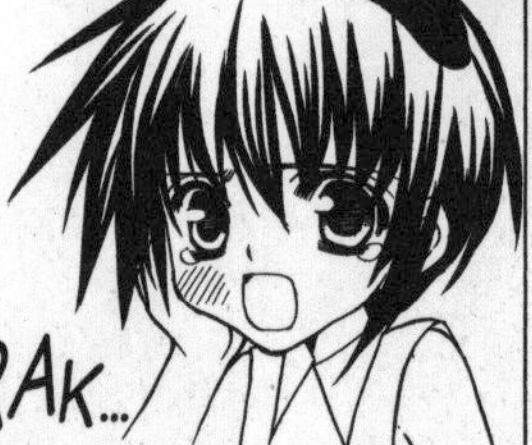

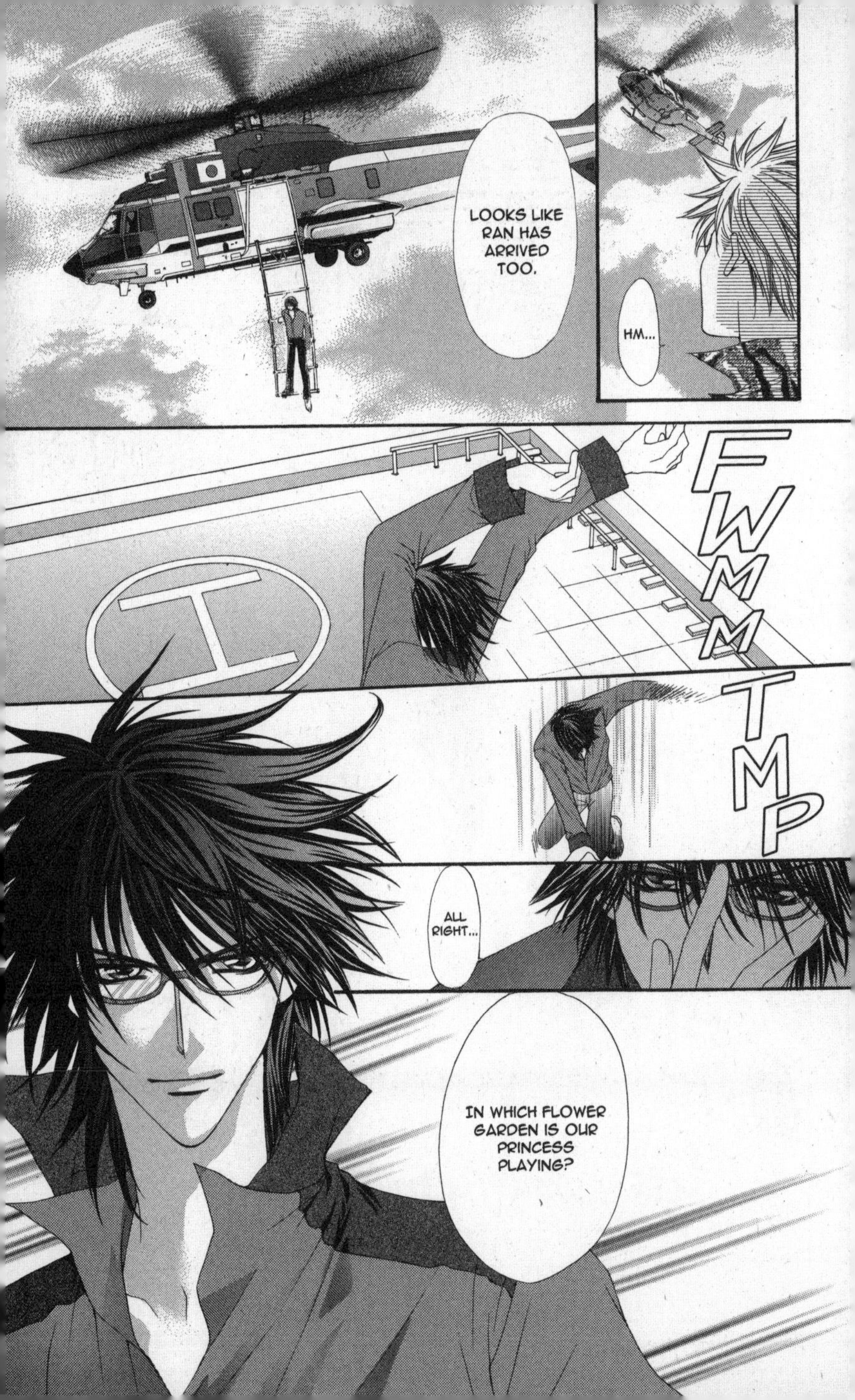
LOOKS LIKE RAN HAS ARRIVED TOO.
HM...
FWMM
TMP
ALL RIGHT...
IN WHICH FLOWER GARDEN IS OUR PRINCESS PLAYING?

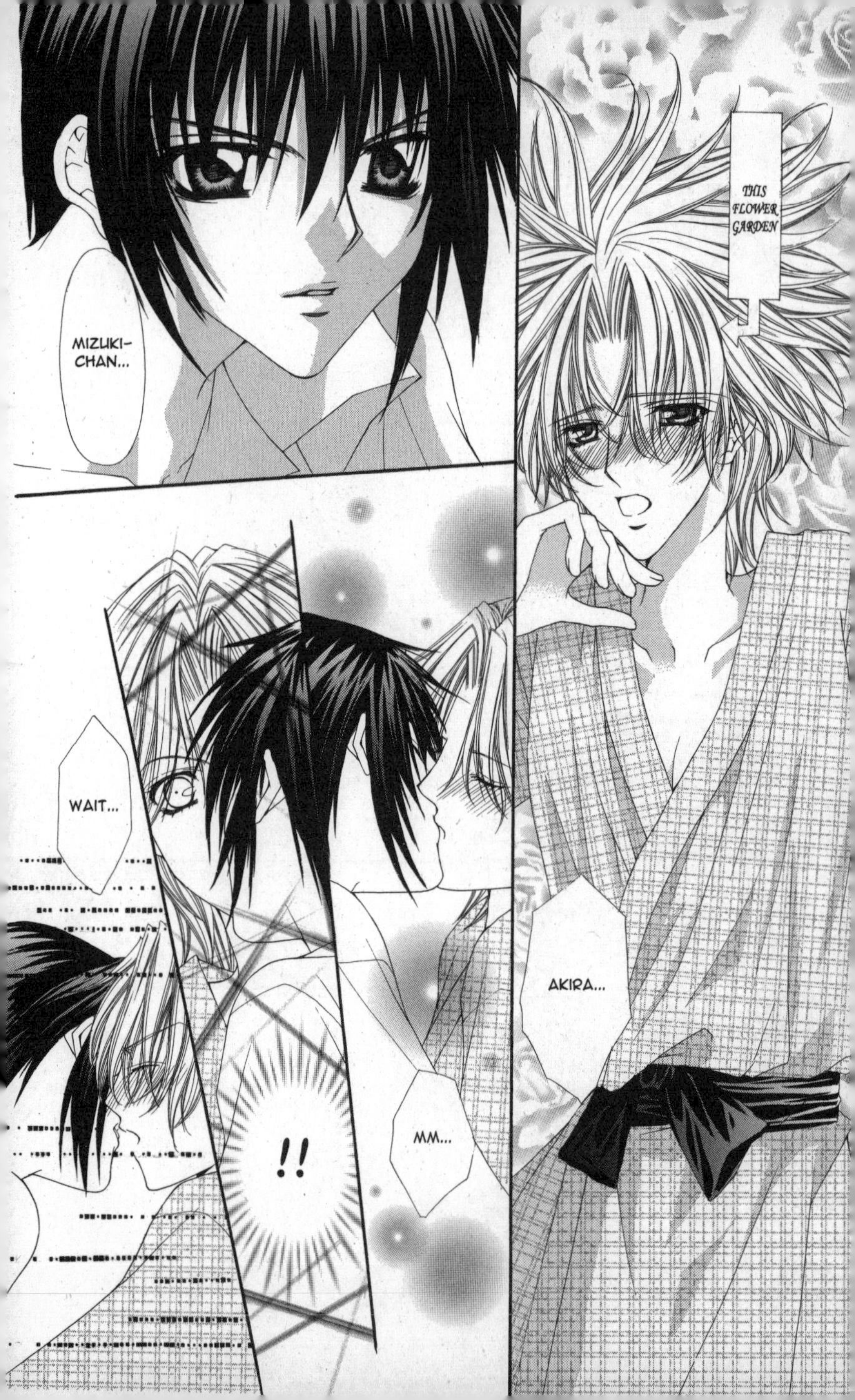
THIS FLOWER GARDEN
AKIRA...
MIZUKI-CHAN...
WAIT...
!!
MM...

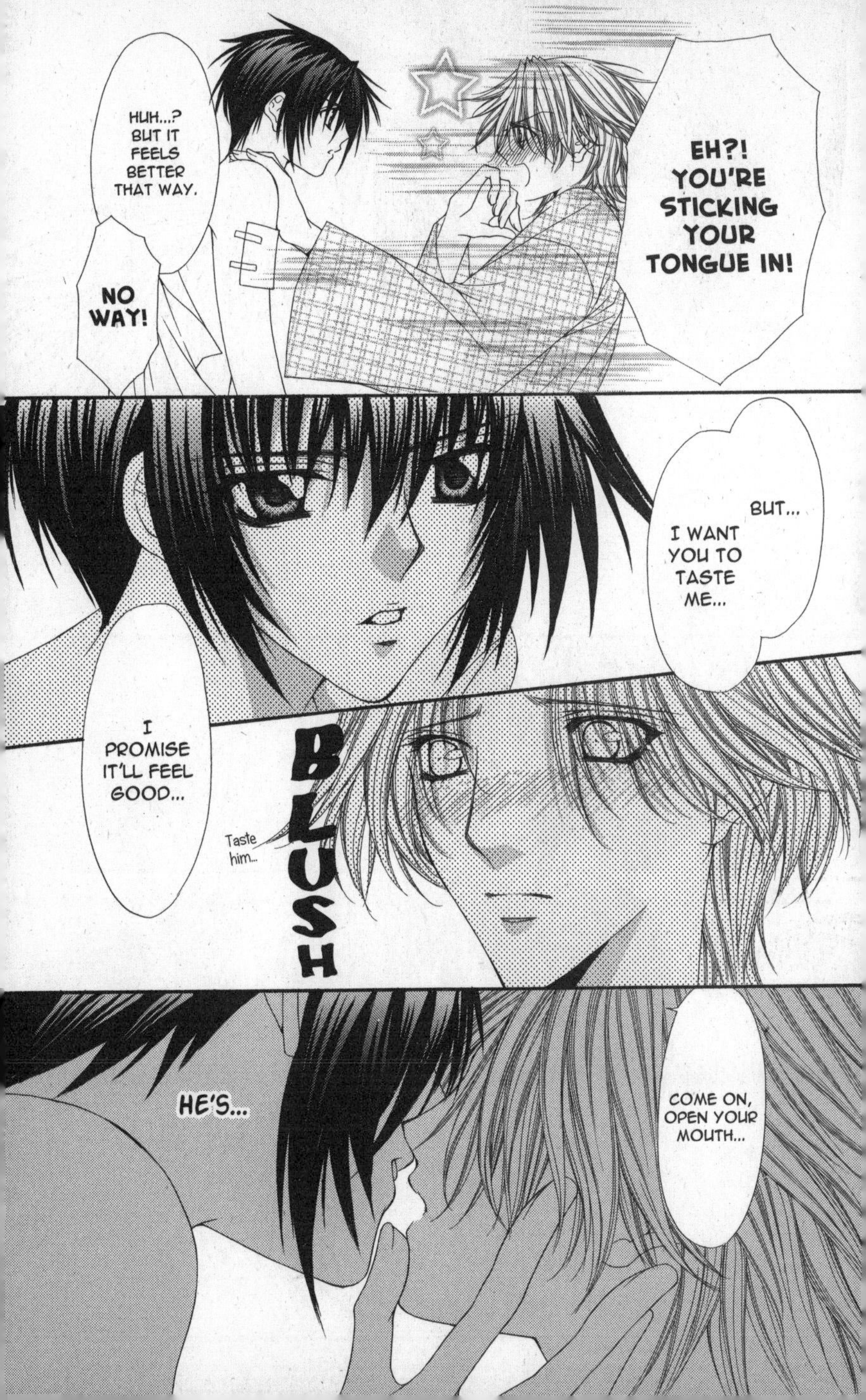
EH?! YOU'RE STICKING YOUR TONGUE IN!
HUH...? BUT IT FEELS BETTER THAT WAY.
NO WAY!
BUT... I WANT YOU TO TASTE ME...
I PROMISE IT'LL FEEL GOOD...
BLUSH
Taste him...
COME ON, OPEN YOUR MOUTH...
HE'S...

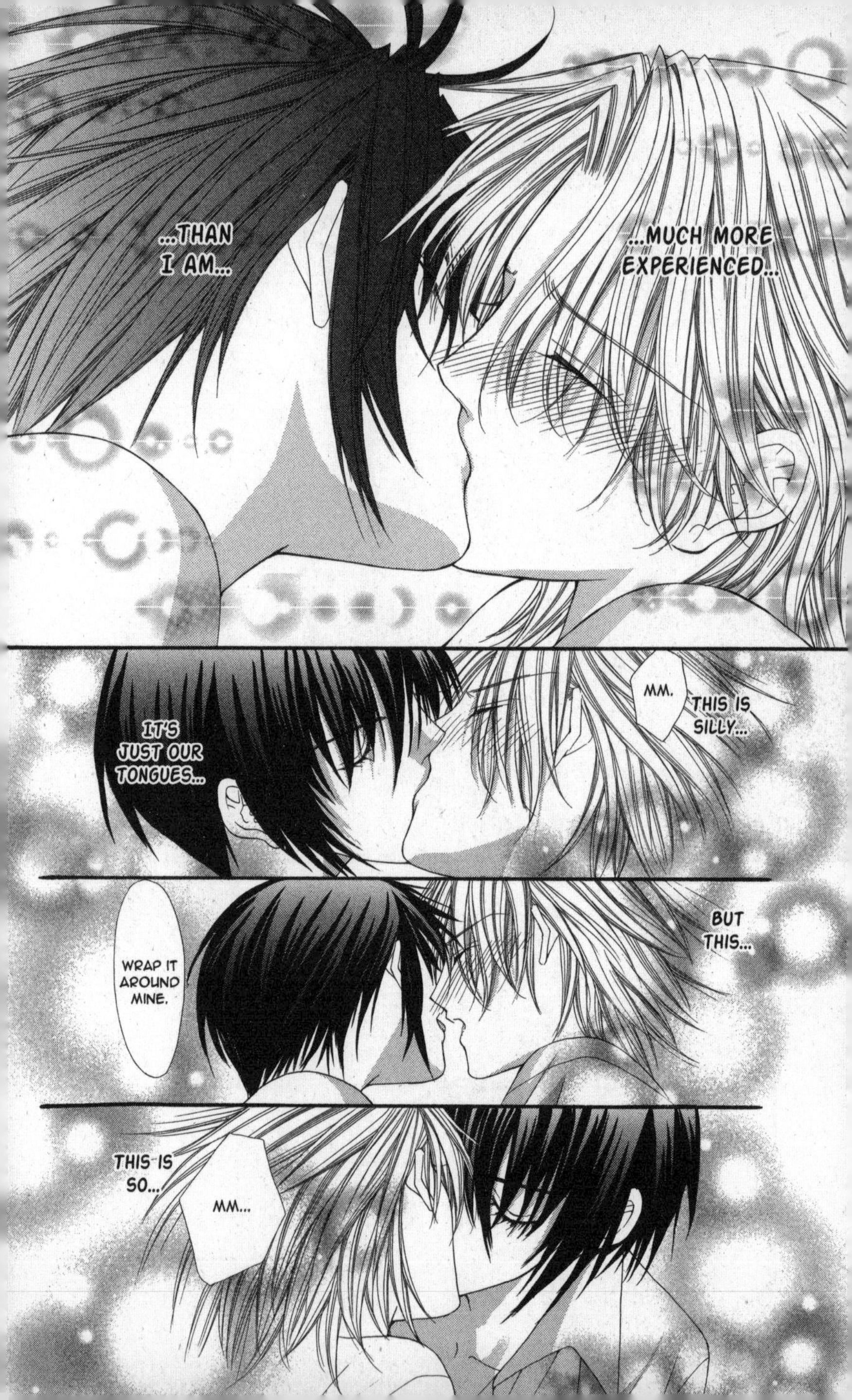
...MUCH MORE EXPERIENCED...
...THAN I AM...
MM.
THIS IS SILLY...
IT'S JUST OUR TONGUES...
BUT THIS...
WRAP IT AROUND MINE.
THIS IS SO...
MM...

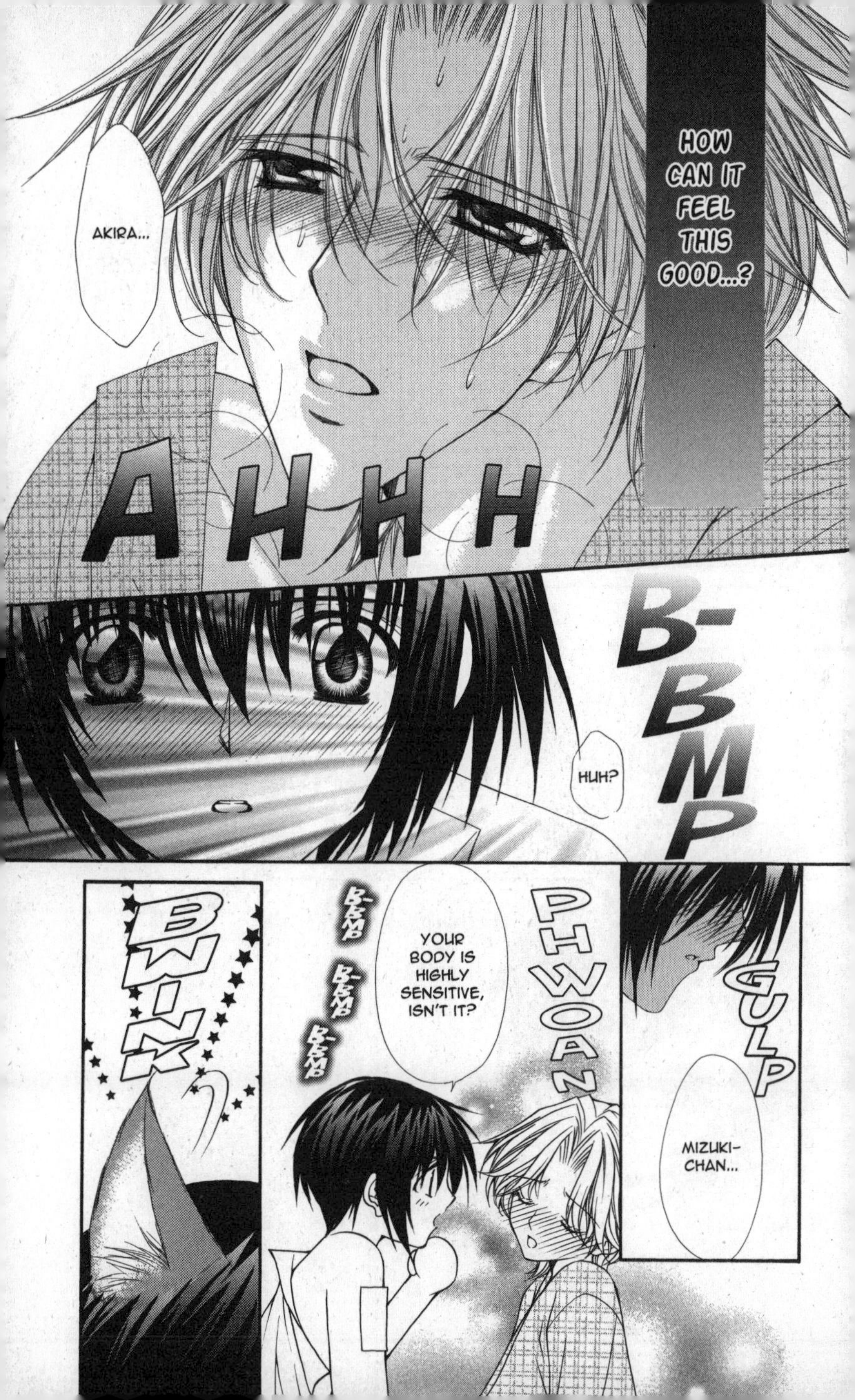
HOW CAN IT FEEL THIS GOOD...?
AKIRA...
AHHH
B-BMP
HUH?
GULP
MIZUKI-CHAN...
PHWOAN
YOUR BODY IS HIGHLY SENSITIVE, ISN'T IT?
B-BMP
B-BMP
B-BMP
BWINK

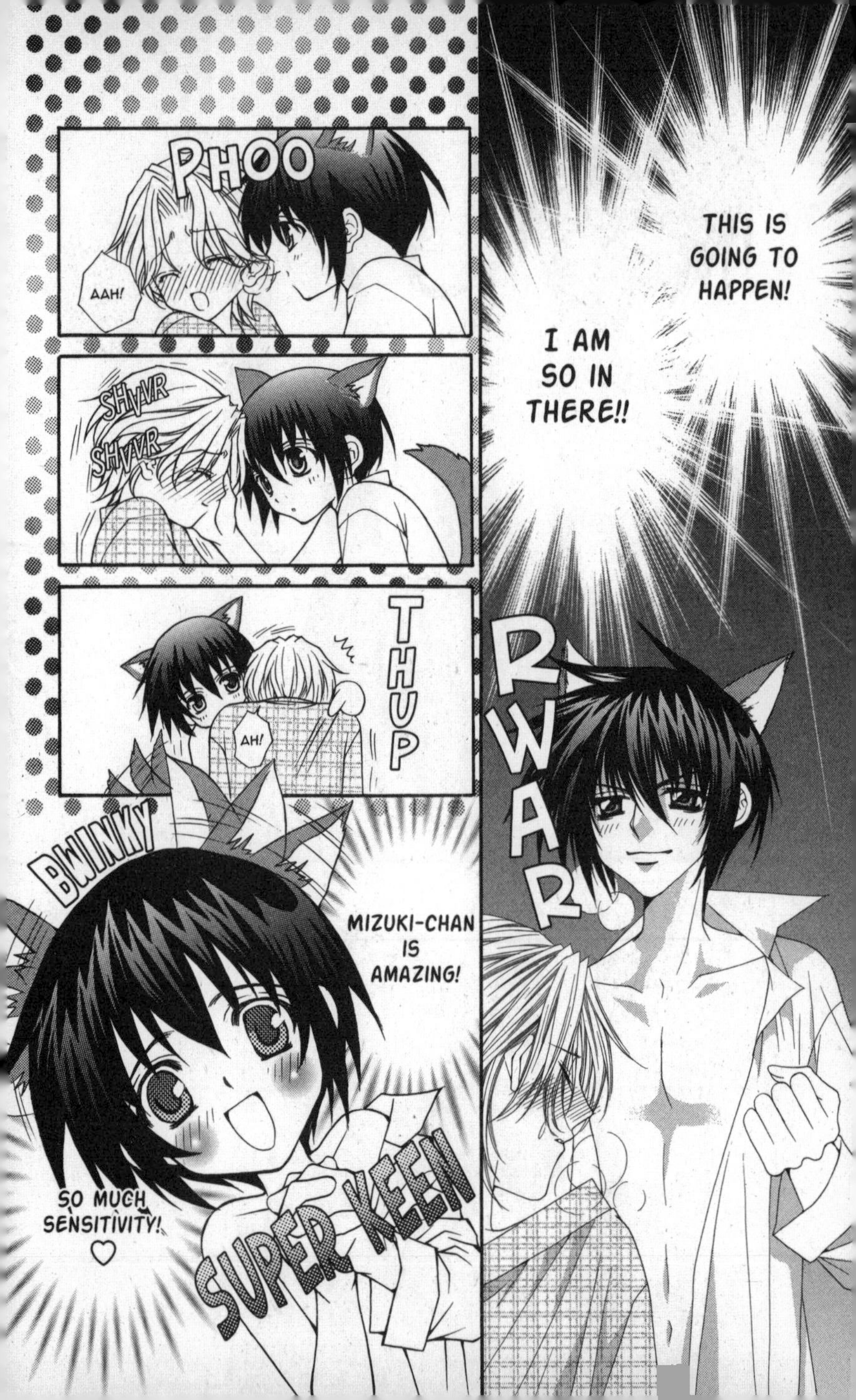
THIS IS GOING TO HAPPEN!
I AM SO IN THERE!!
RWAR
PHOO
AAH!
SHVVR
SHVVR
THUP
AH!
BWINKY
MIZUKI-CHAN IS AMAZING!
SUPER KEEN
SO MUCH SENSITIVITY! ♡

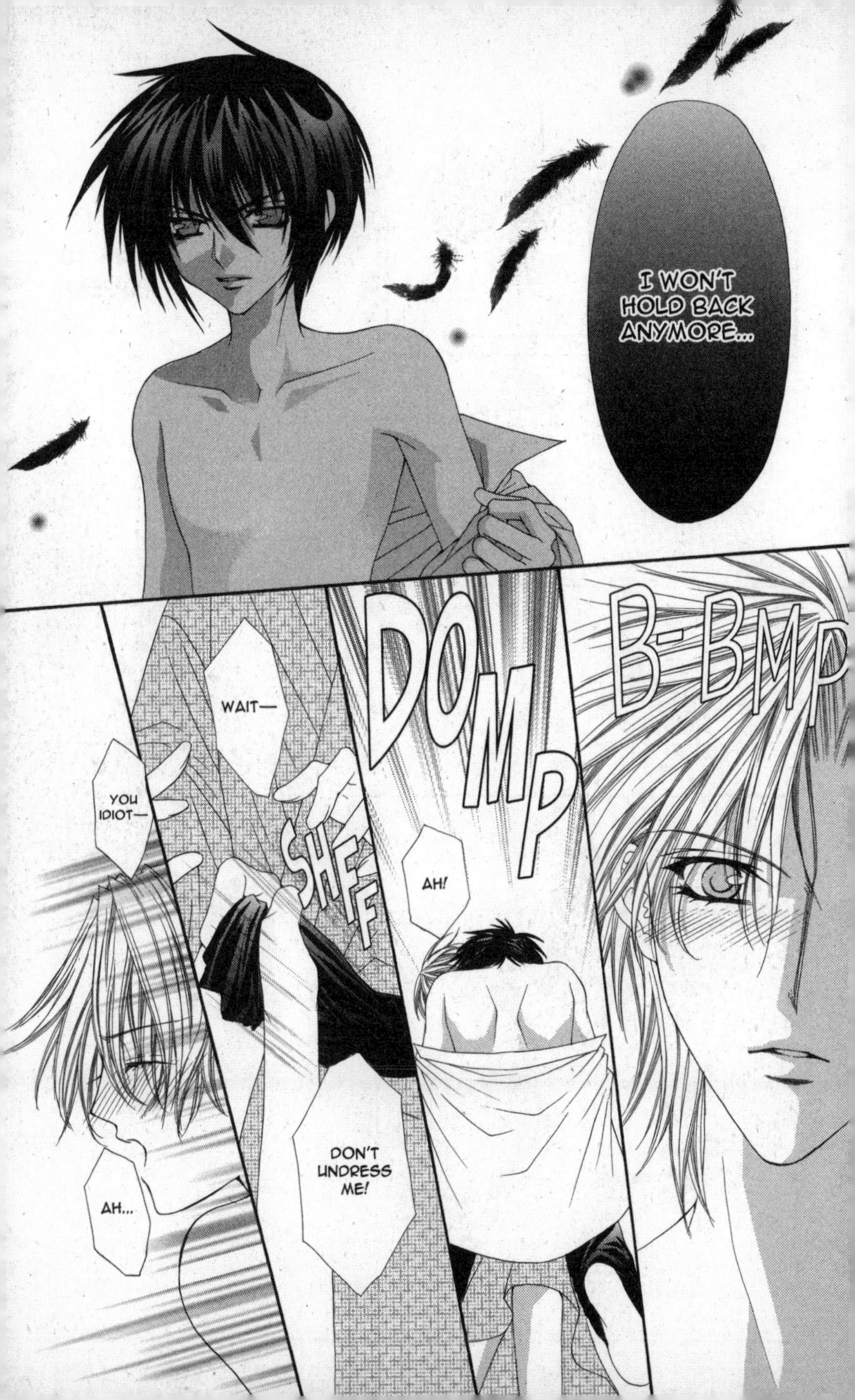
I WON'T HOLD BACK ANYMORE...
B-BMP
DOMP
AH!
SHFF
WAIT—
DON'T UNDRESS ME!
YOU IDIOT—
AH...

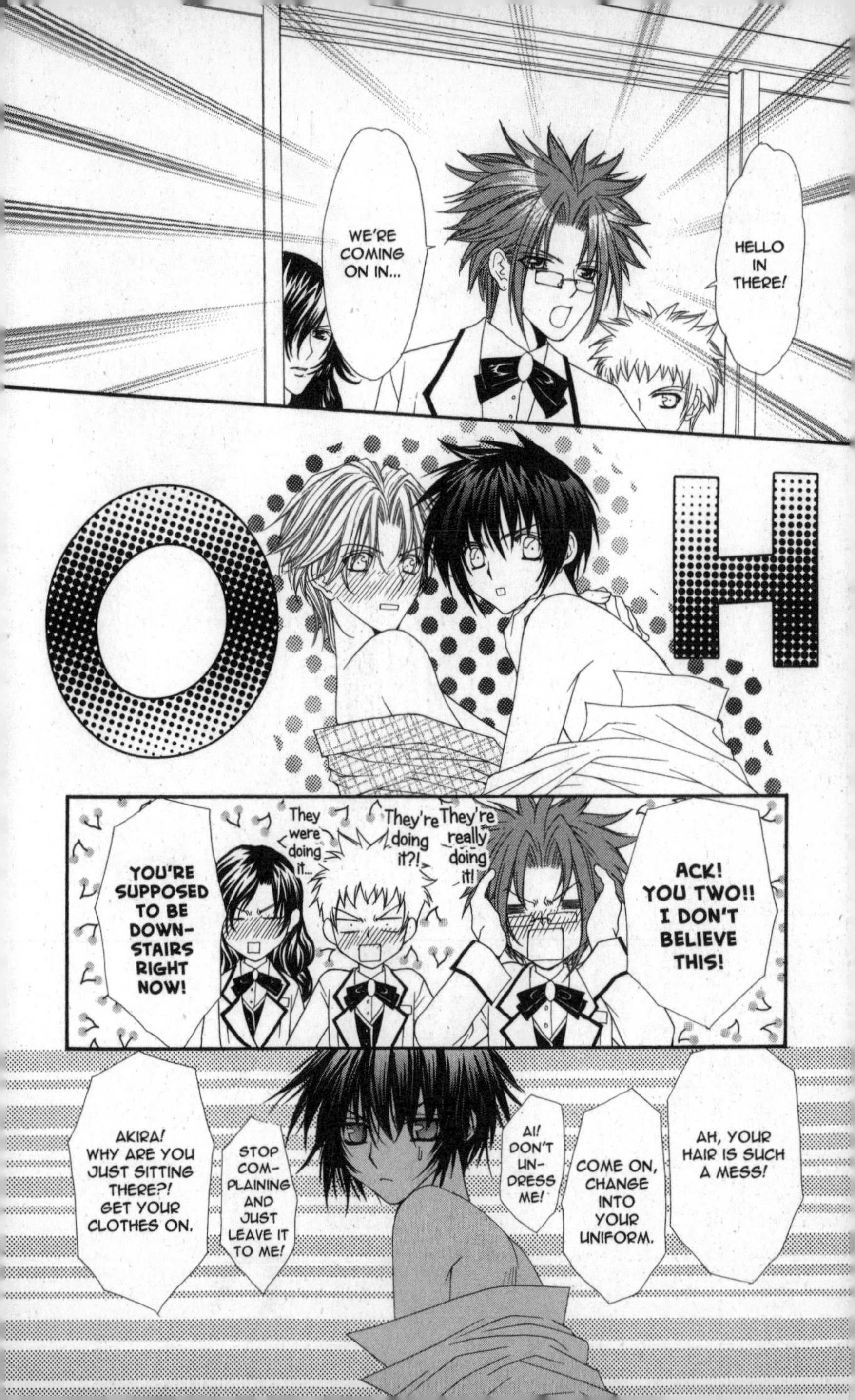
HELLO IN THERE!
WE'RE COMING ON IN...
OH
ACK! YOU TWO!! I DON'T BELIEVE THIS!
They're really doing it!
They're doing it?!
They were doing it...
YOU'RE SUPPOSED TO BE DOWN-STAIRS RIGHT NOW!
AH, YOUR HAIR IS SUCH A MESS!
COME ON, CHANGE INTO YOUR UNIFORM.
AI! DON'T UN-DRESS ME!
STOP COM-PLAINING AND JUST LEAVE IT TO ME!
AKIRA! WHY ARE YOU JUST SITTING THERE?! GET YOUR CLOTHES ON.

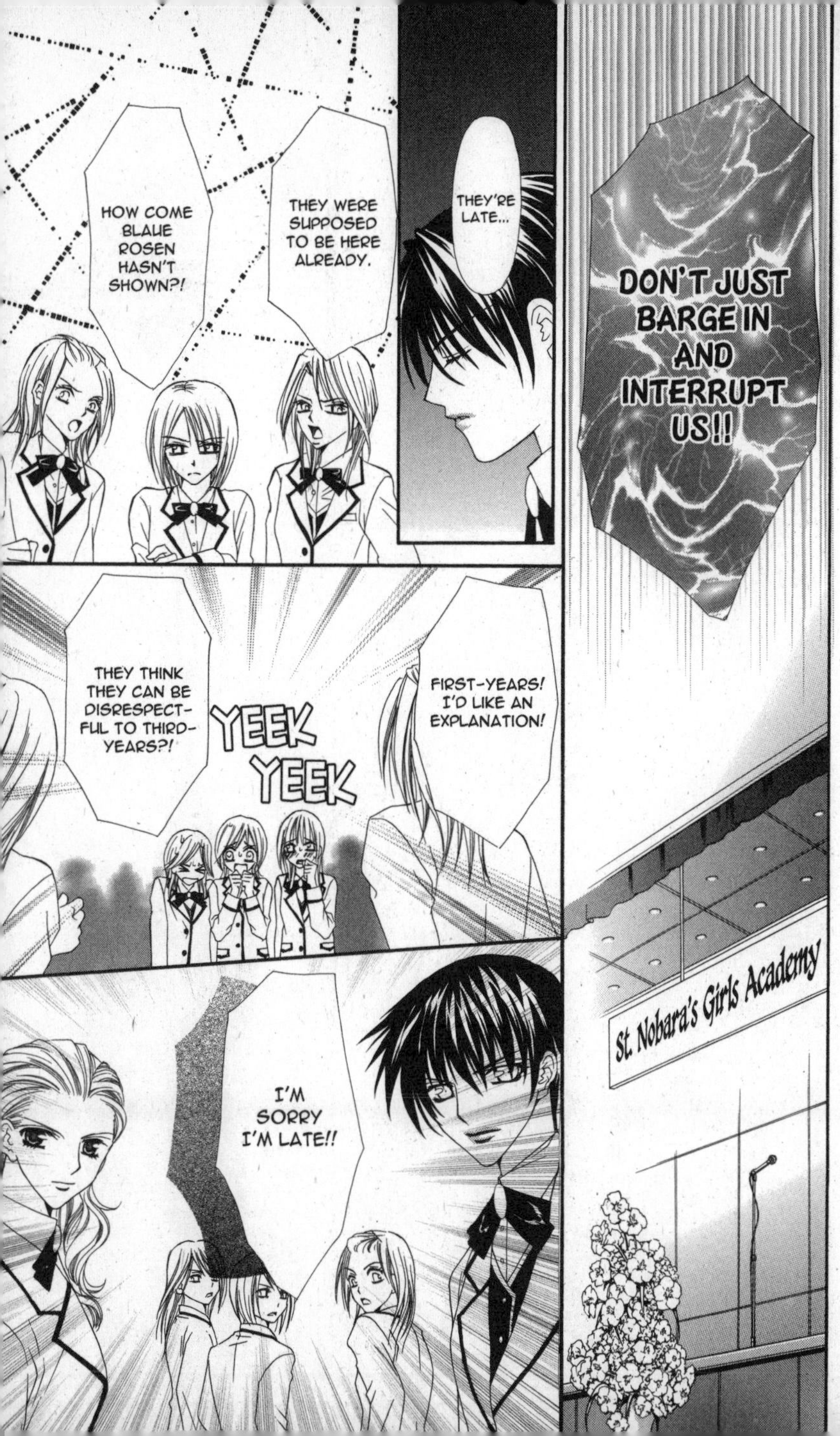
DON'T JUST BARGE IN AND INTERRUPT US!!
St. Nobara's Girls Academy
THEY'RE LATE...
THEY WERE SUPPOSED TO BE HERE ALREADY.
HOW COME BLAUE ROSEN HASN'T SHOWN?!
FIRST-YEARS! I'D LIKE AN EXPLANATION!
YEEK YEEK
THEY THINK THEY CAN BE DISRESPECTFUL TO THIRD-YEARS?!
I'M SORRY I'M LATE!!

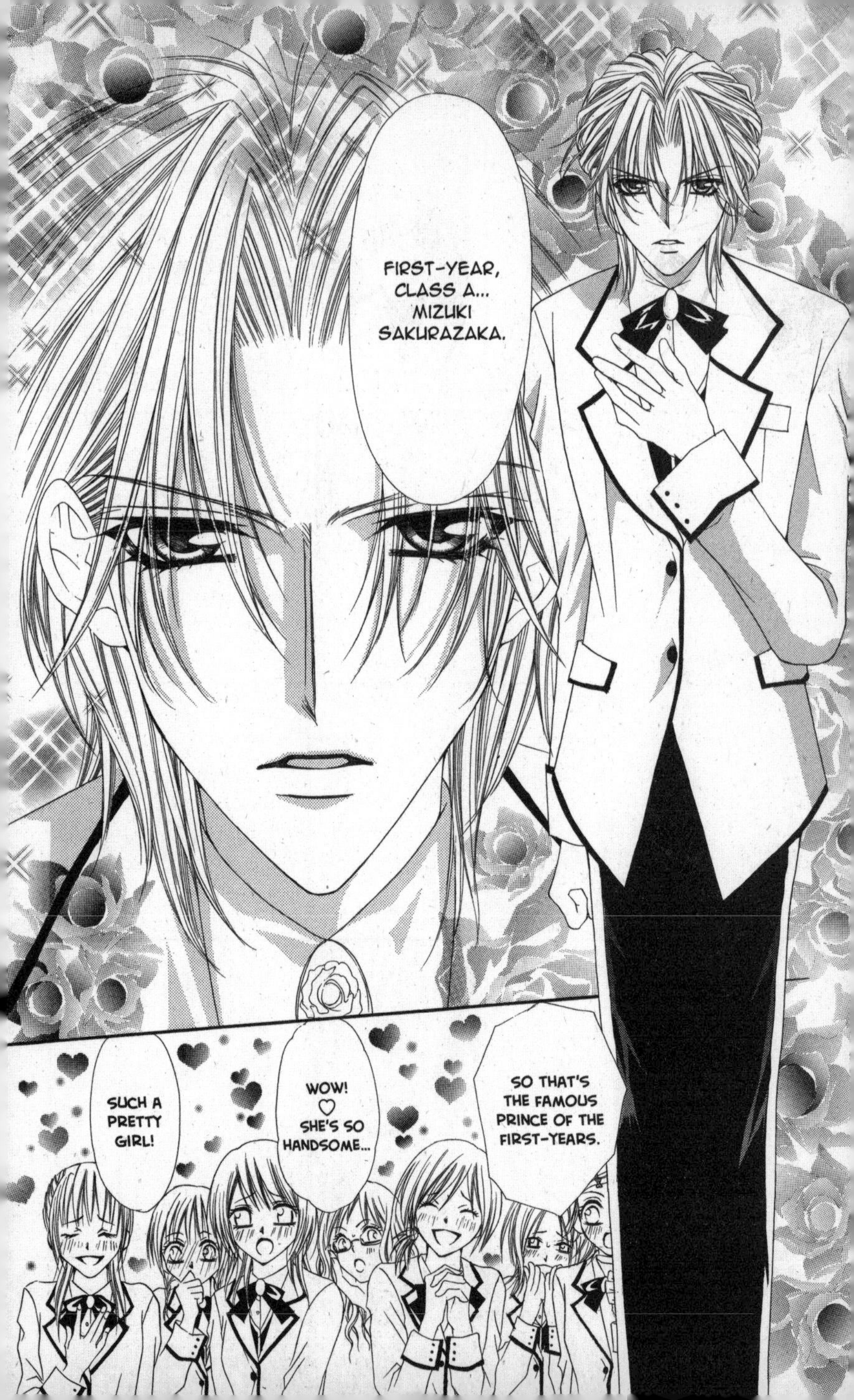
FIRST-YEAR, CLASS A... MIZUKI SAKURAZAKA.
SO THAT'S THE FAMOUS PRINCE OF THE FIRST-YEARS.
WOW! ♡ SHE'S SO HANDSOME...
SUCH A PRETTY GIRL!

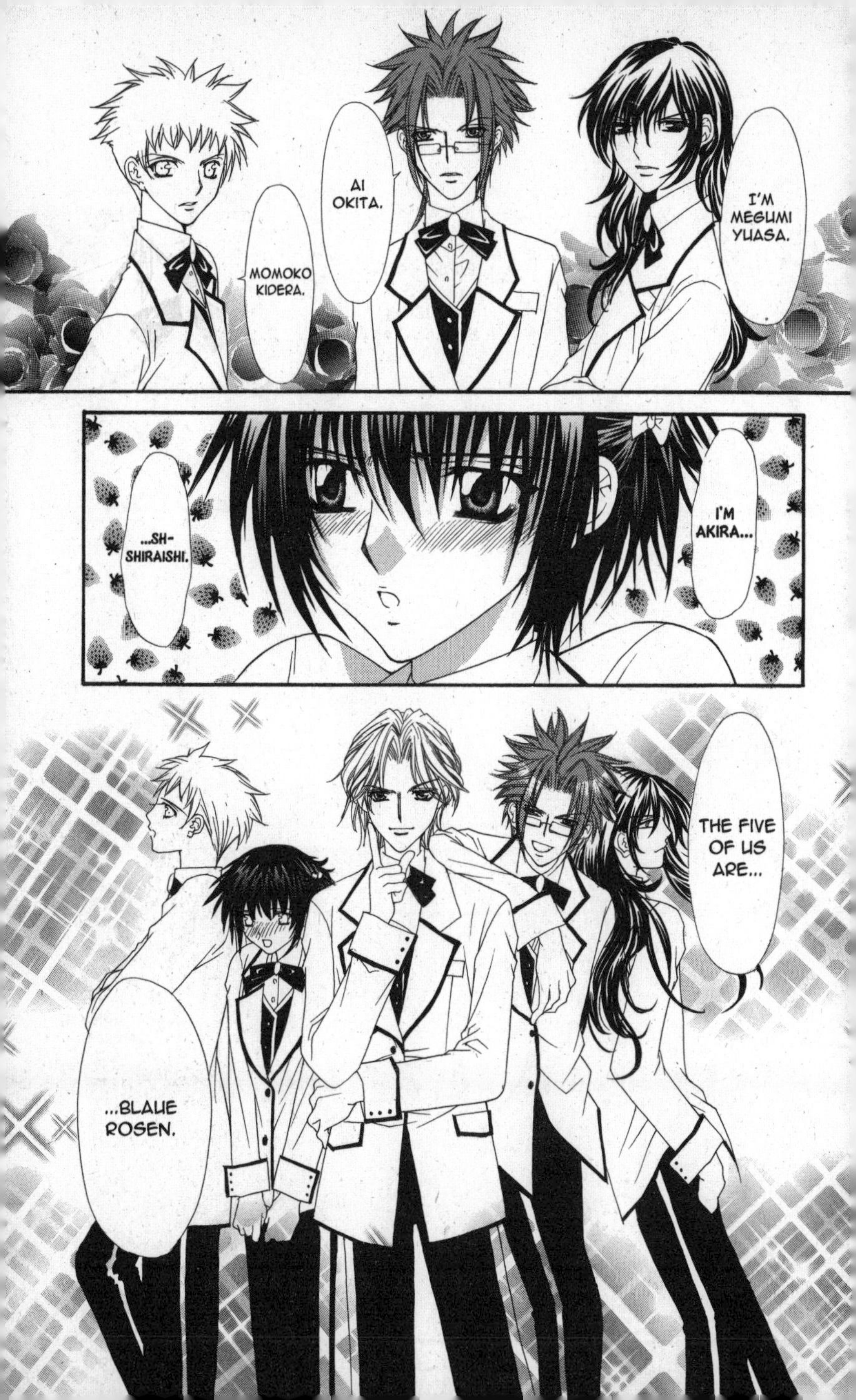
I'M MEGUMI YUASA.
AI OKITA.
MOMOKO KIDERA.
I'M AKIRA...
...SH-SHIRAISHI.
THE FIVE OF US ARE...
...BLAUE ROSEN.

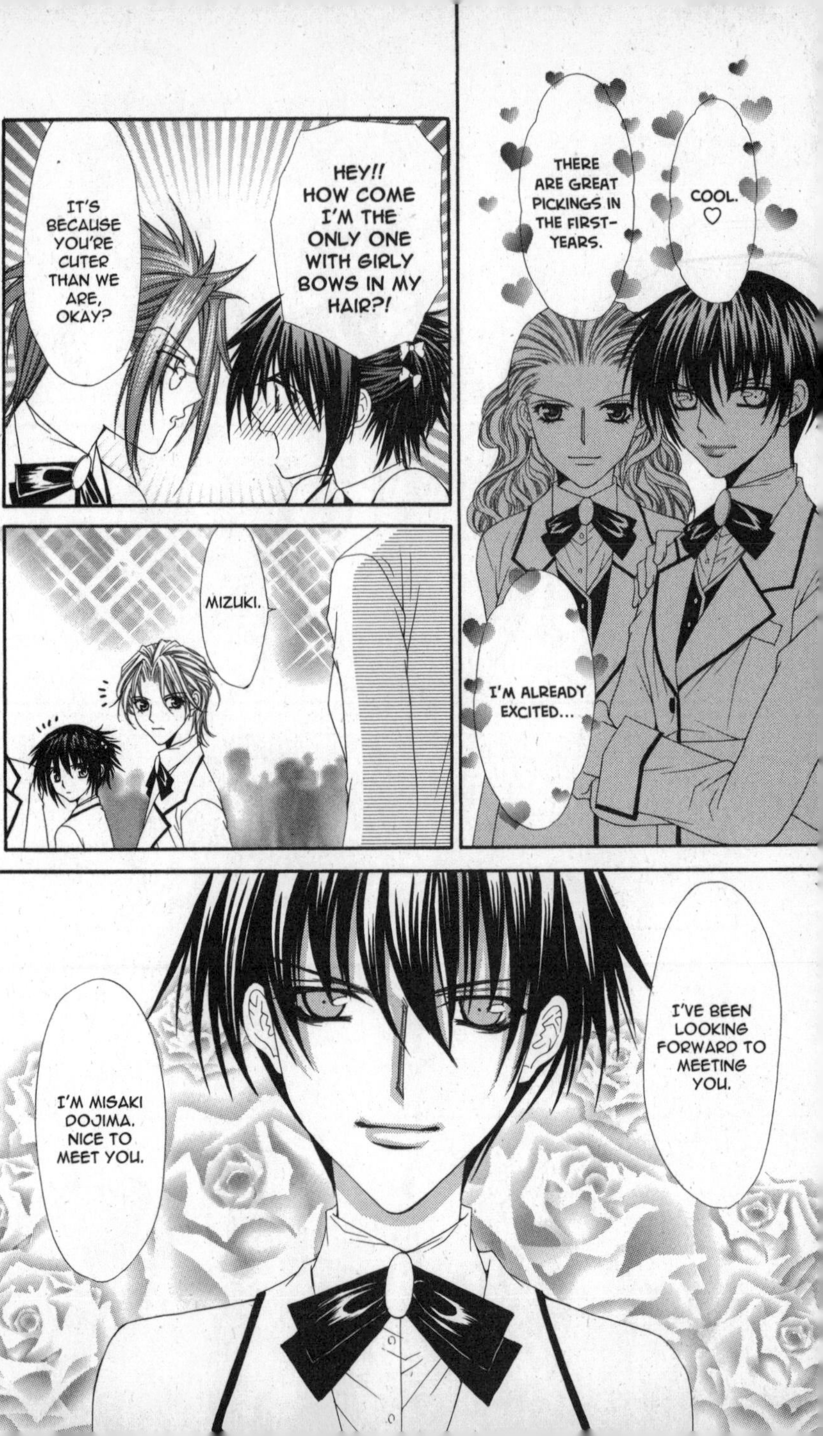
COOL. ♡
THERE ARE GREAT PICKINGS IN THE FIRST-YEARS.
I'M ALREADY EXCITED...
HEY!! HOW COME I'M THE ONLY ONE WITH GIRLY BOWS IN MY HAIR?!
IT'S BECAUSE YOU'RE CUTER THAN WE ARE, OKAY?
MIZUKI.
I'VE BEEN LOOKING FORWARD TO MEETING YOU.
I'M MISAKI DOJIMA. NICE TO MEET YOU.

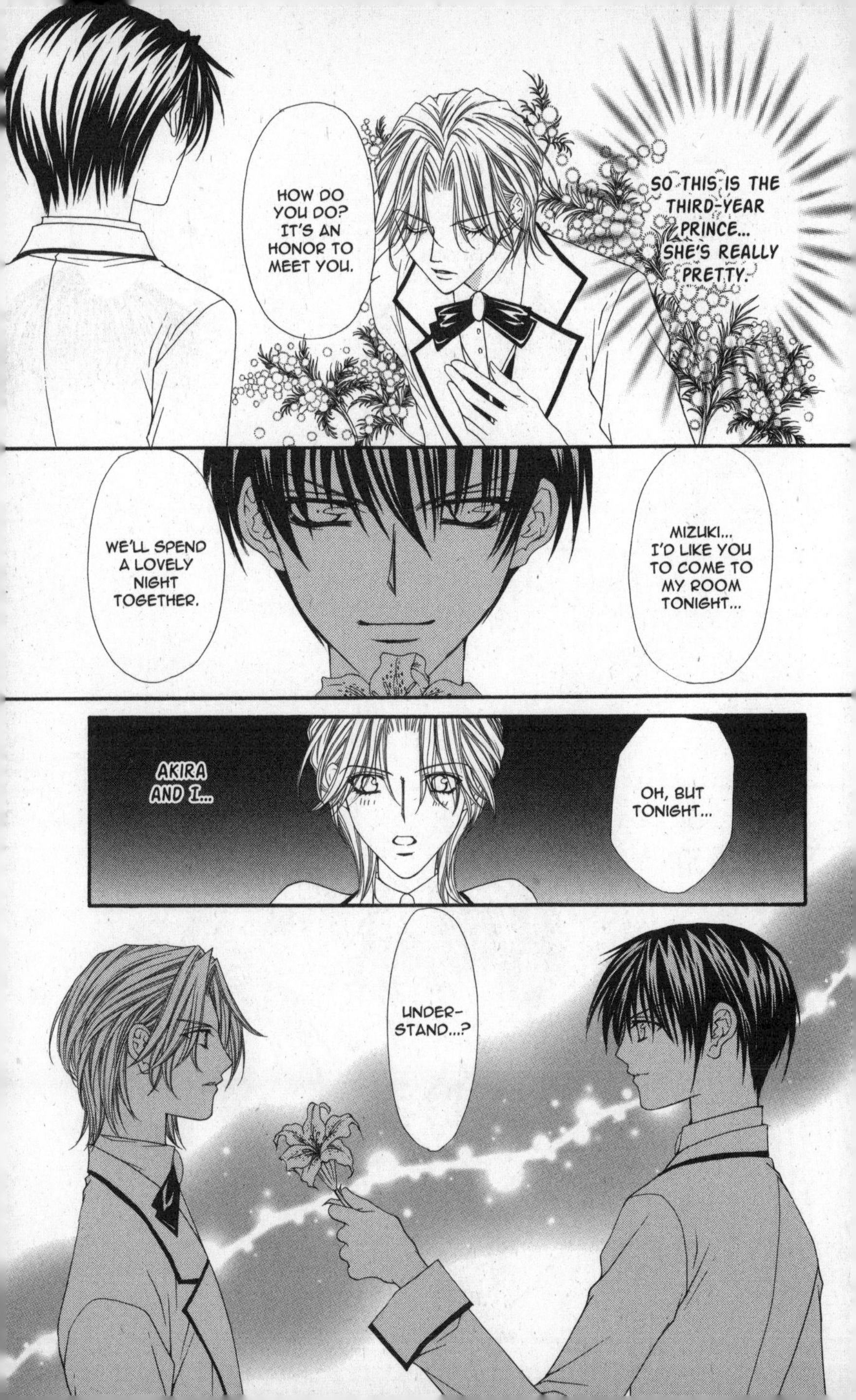
SO THIS IS THE THIRD-YEAR PRINCE... SHE'S REALLY PRETTY.
HOW DO YOU DO? IT'S AN HONOR TO MEET YOU.
MIZUKI... I'D LIKE YOU TO COME TO MY ROOM TONIGHT...
WE'LL SPEND A LOVELY NIGHT TOGETHER.
OH, BUT TONIGHT...
AKIRA AND I...
UNDER-STAND...?

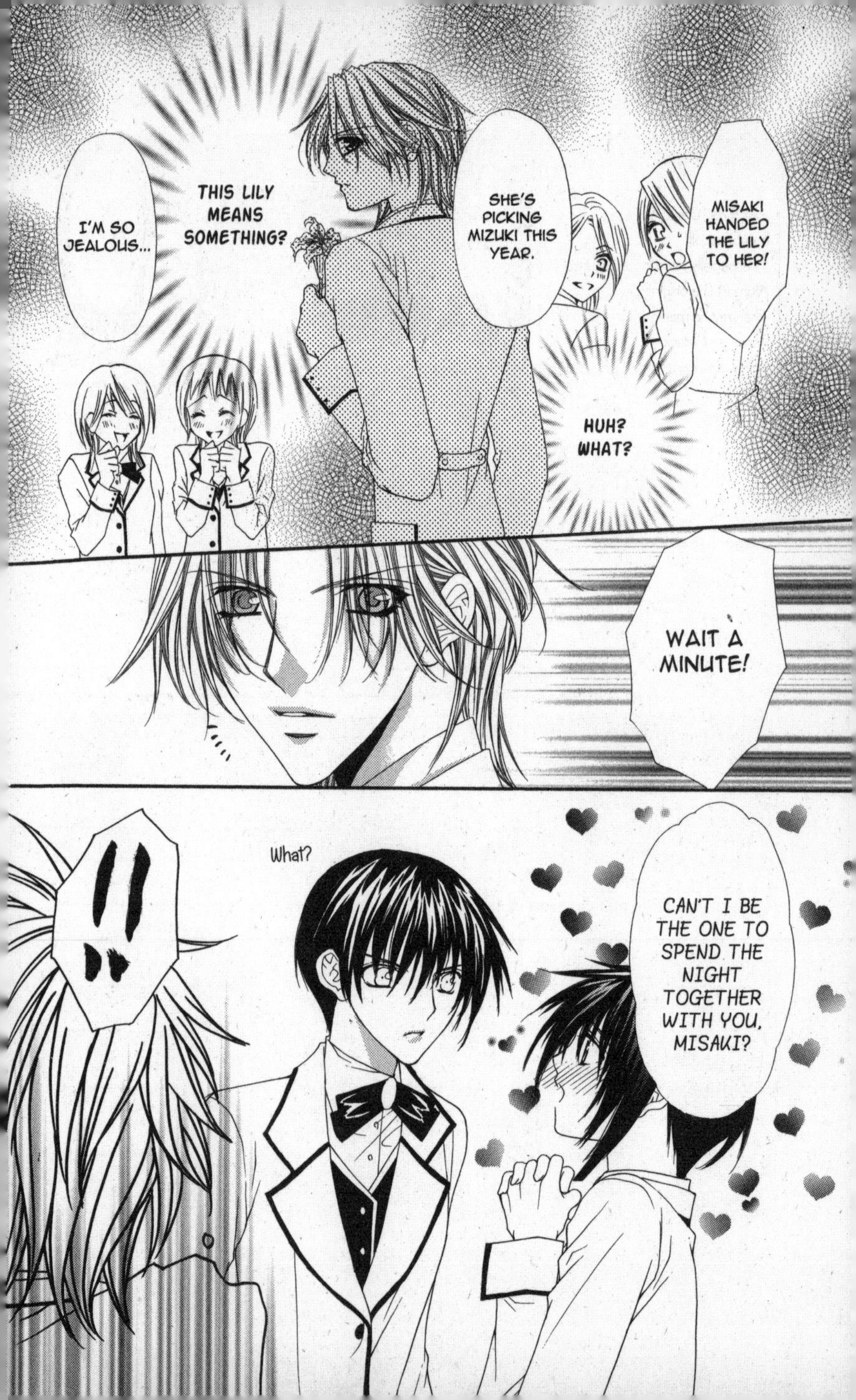
MISAKI HANDED THE LILY TO HER!
HUH? WHAT?
SHE'S PICKING MIZUKI THIS YEAR.
THIS LILY MEANS SOMETHING?
I'M SO JEALOUS...
WAIT A MINUTE!
CAN'T I BE THE ONE TO SPEND THE NIGHT TOGETHER WITH YOU, MISAKI?
What?
!!

So that's how Hoshi-san was. (What?!)

And his "Dark Akira" is unbelievably cool!

I especially recommend Dark Akira in the original bonus story! The way he manipulates Rui and Ran is just hilarious.

Shinjo's selection of moe lines said by Akira:

"Do you want to see...my boobs?"

"I'll let you do...whatever you want to me."

"Hey, I want to mess around. I want to mess around."

Next is Mizuki. I actually asked Saiga-san, "Please give me a hug later!" She remembered and came over to me with open arms saying, "I promised you, didn't I?" I leapt into her arms without thinking twice!!

Aah, she's a woman... She's a woman. Why is my heart beating so fast?!

By the way, I was screaming "Hug me...!!" in the dubbing booth because Mizuki sounded so cool, and the director of audiography (female) was saying "Mitsuki is better looking and manlier than any man you'd meet." I agree. She really is handsome!

It was very rare for Saiga-san to do the voice for a female role, and she told me "I've never done such a cute role before..." To which Kaida-san and the other female voice actresses replied, "We think so too. Mizuki is cute..."

(Continues)

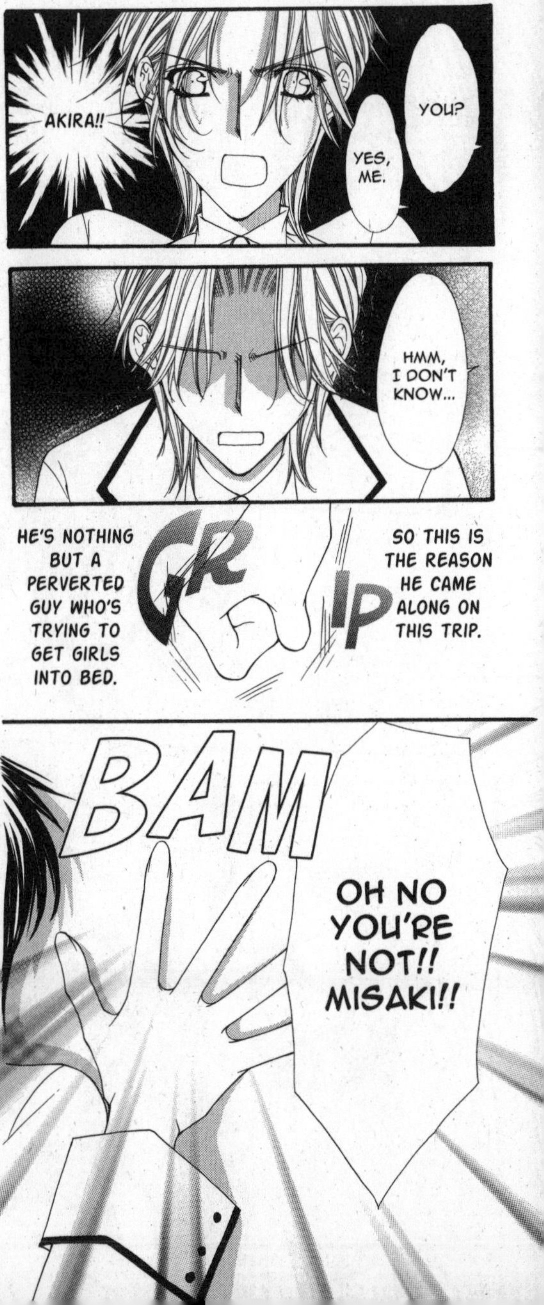
YOU?
YES, ME.
AKIRA!!
HMM, I DON'T KNOW...
SO THIS IS THE REASON HE CAME ALONG ON THIS TRIP.
GRIP
HE'S NOTHING BUT A PERVERTED GUY WHO'S TRYING TO GET GIRLS INTO BED.
OH NO YOU'RE NOT!! MISAKI!!
BAM

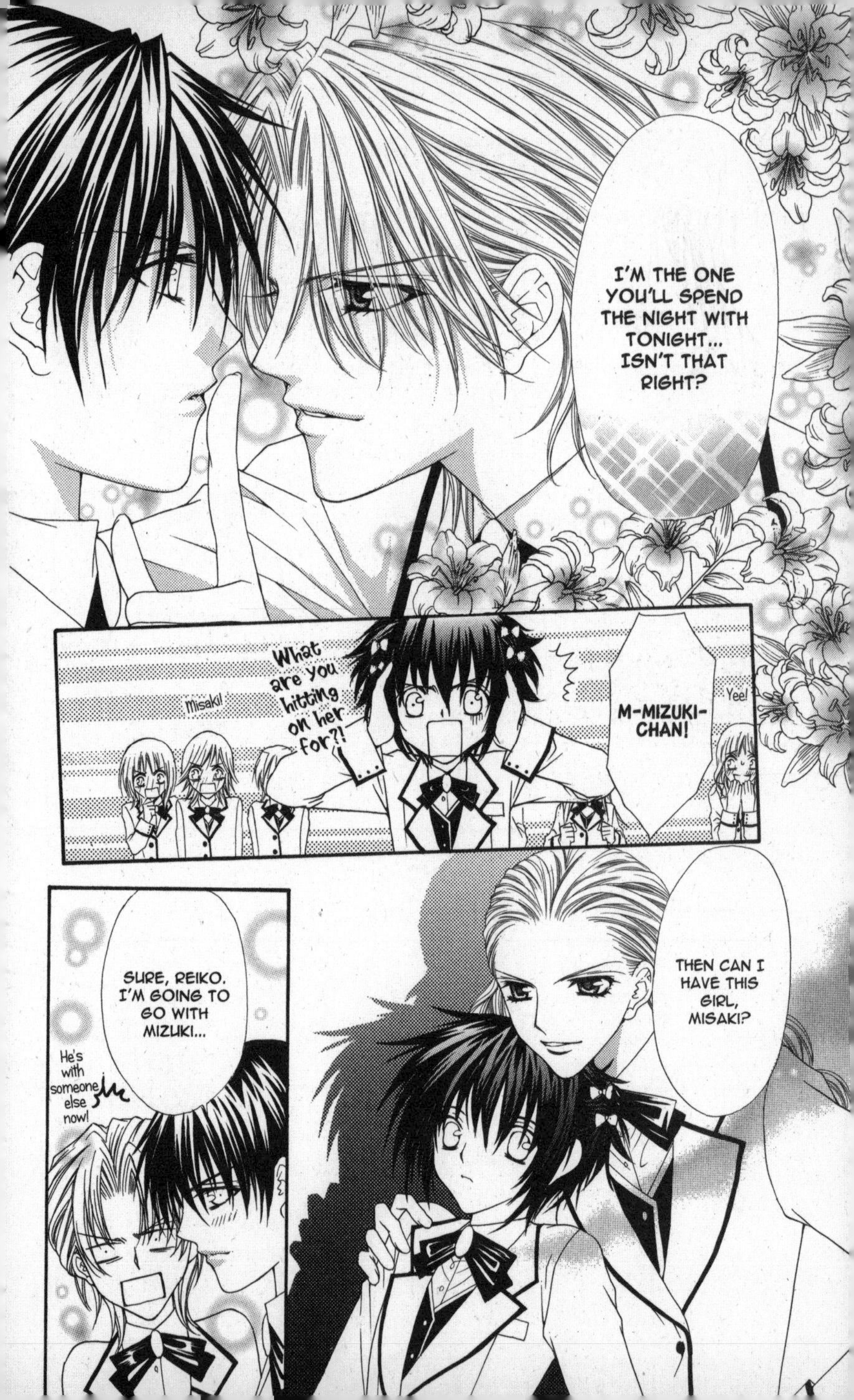
I'M THE ONE YOU'LL SPEND THE NIGHT WITH TONIGHT... ISN'T THAT RIGHT?
Yee!
M-MIZUKI-CHAN!
What are you hitting on her for?!
Misaki!
THEN CAN I HAVE THIS GIRL, MISAKI?
SURE, REIKO. I'M GOING TO GO WITH MIZUKI...
He's with someone else now!

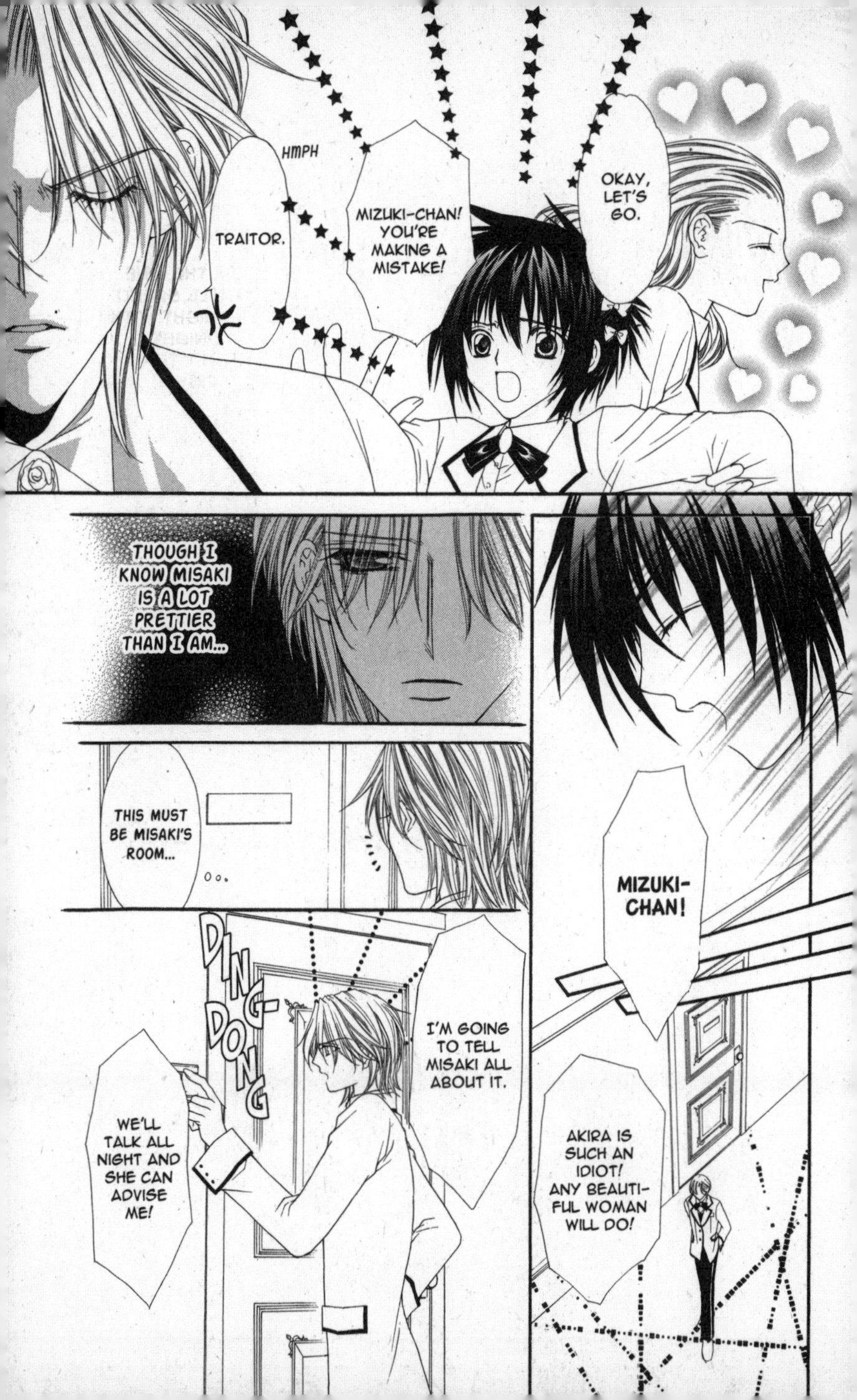

OKAY, LET'S GO.
MIZUKI-CHAN! YOU'RE MAKING A MISTAKE!
HMPH
TRAITOR.
MIZUKI-CHAN!
AKIRA IS SUCH AN IDIOT! ANY BEAUTIFUL WOMAN WILL DO!
THOUGH I KNOW MISAKI IS A LOT PRETTIER THAN I AM...
THIS MUST BE MISAKI'S ROOM...
DING-DONG
I'M GOING TO TELL MISAKI ALL ABOUT IT.
WE'LL TALK ALL NIGHT AND SHE CAN ADVISE ME!

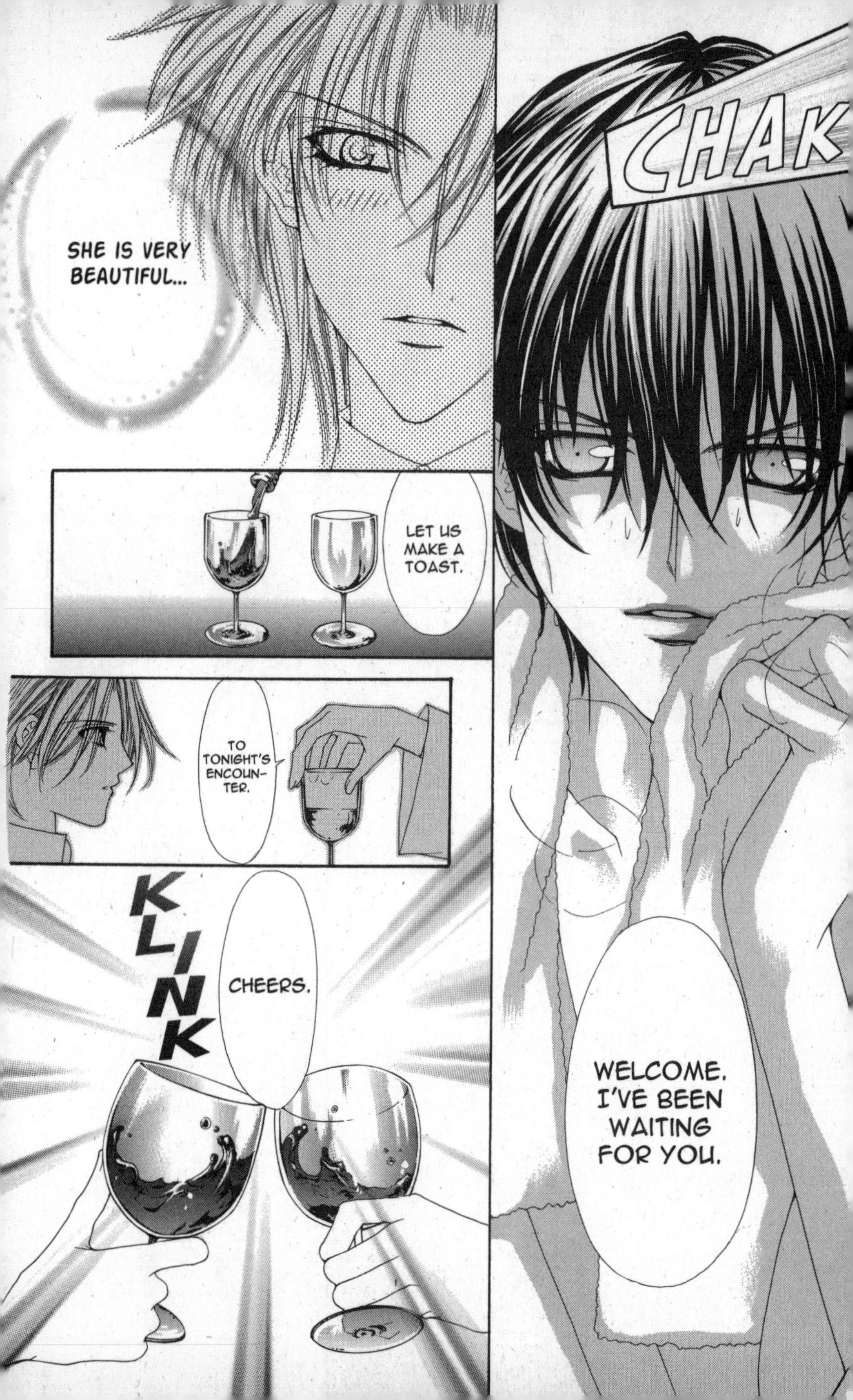
CHAK
WELCOME. I'VE BEEN WAITING FOR YOU.
SHE IS VERY BEAUTIFUL...
LET US MAKE A TOAST.
TO TONIGHT'S ENCOUN-TER.
KLINK
CHEERS.

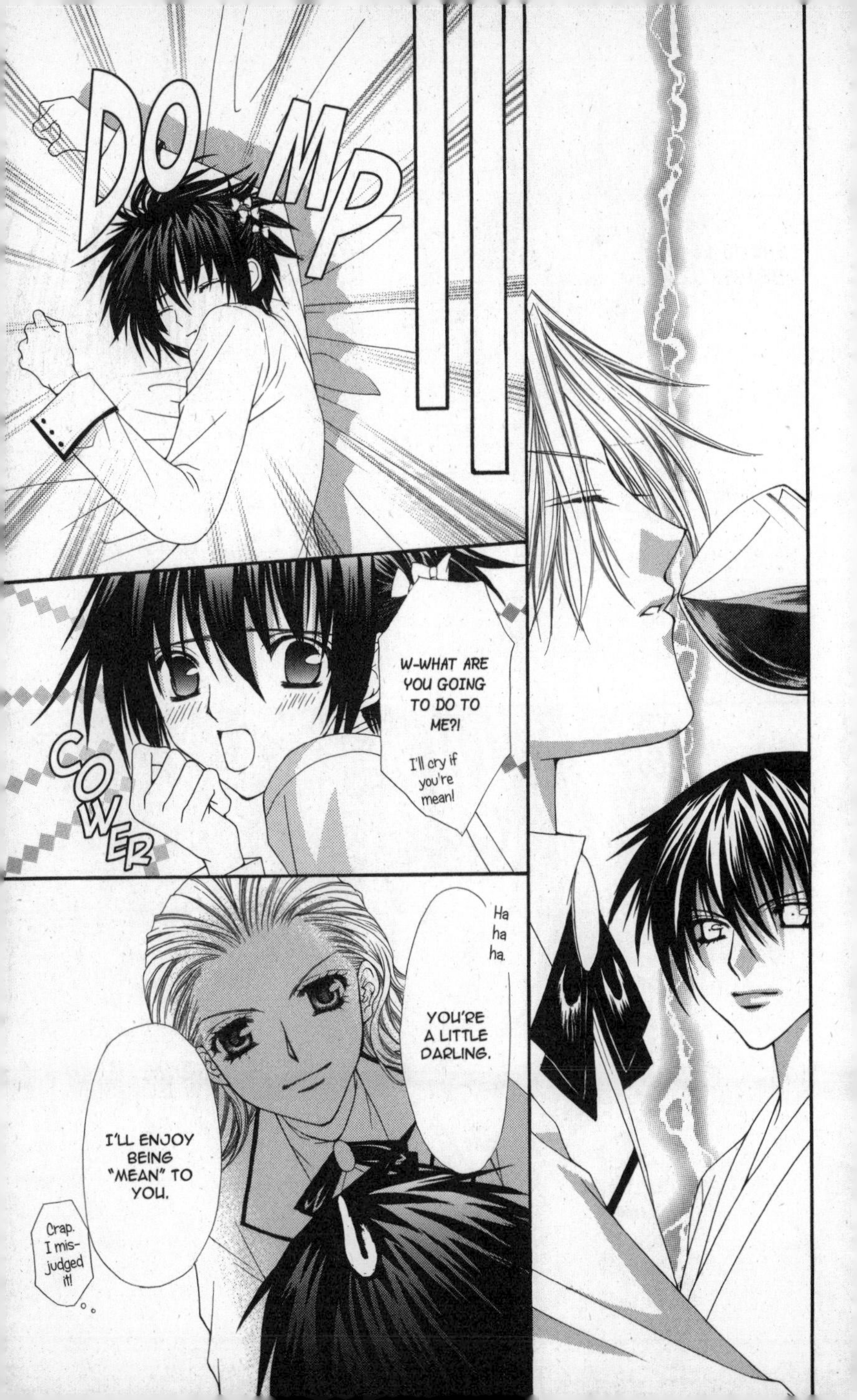
DOMP
W-WHAT ARE YOU GOING TO DO TO ME?!
I'll cry if you're mean!
COWER
Ha ha ha.
YOU'RE A LITTLE DARLING.
I'LL ENJOY BEING "MEAN" TO YOU.
Crap. I mis-judged it!

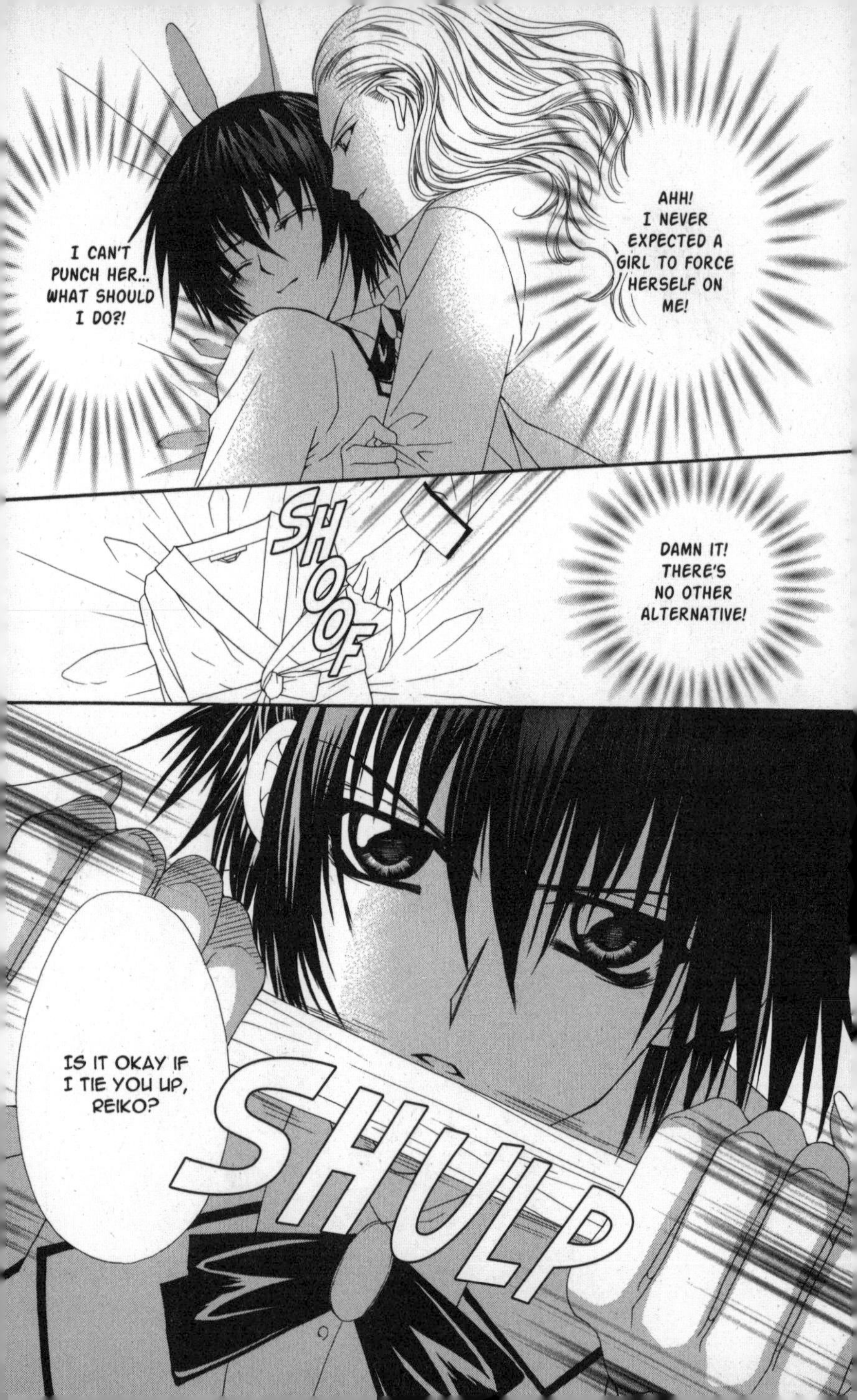
AHH! I NEVER EXPECTED A GIRL TO FORCE HERSELF ON ME!
I CAN'T PUNCH HER... WHAT SHOULD I DO?!
DAMN IT! THERE'S NO OTHER ALTERNATIVE!
SHOOF
IS IT OKAY IF I TIE YOU UP, REIKO?
SHULP

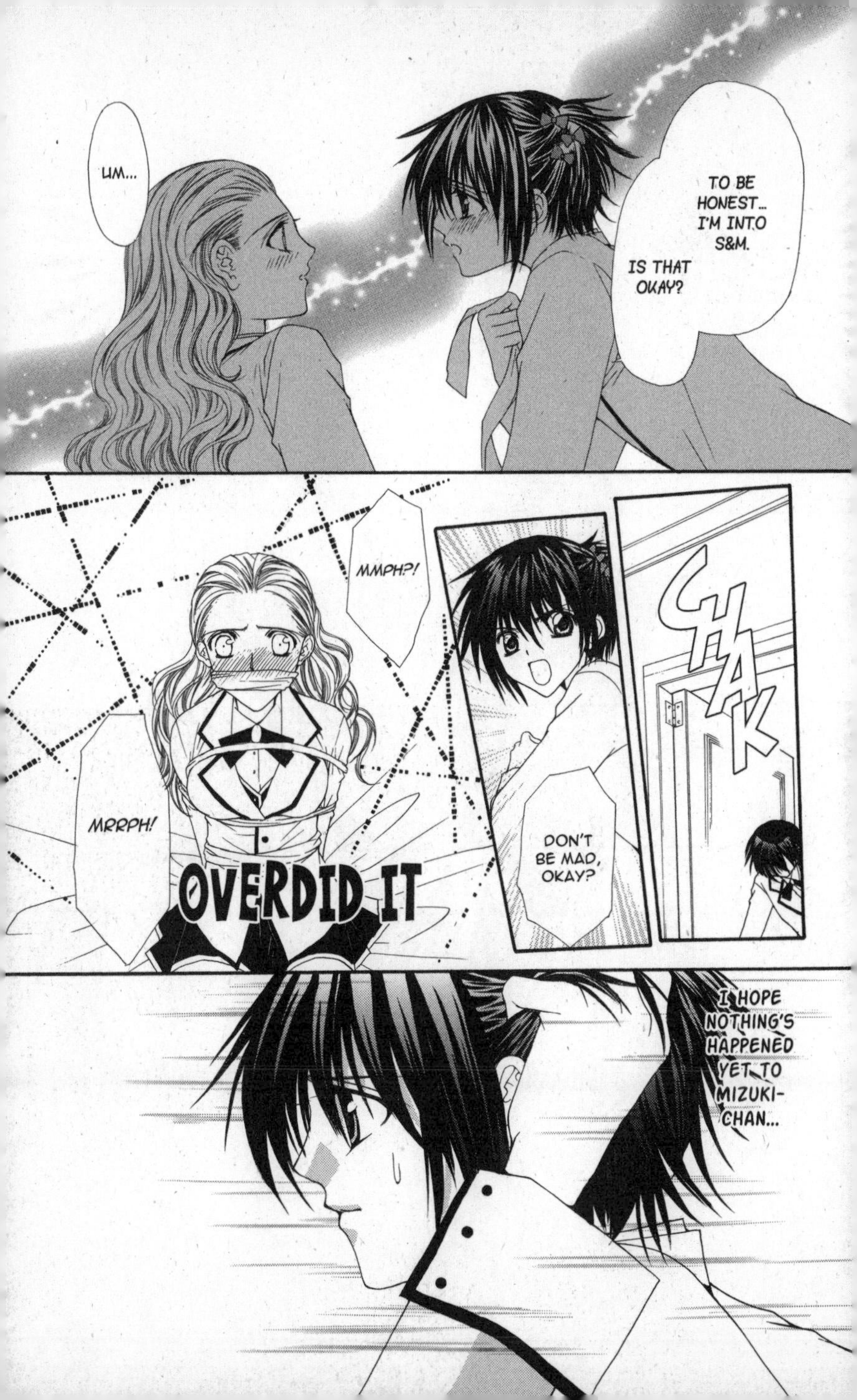

TO BE HONEST... I'M INTO S&M.
IS THAT OKAY?
UM...
CHAK
DON'T BE MAD, OKAY?
MMPH?!
MRRPH!
OVERDID IT
I HOPE NOTHING'S HAPPENED YET TO MIZUKI-CHAN...

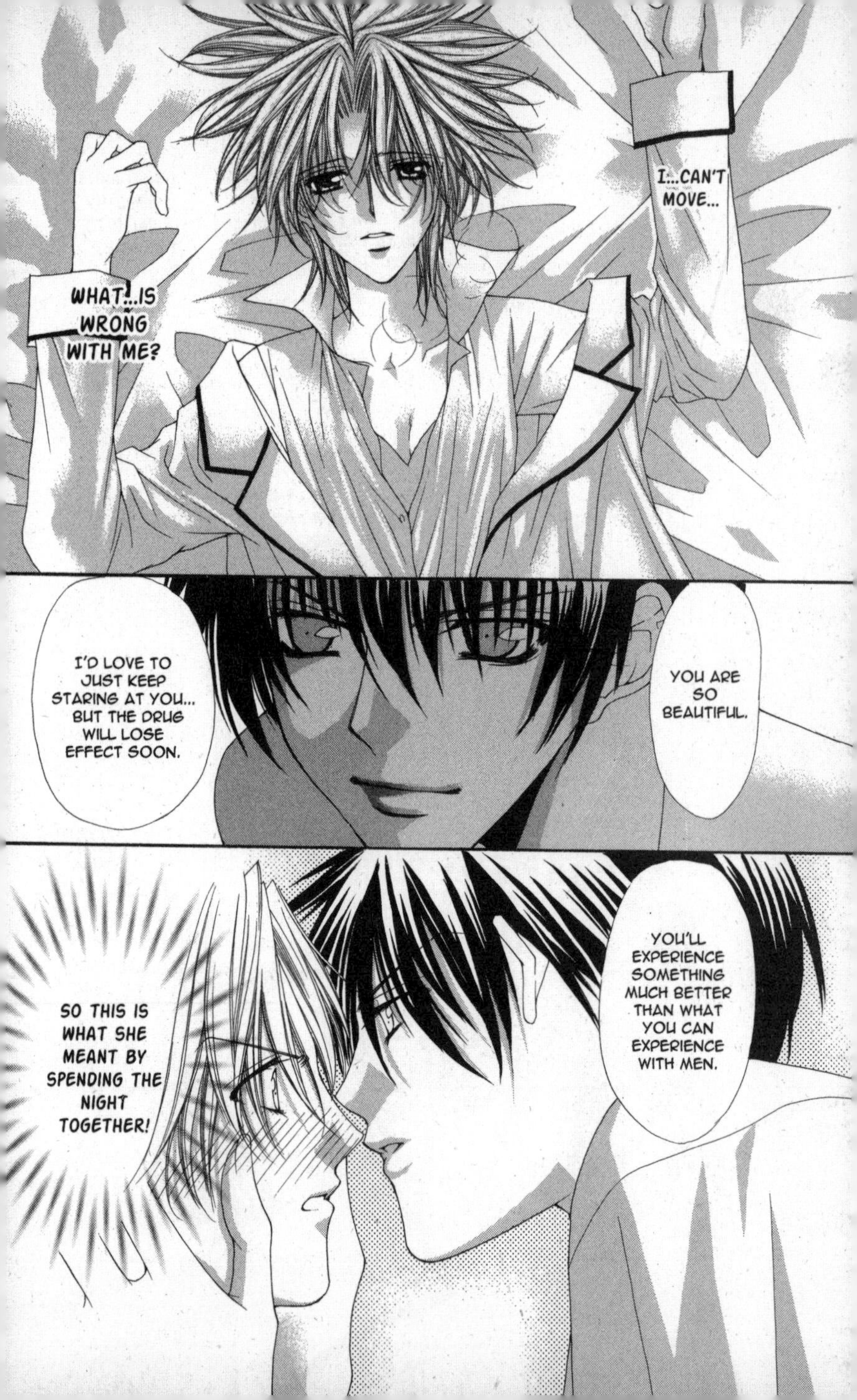
I...CAN'T MOVE...
WHAT...IS WRONG WITH ME?
YOU ARE SO BEAUTIFUL.
I'D LOVE TO JUST KEEP STARING AT YOU... BUT THE DRUG WILL LOSE EFFECT SOON.
YOU'LL EXPERIENCE SOMETHING MUCH BETTER THAN WHAT YOU CAN EXPERIENCE WITH MEN.
SO THIS IS WHAT SHE MEANT BY SPENDING THE NIGHT TOGETHER!

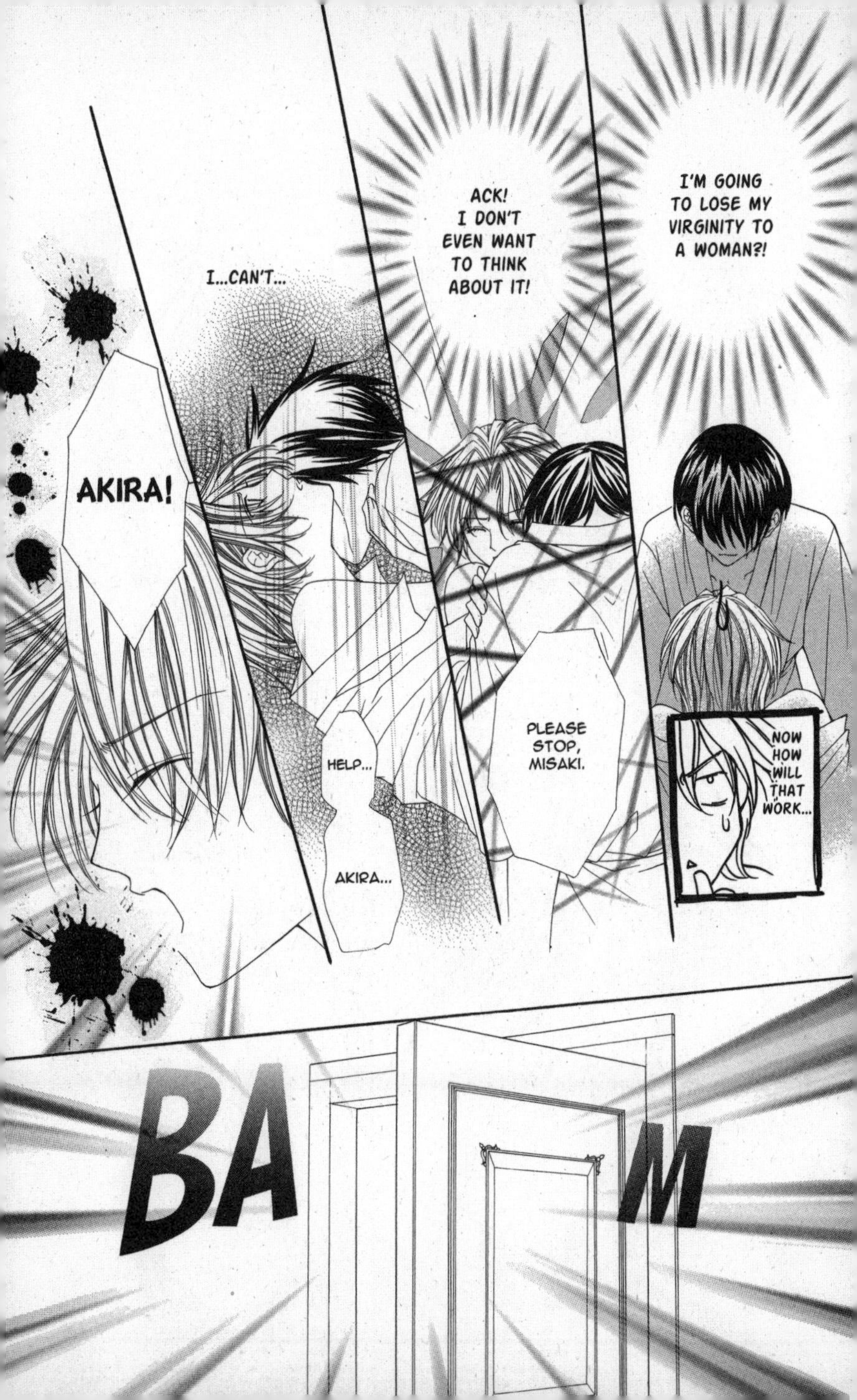
I'M GOING TO LOSE MY VIRGINITY TO A WOMAN?!
NOW HOW WILL THAT WORK...
ACK! I DON'T EVEN WANT TO THINK ABOUT IT!
PLEASE STOP, MISAKI.
I...CAN'T...
HELP...
AKIRA...
AKIRA!
BAM

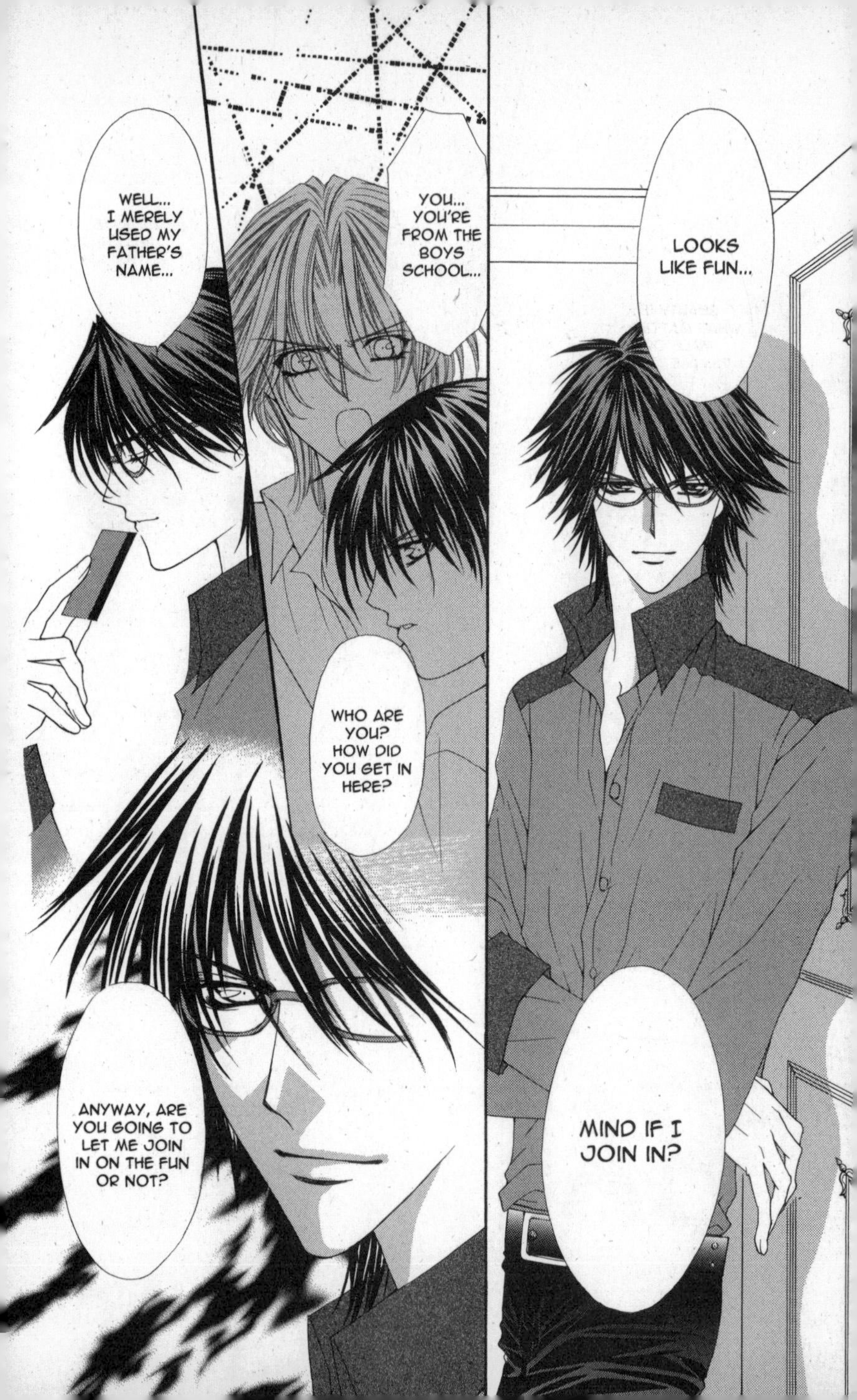
LOOKS LIKE FUN...
MIND IF I JOIN IN?
YOU... YOU'RE FROM THE BOYS SCHOOL...
WHO ARE YOU? HOW DID YOU GET IN HERE?
WELL... I MERELY USED MY FATHER'S NAME...
ANYWAY, ARE YOU GOING TO LET ME JOIN IN ON THE FUN OR NOT?

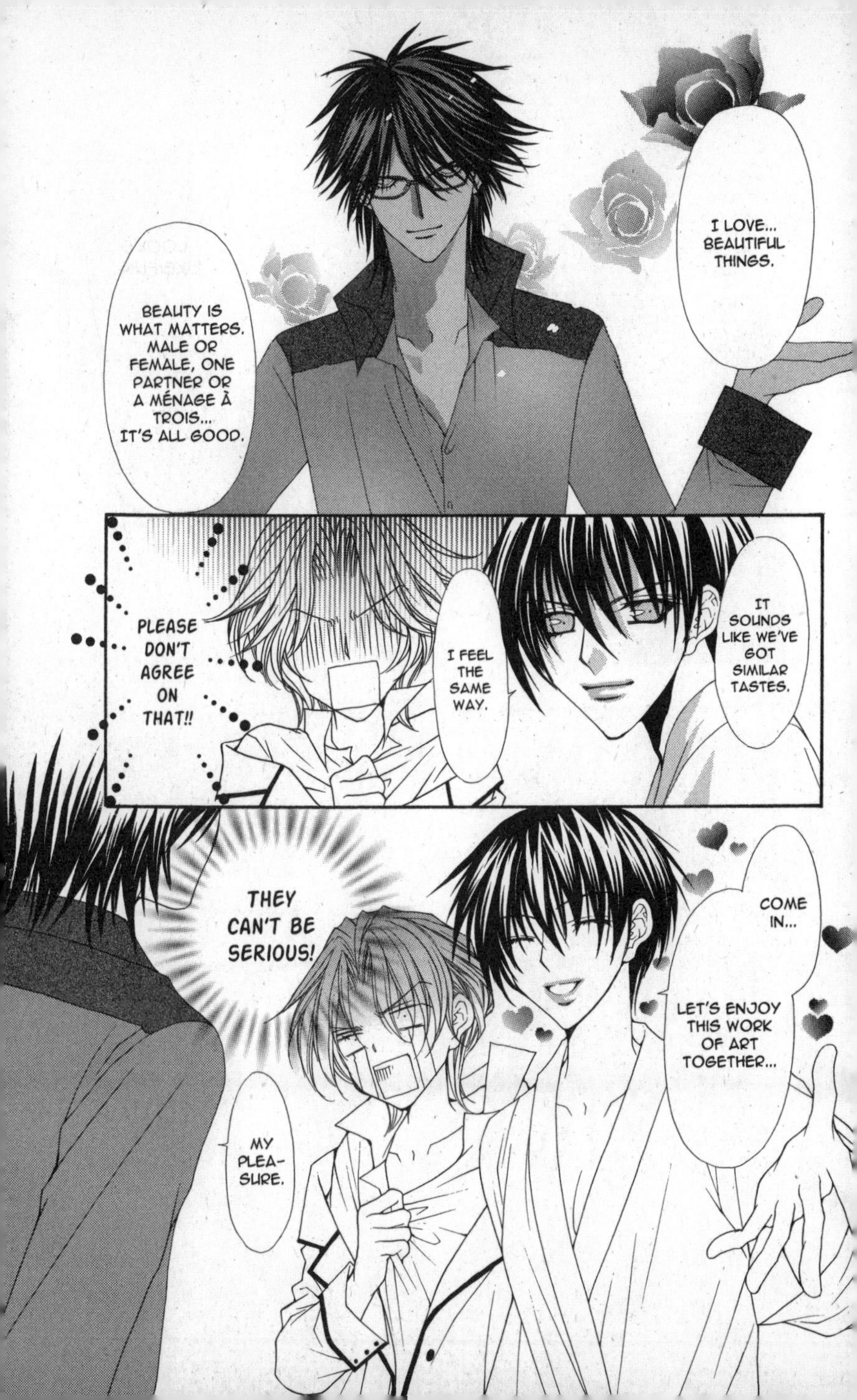
I LOVE... BEAUTIFUL THINGS.
BEAUTY IS WHAT MATTERS. MALE OR FEMALE, ONE PARTNER OR A MÉNAGE À TROIS... IT'S ALL GOOD.
IT SOUNDS LIKE WE'VE GOT SIMILAR TASTES.
I FEEL THE SAME WAY.
PLEASE DON'T AGREE ON THAT!!
COME IN...
LET'S ENJOY THIS WORK OF ART TOGETHER...
THEY CAN'T BE SERIOUS!
MY PLEA-SURE.

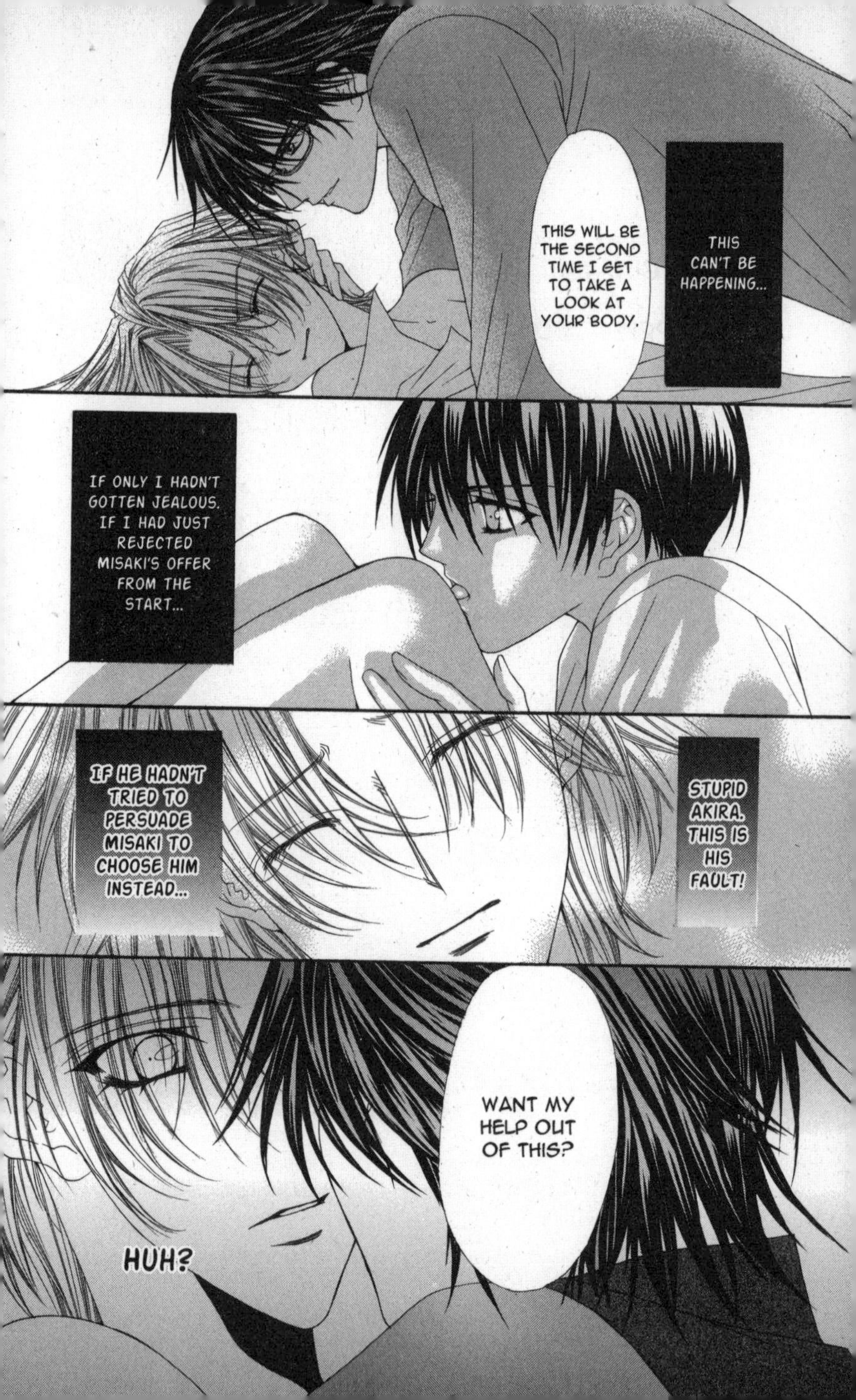
THIS CAN'T BE HAPPENING...
THIS WILL BE THE SECOND TIME I GET TO TAKE A LOOK AT YOUR BODY.
IF ONLY I HADN'T GOTTEN JEALOUS. IF I HAD JUST REJECTED MISAKI'S OFFER FROM THE START...
STUPID AKIRA. THIS IS HIS FAULT!
IF HE HADN'T TRIED TO PERSUADE MISAKI TO CHOOSE HIM INSTEAD...
WANT MY HELP OUT OF THIS?
HUH?

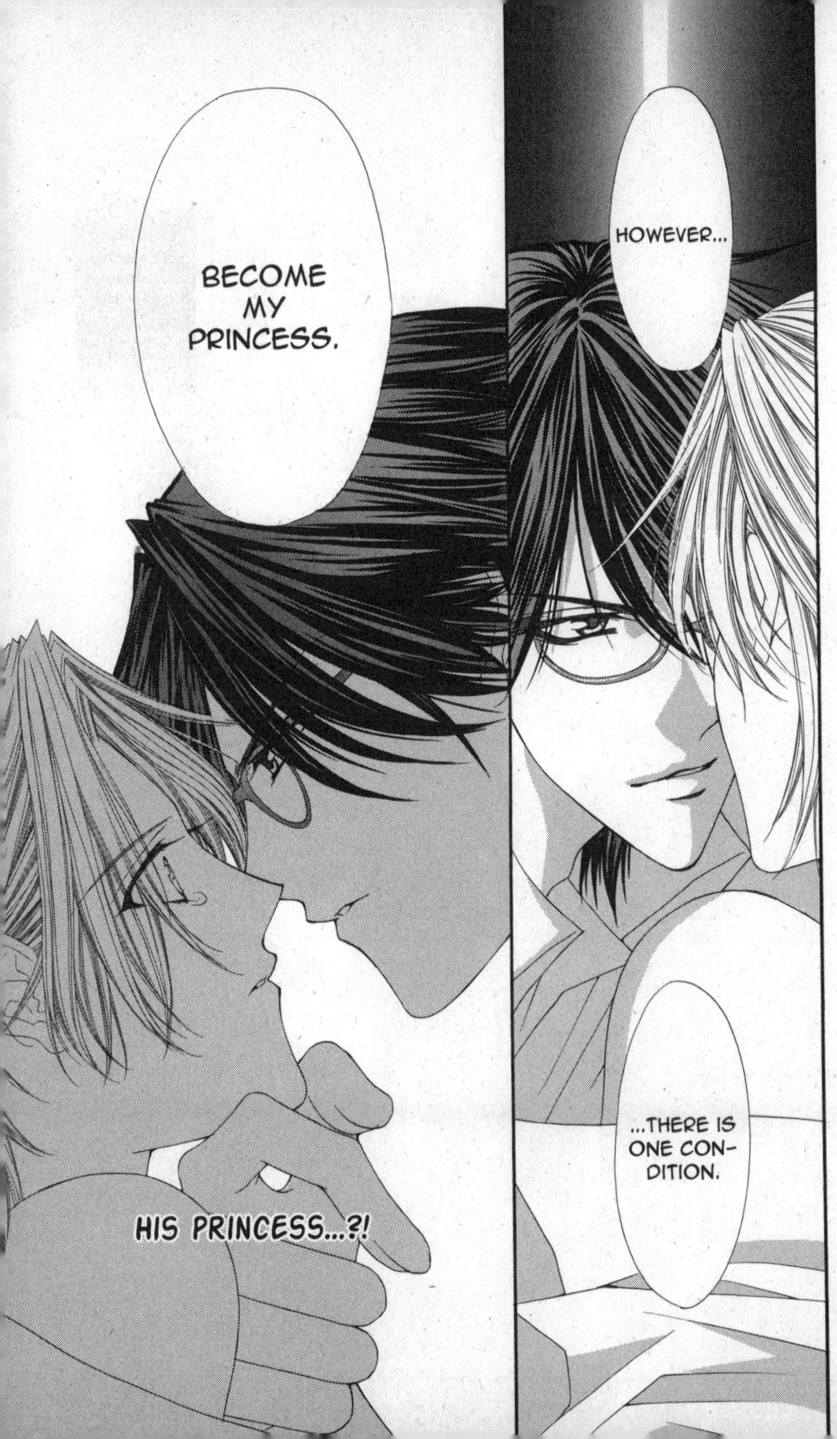
HOWEVER...
...THERE IS ONE CON-DITION.
BECOME MY PRINCESS.
HIS PRINCESS...?!

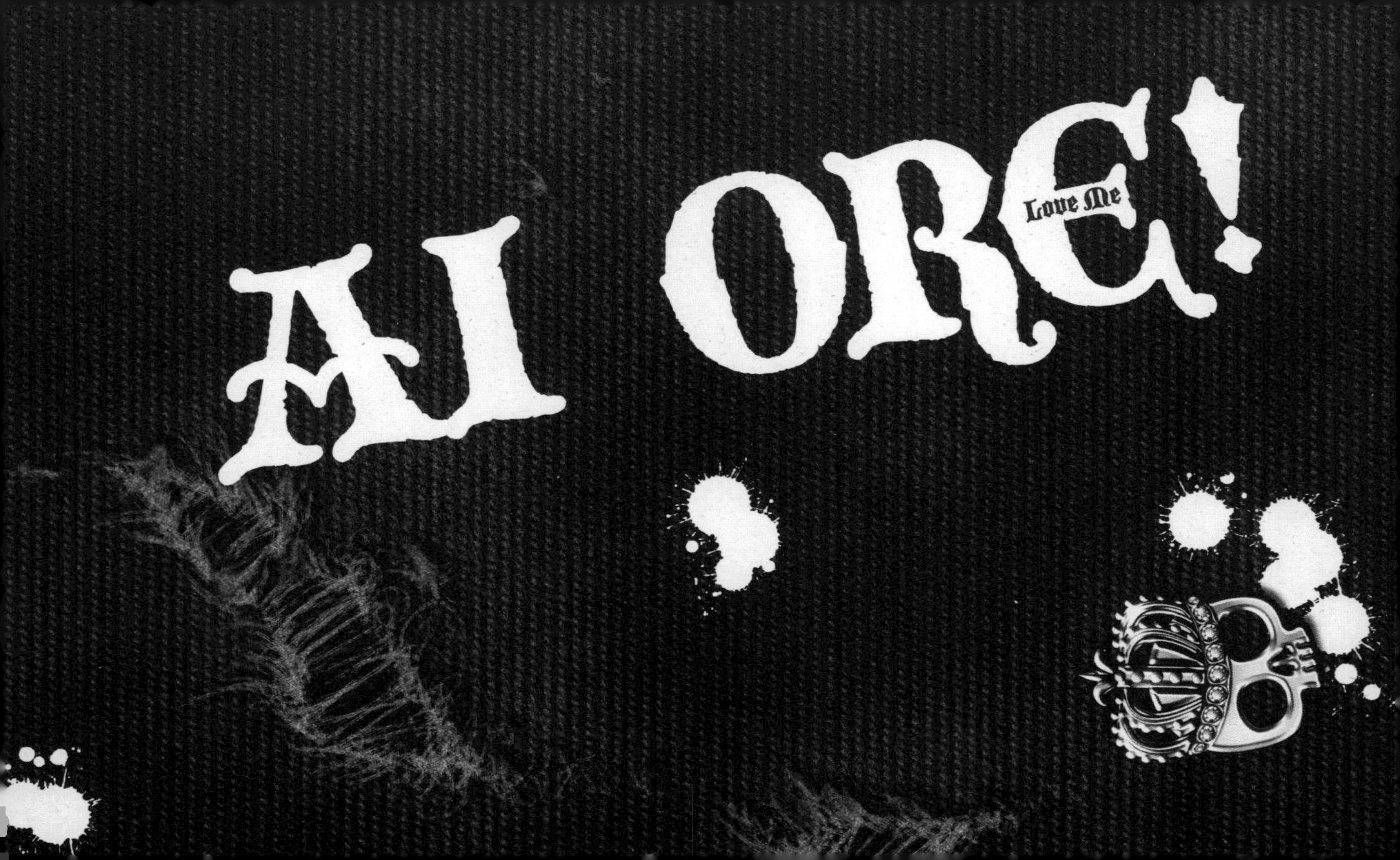
AI ORE!
Love Me

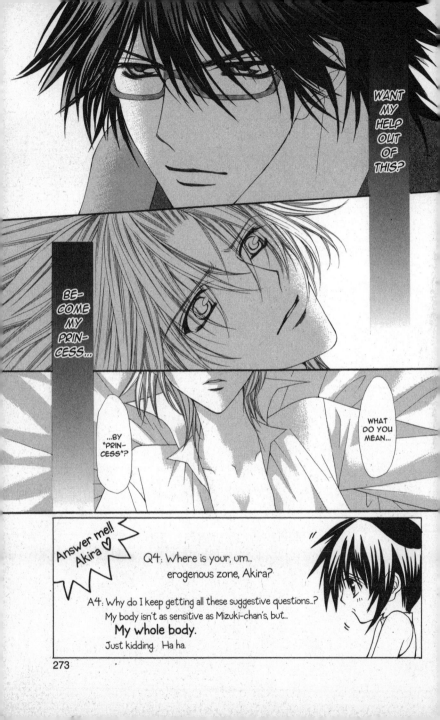

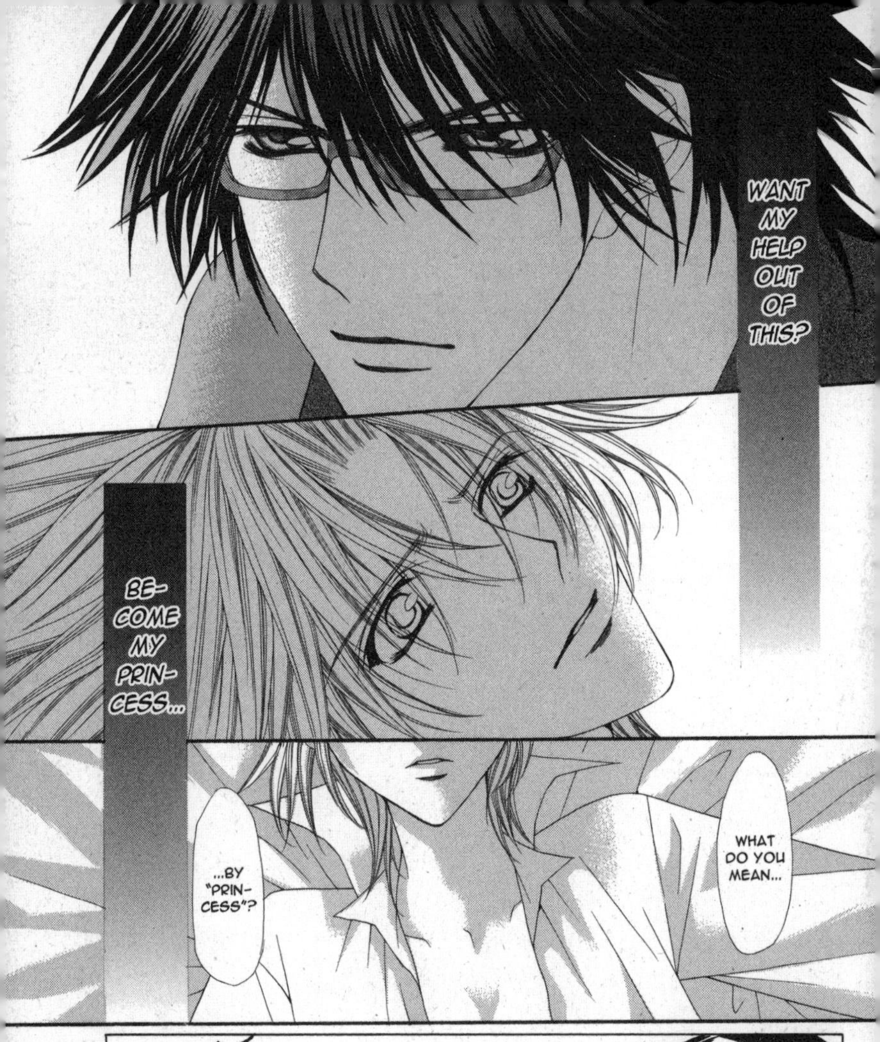
WANT MY HELP OUT OF THIS?
BE-COME MY PRIN-CESS...
WHAT DO YOU MEAN...
...BY "PRIN-CESS"?

Answer me!! Akira ♡

Q4: Where is your, um... erogenous zone, Akira?

A4: Why do I keep getting all these suggestive questions...? My body isn't as sensitive as Mizuki-chan's, but...

My whole body.

Just kidding. Ha ha.

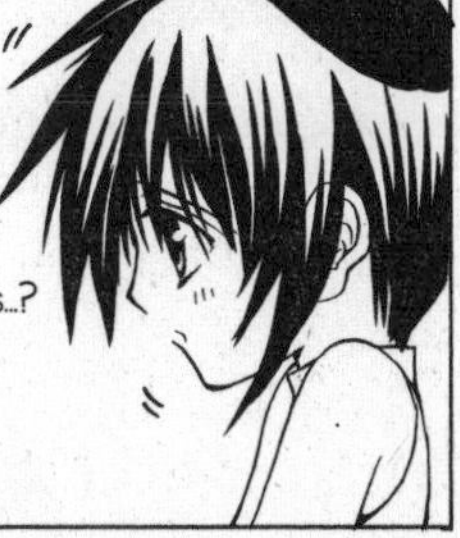

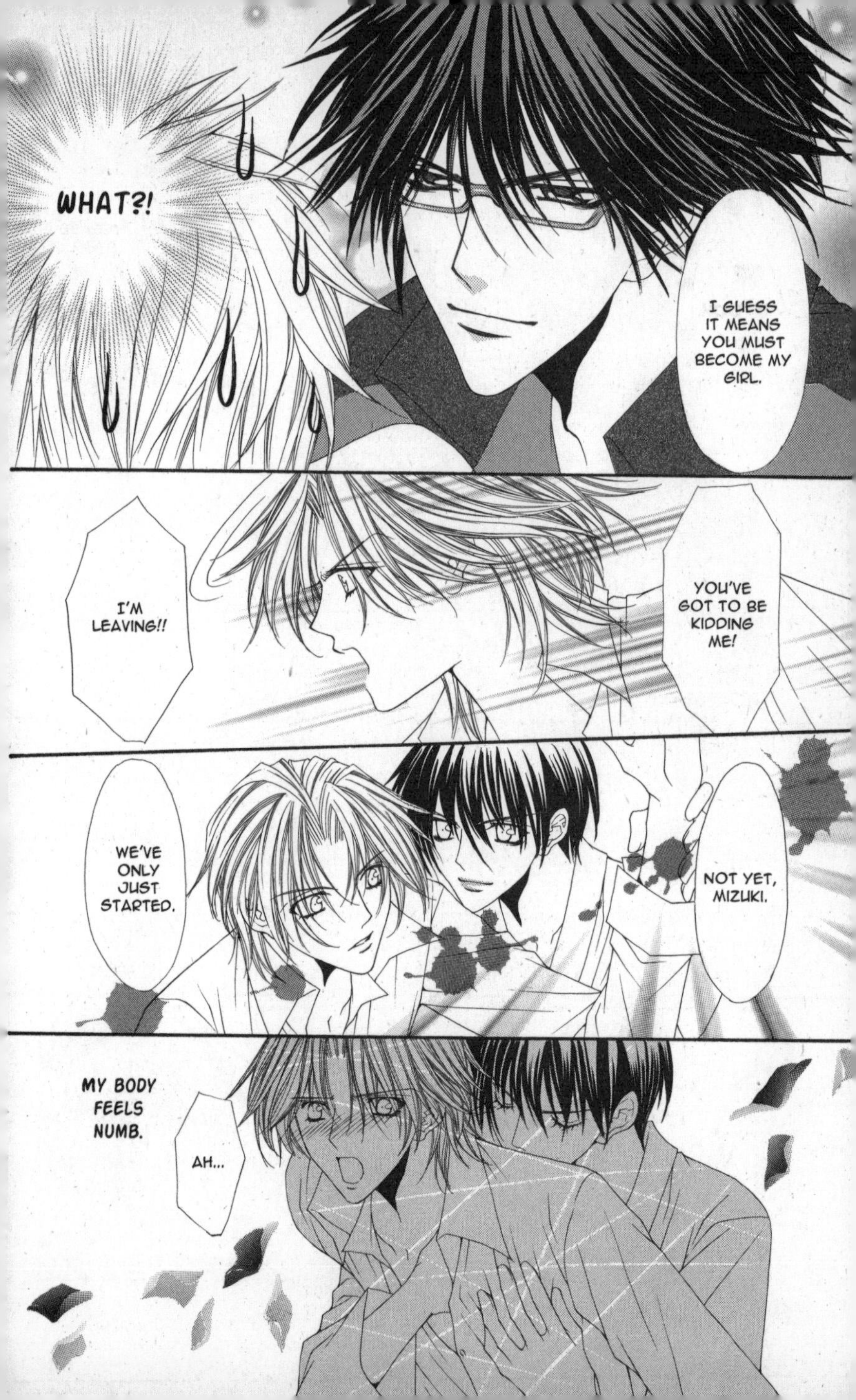
I GUESS IT MEANS YOU MUST BECOME MY GIRL.
WHAT?!
YOU'VE GOT TO BE KIDDING ME!
I'M LEAVING!!
NOT YET, MIZUKI.
WE'VE ONLY JUST STARTED.
AH...
MY BODY FEELS NUMB.

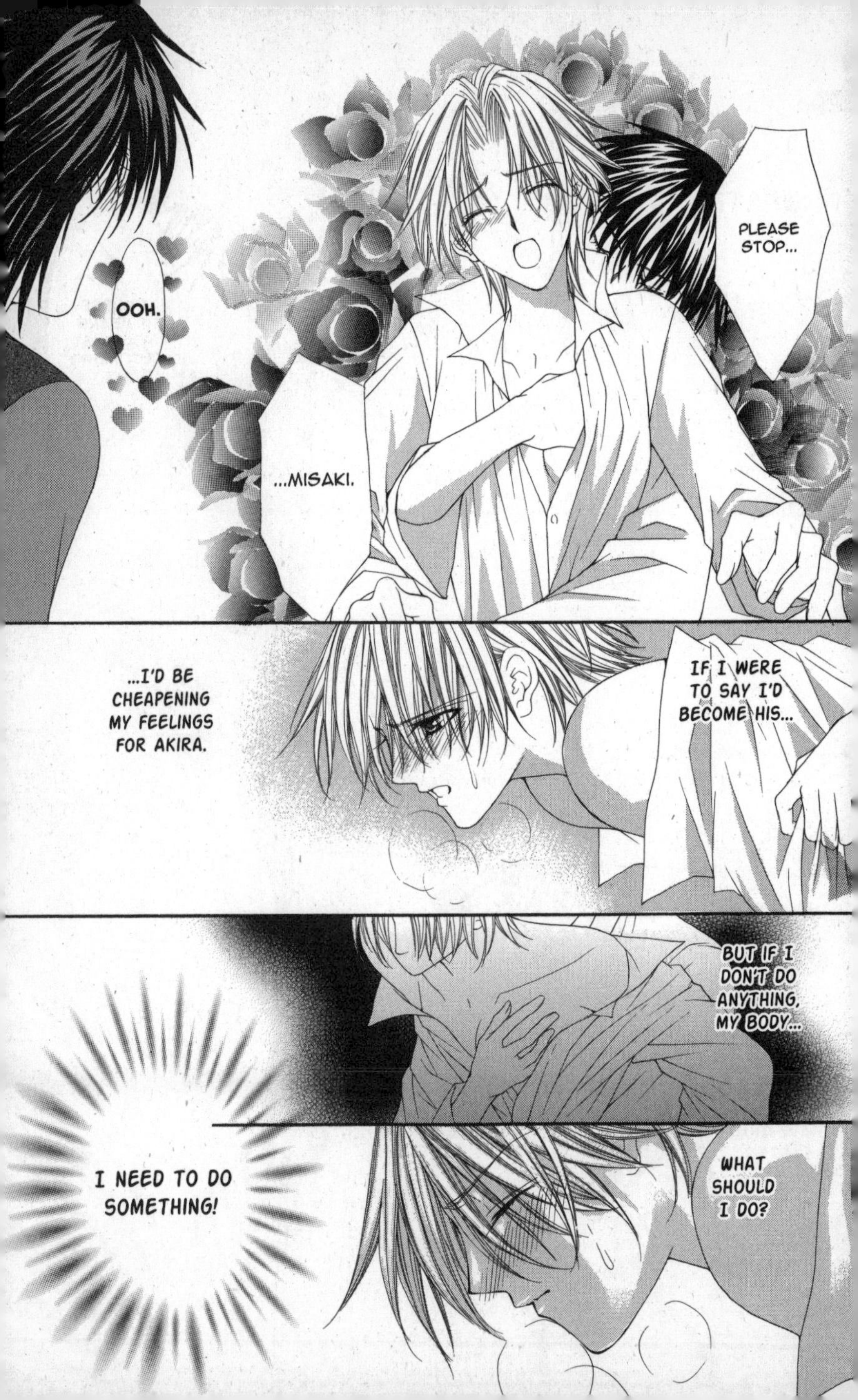
PLEASE STOP...
...MISAKI.
OOH.
IF I WERE TO SAY I'D BECOME HIS...
...I'D BE CHEAPENING MY FEELINGS FOR AKIRA.
BUT IF I DON'T DO ANYTHING, MY BODY...
WHAT SHOULD I DO?
I NEED TO DO SOMETHING!

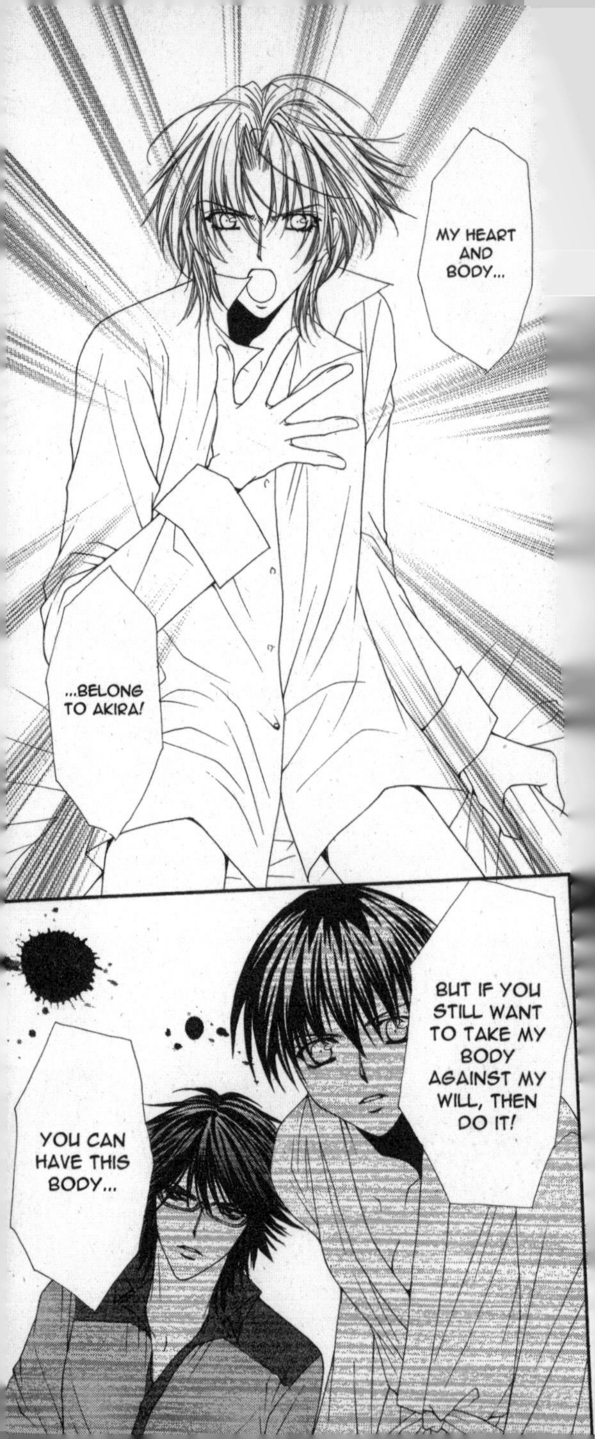
MY HEART AND BODY...
...BELONG TO AKIRA!
BUT IF YOU STILL WANT TO TAKE MY BODY AGAINST MY WILL, THEN DO IT!
YOU CAN HAVE THIS BODY...

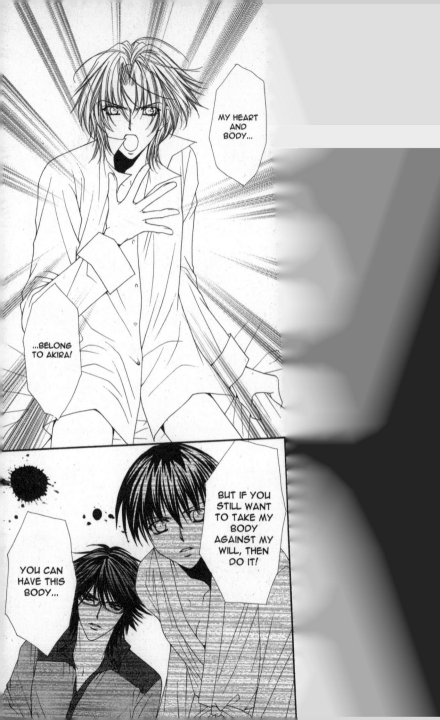

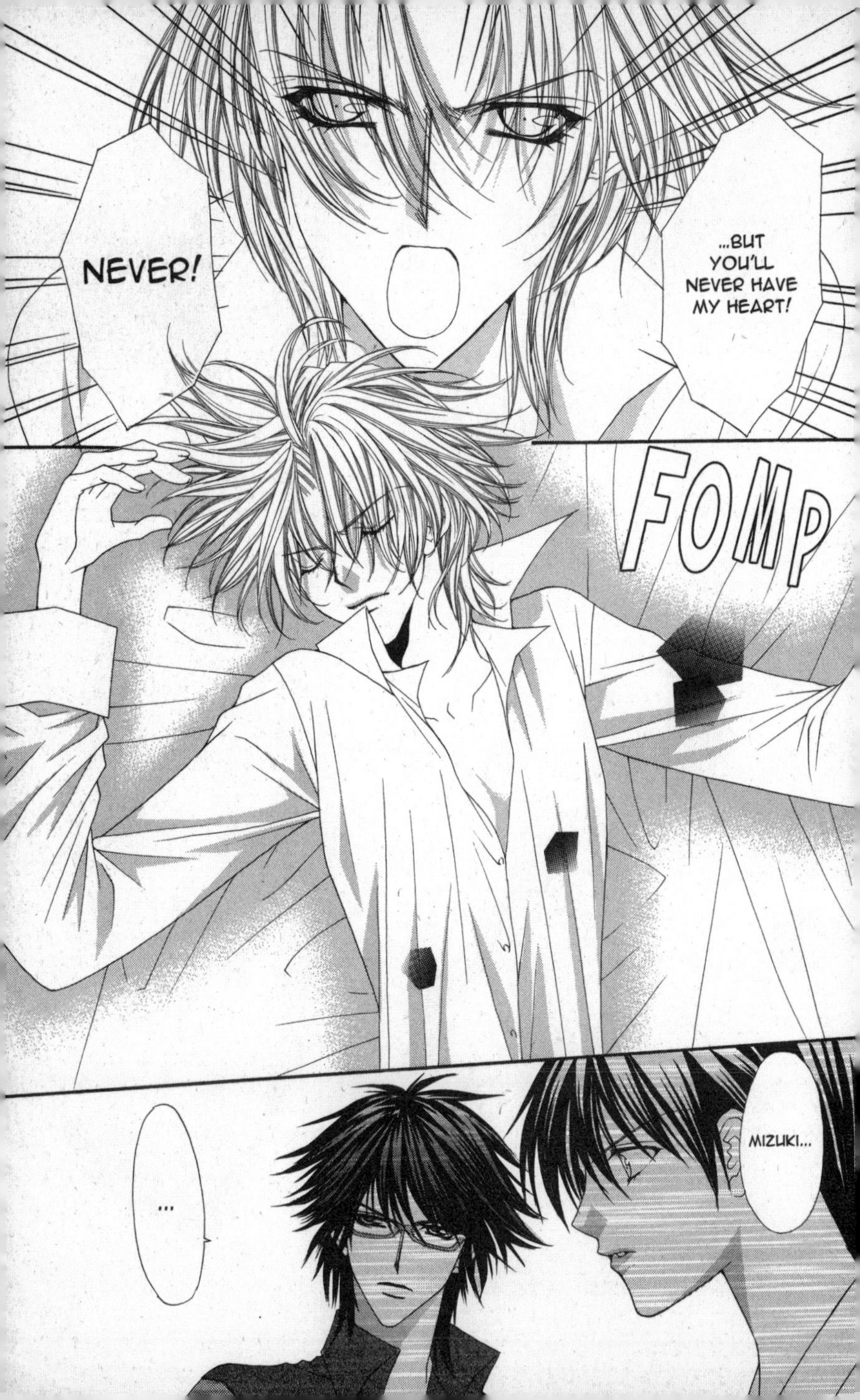
...BUT YOU'LL NEVER HAVE MY HEART!
NEVER!
FOMP
MIZUKI...
...

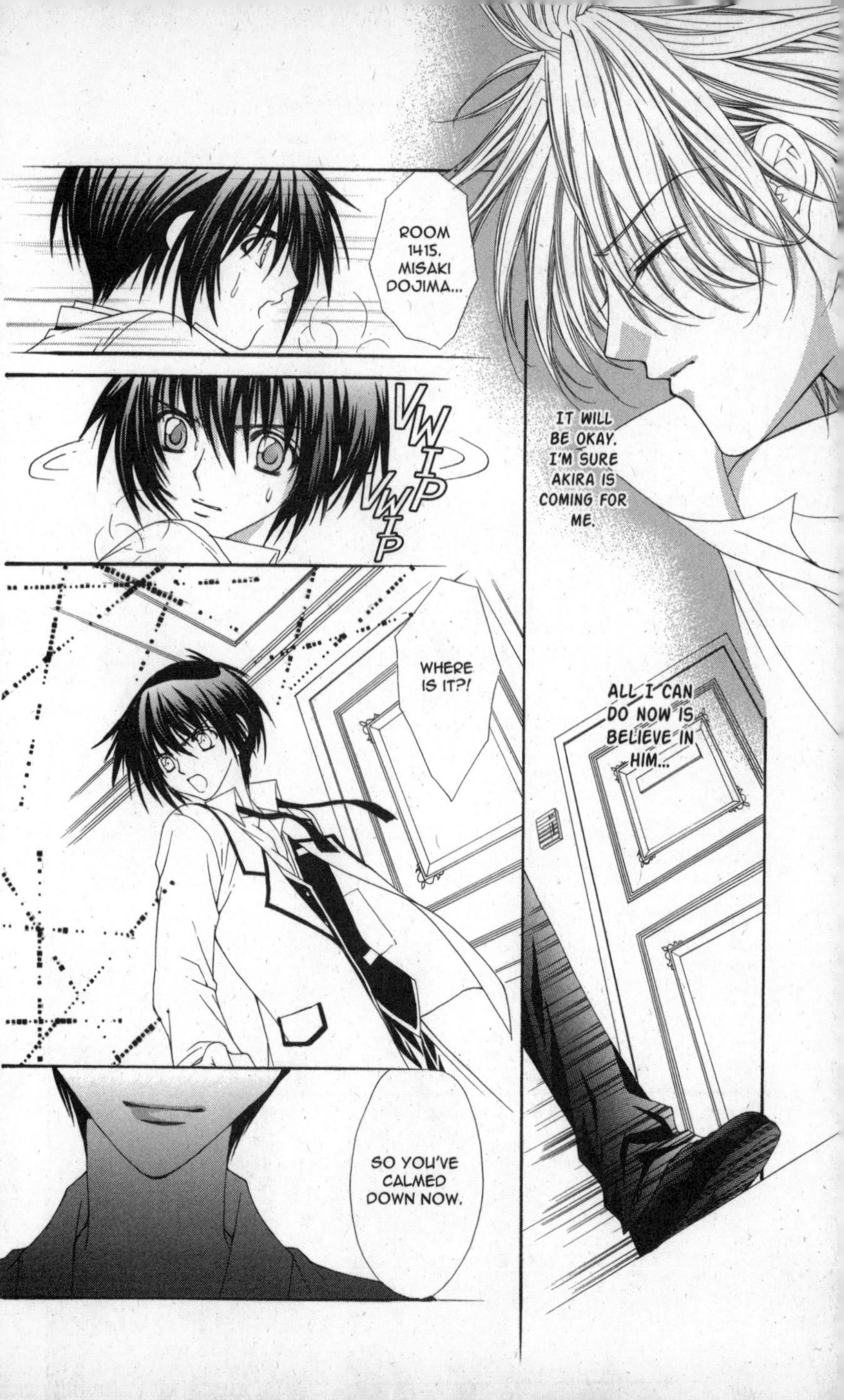
IT WILL BE OKAY. I'M SURE AKIRA IS COMING FOR ME.
ALL I CAN DO NOW IS BELIEVE IN HIM...
ROOM 1415. MISAKI DOJIMA...
VWIP VWIP
WHERE IS IT?!
SO YOU'VE CALMED DOWN NOW.

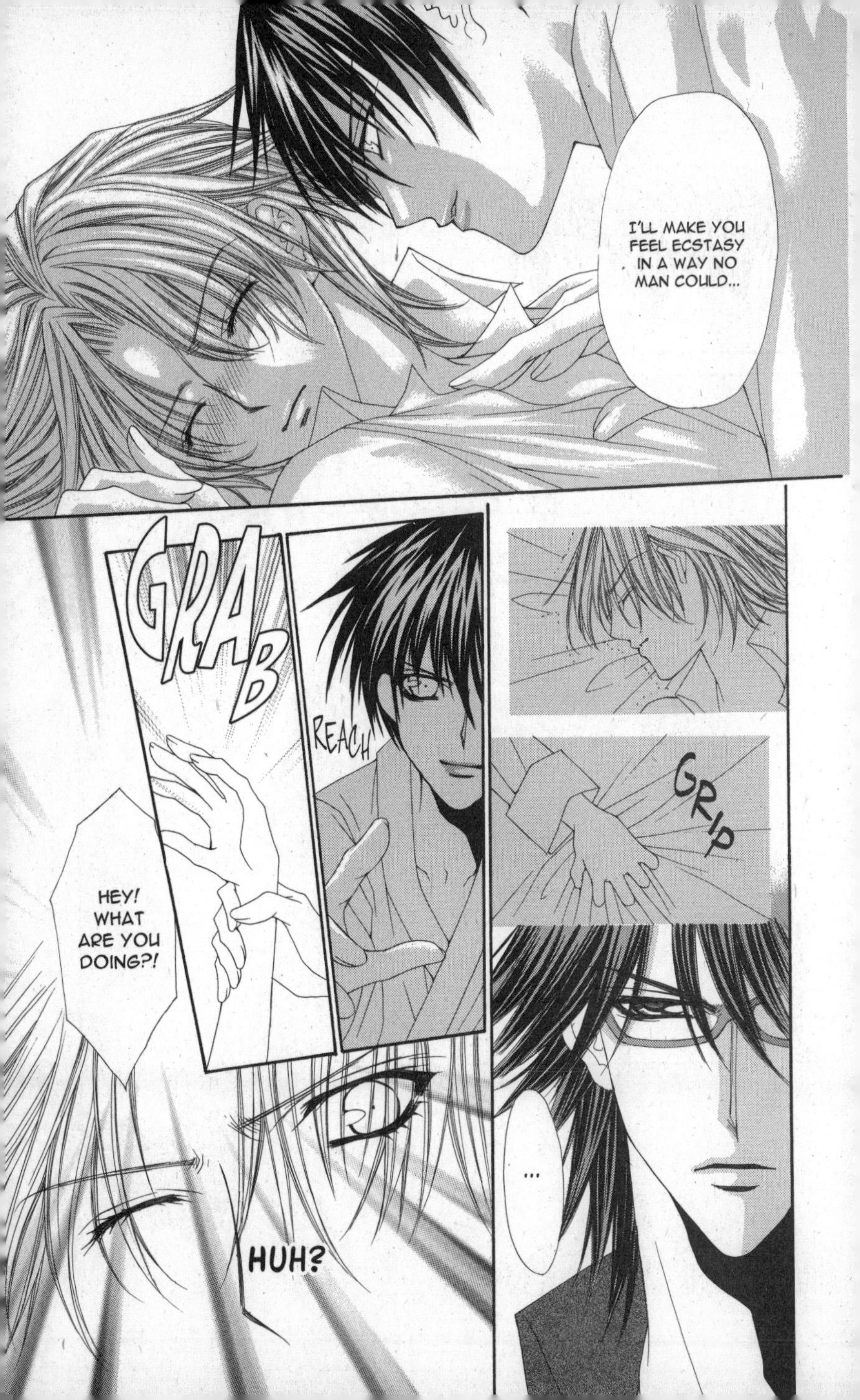
I'LL MAKE YOU FEEL ECSTASY IN A WAY NO MAN COULD...
GRIP
...
REACH
GRAB
HEY! WHAT ARE YOU DOING?!
HUH?

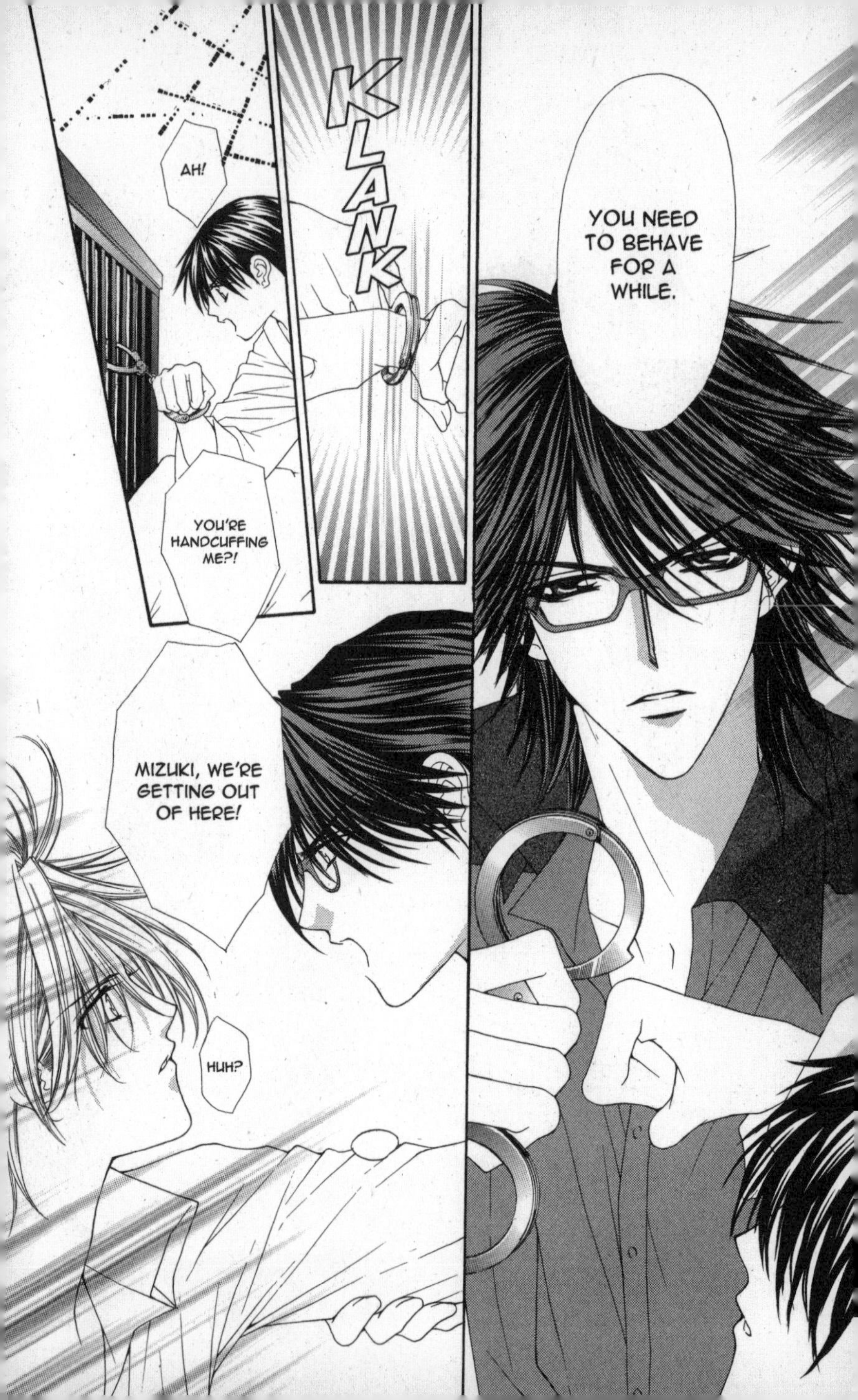
YOU NEED TO BEHAVE FOR A WHILE.
KLANK
AH!
YOU'RE HANDCUFFING ME?!
MIZUKI, WE'RE GETTING OUT OF HERE!
HUH?

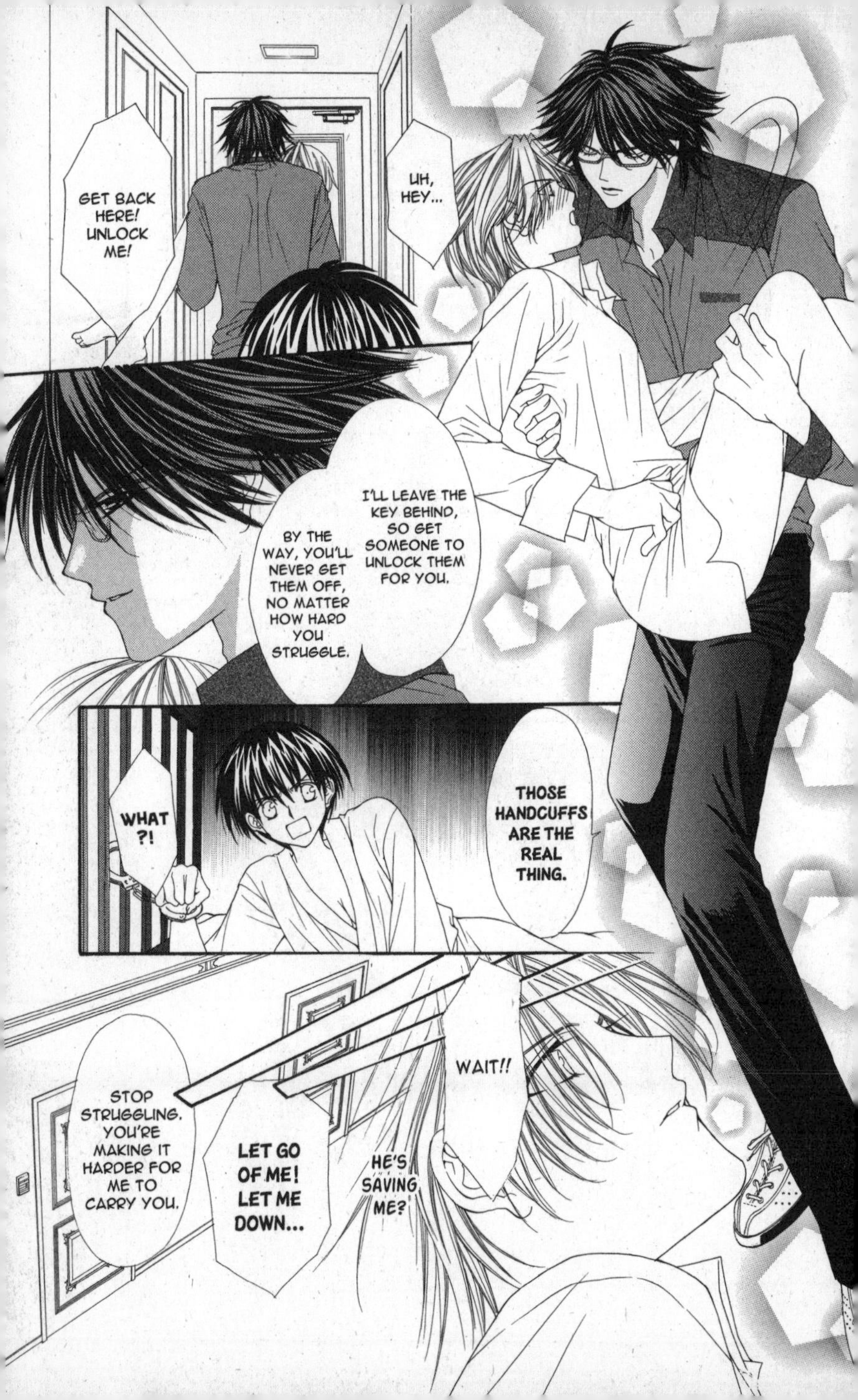
UH, HEY...
GET BACK HERE! UNLOCK ME!
I'LL LEAVE THE KEY BEHIND, SO GET SOMEONE TO UNLOCK THEM FOR YOU.
BY THE WAY, YOU'LL NEVER GET THEM OFF, NO MATTER HOW HARD YOU STRUGGLE.
THOSE HANDCUFFS ARE THE REAL THING.
WHAT?!
WAIT!!
HE'S SAVING ME?
LET GO OF ME! LET ME DOWN...
STOP STRUGGLING. YOU'RE MAKING IT HARDER FOR ME TO CARRY YOU.

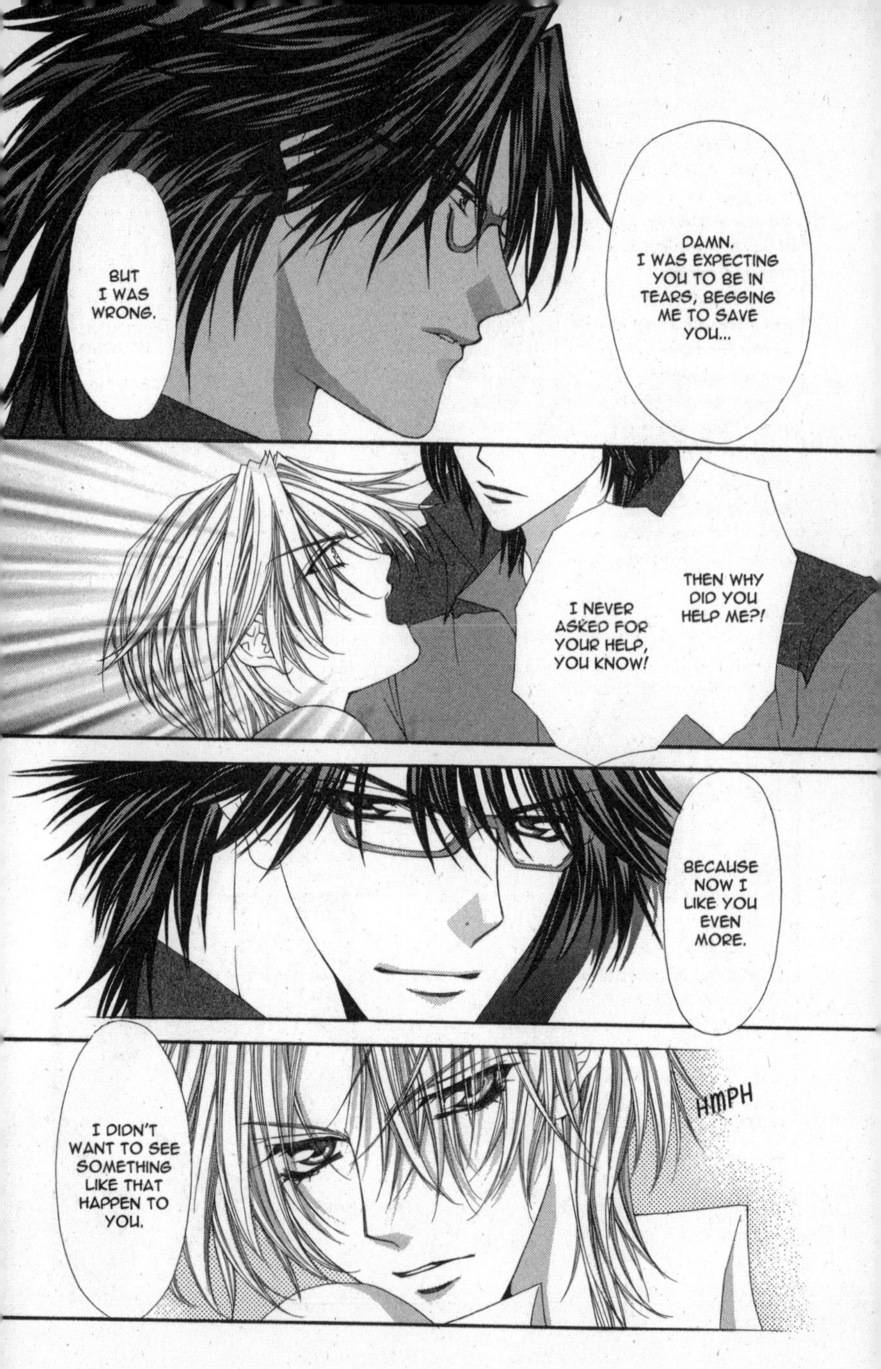
DAMN. I WAS EXPECTING YOU TO BE IN TEARS, BEGGING ME TO SAVE YOU...
BUT I WAS WRONG.
THEN WHY DID YOU HELP ME?!
I NEVER ASKED FOR YOUR HELP, YOU KNOW!
BECAUSE NOW I LIKE YOU EVEN MORE.
HMPH
I DIDN'T WANT TO SEE SOMETHING LIKE THAT HAPPEN TO YOU.

This drama CD has many voice actresses in it, but they all usually specialize in male roles, so they're all slightly...uh, moderately...uh, extremely(?) mannish.

Since I was there in my usual girly attire with a miniskirt and an Alice Band, they took great care of me. (laugh)

Shinjo's selection of moe lines said by Mizuki:

I'm the one you'll spend the night with tonight... Isn't that right?

Mizuki hitting on a girl with everything she's got! She's so cool!!

All right then... Next is Akira Ishida doing the role of Ran. He is normally very poised and quiet, but once the dubbing starts, he's all over the place! I had been told he liked to ham it up, but I never thought he'd be this extreme... (laugh) He is just hilarious! His adlibs are so funny. And!! He has perfect chemistry with Sakurai-san! Most of their lines are with each other, and as they start to get hyped up, the dialogue just gets better and better! The people in the booth were all roaring with laughter!!

The various voice actor magazines were not going to stay quiet when so many skilled voice actors and actresses had come together, so we were bombarded with interview requests, and the cool Ishida-san would keep making humorous replies!! Please read all about it in those magazines...

(Continues)

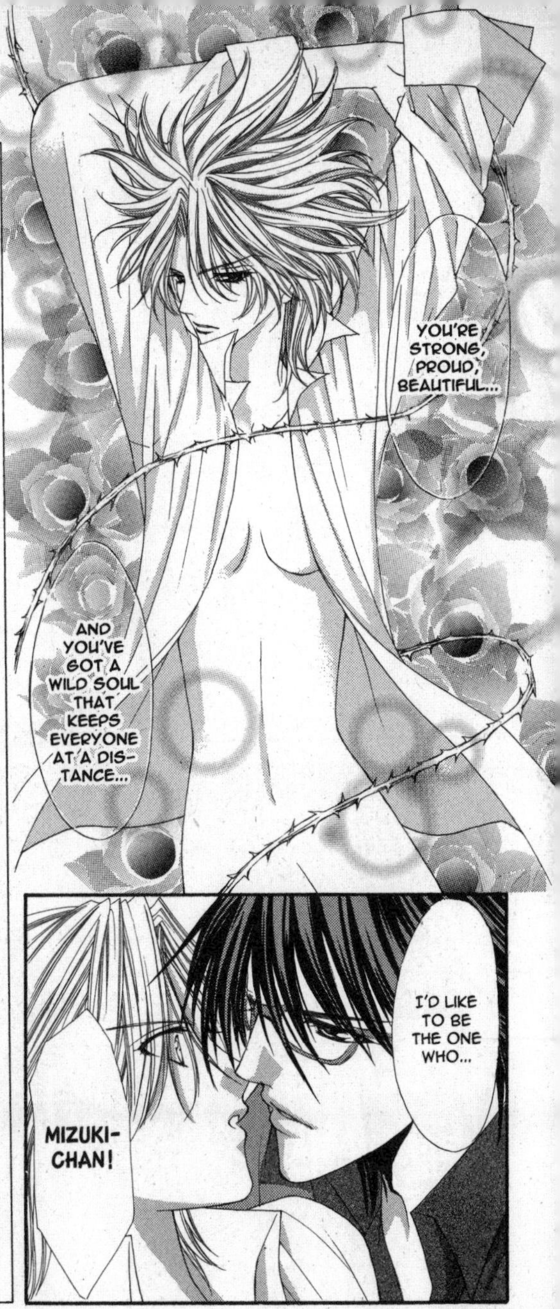
YOU'RE STRONG, PROUD, BEAUTIFUL...
AND YOU'VE GOT A WILD SOUL THAT KEEPS EVERYONE AT A DISTANCE...
I'D LIKE TO BE THE ONE WHO...
MIZUKI-CHAN!

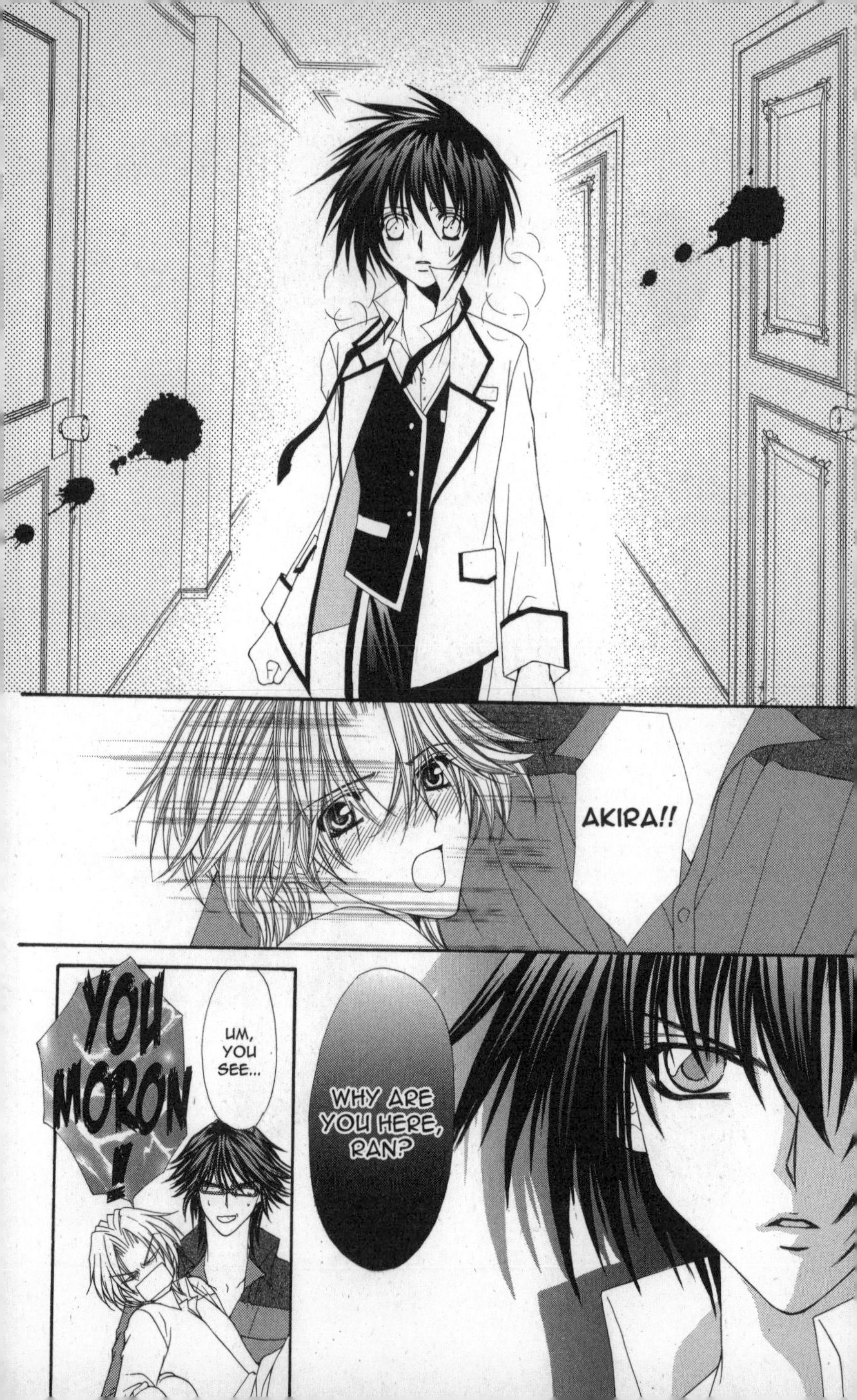
AKIRA!!
WHY ARE YOU HERE, RAN?
UM, YOU SEE...
YOU MORON!

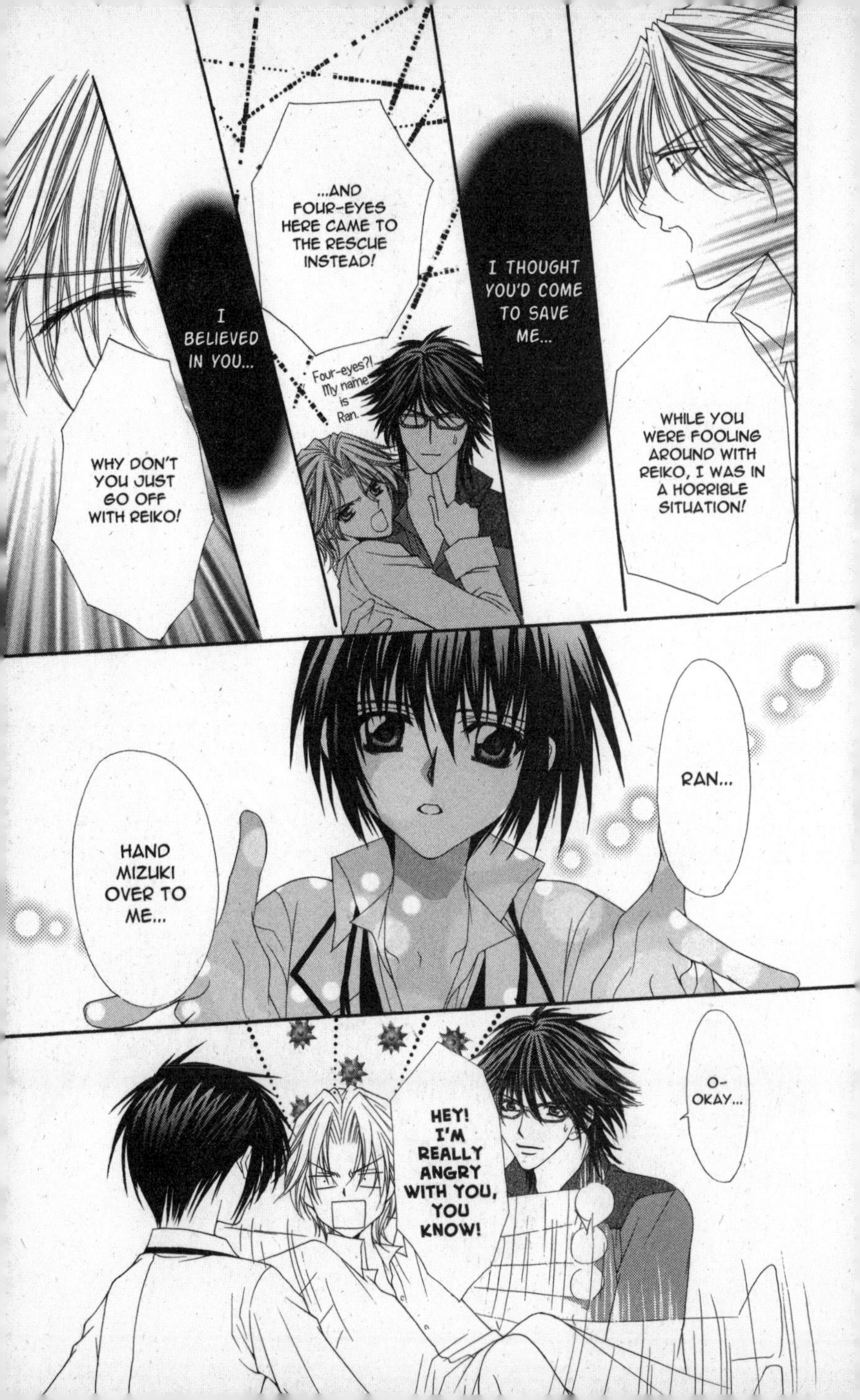

WHILE YOU WERE FOOLING AROUND WITH REIKO, I WAS IN A HORRIBLE SITUATION!
I THOUGHT YOU'D COME TO SAVE ME...
...AND FOUR-EYES HERE CAME TO THE RESCUE INSTEAD!
Four-eyes?! My name is Ran.
I BELIEVED IN YOU...
WHY DON'T YOU JUST GO OFF WITH REIKO!
RAN...
HAND MIZUKI OVER TO ME...
O-OKAY...
HEY! I'M REALLY ANGRY WITH YOU, YOU KNOW!

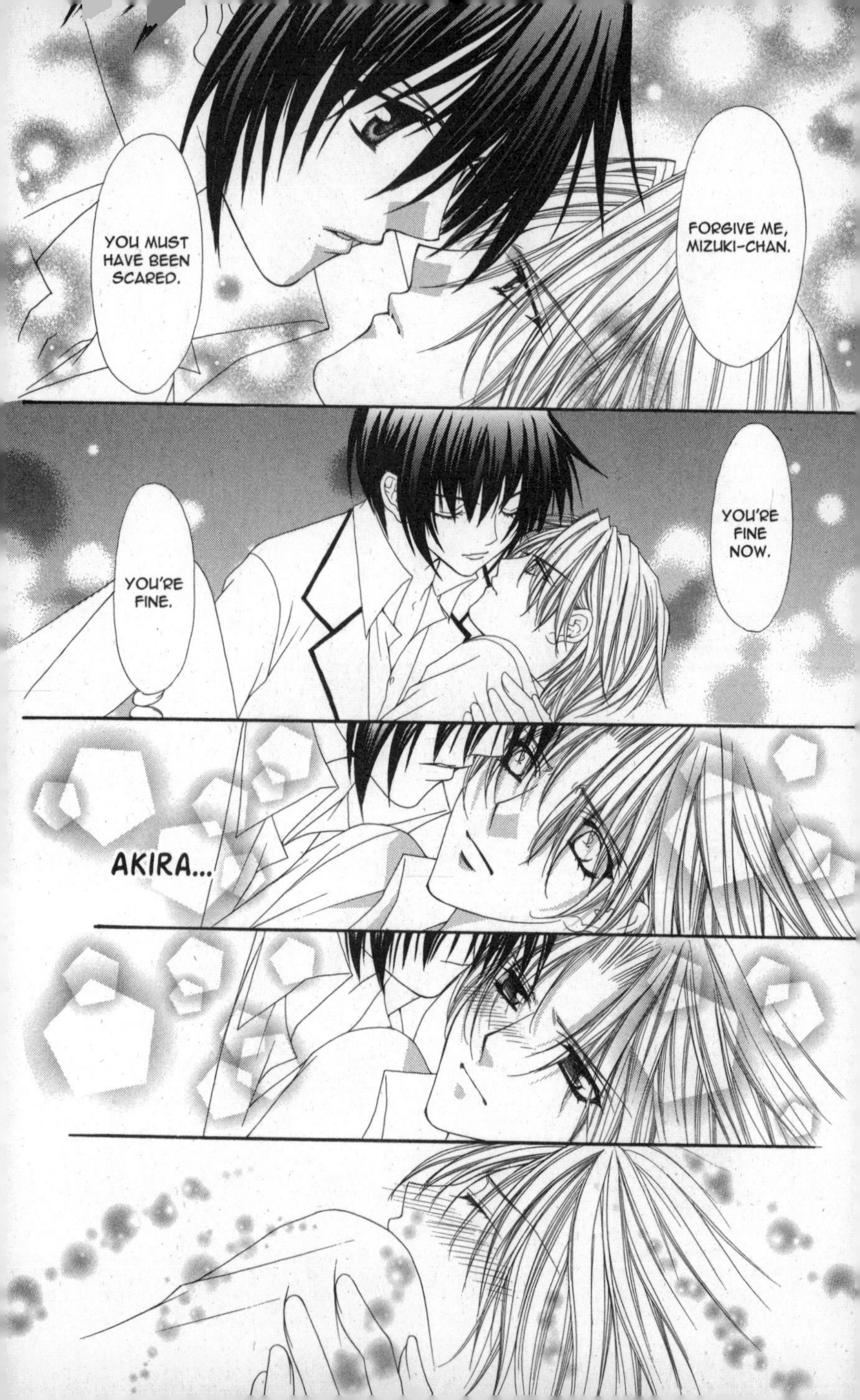
FORGIVE ME, MIZUKI-CHAN.
YOU MUST HAVE BEEN SCARED.
YOU'RE FINE NOW.
YOU'RE FINE.
AKIRA...

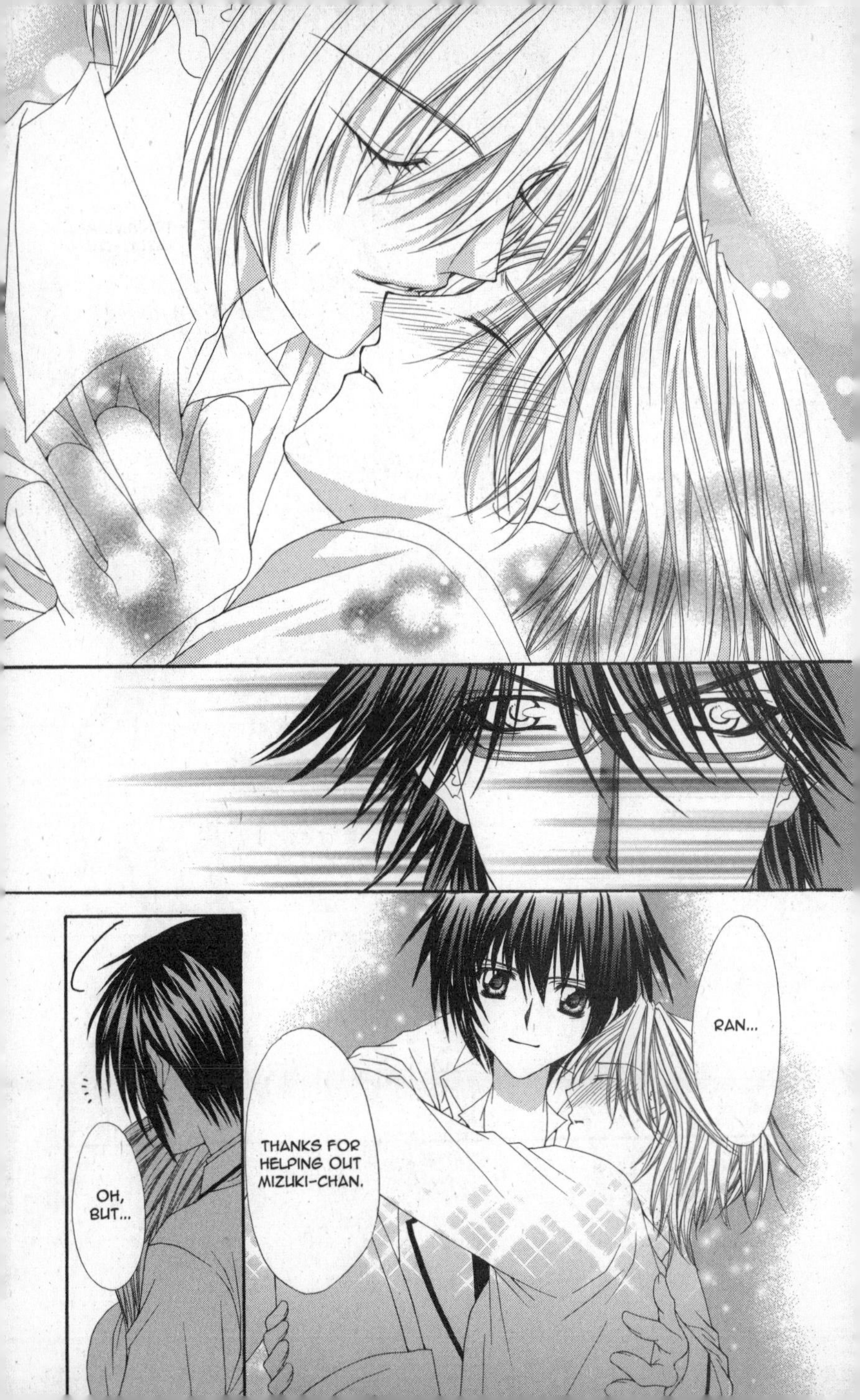
RAN...
THANKS FOR HELPING OUT MIZUKI-CHAN.
OH, BUT...

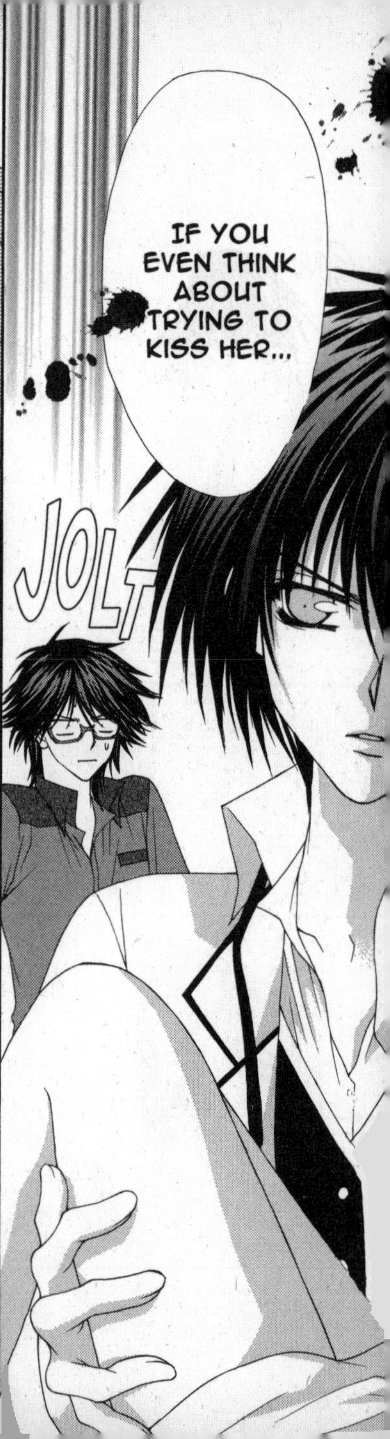
IF YOU EVEN THINK ABOUT TRYING TO KISS HER...
JOLT

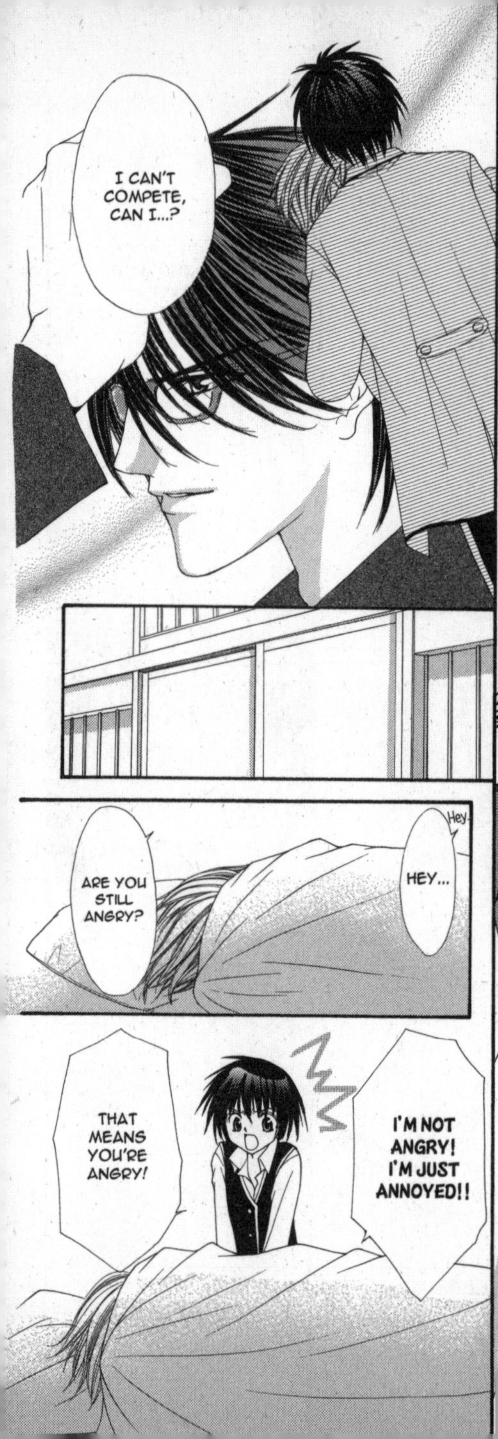
I CAN'T COMPETE, CAN I...?
Hey-
HEY...
ARE YOU STILL ANGRY?
I'M NOT ANGRY! I'M JUST ANNOYED!!
MMM
THAT MEANS YOU'RE ANGRY!

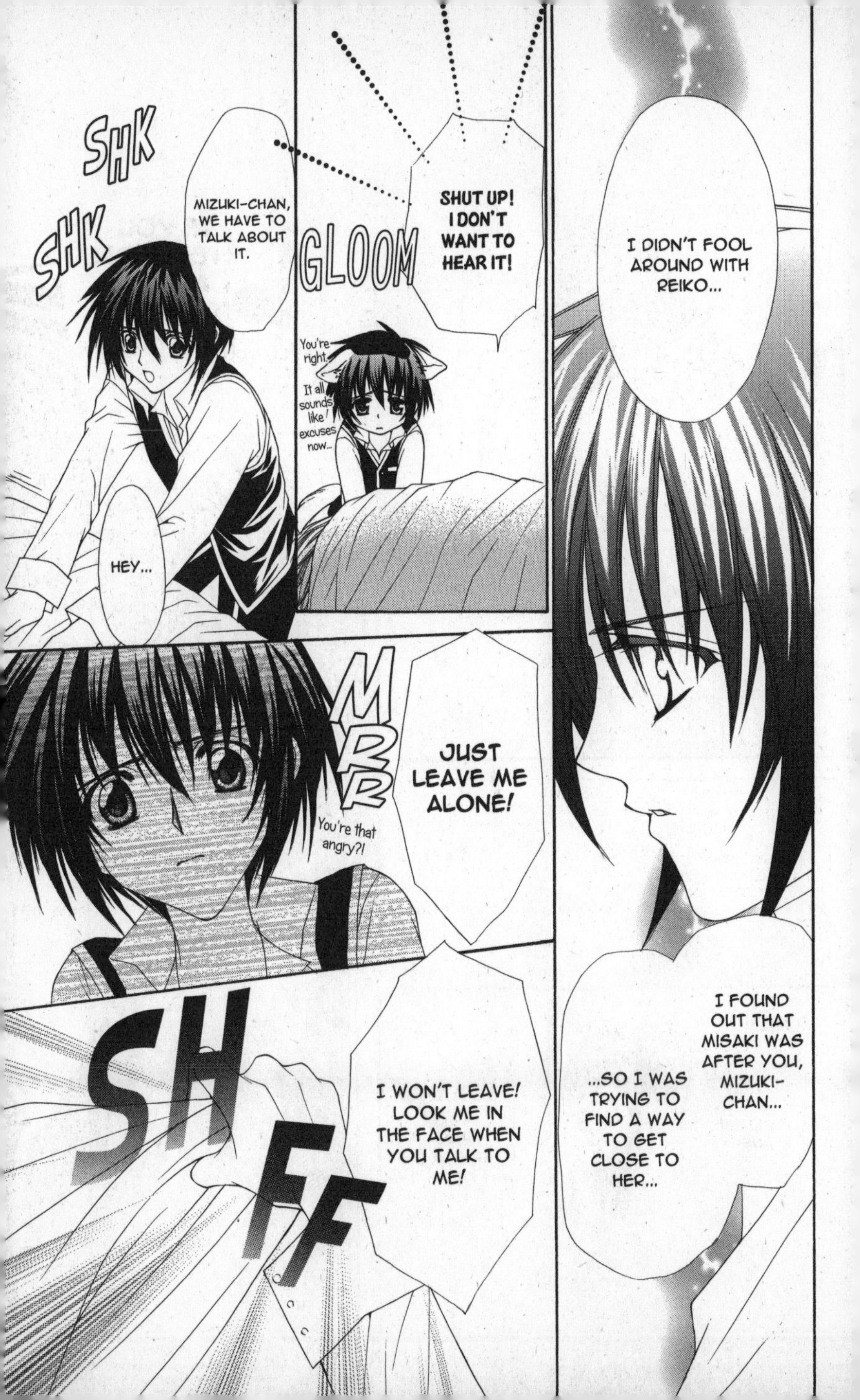
SHK
SHK
HEY...
MIZUKI-CHAN, WE HAVE TO TALK ABOUT IT.
GLOOM
SHUT UP! I DON'T WANT TO HEAR IT!
You're right. It all sounds like excuses now...
MRR
JUST LEAVE ME ALONE!
You're that angry?!
SHFF
I WON'T LEAVE! LOOK ME IN THE FACE WHEN YOU TALK TO ME!
I DIDN'T FOOL AROUND WITH REIKO...
I FOUND OUT THAT MISAKI WAS AFTER YOU, MIZUKI-CHAN...
...SO I WAS TRYING TO FIND A WAY TO GET CLOSE TO HER...

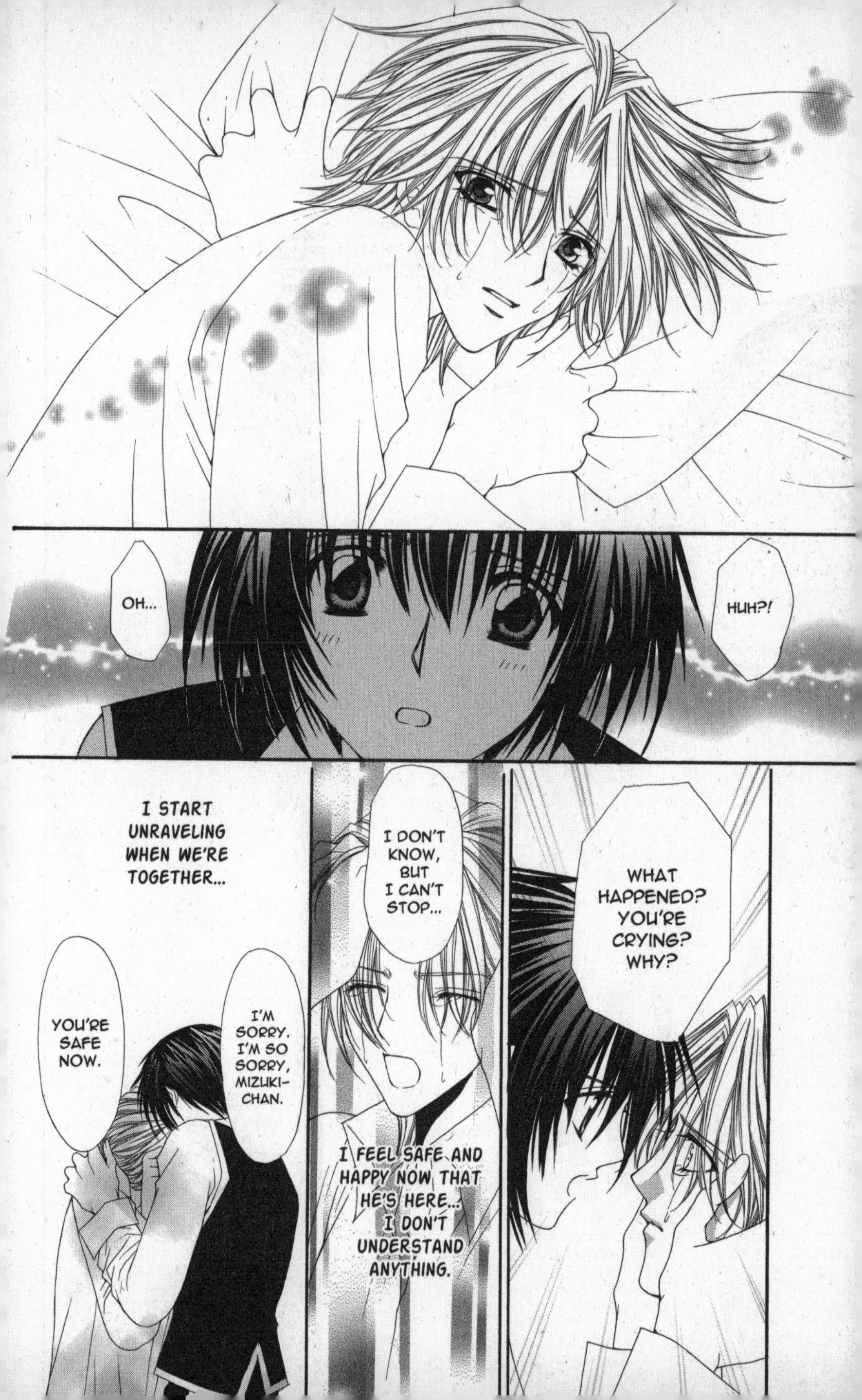
HUH?!
OH...
WHAT HAPPENED? YOU'RE CRYING? WHY?
I DON'T KNOW, BUT I CAN'T STOP...
I FEEL SAFE AND HAPPY NOW THAT HE'S HERE... I DON'T UNDERSTAND ANYTHING.
I START UNRAVELING WHEN WE'RE TOGETHER...
I'M SORRY. I'M SO SORRY, MIZUKI-CHAN.
YOU'RE SAFE NOW.

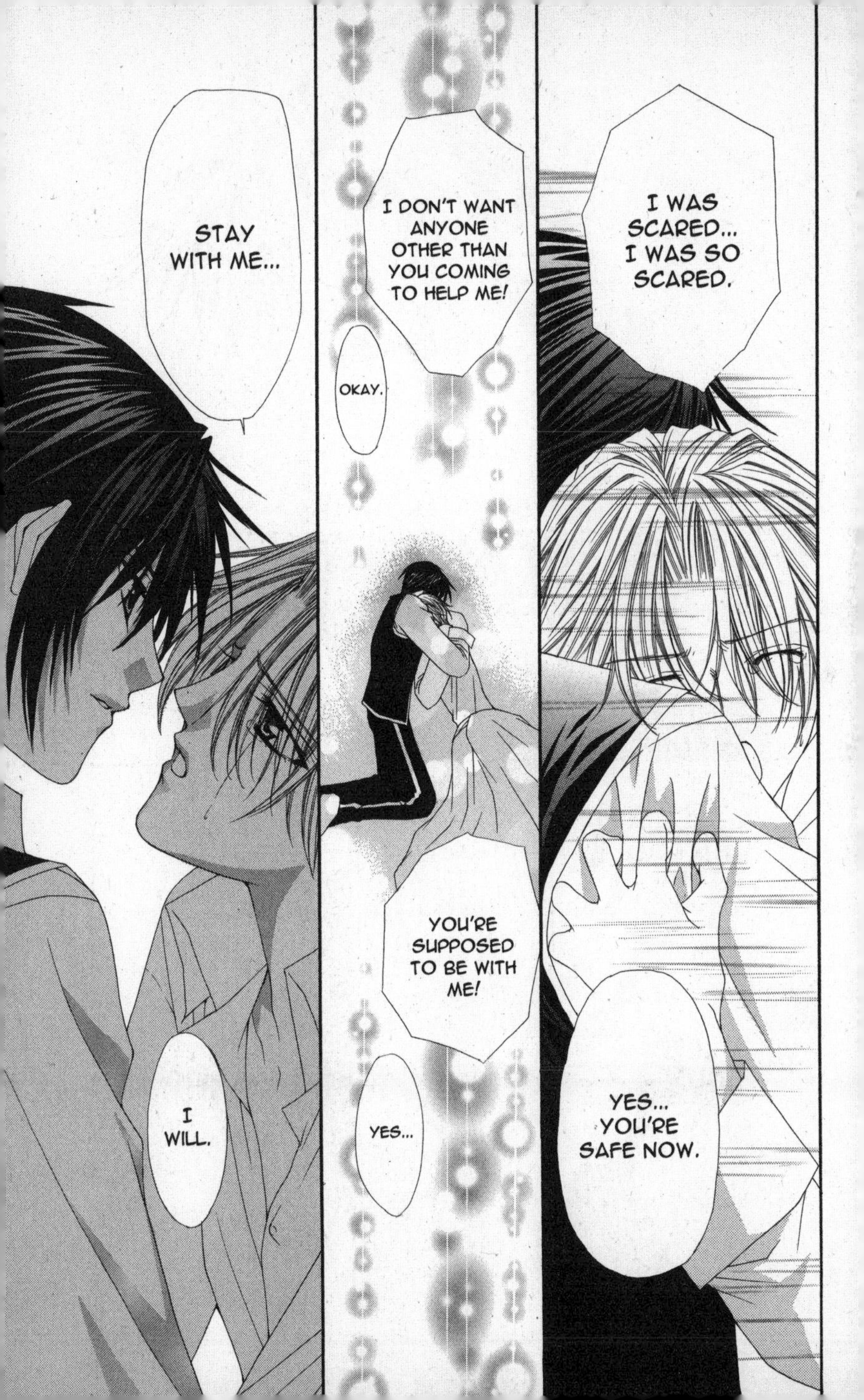
I WAS SCARED... I WAS SO SCARED.
YES... YOU'RE SAFE NOW.
I DON'T WANT ANYONE OTHER THAN YOU COMING TO HELP ME!
OKAY.
YOU'RE SUPPOSED TO BE WITH ME!
YES...
STAY WITH ME...
I WILL.

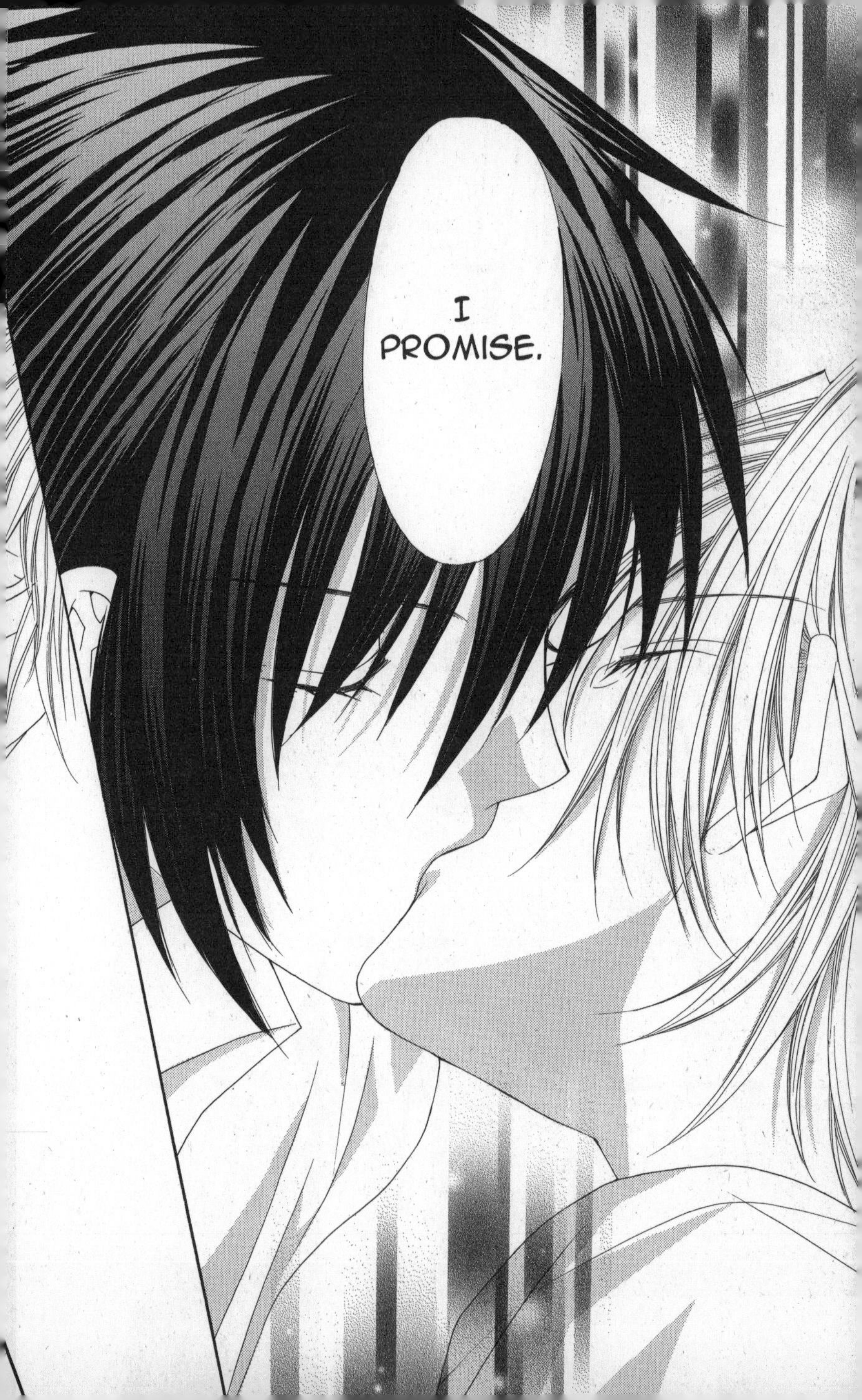
I PROMISE.

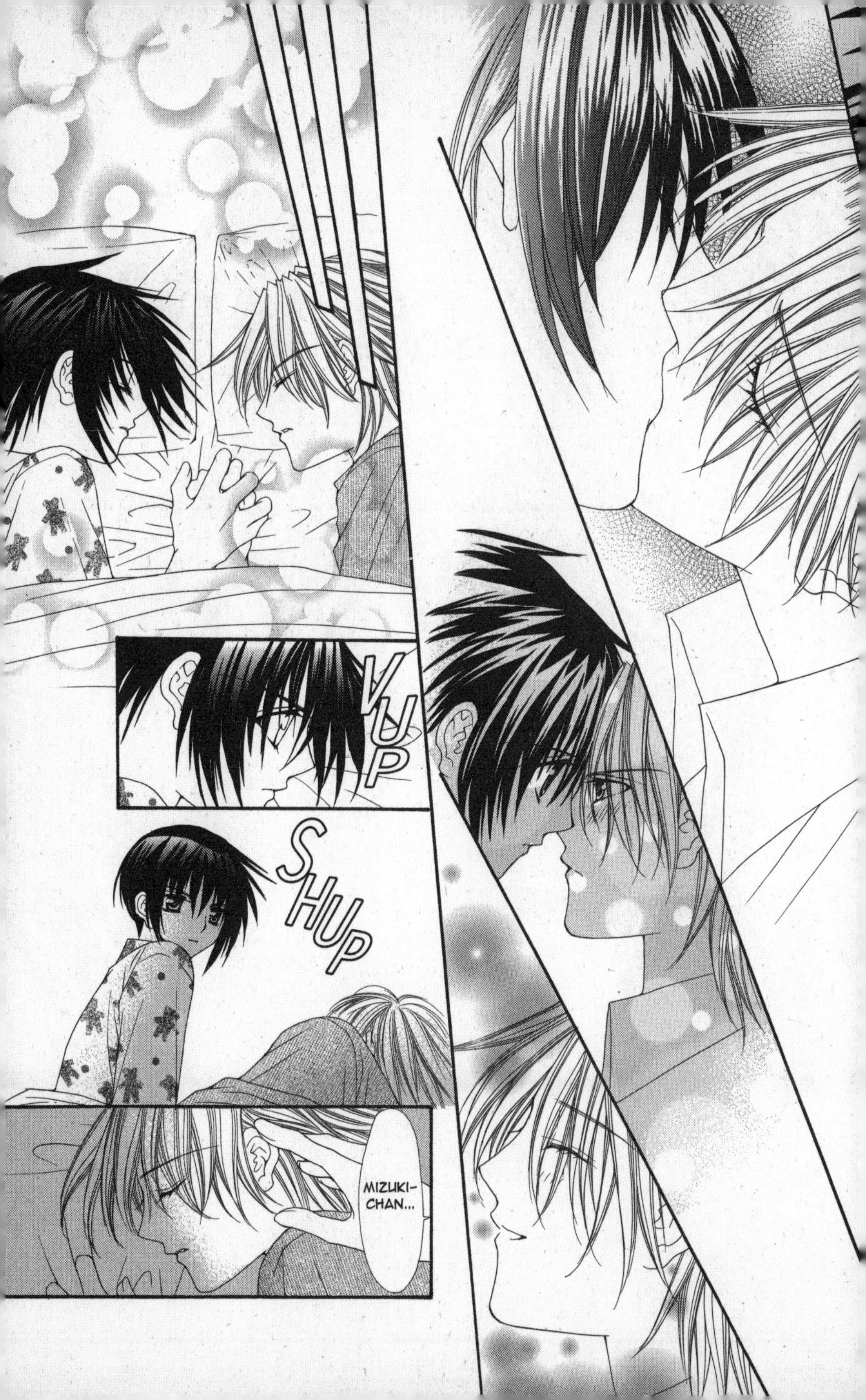
VUP
SHUP
MIZUKI-CHAN...

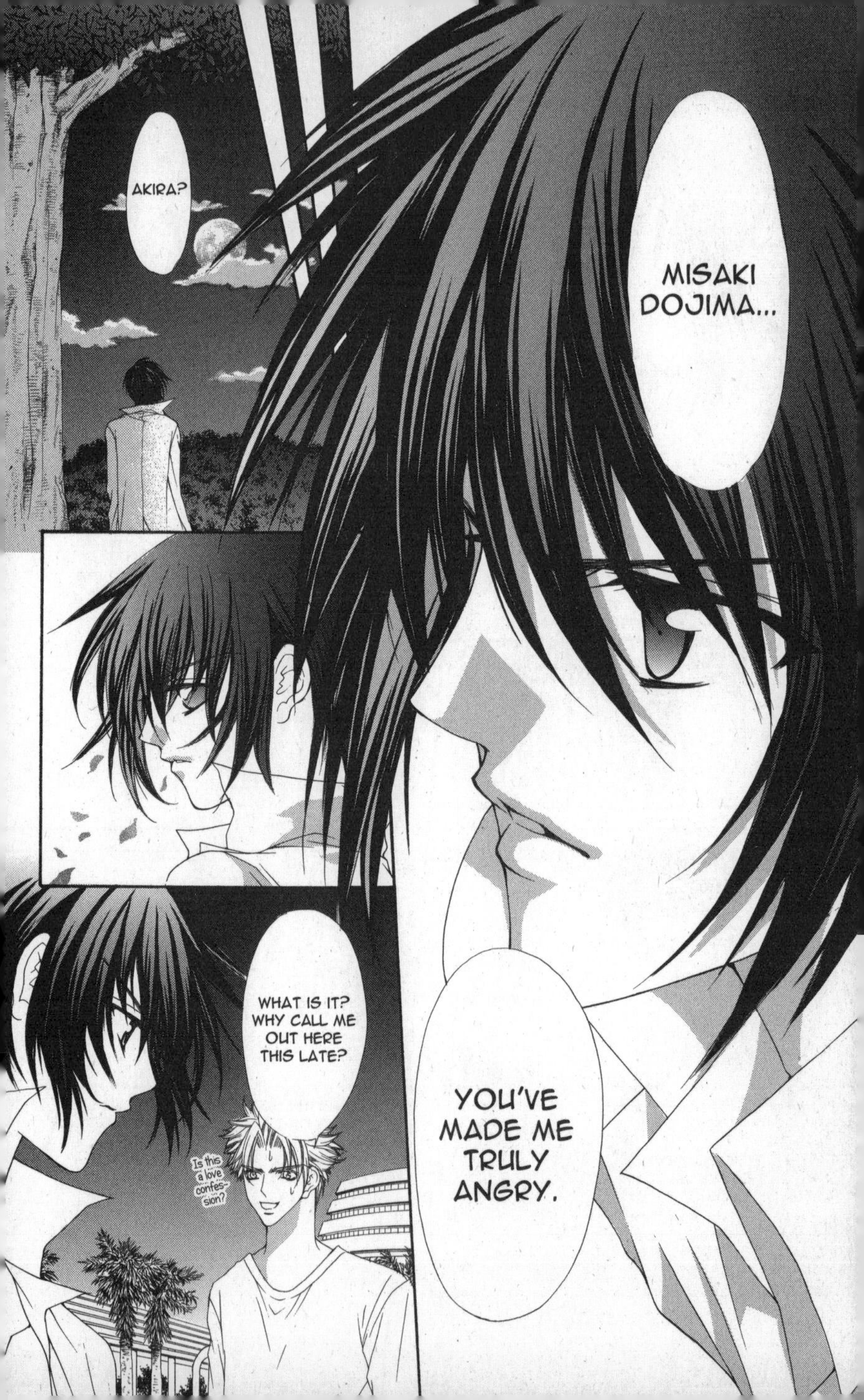
MISAKI DOJIMA...
YOU'VE MADE ME TRULY ANGRY.
AKIRA?
WHAT IS IT? WHY CALL ME OUT HERE THIS LATE?
Is this a love confes-sion?

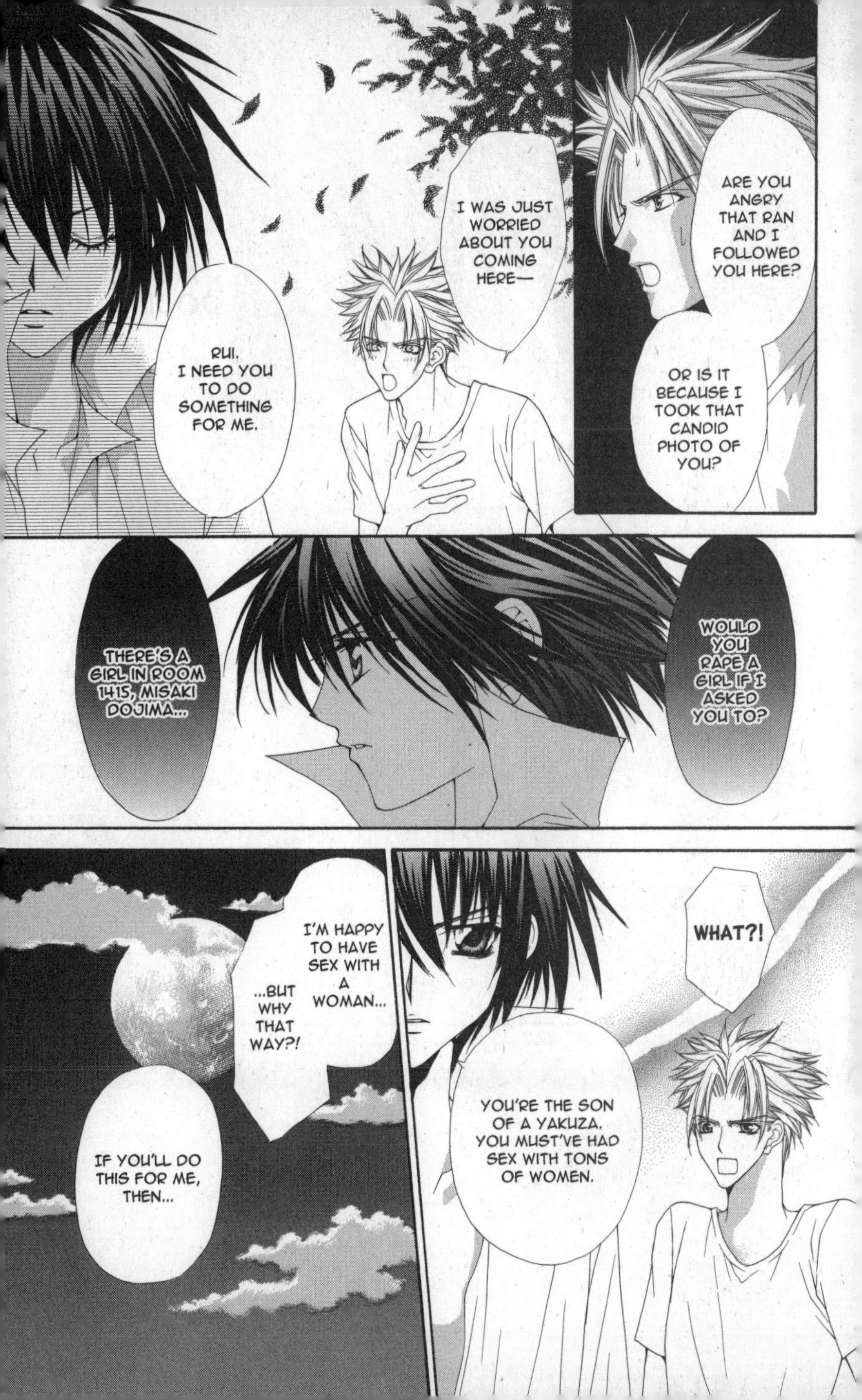
ARE YOU ANGRY THAT RAN AND I FOLLOWED YOU HERE?
OR IS IT BECAUSE I TOOK THAT CANDID PHOTO OF YOU?
I WAS JUST WORRIED ABOUT YOU COMING HERE—
RUI. I NEED YOU TO DO SOMETHING FOR ME.
WOULD YOU RAPE A GIRL IF I ASKED YOU TO?
THERE'S A GIRL IN ROOM 1415, MISAKI DOJIMA...
WHAT?!
YOU'RE THE SON OF A YAKUZA. YOU MUST'VE HAD SEX WITH TONS OF WOMEN.
I'M HAPPY TO HAVE SEX WITH A WOMAN...
...BUT WHY THAT WAY?!
IF YOU'LL DO THIS FOR ME, THEN...

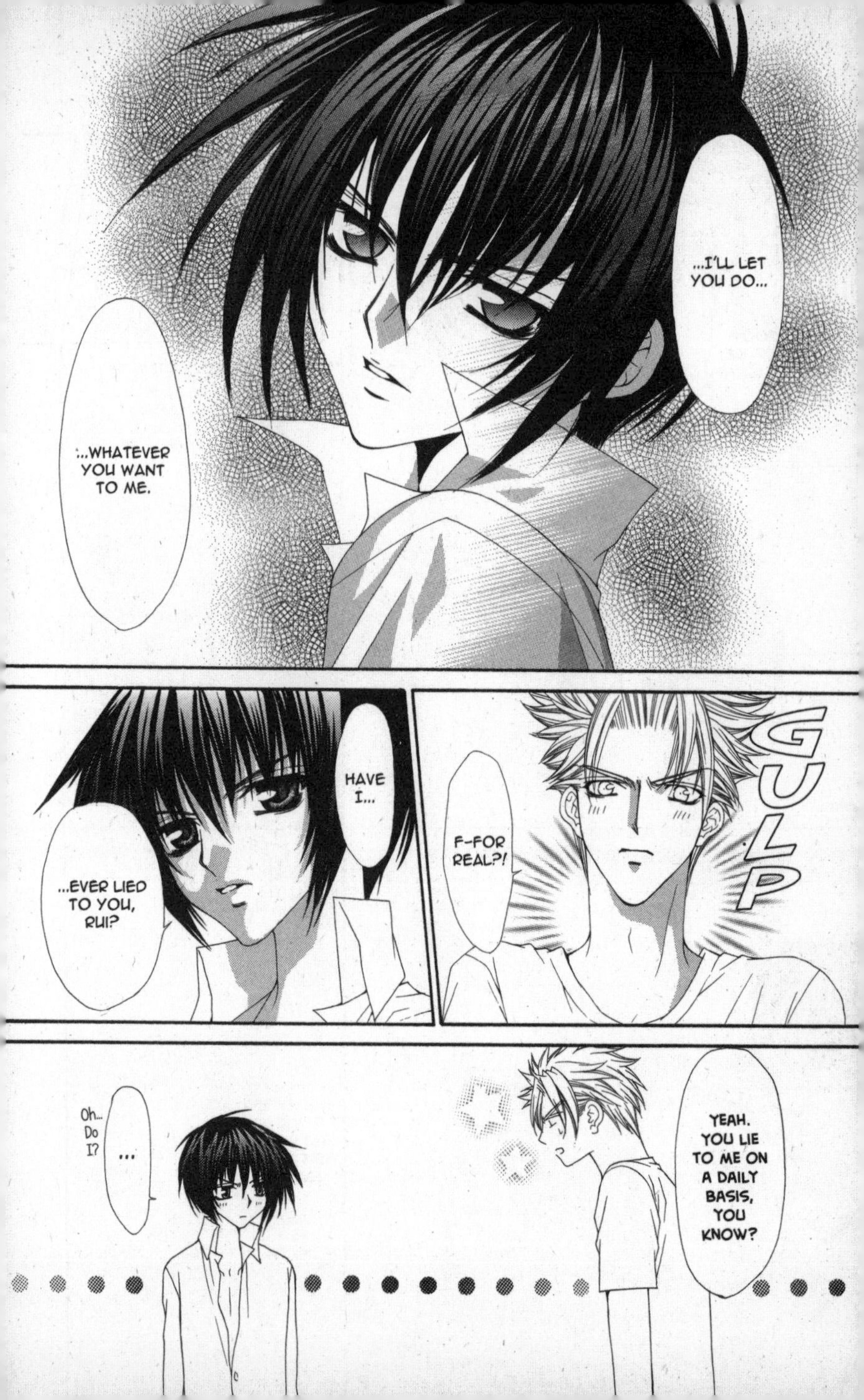
...I'LL LET YOU DO...
...WHATEVER YOU WANT TO ME.
F-FOR REAL?!
GULP
HAVE I...
...EVER LIED TO YOU, RUI?
YEAH. YOU LIE TO ME ON A DAILY BASIS, YOU KNOW?
...
Oh... Do I?

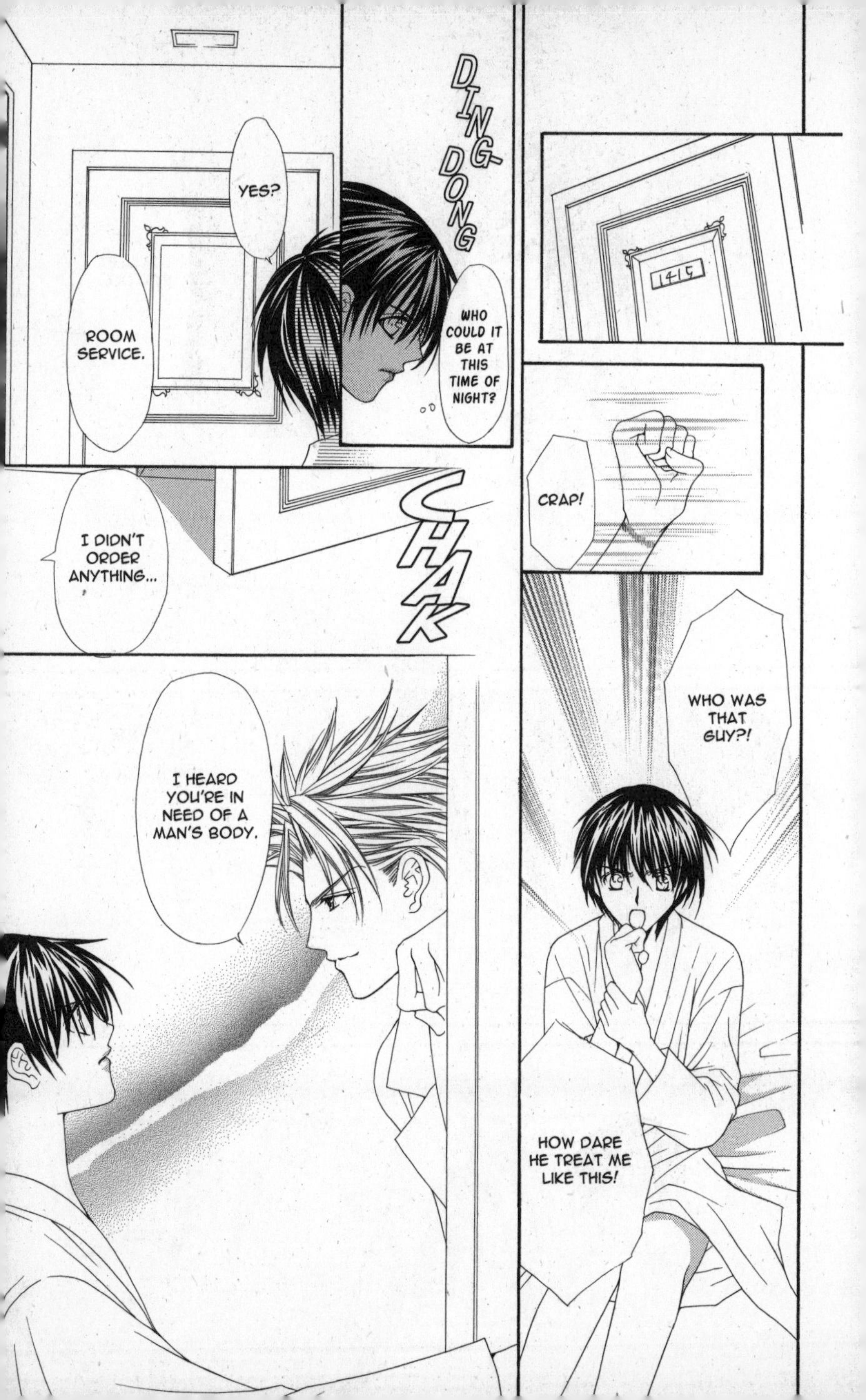
CRAP!
WHO WAS THAT GUY?!
HOW DARE HE TREAT ME LIKE THIS!
DING-DONG
WHO COULD IT BE AT THIS TIME OF NIGHT?
YES?
ROOM SERVICE.
CHAK
I DIDN'T ORDER ANYTHING...
I HEARD YOU'RE IN NEED OF A MAN'S BODY.

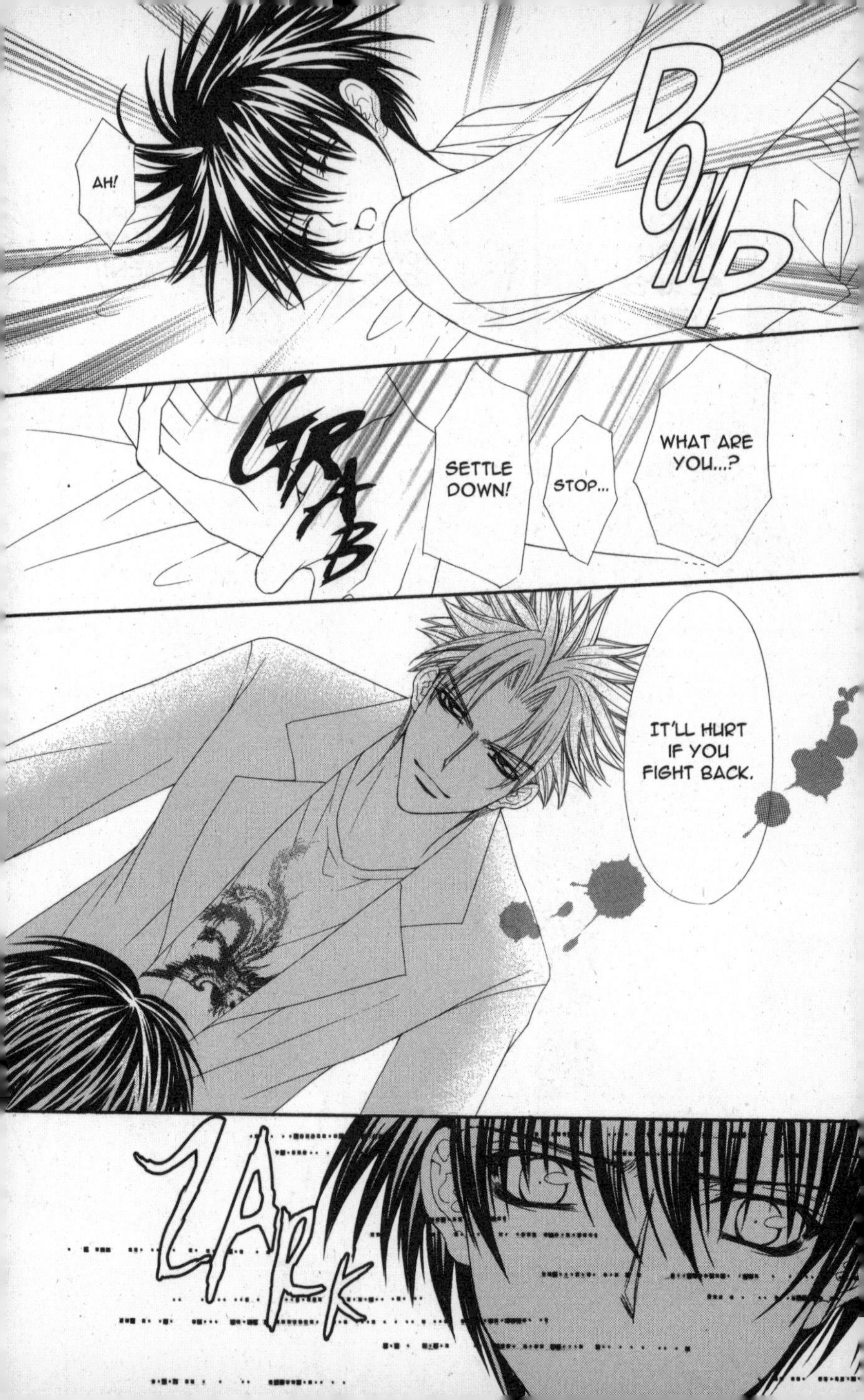
DOMP
AH!
WHAT ARE YOU...?
STOP...
SETTLE DOWN!
GRAB
IT'LL HURT IF YOU FIGHT BACK.
ZARK

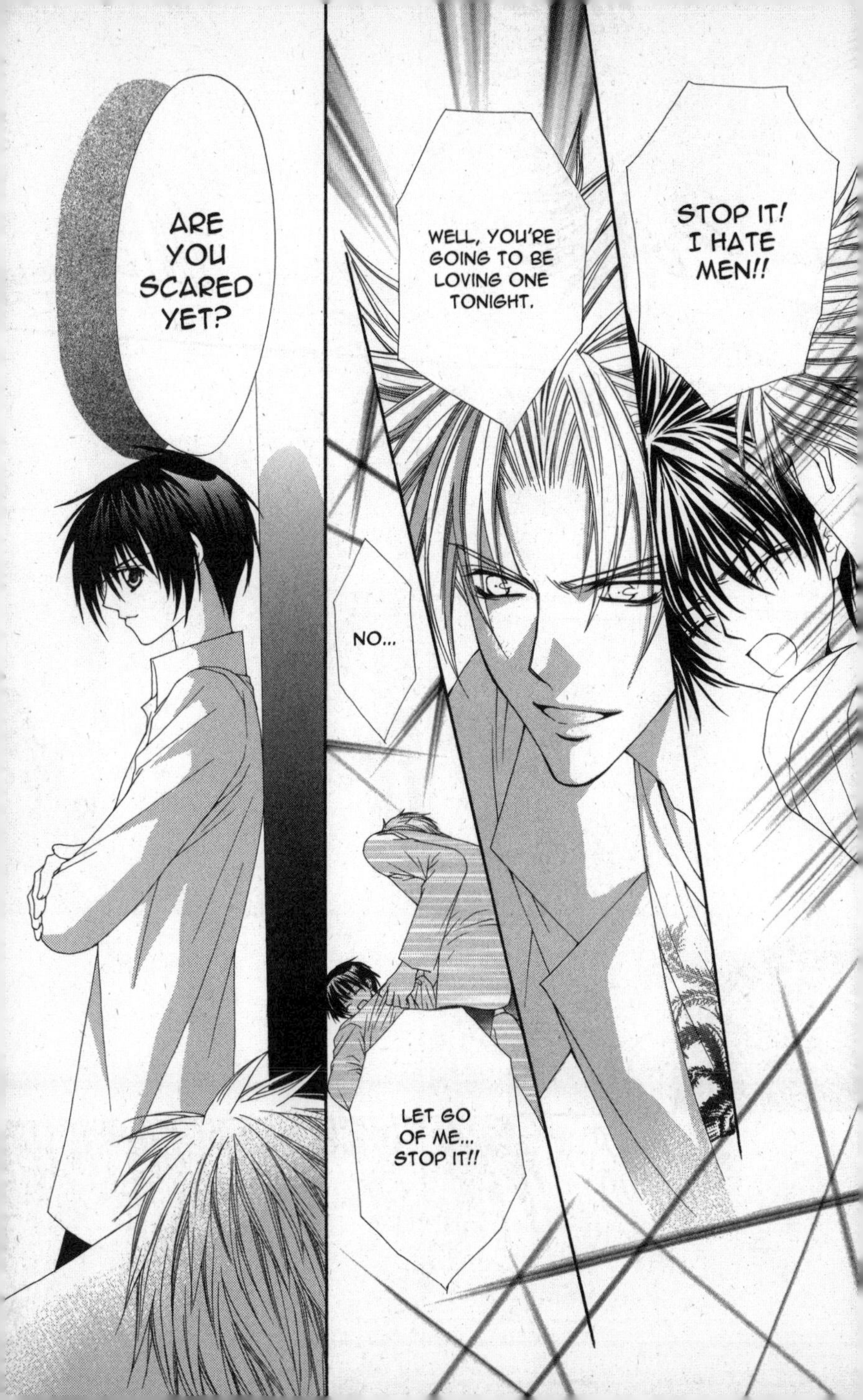
STOP IT! I HATE MEN!!
WELL, YOU'RE GOING TO BE LOVING ONE TONIGHT.
NO...
LET GO OF ME... STOP IT!!
ARE YOU SCARED YET?

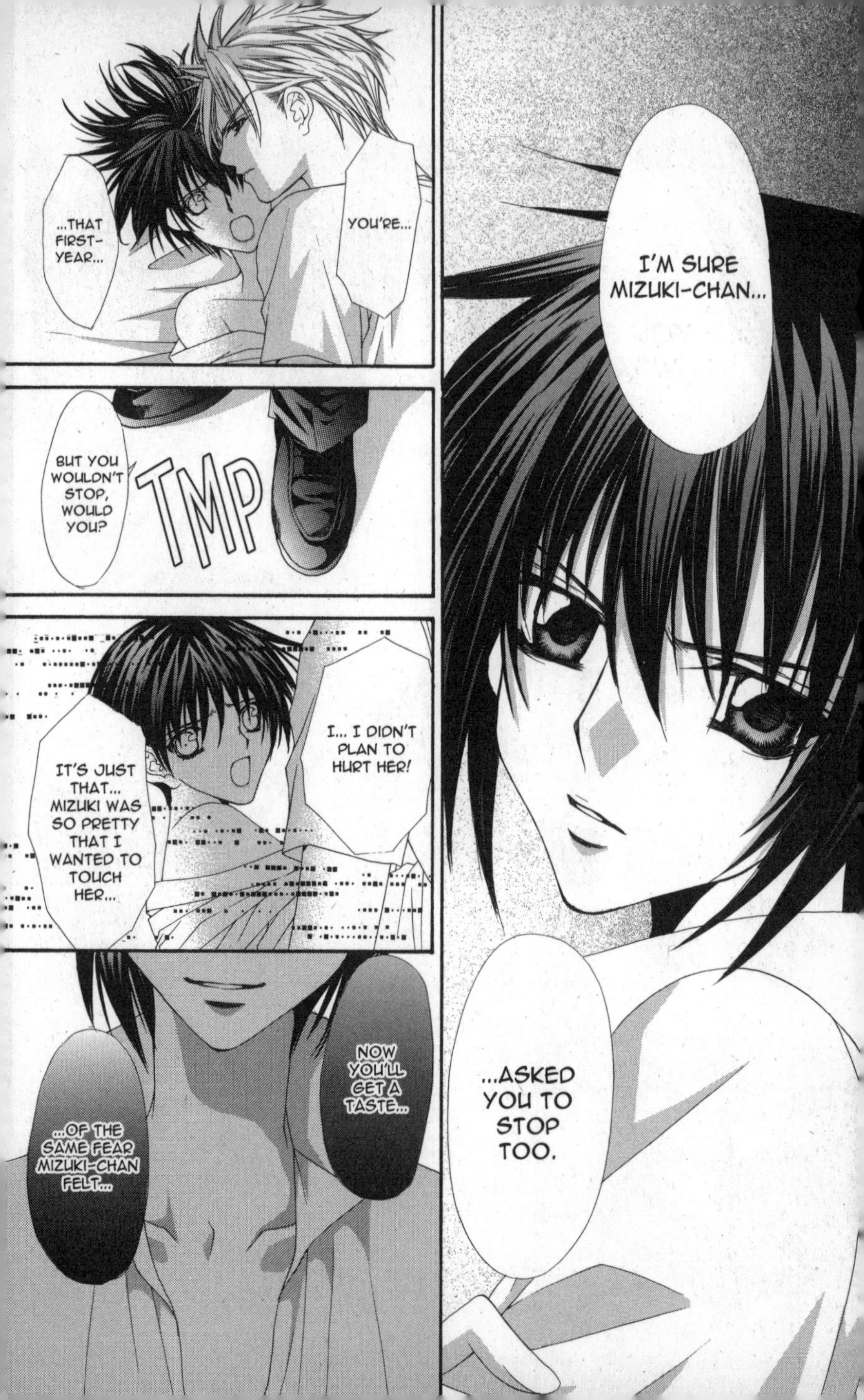
I'M SURE MIZUKI-CHAN...
...ASKED YOU TO STOP TOO.
YOU'RE...
...THAT FIRST-YEAR...
TMP
BUT YOU WOULDN'T STOP, WOULD YOU?
I... I DIDN'T PLAN TO HURT HER!
IT'S JUST THAT... MIZUKI WAS SO PRETTY THAT I WANTED TO TOUCH HER...
NOW YOU'LL GET A TASTE...
...OF THE SAME FEAR MIZUKI-CHAN FELT...

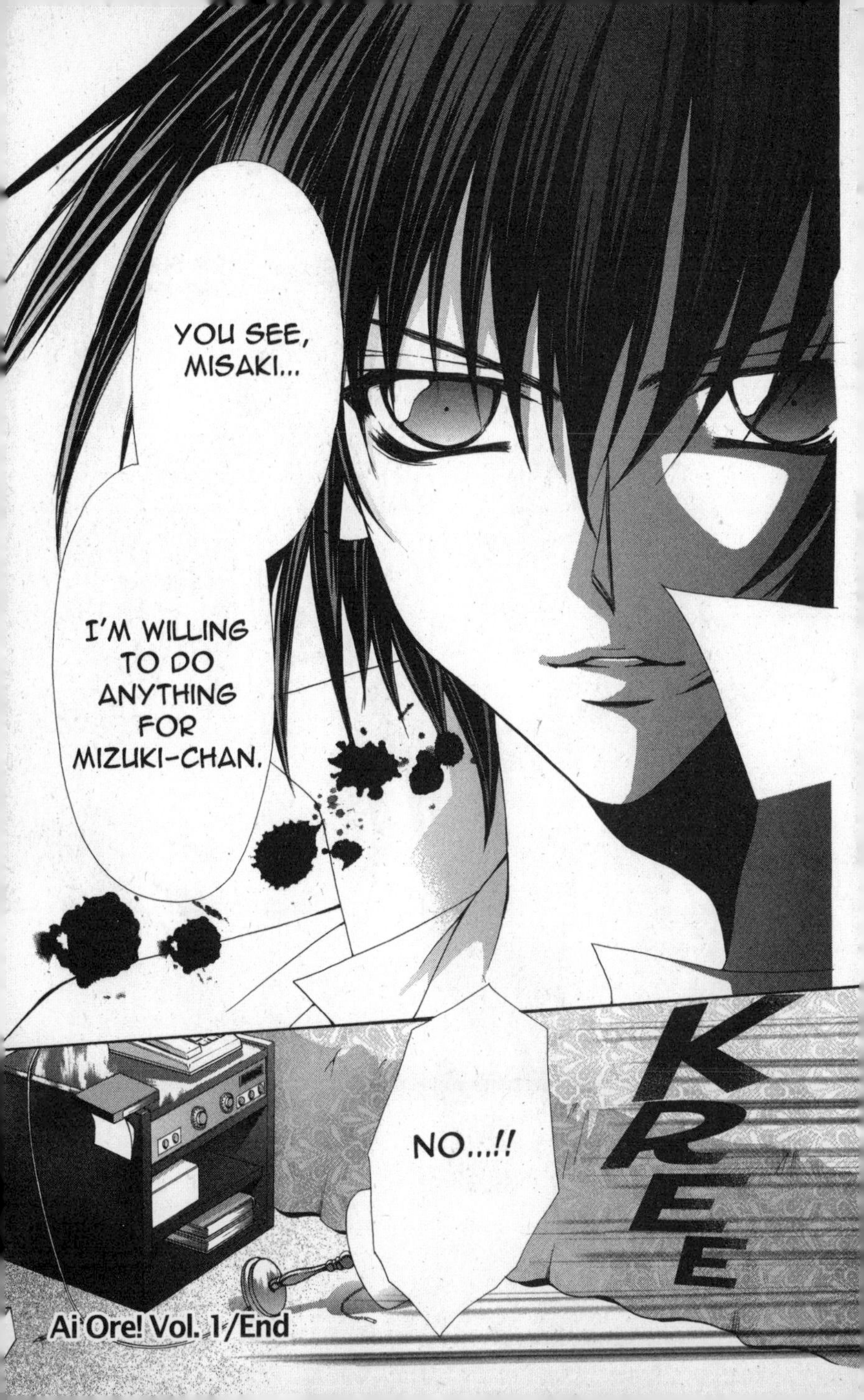
YOU SEE, MISAKI...
I'M WILLING TO DO ANYTHING FOR MIZUKI-CHAN.
KREE
NO...!!
Ai Ore! Vol. 1/End

Illustration Gallery

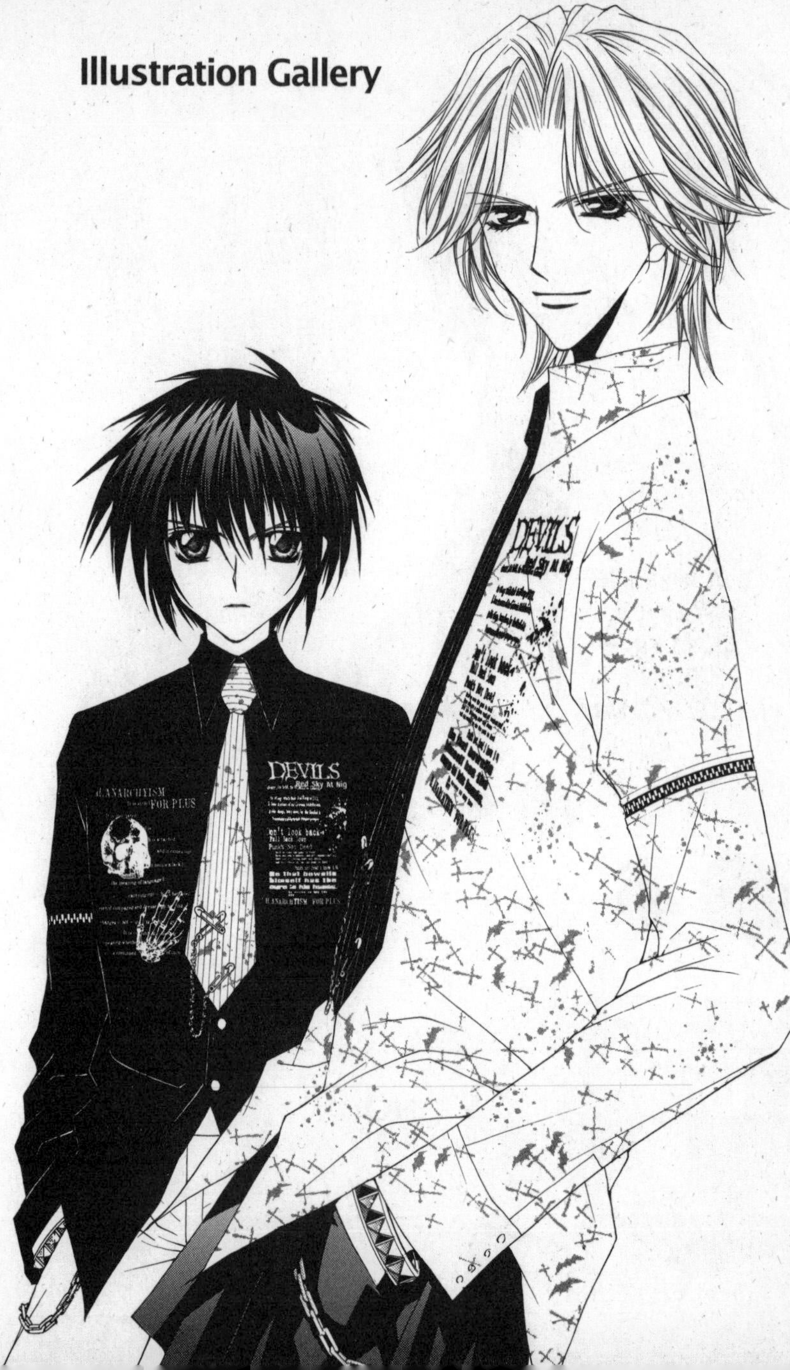
DEVILS
Red Sky At Nig
FOR PLUS
DEVILS

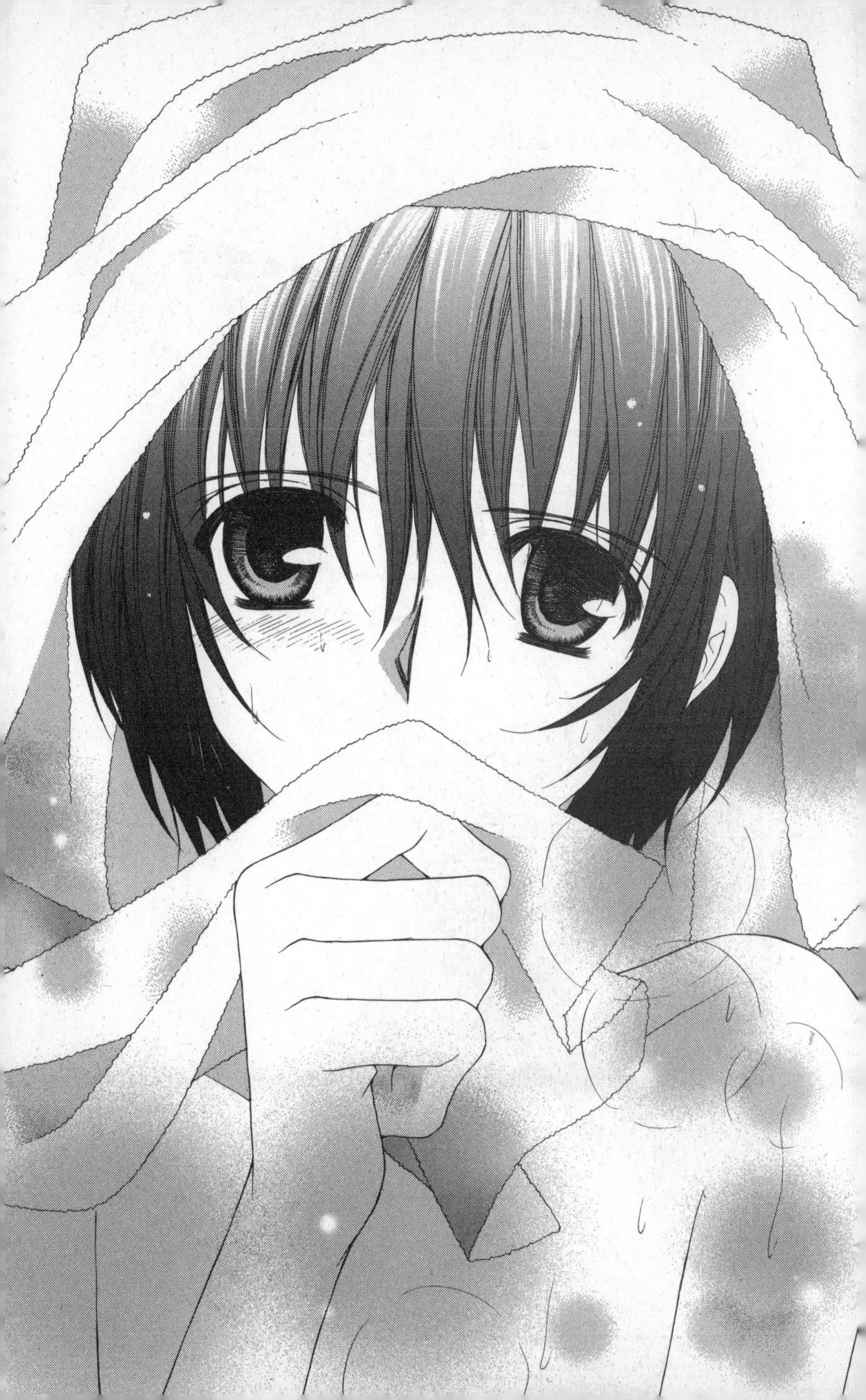

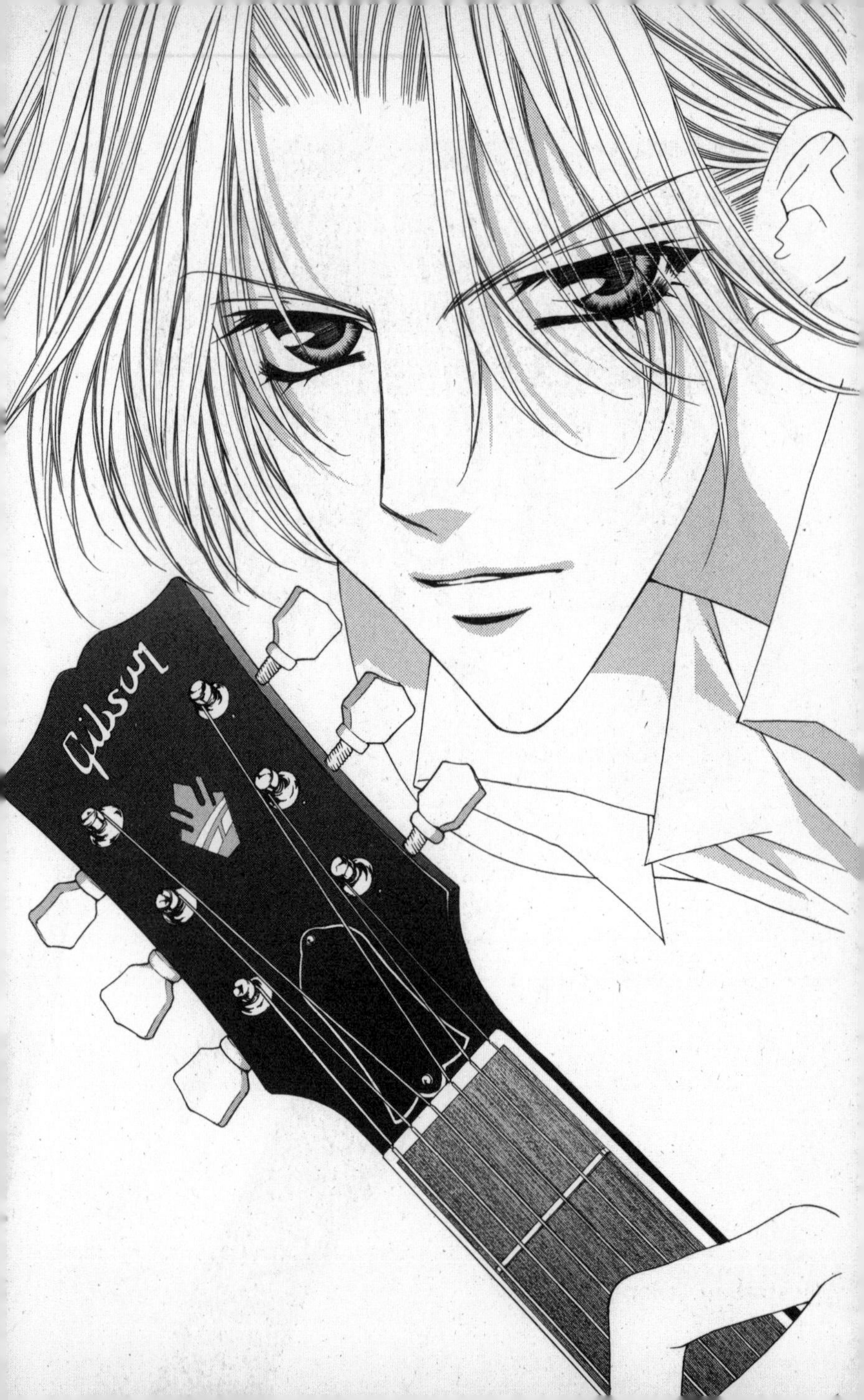
Gibson

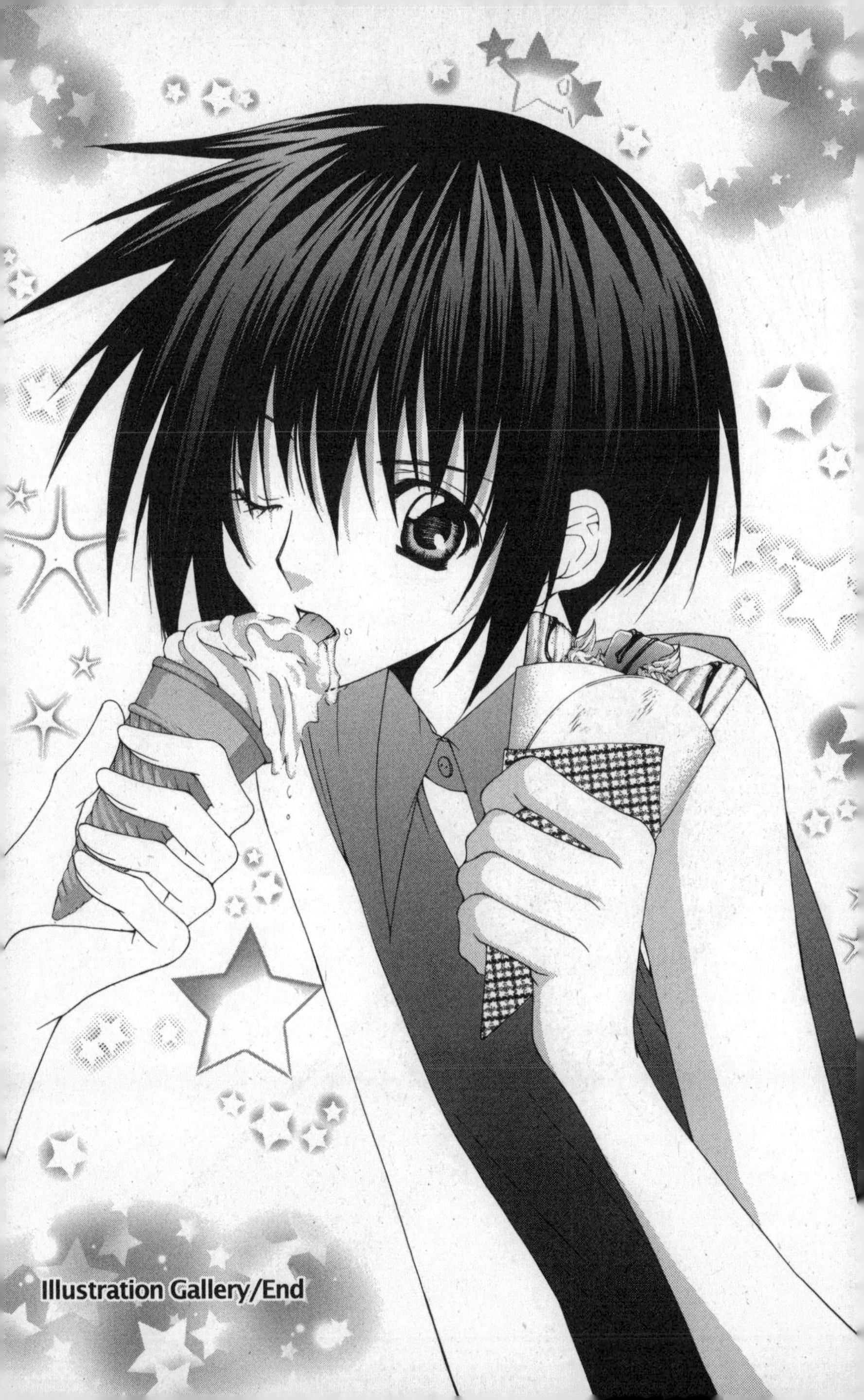
Illustration Gallery/End

This beleaguered piece of work has finally made it out into the open again! The years have passed, and there's a cross-dressing fad going on right now! I couldn't be any happier. I hope you enjoy the origin of the *Ai Ore!* series.

-Mayu Shinjo

Mayu Shinjo was born on January 26. She is a prolific writer of shojo manga, including the series *Sensual Phrase*. Her current series include *Ai-Ore!* and *Ayakashi Koi Emaki*. Her hobbies are cars, shopping and taking baths. Shinjo likes The Prodigy, Nirvana, U2 and Glay.